D0915350

Their Horses Climbed Trees

A Chronicle of the California 100 and Battalion in the Civil War, from San Francisco to Appomattox

Poking Fun at the California Hundred at the East - The Boston *Transcript* of 10th February says:

Our citizens have done well to give the excellent cavalry company from California a fitting welcome. The members of the company are fine fellows, every inch men, and true lovers of their country, for the service of which they have left remunerative employment in California, which is entirely out of the draft, and buckled on the harness of war. Their arrival here, and especially their appearance in the streets of Boston, have excited the liveliest curiosity of our citizens, who have been full of wonder to know what the Californians were like, how many Indians they are in the habit of killing before breakfast, and whether they are themselves white men or aborigines of the Western coast. Consequently, we have heard the most marvelous stories about our guests. It has been currently reported in one place of popular resort, that every man in the company could pick an apple from the ground on the point of his sword, while riding at a breakneck gallop. In another place we heard that the men were native Californians, very expert with the lasso, and that they had been brought East to get Jeff Davis, Bob Lee and Stonewall Jackson "on a string;" that they certainly brought their lassoes with them, one of them having been seen by a member of the Charlestown surprise party. It is common talk that the men ride with equal facility and grace on the top or the bottom of a horse, and that when they make a charge nothing will be visible but the tails of the horses. We have heard an absolute statement, moreover, that when the rolls for enlisting the company were opened, two hundred thousand men put their names down, and this hundred were chosen after a trial in a grand tournament, in which they overthrew all competitors, killing many. Our fellow citizens seem to be so well informed, we can tell them little that will be new about the Californians. We desire to add, however, on indubitable testimony, that each of these gallant fellows has a thousand scalps, which he has taken from the wildest Indians of the mountains, without the consent of the owners, and that their favorite sport is to go bird-nesting, mounted upon the agile mustang, which climbs a tree with perfect ease and safety. The bad feature of the case is this - they have been so accustomed to riding horseback that they cannot walk a step, and if one has a horse killed under him he is obliged to throw his lasso and catch another before he can do the enemy further injury. With this slight drawback the men are all that can be expected of civilized white men who were born in houses.

Evening Bulletin, San Francisco, Saturday, March 28, 1863

Their Horses Climbed Trees

A Chronicle of the California 100 and Battalion in the Civil War, from San Francisco to Appomattox

Larry Rogers and Keith Rogers

Schiffer Military History
Atglen, PA

ACKNOWLEDGMENTS

The very nature of our book makes it difficult to give credit to those who have been so helpful in researching and locating the many primary sources that have gone into this book. All we can say is thanks to all the Librarians, Members of the many Historical Societies, Museums and Cemetery Personnel throughout the United States who have responded to our personal queries, as well as our letters and emails asking for information. All have responded so graciously. We wish we could acknowledge them all by name.

However, we feel we must acknowledge the following by name who took their personal time to review, critique and lend their encouragement:

Robert Chandler, John Langellier, Paul Loane, and Ben Ritter.

And last but not least to those fellow reenactors and researchers who are helping to keep history alive.

Book design by Ian Robertson.

Printed in China.
ISBN: 0-7643-1391-6

We are always looking for people to write books on new and related subjects. If you have an idea for a book, please contact us at the address below.

Published by Schiffer Publishing Ltd.
4880 Lower Valley Road
Atglen, PA 19310
Phone: (610) 593-1777
FAX: (610) 593-2002
E-mail: Schifferbk@aol.com.
Visit our web site at: www.schifferbooks.com
Please write for a free catalog.
This book may be purchased from the publisher.
Please include $3.95 postage.
Try your bookstore first.

In Europe, Schiffer books are distributed by:
Bushwood Books
6 Marksbury Ave.
Kew Gardens
Surrey TW9 4JF
England
Phone: 44 (0)208 392-8585
FAX: 44 (0)208 392-9876
E-mail: Bushwd@aol.com.
Free postage in the UK. Europe: air mail at cost.
Try your bookstore first.

Contents

Foreword

This book is dedicated to Abraham Loane, Company A, The California Hundred, his fellow veterans in the Company and in the California Battalion.

Vallejo Naval & Historical Museum

<u>ABRAHAM LOANE</u>
1839 - 1920

(Great and Great, great Grandfather of the Editor/Compilers)

Introduction

Many words have been written on the American Civil War of 1861-1865. Few, however, have been compiled focusing on the men from California. Their story begins in 1862 when James Sewall Reed of San Francisco received a dispatch from Governor Andrew of Massachusetts. This authorized Reed to raise a cavalry company of 100 men to go East as substitutes to fill the quota of men required from the State of Massachusetts.

This is the story of those men, their recruiting, training, drill, voyage to the East and service in the war as the "California Hundred", Company A, 2d Massachusetts Cavalry. The subsequent recruiting of an additional 400 men by DeWitt Clinton Thompson of San Francisco, to become the "California Battalion", joined with the "California Hundred" in the service of Massachusetts as Companies E, F L, & M of the 2d Massachusetts Cavalry Regiment.

A traditional approach to present this history would have been to take all that has been written on this group, update it, and print out our version. We have taken a different and we hope a more faithful approach to tell the story of this little known group's participation in the Civil War. We have searched as many of the California sources as we could and a few out of state sources as well, for newspaper accounts, diaries, and letters (many published in the newspapers of the time). At the time of the Civil War, people were much more eloquent and descriptive in their usage of English. We felt that any attempt to rewrite these words would only result in the loss of the immediacy and vibrancy of those times that we wanted to convey. After sifting through a surprisingly large amount of information, we hope to tell here the story of these men from the best sources of all, the people who were actually there.

The story is told as a chronological history, as opposed to a narrative history. All entries are given by date and source. Due to space considerations, newspaper articles are not shown in their columnar format; however, we have tried whenever possible to keep the format of the hand written documents. *No attempt has been made to correct these accounts either to conform to proper spelling or historical text.*

Initially, there were numerous newspaper references, both here in California and in the East, as to the whereabouts and activities of the Californians; but as the war progressed, attrition, whether by death or promotion and transfer to other units took its' toll. The California units pretty much lost their identity within the written accounts of the larger units to which they were attached.

These were men who had made California their home and many of them returned to live out their lives in California. We have included information on these men after the war to give an often untold glimpse of a Civil War veteran's life.

The account presented here is by no means complete, there are many gaps and unanswered questions, and the "Editors/Compilers" hope that their efforts will encourage other descendants, historians and those with more than a passing interest in the Civil War to continue the story; for, when doing historical research, the more one digs, the more one finds.

Larry and Keith Rogers, Editors/Compilers

Cavalry Company for the East.

THE UNDERSIGNED HAS BEEN authorized by the Secretary of War to raise a Company of Cavalry for service in the East to make a part of tho Massachusetts quota.

A Roll of the Company is at Assembly Hall, corner Post and Kearny streets where persons desirous of joining can enroll their names

No one need apply who is not a good horseman and in good health. Men from the country preferred. The Roll will be kept open a reasonable time before selections are made.

All expenses will be paid as soon as accepted.

Further particulars apply to Office, corner Post and Kearny street.

oc28-2ptf   J. SEWALL REED.

Alta California

1862

On April 24, 1861, the Pony Express and telegraph brought the news of the surrender of Fort Sumter to California. The people of California, reflecting their many places of birth, took an active part in the issues that confronted the Nation. This meant that both Northern and Southern sympathizers could be found in close proximity. Copperheads paraded in the streets of San Francisco, their bands playing "Dixie" while a minister, Reverend William Scott of Calvary Pres. Church preached for Jeff Davis, and the next day dangled in effigy from a Bush Street lamp post.

Secessionists raised the palmetto flag in San Francisco, and the Bear Flag at Sonoma, and clamoured for a Pacific Republic loyal to the Confederacy. Unionists pulled the flags down and swore that a 100,000 Californians would have to be put to the sword before the State would desert the North.

In August of 1861, the Governor of California, John Downey, issued an order calling for the recruitment of California troops for the Union. While many of the volunteers had hoped for active service in the East, they were for the most part stationed in the West. They replaced the Army regulars in the various Army posts in the western territories, as the regulars were called to the Eastern front. The main effort of these volunteers was to keep the peace in the Far West; not by fighting rebels, but by protecting the emigrant routes and the overland mails from hostile indians who had become aggressive after the removal of the regulars.

As the war in the East progressed, so did the political division of Californians who were subjected to the Secessionist viewpoint of the southland, and of some of the inland valley towns, and the strong Unionist viewpoint of the northland. Fortunately, at this time, both the political and economic strength of California was in the North. With the inauguration in 1862 of Leland Stanford as the first Republican Governor, California's course was set, although Secessionist movements continued to excite the state throughout the war.

At this time, there were active Federal units posted in California and recruiting for these units was ongoing. Men living in California who came from the East, were returning there to fight in the Civil War on their own. It wasn't until the late summer, early fall of 1862 and continuing into the spring of 1863, that an organized effort was made to recruit men then living in California for service in the East. Contrary to their hopes, these volunteers would not become an official California unit but would instead become a part of a Massachusetts Volunteer Cavalry Regiment, and be accounted for in the quota of Massachusetts. Numbering 500 in all, the first 100 left San Francisco December 11, 1862; known as the California Hundred they would become Company A, of the 2d Massachusetts Cavalry Regiment.

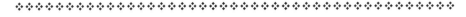

SEPTEMBER, 1862

1   Battle of Chantilly
5   McClellan takes command of the Army of the Potomac
13 Copy of Lee's "Lost Order of Antietam" found by Union men
15 Harper's Ferry falls to the Confederates
17 Battle of Antietam
22 Preliminary Emancipation Proclamation Announced

California Regiments for the War.

We understand that Col. Hungerford, but recently returned from the Army of the Potomac, has applied to the Governor for permission to raise one or more regiments of volunteers, to be conducted directly to the field in Virginia. If at all within the power of Gov. *[Leland]* Stanford, we have no doubt that the application will be successful. With the assurance that the men will be taken directly to the scene of war, there will be no difficulty in procuring enlistments. The main difficulty last fall was, that the volunteers expected what afterwards occurred-that they would be kept in inactivity on this coast.

Col. Hungerford has a reputation as a military man; has come directly from the hard fought fields of the Peninsula, and is desirous to return with a regiment or two of *California fighting men.* Whoever goes with him will have no difficulty in getting into business, or in getting sight of the belligerent elephant. We earnestly hope his application may be successful. We don't think any military leader could be found more competent-certainly none braver or more effectually tried, both in the hottest fires of Mexico, and in Virginia.

The Sierra County News, Downieville, Saturday, September 8, 1862.

Custom House, San Francisco
Collectors Office, Sept. 15, 1862

His Excellency
John A. Andrew
Gov. Massachusetts

My Dear Sir.

The State of California, though by a large extent as thoroughly loyal as any in the Union has not on account of her position been called upon for any active service in the suppression of the rebellion. Last year about 6000 troops were called for, was promptly furnished and are now in the service - some of them in garrison - some in the Indian Territory, some in Arizona and New Mexico, and about 1500 have recently gone to Utah. Our men have cheerfully and loyally gone where they have been ordered, but the duty to which they have been called is not that which they would have chosen. There are thousands of our citizens who would gladly enlist were it judged prudent to send them out of the State, if they could go to the other side and take part in the war directly.

Among such persons is Captain J. Sewall Reed, commander of a cavalry company in this city, and friends of his, all like himself natives of Massachusetts, who are earnestly desirous of making up a troop of cavalry of 100 men, to go immediately east, and make a part of the Massachusetts contingent. It is at the request of Captain Reed and his friends that I write to you and offer their services. They are true men, skilled as horsemen by the habits of the country, as few men in the Atlantic States ever become, and if they can have an opportunity they will certainly make their mark. They propose to uniform themselves, provide saddles, sabres, revolvers, and all equipments except horses, if provision can be made for their passage by steamer from here to New York.

Is it possible for you to make such provision? If so, and it is possible for you to accept them and take them into the service in the manner I have indicated, it would gratify large numbers of the sons of the Old Bay State here, and I think make a pleasant and useful impression at home. Probably an arrangement can be made with the Mail Steam Ship Co. in New York by which such a company can be carried through at a reduced rate of fare.

Mr. Reed suggests that if the thing can be done, you notify me of the fact immediately by Telegraph, and he will go to work at once - then if you will so far trust me as to send to me by mail his commission and blank commissions for first and second Lieutenants, he will be immediately organized.

I can manage so as to have the officers examined as to their qualifications by the Examining Board of the Army here, and the men passed upon by the proper Army Medical officers.

It is quite possible that the whole plan proposed is inadvisable, but if it is in your power, and it should seem to you expedient to adopt it you will gratify the patriotic feelings of some good and loyal men as you will also oblige

Yours very sincerely

(signed) Ira P. Rankin

Massachusetts State Archives, Boston, Massachusetts
[Ira P. Rankin, Collector of the Port of San Francisco, the highest Federal patronage position, and proprietor of the Pacific Iron Foundry]

LOCAL MATTERS

A California Regiment. - By a dispatch received this morning from the Bay, it appears that the War Department has accepted the tender of a regiment from this State, and measures are being taken to have the force immediately organized and sent to Panama. Probably this will be the only California regiment that will have an opportunity of sharing in the perils and honors of the battles yet to be fought in this war for the Union, and for this reason we would like to see Nevada county represented, and if an effort is made we think one company at least, can be raised here in a short time, and fully equipped.

LOCAL MATTERS

Offer of a Regiment. - A San Francisco dispatch of the 14th inst., to the Union, says that Wm. M. Lent and Wm. Chapman have telegraphed to the Secretary of War, offering one thousand or twelve hundred men for the war, to be landed at Aspinwall, all expenses paid. Four of the subscribers to the fund for these troops will give $10,000 each, and one of them agrees to give $10,000 and serve as a private in the regiment. Chapman is said to be the man who makes this offer. We shall probably have an answer from the War Department in a day or two, and if the offer is accepted, there is no doubt that the regiment will be rapidly filled.

Nevada Democrat, Nevada City, Tuesday, 16 September 1862.
[William M. Lent, Commission Merchant; William D. Chapman, Capitalist]

California's Contribution of Troops.

A number of our loyal citizens are not only desirous of sending money, but good fighting men to the scene of conflict in the Atlantic States. On Monday of last week, the following named gentlemen addressed a telegram to the Secretary of War, inquiring if in the event of one thousand men being raised, armed, equipped, and landed in Panama, whether transportation would be provided for them to New York. Last evening the following answer was received:

Washington-sent 13th, received 15th.

Wm. M. Lent, R. M. Jessup, Eugene L. Sullivan, Wm. D. Chapman:

If 1,000 men for the war are placed at Panama, from California, passage will be provided thence for them.

By order of
Secretary of War,
C. R. Buckingham, Brig. Gen., Ass't. Adj't. Gen.

There is no more doubt that the one thousand troops can be raised, and will be forwarded at the expense of our citizens, than that the sum of $250,000 will be sent hence to the Sanitary Fund. The great difficulty will be in knowing whom to select from the thousands who are sure to proffer their services.

Alta California, San Francisco, Tuesday, September 16, 1862.
[Richard M. Jessup, Vice President, California Steam Navigation Co.; Eugene L. Sullivan, President, Spring Valley Water Works]

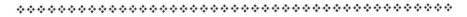

CITY ITEMS.

Rush of Volunteers For Service. - As might be expected, the rush of candidates for enlistment in the California regiment to go Atlanticward, is great, and throughout yesterday the Committee who had received the dispatch satisfactory from the War Department, were overrun with applications. They are powerless in the premises, and so in fact is General Wright, until he receives orders, authority, and instructions relative thereto, from the Home Department at Washington. Meanwhile it has been very prudently suggested that loyal and impatient spirits in the country, who are panting to enlist in the proposed corps, keep cool until the proper authority is received for organizing the regiment. Already Yuba county is heard from. She desires a fair show, and Marysville insists on furnishing one company. Other counties will doubtless offer men enough, and thrice over, for active service in the Atlantic States. But we can't spare them all, so long as John Bull frowns on us from his Asiatic fleet, or in fact so long as his press and politicians unblushingly avow their hearty sympathy with this internal rebellion. Already the names of several gallant and experienced officers are mentioned in connection with the new regiment. It is stated to us on the best authority, that Col. J.D. Stevenson will consent to accept the Colonelcy of the regiment. David Scanlon, Chief Engineer of the Fire Department, and an officer of the Mexican war has been suggested as Lieutenant Colonel. Our former Chief of Police, James F. Curtis, and who early enlisted in the present war, is favorably mentioned in connection with the office of Major. A number of our most talented and esteemed business young men have expressed not only a willingness but an ardent desire to become attached to this regiment, either as officers or privates. We cannot doubt that a body of troops will be sent to the field of battle from California which will show to the world that although residents of a State far removed from the scene of strife, they represent one whose every pulsation is in unison with that of the undivided Union.

Alta California, San Francisco, Wednesday, September 17, 1862
[General George Wright became Commander of the Pacific Department, comprising the States of California and Oregon, the Territories of Washington, Nevada and Utah and the District of Arizona September, 1861. The General, his wife and staff were lost at sea July 30, 1865, when the <u>Brother Jonathan</u> hit an uncharted rock near Crescent City, California. Colonel Jonathan D. Stevenson brought the 1st New York Volunteers to California in 1847].

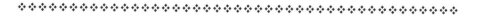

LOCAL MATTERS
A Volunteer, - Mr. Henry Hall, who has been mining on Rock creek for some years started below this morning, with the intention of joining the regiment now being organized to go East. We are informed that he owned claims worth six or seven hundred dollars, which he sold for two hundred, in order to get away immediately.

Nevada Democrat, Nevada City, Thursday, 18 September 1862.

California Regiment. - Some parties in San Francisco propose to fit out a regiment of California Volunteers, and deliver them at Aspinwall for the use of the Government-The Steamship Co. offer to take them for $83,000. It is doubted whether so large a sum can be raised.

The Colusa Sun, Colusa, Saturday, September 20, 1862.

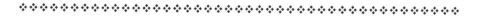

How to Escape the Draft. - The Philadelphia Press relates the following:
One day, recently, an adroit speculator calculating on the fears as well as the curiosity of those liable to military service, advertised in one of our city papers that, in consideration of the sum of one dollar, sent to him by post to a certain given address, he would directly communicate an infallible method by which each person receiving this valuable information could avoid the draft. As many as four hundred letters, each inclosing a dollar, reached the ingenious advertiser within twelve hours. In every instance, he conscientiously performed his promise, and, without delay or evasion, communicated how to evade the draft. The secret, which is well worth knowing was communicated in the single word-enlist.

LOCAL MATTERS

Volunteers. - A movement is on foot to raise a company in this county, to join the regiment that is now talked of being raised to go East. Some eighteen or twenty persons have signed the roll, and they are now only waiting for the movement to get into shape below, when the work of recruiting will begin in earnest. A meeting of the recruits will be held at the Cadet's Armory, head of Broad street, at eight o'clock this evening, and all desirous of joining the company are invited to attend.

Nevada Democrat, Nevada City, Saturday, September 20, 1862

LOCAL MATTERS

The Proposed New Regiment.- In answer to an inquiry, as to whether a company from Nevada would be accepted, in the regiment it is proposed to raise to go East, we received a dispatch from Mr. Lent, yesterday, stating that they were waiting orders from Washington, when they would let us know. We do not know the nature of the orders for which they are waiting, but it seems that no movement has yet been made below towards recruiting. We learn, however, from other sources, that if a regiment is raised, there will be no difficulty in having a company from this county accepted. It is expected that three or four companies will be organized at San Francisco, one at Marysville, one at Sacramento, and the remaining companies in the mines; but it is calculated that a large proportion of the men composing the companies organized in the cities will come from the mountains.

Nevada Democrat, Nevada City, Tuesday, September 23, 1862

LOCAL MATTERS

The New Regiment.- We have heard nothing, since our last issue, relative to the new regiment it is proposed to raise in this State, to go East. Companies are being recruited at Sacramento and Marysville, as well as one at Nevada, but recruiting has not yet commenced at San Francisco. Some thirty-eight names are already signed to the roll of the company proposed to be raised in this county, and a number of others have signified their intention to join. There will be no difficulty in raising the company; but as the men who propose to join are all working men, it is not deemed advisable to break up their business and go to drilling, until it is known for a certainty that the regiment will be raised. We expect to get some further information on the subject this evening.

Nevada Democrat, Nevada City, Thursday, September 25, 1862

California Should be Represented in the War.

Now that the war has assumed such colossal proportions, and there is every prospect that it will continue at least for one or two years longer, many of the loyal citizens of California are anxious to have a hand in it, and only await orders from the War Department to enrol themselves in the Union army. The late reverses to the Union cause, instead of disheartening, but renders them more determined to sustain the Government; and if need be, and the movement is set on foot, we think a regiment can be raised in the State, of men who will pay their own passage to New York, provided they can have the assurance of being mustered into the service when they get there. A few are preparing to go, with the view of joining regiments from other States, but they would much prefer to be with a regiment made up exclusively of Californians.

We notice by the San Francisco papers, that the 3rd and 4th regiments, of California Volunteers, (Col. Connor's and Col. Forman's,) have each made application to be taken East, and the officers and men of the 3d have subscribed some $30,000 towards paying their passage. Why not send both of these regiments, and raise another of picked men to go with them? The three regiments would make a brigade; and California could certainly send 3,000 men to the war, and have enough left to keep peace on this coast. It would probably take three or four months to make the necessary arrangements to supply the places of the two regiments, bring them to San Francisco, and recruit and drill the new regiment. In the mean time efforts could be made to raise money by subscription to pay the passage of the men to New York. Doubtless the officers and men of the regiments would all subscribe one or two months of their pay, and if any thing was lacking when the Legislature met, the State might be called upon to make up the deficiency. Other States have contributed largely towards the expenses of war, and California should be as liberal as her sisters. The brigade could thus be landed in New York by the middle of February, without extra expense to the Government, and be ready for active operations in the spring.

The arrival of such a force from this State would have a happy effect at the East, particularly if they should arrive during a period of reverses to the Federal arms. Their numbers, it is true, would not be sufficient to make any material difference in the result of the contest, but the fact of their coming such a distance to the support of the Government would have an encouraging effect.

[Col. P. Edward Connor, 3rd Infantry; Col. Ferris Foreman, 4th Infantry, Cal. Volunteers]

The Proposed Regiment.-A San Francisco dispatch to the Appeal *[Marysville]*, dated the 25th, says a telegram was received that day from Washington, refusing to grant permission to raise a regiment for the East. The same dispatch says Gen. Wright has telegraphed to the War Department, that in his opinion the regiment had better not leave here. What Gen. Wright's object can be in making such representations we do not know; but we infer that he wants it to appear that there is a large Secession element in California which requires the presence of all the Union men to keep down. But if his purpose is to keep men in this State, for fear of an uprising, it will be a failure. It is impossible to keep men here when so much excitement is going on at the East, and such tremendous issues are to be decided upon the battle field. Those disposed to go, who have the means, will pay their own passage, and many other good men would go if they could raise the money. We have no doubt that enough men to make up a regiment will leave here for the war in the next two or three months. But arriving at different times, they will of course join different regiments, and their identity as Californians will be lost. They would all prefer to join a California regiment, or brigade, and we earnestly hope that arrangements may yet be made to send an organized force from this State.

Nevada Democrat, Nevada City, Saturday, September 27, 1862

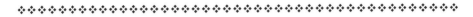

No Soldiers Needed.-A dispatch from San Francisco, published in the Marysville Appeal of yesterday, reads:

"A telegram was received from Washington to-day, refusing to grant permission to raise a regiment for the East. Gen. Wright telegraphed to the Department some days since, that in his opinion the regiment had better not leave here."

If this be so, those gentlemen who offered to subscribe so liberally to the proposed regiment to Washington, can now have a glorious opportunity of paying over the amount to the Patriotic Fund *[U.S. Sanitary Commission]*, where it will do the cause just as much good. Abundance of troops can be had at the East, but the sick need comforts.

The Daily Bee, Sacramento, Saturday, September 27, 1862.

OCTOBER, 1862

    3-4 Battle of Corinth, Mississippi
       8 Battle of Perryville, Kentucky

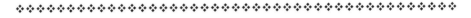

No Regiment from California.- A dispatch from San Francisco to the Sacramento *Union* says that a telegram was received from Washington on the 24th, refusing to grant permission to raise a regiment for the East. Gen. Wright telegraphed to the Department some days since that, in his opinion, the regiment had better not leave here. The 3d Infantry has telegraphed from Ruby Valley to be sent East, stating that $30,000 now due the regiment by the Government will be subscribed towards the expense, and double the amount will be raised, if necessary.

No Soldiers from California.

A short time ago an effort was made by several citizens of this State to raise a regiment for service in the East, and forward it on the route as far as Aspinwall, free of any expense to the Government. The Department at Washington has refused to accept the regiment. The reason of the refusal does not appear. Some have surmised that the War Department fears it may be required on this coast-to keep down secessionists. We will not give the Department discredit for any such foolishness; but it is possible, and probable, that it is believed that the militia of California may be needed to defend the coast from foreign aggression. The present condition of matters does not look very favorable for a long continuance of peace with European powers.

The recent appearance of Edward Everett at Washington, and the reported disagreement of Seward, with the President, in relation to our foreign affairs, indicate the existence of disturbing elements, the nature of which the public have yet to learn. Could the files of the Department of the Secretary of Foreign Affairs be unfolded, it is very probable that we should find ourselves very near the beginning of another and a greater war. With the knowledge of the imminency of difficulties with European nations, the refusal to receive the California Regiment is amply justified. They will be needed nearer home. The following statement of the force of the United States on the Pacific coast, as stated by the N.Y. *Post*, a paper intimately connected with the Administration, shows how completely defenceless California will be in the event of foreign hostilities:

Our present Pacific squadron nominally consists of six vessels, and of these two are gunboats. Annexed is a correct statement of the entire force of the United States, England and France in the Pacific ocean:

	Vessels.	Guns.	Men.
United States	6	84	1,210
England	16	300	3,100
France (about)	9	101	2,000
Total	31	485	6,310

Thus it will be seen that England and France has five times our usual force adjoining one of our most prosperous States.

The Colusa Sun, Colusa, Wednesday, October 4, 1862.
[The Colusa Sun was a strong supporter of the Southern Cause. Edward Everett, orator, statesman and scholar, was the principal speaker at the dedication of the Gettysburg Cemetery, November 19, 1863. William H. Seward, Secretary of State]

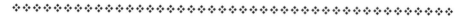

A California Cavalry Company to be raised for the East.

To-day Collector Rankin wrote to Capt. Reed as follows:

San Francisco, October 24, 1862

Capt. J. Sewall Reed-Dear Sir.-I have received from the Governor of Massachusetts a telegram accepting, by authority of the Secretary of War, your offer to raise here a cavalry company of 100 men to form a part of the Massachusetts quota of troops, to go to the East and into active service in the suppression of the rebellion, upon the terms proposed by you through me, to wit: that the company uniform themselves, provide saddles, sabres, revolvers, and all equipments, horses excepted, transportation to the East being provided for them.

Gov. Andrews informs me that the Mayor of Boston agrees to pay $200 for each man which will more than cover the cost of passage.

I congratulate you upon the acceptance of your offer, and have no doubt you will be able in a few days to enlist the number of men you desire of such a character as will do credit to the field and elsewhere to the loyal citizens of California, and be worthy of the well earned fame of the glorious old Bay State. Yours very respectfully,   Ira P. Rankin

The telegram alluded to ran thus:

Commonwealth of Massachusetts
Executive Department
Boston, October 22d, 1862.

Hon. Ira P. Rankin.-The Secretary of War authorizes Massachusetts to accept a cavalry company, subject to the provisions of your letter. The Mayor of Boston agrees to pay $200 each for men, which will cover the cost of transportation.

I await your telegraph that a full company shall be sent. The company should number 100, officers and men, all medically examined and mustered. When can they start? Thanks, and honor to California.

John A. Andrew.
Governor of Massachusetts

So it will be seen that Capt. J. Sewall Reed, of the 1st Light Dragoons of this city, is authorized to raise a company of cavalry to go into service at the East, at once, under the auspices of old Massachusetts. For light cavalry service no better riders or braver men can be found than are in this State; and we may expect to hear great things from them when they go. Capt. Reed will at once commence enlisting his company. To pass examination, every candidate must be a first-class rider, strong, healthy, of about 160 pounds weight, capable of enduring fatigue and the hardest service they may be called on to perform. A Committee, consisting of Collector Rankin, Mayor Teschemacher, Major-General Allen, Assistant Adjutant-General Thompson, Captain C.L. Taylor, James Otis and Dr. Isaac Rowell, will have charge of fitting out the company, and looking out that the proper clothing and equipments are furnished. Captain Reed, who has been actively connected with our State militia for the past ten years, is considered by military men to be well fitted for the command of such a company in the dangerous and honorable duties it will have to perform.

Capt. Reed intends, if possible, to start for the East with his company on the steamer of November 21st.

Evening Bulletin, San Francisco, Friday, October 24, 1862
Alta California, San Francisco, Saturday, October 25, 1862.
The Daily Bee. Sacramento, Saturday, October 25, 1862.
[The First Light Dragoons were organized in San Francisco June 24, 1852.]

The Cavalry Company For The East. - The Committee having in charge the matter of raising a cavalry company for the East, have received a great number of applications from persons in the city, and any number of them from the interior. Assembly Hall at the [Northwest] corner of Kearny and Post streets has been hired, and recruits will be well provided for in every way. The company will be full in a short time; but the very best material stands the only chance.

Evening Bulletin, San Francisco, Monday, October 27, 1862

THE CALIFORNIA CAVALRY COMPANY.- The roll of the Cavalry Company for the East, which is kept at Assembly Hall, will probably be full in less than a week. None but good horsemen, in good health and of fair size need apply. Men from the interior are preferred and the roll will be kept open a reasonable time before selections are made from it. All expenses will be paid as soon as the men are accepted.

Evening Bulletin, San Francisco, Tuesday, October 28, 1862.

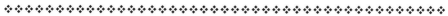

- The Cavalry Company.-We learn from Lt. Staples, recruiting officer in this city, that a dispatch was received from San Francisco yesterday stating that five hundred applications had already been made for admission to the cavalry company now forming to go East. Of this number, some 400 must necessarily be disappointed.

Sacramento Union, Sacramento, Tuesday, October 28, 1862

- News of the Morning.-Those who are engaged in recruiting a cavalry company for service in the East advertise that they would prefer men from the country, accustomed to riding and in robust health. This is a fine chance for good horsemen.

Sacramento Union, Sacramento, Wednesday, October 29, 1862

Aid To The Cavalry Company.

The Committee having in charge the fitting out of the light cavalry company for the East, held a meeting at the Mayor's office on Tuesday afternoon. Mayor Teschemacher was chosen Chairman, James Otis Treasurer, and Lieut. Col. Thompson Secretary.

The following sub-committees were appointed:

Mayor Teschemacher and Collector Rankin to arrange a plan to collect sufficient funds to uniform, arm and equip the Company and defray necessary expenses.

Maj. Gen. Allen and Mayor Teschemacher to contract for the transportation of the Company to New York.

Collector Rankin to correspond with the United States and Massachusetts State authorities at the East, in relation to the movements of the Company.

Major General Allen to contract for uniforms, blankets, etc.

Captain Taylor and Dr. Rowell to assist and advise in relation to men to be enlisted in the company.

The uniforms, arms, horse equipments and camp equipage for the company will be of the best and latest approved patterns, and will be obtained at the government prices. It will cost about $20,000 to place this company in the field ready for service besides the passage money.

Evening Bulletin, San Francisco, Thursday, October 30, 1862
Alta California, San Francisco, Friday, October 31, 1862.

A Suggestion about a Cavalry Company to go East, from a Volunteer in Service.

San Francisco, Oct. 30th, 1862.

Editors Alta—Permit me, through your columns, to propose a plan which I think will meet the approbation of the General Government, the public and the volunteers, of calling into active service at least one company of cavalry, who shall have been raised, and which shall have the honor of bearing arms, from California, *as Californians,* to whom the honor of this State shall be entrusted. In proposing this I do not wish to be understood as wishing to throw any slur against the noble and patriotic men enlisting now under Captain Reed, who, I understand are to belong to the Massachusetts quota, but simply to make a proposition which will chime in and harmonize with all parties.

My proposition is this, that nine men, selected from the *best drilled* ones of each of the twelve companies of the Second Regiment of Cavalry, California Volunteers, be selected as members of the company. Officers to be elected or appointed out of these, from Captain down to eighth Corporal, the balance to be privates in this company. Thus we would have a company of drilled men ready for the field at once, fully armed and equipped. So much as to raising the men. The public of California, or at least the loyal portion, no doubt would feel a pride and honor in raising the means to pay their passage to the States. A very small sum from the many loyal men of California would be sufficient, at any rate to transport them to the States without horses. The General Government would, doubtless, mount them again on their arrival, and give California a chance to strike a blow for the Union.

I know that some may be inclined to cavil and say that our regiment is dispersed, and it would take sometime to call the men. This is the most difficult part of the plan, but still it is not unsurmountable. It will take some little time to collect the men, but the advantages are so great, in my humble opinion, as to make it desirable.

Cavalry to be of much use and to be effective in the field, require from one year to eighteen months drilling before being *fit for active service.* This Company would have been drilled from fourteen to fifteen months, and consequently ready for action as soon as landed in New York. Besides this they would mostly be composed of men inured to camp life, and consequently not so likely to suffer much from disease usually incident to a camp life. Further, as they would be the only troops sent actually as Californians from their State, they would naturally feel a pride which would go far to make them distinguish themselves in action.

Should these remarks suit your columns you would much oblige my fellow soldiers and myself by giving them publicity. I am, sir,

A CALIFORNIA VOLUNTEER.

Alta California, San Francisco, Saturday, November 1, 1862

NOVEMBER, 1862

1 Union begins campaign to capture Vicksburg, Mississippi
7 Major General Burnside replaces McClellan as commander of
the Army of the Potomac

The California Cavalry Company.

Over 100 names of men who have offered themselves for service in the California Cavalry Company now organizing in this city, for service in the East, are now on the muster roll; but this need not deter others from offering, for from all who offer it is determined to select the best men-men in robust health, accustomed to the use of firearms, and expert riders. Recruits from the country will be preferred over those from the city, for the countryman, although not possessed of more courage than the city, is generally healthier and stronger. Drilling is daily going on in Assembly Hall, and the company will soon be advanced sufficiently to be drilled on horseback at the Presidio. Capt. DeMerritt, of the Sacramento Rangers, intends to resign and join this company, if his resignation is accepted, as he says he wants to go into active service, even if he has to go as a sergeant. It was the intention to have sent the company to the East by the steamer of the 21st instant, but it has since been thought better to wait until December 1st, as the men should be drilled as much as possible before they go. Negotiations are now in progress as to their passage East.

Evening Bulletin, San Francisco, Monday, November 3, 1862

BOARD OF SUPERVISORS.

———————

$20.000 For The Cavalry Company - Mr. Redington offered the following resolution which after some discussion was passed to print:

Resolved, That this Board apply to the next Legislature for power to appropriate from the General Fund a sum not to exceed $20,000 for the equipment and transportation East of the California Company of 100 men now being raised in this city.

Alta California, San Francisco, Tuesday, November 4, 1862.
[John H. Redington, Supervisor, 10th Ward and wholesale druggist]

The California Company to Join Banks.

    Collector Rankin has received a despatch from Gov. Andrew of Massachusetts, stating that the cavalry company to be raised here for Massachusetts, is to join Gen. Banks's forces in Texas. The route by which they are to be conveyed thither is not yet settled upon.

Evening Bulletin, San Francisco, Thursday, November 6, 1862

    The California Cavalry Company.-We spoke yesterday of a despatch received to the effect that the California Cavalry Company is to serve under Gen. Banks, in Texas. As the Mayor of Boston has $200 credited for the traveling expenses of each member, it will be at the option of Massachusetts to have a transport ready at Aspinwall to proceed thence to Galveston, or they may keep on direct to Boston. This company, though originating in the Old Bay State, is not altogether a Massachusetts contribution to the war, since the bone, muscle and outfit is furnished by California. It should therefore be a matter of State pride with us to equip them for their approaching service. The proposition to this effect is already before the city authorities. A memorial from the Supervisors to the Legislature for an appropriation of $20,000 for this purpose would undoubtedly be promptly responded to on the assembling of that body, and meantime the requisite funds might be raised by private subscription, among San Franciscans, as a loan, to be repaid on the meeting of the Legislature. A project is on foot for a grand military ball as one means to swell the finances for so laudable a purpose.

Evening Bulletin, San Francisco, Friday, November 7, 1862

    "LEFT OUT IN THE COLD." - The $20,000 appropriation order for the fitting out of the Cavalry Company of former citizens of the Bay State, was indefinitely postponed in the Board of Supervisors, last evening, by the nearly unanimous vote of 11 to 1. One of the most spicy and really entertaining discussions we have heard for a long time occurred on the motion to finally adopt the order calling upon the next Legislature to make the above named appropriation. Mr. Sweeney reiterated the objections urged by him at the last meeting. He believed the proposition emanated with those desirous of making capital for Massachusetts. It was a sectional move, and he denounced it as such. If this Board authorized this appropriation it might do the same for the benefit of other individual States. He would vote the last dollar for the National Army, and if 999 men were raised he would cheerfully offer himself as the thousandth volunteer. He was not afraid of powder. He had smelt it before, and if any man thought otherwise, he had better try him. California had already sent five regiments hence to the field. These had encountered hardships on arid plains, and desolate deserts, but had not received a dollar's compensation from the State. If this money had to be appropriated, it should go to them, rather than to the fitting out of Massachusetts' quota. Mr. Sweeney proceeded to comment on the almost universal condemnation of this proposition by the press, and in bitter terms animadverted on the conduct of those who go counter to enlightened and unbiased public opinion. He beseeched the Board to pause, before endorsing so unjust and unfair a proposition. Mr. Redington retorted in strains ironical, on the speech of the preceding speaker. The motion made at the last meeting to pass the order to print, was made with the intention of giving time for deliberate thought over the feasibility of the proposition. If the same was to be favorably entertained, he desired that there should be no division in the Board on the question. He himself did not think it prudent to send any more troops from the State; but he doubted the idea advanced, that this enterprise was gotten up for the sole benefit of Massachusetts. The troops were to go to Texas, to fight for the Union. He, therefore, in consonance with the views consistently entertained heretofore, moved the indefinite postponement of the resolution.

Mr. McCoppin opposed the authorization of the appropriation, and in the course of his remarks, hit Governor Andrew, of Massachusetts, a very hard blow by referring to his virulent opposition to McClellen. He furthermore insisted that California should keep the remaining force in the State, as an emergency might speedily arise, which would require all of the available force.

The discussion terminated with the decisive and killing vote above given.

Alta California, San Francisco, Tuesday, November 11, 1862.
[Myles D. Sweeny, Supervisor, 2nd Ward, wholesale liquor dealer; Frank McCoppin, Supervisor 11th Ward, Supervisor of the Market Street Railway Co.]

❖❖

At the last meeting (Board of Supervisors) a resolution was passed to print, asking the next Legislature to authorize the Board to appropriate from the General Fund $20,000 to equip and transport Capt. Reed's company of cavalry to Panama, on their way to the East to join a regiment - the Mayor of Boston having agreed to expend the $200 bounty money to each of the 100 men, or $20,000 in all, in paying their passage from the Isthmus to Massachusetts. This resolution now came up for final passage and was opposed in the main by Messrs. Gaven, Sweeny, Redington and McCoppin. It was advanced in debate that Massachusetts having to pay $300 bounty to volunteers or for substitutes, would make a shrewd bargain by getting 100 Californians for only $200 each. Some didn't believe in sharp practice or "shenanigan" of this sort. Let Massachusetts fill her quota with her own citizens, and not come to California for them. The State of California will fill her own regiments with her own citizens. Others said there was nothing mean in this affair. Capt. Reed wanted to raise a company for service at the seat of war. Through Collector Rankin he offered to do so, and Gov. Andrew replied: "If you want to fight come on, and Boston will pay your passage." At last the resolution was indefinitely postponed - Mr. Merrill alone voting "no." (This is the second occasion where individual citizens have earned, very cheaply, a reputation for ultra-patriotism by sending buncome telegrams to the East, pledging the *State*, in name, first for a regiment and next for a company. They ought to have first counted the cost, and been sure of raising the necessary funds out of their own pockets, if by no other way. They may make fools of themselves, but they should not be permitted to throw ridicule on California. - Ed. Bulletin.)

Evening Bulletin, San Francisco, Tuesday, November 11, 1862
[Dominick Gaven, Supervisor, 5th Ward, Real Estate]

❖❖

California Cavalry Company — It is a matter of congratulation that the cavalry company now organizing in this state for active duty in the very heart of the rebellion, will be speedily armed and equipped, and on their way to the seat of the war. Although (and very properly too) no aid is afforded by the State authorities, still loyal and moneyed men are found here, ready and willing to fit the Company out in as complete a manner as are the pet regiments of the Atlantic States. In this connection it is pertinent to quote the remarks made by Mr. Gaven, in the Board of Supervisors, on this subject, which were inadvertently omitted from our report. The gentleman, although a consistent and ardent Union man, and favoring the sustaining of the Government, in all legitimate ways, for the suppression of the rebellion, did not authorize the appropriation of moneys out of the State Treasury for the assistance of men whose identity as Californians will be lost, as it must be, were they incorporated into a regiment from another State. Mr. Gaven declared at the outset of his remarks, that he was for the Union, now and forever. He would cheerfully give his money, and himself, if need be, to maintain the Union. But the Board was called upon to appropriate $20,000 to fit out the quota of Massachusetts. This looked like a speculation. San Francisco is not only to furnish the men, but pay the bounty also. The speaker entertained no animosity against Massachusetts. He could not approve such an appropriation, come from what state it might. We had already sent thousands of our men to Texas, and elsewhere beyond the borders of this State, which regiments are deficient in numbers. We ought to relieve our own troops first. He would vote for forwarding more men at the public expense, and if called upon, would cheerfully contribute his quota, but he did think the present movement savored of local prejudice, a thing proposed by Supervisors hailing from the old Bay State.

Alta California, San Francisco, Friday, November 14, 1862.

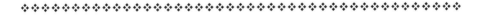

The Cavalry Company. - Over 200 persons are said to have applied to be received into the Cavalry Company for service in the East. The uniforms, saddles, etc., are now being made in this city. Drills are going on nightly at Assembly Hall.

Evening Bulletin San Francisco, Wednesday, November 12, 1862
Sacramento Union, Sacramento, Friday, November 14, 1862

A New Cavalry Regiment In Massachusetts.
The following extracts from a special order issued from the Adjutant General's office, give some information of interest respecting a new cavalry regiment in this State:

It has been decided by the Commander-in-Chief to raise another regiment of cavalry, to be called the Second Massachusetts Cavalry. Captain Charles R. Lowell, of the Sixth United States Cavalry, has been designated as the Colonel: Captain Caspar Crowninshield, of Boston, of the First Massachusetts Cavalry, as Major of the First Battalion, and Captain Frederic Barton, of Springfield, as Major of the Second Battalion.

The Hon. Amos A. Lawrence, of Boston, has been appointed agent to superintend the recruitment of the first battalion, which it is hoped will be filled up from the city of Boston and the Eastern part of the State.

The Hon. Eliphalet Trask, of Springfield, has been appointed to superintend the recruitment of the second battalion, which will be formed in the Western part of the State. It is desirable that these battalions be recruited with all possible despatch.

A company has been offerred to the Commander-in-Chief of Massachusetts, of men residing in San Francisco, in the State of California, and accepted by him, which is now full, and will be designated as Company A, of the first battalion.

The arrangements for beginning the recruitment of the third battalion are not complete, but will be seasonably announced. The work of recruiting the first and second battalions will be immediately begun.

Evening Transcript, Boston, Thursday, November 13, 1862.

❖❖

Lecture By The Rev. Starr King. - The Rev. Mr. King will deliver a lecture in the Music Hall on the evening of Tuesday next for the benefit of Capt. Reed's new Cavalry Company for the East.

Evening Bulletin, San Francisco, Thursday, November 13, 1862

❖❖

The "California Rangers. "-The cavalry company for service in the East will be called the "California Rangers." They expect to sail on the 1st December.

Alta California, San Francisco, Friday, November 14, 1862.
Evening Bulletin, San Francisco, Friday, November 14, 1862

❖❖

The Second Massachusetts Cavalry. Our State [Mass.] has already sent into service a regiment of Cavalry, which compares favorably in discipline and efficiency with even the best Regular Cavalry. The Government now authorizes the recruiting of a second, which it is understood will join the great expedition of Gen. Banks: and we now call attention to the advertisement of our respected fellow citizen, Hon. A. A. Lawrence, who has consented to act as chief recruiting agent for the first battalion.

There is now a chance for such of our young men as have the requisite dash and horsemanship to join a regiment started under the best auspices and intended to be under the command of our Massachusetts General. The officers already named are Colonel, (Captain) Charles R. Lowell, of the 6th Regulars, who distinguished himself at Antietam, while serving on General McClellan's staff, and was, in compliment to his gallantry, sent to Washington with the trophies of that hard fought field. He has already made a name in the regular army, and cannot fail to give a high tone to the regiment he is now to command.

The Major of the 1ˢᵗ is Caspar Crowninshield, of the 1st Mass. Cavalry, well known to those who have watched the war by his gallantry at Ball's Bluff, where he stood beside General Baker when he was killed, and after fighting to the last, swam across the swollen Potomac. He has also been in the most active part of all the late operations on the Potomac, including South Mountain, Antietam, Snicker's Gap, and various skirmishes and reconnoissances. Those who know him best have most confidence in his capacity, valor and coolness. It is believed that the other officers will be selected with reference to services already performed, and to their merit.

The impression has prevailed that cavalry is the most hazardous as well as the most exciting arm of the service, but the experience of our first cavalry does not confirm this view.

They have been in some of the most severe actions of the war, and have thus far lost but one officer killed-the gallant Capt. Pratt. No privates are known to have been killed, although a few are missing-probably prisoners. Two officers and a few men have been made prisoners and released on parole.

Although exposed to the climate of South Carolina, and lately to an active campaign without tents or trains, their health has been wonderfully good on the whole, which may be partly referred to the excellent medical staff, and to the strict discipline of both camp and hospital. With the help of some little recruiting their ranks are now nearly full. May the Massachusetts Second be equally fortunate.

Evening Transcript, Boston, Saturday, November 15, 1862.

❖❖

Capt. DeMerritt, who tendered his resignation as Captain of the Sacramento Rangers, to join the Cavalry Company to go East, was refused the liberty by Gen. Wright.

The Colusa Sun, Colusa, Saturday, November 15, 1862.

❖❖

The New Cavalry Company.- Last evening over fifty of the new cavalry company, now being organized in this State for active service in the East, made their first appearance on the street, under the command of their Captain, J. Sewall Reed. All of them appear to be stout, able-bodied men, worthy representatives of the fighting element of California. They marched very well to the music of the drum and fife. The company is so nearly full that they will be enabled to leave, without doubt, for the seat of war by the 1st proximo. This evening a lecture for the benefit of this cavalry company will be delivered in Platt's Hall *[present day site of the Mills Building]*, by Rev. T. Starr King. The theme selected for the occasion is "Patriotism-its Privileges and Duties." The friends of this movement will doubtless exert themselves to render the benefit a substantial one to the company, and such as will redound to the credit of a State, the loyalty of which has been so frequently attested by its contribution of fighting men, of money, and at the ballot box.

Alta California, San Francisco, Tuesday, November 18, 1862.
Evening Bulletin, San Francisco, Tuesday, November 18, 1862

❖❖

Lecture on Patriotism.-Rev. Starr King redelivered his former lecture on "Patriotism," with very many alterations and additions, last evening at Platt's Hall. There was a large attendance; and the new cavalry company, for whose benefit the entertainment was given, must find their finances materially improved thereby. During his discourse the reverend gentleman recited a very eloquent and elegant poem on the "Rebellion," the author of which is Mr. F.B. Harte. In dwelling on the necessity of California contributing still further to the various calls of patriotism, Mr. King cited not only the cavalry company, but the Matheson Testimonial, Baker's Monument, and the Ladies' Patriotic Fund, as deserving of support. The speaker also made the gratifying statement that probably the next steamer would carry hence to the Sanitary Committee a sum sufficient to swell the total contributions of this State and Nevada Territory to $400,000, being twice as much as had been donated by all the Eastern States combined, although they had contributed to the cause in other ways six or eight times this sum. The lecturer descanted at length on the efforts of politicians at the East to patch up a peace, offering compromises to traitors in arms, etc. He came down savagely on Fernando Wood and his brother Ben, *ex id omne genus*. The War Democrats would never tolerate any tampering with the rebels. The ballot-box should be carried to the camp, and then what a rebuke would be administered to the stay-at-home cowards. This portion of the address was vociferously applauded. The lecture in fact, as an entirety, gave great satisfaction to the audience.

Alta California, San Francisco, Wednesday, November 19, 1862.
[Fernando Wood - former Mayor of NY & reputed leader of the Knights of the Golden Circle.
F.B. Harte aka Bret Harte, writer]

❖❖

The Rev. T. Starr King on Patriotism

The Rev. T. Starr King repeated his lecture on *Patriotism* last evening, for the benefit of the new cavalry company which is recruiting to join Gen. Bank's army in Texas. The house was not well filled - that is, it was a much smaller audience than Mr. King usually lectures to, yet it was comfortably large, and the empty seats would not have been remarked if some less universally popular lecturer had been the speaker of the evening. The night was glorious, and pedestrians felt it cruel to turn in under any roof; there were unusual attractions at the places of amusement, and, we suspect, there is some lukewarmness toward the enterprise itself. The idea of fitting out a Massachusetts company is distasteful to some - the greater the pity for the lack of taste - and those who believe it is noble have not waked up very generally.

Mr. King was introduced by a gentleman whose name we did not obtain, in a neat, brief statement of the objects of the meeting - to help fit out a company to fight the battles of our country, not of Massachusetts, as some would have it.

Mr. King opened with a broadside of hot shot into the Supervisors for their refusal of municipal aid to fit out the company. One of the Supervisors, who made a big speech against the appropriation was there and wears a fiery face ever since. Of the lecture itself we need not speak, as it has been heard by hundreds in the city already. To one who never heard the lecturer before it was magnificent. To the public generally we suspect it was more dry than usual, with more repetitions of the choice things in his other good lectures than usual, and it was too long......

Evening Bulletin, San Francisco, Wednesday, November 19, 1862

❖❖

Capt. Reed's Company. - Captain Reed's Rangers are to be mustered into active service in the U.S. Army forthwith, in accordance with an order received by Gen. Wright from headquarters.

Evening Bulletin, San Francisco, Thursday, November 20, 1862

❖❖

Capt. Reed's California Rangers. - Sixty men have so far been accepted by the U.S. Army Surgeon. There is an opportunity for a few more first-class men if they apply immediately.

Evening Bulletin, San Francisco, Tuesday, November 25, 1862

Presentation to Capt. J. Sewall Reed. - Last evening the Light Dragoons, at a reunion at Assembly Hall, presented some beautiful and serviceable gifts to the commander of the California Rangers. The first was a saddle, with complete equipments for service in the field. It was presented, with an address by private Kimball, of the Light Dragoons, in behalf of the donors, Main & Winchester, who are members of this old company. After Capt. Reed had returned thanks, briefly, ex-Capt. Taylor, for the Light Dragoons, presented him with a pair of Colt's army revolvers, silver and ivory mounted, with this inscription engraved on the handle of each weapon: "To Capt. J. Sewall Reed, from the First Light Dragoons. San Francisco, Nov. 26, 1862."

Capt. Taylor said in his remarks that he had hoped that the Rangers would have been equipped at the expense of the city, which would have been after all but a drop in the bucket compared to what the Eastern cities and towns have been doing since the commencement of the war; and he thought that the citizens of San Francisco would have been much better pleased if the City Government had appropriated a sufficient sum for this purpose, instead of expending so much for what generally proved to be unworthy objects. Capt. Reed, for these, too, responded happily, and then the Rangers and Dragoons sat down to dinner. Capt. Reed's company is now nearly full of as good material as the State can furnish.

Alta California, San Francisco, Thursday, November 27, 1862.
Evening Bulletin, San Francisco, Friday, November 28, 1862
[Charles Main & Ezra Winchester, Leather & Harness Makers, est. 1849]

Gov. Andrew has again postponed the draft in Massachusetts-this time to the 15th inst. This we believe is the fifth postponement he has ordered. Massachusetts is the most backward of all the Eastern States in the matter of volunteering, notwithstanding the enormous bounties-larger than those of any other State-which have been offered.- We wait patiently to hear of those thronged roads and crowding recruiting offices which Gov. Andrew promised us if an emancipation proclamation should be issued. We wait patiently also for Mr. Greely's "thrice three hundred thousand." - *N.Y. World.*

The Weekly Colusa Sun, Colusa, Saturday, November 29, 1862.

For The Wars. - Chas. P. Briggs, William McNeil and Frederick Quant, of this town, have joined the new Cavalry Company, which will leave San Francisco per steamer on Monday, for the East. Charley has been sporting a military cap, and making a military appearance for some time, and it is well, perhaps, that he can now do so by authority.

The Pacific Echo, Napa, Saturday, November 29, 1862.

❖❖❖

DECEMBER, 1862

13 Battle of Fredericksburg, Virginia.
27-29 Battle of Chickasaw Bayou, Mississippi.
31-2 Battle of Murfreesboro, Tennessee

❖❖❖

California Rangers. - Ninety men were mustered into service to-day There are plenty of applicants, and none but the best are selected.

Evening Bulletin, San Francisco, Monday, December 1, 1862

❖❖❖

Hd. Qrs. Cal. Hundred Mass Vol. Co. - Regiment

Special Order
____No. 1
The Company will assemble at Armory on Tuesday December 2nd 1862 at 3 P.M. to be Mustered into Service for 3 years or during the War.

By Order
J. Sewall Reed,
San Francisco   Comdg Co
Dec. 1st 1862.

Regimental Record Books, National Archives, Washington, D.C.

❖❖❖

The California Rangers.-Seventy-four applicants for admission into this company, in San Francisco, have passed the medical examination.

Sacramento Union, Sacramento, Tuesday, December 2, 1862

❖❖❖

California Rangers.- At 2 o'clock yesterday the California Rangers, numbering 86 men, were mustered into the United States service by Col. Ringgold. The company are now quartered at Assembly Hall and are performing garrison duty. Part of the uniform, consisting of caps, blouses, and blankets, have arrived, and the rest will come in to-day. The clothing outfit of the company is furnished by the subscriptions of citizens of this city and will cost $4,000. The $20,000 appropriated by the State of Massachusetts will be used to pay the passage of the company East, and to purchase arms, horse, equipments, etc. on their arrival East. Only 14 more men are required to fill up the ranks to the proper standard.

Evening Bulletin, San Francisco, Wednesday, December 3, 1862
[Lt. Col. George H. Ringgold, Deputy Paymaster, Department of the Pacific]

❖ ❖

Help to the "California Hundred" - The Captain of the Summer Light Guard has sent the under added communication to the Captain of the California Cavalry Company:

Headquarters Company I,
First Regiment C. M.
San Francisco, December 2, 1862

J. Sewall Reed, Captain California Rangers - At the regular monthly meeting of the Summer Light Guard, held last evening, a resolution was unanimously adopted, donating to the California Rangers $100 to aid in their outfit.

Enclosed you will find a check for said amount, which though but a small sum, please accept as an expression of our appreciation and encouragement of your patriotic corps, who so nobly go forth as representatives of California in our nation's struggle.

T. R. Ludlum
Captain Commanding Summer Light Guard,

The Company numbers now eighty five men, stalwart, healthy, and in every respect suitable for active service. They were mustered into service yesterday, by Colonel Ringgold. The full quota will be made up before the departure of the next steamer. It is expected that the Company will leave by the steamer of the 21st, for the Atlantic States. Most of the uniform of the Company is already in their possession. The future career of this corps will be watched with eager anxiety by Californians.

Alta California, San Francisco, Thursday, December 4, 1862.

❖ ❖

Full Ranks.-Capt. Reed's California Rangers received an accession of eight more men today, which brings the company up to the full standard of 100.

Some two weeks ago, 100 yards of cloth belonging to the Company were stolen from the State Prison, where it was being manufactured into uniforms. This delayed the company over one steamer. The Mission Woolen Mills, however, soon made up the deficiency, and they will be able to get away on the 11th December. Kidd's Band have volunteered to escort the Rangers to the steamer on Thursday next.

Evening Bulletin, San Francisco, Friday, December 5, 1862
[San Quentin Prison established 1852.]

❖ ❖

The Cavalry Company Review- Presentation of a Sword to The First Lieutenant-A Theatrical Benefit Tendered.-The California Cavalry Company is now full, mustered into active service, and will be ready to leave for the Atlantic States on the steamer of the eleventh instant. They paraded through Montgomery street yesterday afternoon in their new and neat uniform, and with sabres. Their martial bearing and regular soldier-like movements elicited the heartiest commendations from the bystanders. The company was reviewed on the Plaza by General Wright at three o'clock, and that officer expressed himself as highly gratified at their appearance on parade. In the evening the company met for drill at Assembly Hall on Kearny street. While they were going through their evolutions, the First Lieutenant was called out and presented with a magnificent sword and paraphernalia, all of the latest style and most exquisite workmanship. A massive gold plate on the scabbard, bears the following inscription: "Presented to Archibald McKendry, by his friends, December 6th, 1862." The sword and scabbard are both elaborately carved. A steel hilt with three handsomely turned ribs, and ornamented with a beautiful piece of California quartz, sets off the sword to perfection. Besides the sword and scabbard, are splendid gauntlets, sash, belt, and sabre knot, all rich and tasteful. The total value of sword and accoutrements is not less than one hundred and fifty dollars. The presentation speech was made in very appropriate terms by Hon. Geo. Amerige, and felicitously responded to by the recipient. The company is now doing regular garrison duty, and we sincerely believe that California will be proud of their conduct whenever confronted by the foes of the Union. As an agreeable *Addendum* to this article, it may be stated that the loyal theatrical manager, Mr. W. H. Leighton, tendered a benefit to the Company, which will take place at the American Theatre on Tuesday or Wednesday of this week.

Alta California, San Francisco, Sunday, December 7, 1862.
[George Amerige, printer and San Francisco Assemblyman, 1862 Session]

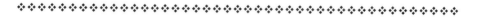

The Pirate's Doings.

News reached San Francisco on Saturday last that the steamer *Ariel*, engaged in the California trade, and running between New York and Aspinwall, had been captured by the pirate ship *Alabama*. The particulars are as follows: On Sunday, Dec. 7th, the *Ariel* was off the southwestern end of Cuba. At 1 o'clock, P.M., when about fifteen miles distant from land, she sighted the rebel cruiser, which was under easy sail. She was heading for Cuba, but in about an hour altered her course and ran down toward the Ariel - the latter having kept steadily on her course, not having suspected the character of the other vessel. The Alabama kept the stars and stripes at the fore, and, when she came near enough to make out that she was a steamer, it was supposed that she was a United States cruiser. As the Ariel got within range the rebel hauled down the gridiron, and hoisted the stars and bars, at the same time firing a blank cartridge across the Ariel's bows, which is plain English for "come to." As the Ariel did not stop her engines when requested, the pirate sent his compliments in the shape of two shots - a 100 lb. and a 68 pounder, it is said. The latter struck the mainmast and splintered it. When the shots were fired the Ariel's flag was hauled down and the engines stopped; presently she was boarded by a boat's crew under command of Lieut. Lowe, who demanded from Capt. Jones the ship's papers, passenger list, treasure and arms, and took possession of the vessel as a prize to the Confederate Government. The U.S. Marines, who were designed to garrison Mare Island, were stripped of their arms and paroled "not to serve against the Confederate States during the war." The Lieutenant took in the way of treasure $1500 in coin and $8,500 in green-backs. All Sunday night the steamers lay to with signal lanterns to avoid collision. The next morning the pirate signaled the Ariel to follow her, and they steamed back toward San Domingo. About "six bells" in the afternoon watch they made out a steamer in the distance in which they had been looking for the steamer *Champion* with the California treasure. The sails of the Ariel were unbent and thrown overboard by order of the rebel, and they carried off one of the valves of the engine to prevent the steamer from getting away while they were in pursuit of the Champion. The sail in sight proved not to be the Champion, and the pursuit was abandoned. At night the valve was returned and replaced, and the Ariel was then ordered to follow, heading for Jamaica. Same night, the cruiser overhauled a Dutch craft, but when her nationality was discovered she was allowed to pass on. Next day, off Jamaica, another Dutch vessel was spoken, and Captain Semmes obtained information which led him to abandon his intention of landing the passengers at Kingston and burning the vessel. He said he had ascertained that the yellow fever was raging at Kingston, and he would not expose the lives of the passengers, but it is more likely that he learned of the presence of U.S. cruisers in the vicinity, and did not dare to linger. Capt. Jones was then compelled to give bond for the value of the ship, cargo and freight - in all, $250,000 - to be paid within thirty days after the independence of the Confederate States shall have been gained. The Alabama then shut off steam, hoisted her propeller, made sail, and was soon hull down away to the eastward.

Marin County Journal, San Rafael, Saturday, January 3, 1863.
[Piracy was to be of concern to the Californians' voyage as well, see C.P. Briggs letter of Dec. 23, 1862]

❖❖❖

THE CALIFORNIA HUNDRED before leaving San Francisco were the recipients of many attentions and an abundance of patriotic good wishes. On the morning of Sunday, Dec. 7th, 1862, they attended the First Unitarian Church, the pastor of which, Rev. T. S. King, preached an appropriate discourse from the text, " Be not weary in well doing, for in due season we shall reap if we faint not." Capt. Reed has furnished us for publication the following extracts from this production, in which his noble command was specially addressed.

———

There is another appeal to us in the church today, not to be weary in well-doing. It is the presence of soldiers who offer, not something of their income, but their capital,-not a word merely, or a vote, a speech, a subscription, but *themselves* to their country and to freedom, for your cause and mine, and for the good and honor of our children. Each of them dedicates his whole personality.

They are not drafted; they are not even *asked* to volunteer. They do not wait for the pressure of a request. They were moved from within. They hear from afar the thunder of the captains and the war-shout. They see across the continent the peril of the flag. They leave all, and follow the beckoning of an idea.

God bless you, brother Americans, for your readiness, for your zeal, for your pure offering of devotedness, which today add force as well as illustration to the pleading of the Gospel with our hearts! You are not "weary" of the call and the strain of patriotism. There are those at the East who are. They wear no wounds nor scars. They have not exposed their lives. They have not scented the sulphur of battle. They scent only the war-tax. They ache for more prosperity, though it be bought with infamy. They fear that their country may be pledged to an idea, and that freedom, the sound of whose syllables they hate, may become continental. Once, months ago, they were swept into a nobler mood. But they now go to the ballot box and vote that they are "weary of well-doing;" vote peril to their country; vote the entering wedge of a base compromise; vote their own lasting shame.

And you, in these same hours, *seek the opportunity* of pledging strength and skill, and blood and breath, to our country's integrity and honor. Heaven hear our prayers for you and cover you with its benediction! You are to use the sabre. May the flash of your blades, if you are called into battle, be part of the dawn of a better age for your country! You will ride into conflict. God give your horses strength, and clothe their necks with thunder! May the glory of their nostrils be terrible; may they swallow the ground with fierceness and rage, when they smell the battle afar off! And may they help, in the crisis of the struggle, when the hope and future of the country, are at stake, to put to flight the army of the aliens!

Go, brethren, to your tremendous duty with dedicated hearts,-in the fear of God, which roots out all other fear; in allegiance to Christ; with the New Testament very near your hand, and its appeal very sweet to your souls! "Be not weary with well doing," though your marches be long, and your hope of speedy success be denied. In due time you shall reap if you faint not, and if those you leave at home be not cowards and traitors both. You shall reap, though you bleed; though be maimed; though you die; you shall reap in your country's redemption and renewal,-in the honor that will invest your names in future years,-in your reward in the better world.

Evening Transcript, Boston, Wednesday, January 14, 1863

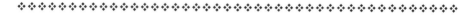

The California Rangers

Captain Reed's company of cavalry appeared on Saturday afternoon, for the first time, in their new uniforms. They marched through some of the principal streets to the Plaza, where they were informally reviewed by Gen. Wright and staff. The General told the Rangers they were the finest company he had ever seen. "Your marching is splendid," said he, "and I would like to command 1,000 men like you upon the field of battle." Mayor Teschemacher and several prominent citizens have been named a committee to make arrangements for giving the company a complimentary ball and supper, to take place on Wednesday evening, at Platt's Hall. The proceeds of the entertainment will be appropriated to the outfit of the troop.

The principal theatrical talent of the city, too, has volunteered to give the company a benefit, which will take place at the American Theatre, some evening this week.

An effort is now being made in the city to raise sufficient funds to enable the company to purchase a complete outfit, in every particular, so that they will not be under the necessity of drawing upon the Government for anything but their rations.

On Saturday evening Capt. Reed received from his friends a $50 regulation sash, and the 1st Lieutenant of the Company, A. McKendry, was presented with a fine sword and its equipments.

Yesterday morning the rangers attended in a body divine service at the church of the Rev. T. Starr King.

After the return of the company to their quarters about 1 o'clock P.M., they were supplied, each man, with a copy of the New Testament, by the California Bible Society. The company were drawn up on three sides of a hollow square, and gave the strictest attention while they were addressed by the Agent, the Rev. Mr. Buel.

PRESENTED WITH TESTAMENTS

The design of the remarks was to impress the volunteers that the worth of the book was not to be estimated by them in its pecuniary value, but as a testimony of the interest which was felt in them by good men, so that whenever they held the book in their hands they might look upon it as a pledge that the sympathy and prayer of Christian men followed them wherever they might be, in the camp, on the march and on the battlefield; that the book was given them to make them better men, for the teachings of the book would lead them in the path of virtue, honor and truth, and to make them better soldiers, for it set forth the government, not a mere creature of human caprice, but the ordinance of God, and, while they fought for the support of the Government, which their fathers gave their blood and lives to found, taught by the truths of the Holy Book, they would do it with the advantage that as the God of their fathers would honor His own ordinance and bless with His favor those who periled their lives for the defense of the Government; better soldiers, because discipline gives to a military body its joints and bones, united efficiency and solidity; a company of soldiers disciplined is like a bludgeon, with which one may strike a deadly blow-undisciplined, it is a mass of shavings, and the teaching of the Word was, "Let every soul be subject to the higher powers," better soldiers, for, led by the truth of the Gospel to commit his soul to the keeping of the Lord Jesus Christ, the soldier is ready for all things, for life or death-to die on the field of battle if there the path of duty leads him.

The idea that religion unfits a man for a soldier was a delusion. Commodore Foote says that on the night before the battle of Fort Donelson, he wrestled with God in prayer until he was assured of victory, and where was he on the day of that fight? In the pilot house of the flagship of the flotilla, in the most exposed position of the whole battle, and when his pilot was shot at the wheel he was sprinkled by his blood, and himself severely wounded by the same discharge.

In conclusion, the blessing of God was invoked on the company in all their marches and exposures on the field of battle. Then some little boys and girls, who were present, with ready hands and nimble feet entered on the distribution of the books, and very briefly every soldier was supplied with a copy of the New Testament.

In the evening 43 of their number

JOINED THE DASHAWAYS

They proceeded to Dashaway Hall and signed the pledge in accordance with a mutual agreement of which the following is a copy:

We, the undersigned, members of the Cavalry Company known as the "California Hundred," do hereby agree to join the Dashaway Association on the evening of the 7th day of December, 1862.

James Freeman	G. I. Holt
Samuel Corbell	G. O. Grindle
C. H. Willis	W. H. Hussey
H. G. Burlingham	J. H. Williams
John Winship	M. C. Pool
Peter E. White	Frank Baker
R. S. Ellet	J. F. McNutt

W. H. Bumgardner
C. W. Hill
James Pelham
Henry H. Tillebrown
George Plummel
E. W. Woodward
W. Chandler
H. Rice
W. Cunningham
William Hammerberg
J. C. Ross
G. F. Davis
Frank Knowles
Charles Rhone

W. W. West
John Fletcher
Hugh Armstrong
G. W. Vierick
J. W. Owen
F. J. Quant
J. Blaker
N. A. Beach
R. M. Parker
Mr. Tubbs
J. D. Barnstead
F. Libby
I. Nixon
J. I. McCarty

The agreement was kept and all of the above are Dashaways; they will go sober men to the field and through its perils. California may well be proud of them.

The sympathies of all Californians should most assuredly go with this company for in their appearance and demeanor, both officers and men, they seem worthy of it.

Evening Bulletin, San Francisco, Monday, December 8, 1862
Alta California, San Francisco, Tuesday, December 9th, 1862
[The Dashaway Association was a temperance society that appears to have been organized in San Francisco early in 1849 by the Howard Engine Co., a volunteer fire company who after an evening of overindulgence and undoubtedly hung over, pledged itself to total abstinence cementing the vow by smashing all remaining supplies of alcoholic beverages. Names have been left as published]

Monday, December 8, 1862.

At a meeting of the friends of Captain Reed's Cavalry Company, it was resolved to give them a SUPPER AND BALL, prior to their departure for the Seat of War, on THURSDAY NEXT.

The following gentlemen were named as a Committee, to complete arrangements, and are requested to meet at the Room of the Board of Supervisors THIS DAY, Monday, Dec. 8th, 1862, at 12 o'clock.

H F Teschmacher
G C Shreve,
John C Merrill,
O V Sawyer,
G W Blake,
N Holland,
P W Shepheard,
W H Sharp,
John W Tucker,
H S Brown,
James Otis,
S H Parker,

Fred Billings,
T W Park,
Cyrus Palmer,
A P Stanford,
E H Washburn,
G C Potter
Albert Dibblee,
E L Sullivan,
Robt J Tiffany,
M S Whiting,
A S Tubbs,
Sam'l Cowles

Walter S Denio,
S C Bigelow,
Chas A Crane,
F MacCrellish,
O L Shalter,
George Tait,
C Watrous,
Franklin Tuthill,
Jacob Underhill,
Frank Soule,
T L Barker.

R G Sneath,	A T Lawton,	G W Rand,
R Chenery,	J B Thomas,	W Cheesman,
J Britton,	H Baker,	Wm C Ralston,
E F Beale,	Peter Donahue,	G Amerage,
Jacob Bacon,	M C Blake,	George Reed,
S C Ellis,	C B Marvin,	E W Bourne,
A G Abell,	J McM Shafter,	J H Catten,
H P Coon,	G H Moore	H B Williams,
A J Pope,	O F Willey,	John Whitman,
John White,	Henry Webb,	Joseph Hobart,
H L Dodge,	Ogden Hoffman,	R L Ogden,
C S Hobbs,	G W Gilmore,	C W Hathaway,
W A Macondray,	C T Fay,	S C Harding,
J C Johnson,	Chas Main,	Wm Sherman,
H M Hale,	B A Sheldon,	Thos Young,
H L Davis,	I P Rankin	Wm G Patch,
Wm H Keith,	H M Newhall,	R B Swain,
Henry Seligman,	Samuel Soule,	C C Webb,
Daniel Norcross,	C L Taylor,	B H Freeman,
W C Hinckley,	Wm H Stevens,	David Dwyer,
D B Northrop,	Wm B Farwell,	John J Kelly,
J H Stearns,	L T Lander,	George J Brooks,
S H Wetherbee,	J P H Wentworth,	A J Ellis
James Jayres,	Jn E Kincade,	

Alta California, San Francisco, Monday, December 8, 1862.
[All leading officials, merchants and financiers]

Farewell Ovation to the Calvary Company.

The gallant fellows who have enlisted in the Cavalry Company, to go hence on the 11th instant, for the purpose of aiding the Government in the suppression of the rebellion, will be the recipients of a complimentary testimonial from our citizens prior to their departure. Initiative steps were taken yesterday at the City Hall, where a number of our leading men assembled and resolved to extend to the California Rangers a musical festival. The Collector of the Port, Ira P. Rankin, was appointed Chairman of the meeting, and E. H. Washburn, Secretary. The following named gentlemen were elected as a Committee of Arrangements to carry out the details of the proposed festival, *i.e.* E.H. Washburn, W.A. Macondray, G.W. Blake, J. Brittan, George Amerige, O.F. Willey, C.C. Webb, W.S. Denio, W.C. Hincley, and Col. Wood. The festival will take place this evening at Platt's Hall. Tickets can be procured at Blake's hat store, and we hope that our loyal citizens generally will purchase them freely, inasmuch as the "Rangers" ought to be handsomely fitted out by the people of a metropolis who are, and have been, benefited pecuniarily, rather than injured, by the war now raging on the other side of the continent.

Evening Bulletin, San Francisco, Monday, December 8, 1862
Alta California, San Francisco, Tuesday, December 9, 1862.

CITIZENS' DEMONSTRATION !

In Honor of

CAPTAIN REED'S COMPANY

....OF

CALIFORNIA RANGERS.

Promenade. Musicale and Ball,

....AT....

PLATT'S MUSIC HALL,

....ON......

Tuesday Evening, Dec. 9th.

THIS ENTERTAINMENT is tendered to this company on occasion of their departure for the seat of war. Citizens generally, and the military especially, are invited to participate.

C I Drumm has generously tendered the services of the Presidio Band, and the Rev, T/Hiarr King and other speakers will d-ll er addresses on the occasion.

TICKETS   ONE DOLLAR

The military are requested to appear in uni orm.

H. N. BLAKE,

Jnh.2t   Secretary Committee of Arrangements.

Alta California, San Francisco, Tuesday, December 9, 1862.

MILITARY ELECTION.-The following officers were elected last evening by the First Light Dragoons: Captain-C. L. Taylor; First Lieutenant-David Moore; Second Lieutenant-M. E. Fitz-Gibbon; Brevet Second Lieutenant-J. Browning; Orderly Sergeant-H. Kruse; The Company also passed the following:

Resolved, That this Company tender the Rev. Thomas Starr King a vote of thanks for his liberality and kindness, in tendering his services to this Company, in a lecture for the benefit of Capt. Reed's new Cavalry Company, and that the Secretary be instructed to communicate the same to Mr. King.

PROVOST GUARD.-Captain DeMerritt's Company, which has been doing Provost Guard duty here, having been ordered to Sacramento, a detachment of equal numbers, of late recruits, rode in from the Presidio camp yesterday, and will be detailed for service in this city.

Alta California, San Francisco, Tuesday, December 9, 1862.
[Sacramento Rangers]

One Hundred Men for One Woman!

- A French novel by Chevalier has just reached town with the startling title "Fifty Men for One Woman." But truth in San Francisco is almost three fold stranger than French fiction. See the proof. At Post Street Hall, Captain Reed's new cavalry Company, destined for the East, were reviewed and inspected last night by Lieutenant Colonel Thompson, after which the Reverend T. Starr King came forward to address the soldiers, which he did of course, most felicitously. He then read a communication from the President of the "Ladies Patriotic Fund Society," offering to care for the families of each of the soldiers present as might need their aid and council. Then Captain Reed desired that all the married men step one pace to the front. This order was obeyed by but one man only, and upon inquiry his wife was found to be with her own family at the East. So suitable a circumstance as this must attract the attention of our fair countrywomen at the East and induce a liberal emigration at once.

Evening Bulletin, San Francisco, Tuesday, December 9, 1862
The Weekly Colusa Sun, Colusa, Saturday, December 20, 1862
[The married man was Joseph Burdick - he was the first unit fatality- South Anna Bridge, June 1863. Lt. Col. DeWitt C. Thompson, Assistant Adjutant General of California and subsequent organizer and Commander of the California Battalion.]

The Ovation to the California Rangers-

Platt's Music Hall was very tastefully and generally dressed in flags, streamers, &c., for the occasion of the festival given last evening, in honor of the speedy departure to the scene of hostilities in the East, of the California Cavalry Company. Owing to the inclemency of the weather the attendance of ladies was not as numerous as it would certainly have been had the elements been more propitious. The band of the Ninth Regiment played at intervals some choice selections of music. Then marched in the "one hundred," (lacking a dozen or so, absent on guard duty,) who went through various evolutions, under command of Captain Reed. The very flattering encomiums passed upon their proficiency in drill, on former occasions, were repeated continually throughout the evening. Certainly a more intelligent and fine-looking body of soldiers, of equal numbers, we have never seen.

E. H. Washburn, Esq., mounted the rostrum and briefly stated the order of the evening's entertainment, the programme consisting of music, dancing, addresses, etc. Mr. Rankin subsequently introduced Mr. Washburn who made a most felicitous, feeling and eloquent speech to the troops drawn up in a hollow square in front of the stage. He exhorted them to remember that the eyes of the civilized world would be fastened upon them; that they were destined to achieve imperishable renown, or endure hereafter ignominy and disgrace if they failed to do their duty to their country and themselves. But he would not insult them by harboring the latter suspicion, for he knew them to be gallant, brave, and in fact the picked men of California. After wishing for them a speedy trip, glorious victories and a safe return to their adopted State, he bade them farewell. Nathan Porter, and Edward Tompkins, Esqs., also spoke words of encouragement, and complimented the men on their soldierly appearance. The following note was read to the assemblage by Mr. Washburn at the opening of the exercises:

"*To the Committee of Arrangements for the Festival in honor of the California Rangers*:

"Gentlemen-I regret to inform you that a duty which I cannot postpone will prevent my attendance at the entertainment this evening, in honor of the Cavalry Company, until an hour that, probably, will be too late for speaking.

"As for the soldiers, they speak for themselves to every American who has an eye for noble symmetry and strength. Never was patriotism more worthily embodied. If the Government desires to see them fitly mounted for duty, it should provide for them a hundred full blood Black Hawks-horses such as Shakspeare describes, that 'bound from the earth as if their entrails were hairs,' horses that 'trot the air,' horses that 'make the earth sing when they touch it,' horses 'whose neighing is like the bidding of a monarch.'

"Wherever these men serve the country's cause-whether in Texas or in Virginia-may Heaven's blessing attend them, and invigorate their hearts and arms and steel against the enemies of the hope and honor of the American Republic! And may God grant them health and victory!

"With sincere regret that I cannot be with you in the early part of the entertainment, I am

Yours cordially,

T. S. King.

San Francisco Tuesday, Dec. 9th, 1862.

The festivities were prolonged until a late hour, and the "Rangers" entered into the spirit of the dance as enthusiastically as they executed their more martial manoeuvrings.

It is understood that this Company will report for duty at Boston direct, and will constitute one of four companies allotted to Massachusetts, under the new cavalry regiment raising for service in the Eastern States.

This evening a grand theatrical entertainment is to be given by the Leighton troupe for the benefit of the "One Hundred." We hope it will be all the more substantial from the fact of the attendance being so slim last evening, for the reason stated above. The Ellsworth Rifles have tendered their services, and will enhance the attractions of the festival by going through their skirmishing drill. The Cavalry Company will appear in full uniform. On Thursday morning they take their departure on the Panama steamer.

Alta California, San Francisco, Wednesday, December 10, 1862.
Evening Bulletin, San Francisco, Wednesday, December 10, 1862
Evening Transcript, Boston, Saturday, January 10, 1863
[Nathan Porter, City & County District Attorney; Edward Tompkins, Attorney]

❖❖

AMERICAN · THEATRE !
Corner of Sansome and Halleck streets.

W: H. LEIGHTON,................................MANAGER

COMPLIMENTARY BENEFIT
....TO THE....

CALIFORNIA HUNDRED,

Prior to their Departure for the Seat of War.

Tendered by Mr. W. H. Leighton,

On which occasion the following talented Artistes will
appear, (having kindly volunteered:) Mrs. W. H. Leighton, Mrs. W. C. Forbes, D C. Anderson, W. Barry, J. H.
O'Neil, Yankee Locke, W. C Forbes, William Aymar, A.
Fischer, and a host of others.

The celebrated ELLSWORTH RIFLES, Capt. McDonald,
will appear in their famous Zouave Drill, (having kindly
volunteered for the occasion)
The CALIFORNIA HUNDRED will attend in full uniform.

WEDNESDAY EVENING, DECEMBER 10,
Will be performed the elegant comedy of

PERFECTION.

Kate O'Brien............................Mrs W C Forbes
Susan, Miss I Land....Str Lawrence Parnyon, W H
Leighton... Sam, W Barry.

After which, Grand Drill by the Ellsworth Rifles, in
which they will introduce many new and interesting
movements.
Operatic and Dramatic Jig.....................J H O'Neil
Advice to Husbands.......................Mrs W C Forbes
To conclude with the ever welcome

FOOL OF THE FAMILY.
Betty Saunders, with songs.............Mrs W H Leighton

Admission,...................... One Dollar.
de10 lt

Alta California

❖❖

Review of The California Rangers.-At 3 o'clock to-day there was to be on the Plaza a review of the California Rangers by Gen. Allen, at which time it was expected that there would be presented to the company a beautiful silk guidon, with the letters "U.S." and a picture of a grizzly bear painted in the centre. The company have all their baggage packed up, ready to start. They will be escorted to-morrow morning to the *Golden Age* by the 1st Light Dragoons, on foot, headed by Kidd's band of 20 pieces. The members of the band will be attired in their new uniform. The Light Dragoons have loaned the Rangers their sabres to drill with on the voyage to New York.

Evening Bulletin, San Francisco, Wednesday, December 10, 1862

❖❖

Special Order
    No. 3
Until further orders Private Hugh Armstrong is hereby detailed and will act as First Sergeant, Private James L. Wheat is hereby detailed as acting Quarter Master Sergeant, Private Henry G. Burlingham is hereby detailed as acting Commissary Sergeant. They will be respected accordingly.

                        By Order
Assembly Hall   J. Sewall Reed
    San Francisco Cal. Captain
        December 10th 1862   Commanding Co.

Special Order
    No. 4
                    Until further orders there will be detailed from the Guard one Sergeant and one Corporal to be announced daily by the Orderly Sergeant when guard is detailed.

                    Said Sergeant and Corporal to rank as Lance Sergeant and Corporal, and will be obeyed accordingly.

                        By Order
Assembly Hall   J. Sewall Reed
    San Francisco, Cal.   Capt. Comdg. Co.
        December 10th 1862

Special Order
    No. 5
                    This Company will assemble at the Armory on Thursday Dec 11th at 9 Oclock A.M. for embarcation on Steamer Golden Age for New York. All Company freight & Baggage will be taken charge of By Act. Quarter Master Segt. & provide transportation to Steamer.

                        By Order
                        J. Sewall Reed
                            Capt. Commanding

Special Order
    No. 6
                    The Cap & Blouse will be worn on Steamer as uniform at Guard. Mounting the Guard will appear in full uniform.

                        By Order
                        J. Sewall Reed
                            Captain

Special Order

           The following are the Non-Commissioned Officers of Co. "A" (California Hundred) 2nd Mass. Cavalry.

Orderly Sergt		H. Armstrong
Quarter Master	do	Chas. M. Kinne
1st Duty do		H. Burlingham
2nd do	do	G. C. Doane
3rd do	do	H. Crum
4th do	do	J. L. Wheat
5th do	do	C. E. Allen
6th do	do	C. Powers
1st Corporal		I. R. McIntosh
2nd do		C. Dewey
3rd do		W. N. Percy
4th do		F. J. Quant
5th do		B. Locke
6th do		J. A. Hill
7th do		E. R. Sterling
8th do		W. Woodman

           By Order J. Sewall Reed
                Capt.

Regimental Record Books, National Archives, Washington, D.C.

    Review of the California Hundred.-Captain Reed's cavalry company of California Rangers, or as they are at present, and will be in the future, best known, "The California Hundred," were reviewed on the Plaza (Portsmouth Square) yesterday afternoon, by Mayor Teschemacher and other prominent citizens. They were also inspected by Lieut. Col. Thompson, after which they paraded through the principal streets and returned to their headquarters at Assembly Hall. The company were presented yesterday with a fine guidon by D. Norcross, Esq. It is composed of white and crimson silk, having the letters U. S. in gilt over a California grizzly bear, which latter, we presume, will be adopted as an appropriate emblem by the troop. It will not be the first time that the "Bear Flag" has been borne on the battlefield. The guidon is beautifully mounted, and reflects great credit upon Mr. Norcross' taste in getting it up in the nick of time, and his liberality in bestowing it upon the gallant fellows who are to carry it when doing battle for the Union. A visit to their barracks showed that they were all in readiness for their departure to the East, by the steamer *Golden Age* today. Blankets, overcoats, trunks and traveling sacks were piled in order; and some few, who are disposed to "be jolly" under all circumstances, carry with them musical instruments, with which to beguile the monotony of the sea voyage. A lighter and more serviceable sabre than that now used (by the kindness of the First Light Dragoons) will be provided them on their arrival at their destination, Boston. The company attended the theatrical entertainment given for their benefit by the Leighton troupe, at the American Theatre, last evening, and which was well patronized by the public. The drill of the Ellsworth Rifles, Capt. McDonald, called forth the admiration of the audience. The "Hundred" will be escorted to the steamer this morning by the Vallejo Rifles, Captain Frisbie, (which company arrived last evening) the Light Dragoons, Kidd's Brass Band of 20 pieces, and a Committee of citizens. Accommodations have been provided expressly for the Company on board the steamer, equal to those of the second cabin class of passengers, for which they pay at the rate of $60 per man. May they have a prosperous voyage and have an early chance to distinguish themselves as Californian horsemen upon the battlefield, and the day will come when that grizzly guidon will take its place as one of California's proudest momentoes of the times that tried men's love for the union.

The Military Academy of California.-Although we have no State Military Academy, San Francisco possesses a military school-the Old Guard-the First California Guard, (artillery), Captain Bluxome. Two more graduates leave on the steamer to-day, members of the "California One Hundred," Capt. Reed, John W. Sim, Second Lieutenant and *twenty-sixth* member of the Old Guard, now holding a commission from the United States Government, and Private Chas. M. Kinne, the thirty-first member of the Old Guard in the United States service. We believe that this record is unsurpassed-that no militia organization in the Union can show an equal list of commissioned officers in the regular service, or so many who have distinguished themselves. All honor to "The Old Guard." May she prove the West Point of California! The military record of Mr. John W. Sim, late one of the Deputy Sheriffs of this county, is as follows: was elected a member of the First California Guard (light battery) November 10th, 1859; elected 3d sergeant, May 3d. 1860; appointed 2d sergeant, July 26th, 1860; appointed first sergeant, May 16th. 1861; resigned from the company, May 30th, 1861; reelected a member of the company, September 26th, 1861; elected Junior First Lieutenant, Nov. 21st. 1861; resigned from the company August 5th. 1862; transferred to active roll, Oct. 14th. 1862; elected an honorary member, August 5th. 1862; elected Senior First Lieutenant, Nov. 4th 1862; Second Lieutenant cavalry company (California Rangers) going East, Dec. 1st.

The military record of Charles M. Kinne, late bookkeeper for Thomas Ogg Shaw, is as follows; was elected a member of the First California Guard on May 17th, 1859; appointed fourth corporal, July 26th, 1861; by Capt. Ellis, now Brigadier General, C. S. M.; appointed third sergeant, May 16th, 1861, by Capt. Ellis; elected Secretary of the company, Sept. 26th, 1861; appointed first sergeant, October 10th, 1861, by Capt. I. Bluxome, jr.; elected Second Lieutenant, Sept. 2d, 1862; goes East as a member of Capt. Reed's cavalry company, Dec. 11th, 1862.

The First California Guard will take out one section of their battery (two guns) this morning, and salute their old comrades. May success attend them.

Alta California, San Francisco, Thursday, December 11, 1862.
[Daniel Norcross, Lt. Col. & Paymaster, 2nd Division, California Militia also Merchant providing military goods and regalia. Captain Reed's wife, Hattie L. and although not mentioned, their son Walter Sewall who was born in California Jan. 25, 1861. The bear "roundel" was painted on both sides by Frederick Nutz, a signpainter in San Francisco.]

PACIFIC MAIL STEAMSHIP CO.

THE FOLLOWING

 Steamships will be dispatched in the Month of December, 1862:

Dec. 11th—GOLDEN AGE, W. H. Hudson, Com.
Dec. 20th—SONORA, W. F. Lapidge, Com.

From Folsom street Wharf, at nine o'clock A. M., punctually,

FOR PANAMA.

Passengers will be convoyed from Panama to Aspinwall by the Panama Railroad Company, and from Aspinwall to New York by the Atlantic and Pacific Steamship Company.

A. B. FORBES,
Agent P. M. S. Co.,
no21-tf   Cor. Sacramento and Leidesdorff sts.

Alta California

The California Rangers

The California Rangers were reviewed yesterday afternoon in the Plaza by Major-General Allen. The Mayor and other city officials were present. A handsome silk "guidon" was presented to the company from a number of citizens, which was received in behalf of the company by Capt. Reed. They visited the American Theatre last evening, at which place a benefit was tendered them by the Leighton troupe. The house was filled and about $600 was netted, after deducting the expenses, which were very light. They were escorted to the steamer *Golden Age* this morning, on which they left for the East. The escort was composed of the following companies preceded by Kidd's Brass Band: California Guard, Ellsworth Rifles, Vallejo Rifles, one detachment of the Black Hussars, and the Light Dragoons. The column marched down Post street to Montgomery, Montgomery to Washington, Washington to Front, Front to California, California to Sansome, Sansome to Market, Market to Second, Second to Folsom, Folsom to the steamship wharf, which was crowded with people. As the column, headed by Capt. Reed, filed through the steamer's gangway, three tremendous cheers were given for the California Rangers. The company ranged themselves in a line on the hurricane deck where they had an opportunity to bid their friends on the wharf farewell. Shortly before the sailing of the steamer, the Rangers gave three lusty cheers for the escort, and three for the band. A person in the crowd proposed three cheers for the Union, which were given by the soldiers and citizens with hearty good will. The band played *Sweet Home, Hail Columbia*, etc.

At 12 o'clock M., the steamer cast loose from the wharf, and turned her prow in the direction of the Golden Gate. The California Guard fired a salute of 13 guns in honor of John W. Sim and Charles McKinnie [Kinne], who were formerly members of that company. The former gentleman is a second lieutenant of the Rangers and the latter a private. The wife and child of Capt. Reed accompany him.

Evening Bulletin, San Francisco, Thursday, December 11, 1862
The Golden Era, San Francisco, Sunday, December 14, 1862.

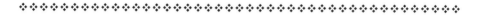

"The California Rangers on the War Path"

Before these lines fall under the eyes of the reader, the 'California One Hundred' will be far down the coast on their way to the battle fields on the Eastern slope of the continent. On Thursday morning their fellow soldiers in arms repaired to the headquarters of the 'Rangers', for the purpose of escorting them to the steamer. These were the Vallejo Rifles, detachments from the Light Dragoons, Hussars, Ellsworth Rifles, Light Guards, and the Old California Guard, the latter with two field pieces. The procession formed on Post street, at the corner of Kearney, at 10 o'clock, and preceded by Kidd's brass band, escorted the Cavalry Company through Montgomery, Washington, Front, Market, Second and Folson streets to the wharf of the P.M. Steamship Company. The streets through which the procession marched were thronged to suffocation, and the windows and doors of every building along the line of route occupied with ladies and children enthusiastically waving their kerchiefs in compliment to the 'Hundred', who marched in the rear of the line. Two big trucks laden with knapsacks, trunks, boxes, bundles, and various military trappings followed the Company, and attracted no little attention. They were suggestive of the speedy departure of the 'Hundred' on the war path.

Arriving at the wharf, the scene presented attested the universal interest prevailing throughout the community. Continuous cheers from thousands of throats went up for the 'Hundred', the Captain, Lieutenants, etc. The Old Guard stationed themselves at the upper end of the wharf, ready to thunder forth their adieus, whilst the other portion of the military escort ranged themselves along the edge of the pier, opposite the after gang plank. The 'Rangers' marched aboard and up to the quarter deck, where, arranged in line, cheers and partings were interchanged. At intervals, the band played 'Auld Lang Syne' and 'Home Sweet Home', and numerous national airs. A drizzly rain of an hour or more did not drive away the crowd; but the weather cleared up some time before the *GOLDEN AGE* cast off her hawsers, and turned her prow toward the 'Gate'. As the steamer pushed from the wharf, the California Guard fired a salute in honor of the two lieutenants. (Sim and private Kinne), who were at one time attached to their company, as was stated in yesterday's issue. Cheers and waving of pocket handkerchiefs were kept up, by the soldiers and the friends they left behind, until the steamer disappeared amidst the shipping of the lower wharves.

Alta California, San Francisco, Friday, December 12, 1862

DASHAWAYS. Forty-two of the cavalry company, known as the California Rangers, joined the Dashaway Association, in San Francisco. Of our three Napa members, Quant was the only one to give his signature. We commend the effort at abstaining from bad whiskey, but suggest that camp-life is lightning on sober resolutions, as witness the fact that whiskey rations are dealt out every day to the Federal troops.

The Pacific Echo, Napa, Saturday, December 13, 1862.

The California Rangers.-The company of volunteer cavalry under Capt. J. Sewall Reed, consisting of 103 men, left San Francisco on the 11th inst. Among the names of these men, who will undoubtedly carve for themselves names high in the niche of Fame's temple and do credit to the State they represent, we notice the names of the following, heretofore residents of this county: C.H. Ackerman, J.B. Ackerman, E.B. Campbell; C.F. Demsey, J. Fletcher, W.H.H. Hussey, A. Lee, J. Mariam, of Vallejo, C.B. Benjamin, of Rio Vista, and G.O. Grindell of Benicia. The Vallejo Rifles assisted in seeing them off.

The Solano Herald, Suisun, Saturday, December 13, 1862

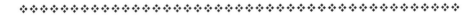

California Rangers.-This company, composed of one hundred and three members, left San Francisco on the 11th, to join a Massachusetts regiment of cavalry, and are to proceed immediately into active service. We notice among the list of members the name of I.R. McIntosh, formerly of Whiskey Creek, in this county.

Shasta Courier, Saturday, December 13, 1862

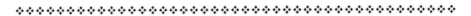

A FULL REPRESENTATION.-Of the "California One Hundred" who left the other day for the wars, no less than eight hailed from Vallejo. The Ladies of the *quondam* capital, who belong to the Patriotic Fund Society, contributed many things for the comfort and convenience of their gallant townsmen. Prior to the company's going down to the steamer on the morning of their departure, Messrs. Tubbs & Patten, of the Lick House, furnished them with an elegant and substantial breakfast, the last that many of them could do justice to for many days thereafter, even though set before them in the steamer's cabin. It is almost superfluous to remark that soldiers have as sensitive stomachs at sea as does a bilious rustic, "or any other man."

Alta California, San Francisco, Sunday, December 14, 1862.
[Micol Tubbs & David R. Patten, proprietors of the Lick House. From Vallejo: C. Ackerman, J. Ackerman, E. Campbell, W. Hussey, A. Lee, J. Fletcher, F. Quant, J. Merriam.]

The "One Hundred," - Among the members of the Cavalry company which left for the East on the 14th, were R.G. Samuels, Hugh Armstrong, and James Watson of this county.

Marin County Journal, San Rafael, Monday, December 15, 1862.

Off For the War.-A young native Californian, by the name of "Santiago," or James Watson, left here on the last steamer as a volunteer in Captain Reed's "Hundred from California." This is the first instance, we believe, of a native Californian joining the Union Army. A friend assures us, from a personal acquaintance with the young "native" for several years past, that he will make his mark, and also be found one of the most useful men in the command. Young Watson was born in Monterey, Cal., is now about 22 years old; has lived for the past ten years in Baulines [Bolinas] township, Marin county; is athletic and active, expert with a lasso, and one of the best horsemen and vaqueros in the State.

Alta California, San Francisco, Tuesday, December 16, 1862.

Off To The Wars. - In Capt. Reed's cavalry company, which left for the East on the 11th inst., were two citizens of Ukiah Valley. James B. and William Ackerman, the former late Deputy Sheriff. It is currently reported that certain parties have, or are about to, obtain permission to raise a company in this county. Should Gen. Wright forward the necessary documents, which we have no doubt he will do, a company will be raised in this county which will be an honor to the State. The parties who have taken the matter in hand are old soldiers and know how to attend to such things.

Mendocino Herald, Ukiah, Friday, December 19, 1862.

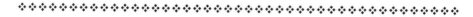

CALIFORNIA BATTALION

How Californians Can Best Show Their Loyalty - Another Call For Volunteers. - Thus far the Federal Government has not appealed in vain for troops from the Pacific side, to aid in putting down the civil war, now raging so frightfully in the Atlantic States. They have not only fulfilled all required of them in the way of furnishing men, but given freely of their treasure to relieve the wants and sufferings of their battle-stained brethren in the East. We firmly believe that this state, loyal to the core as it is, not only can, but will, respond with alacrity and enthusiasm to the second call herewith annexed. Disease, exposure, and the casualties of conflict have in the natural course of revolutions, destroyed many valuable lives, and the ranks of some regiments are decimated to-day. The opportunity is now afforded loyal citizens to enlist in the Union army; and we have the word of the commanding officer at this station that they shall be led by competent officers, and pushed forward at once to the post of danger. The official circular reads as follows:

"Headquarters Department of The Pacific,}
"San Francisco, Cal., Dec. 16, 1862}
"The undersigned, commanding the Military Department of the Pacific, takes great pleasure in announcing to the patriotic citizens of California, that he has been authorized by the Honorable Secretary of War to call upon His Excellency the Governor, for an additional regiment of infantry and seven companies of cavalry to be mustered into the service of the United States.

"The troops called for are designed for distant service in the field, and will be commanded by able and experienced officers.

"Californians: You have already exhibited a noble devotion to the Union. Ten thousand men furnished by your state, and the magnificent voluntary contributions in money and supplies which you have sent forward to aid our sick and wounded soldiers in the East, bear witness to your love for that Old Flag.

"Knowing, as I do, the people of this State, their love of country, their intelligence, their zealous and holy attachment to the Union, I appeal to them with confidence.

"Respond promptly to the call; rally under the protecting folds of the glorious star-spangled banner, and swear fidelity to the Union,
G. Wright
"Brigadier General U. S. Army, Commanding."

Alta California, San Francisco, Friday, December 19, 1862.

❖ ❖

Off For The War. - Santa Cruz county has a representative in Capt. Reed's Company in the person of Mr. H.C.S. Tubbs, of Watsonville.

We desire to correct the Alta in one particular, there are several native Californians in the Union army, both in Capt. Brown's Cavalry Company, and Capt. Tidball's Co., 5th Infantry.
The Sentinel, Santa Cruz, Saturday, December 20, 1862.

[Capt. Albert Brown, Co. L, 2nd Cav. California Volunteers; Capt. Thomas Tidball, Co. K, 5th Infantry, California Volunteers, both organized in Santa Cruz]

❖ ❖

General News Items.
The festival given in San Francisco for the benefit of the cavalry company raised to help patriotic, warlike, volunteer overflowing Massachusetts was a humbug. There was the usual amount of "war meetin' gas,' but when it came to diving into their pantaloons for mint-drops, their stingy souls failed them.

The Weekly Colusa Sun, Colusa, Saturday, December 20, 1862.

❖ ❖

The California "One Hundred."

The Cavalry Company, of one hundred, organized in San Francisco for actual service East, departed from this State on the last ocean steamer. This Company will be heard from. The "Rangers" are composed of picked men, and the most of them have seen service. Below we publish the roll:
OFFICERS.
Captain, J. Sewall Reed, San Francisco.
First Lieutenant, A. McKendry, San Francisco.
Second Lieutenant, John W. Sim, San Francisco.

PRIVATES.

Armstrong, H., Tomales.
Ackerman, C.H., Vallejo.
Ackerman, J.B., Vallejo.
Allan, H.W., Victoria, V.I.
Allen, C.E., San Francisco.
Allen, H., San Francisco.
Anderson, George, San Jose.
Anthony, W.G., Auburn.
Burdick, J.B., Napa.
Benjamin, C.E., Rio Vista.
Barnstead, T.D., San Francisco.
Balton, D.O., Chico.
Burlingham, H.G., San Francisco.
Bumgardner, W.H.H., Iowa Hill.
Balke, C., San Francisco.
Baker, A.F., Nevada.
Beach, N.A., San Francisco.
Briggs, C.P., Napa.
Blake, J., Fiddletown.
Campbell, E.B., Vallejo.
Carey, J., Dalles, Oregon.
Collins, W.W., Half Moon Bay.
Corbet, S.J., Sacramento.
Cunningham, W., San Francisco.
Chalmers, J.M., San Francisco.
Chanlee, S., Sacramento.
Crum, H., Howland Flat.
Crumpton, W.R., San Francisco.
Davis, G.F., San Francisco.
Dewey, Charles S., Virginia City.
Dearborn, Valorous, San Francisco.
Demsey, C.F., Vallejo.
Ellet, R.S., Alameda.
Forbes, A.C., Yolo.
Freeman, J., Sacramento.
Fillebrown, H.H., San Francisco.
Fletcher, J., Vallejo.
Gibbs, B.D., Shellings.
Golding, Geo.
Hall, Fred., Empire City, N.T.
Hanscom, S., Port Madison, W.T.
Hammerburg, W., San Francisco.
Hill, C.W., San Francisco.
Hill, J.A., San Francisco.
Hilliard, W.H.J., San Francisco.

Kinne, C.M.
Knowles, F., Virginia City.
Leighton, San Francisco.
Lee, A., Vallejo.
Legler, C., San Francisco.
Loane, A., San Francisco.
Libbey, T.O., Howland flat.
Locke, B., San Francisco.
Mazy, H., Contra Costa.
Magary, J.
Mariam, J. Vallejo.
McCarty, John, Marysville.
McCarty, J.D., Portland, O.
McIntosh, J.R., San Francisco.
McNeil, W.H., Napa.
Nellis, C., San Francisco.
Nelson, H., San Francisco.
Nixon, J., Oroville.
Owen, J.W., Virginia City.
Parker, R.M.
Pelham, J.W., San Francisco.
Percy, W.N., San Jose.
Pool, M.G., Sacramento.
Powers, C.H. San Francisco.
Plummer, G.., San Pedro.
Quant, F.J., Napa.
Rice, H., San Francisco.
Robinson, W.A., San Francisco.
Ross, J.C., Sacramento.
Rowe, C., Portland, O.
Samuel, R.C., Tomales.
Schrob, H., Mormon Island.
Sherwin, H.C., Petaluma.
Sivalls, B., Santa Clara.
Smith, S., Jr., San Francisco.
Spreight, C.L.S., Mariposa.
Starr, W., Placerville.
Sterling, E.B., Murphy's.
Towle, G.W., San Francisco.
Thompson, G.M.
Tubbs, H.S.C., Watsonville.
Vierieck, G.W., San Francisco.
West, W.W., Dry Town.
Wheat, J.L., San Francisco.
White, P.E., San Francisco.

Holt, George I., San Francisco.
Hunt, J.A., San Francisco.
Hunter, J.L., Volcourville.
Hussey, W.H.H., Vallejo.
Johnson, G.M., Marin.

Williams, J.H., San Francisco.
Winship, J., Florence, W.T.
Woodman, H.F., San Francisco.
Watson, James.

Santa Cruz Sentinel, Santa Cruz, Saturday, December 20, 1862

Letter from C. P. Briggs.
_____

On Board Steam-Ship Golden Age.

December 23rd, 1862.

Eds. Reporter: - As I cannot write to you all, I try to scratch a few lines to you all in common. We are now going up the Bay of Panama after 12 days sail. Capt. Hudson said he had made twenty trips without so much bad weather. All the California Hundred were accommodated with free baths of salt water. I have not taken off my clothes but once since I left San Francisco, and that was only to change. I did go so far as to take off my boots at nights some times. All the main deck forward of the fore hatch is allotted to the Hundred, and woe to the steerage passenger that crosses the line. Our grub was horrible the first and second day out, and we made complaint and also began to make some preparations to seize the galley and butcher shop; but Capt. Hudson told us to keep quiet and all should be well, and so it was. We then mounted guard over the tables from that time on, and kept all but the One Hundred from them until we were through. Our Company paid more than most of the others, and was of course entitled to better fare. Our Company consists of 1 Captain, 2 Lieutenants and 101 Privates, two of the 104 are married men. Capt. Reed and one Private who has a wife in Massachusetts. What a commotion it will create among the Boston gals to have 102 bachelors and widowers to arrive at once among them. We have had only two deaths on board, and those were in the Cabin. There is one man aboard running away from his wife, with all the money and three children, and also two women running away from their dear husbands; one with a man, and the other with her sister. It takes us to find out secrets.

I should not have written until I went ashore, but the Captain told us it was uncertain if we remained at Panama any time at all. The vessel shakes and rolls so, that I don't know if you can read this. We got news of the Constitution as she passed us; of the Ariel being taken by the Alabama, and of her passengers being paroled. Heaven and Earth, won't we be the sickest set of boys if she comes in our wake and takes us prisoners and no show whatever to fight. We have no arms of any kind, for we have sent back the sabres we had, and we are to get ours in Boston. It will depend upon our officers whether we take the oath or go prisoners. I will write the first time I get an opportunity. Tell all the boys if they will write, I will answer them. Direct all papers or letters to Capt. Reed's California Hundred, Boston, as they will be forwarded to us wherever we are.

C.P. Briggs.

The Napa County Reporter, Napa, Saturday, January 24, 1863.
[Charles P. Briggs, Company A, California Hundred, first came to California in 1843; he was attached to Fremont's Battalion; after the war he returned to Massachusetts and in 1882 returned to California and settled in Napa where he died January 3, 1885.]

Battalion

SWORD PRESENTATION.-The members of the National Guard presented their Captain, at the Armory on Christmas morning, with a very handsome regulation sword. The blade is of highly polished steel, perfectly tempered, and of suitable length. The scabbard is richly mounted, and the large gold plate in the centre bears the following inscription:

"Presented to Captain Z. B. Adams, by the Members of the National Guard. December 25, 1862."

The gift was accompanied with some very suitable and feeling remarks on the part of the Company, through Sergeant George Humphrey, and were appropriately responded to by the officer so highly and justly complimented. The sword is no "holiday toy," but made for active, and, if need be, sanguinary service. It has a massive hilt, completely shielded by the guard, and constructed in the strongest manner. The sash, belt and heavy gold tassel, presented with the sword, are really elegant and tasteful, and serve to set off both the officer and his testimonial to the finest advantage. The total cost of sword and equipments was $100.

Alta California, San Francisco, Saturday, December 27, 1862.
[Captain (Zabdiel) B. Adams, Co. L]

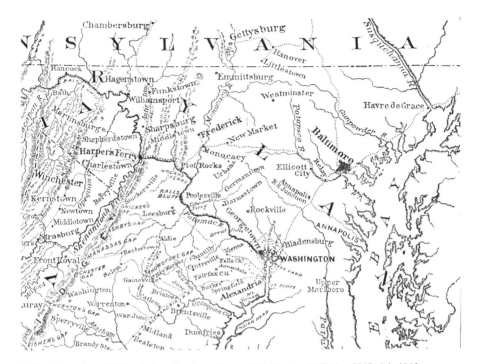

Field of Operations: California Battalion in and around Washington, D.C. May 1863- July 1863

Field of Operations: California Hundred in and around Gloucester Point, VA. February 1863- July 1863

1863

The New Year found the California Hundred at Camp Meigs, Readville, near Boston, Massachusetts. Soon after their arrival came the news that an additional 400 men would be recruited to serve under the Massachusetts quota. Raised in California as companies A, B, C, D, these men would become known as the California Battalion, Companies E, L, M, and F respectively, of the 2d Massachusetts Cavalry Regiment.

After some basic training, the California Hundred along with four additional companys organized and recruited in Massachusetts were sent to Fortress Monroe, Virginia. for further instruction. They would soon encounter the confederate troops in that general area. On June 1863, at the South Anna Railroad Bridge, Virginia., they had their first major engagement and their first loss, with the death of Joseph Burdick.

By this time, the California Battalion, having arrived at Camp Meigs, Massachusetts in March and April of 1863, were engaged in the defences of Washington, D.C., as a part of the cavalry force for the Department of Washington. There they encountered the guerrilla forces of Colonel John Mosby and Colonel E. V. White, and soon became well acquainted with their tactics. In mid June the California Battalion made their first raid into Virginia. Then in July, they were engaged in harassing Stuart's cavalry as he made his way thru Maryland. They were somewhat responsible, certainly, for delaying his getting to the field at Gettysburg. August brought the California Hundred and the Battalion together at last, at Centreville, Virginia. and from this time on, the story is a combined one.

The balance of 1863 found the 2d Massachusetts Cavalry, together with the 13th and 16th New York Cavalrys, under the command of Colonel Lowell, Department of Washington, and actively engaged in countering the raids of Mosby and White's guerrillas.

❖❖❖

JANUARY, 1863

1 Lincoln signs the Emancipation Proclamation.
8 Ground broken in Sacramento for the Central Pacific Railroad.
26 Major General Joseph Hooker replaces Burnside as commander of the Army of the Potomac.

❖❖❖

THE CALIFORNIA CAVALRY COMPANY FOR MASSACHUSETTS. Adjutant General Schouler has received the muster roll of this company, which is composed, for the most part, of young men. The corps has been mustered into the service of the United States. It will probably arrive in this city on Monday or Tuesday of next week. J. Sewall Reed is the Captain; Archibald McKendry, 1st Lieutenant. Capt. Reed was asked who he should report to in New York and he replied, "I report, sir, to Governor Andrew on Boston Common". Let the company have a warm reception on its arrival in this city.

Evening Transcript, Boston, Friday, January 2, 1863

❖❖❖

From the N. Y. Times of January 2, 1863

The "California Hundred" at New York.

The steamer *Champion* came in this morning with the California mails and treasure all safe and sound, much to the agreeable disappointment of the croakers, who were silly enough to believe that the pirate Semmes would be so unwise to remain on the California route after his outrage upon the *Ariel*. As soon as she had touched the dock, a Committee of the Sons of Massachusetts took possession of the California "One Hundred," and escorted them to the New England Rooms, where they provided them with a bountiful breakfast. They dined at the same place at noon, where they partook of a still more bountiful meal, and received the congratulations of many distinguished gentlemen, military and otherwise, including Gen. Andrews and staff, of Bank's expedition, who still remain here, closing up their business. The Californians will leave this evening for Boston, and be escorted to the boat by the 53d Massachusetts Regiment. The Massachusetts 2nd Cavalry, for which the Californians have been recruited, is now nearly full, the last accounts giving them 800 men in camp.

Evening Bulletin, San Francisco, Monday, February 2, 1863.
[Paper in error, arrival on the Ocean Queen. Raphael Semmes, Captain of the CSS Alabama]

❖❖

California Soldiers Want to Fight.-The following is the text of the communication sent to General Halleck by Col. Connor, on behalf of the soldiers under his command, now in Utah Territory. It has but just now found its way into print:

Maj. Gen'l. Halleck, General-In-Chief of the U.S. Army, Washington, D.C.—The 3d Infantry California Volunteers has been in the service one year and marched 600 miles. It is well officered and thoroughly drilled; it is of no service on the Overland Mail routes as there is cavalry sufficient for its protection in Utah District. The Regiment will authorize the Paymaster to withhold $30,000 of pay now due if the Government will order it East; and it pledges Gen. Halleck never to disgrace the flag, himself, or California. The men enlisted to fight traitors, and can do so more effectively than raw recruits; and ask that they may be placed, at least, on the same footing in regard to transportation East. If the above sum is insufficient, we will pay our own passage from San Francisco to Panama.
        By request of the Regiment.
        P. Edw. Connor, Col. Commanding

Marin County Journal, San Rafael, Saturday, January 3, 1863.

❖❖

[Meanwhile in Boston, Massachusetts]

Military. The 2d Massachusetts cavalry is meeting with good success. Fifty or sixty men have been enlisted, sworn in and sent to camp. They occupy barracks at Readville, and are now temporarily in command of Lieut. Richards. The sabre exercise is daily practiced, and the mounted drill will soon be introduced. The California company is expected in Boston the present week, coming by way of New York, and they will probably join this regiment at Readville.

Evening Transcript, Boston, Monday, January 5, 1863.

Arrival in New York of the California Cavalry Company.-As the public are aware, the California "Hundred" left this city on the 11th of December, in the steamer *Golden Age*. Letters from Acapulco had already been published, giving descriptions of the rough weather experienced shortly after leaving this port. The *Age* connected with the *Ocean Queen*, on the Atlantic side, and the numerous friends of the company as of other passengers aboard, will be pleased to learn that this latter vessel has safely reached her destined haven. The subjoined telegram furnishes this information.

New York, Saturday, January 3d., 1863.
Received S. F., January 3d. 7 P. M.}

Colonel D. W. C. Thompson;

California's "Hundred" came through all right. They will go on to Boston to-night.
J. Sewall Reed, Captain.

Alta California, San Francisco, Sunday, January 4, 1863.
The Napa County Reporter, Napa, Saturday, January 10, 1863.

FROM ASPINWALL

Arrival of the California Cavalry for Boston.

New York, 3d. The steamer Ocean Queen, from Aspinwall 24th. She has $1,300,000 in treasure, and a large number of passengers and a company of Cavalry for the Mass. 2d Regiment.

New York, 3d. The California company of cavalry for a Massachusetts regiment will arrive in Boston Sunday morning. They are receiving attention from the Massachusetts Agent and others today. They are a fine looking body of men.

Evening Transcript, Boston, Saturday, Jan. 3, 1863
[Aspinwall- Colon, Panama]

**Public Dinner to the "California Hundred"
in New York.**
(From the N.Y. "Post" of 3d January)
The "California Hundred." Captain Reed's brave little band, who have come so many miles to join the army of the Union in the East, are receiving the most gratifying attention from the New England Soldier's Association under the management of Col. Frank Howe. This afternoon a good substantial dinner was served to them at the rooms of the Association, and after it the soldiers were addressed by Col. Howe, who bade them welcome to New York, and in-

formed them that in 90 minutes this reception and repast had been prepared for them, while some of our soldiery now in town were waiting to receive them at the Park. James T. Brady made a telling little speech replete with humor. He alluded to the fact that only one man of the entire company was married, and was heartily cheered by the soldiers. Major Barnes made a few remarks eulogistic of California and her sons. Charles Gould followed, introducing Col. Bartlett of the 49th Massachusetts Regiment, who had lost a leg at Yorktown. Gen. Prosper M. Wetmore also made some remarks. Capt. Reed returned his thanks for the unexpected and cordial reception awarded to his men in New York. They had come 5,000 miles to fight for the Union, and did not know the result, but were determined to do the best they could. After the dinner, which was enlivened by the music of the 7th Regiment band, and the speeches, the "California Hundred" marched to the Park, where they were reviewed by the Mayor, before a large assemblage of military men and citizens.

Evening Bulletin, San Francisco, Saturday, January 31, 1863
Alta California, San Francisco, Monday, January 5, 1863.
The Napa County Reporter, Napa, Saturday, January 10, 1863

CALIFORNIA VOLUNTEERS.

They are Entertained at the New England Rooms - Speech of James F. Brady, Esq.

One Hundred picked men from California, all of whom are peculiarly qualified for cavalry service, arrived in this city yesterday forenoon per steamer *Ocean Queen* having left San Francisco on the 11th ultimo, on their way to Boston, where they are to be incorporated into the Second Massachusetts Cavalry, Col. C. R. Lowell, now forming there. The "California Hundred," as this company is termed, is composed of representatives from every Northern State, who have been residents of California, as also Kentuckians, Virginians, Tennesseans and Missourians, and presents the finest appearance of any detachment that has ever passed through our City. Recruiting for the "Hundred" was commenced on the 28th of October last and the required number was recruited, of picked men, before the end of the month. Having obtained governmental permission to join the Second Massachusetts Cavalry, the expense of coming here (about $20,000) was borne by the company.

The following are the officers of the "Hundred;"
Captain –J. Sewall Reed.
First Lieutenant – Arch. McKendry.
Second Lieutenant – John W. Sim.

New York Times, New York, Sunday, January 4, 1863

RECEPTION OF THE CALIFORNIA COMPANY FOR MASSACHUSETTS IN NEW YORK.- *New York, Jan. 3.* The reception of the California Company to-day was one of the most successful impromptu affairs ever accomplished in this city.

On arrival of the California hundred they were stationed in the Park Barracks, where numerous calls were made upon them.

Col. Howe, as Agent for the State of Massachusetts, immediately tendered them a dinner at the New England Rooms, and the 4th, 49th and 53d Mass. regiments were tendered them as an escort on their departure. Capt. Reed accepted the courtesies for his command.

Prior to attending dinner the California hundred were received at the City Hall by the Mayor, who welcomed them to the city.

They dined at 2 o'clock at the New England Rooms. After the cloth was removed, Col. Howe made a most feeling welcome speech, and introduced James P. Brady who addressed them a few words of welcome. He said in substance: It seemed appropriate that this welcome to the Soldier's Home should be brief, as the dinner had been gotten up *impromtu*. He was glad to see so fine a body of men from California eager to join with Massachusetts in an endeavor to sustain the Government. Many of those present were Yankees, and the events of this war had made him (the Speaker) as good a Yankee as any of them. He was glad to learn there was but one married man among the "Hundred" – that fact was gratifying to his bachelor heart and habits; but, if single they could, like Richelieu of France, call the nation their "wedded wife," meantime he would say God bless and sustain that sole married man, whose duty it would be to look after the morals of this "Hundred." (Great laughter.) Mr. Brady again extended a welcome to the soldiers, and paid a glowing compliment to the New England Relief Association, after which he closed his remarks, his peroration being a strain of patriotic sentiment, delivered with great emphasis and beauty of diction. When the war closed, and the power of the Union was reestablished, he hoped to welcome them all again to this Metropolis as soldiers who had done a noble duty, and won immortal honor.

The "boys" evidently appreciated Mr. Brady's patriotic sentiments, and when he had closed, his remarks were vociferously applauded. Captain Reed appropriately responded. Other excellent speeches were made by Col. Barnes, Lieut. Limes, Chas. Gould, Judge Bonney, and others. Col. Bartlett, of the Mass. 49th, and other officers of the 49th and 53d Mass. Regiments, and members of Gen. Andrews staff were present, and gave a soldiers welcome to the California brothers in arms.

After dinner, during which a salute was fired from the roof of the New England Rooms, the Company proceeded to their quarters, where their escort soon after arrived. The column proceeded up Broadway as far as the Metropolitan Hotel, where they countermarched and proceeded down Broadway through Courtland street, and embarked on the Stonington route, Grainlad's band playing Yankee Doodle, and left for Readville.

Their march on Broadway was a perfect ovation, thousands lining the sidewalks and drowning the music of the band with deafening cheers, and so on till the boat left the pier.

As they passed the New England Rooms, they were again saluted by the Mass. six-pounder, and the windows were filled with the daughters of the old Bay State, who waved flags and handkerchiefs.

The hundred are composed of young, stalwart men, only the captain and one private being married. They have paid all their own expenses of travel, and intend purchasing their own steeds.

The whole reception was designed and most effectually carried out on two hours' notice for preparation by Col. Howe, and his energy and patriotism on this occasion received the most hearty appreciation and thanks of Capt. Reed, his officers and men, as well as the sons of Massachusetts resident in this city.

New York Herald, Sunday, January 4, 1863
Evening Transcript, Boston, Monday, January 5, 1863
Sacramento Daily Union, Saturday, January 31, 1863

❖❖❖

Arrival Of The California Cavalry Company.-The California Company of Cavalry arrived at Readville yesterday morning, where they went into barracks at Camp Meigs. They were recruited in San Francisco by J. Sewall Reed, who commands them. They are a fine body of men, and will unquestionably perform good service. The company numbers 100 men, besides three officers and were all recruited between Oct. 28 and Dec. 10, the day the men were mustered into the service for three years by Col. George H. Ringgold, Deputy Paymaster General, U.S.A., at San Francisco. There are some half dozen of the men 35 years of age, and about four 19 years old, and those are the two extremes-the main body of the company being from 25 to 30 years of age. The following are their names from the muster roll:-

J. Sewall Reed, Captain; Archibald McKendry, 1st Lieut.; John W. Sim, 2d Lieut.

Privates Charles H. Ackerman, William G. Anthony, George Anderson, Henry E. Allen, Hugh Armstrong, Henry W. Allen, Charles E. Allen, James B. Ackerman, Joseph B. Burdick, Nathan A. Beach, Josephus Blake, Chas. E. Benjamin, Thomas D. Barnstead, Hugh G. Burlingham, Darnley O. Balcom, Chas. P. Broggs, Wm. H.H. Bumgardner, Charles Balke, A. Frank Baker, Edw. B. Campbell, John M. Chalmers, Wesley R. Crampton, Henry Crum, Stoander Chanlee, Wm. W. Collins, Wm. Cunningham, Samuel J. Corbett, Jeremiah Carey, Charles S. Dewey, Cyrus S. Demsey, George F. Davis, Valorus Dearborn, Rochard S. Ellet, Alexander C. Forbes, James Freeman, Henry H. Fillebrown, John Fletcher, Byron G. Gibbs, George M. Goulding, Charles W. Hill, William H.H. Hussey, John A. Hill, John L. Hunter, William H.J. Hilliard, James A. Hunt, George I. Holt, Frederick Hall, Samuel G. Hanscom, William Hammerburg, G.M. Johnson, Frank Knowles, C.M. Kinne, B. Locke, G. Legler, F.O. Libby, Alfred Lee, Abra'm Loane, Alfred Laighton, William H. McNeil, Issac R. McIntosh, Jonathan Merriam, John McCarty, John D. McCarty, Henry Mazy, Albert Magary, Joseph Nixon, Colburn Nellis, Henry Nelson, John W. Owen, James Pelham, William N. Percy, Geo. Plummer, Charles H. Powers, Milburn Z. Pool, Robert M. Parker, Frederick I. Quant, Wm. A. Robinson, Joshua C. Ross, Hamilton Rice, Carlos Rone, Richard C. Samuel, Charles L. Speight, Wm. Star, Samuel Smith, Jr., Henry Schroh, Edward R. Sterling, Benson Sivalls, Henry C. Sherwin, Geo. W. Towle, Henry S.C. Tubbs, George E. Thompson, George W. Viereck, Edwin W. Woodward, Henry F. Woodman, James L. Wheat, John Winship, Wells W. West, John H. Williams, Peter E. White and James Watson.

It was expected that the company would report in Boston, but this arrangement was not regarded as the best to pursue. They will, however, have a public reception in Boston soon; probably this week. The occasion will no doubt be one of no little interest. A meeting of Californians, and others interested in giving the California cavalry company a proper reception held a meeting Saturday forenoon at the office of Messrs F.H. and J.S. Bacon, No.76, State street. On account of the intention of the authorities to have the company proceed at once to camp at Readville, a demonstration upon their arrival was thought to be impracticable, but the idea will probably be carried out before their departure.

The company were honored with a grand farewell entertainment before leaving San Francisco.

Boston Post, Monday, January 5, 1863.
Evening Transcript, Boston, Monday, January 5, 1863
Boston Herald, Monday, January 5, 1863.

❖❖❖

Letter from C.P. Briggs.
_____

NO. 2
_____

Camp Meigs, Reedville,
January 5th, 1863.

Eds. Reporter: - We arrived in Panama on the 22nd of December at daybreak, and immediately went ashore, marched into the cars, and by 2 o'clock reached Aspinwall, being 22 hours
without anything to eat. Whereupon we charged furiously upon two restaurants and put all the
provisions to flight. We had been half-starved on the Golden Age, and all were crazy for good
cheer. I did not eat as much as some: only one large steak, two boiled eggs, ham, kidney stew,
two cups of tea, half a loaf warm bread, two plates apple sauce, some turnips and began to look
around for some pie, but could discover none, and so I concluded to pay my dollar and vamose.

We went aboard the Ocean Queen, and sailed at 3 o'clock, P.M. We struck out for the
nearest point off the coast of Florida, running about 300 miles out of the old line to avoid the
Alabama. The Alabama was sure she would catch her that trip. She has an old grudge against
Capt. Tenklepaugh-commander of the Ocean Queen, and would hang him if ever they catch
him, but this was his last trip in the civil service, for he has had an appointment in the Navy. We
were delayed eight hours at Key West, and it was here that we first heard of the defeat of
Burnside, and you may believe it did not set well on our minds. We had beautiful weather on
the Atlantic, until we reached Cape Hatteras, and great guns! how it blowed, but we were
happy, and little thought that the Monitor was some where near us in the same gale, or at the
bottom, (for we hugged the shore pretty close) Poor Monitor, noble craft, she has gone to the
bottom!

We arrived in New York on the 3rd, at day-light, marched to the Park, where we were
reviewed by the Mayor. The New England Relief Association invited us to dinner at their Hall
on Broadway, where we were addressed by some eminent speakers, such as Chas. Gould,
Brady, Mayor Barner, Col. Bartlet, of the Mass. 9th, with one leg shot off, Gen. Wetmore,
Judge Barney and others. We marched through the Sick Rooms and received hearty cheers
from the poor sick and wounded. We then marched up and down Broadway with part of a
Regiment of Massachusetts Volunteers that are quartered there, they then escorted us to the
Stonington Road, and off we went at 4 o'clock P.M. We arrived in Camp at day-light, Sunday
the 4th, we should have gone direct through to Boston had it not been Sunday as we thought
they would not be able or ready to receive us. But we were mistaken, two separate parties
prepared a grand dinner and supper for us. We are to go to Boston on Thursday to show ourselves, and be received and have a good time generally. - This Company surely beats any
company of men I ever saw together; there has been but one man drunk since I joined, and that
was in San Francisco; there has not been a quarrel or a blow passed among us.

There are about five hundred men in this Camp besides ourselves, and they can't be trusted
out of sight, for some that drink get so drunk that they forget to come back. In our barracks
there is a large poster stuck up, to this effect, that if any man wished to leave the Company, not
to run away, and disgrace the Company, but to go to the Captain who will do his best to procure
his discharge. But there is no danger of any applications. I don't think any one would take two
hundred dollars for his chance. I had rather be a Private in this Company than Lieutenant in any
other company I see here. The other companies are red-hot with jealousy, we are so much
better dressed; more uniform in size; more particular in our dress when on duty; more particular to salute officers, etc. Farmers and their wives coming in from the country, call us together,
and load us with Yankee apples, and all kinds of "goodies," while they have to be satisfied with

looking on. Orders have arrived making us Company A, 2nd Regiment Massachusetts Volunteers, but we still go by the name of the California Hundred, all our clothing, blankets, baggage are marked "Cal 100."

C.P. Briggs.

The Napa County Reporter, Napa, Saturday, February 7, 1863.
[Shortly after midnight, Dec. 30, the Monitor *foundered in a storm off Cape Hatteras with the loss of four officers and twelve men.]*

❖❖

THE CALIFORNIA CAVALRY COMPANY. The interest taken by Rev. Mr. King and other New Englanders on the Pacific, in this corps, which has come five thousand miles to identify itself with Massachusetts in fighting for the Union under her banner, is in part explained by its composition. "Ninety-five of the one hundred are Northern men by birth. Nearly one half are natives of New England. One only came from a State which has been even partially in rebellion-Tennessee; and but one was born in California."

The company has already been welcomed by those immediately connected with the Second Cavalry as a noble contribution to the Regiment. The men are all that could be asked for, in the opinion of those most interested in and competent to judge of their soldierly bearing and qualities.

This addition to the Second has been eagerly expected, and its coming will give new prestige to what promises to be one of the most efficient commands the Old Bay State has sent to the rescue of the endangered nation.

Evening Transcript, Boston, Tuesday, January 6, 1863
[Hugh Armstrong, from Rogersville Tenn.; James Watson, Monterey, Ca.]

❖❖

RECEPTION TO THE CALIFORNIA CAVALRY COMPANY. The natives of California resident in Boston, feeling that some public notice was due to their brethren who have enlisted in a Massachusetts Volunteer Cavalry regiment, held a meeting this morning at the office of T. H. Bacon, No. 76 State street, to take proper measures for giving them a public reception. After giving the matter full discussion, it was proposed to celebrate their arrival by an oration in Faneuil Hall, and other ceremonies. A committee was appointed to perfect the necessary arrangements for the occasion, and they are to attend to their duties forthwith and report as soon as possible. It is probable that they will be released for a day after going to camp at Readville, that they may receive the welcome their patriotism deserves.

Evening Transcript, Boston, Monday, January 5, 1863
Evening Transcript, Boston, Wednesday, January 7, 1863
Boston Herald, Thursday, January 8, 1863

❖❖

Battalion

A BATTALION OF CAVALRY OFFERED FROM CALIFORNIA. We learn that Gov. Andrew has received the proffer of a cavalry battalion of four companies from California. The question of their acceptance is now pending before the War Department. Should the General Government accept the services of these loyal Californians, Gov. Andrew will appoint Col. Thompson of California, formerly of Gen. Halleck's staff to lead the patriotic volunteers from the Golden State.

Evening Transcript, Boston, Thursday, January 8, 1863

SECOND MASSACHUSETTS CAVALRY

The cavalry company from California, which arrived in Massachusetts during the last week, does credit to the noble young State of the Pacific coast. A finer body of men we have not seen in long time, and we are told that they all know how to ride a horse, which is more than can be said of some of our cavalry, for which reason we have been on the whole, very deficient in that arm of the service. We understand that a whole battalion of cavalry from California has been offered to Massachusetts, and it will be accepted if the consent of the Government can be obtained. The roll for this company was signed by nearly three hundred good men, and those who could not come were greatly disappointed. Recruits are not plenty in California because men lack employment. Business is good in that State; nearly every man of this company left remunerative employment, and will return when they have performed the service for which they have volunteered. They were undoubtedly moved by a commendable pride in their gallant young State to show what they were willing to do for the country for whose blessings they are content, and we should give them a hearty welcome when they pay us a visit.

Boston Herald, Saturday, January 10, 1863

RECEPTION OF THE CALIFORNIA CAVALRY COMPANY. This fine body of men are to have a grand public reception on Wednesday next, the arrangements for which have been completed by committees from the City Government and Californians resident in Boston.

The company is expected to arrive at the Providence depot, from Readville, about ten o'clock on Wednesday morning. Here they will be received by an escort consisting of the Boston Light Dragoons, Major Wilder, with music, and a delegation of Californians with Gilmore's Band, beside several members of the City Government, and probably a procession of citizens. From the depot the procession will move to the Mayor's office, corner of Bedford and Chauncy streets, where they are to be received by His Honor Mayor Lincoln. The next place visited will be the State House and a call there made upon the Governor who will probably make them an address. The day's programme will conclude with a collation served in Faneuil Hall.

The two flags sent from California a few months since to Bunker Hill and presented to the Charlestown City Guard and Charlestown Artillery, will perhaps figure in the procession.

The guests will appear in the cavalry uniform complete. It was all made to order, and each garment by measure, in San Francisco, previous to the departure of the company from home, and the cloth is made from California wool, grown in the State and manufactured at the San Francisco Woolen Mills.

Owing to the verdancy of the government horse at Readville, it has been thought advisable to do away with the animal entirely on this occasion, and consequently both guests and escort will execute movements about the city on foot.

Evening Transcript, Boston, Monday, January 12, 1863
Boston Herald, Tuesday, January 13, 1863

SECOND REGIMENT

MASSACHUSETTS CAVALRY

$175 BOUNTY !

MAJOR CASPAR GROWNINSHIELD
Is authorized to receive recruits for the 1st Battalion for three years service or the war.

His Headquarters will be at No. 118 Washington street, where he will place one or more officers duly appointed.

The inducements to enlist are as follows:

$100 BOUNTY
by the United States Government (viz: 25 dollars upon being mustered into service and 75 dollars upon honorable discharge.)

$75 BOUNTY
WILL BE PAID BY THE CITY OF BOSTON
13 Dollars advance pay will become due when the Regiment marches.

In addition, the advantages of State aid to the families of recruits.

Horses, arms, accoutrements, uniforms, clothing, rations and medical attendance are furnished by the United States Government.

The sum of $5 will be paid to any one who will bring a suitable recruit to this office..

AMOS A. LAWRENCE,

Recruiting Officer.

The Boston Herald, Tuesday, January 13, 1863.

PRESENTATION OF A FLAG TO THE CALIFORNIA COMPANY. A very interesting ceremony took place at Readville last evening, when a flag, the gift of Miss Abbie A. Lord of Charlestown, was presented to the California Cavalry Company. Miss Lord is a patriotic young lady who has taken a deep interest in the national cause, and who was enrolled as a volunteer army nurse last August, although her services have not yet been demanded. Some three hundred ladies and gentlemen of Charlestown were present last evening. The ladies, with the committee of arrangements, of which C. A. Wellington, Esq., was chairman, went out in the afternoon, and arranged a bountiful supper, which was ready on the arrival of the gentlemen in an evening train. One of the empty barracks had been handsomely ornamented with evergreens by the soldiers and in this the tables were spread. About seven o'clock when the California Hundred had marched in and taken their places the meeting was called to order by Mr. Wellington, who introduced Rev. Mr. Graves as Chairman, Rev. Mr. Miles asked a blessing, and the Company and their friends at once made an attack on the viands, but such was the supply, that the fierce onset produced no sensible reduction of the enemy's forces. When the feast was concluded, the Chairman introduced in a few pithy remarks, Miss Lord, who, in presenting the flag spoke as follows:

Mr. Commander-It is my privilege to present to you and the noble men of your command, this American flag. (Cheers.) It is, as you see, of the regulation size, and composed of the best materials. Upon the ferrule, which is heavily plated with silver, is engraved the name of your Company and its Captain. Beneath this inscription there appears the coat of arms of our beloved Massachusetts with its liberty-speaking motto and joined to this the coat of arms of your golden State of California. Between those there is a representation of the Bunker Hill Monument. The whole is designed to illustrate how you and the brave men of your command have nobly rallied to support the principles for which the heroes of the Revolution fought and fell on that sacred height, and how in you, Massachusetts and California strike hands together for the same undying purpose. (Applause.) Accept, sir, this flag, and with it the sincere prayer that it may never trail in the dust at the feet of rebels (cheers), and that, protected by our Heavenly Father, you may speedily return with these starry folds gleaming with the emblems of conquest and victory. (Cheers and applause.)

Capt. Reed replied as follows: Soldiers of the California Hundred, do you see that flag? Will the rebels ever get that flag? (Never, never.) Miss Lord, I wish I had the eloquence of Webster to express my feelings or my thoughts. Since I came into this hall I have been filled with admiration and wonder. I have never before gazed on so much beauty and intelligence. Miss Lord, in behalf of the California Hundred I accept your beautiful, noble gift. We will carry it as representing one of the cities sacred in American history, and when we behold it fluttering in the breeze we will remember that a lady of that noble city presented it to us. If ever we live to come back to this place, that flag shall come back. It shall come, if there is only one man left to bring it. And that one I hope will come as a suitor. (Great applause.)

The song of "Stand by the Flag" was then sung by Mr. S. D. Bassett, the choir of the 1st Baptist Church of Charlestown singing the chorus. Brief and appropriate addresses were made by Rev. Mr. Miles, Alderman Childs, Councilman Morse, Andrew J. Locke, Lieut. Hodgkins of the 36th Regiment, Lieut. Geo. Childs who was a prisoner several months in Richmond, and Lieut. Ripley of the 29th Regiment. Mr. Prescott sung with effect "The Sword of Bunker Hill." The remaining time was spent in social conversation and in listening to the music of the band. The party were escorted to the railroad station by the Hundred, and left in an extra train, at 10 o'clock, amidst the cheers of the soldiers. To-day the company are to visit this city.

Evening Transcript, Boston, Wednesday, January 14, 1863
Boston Herald, Wednesday, January 14, 1863
Boston Post, Wednesday, January 14, 1863
[The flag presented by Miss Lord is preserved at the California State Archives, Sacramento]

RECEPTION OF THE CALIFORNIA COMPANY

The California Cavalry Company, Captain J. Sewell Reed, which was enlisted in that State to aid in filling the quota of the city of Boston, made their promised visit to the city today. The weather has not been of the best, but notwithstanding this fact, they have met with a most enthusiastic reception from our citizens, and also from the city and State authorities. The company reached the city about ten o'clock, and were met at the depot by the First Battalion of Light Dragoons, Major Charles W. Wilder, comprising Co. A, (National Lancers), Capt. Lucius Slade, numbering about 100 men, and Co. B, (Boston Light Dragoons), Capt. Charles T. Stevens, about 60 men; and also by a committee of resident Californians, accompanied by Gilmore's Band. The Battalion of Dragoons was accompanied by the Boston Brigade Band. The customary reception ceremonies were gone through with in Park Square and Boylston Sts., and the procession then took up its line of march through Boylston, Tremont, West and Bedford streets to Mechanics' Hall, to be received by the City authorities.

During this and their subsequent marches through our streets, the Californians made a soldierly appearance, and were the recipients of many enthusiastic greetings. They are a fine, manly looking company of men, and their appearance has never been excelled in this city. The Californians carried in their ranks the handsome American flag presented to them last evening by the ladies of Charlestown, and also a beautiful banner presented to them before they left their own State.

The reception at Mechanics' Hall took place at eleven o'clock. The company and their escort were assembled in the upper hall, now devoted to the use of the Common Council, and were addressed by Ex-Mayor Wightman.

Mr. Wightman said that in addition to his regular duties as Mayor of the city for the past year, he had also to attend to the raising of the men as the quota of Boston. While these men were being raised he received a communication from the Governor of Massachusetts, stating that a company of Californians desired to enroll themselves in the quota of Boston. The company tendered had been gladly accepted, and he was happy to greet them on this occasion. They had come not as citizens of California but as citizens of our common country. He would greet them as friends and brothers and as citizens.

He closed by introducing His Honor Mayor Lincoln, who extended a welcome in behalf of the city. He alluded to the peculiar circumstances under which they were met. Men from the golden shores of California had come to fight by the side of our own sons. He hoped they would meet the enemy in personal encounter. He spoke of the need which had been felt in the present war of cavalry, and of the fact that in past times nearly all the great battles have been won by the aid of cavalry.

Captain Reed replied briefly, saying he had brought one hundred Californians. They had not come as citizens of California, nor as citizens of Massachusetts, but as citizens of the United States. They were proud to enrol themselves under the quota of Boston.

From Mechanics' Hall, the company were escorted through Chauncey, Summer, Winter, Tremont and Park streets to the State House, where they were met by Governor Andrew. The three companies were assembled in Doric Hall, and His Excellency was introduced by His Honor Mayor Lincoln.

The Governor said it had given him unalloyed satisfaction and filled his heart with pride to greet them as soldiers of the Union. They had crossed from the shores of the Pacific to those of the Atlantic to defend the country's flag, and to fight for the right, honor and perpetuity of our Union. Who can doubt of the success of our cause, when soldiers and citizens like these desert their golden mines and their peaceful homes and hurry to our defence. He was proud that their names were to be enrolled with our own contingent. But they were no longer of Massachusetts, of New York, of Illinois, of California, when a common hope, a common joy and a common interest were at stake. The flag which they bore was the standard our fathers had erected, the flag which we all loved, and which every good citizen would lay down his life to defend.

His Excellency said that it gave him much pleasure to announce that the War Department had this day authorized him to accept in behalf of the State, the whole Battalion of Californians, which had been tendered. This announcement was received by the members of the California company with loud and prolonged cheers.

Governor Andrew continued, saying that the history of this war had revealed to us changeful scenes-disaster as well as victory-and it had also shown that the love of country and the firmness of heroic duty, cannot be doubted among those who have gone forth for our country's defence. Disaster can only be the trial of our mettle, delay the test of our patience, while victory can only be honorable when fairly won. He had been proud to commit to the keeping of Capt. Reed and his associates the commissions by which they had become enrolled under the white flag of Massachusetts as well as under the starry banner of our country, and he did it with the utmost confidence that our common cause would be bravely defended, and that the flag would never be surrendered to any enemy. Unnumbered as were the battle-fields whereon the sons of Massachusetts had spilled their blood, no banner had yet been wrested from the hands of Massachusetts soldiers.

Soon after 12 o'clock the company were escorted to Faneuil Hall to partake of a collation.

After the collation was disposed of, the visitors went through a series of military evolutions in a style which elicited the most enthusiastic applause of all the spectators. They also passed in review before His Honor Mayor Lincoln, Major Wilder (of the Dragoons), and Adjutant General Schouler.

Short speeches were made by Adjutant General Schouler; Hon. D.C. McRuer, of San Francisco, who is on a brief visit to Boston; Major Wilder, of the Dragoons, and Ex-Mayor Wightman.

Shortly before three o'clock, Captain Reed's company were escorted to the Providence depot there to take the cars for Readville.

Evening Transcript, Boston, Wednesday, January 14, 1863
Boston Courier, Thursday, January 15, 1863

❖❖

NEWS OF THE DAY

Ovation to The California Rangers.-

Our latest files of Boston papers contain minute descriptions of the reception of the "California Hundred" in the "City of Nations." Previously, however, the ladies of Charlestown gave an entertainment to the Company at their barracks in Readville. On this occasion, a young lady named Abbie A. Lord presented the Company with a beautiful flag. Speeches were subsequently made by distinguished personages, and the festivities closed by singing "Auld Lang Syne." On the following day, (Jan. 14th,) the Company was received at the Boston depot by a battalion of cavalry on foot, and a large number of old Californians. A procession was formed which moved through the principal streets to the city government rooms, where the Company was formally welcomed to the hospitalities of the city. Here they were addressed by ex-Mayor Wightman and Mayor Lincoln. To the latter, Captain Reed responded in the following brief and sententious language:

"*Mayor Lincoln*: I bring you one hundred Californians. We come not as citizens of California, neither as citizens of Massachusetts. We come as citizens of the United States, (cheers) and we are proud to enroll ourselves under the quota of Boston." (Renewed cheers.)

Subsequently Governor Andrews made the Company a patriotic and complimentary speech in the State House. A banquet was partaken of in Faneuil Hall, of which the *Journal* says:

"The bountiful collation at Faneuil Hall received ample justice between 12 and 1 o'clock, and afterward the Rangers, as well as the Battalion escort, were dismissed for half an hour. The time was pleasantly occupied in social commingling and cultivating those finer feelings which have ever existed between the loyal citizens of the Atlantic and Pacific coasts.

"The occasion was one of delightful interest, and one that will not soon be forgotten by those that participated in it. The Californians will remember it as a fit testimonial of their patriotism and bravery, and those who tendered it will have the pleasant satisfaction of knowing that their courtesies were heartily appreciated. During the pleasant half-hour of friendly intercourse, the occasion was greatly enhanced by music from the band, and several of the tables were removed, and the Atlantic and Pacific selected partners and joined in merry dances and waltzes.

"After the Rangers had been summoned into ranks, at the expiration of the half-hour, they went through a series of drilling exercises under command of Capt. Reed, and were reviewed and inspected by Mayor Lincoln and Major Wilder, commanding the battalion of escort, and Adjutant-General Schouler. The manner in which the company performed their drill and passed the review elicited the hearty applause of all."

Before leaving the Hall, Mayor Lincoln spoke again, and then D. C. McRuer, of this city made a speech. He said that the events that are now daily transpiring make these times demand men of action and not of words, and he rejoiced that the State of his adoption is represented here to-day by so many stalwart men of action, and thanked the State of Massachusetts for bringing so many of the citizens of California into the field. He said he had been often asked, since his visit here, if California would not secede on its own hook, and he was proud to stand in Faneuil Hall and say-No!

Although her geographical position leaves her on the side of Secession, he was sure there is no more loyal city and State existing than those which he was so proud to represent. California, he said, claims a heritage in Bunker Hill, Concord, Lexington, and this grand old Faneuil Hall, the Cradle of Liberty and Union. To this gallant company he would say, as a citizen of San Francisco, that he greeted them with mingled feelings of pride and confidence. Your position, he concluded, is nominally conspicuous. You have two godfathers-California and Massachusetts. You will do honor to both.

Major Charles W. Wilder, commander of the escort, who was next introduced, said that although speaking was not of his vocation, he felt as if he must say one word in behalf of his command. He could say nothing better than was conveyed when two hundred sabres were presented at the depot this morning, having behind them, as they did, two hundred loyal hearts to greet you from the far-off Pacific. He trusted this pleasant meeting and greeting of the Atlantic and Pacific is but the harbinger of future meetings, as social and pleasing in character, that shall come when this great war passes away, and the national ensign shall float over every capital in the country. In concluding he said he could not utter what he felt. Our parade to-day is the best representation of our feelings that I can present.

The concluding speech by ex-Mayor Wightman reviewed the tributes that had been paid the Company during the day by the Mayor, the Governor, and their fellow soldiers, and said that, as the representative of the city of Boston, he stood before them-not officially-to give them hearty welcome to this sacred canopy.

At the conclusion of Mr. Wightman's remarks, the Company was re-formed and escorted directly to the Providence depot, from which place they returned to their camp at Readville, all evidently highly gratified and satisfied with the day's entertainment.

Evening Bulletin, San Francisco, Thursday, February 12, 1863
Alta California, San Francisco, Friday, February 13, 1863
The Daily Bee. Sacramento, Friday, February 13, 1863.

❖❖
Battalion

The California Cavalry Battalion for the East.
The following letter explains itself:

Custom House, San Francisco
Collector's Office, January 14, 1863.

Major D. W. C. Thompson-Dear Sir-I have the pleasure of informing you that your proposition communicated through me to the Governor of Massachusetts, to raise four companies of Cavalry under your command as Major, for service at the East during the war, has been accepted by Gov. Andrew and approved by the War Department.

The question of your fitness for such a command was, in accordance with your request, submitted to Major-General Halleck, the General-in-Chief of the United States army, and decided in your favor. I am informed by telegraph that "Massachusetts meets the California Hundred" in Faneuil Hall to-day, In that Hall, sacred to the heroes and patriots of the Revolution, their patriotic fervor will be quickened and invigorated, and wheresoever the call of duty may take them I have no fear that they will discredit this Golden State in which they were organized, or the venerable Mother of States under whose patronage they enter the service.

There are, however, many thousands of equally worthy and patriotic young men still left in this State who are eager to be placed where they can strike a blow in defense of the Government and institutions under which they live. From among them you will be able, without difficulty and without delay, to select the number of men you desire; all of whom should be true men, sober, intelligent, and patriotic, their hearts in the work, and their efforts and their lives at the service of their country.

Wishing you entire and speedy success in completing your organization,
I am, very truly, your obd't serv't,
Ira P. Rankin

Major Thompson, who has been appointed to raise and command these companies, has been connected with the militia in this State for about 13 years-being one of the founders of the First California Guard in 1849. In 1859 and 1860 he was Assistant Adjutant-General of the Second Brigade, on the staff of Brig.-Gen. Cobb. On the appointment of Maj.-Gen. Halleck to command the Second Division, California Militia, he was made Division Inspector on that General's staff. When our State Militia was reorganized last spring Major-Gen. Allen appointed Major Thompson his Assistant Adjutant-General and Chief of Staff, which position he has held to the present time.

Gen. Wright has already received orders to muster in and fit out the four companies. They intend leaving on the 11th February on the steamer *Constitution*, connecting with the *Ocean*

Queen-both fine ships, with ample space to drill. An advertisement calling for enlistments will be found in to-days *Bulletin*.

Evening Bulletin, San Francisco, Thursday, January 15, 1863

❖❖❖

Head Quarters Second Regiment Mass. Cavalry,
113 Washington Street,
Boston, Jany. 15th 1863

Colonel
          Sir
                    I have the honor to inform you that I have two recruits whom I have every reason to believe intend deserting - and therefore ask your permission to send them to Fort Warren for safekeeping - It is the wish of Capt. C.R. Lowell - commanding 2nd Mass. Cavalry -

Respectfully &c
I am your obt. servt.
W. M. Rumery
2nd Lt. and Rect. officer

Col. Day   {One of these men has publicly threatened to desert - the other, apparently a <u>German</u> enlists under an <u>Irish</u> name.}
    U.S.A.   C.R. Lowell, Jr.
                                                      Capt. 1st Cavy.
                                                      Comdg 2nd Mass Cavy

Regimental Record Books, National Archives Washington, D.C.

❖❖❖
Battalion

Cavalry Battalion.-D.W.C. Thompson, a good military man, who has been connected with our State militia since the earliest days of California Americanized, proposed to Governor Andrew, through Collector Rankin, to raise four cavalry companies here, to be mustered into the service under the Massachusetts quota, and to serve three years or during the war. Governor Andrew accepted the proposition, and the War Department consented, while General Halleck approved the suggestion of making Thompson Major,-and this from a personal knowledge of his fitness. If these companies can be raised in time, it is proposed to send them East by the steamer of February 11th. A rendezvous has been established in San Francisco and Collector Rankin has had ample funds placed in his hands for all sustenance, equipment, etc., and Gen. Wright has received orders in conformity with this programme.

The Daily Bee, Sacramento, Friday, January 16, 1863.
Stockton Daily Independent, Friday, January 16, 1863.

❖❖❖

Battalion

Boston, January 15th - Governor Andrew in an address at the reception of the California Cavalry Company yesterday, said that he had received assurances from Washington that the tender of a whole cavalry battalion from California was accepted, and that the battalion will be counted as a part of the Massachusetts contingent.

(If a battalion of cavalry is accepted by the Federal Government coming from this State, we would rather have California receive the credit thereof than Massachusetts or any other State.-Eds. Alta.)

Alta California, San Francisco, Friday, January 16, 1863.

❖❖

Battalion

More Cavalry from California. - We learn that another draft is to be made upon California for four companies of light cavalry, to fill out the Massachusetts quota. Lieutenant Colonel D.W.C. Thompson, at present chief of Major General Allen's staff, has been appointed Major of Cavalry by the Governor of Massachusetts, on the unqualified approval of Major General Halleck, and will command them. Colonel Thompson is of good old Revolutionary stock. His grandfather was a Lieutenant Colonel in the Continental army. Col. Thompson has been connected with the State Militia since 1849. Orders have already been received at General Wright's headquarters from the U. S. Government to muster these Companies into the service; and furnish them with uniforms, clothing, subsistence, etc. The greatest care will be taken to select the officers, and none but healthy, active men will be accepted. There will be no delay, and as soon as mustered in, they will leave for the seat of war. For further details, our readers are referred to the advertisement.

Alta California, San Francisco, Friday, January 16, 1863

❖❖

LIGHT CAVALRY WANTED.

WITH THE APPROVAL OF the War Department, the undersigned has been authorized to raise four companes of Cavalry for active service in the war at the East.

These companies will be mustered into the United States service for three years or the war, under the Massachusetts quota, and will leave for New York on the 11th of February next.

Transportation has been provided, and sufficient funds are now under the control of Hon. Ira P. Rankin to pay the expenses of organization, uniforms, subsistence, and quarters will be furnished men as soon as accepted.

The commissioned officers will be appointed from the best military men that can be obtained in this State, and the non-commissioned officers from the best qualified of the enlisted men.

Every man joining these companies must be in good health, intelligent, active, and capable of performing the hardest light cavalry service. Companies will be immediately organized at headquarters, ASSEMBLY HALL, corner Post and Kearny streets.

D. W. C. THOMPSON, Major Commanding.
San Francisco, January 15, 1863.   ja17-1m1p

Alta California

❖❖

[Telegram]

Hdqrs. 2d Mass. Cavalry
Boston, Jan. 16, 1863

His Excelcy. John A. Andrew,
Governor of Massachusetts

Governor,
Sometime since Commissions in the 2nd Mass. Cavy were offered to Capts. Russell and Shaw of the 2nd Regiment Infantry - those Commissions were declined - but I have since learnt that they were declined upon a <u>misunderstanding</u> of the circumstances.
I have now the honor to request that you will again offer to Capt. Russell the place of Lt. Colonel, and to Capt. Shaw a Squadron Captaincy. I sincerely believe that the good of the Regiment and of the Service will thereby be promoted.
I am, Governor, Respectfully yrobdtsvt,
C.R. Lowell, Jr.
Capt. 6th Cavy
Comg 2nd Mass. Cavy

Jany 16th, '63.

Captain Robert G. Shaw
2d Regt Massachusetts Vols.

I again offer you a Captaincy in Second Massachusetts Cavalry. The order giving you leave I presume is outstanding. Come immediately to Massachusetts.

John A. Andrew
Governor of Mass.

[Telegram]

Jany 16th, '63

Captain Henry S. Russell
2d Regt Massachusetts Vols.

I again offer you Lieutenant Colonelcy Second Massachusetts Cavalry. The order giving you leave I presume is outstanding. Come immediately to Massachusetts.

John A. Andrew
Governor of Mass.

Massachusetts State Archives, Boston, Mass.
[Captain Robert G. Shaw, subsequently made Commander of 54th Mass. Colored Infantry]

Battalion

THE ACCEPTANCE OF THE CALIFORNIA BATTALION to join the 2d Mass. Cavalry Regiment is a gratifying fact. The specimen that "The Hundred" have given of the kind of men that may be expected from the "Golden State," should inspire Massachusetts to fill up the corps at once with fitting material to be their companions in camp and field. Surely there are enterprising and daring young men amongst us who should eagerly accept this opportunity to serve their country in this new command; uniting the Pacific and the Atlantic "for the Union."

Evening Transcript, Boston, Friday, January 16, 1863

OUR LETTER FROM ST. LOUIS.
(From Our Resident Correspondent of the Alta California.)
St. Louis, January 16th, 1863.

The Cavalry Question - Late Successful Cavalry Raids.
A full battalion of cavalry having been authorized to be raised in California, something extra in the cavalry line must be expected in order to outdo the Union cavalry now in the field. The truth is, that as our troopers are becoming more used to cavalry life, they are rapidly improving. The rebels have by no means of late monopolized the cavalry raids upon the enemy. Several very successful raids have taken place within a few months. At the head of the list is Gen. Carter's raid into East Tennessee, for the destruction of the East Tennessee and Virginia Railroad, which was successfully accomplished with a comparatively small force. Gen. Blunt and Gen. Herron's dash into Van Buren is likewise an important affair. Added to these, Col. Dickey's destruction of the Mobile and Ohio Railroad, sixty-five miles south of Corinth; the raid upon the York River Railroad, between Westpoint and the Pamunkey, within a few miles of Richmond; Col. Lee's raids toward Grenada, and other smaller affairs - all show that our cavalry is rousing itself gradually to the understanding that they must do something to sustain their reputation. Californians will, of course, perceive as quickly as anybody, that cavalry regiments which have been in the service fifteen months should know something of their business. Californians therefore need not send inferior horsemen as part of the new battalion. The men must be superior riders, and able to astonish the natives on this side with their equestrian powers. Hereaway, a ride of 200 miles in six days is considered a big thing. The California vaqueros would not mind riding that distance in four days, but even in five days it would frighten the nerves of the cavalry raised east or west on this side of the Rocky Mountains. Send us expert horsemen and brave men, and California will be honored by them, even if the late raids have demonstrated that our present cavalry force is worth something.

Alta California, San Francisco, Thursday, February 12, 1863.

Battalion

The New Cavalry Companies - The officers selected for the companies of light cavalry now being raised for active service in the East, are to be commissioned by the Governor of Massachusetts. The pay of officers and men commences from the date of their entering the service.

The men are entitled each to one hundred dollars bounty from the Federal Government. The uniforms, subsistence, sabres and belts, are supplied here, and are now ready for the recruits. Other arms, horses and horses equipments, will be furnished on the arrival of the companies on the Atlantic side. Some forty or fifty applications, in all, have already been made for admission into the ranks.

Only those able to ride, and sober men, will be received. Col. Ringgold, U.S.A., is the mustering officer; and Dr. Christian, U.S.A., Medical Examiner.

Alta California, San Francisco, Monday, January 19, 1863.

❖❖❖

Battalion

Massachusetts Contingent. - The San Francisco *Herald*, in speaking of the proposition to raise six companies of cavalry in California to serve as a part of the quota of Massachusetts, says that it cannot see that there are any good grounds for hostility to the measure. If our citizens volunteer to go to the war, they will go to fight the battles of the country, and it matters not whether they fight alongside of Massachusetts men, their service will be given to the whole country and not alone to the Bay State. Whenever our cavalry get a chance for glory we may be certain that we shall hear from them to the credit of California. And if the Massachusetts cavalry gains any more character on account of association with California cavalry, why it won't hurt the cause of the Union at all.

The Daily Appeal, Marysville, Tuesday, January 20, 1863.

❖❖❖

Battalion

By Telegraph to the Union.-About 50 men have enrolled in the Light Cavalry to join the Massachusetts Regiment.

Sacramento Union, Tuesday, January 20, 1863

❖❖❖
Battalion

CITY ITEMS.

California Cossacks.-Charles S. Eigenbrodt, one of the Supervisors of Alameda County, and Major on the Staff of Brigadier General Ellis, has been appointed Captain of Company A, "California Cossacks," one of the four Companies now organizing in this State, under Major Thompson, for active service in the war at the East. Capt. Eigenbrodt will immediately organize his Company at headquarters in this city, and obtain his men chiefly from the agricultural counties, which can furnish the most daring and skillful horsemen in the Union. Captains of Companies B, C and D, will soon be appointed, and the Companies organized are to go East on the 11th of February next. If the "California Cossacks" prove as troublesome to the rebels as the Russian Cossacks have to the enemies of that great Empire, California will not regret sparing these four Companies from her peaceful pursuits.

Alta California, San Francisco, Wednesday, January 21, 1863.

THE NEW TROOPS.

The San Francisco Call, of yesterday, publishes a letter written in that city and addressed to itself in relation to the new troops being raised here. In that letter we find the following:

"The collector of the Port, Ira P. Rankin, Esq., has taken upon himself to raise four companies of cavalry to go into a *Massachusetts Regiment*, in order that he and his friend, the 'Merry' Andrew, of Massachusetts may save their friends in Boston from being drafted into the ranks of the 'bullet-stoppers' for the rifles of the 'butter-nut adherents' of 'Foot-ball' Jackson. Now, it is said that D.W.C. Thompson is to command the squadron, and the other commissioned officers are to be appointed by the aforesaid Governor Andrew. It is high time that Governor Stanford interposed his authority in this matter, and stopped the recruiting for any regiments but those of California, who really needs them in the Texas expedition."

The recent course of the Call upon this subject and others of a somewhat similar nature, is strange for a Union paper. It may be that certain etiquette due the Governor of California has been overlooked in this matter. Of that we do not now judge; but the Governor has not publicly complained, nor do we know that he has done so privately. Aside from that, what matters it to Union men whether Californians fight in Massachusetts regiments or California regiments under the national banner? The cause is one-the suppression of rebellion, the reestablishment of the national authority over all the territory of the Republic. The glory will belong alike to all, and the benefits accrue alike to each.

This State has thus far been called upon for but few men, and yet she is able to furnish her quota when that duty is demanded of her; but in that case these troops will doubtless be included in her portion. It is not, however, likely that such call will be made upon her; but whether or not, it is unbecoming in the loyal people of a State that has been so highly favored by the National Government to object, by word or deed, to her citizens volunteering to go forth to battle in defense of that Government. Because they cannot go in California regiments, or because they do not choose to enter a department of the service where they will be kept distant from the theater of war, but choose rather to enlist in such manner as to be sure of active service in the field, where there will be a chance of honor and promotion, shall these facts be urged against them and they be denied the opportunity of assisting to put down treason? Surely not! And yet the quotation from the Call, the substance of which it has on several occasions editorially indorsed, amounts to this. It is a small thing in Union men to endeavor to excite an antipathy of this kind between loyal States. Such course is pursued by rebels and their sympathizers, but it is wholly unbecoming in any others. Californians should be the last people on the continent to favor any such heresy.

There is, we believe, a law for punishing those who discourage enlistments; and we should be sorry to learn that any man or journal upon this coast had violated it. The quotation may not come within the letter of that law, but does it not encroach upon its spirit? And even then this correspondent does not halt, but appeals "again" to Gov. Stanford to stop this recruiting for "Bosting," until the ranks of the reinforcements to Gen. Carleton be filled up. For ourselves, we cannot see why those who desire to volunteer to fight the battles of the country should be hindered from so doing. There are those who do not choose to volunteer in California regiments, because they fear they may not have any fighting to do, hence the earnest Union men, who wish to have a hand in this great struggle, prefer to enlist so that they are certain of being led into the war. Should such men be prevented from entering the National service? Yet the writer referred to proposes that very thing. Surely the Call, when it considers this subject with a sober second thought, will make amends for the error it has been guilty of.

The Daily Bee, Sacramento, Thursday, January 22, 1863.

❖❖

MEAN TO DOUBLE THEIR NUMBER. Captain Reed of the California Hundred has been authorized to recruit in this State another company to form with his present command the first squadron of the first battalion of the Second Regiment of Cavalry. He will be assisted by his men, and no doubt will meet with entire success. This new movement, together with the expected additional quota from the Pacific, will make it necessary for our Massachusetts young men to be prompt to enrol themselves in what gives every promise of being a "crack" corps.

Evening Transcript, Boston, Friday, January 23, 1863

❖❖
Battalion

California Cossacks. - The headquarters of the new cavalry companies now raising for service in the East have been removed from Assembly Hall to Platt's Music Hall, on Montgomery street. The four companies will be quartered in this spacious building. The main floor of the large hall is to be used for battalion and company drills, and the galleries set apart for visitors. The basement of the hall will be used for squad drills, and, in connection with the well arranged kitchen and storerooms, for the subsistence department. The front hall in the second story will be occupied by the commissioned officers for headquarters, and the adjoining rooms for sleeping apartments. The upper story and other parts of the building will be assigned to the men for their quarters. The Cossacks will commence their drills and garrison duty next week, and fill up the companies to the full quota as soon as possible. It is the intention of those having the fitting out of these companies that none shall enter them who cannot ably and honorably represent California in the great war in the East. The total number of applications thus far is about one hundred. Recruiting stations have been opened in the interior. There will be no difficulty experienced in getting the ranks filled, but very serious doubts are expressed by true and loyal men as to the policy and propriety of sending away more men of the State, in view of the probable or possible interruptions of amicable relations with foreign powers.

Alta California, San Francisco, Friday, January 23, 1863

Battalion

The following officers have been selected: Company A-Captain C. S. Eigenbrodt, Alameda County; 2d Lieutenant-J. T. Campbell, Alvarado; Company B-Captain Z. D. Adams, San Francisco; 2d Lieutenant I. J. Harris, San Francisco; Company C-2d Lieutenant A. W. Stone, San Jose.

Evening Bulletin, San Francisco, Friday, January 23, 1863

Battalion

The roads in Massachusetts being impeded by the "varst numbers" of volunteers crowding to the army, Thompson has been appointed Major and authorized to raise four more companies of cavalry in this State, as a help towards relieving the pressure.

The Colusa Sun, Saturday, January 24, 1863.
[The Colusa Sun was a strong proponent of the Southern cause in California.]

Battalion

THE CALIFORNIA CAVALRY BATTALION.- General Wright has received orders to muster into service four additional companies of Cavalry, to form a part of the Massachusetts complement. It is intended they shall be ready to depart for the East on the 11th of February on the steamer Constitution. Major D.W.C. Thompson has been appointed to command. The California Hundred has arrived at Boston, and been honored with a public reception, and addressed by Governor Andrew in behalf of the State.

We are opposed to California's filling the Massachusetts's quota, as long as our own regiments want men. Officers are constantly recruiting in this State for our regiments, and for the regular service and the Oregon regiment, and after furnishing one hundred men for Massachusetts, we are called upon for four hundred more; and this, too, in the face of a requisition on this State for one regiment more of infantry and five companies of cavalry, which has been called for by Gen. Wright, and not yet responded to by Gov. Stanford of the State.

The Sentinel, Santa Cruz, Saturday, January 24, 1863.

GOVERNOR STANFORD'S LETTER TO
GENERAL WRIGHT
Executive Department,
January 24, 1863

General: - I have the honor to acknowledge the receipt of yours of the 23d inst., inclosing a dispatch from W. Scott Ketchum, Brigadier General and Assistant Adjutant General, ordering the mustering into the service of the United States of *four companies of cavalry, to be raised in this State, for service in the contingent of the State of Massachusetts.*

The proceedings under and by force of which these troops are to be raised are clearly irregular and in violation of the rights of this State. I know of no authority by which the *Governor of Massachusetts can raise volunteers in California*, either through the orders of the War Department or the inconsiderate and officious action of citizens of this State.
LELAND STANFORD,
Governor of California.

The italics are ours;-[Ed.]
Weekly Butte Record, Oroville, Saturday, April 4, 1863.

Head Quarters Second Regiment Mass. Cavalry,
113 Washington Street,
Boston, Jany 24, 1863

To
  Brig. General Geo. H. Andrews,
      Comg. Remainder of Banks Expedition.

General,
  I was sorry not to find you in New York last week - and to miss you again in Boston on my return.
  Capt. McKim, A. Q. M., tells me that he had some conversation with you about shipping the 1st Battalion of my Regiment - and that you proposed to send it from New York. Of course this is quite inmaterial to me - but I sincerely hope that you may find it possible to delay the shipment till say Feb 10th, in order that I may complete their equipment, and may send them off with a feeling that they know a little at least about the care of horses. I hope too that you will give me such notice of your intentions, that either my Q Master or myself may go to New York & personally superintend the preparation of the vessels. I have no wish to have my Regiment crippled by such a loss as the 12th Battery met with.
  I am, General, Respectfully Your obdtservt.
      C. R. Lowell, Jr.
      Capt. 6th Cav, Comg 2d Mass. Cav.

(We hear from San Francisco that the
3rd Battn is gettting on well-and will
probably sail on Feb 11th from there.)

Regimental Record Books, National Archives, Washington, D.C.

❖❖
Battalion
CITY ITEMS
_____

  Cavalry Commander.-Captain Z.B. Adams, of the National Guard of this city, has assumed command of Company B of the California Cossacks, and is now enlisting his company at Platt's Hall. Already has the National Guard sent five officers to aid in crushing out this infamous rebellion, and now goes a sixth. These are Captains Moore, Potts, Johns, Ropes and Pollock.

Alta California, San Francisco, Sunday, January 25, 1863
❖❖

  We agree with our neighbor [The Bee], that to fight under the National banner, no matter for what State, is an honor and a service; but why is it that Massachusetts alone, of all the loyal States, resorts to California for fighting men to fill up her quota?-[San Francisco Call].
  Massachusetts did not resort to California for fighting men to fill up her quota. She has never yet been behind any of her sister States in furnishing men to the battle for the nation.

Her men have always been there, if not in the van, then certainly in full numbers. She was first in the war of independence, first to rush to the defense of the Capitol when Sumter was assailed, and hers was the first blood shed in this great struggle! It comes with but a poor grace from a young and beardless State like California, whose maiden sword has not yet been fleshed, to talk to the old patriot and hero Bay State of *our* great valor and *her* want of it! It is childish – if it do not arise from innocence of history. Massachusetts did not ask California for troops. Some respected citizens of this State asked Massachusetts if she would accept a few of our superior horsemen and give them a place in her gallant cavalry, and she answered "yes;" and not only that, but said she would bear their expenses hence to the field of muster. If some had asked New York or Pennsylvania or Illinois a similar question, and they had answered as Massachusetts did – which, by the way, they would have done almost without doubt – would the Call have thrown obstacles in the way of recruiting for such purposes? We can spare a few hundred or thousand of our brave fellows to battle for the nation and liberty. It is not long since a whole regiment was offered the Government, and the Call was loud in its denunciations, because the parties proposing backed out and would not send it; and now because other parties are expending their means and sending troops to the battle-field, for precisely the same purpose, that journal growls and snaps at them all the while, as if they were doing some evil thing, or as if it desired to prevent men from enlisting in the Union cause. We are not defending Massachusetts. She needs it not from us – nor did she need any from the great Webster – "there stands her history; look at it." But we grieve to see a good and loyal journal so blind to facts as to say that Massachusetts asked California for troops, and that she cannot raise her quota at home. She never yet failed to do her share, nor will she fall now. A few Californians made her a free will offering, and she accepted it. "Her offending hath this extent – no more."

The Daily Bee, Sacramento, Monday, January 26, 1863.

❖❖❖
Battalion

California Cavalry Battalion.-The cavalry battalion organizing for the war at the East under Major Thompson, at Platt's Hall, will consist of four companies, A, B, C, and D. Each company will comprise the following officers, non-commissioned officers and privates: Captain, first and second lieutenants, first sergeant, quartermaster, commissary sergeant, 5 sergeants, 8 corporals, 2 teamsters, 2 blacksmiths, wagoner, 2 trumpeters and 76 privates-in all 103 officers and privates.

Evening Bulletin, San Francisco, Monday, January 26, 1863
Stockton Daily Independent, Wednesday, January 28, 1863.

❖❖❖

The California Hundred have received a furlough for one week, to visit their relatives and friends. They are from nearly every loyal State. Capt. Reed has the most implicit faith in them, and says every one will return at the time appointed. - *Boston Journal Jan. 30th.*

Alta California, San Francisco, Wednesday, February 25, 1863
[In spite of Reed's faith, 7 men deserted although 2 subsequently returned.]

❖❖❖

Battalion

SECOND MASSACHUSETTS CAVALRY. Lieut. Blagden, son of the Rev. Dr. Blagden of this city, has reached home from the 1st Mass. Cavalry, and is engaged in recruiting the company of which he is to be Captain in the 2d. This last named corps only wants two or three companies to be full. These should be forthcoming at once, so that on the arrival of the Battalion from California, the Regiment may be ready to render the efficient services so greatly needed, and which it will be so able to perform.

Evening Transcript, Boston, Saturday, January 31, 1863
[George Blagden, Co. K]

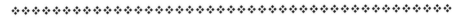

FEBRUARY, 1863

16   U.S. Senate passes the Conscription Act.
25   Lincoln signs an act for creating a national bank system and national currency.

Battalion

By Telegraph to the Union.-Over seventy men have enlisted in the new cavalry battalion.

Sacramento Union, Tuesday, February 3, 1863

Battalion

Samuel F. Barker states, in a published card, that Major D.W.C. Thompson, now raising a battalion of cavalry for service in the East, had an interview with him about December 11th, 1862, and offered him a position in the command. He was duly appointed First Lieutenant of Company B by Captain Adams; but through Major Thompson's influence, he was removed and appointed Second Lieutenant, Major Thompson in the meantime telling him to be prepared to leave on the shortest notice. Now he is told that he cannot hold even his Second Lieutenancy, because he is a man of family which fact, he says, Major Thompson knew from the first; and he moreover states that Thompson is himself a family man. He has recruited twenty to thirty men, settled his business here, and now to be told that because he has a family he cannot serve his country, is more than provoking, This, he thinks, is not the true reason.

The Daily Bee, Sacramento, Wednesday, February 4, 1863.

Letter from Boston (From our Special Correspondent)
Boston, February 4, 1863.

The California Hundred

Were the subject of a very pleasant and very hearty ovation a few days ago. This compliment was tendered them by the former Californians now resident or visiting in Boston, and the occasion was one of much gratification to all participants. The only drawback was a pouring rain, which made the march through the streets a most disagreeable job, but it was not without its advantages, as it enabled the company to display a most excellent article of top boots, with which a skillful artisan in this burg had provided them. The sight of a hundred pairs of top boots on the extremities of a hundred stout men, does much to reconcile one with the most disagreeable dispensations of Providence in the way of weather. It is such an admirable illustration of the fitness of things that the artistic sense is deeply gratified. No single article of human apparel exerts a greater reflex influence upon the wearer than boots. A man shod with well fitting, substantial and reliable boots is thrice a man. The friends at home of our hundred Californians will no doubt be gratified when I tell them that the hundred pairs of boots made a great sensation-great enough to reconcile everybody to the absence of the horse element in the parade.

Hurry up the balance of that battalion, sister California! The Bay State is grateful for favors received, but, Twist-like, she looks over her shoulder for more. Enlistments are not progressing with great rapidity in the Second Cavalry, and the Pacific battalion is needed. The arrival of Captain Reed's company gave a stimulus to recruiting, and the advent of another goodlooking body of men on our shores would be a real blessing to the authorities at the State House.

Sacramento Daily Union, Wednesday, March 4, 1863.

News and Miscellaneous Items.

Insulted Californians. A few nights ago, at eleven o'clock, at the corner of Court and Howard streets, (a place no city government has yet been able to station police force enough to protect men and women from insult,) two "roughs" were standing as three sober and well-behaved soldiers of our California company were passing. The two bullies jeered them by singing "the raw recruit," and by all kinds of insulting speech, to which no reply was made. At last one of the three Californians went back and said to the two men, "You must stop this or I shall." As soon as his back was turned the insults were renewed. He went back and struck one a blow in his face as severe as it was deserved, which sent him from the sidewalk flat into the street. His companion picked him up, with a mark upon his face which will make him remember California for a long while. It is somewhat surprising that a police officer did not arrive in time to arrest the wrong man.

The Colored Regiment will probably go into camp at Worcester. It will be numbered the 54th Mass. Vol. Infantry. Capt. N.P. Hallowell, of the Mass. 20th, will be promoted to be one of its field officers, and Capt. Robert G. Shaw, of the Mass. 2d Regiment, another field officer.

John Wilkes Booth commences tonight the fourth and final work of his truly extraordinary engagement at the Boston Museum. The announcement of this fact will doubtless make the rush greater than ever and enhance the importance of making early application for seats. The piece reserved for his farewell effort is "The Corsican Brothers," an intensely effective drama, in which the young tragedian must appear to excellent advantage, and we are assured of an admirable performance in the fact that the piece has been in preparation several weeks. Mr. Booth appears on Wednesday afternoon.

Evening Transcript, Boston, Monday, February 9, 1863.

❖❖❖
Battalion

The Massachusetts Contingent.-Major Thompson who is enlisting a battalion of cavalry, on behalf of the State of Massachusetts, for duty in the East, has about one hundred and fifty men enrolled.

Alta California, San Francisco, Saturday, February 7, 1863
Sacramento Daily Union, Monday, February 9, 1863

❖❖❖
Battalion

CITY INTELLIGENCE
Recruiting Office.-Lieutenant J.W. McMadden, who stands six feet five inches in his stockings and may therefore be expected to do some tall fighting when he meets the enemy, has opened a recruiting office at the Western Hotel, on K street between Second and Third streets. Lieutenant McMadden is recruiting for Company A of the California Battalion for Massachusetts. He expects to remain in the city about a week.

Sacramento Daily Union, Monday, February 9, 1863

❖❖❖
Battalion

California Volunteers. - Last week 100 men were sworn into service to serve with the California Cavalry battalion now forming at Platt's Hall. 100 more men are ready to join, and will be examined and passed speedily. The men are furnished with meals and quarters after a satisfactory inspection by the surgeon, and when sworn they receive their uniforms. A cavalry battalion consists of 4 companies, of 100 men each. The following officers have already been selected: Captain of Co. A, C.S. Eigenbrodt, of Brig. Gen. Ellis's staff; Captain of Co. B, Z.B. Adams, of the National Guard, San Francisco; 1st Lieutenant, Co. A, George A. Manning, of the Sacramento Rangers; 1st Lieutenant, Co. B, H.W. Smith, of the Light Guard, San Francisco; 2nd Lieutenant, Co. A, Alvin W. Stone, of the Union Guard, San Jose; and 2nd Lieutenant, Co. B, Henry H. Crocker, of the Oakland Guard, Alameda county. It is the intention of Major Thompson to select most of the officers of this battalion from the uniformed companies of this State.

Captain DeMerritt, commander of the Sacramento Rangers, resigned his position on Saturday, and will be appointed as one of the Captains of this battalion. The drill-room is in the basement under Platt's Hall, entrance on Bush street, where the men already enlisted are receiving instructions in regard to military evolutions at various hours of the day. The officers' room is in the same building, up stairs, entrance on Montgomery street. This battalion will form a portion of the Massachusetts quota of troops for the war, and will leave in the steamer for Boston about the 1st or 19th of March. Ira P. Rankin, U.S. Port Collector, received by the steamer just arrived, funds from Massachusetts to pay all the expenses of fitting out this battalion and their passage East.

Evening Bulletin, San Francisco, Monday, February 9, 1863
The Daily Bee, Sacramento, Tuesday, February 10, 1863.

Battalion

Massachusetts Cavalry Battalion. —

The four companies of this Battalion are now quartered at Platt's Hall. Captain Eigenbrodt's and Captain Adams' companies have sixty-five men each. Company C, Lieutenant Stone commanding, has thirty-three, and Company D, Lieutenant Smith, commanding, has twenty-one. On Thursday last, 100 men were sworn into service by Captain Woodruff, U.S. Army, and were furnished with a complete outfit for field service. It is expected that one hundred men a week will be mustered into service and uniformed until the Battalion is full. Captain Van Voast, of the Ninth Infantry, a graduate of West Point, has been, by permission of General Wright, detailed to act as military instructor for the Battalion, until its departure. One company, we learn, is to be composed of native Californians.

Alta California, San Francisco, Tuesday, February 10, 1863.

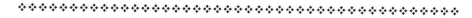

Battalion

NEW COMPANY FOR 2D MASS. CAVALRY. Lieut. McKendry of the California Hundred, has received authority to raise a company of Cavalry, which, with the California Hundred, will make the first Squadron attached to the first Battalion of 2d Mass. Cavalry.

Among returned Californians, and among those who have friends already in the Cal. Co., or those who know the character of that organization, and would wish to serve with it, he is confident he can find in his native State another Hundred equal to those who came with him from the Pacific. This Squadron will be in the first Battalion, and will be the ranking Squadron of the Regiment.

Lieut. McKendry wants active, patriotic young men. None others need apply.

As the first Battalion may be ordered away within the present month, those who wish to join must apply at Camp Meigs, Readville, and at other points to be designated hereafter.

Col. C.R. Lowell,
Com'd 2d Mass. Cavalry.

Advertisement, Evening Transcript, Boston, Tuesday, February 10, 1863.

The First Battalion of the 2d Mass. Cavalry, Major Caspar Crowninshield, will start for Fortress Monroe tomorrow. The battalion numbers five full companies, and will take nearly all the men now at Readville. They will go by rail to Baltimore, and will start directly from camp without coming to this city. The intention is to form a camp of instruction at Fortress Monroe, where there will be no trouble in keeping the men. The deserters were all brought up from Fort Warren yesterday.

Evening Transcript, Boston , Tuesday, February 10, 1863.
[Co.'s A,B,C,D & K]

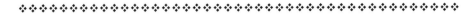

DEPARTURE OF THE CAVALRY BATTALION FROM READVILLE CAMP. THE CAV-ALRY CO. IN ROUTE FOR THE SEAT OF WAR. The First Battalion of the 2d Massachusetts Cavalry left Readville yesterday afternoon for the seat of war. The following is the roster so far as completed:

Major-Caspar Crowninshield.
Acting Adjutant-G. A. Stone.
Quartermaster Sergeant- —Files.
Co. A (California)-Captain J. Sewall Reed;
1st Lieut. W. H. Rumery (acting), 2d do. John W. Sim.
Co. B-1st Lieut. L. S. Dabney (acting Captain); 2d do. W.F. Ball.
Co. C-Captain C. E. Rice; 1st Lieut. John T. Richards.
Co. D-Captain, Francis Washburn; 1st Lieut., —Payson.
Co. K-Captain, Geo. F. Holman (acting); 2d Lieut., —Allwood.

The above companies have each about 64 men, the minimum, except the first, which is 100 (California), thus making 350 men in all. Ten men are left behind at camp in the hospital, several of whom have been injured by their horses, and two of whom are seriously ill with fever. The battalion is fully equipped with the exception of carbines and pistols. They have a complete uniform, and are armed with sabres only, at present. The horses are the same as have been used at camp, in drill, and 350 were taken with the battalion. Saddles and other trappings are also complete. Six days' rations were taken by the men. The regimental Quartermaster, J. N. Brown, will accompany the battalion to its destination and then return to look after the other battalions. The route to be taken is a land route, by way of the Providence, Hartford and New Haven roads to New York, where they will arrive this morning. Thence by ferryboat, they will go to Elizabethport, N.J., and again enter the cars, which, without another change, will convey them west to Harrisburg, and thence southeast to Baltimore. From Baltimore, by steamer, they will proceed to Fortress Monroe and report to General Dix. They are expected to arrive at Baltimore tomorrow night or Sunday morning. The reason for going by way of Harrisburg is, that by the other route it would be necessary to change cars at Philadelphia, and transfer all the men, horses and baggage across the city. There was a large gathering of the friends of the soldiers at Readville to bid them adieu. They all left in good spirits. We expect to hear well of the gallant boys; and the country will particularly watch the California One Hundred, as fine a body of soldiers as has gone forth to aid the Union cause.

A beautiful flag, recently arrived from the Golden State, was presented to the California Company before its departure. The presentation speech was made by Hon. Amos A. Lawrence, and appropriately responded to by the soldiers of the Company.

Evening Transcript, Boston, Friday, February 13, 1863
Boston Journal, Saturday, February 14, 1863
[Flag of the Dashaway Society, whereabouts unknown.]

Battalion

The Massachusetts Contingent - Maj. Thompson, who is enlisting a battalion of cavalry, on behalf of the State of Massachusetts, for duty in the East, has about one hundred and fifty men enrolled.

Alta California, San Francisco, Thursday, February 12, 1863.

❖❖❖
Battalion

AMUSEMENTS.

Metropolitan Theatre.-The National Guard tender a benefit this evening at the Metropolitan Theatre, to Capt. Z. B. Adams, their commander, who is now raising a company for the Massachusetts Cavalry Battalion, when the "School for Scandal" will be played, with Mr. J. H. Taylor as Charles Surface, and Mrs. Hayne as Lady Teazle, to be followed by a song and dance by Miss Lotta and a *pas de deux* by the Misses Worrell, and to conclude with the farce of "Nan, the Good for Nothing," with Little Jennie Worrell as Nan.

Alta California, San Francisco, Friday, February 13, 1863.

❖❖❖

METROPOLITAN THEATRE,

Montgomery street, bet. Washington and Jackson

BENEFIT OF CAPT. Z. B. ADAMS

TENDERED BY THE

National Guard,

ON

FRIDAY EVENING,...... ...FEBRUARY 13,

On which occasion,

Julia Dean Hayne,

MISS LOTTA,

THE STAR SISTERS WORRELL,

SOPHIE, JENNIE AND IRENE,

MR. JOHN WOODARD,

MR. J. H. TAYLOR.

The performance will commence with the great comedy of

SCHOOL FOR SCANDAL.

For characters see bills of the day.

Song and Dance.......................................Miss Lotta

Dance.............................Sophie and Irene Worrell

To conclude with the farce of

NAN, THE GOOD FOR NOTHING.

Nan..Jennie Worrell

Box office open at 10 o'clock on Friday morning. NoT.cs—Only six seats will be reserved to any one person.   fe12

METROPOLITAN THEATRE.

Alta California

❖❖❖

CAVALRY WANTED.-It is undoubtedly true that the Federal army is deficient in quantity and quality as to this arm of the service among the volunteers, and needs strengthening. There are five regiments, diligent and daring, but, they are few and far between. Massachusetts can do no better thing, just now, in the military line, than contribute promptly her second corps of efficient light dragoons. One battalion of the 2d regiment, including the California Hundred, has just left for a camp of instruction, near Fortress Monroe. A second battalion is expected in March from the Pacific. Before that arrives the third to be raised here should be all recruited, armed and equipt. Then the State will have under its auspices a mounted force to be proud of.

Evening Transcript, Boston, Friday, February.13, 1863

❖❖❖

LETTER FROM NEW YORK
From Our Own Correspondent
New York February 17, 1863

The California Hundred already in Active Service.
The first battalion of the 2d Regiment of Massachusetts cavalry passed through this city on Saturday, *en route* for Fortress Monroe. It includes the California Hundred, who led the van, having their State flag, which was greeted wherever recognized by enthusiastic cheering. The battalion was in the command of Major Caspar Crowninshield.

Evening Bulletin, San Francisco, Tuesday, March 17, 1863
The Marin County Journal San Rafael, Saturday, March 21, 1863
[Harrisburg, Pennsylvania, Saturday, February 14, 1863.]

❖❖❖
Battalion

The Massachusetts Battalion. - Here is what the Santa Cruz *Sentinal* says relative to the efforts in progress for filling the Massachusetts quota of troops: "We have a letter from a person who signs himself J. Wing Oliver, Lieutenant Company A, California Light Cavalry, asking us to do what we can to assist in raising the four companies for service in the Massachusetts regiments. We beg to decline, for reasons heretofore expressed. The regiments of our own State want more men to take the place of those sick or disabled. There has been a call upon this State for one regiment of infantry and seven companies of cavalry, which has not yet been responded to. When California fills the requirements of the General Government then we have no objection to furnishing Massachusetts with a few substitutes."

Santa Cruz Sentinel, Saturday, January 24, 1863
Alta California, San Francisco, Monday, February 16, 1863

❖❖❖

HKAI QUARTERS CALIFORNIA CAV. BATTATION,
Platt's Hall, 216 Montgomery street,
San Francisco, Feb. 14, 1863.

Wanted.

BUGLERS, BLACKSMITHS, FAR-
riers, saddlers and good light cavalry soldiers, to fill Companies A, B, C, and D, of
this battalion.

Transportation has been paid to New York, and
ample funds are now here to pay all expenses, and
the battalion will leave for the war at the East in
March next.

This battalion is being organized and fitted out
under orders from the War Department at Washington, and is intended for light cavalry service,
and will be assigned to most active and brilliant
position in the war.

Uniforms, subsistence and quarters will be furnished men as soon as accepted, and one hundred
dollars bounty, monthly pay, &c., as allowed by
army regulations.

Young men who desire to help maintain the Government of the United States, and participate in
the great and stirring events at the East, can have
no better opportunity than to enlist in this battalion.

fe15-tf

D. W. C. THOMPSON,
Major Commanding.

Alta California

❖❖❖

Coleman's Eutaw House

Baltimore, Feb 18th 1863

My Dear Mammy

This is the first opportunity I have had, since I left Readville, of writing to you. From the time we left the station at Readville until the present moment desertions have been going on at sufficiently rapid a rate quite a large part of the Battalion are at the present moment scattered along the road between this place and Boston. It was impossible to prevent it in the confusion of loading & unloading the horses the men got away & when I posted a guard the guard gener- ally deserted - With the exception of the Californians the men are a disgrace to the name of soldiers and to the state which sent them. They get beastly drunk & fight among themselves draw the sabres & pistols & cut & slash each other. Two men have already been severly hurt. We have been detained here for some time owing to a want of transportation & the men have been quartered in a stone house there was a guard of some 15 infantry men put over them & I left Lieut Payson also to look out for them. While he was gone to get his supper the men attacked the guard disarmed them & went out of the building & were drunk & fighting all night long round town during that night & the next day most all of them were arrested & brought back but some have still remained absent & have I suppose deserted. Yesterday I sent most all of them down on two transports to Fortress Monroe. The Californians & about twenty men of Co B still remain here & I shall probably get off with them tomorrow but there is a scarcity of boats here & I may be kept still longer. I cannot say that I have enjoyed myself much so far but when I once get the men in camp down at the Fortress I hope to be able to make something like soldiers out of them - though like enough many will desert to the enemy. And as they are a most expert set of thieves perhaps they will be more servicable to us in that capacity than they could possibly be as soldiers. It would give me real pleasure to see 100 of them, whom I could pick out, hanged all in a row. Well enough of this I hope I shall be able to give better accounts of them when next I write, but just to illustrate what a class of men they are - two of them had a dispute & one of them drew his sabre & stabed the other in the stomach the sword glanced & only a slight wound was inflicted I happened to be near by & I ran up & knocked the man who had the sabre down & had him secured - well I have come to the end of my paper so I must say goodby - I will write again soon & I hope in better spirits - give my best love to grandfather & mother - Cousin John & Fanny - your affectionate son Caspar

Caspar Crowninshield, Letters, Massachusetts Historical Society

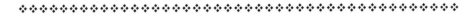

Whereabouts of the California Hundred-Their
Arrival at Gloucester Point.

The *Boston Journal*, of March 1st, contains a letter dated Gloucester Point, February 23, which gives some particulars of the whereabouts of the cavalry company raised in California, for the Second Massachusetts Cavalry. The letter says: "The detachment which left Camp Meigs, Readville, on the 12 inst., consisting of companies A B C D and K, is now encamped at this place.

"We came by rail *via* Providence and Hartford to New York; there we took the boat to Elizabethport, N. J., arriving at 7 P. M. on the 13th; again by land to Baltimore early on the morning of the 15th. The Ninth Army Corps having been just carried to Fortress Monroe, we had to wait the return of transports. On Tuesday afternoon we went on board the United States steamers *Kennebee* and *Express* and started for Fortress Monroe. The *Kennebee* arrived first at the fortress, and Capt. Holman, the senior officer on board, reported to Gen. Dix. We were ordered to proceed to Yorktown and report for duty to Major General Keyes, commanding the Fourth Army Corps. Captain H. *[George F. Holman, Co. K]* reported his detachments at Yorktown on the 19th, and Gen. Keyes encamped us here. The balance of officers and men arrived two days later.

"Gloucester Point is on the York River, directly opposite Yorktown. It is a beautiful spot, a sandy plain thirty feet above the river. We are the outposts on this side of the river. The outer pickets are less than a hundred rods from camp. There is a small earthwork on the point called Fort Keyes, a battery and some regiments besides ourselves. On the Yorktown side the fortifi-cations are extensive and extend thirteen miles up the river.

"The infantrymen here were evidently glad to see us, having been troubled by occasional dashes of rebel cavalry on our pickets. This we hope to stop and then return the compliment."

"The officers here with us are as follows, named in order of their rank and seniority:

Major Casper Crowninshield; Captains J. Sewall Reed, Co. A; Francis Washburn, Co. D; Chas. E. Rice, Co. C; 1st Lieutenants, G. A. Stone, I. T. Richards, Henry E. Alvord, W. J. Ball, John W. Sim, Chas. Payson; Assistant Surgeon, Gamwell.

"It is thought pretty generally that it was a mistake undertaking to send on the men from Massachusetts by land after paying the large bounties. Several deserted on the route. It is to be hoped that the next detachment will go on board transports at Boston, there paid their bounties and sail at once."

Boston Journal, February 28, 1863. From a letter signed Cadet.
Alta California, San Francisco, Wednesday, April 8, 1863.
[Deserters: Co. B - 9; Co. K - 8]

❖❖
Battalion

Washington's Birthday Celebration- Grand Military Parade and Review.

The one hundred and thirty-first anniversary of the birth of George Washington was universally celebrated by the loyal citizens of this metropolis. The feeling of the patriotic masses of this community in this eventful period of their country's history found vent in demonstrations which must convince the deluded adherents to the policy of rebeldom in our midst that the spirit of "76" still exists as strong as in those early days of the Republic that tried the heroism of their sires.

The Military Parade and Review. - The parade of the California 2d Brigade yesterday, and its review at the Mission by Gen. Allen, was a pleasing sight. The Brigade was composed of the following regiments, battalions and companies:

1st Regiment-City Guard, National Guard, San Francisco Hussars, California Fusileers, San Francisco Light Guard and Ellsworth Rifles.

2d Regiment-Montgomery Guard, McMahon Guard, Shields Guard, Wolf Tone Guard, Irish Invincibles, Emmet Rifles and Emmet Life Guard.

1st Infantry Battalion-Union Guard, Ellsworth Guard, Oakland Guard, Washington Light Infantry and Franklin Light Infantry.

With the above was the California Cavalry Battalion making a total number of officers and privates of about 900 men.

The entire brigade was commanded by Brig. Gen. John S. Ellis, the 1st Regiment by Col. James Wood, the 2d Regiment by Col. T.N. Casneau, the 1st Infantry battalion by Col. J.W. McKenzie and the Cavalry battalion by Maj. D.W.C. Thompson.

There was a very large concourse of spectators, who were much pleased with the military evolutions.

Alta California, San Francisco, Tuesday, February 24, 1863.
Evening Bulletin, San Francisco, Tuesday, February 24, 1863

❖❖
Battalion

FOR FREEDOM.- Among those who have lately enlisted for the war from this county is B. F. Hoxie, for a number of years a resident of this town. We are sure that the Massachusetts Battalion can boast of no abler man than Ben, whom the enemy will find a rough fellow to handle. John McKinney, Amos Howard and John Taylor, also of this town, left Suisun on Friday for the purpose of enlisting. Honor to the brave ones who buckle on their armor in defense of their country! She needs them more than ever.

Solano County Herald, Saturday, February 28, 1863
[All of Company L. Benjamin F. Hoxie was specially detailed as one of Sheridan's scouts in Dec., 1864.]

Gov. Stanford sent to Gen. Wright a kind of semi-protest against the mode by which it was proposed to raise troops in California for Massachusetts, saying, however, that while he would not interfere with it now, his silence must not be taken as a precedent or as an evidence that he was content. General Wright sent this letter to the War Department, and one of his own with it, in which he says:

"I deem it proper to say to the Department that the authority given to individuals to raise troops in this State, independent of the Executive authority, and to send them to the theater of war as a portion of the quota from another State, has not been regarded favorably by the people. This feeling, however, will not prevent the prompt organization of the companies called for. The great anxiety among these people is for active service in the field, and if they cannot go as California troops, they will seek service under any call which will carry them to the battle-field."

The Daily Bee, Sacramento, Saturday, February 28, 1863.

MARCH, 1863

3   Lincoln signs act for first Federal Draft.
8   Mosby captures Brig. Gen. E. H. Stoughton while in bed at Fairfax County Court House, Va.

LETTER FROM A CALIFORNIAN IN THE ARMY OF VIRGINIA.

(We are permitted to extract the following from a letter received by a gentleman of this city from his son in Virginia.- Eds. ALTA.)
GLOUCESTER POINT, (opposite Yorktown March 1, 1863.)

DEAR FATHER: It having been some three weeks since I last wrote you, and today being Sunday, having the day to myself, I improve the opportunity offered by writing to you, knowing that I could not be engaged in anything more beneficial.

Since the date of my last letter, a great change has taken place in our situation, being now encamped on the "sacred soil of Virginia," within seventy-five miles of Richmond; but it is not expected that we will take any active part in fighting for some time yet. It is reported that a thousand rebel cavalry are within five miles of our camp; but there are so many false reports always circulating around a camp that I do not place much faith in it, though our officers do- so much indeed that we are obliged to sleep with all our clothes on, including boots and spurs, with our arms within reach, and our saddles placed, so that in three minutes after an alarm being given we can be saddled up and ready to repel the attack of an enemy.

We are encamped about a mile below Yorktown, on the bank of the York river on what appears to be very fertile soil, and the country well watered and timbered. The camp is protected by a gunboat lying in the river some two hundred yards from the bank, and by heavy guns in the fort at Yorktown, capable of throwing shot and shell a distance of five miles. Besides this, there are picket guards stationed out in the country some two miles from camp, and completely surrounding it, who, in case of a surprise, will throw up rockets, which can be seen by the camp guard, who alarm the camp, which is expected to be ready to do some fighting in three minutes after the alarm being sounded. The tents which we occupy are what are called here the Sibley tent; but the pole is different from those which you have seen. At the bottom of these poles there is an iron-tripod, the legs of which are some four feet long, and on the top of this tripod there is a socket, into which a common upright tent pole is fitted, and, with this contrivance a tent can be stretched to its utmost capacity. The tents are occupied by from fifteen to twenty men each, and with the bottom of the tent spread with pine foliage, we get along very comfortably indeed. The food we receive, although not of the best, is wholesome and substantial, and I manage very easily to keep up my weight on it, having just now unbuttoned my coat on account of the hearty dinner I have just devoured.

Before I enlisted, I had read in the papers of the great hardships which soldiers had to undergo, being deprived of sleep and food for forty-eight hours at a time; but I have seen nothing of it as yet, and I think the instances are very rare where such deprivations have occurred. There are grumblers in all classes, but the army furnishes more than any other, and the less the majority of soldiers have to do the more they growl when they are ordered to do anything. As for me, I like a soldiers life first-rate - it being surrounded with plenty of excitement and very little to care for, with a great deal to be seen and a great deal to be learned; and a private is treated like a white man as long as he behaves himself and carries himself the same as he would in any other situation.

T. D. B.

Alta California, San Francisco, Sunday, April 19, 1863.
[Thomas Delap Barnstead, Company A, California Hundred. Born in Philadelphia, Pa. Returned to San Francisco at war's end and joined the police force, from which he retired as a Sergeant. He died at San Francisco, October 18, 1903. A thorough search of the Alta prior to this letter failed to turn up a letter of three weeks ago, apparently it was never published]

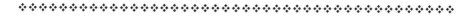

Massachusetts and the California Recruits.

Editor Bulletin.-A morning paper does not do the State of Massachusetts justice in an article respecting "Governor Stanford", etc. It would be well for Gov. Stanford to bear in mind that Massachusetts does not seek to fill up her regiment by application to California. The gist of the matter is that many of "our boys" not seeing any opportunity to get to the wars as a California regiment, induced Mr. Rankin and others to solicit-to beg-to **ENTREAT**, that Gov. Andrew or some other good Eastern governor would let them enlist and come on as part of the Massachusetts (or some other State) quota. After much persuasion, Gov. Andrew, in admiration of their patriotism, consented to receive them as part of the Massachusetts quota. This was wholly unsought by Massachusetts, (she does not need soldiers from beyond her own boundaries,) and was done only to give the boys a chance. It seems to be commonly believed that Massachusetts sent here to recruit her armies. It is not so, and Gov. Stanford need give himself no uneasiness that "the thing will be repeated." The war record of Massachusetts is before the world, and, thank God! she needs not to go out of the limits of the Bay State to raise men or money. If a few devoted men ask her to receive them in her ranks that they may strike a blow for freedom, I honor her for allowing them the opportunity. Understand it, then, as it is: Massachusetts has not asked California for men, but California has asked Massachusetts the privilege of marching in her ranks.

A Massachusetts Man,
And a Californian of 14 Years Standing.

Evening Bulletin, San Francisco, Tuesday, March 3, 1863

❖❖❖

The "California Hundred". - We learn that Captain Reed's one hundred California Cavalry Company has been organized into two companies, the commissioned officers of the second company being promoted from the original one hundred. Captain Reed has command of the two companies. The California soldiers stand deservedly high in the estimation of their Atlantic brethren.

Alta California, San Francisco, Wednesday, March 4, 1863

❖❖❖

The Brave Old Bay State and the California Volunteers who Join her Troops.

EDITOR BULLETIN. - The communication in your paper of Tuesday evening, signed "A Massachusetts Man," led me to inquire whether, seriously Governor Stanford, or any other man, was innocent enough to imagine that the State of Massachusetts wished to recruit in California. It would seem that any public citizen who would indulge in such a supposition was worthy a niche alongside of that of the late highly esteemed Chief Magistrate of Barrataria. For the enlightenment of those yet groping in darkness respecting the California troops for the Massachusetts quota, let them be assured, one and all, that the brave men here who have volunteered, go of their own free will and accord. As your correspondent justly observes, Massachusetts need not go beyond her own borders for men to fill her ranks; for the gallant old Bay State has at this moment in the field 50 regiments of infantry, 11 batteries of artillery and 2 regiments of cavalry, besides 12,000 seamen in the navy. At the risk of incurring the charge of prolixity, allow me further to say that Massachusetts herself has furnished largely troops for other States. She has 900 men serving in the 3d N.Y. regiment; 4 companies in the Mozart N.Y. regiment; 2 companies in Sickles' N.Y. brigade; 1 company in the N.Y. "Ira Harris" cavalry; a large number of men in the N.Y. D'Epineull Zouaves; while the 3d *Maryland* regiment is made up entirely of Massachusetts men.

Yet in the face of all these facts, individuals are found obtuse enough to suppose that Massachusetts sends 5,000 miles to recruit for a single battalion! I can imagine the old State indulging in one of those broad grins she is wont to reserve for the neighboring empire of South Carolina; at the bare idea.

Evening Bulletin, San Francisco, Thursday, March 5, 1863

CALIFORNIA COSSACKS

The State of Massachusetts—the moving spirit for the twenty years past in all the theories and practices that have undermined the confidence of the people in our government, and poisoned the minds of men against the union of the free and slave States—the one against the other—that has corrupted the public judgment into a disregard of law and constitutional rights; through which means this unhappy civil war has been set on foot and the land drenched in fraternal blood, despotism practised and usurpation attempted to be established as the rule in this heretofore prosperous and devoted country—Massachusetts, with this responsibility resting upon her shoulders—with the evils and misery she has thus wrought plainly before her—*fails to furnish her quota of soldiers in the field!*

She is numerously represented among the officers of higher grade and fat contractors, but is not up to the mark in the number of her enlisted or drafted men for the ranks. She does not lack in her representation in Congress or in other civil departments, and these representatives delight much in vaunting the prowess of the great "Bay State," but her people do not verify their boasting by appearing in the field.

Her "Emigrant Aid" societies sent many an able-bodied soldier, with Bible and Sharp's rifle, into Kansas; in times gone by, they even contributed the sinews of war which enabled old John Brown's party to invade Virginia—but then it must be borne in mind that these things were done when fraternal love and common interest bound the States together, and at a time of profound peace. The *pay* of war Massachusetts likes, and the higher the office and fatter the contract, the more patriotic and better pleased are her chosen people. Shoddy clothing and pasteboard shoes are articles of export from that proud old State, for the benefit of the army.

As to the hard knocks of war, her people are not so covetous, indeed they seem willing that almost any one else may take them—she is so very liberal. A similar state of feeling existed among these good people during our war with Great Britain in 1812, when signal lights were burned along her hospitable shores, telegraphing the enemy such information as was deemed to their advantage. Their burthens, however, in that war became so intolerable as to induce some of her statesmen to propose secession from the Union.

Still less were they inclined to vindicate our national rights upon the plains of Texas, or in the passes of the Sierra Madre, during the more recent war with Mexico. But one regiment of patriotic men were found in that State volunteering for that service, and those who composed it were not regarded with favor by their fellow citizens for so doing.

The great majority of that good people, with honest John Davis at their head, inveighed against the war as sinful and as discreditable, it being "old Polk's unjust and God-ahorring war," and the Massachusetts members in Congress voted against supplying our soldiers with food and clothing while they were upon the battle field.

One of the results of that war was the acquisition of California, a measure most vehemently denounced by Massachusetts men. The purchase, they said, was a fraud and swindle upon the nation; the territory acquired they declared barren, sterile, covered with rocks and thorns, and only inhabited by rattlesnakes, horned frogs, poisonous vermin and grizzly bear. When, however, the people of that State heard the report about the mines rich with gold in this despised land, "a change came o'er the spirit of their dreams. "All the old rotten whalers belonging to the honest merchants were freighted with passengers and launched upon a journey to California. Most of these adventurers landed safe at their destination, the reputed wealth proved a reality, and she sent us more of her people. Let us do ample justice. Many of those immigrants have made us excellent citizens, and have our utmost respect as such. The censures of this article are not meant for such—we regard them no longer as "Arab of the Arabs."

Massachusetts has planted herself here, and on our shores her children raise their Ebenezers in hosannas to the "Pilgrim Fathers," pious souls, who burned the witches, whipped the Baptists, drove the benevolent Roger Williams from among them because he would not turn Congregationalist, and made the Quakers get up and travel from the State. For doing these things, all to glorify the Lord, as a matter of course they should be kept green in our memories. She sells to us her various whimwhams, manufactured by the over-tasked labor principally of her women and children, and is good enough to receive our gold and silver in exchange. In short, Massachusetts has done well out of California, and California has risen in her estimation. While we continue to send her our gold, she continues to like us, and the more gold we send her, the deeper rooted becomes her affections. For instance, she is quite willing our people may have the paper currency which her policy in national affairs has placed in circulation.

Indeed, we have risen so in the estimation of Massachusetts that she now consents to recruit her skeleton cohorts from among our people-that is her white soldiers-her negro regiments she will fill up, if possible, from among her own more reliable citizens. Recently some enterprising gentlemen sent to her a company of cavalry recruited in this State-the "California Hundred," and they were at once honored with a place among her quota, under the name and style of the

"CALIFORNIA COSSACKS."

This name designates a class of bandit warriors, known in Russia and Turkey, and who are called in their own language "Kazack," which in the Turkish designates robber, and in the dialect of the Tartars, "free light mounted warriors." Several of the papers of California have noticed this new christening of the "Hundred," and appear proud of it. Our weak vision will not permit us to distinguish any cause for pride. The Cossacks have always lived in tribes subordinate to some despotic ruler, roving in nomadic hordes, violating every rule of civilization. Kidnaping children is mentioned as one of their innocent pastimes. As soldiers they are ever ready to enlist under the standard of any commander who will furnish pay, and place no restraint upon the gratification of their passion for "*loot*," which signifies plunder. Their bravest deeds are performed in the murder of fainting soldiers, straggling on the flanks and rear of a retreating army. Their furious charge and wild hurrahs are more terrible to women and children, and to the sick and wounded, than to an army in battle array. The followers of Tecumseh were chivalrous knights compared to the Cossacks of the Steppes of Russia. Neither is the fact of their being mercenaries, a feature in the comparison, to exalt a Californian's pride. The Mahratta of India, were insolent invaders, savage robbers-and ready *mercenaries*. "Wherever," says McCauley, "their kettle drums were heard, the peasant threw his bag of rice on his shoulder, hid his small savings in his girdle, and fled with his wife and children to the mountains or the jungles-to the milder neighborhood of the hyaena and the tiger." The Gaulic mercenaries, whose Captains despoiled the provinces of the Roman Empire, all have their record in history, and the greatest merit they reveal, being bold robbery and savage murder. The Hessian, for a compensation in money paid by the English, consented to fight the people of the American Colonies, in the days our "rebel" fathers struggled for freedom and independence, and even in this day, to be called a Hessian, is an insult. In view of these facts, we are at a loss to see how a Californian prides himself on being called a Cossack.

Our fathers, who framed the government under which we live, in their Declaration of Independence, which is the Bill of Rights prefacing our Constitution, declared that people have a right to choose their own form of government, and to "alter or abolish" that form of government whenever they choose. The people of the free States made war upon one of the most cherished domestic institutions of the South. Abolition emissaries were sent into every

State to excite insurrection and run off slaves from their masters-their soil was invaded, and musket, and pike, and torch, and poison, were employed in the work of murder and desolation-and this sectional party obtained control of the government by virtue of a platform which excluded slaveholders from the common inheritance in the Territories, the effect of which would be to strip them of all political power in the government. Now these were grievances greater than those which impelled our fathers to revolution, and when the people of the South asserted this right, which is nailed to the mast's head in this Bill of Rights, the Declaration of Independence, this immortal "California Hundred," *repudiate* it, turn *Cossack*, and *hire* out their services to kill and slay the aggrieved party, whose only offence was, in imitation of the men of revolution, they resumed the exercise of the inalienable right of self-government!

We observe by the advertisement of Major D.W.C. Thompson that more of these Cossacks to complete the complement of Massachusetts are wanted. This officer says that, with the approval of the War Department, he has been authorized to raise four companies for that service. Any man, "in good health, intelligent, active, and capable of performing the hardest light-cavalry service," by joining one of these companies can get to play Cossack for Massachusetts, three years, unless sooner discharged.

The complement of troops required of California by the administration has never been filled, and we would suppose it the duty of those of her citizens desirous of service, to join her banner before that of Massachusetts. It has, however, become the fashion to repudiate the rights and dignity of States, and why should the young men of California be expected to maintain them, when her highest officers spit upon and deride her most sacred laws?

Here, then, is a most excellent opportunity for a young man who pants for glory. Let him, like the Cossack, the Mahratta and Hessian, become the mercenary. Fill up the ranks of Massachusetts, and go down to posterity upon her muster rolls, with the Caesars and Pompeys of her negro battalions.

Equal Rights Expositer, Visalia, Thursday, March 5, 1863.
[The most openly secessionist newspaper, it's editorials urged support of secession, discouraged enlistment in the Union Army, magnified Union defeats, belittled Union victories & ridiculed President Lincoln as "a narrow minded bigot, an unprincipaled demagogue".]

❖❖

Demolition of the Secesh Organ at Visalia.
Visalia, Tulare county, March 5, 1863.

Editor Bulletin.-This evening, at a little after 9 o'clock, the secession newspaper called *The States' Rights Expositer* was entirely destroyed. You have undoubtedly received a notice of the fact by telegraph, but as your readers may feel interested in the particulars, I hasten to give them. The *Expositer* has been the strongest secesh paper in the State, and by far the bitterest in its denunciations of everything Federal and loyal. A few days ago the "head" man of the establishment, L.P. Hall, withdrew from the temperance society known as the Good Templars, and with malice aforethought, went "on a bust," and during that bust proclaimed his principles freely in sundry places with all possible zeal; and the more he talked the more he imbibed of the ardent, and the more ardent he became in his strongheaded ideas. Last night, somebody-some 12 or 15 persons with bugles and drums-gave him a serenade, which made music of a kind never heard before; and somehow or other, in the course of events, the object of interest was tumbled into a ditch, presumed to be the very ditch he desired as a last place to die in.

Nothing has been heard during the day of the intended "charge," and at 8 o'clock, all soldiers lounging around town proceeded to camp as usual. About 9, a crowd of men came down one street, some up another, some this way and some that, until about 70 or 80 were suddenly in front of the *Expositer* office which had recently been removed from the upper part of a wooden building into a one-story brick, where the "fixins" were easy of access from the street. When the crowd rushed in, the work of demolition commenced, and during about 15 minutes there was heard a continual cracking, and banging, and smashing, and thumping, interlarded with any quantity of glass breaking, seeming as if whole windows were annihilated by single blows. After everything had been "arranged," in apple pie order, the assaulting party came out, and while several men fired a score or so of shots into the air, others sang out, "Where's your secession press now!" Then through the middle of the street they marched off-first giving a number of groans for the traitorous institution-and when opposite the office of the *Delta*, the whole party saluted that loyal sheet with three cheers.

Officers are around as well as a guard patrol, in search of something or somebody, without any expectation of finding anybody or anything connected with the grand charge. J. W. T.

Evening Bulletin, San Francisco, Wednesday, March 11, 1863.

The Suppressed Rebel Journal.

It is said that the troops or somebody else played havoc among the types and material of the Equal Rights Expositer, published in Visalia. We have a copy of that journal March 5th, which we presume was the immediate cause of the suppression. Here are a few extracts from that delicious sheet. Speaking of the California hundred, sent to Massachusetts, and who have been termed "California Cossacks," it says the name designates a class of bandit warriors or robbers who violate every rule of civilization, and kidnap children as an innocent pastime:

"As soldiers, they are ever ready to enlist under the standard of any commander who will furnish pay, and place no restraint upon the gratification of their passion for "loot," which signifies plunder. Their bravest deeds are performed in the murder of fainting soldiers, straggling on the flanks and rear of a retreating army. The followers of Tecumseh were chivalrous knights compared to the Cossacks of the Steppes of Russia. Neither is the fact of their being mercenaries, a feature in the comparison, to exalt California's pride. In view of these facts, we are at a loss to see how a Californian prides himself on being called a Cossack."

"Our fathers, who framed the government under which we live, in their Declaration of Independence, which is the Bill of Rights prefacing our Constitution, declared that people have a right to choose their own form of government, and to 'alter or abolish' that form of government whenever they choose. When the people of the South asserted this right, which is nailed to the mast's head in this Bill of Rights, the Declaration of Independence, this immortal 'California Hundred,' repudiate it, turn Cossack, and hire (the italics are its own) out their services to kill and slay the aggrieved party, whose only offense was, in imitation of the men of the revolution, they resumed the exercise of the inalienable right of self-government!"

"We observe by the advertisement of Major D.W.C. Thompson that more of these Cossacks to complete the complement of Massachusetts are wanted. Here, then, is a most excellent opportunity for a young man who pants for glory. Let him, like the Cossacks, the Mahratta and Hessian, become the mercenary. Fill up the ranks of Massachusetts, and go down to posterity upon her muster rolls, with the Caesers and Pompeys of her negro battalions."

"These negro-worshipping scoundrels may quiet their fears about the possibility of a re-construction of the Union; the Union will never be restored so as to include their sort in it. The same 'slave power' that formed and maintained the old Union, and made it one of the powers of the earth, will rear another structure surpassing the first in strength and magnificence, and all discordant elements will be carefully excluded."

"The Expositer is the only paper in the State that has, without concealment or reservation, opposed the present war and contended that the Southern States had a perfect right to do as they have done."

There is much more such abominable stuff, but this is enough.

The Daily Bee, Sacramento, Wednesday, March 11, 1863.

❖ ❖
Battalion

Massachusetts Cavalry Battalion.-This force, now organizing in California, will leave March 21st, on the steamer Constitution. The battalion consists of 13 commissioned officers, 64 non-commissioned officers, 8 buglers, 336 enlisted men and 14 officer's servants-in all, 435 men. On the arrival of the battalion in Massachusetts, they will be organized into a regi-ment, if the same meets with the approval of the Governor.

Alta California, San Francisco, Wednesday, March 4, 1863
Sacramento Daily Union, Friday, March 6, 1863.

❖ ❖
Battalion

The Cavalry Battalion. -The Bulletin says:
Arrangements have been made for the passage of the California Cavalry Battalion to New York, per steamer Constitution, on the 21st instant. The four companies now average about 70 men each. The full complement of the battalion will be 433 officers and soldiers. There is an opportunity for 150 more men to join and go into the war at once. It is expected that after the battalion is furnished with horses, camp equipage, etc., it will join the army of the Potomac, and give to California's General, "Fighting Joe," a worthy support. No arm of our service is more needed than light cavalry, and perhaps no part of the Union can furnish better than this State. This battalion has been organized, and the men selected especially for that service, and the officers and men are desirous of paying their respects to the "Black Horse Legion" *[6th Virginia Cav.]* of the rebel army as soon as possible. A good supply of lassoes will be taken along, and if the rebels are very obstinate, some of them will be brought up with a round turn by that catching instrument."

The Daily Bee, Sacramento, Friday, March 6, 1863.
The Daily Bee, Sacramento, Wednesday, March 11, 1863.

❖ ❖

The California 100. - Charley Briggs, who belongs to this Company, writes from Boston under date of March 8th, giving a glowing account of the noble reception and kind treatment of the Hundred by the people of Boston. He remains in that city at one of the recruiting offices, while his fellow soldiers are drilling at Fortress Monroe.

The Napa County Reporter, Napa, Saturday, April 11, 1863.
[Unfortunately, the "glowing account" was never published.]

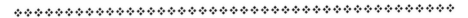

Battalion

Military Display - Massachusetts Cavalry Battalion. - There were hundreds of persons collected in and congregated about the Plaza yesterday afternoon to witness the parade and review of Major Thompson's recruits, who are so soon to leave for active service on the field in the Atlantic States. The day being bright and beautiful, added greatly to the success of the display. There were three companies, "A," "B," and "C," on the field, with pretty full ranks. The men went through with their various evolutions in a prompt, accurate, and soldier-like style, evincing great care and rigid instruction on the part of the officers, and diligent attention to their duties on the part of the men. It is now certain that these troops will leave for the seat of war by the steamer of the 21st. It is hoped and confidently believed that they will at all times and in all places, reflect the highest credit on the State where they enlisted, after leaving these Pacific shores.

Alta California, San Francisco, Monday, March 9, 1863

Native Californian Troops - Forty members of the Native California Cavalry Company raised as one of those to comprise the "Massachusetts Contingent," have arrived in town and are now quartered at the Presidio. This Company has been organized at San Jose, and is the first one of native born citizens of California raised during the war. Amongst their novel weapons of offence are lassos, which they are exceedingly expert at using on horseback. At a meeting held on Tuesday evening last, at their headquarters on the San Jose Plaza, Capt. J.R. Pico spoke in the following soul-stirring strain.

My fellow Countrymen: We convene here tonight on an important matter! The Captain's commission which I here display before you authorizes me to form a company of California cavalry, to be composed of a hundred able-bodied men, to serve the Government of the United States of America. Those among you who are willing to enlist under my command shall not regret their choice. I have sworn to defend this beautiful flag, the Star Spangled Banner, the emblem of Truth, Liberty and Justice, and would also take another oath to guard the personal rights of each and every volunteer under my command.

Sons of California! our country calls, and we must obey! This unholy rebellion of the Southern States' must be crushed; they must come back into the Union, and pay obedience to the Stars and Stripes. United, we will, by the force of circumstances, become the freest and mightiest republic on earth! Crowned monarchs must be driven away from the sacred continent of free America!
Strike for your altar and your fires!
Strike for the green graves of your sires!

Strike for our Union's emblem grand,
Star Spangled Banner, God and your native land!

Alta California, San Francisco, Wednesday, March 11, 1863.
[Whatever the original intent was, this unit ended up serving in the Washington Territory.]

❖❖

The Destruction of the Secesh Newspaper At Visalia. - The Visalia *Delta* of 12th March gives the following version of an accident that has already been once or twice mentioned in our columns:

On Thursday evening last, about 9 o'clock, the town was aroused by the sound of crashing and smashing, which was soon ascertained to proceed from the building occupied as the printing office of the *Equal Rights Expositer*. A crowd at once rushed towards the spot, but they did not get far, for on each street and alley intersecting the block were found sentinels with cocked pistols, who informed them that "no citizens were allowed inside the lines!" and the orders were enforced to the letter. In less than half an hour the establishment was a perfect wreck, the type being thrown into the streets, and the stands, cases and press smashed to pieces. Their work done, the rioters departed whence they came. On entering, Mr. Garrison, the junior partner, was found at work, and a guard was placed over him, with the assurance that no harm was intended him.

The immediate cause of the outbreak is said to have been the publication of an article on the "California Cossacks," which teemed with abuse; but the starting of it is attributable to the almost unintermitted publication, for the past six months, of such compliments as the following:

We wish the people to look this matter boldly in the face, so that they may know when they give their support to the President, they give a vital stab to the Government of their fathers.

We have said Abraham Lincoln has purjured himself, and we have proved it. We now tell those who support this detestable war, to the extent of their support they participate with Lincoln; in the crime of perjury.

Much has been written and said about the spirit of Americans, but that portion of them who sustain the Administration are base cowards; they have the hearts only of does and rabbits-not of men. They are an incumbrance and disgrace to any free country, and are constitutionally fitted only for serfs to some despot. They would cringe and lick the rod as often as it smote them!

Let our State Rights friends look around them, and note the passive slaves of the President, who prate about rebels and traitors, while they hug their chains with the servility of a kicked and cuffed hound!

These insults have been keenly felt, and the result is the destruction of the office. The talk on the street is that the Tuolumne Rangers (Co. E, 2d Cavalry) took the lead in the matter. Not a citizen was allowed to be present, and we do not think a single one was apprized of the design.

Evening Bulletin, San Francisco, Monday, March 16, 1863.
Sacramento Daily Union, Tuesday, March 17, 1863.

❖❖

Battalion

Military Review - At 3 o'clock, yesterday afternoon, a review and inspection of the Massachusetts Cavalry Battalion was had on the Plaza. The companies comprising it, under command of
Major D.W.C. Thompson, appeared promptly on the ground at the appointed hour. Shortly
thereafter the reviewing officer, Brigadier General John S. Ellis, accompanied by the following named officers of his staff, left City Hall, and repaired to the Plaza; i.e., Major John Hill,
Inspector; Major Henry Hasbach, Engineer; and Major S. R. Gerry, Surgeon. The reviewing
officer expressed himself as pleased with the appearance of the troops, who certainly acquitted
themselves excellently well, for men so short a time under arms. Subsequently the battalion
had a drill, which was witnessed by crowds of spectators congregated around the Plaza.

Alta California, San Francisco, Thursday, March 12, 1863
Alta California, San Francisco, Friday, March 13, 1863.

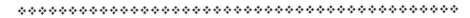

The Mounted Guerrillas.
The Richmond *[Virginia]* Examiner has the following caustic remarks upon these horse-
men robbers of the South;
"There are some people who advocate a heavy increase of the cavalry arm of the service.
Inspired by a transporting patriotism, they plead for a vast increase of horsemen with the zeal
of revival preachers for converted sinners.
The country people have a propensity to suit the orthography of words to the ideas associated with the things which they are intended to designate. They call a Cotswald sheep a
Scotchwood sheep, having the idea that Scotch wool is very long and coarse. The idea of a
most horrible crucifixion is associated in the pious mind with the name of Calvary; and inasmuch as the people and all they have and own are literally crucified when the mounted troops
come about, in the simplicity of the unlettered mind, they confound the technical word designating these troops with the most painful name in all the Scriptures. A few special detachments
of 'our cavalry' have done great service, but if we leave out of view the daring, heroic and
invaluable services of these brigades, the rest have been a scourge to the people and a curse to
the cause. The expense of horse troops is enormous; it is three times as great to the treasury as
that of infantry; and the infliction upon the people of their rapacious and wanton depredations
is tenfold more that that suffered from any other troops.
A faithful description of the general physiognomy of the 'cavalry,' as they are seen in their
camps and upon their strolling marches, might bring a ghastly smile on the rigid lips of the
most impassable ascetic, provided he were off at a safe distance; but the terror which seizes the
people on their approach is overwhelming. They are usually armed with every conceivable
weapon of offense except the saber of the real dragoon. They are as ignorant of the drill as of
the saber practice. They are comfortably clad, but as unwashed and as unkemp as the urchins
that play about the wigwams of Nebraska.
The 'cavalry' accomplish a great deal, but it is a deal of mischief; they perform a vast
amount of service, but unhappily as a general rule, it inures indirectly to the benefit of the
enemy. Their lack of economy is as deplorable as their lack of drill and discipline, and a general disbanding of at least two-thirds of the numerous corps now in the field would be hailed
with joy by the people whom they claim to protect. And as for fighting, when that is to be done,
the order is 'cavalry to the rear,' and then comes up from the infantry a shout of derision and
exultation.

There are a few brigades of splendid mounted troops in the Confederate service; but that prodigious body of strolling horsemen who lead an unsettled gipsy life in the border country, stealing here, robbing there, begging in this place and behaving a little better in that; who are never heard of in the vicinity of the enemy; who are always too late to catch the Yankees when in force, but are dreadfully ferocious on all individuals ever so loyal to the South, whom they choose to denounce as Union men, and who are known among the common people by the horrifying appellation of the 'cavalry.' These troops are a reproach to the Confederate service, a curse to the cause, against which they have raised up thousands of enemies, a scourge to our own people, and a desolation to large districts of wilderness country, which, but for them, would be producing crops for the general support.

If the forage which has been consumed, stolen and wasted by these worse than useless troops had been saved, if the farms which they have desolated were still in cultivation, and if the farmers, whom they have utterly discouraged from producing crops, were still busy in their blessed calling, an additional amount of supplies would be raised over and above what we now have, to support our entire armies in the field; but as long as these licensed plunderers are permitted to run riot over the border country, where crops are most needed for our armies, and which must continue to be the chief theater of our military operations, we shall not cease to hear of scarce provisions, high prices for food, arbitrary impressments, desolated farms and abandoned homes and fields.

Instead of too few, we have far too many cavalry. Gen. Scott held the true idea when he discouraged the undue augmentation of this service. Had the Yankees indulged in the expensive luxury of horses and mules to the extent that we have done in our service, their exchequer would have been bankrupt in a year. An increase of 'the cavalry' force is simply an impossibility. If we have more cavalry, we must consent to have no more corn. The question of cavalry is simply a question of absolute ruin. But, happily, this service cannot be increased. The horses are not to be had at practicable prices; and if they could be, they would have to starve for food."

The Daily Bee, Sacramento, Saturday, March 14, 1863
[A Southern view of the cavalry.]

Battalion

Military Review. - To-day, at 10 o'clock, A.M. the Massachusetts Battalion, consisting of Captain Eigenbrodt, Captain De Merritt, Captain Adams and Captain Manning's companies, under command of Major Thompson, will be reviewed and inspected by General Wright, on the Plaza. After the review the Battalion will perform various evolutions and go through the regulation sabre exercise, in open order, covering most of the Plaza. The military exercises will close with a dress parade. Companies A and B of the Battalion are now full; Company C wants about thirty-five men, and Company D about fifty to make up their hundred. The Battalion will leave for New York next Saturday morning.

Alta California, San Francisco, Wednesday, March 18, 1863.
Evening Bulletin, San Francisco, Wednesday, March 18, 1863.

Battalion

Inspection of the Cavalry Battalion. - The weather partially cleared up on Wednesday
morning which afforded an opportunity for a favorable review and parade by the Massachusetts Cavalry Battalion. At eleven o'clock, the four companies comprising the battalion marched
through Montgomery Street, and up Washington to the Plaza, under command of Maj. D.W.C.
Thompson. Brig. General Wright and staff shortly thereafter came upon the ground and took
up their position at the fountain, in the centre of the Plaza. Here the troops underwent a very
critical inspection by the General, who together with his staff expressed themselves as greatly
pleased at their proficiency in the drill, considering the very brief period they have been in the
service. Both officers and soldiers "put their best foot foremost," knowing that the optics of
military veterans were fastened on their every movement. The various evolutions of the troops
were skillfully and correctly executed and their martial bearing called forth merited encomiums. After the inspection came the parade and the various companies marched to their headquarters. The battalion leaves on the 21st. in the steamer *Constitution*.

Alta California, San Francisco, Thursday, March 19, 1863.

❖❖❖
Battalion
San Francisco, March 18, 1863
Dear Sister
You will also see that I have changed my place of abode but it is
of short duration as I leave day after to morrow (which way you will say) while you are guess-
ing I will tell you the news. of course I am in good health and about eleven years older than
when I saw you last. have been here about two months. I received your kind letter with Moth-
ers which as you say was not unwelcome also one from Warren I answered them by writing one
to Father and one to Mother am really glad to hear that Mothers health is so good. Must say that
I have had a good deal of anxiety on her account she is getting along in years and her health
being poorly I have been afraid she would drop off and I never would see her again I feel that
I have done wrong in not going home expressly to see her but think I will go and see her when
I get to Boston (to Boston gracious me you aint going to Boston are you) indeed I am going to
Boston and to the wars. I have joined a Cavalry Battalion of four Cos bound to the seat of war
the Batt is raised under Mass quota therefore bound for Boston have joined Co. B. Capt Adams.
I send you two copies of a Photograph Likeness of a Bloody soldier standing at a position of
rest. we do not get our horses until we get east. now Mary what do you think am I doing right
or not. dont you think I should have done so long ago. if you dont I do. the fact of the business
is the Union has got to be saved and it can not be done by any means in the world but fighting
for it we can not have peace untill we conquer it in fact peace is not desirable upon any terms
but the crushing out of secesh I am glad to hear to that Jesse has gone and believe me Mary
will not shed a tear to hear of his being cut down battling for the right. fighting for his country
for the Union. for the glorious old flag. Long may it wave. I shall endeavor to get (and think I
shall succeed) a furlough at Boston and go home and see our beloved Mother I dont know why
it is but it is first Mother then Father then I would run to see Lucy then dont know which one
Mary I believe but one day more and we embark on the Constitution on the briny deep O wont
I be good and sick heave up Jonah Y.I. I suppose is sound on the union. could not doubt it. hope
he will be successful in his search for riches I have tried it along time and no fault to find have
made money but when I had it had no inclination to go home but the desire to make more was
uppermost but I must say good bye Mary and perhaps the last time who knows perhaps the

Alabama may run across our track but hope for the best so good bye Mary your husband and little ones. from your Brother

L.P. Washburn

Minnesota Historical Society
[Luman P. Washburn, Co. L, died of wounds, Vienna, Va., Nov. 14, 1863; he was originally from Erie County, New York]

❖ ❖
Battalion

Union Demonstration at Platt's Hall. - A grand entertainment will be given this evening at Platt's Hall, to the California-Massachusetts Battalion, prior to their departure on Saturday for the East. A variety of amusements will be offered. No admission fee; but free to all.

Alta California, San Francisco, Thursday, March 19, 1863.

❖ ❖
Battalion

Complimentary to Soldiers. - The Ladies' Pioneer Temperance Society got up a neat and very creditable impromptu festival for the entertainment of the soldiers who go East on the steamer *Constitution.* The affair took place in Platt's Hall last evening, and consisted of vocal and instrumental music, and addresses by Messrs. Winton, McClellan, Manchester and Delos Howe. A collection was subsequently taken, and as the audience was large, amounted to a very considerable sum. This unexpected compliment to the soldiers reflects great credit on the generosity and patriotism of the fair daughters of Father Mathew.

Alta California, San Francisco, Friday, March 20. 1863.

❖ ❖
Battalion

Enlisted.-Three young men, minors, enlisted lately at San Francisco, in Captain Adams' Cavalry Company of Volunteers, with the consent of Judge Blake, who appointed the Captain their guardian on his giving the requisite bonds therefor. Their names are Eugene Loud, George P. Boyle and Edward Thompson, and have no parents or relations here.

Sacramnento Daily Union, Saturday, March 21, 1863
[Loud and Boyle of Co. L ; Thompson of Co. F.]

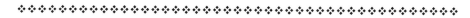

SECOND MASSACHUSETTS CAVALRY.
Gloucester Point, Va., March 21, 1863.
To the Editor of The Boston Journal:
    The hardest storm of the season keeps everyone under cover whose duties allow it-it is just the time to write. "Saint Patrick's Day in the morning" was beautifully bright, warm and pleasant. Early in the afternoon, however, the weather suddenly changed; it became cold and rained at intervals all night. Thursday morning the rain turned to half, at noon to snow. It

snowed then constantly, the wind blowing hard till this morning; a full foot of snow fell. To-day it rains, but the storm is still severe. It must be our equinoctial. The daily boat which generally arrives promptly at 4 P. M. with a good mail from Fortress Monroe, has not been seen since Wednesday; The news in Tuesday's New York papers is the latest we have.

On the last day of February our detachment was inspected by Major Hall of the 6th New York Cavalry, and we had our rolls all prepared for Major Paymaster. That gentleman has not yet favored us with his presence, however; still we hope the infantrymen on one of the picket posts insisted that they heard distinctly, on the night of the 6th inst., the rattle of sabres at a house not far beyond the lines. A reconnoissance by Gen. Keyes with some of our cavalry, proved that the rebels had had a mounted picket at the house where the noise was heard. It was satisfactorily ascertained that Gen. Fizhugh Lee, with his brigade of rebel cavalry, nearly 2000 strong, and a field battery, had bivouacked on the night in question within four miles of this camp. The force returned up country next morning for reinforcements, they said.

Our line of pickets extend along a creek and the edge of a swamp. At only one point can cavalry come in, and there we have adequate defenses.

The enemy is now reported in force at Saluda, twelve or fourteen miles from here. Parties are out foraging or scouting nearly every day, and squads of rebel cavalry are often seen, but invariably retreat on our approach. An attack is thought probable, and Fort Keyes has been strengthened by some large guns. At Williamsburg the enemy press our lines closely and all guards are enjoined to be especially vigilant. Gen. Keyes frequently visits the pickets in person.

It is hardly reasonable to suppose the rebels desire to take the oath while Yorktown is ours and our gunboats are in the river, but they evidently contemplate something, and it is quite probable they intend a "raid," with an eye to our horses and camp equipage.

There are very few cases of sickness in our detachment-none serious. All mail and express matter to any one with us should be directed; 2d Mass. Cavalry, 4th Army Corps, Fortress Monroe.

Sunday, March 22. The boat with three days mail and papers, arrived last night, the storm having abated. Today we have fine weather again.

Cadet.

Boston Journal, Thursday, March 26, 1863

❖❖

LETTER FROM A CALIFORNIAN IN THE ARMY IN VIRGINIA- No. 2.

Pictures of Camp Life - Cavalry Duties- Health of the Men-Weather -Incidents, etc.

GLOUCESTER POINT (Opposite Yorktown)
March 22, 1863.

I have not yet received any letter from you since leaving the golden shores of the Pacific, but I shall keep on writing to you, hoping that you have written to me, and that I may in a short time receive a letter from you, which, I can assure you, would be very welcome. This will make the second letter I have written to you since being here, and the fourth since leaving California. Ever since being here, we have been in continual expectation of an attack from the "sons of the sunny South," and every night. on going to bed, we have saddled up our horses, so as to be ready at a moment's warning to spring into the saddle and fight or run, as the judgment of our officers may dictate. We have also slept with all our clothes on, including boots and spurs, and our arms by our side, consisting of a Colt's revolver and a sabre. Carbines we have not yet received, but expect to in a short time. Without them, we should be able to offer but a feeble resistance to the enemy, in case of an attack, as a six-shooter is soon emptied, and in the excitement of a battle, and on horseback, they could not be very easily or quickly loaded; and as for our sabres, I place but very little dependence on them, they not being sharpened, and it would require a large amount of muscle to make much of a cut with them, dull as they are at present.

We are very comfortably quartered here, (that is, I call it comfortable now, but I should never have thought of calling it by such a name in California,) being sheltered by good tents, and having a small camp stove in each one, which, when kept filled up with wood, throws out heat enough to keep us quite warm and dry. There are from sixteen to twenty men in each tent, and in ours we manage to agree very well, not doing as much growling as the law allows a soldier, and that is saying a good deal, for a soldier generally exceeds his allowance in that respect. Our food consists of fresh beef every other day, alternating with pork and beans, and sometimes rice; one loaf of fresh bread per day, and coffee morning and evening, sweetened with sugar. This is our full bill of fare, and when meal time comes we consume all it calls for. When the weather permits we are exercised in the drill, and we are now able to go through the different evolutions very creditably; our horses now understanding what is expected of them nearly as well as the men. Four hours in each day are devoted to drilling, and the saddles are such easy riding ones that I have never chafed myself, or felt the least fatigue after coming from drill; and this is the first time that I have not experienced such effects after riding any length of time. When our Company left San Francisco we numbered one hundred and one men; but from desertion (of which there has been eight cases,) and sickness, there are now only sixty men fit for duty, which makes it rather hard on the well ones, there being just as much duty to perform as though the whole Company were here to do it. In the whole battalion, consisting of four companies, and which ought to number four hundred men, there are only two hundred and thirty-seven men; fit for duty, one hundred and twenty-seven men. So you can see that the battalion is nearly as well represented in the hospital as it is out of it, and the climate at present is not sickly either; and if they continue going into the hospital as fast as they now are, there will be none left out in a short time to perform any duty at all. However, there is no contagious disease existing among us, the sickness being confined to disarrangement of the bowels, colds, and minor complaints, and the prospect is that in a month there will be more fit for duty than at present. We now perform picket duty every night, twenty men from the battalion being detailed each night for that purpose; so that each man's turn comes every six days. The guard is only kept up at night, two hours on and four off, and is posted some three miles from camp on the roads leading into it; six men being on at a time, and posted within pistol shot of each other, and our duty is to alarm the camp if anything suspicious should be seen. It is a very unpleasant duty sitting on your horse quietly for two hours, in such cold weather as we have had lately, and a person's feet are nearly froze by the time he is relieved. However, the hardship is soon forgotten, half an hour round a good hot fire dispelling all thoughts of it.

It has been storming here violently from noon on the 19th up to this morning; commencing with a snow-storm, which continued up to yesterday morning, covering the ground with a foot of snow, and culminating in a rain storm which ceased this morning, and which succeeded in removing nearly every vestige of snow. Such weather is very hard on our horses, as they have to stand out in it, unprotected by any shelter whatever, except what is afforded by our saddle-blankets thrown over them and buckled on, and consequently one of them "pegs out" occasionally. They are rather a poor lot of horses, there not being one of them a private individual would pay more than a hundred dollars for and the majority of them are not worth more than fifty; whereas, that much abused and imposed upon "Uncle Samuel," has paid $115 for each one. But I suppose he is able to stand it, owning, as he does, any quantity of land with lots of friends in the shape of tax-payers to furnish him with "rhino" and greenback," to pay for them. But it don't come in fast enough to keep the soldiers paid. We have now been in the service four, and some of us, five months and all the money we have received from the U. S. has been twenty-five dollars bounty. There is now due me $52, but it is mighty uncertain when I will receive it. At present, I am "flat broke," (and I have lots of company in the same fix), and have had to beg all the tobacco I have used for the last month. Now I am pretty well "played out," and have to go without most of the time. There is no sutler attached to our battalion, and, therefore, we have no place to go and get trusted. The Captain is also out of money, but he expects to have some in a few days; then, probably, I shall be able to borrow some and get what necessaries I actually need. We have made several incursions into the country of the enemy, but have never went further than six miles from the outer posts; and in those raids we have succeeded in capturing six fine mules, three yoke of oxen, a dozen of sheep, three good wagons, and about one hundred specimens of the barn-yard fowls, consisting of turkeys, chickens, geese, ducks, &c., which went towards comforting our "inner man." The cattle were turned over to Brigadier-General Keyes, at Yorktown, by his order. Four of the mules were given to our Quartermaster, who uses them for the benefit of the Battalion; and the other two mules to our Company, we using them to haul our firewood into camp and doing other jobs which relieves the men of considerable work. All of the above were the property of Secessionists, and we did not feel as though we were doing a wrong action in taking them, knowing full well that if they had the same chance to forage in the North that we have in the South, the indignities committed would be far greater; and if we expect to bring this war to a successful termination, we must make the enemy feel the war in their most tender spot—that is, their pockets. In the houses around this vicinity, outside the lines, there is not to be found any young white men, all those capable of bearing arms being engaged in fighting in the army of the Southern Confederacy. All the persons left on the plantations are men far advanced in years, and women. What slaves there are left appear to be contented to stay where they are. They know of Lincoln's Proclamation freeing them, but all with whom I have conversed with few exceptions, seem to think they are better off where they are, and I take no pains to convince them otherwise thinking likewise. There is but very little land on the plantations being tilled this year, the slaves merely cultivating land enough to raise sufficient corn to keep themselves throughout the next winter, their food consisting of corn cake and oysters, the latter being very plentiful in the waters of this vicinity.

T. D. B.

Alta California, San Francisco, Sunday, April 26, 1863.

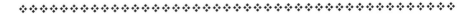

NOTICE.

THE STEAMSHIP

Constitution,

Capt. J. T. WATKINS,

Will be Dispatched

ON

MONDAY,....................**MARCH 23, 1863,**

At 9 o'clock A. M.

Treasure for shipment received on board up to
midnight, Saturday, 21st inst.

mh:0   A. B. FORBES, Agent.

Alta California

❖❖❖

Battalion

Departure of the California Troops for the Seat of War. - On the steamer *Constitution*, which leaves this morning for Panama, go hence to the seat of war the California Cavalry Battalion. The troops will be escorted from their headquarters to the Folsom Street Wharf, at 8 o'clock, by the First Regiment, Col. Wood commanding, and the Pioneer California Guard, Capt. Isaac Bluxome commanding. The escort will be attended by Chris Andres' Band and the battalion by the American Brass Band. The California Guard (artillery) will fire a salute on the wharf for four of their members who leave with the four companies of cavalry. The Old Guard have now sent from their ranks to the war thirty four members, all of whom are officers in the service of the Federal Government. Inasmuch as all of the departing officers and soldiers have either relatives or friends in this State, we herewith subjoin a roster of Companies A, B and C, which leave this morning by the steamer; Company D, Captain DeMerritt, will leave so soon as he has obtained a full complement of men. Major Dewitt C. Thompson commanding:

COMPANY "A."

Captain- Chas. S. Eigenbrodt, New York;
*First Lieut.-*Rufus W. Smith, Maine;
Second Lieut.- Henry H. Crocker, Connecticut;

Privates-
Allen, Geo. H., age 25, New York;   Black, Thos. G., 22, Illinois;
Burnap, Oscar, 23, New York;   Barns, Walter S., 24, Indiana;
Bishop, Geo., 28, Pennsylvania;   Brossamer, Chas., A., 25, Ohio;

Baker, Nelson S., 32, Ohio;
Brickley, Richard T., 26, Washington City;
Blanchard, Oscar, 26, New Jersey;
Burns, Edward, 29, New York;
Cobbey, Thos. W., 31, Illinois;
Chrystler, Hiram, 33, Maine;
Campbell, John, C., 25;
Cottrill, Robert, 24;
Crawford, Josiah H., 30;
Davis, Asa, M., 26, Iowa;
Esten, Stephen H., 33, New York;
Flood, Stephen, 22, Indiana;
Flournoy, Charles H., 22, Kentucky;
Getty, Harry, W., 22, New York;
Heitman, Charles W., 28, New York;
Hood, John, 32, Iowa;
Hamilton, Jasper A., 30, Illinois;
Jones, John, 27, Maryland;
Joy, Maurice, 21, Massachusetts;
Lewis, Stephen, 26, Pennsylvania;
Lunt, Wm. P., 25, Pennsylvania;
Merrill, Daniel, 30, Maine;
Mortimer, Harry W. 21, New York;
Mallory, Abner J., 35, New York;
Moore, Delavan, 20, Illinois;
Manchester, Luman A., 33, Lancaster, Wis.;
Manker, Wm. A., 29, Ohio;
Morris, Wm., 26, Missouri;
Millican, Wm. W., 30, Tennessee;
Ordway, John H., 28, Maryland;
Saunders, Halsey H., 27, Michigan;
Palmer, Wm. T., 25, Illinois;
Paris, Frank, 30, Ohio;
Reese, Jas., 25, Wales, Eng.;
Rhodes, Samuel, 33, New York;
Sheldon, Aurelius B. C., 30, Maine;
Shaw, William, 31, New York;
Silver, Harry, 31, New York;
Shaw, Sylvanus H., 28, Vermont;
Sheldon, Albert, 22, Illinois;
Sarchet, Jos D., 30, Ohio;
Sprague, James E., 27, New York;
Turnham, Alfred B., 22, New York;
Turner, Levi W., 37, Maine;
Vultee, Francis, 26, New York;
Wilcox, Geo., 29, Illinois;
White, Jas. A., 30, Illinois;
Wooster, John A. 19, Connecticut;
Wyatt, Henry, 22, Ohio;

Buswell, John H., 32, New Hampshire;
Buhrer, Geo. W., 28, Michigan;
Brandon, John R., 27, New York;
Blanche, Edgar M., 25, Pennsylvania;
Cain, John A., 30, New York;
Cherry, William, 25;
Campbell, Robert A., 21;
Clark, Wm. W., 24, New York;
Clark, Hiram E. W., 27, Ohio;
Dyer, Andrew B. C., 26, Arkansas;
Enos, Erastus, 26, Pennsylvania;
Fisher, Jackson, 30, Maryland;
Griffing, Charles C., 31, Illinois;
Garrity, Thomas, 22, Kentucky;
Holland, Henry, 33, Pennsylvania;
Hepburn, James W., 25, New York;
Irving, Harry P., 25, Vermont;
Jenkins, Charles M., 23, Ohio;
Kelly, Caius P., 26, Pennsylvania;
Lord, Thomas H., 32, Pennsylvania;
McEwen, Warren, 24, Michigan;
Moore, Wm. H., 28, Maine;
Mihay, Wm. 31, Canada;
Massman, Judson A., 31, Massachusetts;
Miller, Jas. M., 29, Missouri;
Morrison, Wm., 20, Indiana;
Meyers, Randolph P., 19, Canada;
Mitchell, John T., 26, New York;
McCarrak, Joseph, 25, New York;
Osts, John, 27, New York;
Partridge, Benj. F., 26, Maine;
Purvis, Lawrence G., 26, Illinois;
Perry, Albert, 27, Connecticut;
Rodgers, Thos. L., 23, Illinois;
Russel, Alvin H., 26, New York;
Sheldon, Joseph, 22, Maine;
Spaulding, John, 28, Mass.;
Straub, Edward, 23, Germany;
Stevenson, John H., 22, Ohio;
Smith, Leonard F., 27, Pennsylvania;
Smith, John W., 26, Illinois;
Towne, Nathan, 33, Rhode Island;
Thompson, Lawrence, 26;
Turner, Jun.T., 31, Whidby's Island,
Vonnem, Hiram, 26, Illinois;
Williams, Benj. T., 26, Pennsylvania;
Westcott, William, 36, New York;
Walther, Jacob, 23, Germany;

COMPANY "B."

Captain- Z. B. Adams, Massachusetts.
First Lieutenant- Wm., C. Manning, Maine.
Second Lieutenant- Josiah A. Baldwin, Massach'tts.

Privates-

Brunen, Edward D., Pennsylvania;
Abbey, Samuel, Connecticut;
Anderson, John, England;
Beebee, Samuel J., Ohio;
Barron, Francis E., Illinois;
Boggs, David W., Ohio;
Backus, L. W., New York;
Babcock, Samuel B., Pennsylvania;
Coolidge, Harry H., Massachusetts;
Clark, Charles A., Mississippi;
Chaffee, Daniel K., Rhode Island;
Dealing, Charles A., Connecticut;
Ferrell, David C., New York;
Ferdman, Nathan C., New York;
Felch, John H., Wisconsin;
Gudith, John D., Switzerland;
Green, Charles N., New York;
Howe, John W., Massachusetts;
Hatch, Richard A., Kentucky;
Hawkins, James M., Missouri;
Harrington, George, Massachusetts;
Hoxie, Benjamin F., New York;
Hannun, Wm. M., Pennsylvania;
Kimball, Solon D., New York;
Kuhls, Henry, Germany;
Lane, Edward P., Michigan;
Leonard, Partrick H., New York;
Little, Hazen D., New Hampshire;
Loud, Eugene, Massachusetts;
Maguire, Thomas F., Ireland;
McCallen, John C., Kentucky;
McDougal, Daniel, Scotland;
Merry, Thomas H., New York;
Nystrom, Charles W., New York;
Pringle, Wm. H., Pennsylvania;
Parker, George W., New York;
Pewin, Samuel, Illinois;
Randall, James B., Rhode Island;
Reed, George W., Missouri;
Still, Alonzo D., New York;
Seagrave, Edward F., Massachusetts;
Spencer, Ebenezer, Ireland;

Anderson, John, New York;
Ayers, Osborn, New York;
Bard, James, New Jersey;
Barns, John, Ireland;
Baldwin, George F., Massachusetts;
Boyle, George P., Missouri;
Burney, Ezra D., Michigan;
Chamberlain, Richard L., Vermont;
Clawell, Robert, Indiana;
Clark, Levi R., Maine;
Chandler, Seth, Maine;
Enos, Frank, Ohio;
Finley, John L., Ohio;
Fogg, Nathan H., Maine;
Fortman, Henry, Germany;
Gaskill, Aaron A., Ohio;
Hull, Chauncey, Ohio;
Howard, Amos H., Illinois;
Hudson, Charles, New York;
Hunter, James P., Pennsylvania;
Halsey, Wm. F. Jr., New York;
Hardman, Wm. H., England;
Jones, Cyrus B., Texas;
Kingsley, Edward H., Connecticut;
Long, Edward, Maine;
Larrien, Lorenzo D., Illinois;
Levitz, George, Pennsylvania;
Lee, John L. Jr., New York;
Lycan, William M., Illinois;
McLean, Alfred A., New York;
McKinney, John W., Ohio;
McFarlane, Thos., Maine;
Morse, John, New York;
Parker, Wm. E., South Carolina;
Peebles, James J., Kentucky;
Piquet, William, Massachusetts;
Renard, Peter, New York;
Reston, Joseph L., Massachusetts;
Swank. Loima, Ohio;
Smedley, William W., Tennessee;
Spenogle, James W., Ohio;
Smith, Roswell R., Vermont;

Sparhawk, Jared S., New York;
Schroder, Henry, Germany;
Taylor, John, Ohio;
Van Benscoten, Henry, New York;
Weaver, William, New York;
Weaver, Joseph, Pennsylvania;
Washburn, Lyman H., New York;

Smith, Albert J., Missouri;
Townsend, Hiram, Michigan;
Van Hoosen, Jerome, New York;
Waggoner, John H., Pennsylvania;
Wilson, Peter H., Canada;
Wildes, Bradstreet R., Maine;
Wilson, Frederick, Pennsylvania;

COMPANY "C."

Captain- Geo. A. Manning, Maine;
First Lieutenant- Alvin W. Stone, Mass;
Second Lieutenant- John C. Norcross, Maine;

Privates-

Algier, Hugh, Penn;
Byrnes, George L., New York;
Barnett, Thomas, Ohio;
Beals, Merrill C., New Hampshire;
Bixby, Samuel H. Vermont;
Burke, James H., Ireland;
Conley, James, New York;
De Forest, Wm. H., New York;
Dodd, Benjamin, Mass;
Foster, James, New Hampshire;
Gettings, Peter, Ireland;
Gossan, Hammon, Hamburg;
Halstedt, Jacob H., Switzerland;
Miles, Johm W., Ohio;
Kehoe, James, New York;
Lawrence, W. C., Mass.;
Locke, John W., Maine;
McCann, James W., Massachusetts;
Merritt, Gilbert H., New Jersey;
Morris, Samuel N., New York;
Nicholas, Wm., Michigan
Poe, Wm. C., Kentucky;
Larkin, Robert, Michigan;
Negly, Enos. Ohio;
Shiels, Joseph, H., Ireland;
Smith, John P., New Hampshire;
Stocking, Edward, Connecticut;
Taylor, George, Ireland;
Thayer, William, Miss.;
Warren, Isaac S., Massachusetts;
Wilcox, William, Massachusetts;
Wood, Warren, Ohio;
Bluett, Joseph, Pennsylvania;
Bucklin, Henry, New York;
Howe, James W., Pennsylvania;

Allwell, Andrew, New York;
Babcock, Silas B., Vermont;
Belnap, Wm. B., Penn.;
Bell, William, Ireland;
Blanchard, William E., Maine;
Coleman, Thomas F., Mass.;
Cooper, Seth H., Vermont;
Dexter, Henry C., Virginia;
Ford, Milo G., New York;
Foster, Edward, Ohio;
Goodrich, Henry M., New York;
Hackett, Patrick J., Ireland;
Hayford, James B., Maine;
Jones, John, Wales;
Knapp, Jos., Canada;
Lay, Wm. J., New York;
McCann, Thomas, Ireland;
Meadow, Charles E., Maine;
Morris, Joseph, France;
Morris, Jas., Massachusetts;
Parker, Geo, W., New York;
Price, Edward, Ireland;
Robinson, Charles, New York;
Seccion, Joseph, Hungary;
Siminson, Anthony, Pennsylvania;
Smith, Geo, E., Virginia;
Street, Hamilton, New York;
Taylor, Archibald, Scotland;
Van Slyke, Peter, New York;
Watson, David, Ohio;
Withrow, Abel A., Indiana;
Williams, John, New York;
Benniger, Hammon, Pennsylvania;
Eby, James W., Pennsylvania;
Miles, Henry P., Wisconsin;

Stevens, Alfred, Maine;
Varnum, Joseph B., Massachusetts;
Harbich, Henry R., New York;
Thompson, Joseph W., Ohio;
Williams, Charles, Illinois;
Clark, Richard, Massachusetts;
Jennings, William H., Maine;

Stevens, Thomas Z., New York;
Van Vleet, De Witt C., Michigan;
Neimeyer, Valentine, New York;
Dowly, John, Pennsylvania;
Dickson, William C., New York;
Lee, George W., Texas;
Mattox, Henry C., Wisconsin;

Alta California, San Francisco, Monday, March 23, 1863.
[No attempt has been made to correct any misspellings by the Alta. After arrival at Readville the companies were changed- A to E, B to L, C to M and D to F]

❖❖
Battalion

Following are the names of members of <u>Company D</u> who also went in the steamer:

Joseph Bradford, Benjamin F. Booth, Elhanan Wakefield, William Welch, Edward Thompson, Robert H. Williams, George F. Wilsey, George H. Small, James O'Brien, Augustus D. Day, Andrew Williams, Charles Bunn, Warren W. Cochran, Julius H. Whitcomb, James Hill, Goerge Wagoner, John Maler, Louis Munger, William Johnson, William H. Sutton, C. H. Rawson, B. F. Rawson, Dennis Seymour, Chester Case, L. McCarty, J. H. Wilson, William T. Cook, Joseph Shiffer, Oscar G. Shurliff, James Shuler, Hosea Osgood, H.T. Langley, A. M. Tufferty, George W. Gaskell and John Seinler-total 35.

Capt. DeMerritt, <u>Company D</u>, and First Lieut. Stone of <u>Company C</u>, remain in town. The battalion who left in the steamer are under the command of Col. D.C. Thompson. They were escorted to the boat by the National Guard, San Francisco Light Guard, Elsworth Guard, First California Guard, City Guard and California Fusileers.

Sailing of the *Constitution* - Departure of the California Battalion.

The Steamship *Constitution*, Watkins commanding, left her wharf at about half past 11 o'clock this morning, bound for Panama. On board of his vessel were four companies of cavalry, of the California contingent, who leave for the seat of war in the Atlantic States. These companies form part of the battalion which has been raised in this state under the auspices and at the expense of the State of Massachusetts, to whose troops they will be attached. The men and officers, numbering 307, were accompanied to the steamer by a splendid escort of our city uniformed military, which was composed of the following companies, viz: Sigel Rifles, Capt. Ewald; Ellsworth Rifles, Capt. McDonald; City Guard, Capt. Little; Light Guard, Capt. Robbins; National Guard, Capt. Pratt; Sumner Guard, Capt. Ludlum; Fusileers, Capt. Tittle; and a section of the Old California Guard Artillery. After marching through several principal streets, the cavalry companies and the escort proceeded to the steamer and embarked, the escort being drawn up in line on the wharf and saluting the contingent as they passed.

The wharf was densely crowded, a great number of people having been attracted by notice of the military proceedings. In the excitement attending the embarcation the throng pushed a man overboard next the steamer, who was upheld in the water by another man who jumped over after the first, until a boat took on board the pair and landed them safely at the boat steps. After a delay of about an hour the *Constitution's* fasts were cast off and she backed slowly out from the wharf, the band on shore playing *Home, Sweet Home*, the artillery firing a salute in honor of some of their former members who now form part of the departing battalion. While

the steamer lay at the wharf an almost constant succession of cheers was given by those on board and on the wharf. Following is a (Partial) list of the steamer's cabin passengers:
Maj. D.W.C. Thompson, wife and 2 children,
Capt. Adams, wife and child,
Capt. G.A. Manning,
Lieut. J.C. Norcross,
Capt. C.S. Eigenbrodt,
Lieut. H.H. Crocker,
Lieut. W.C. Manning,
Lieut. J.A. Baldwin,
Lieut. R.W. Smith

Evening Bulletin, San Francisco, Monday, March 23, 1863
Daily Bee, Sacramento, Tuesday, March 24, 1863
Daily Union, Sacramento, Wednesday, March 25, 1863
Solano County Herald, Saturday, March 28, 1863

❖❖
Battalion

Light Cavalry.- Capt. DeMerritt wants fifty men for companies C and D, of the California Cavalry battalion who are intended for active service in the East. His recruiting office in this city is in Klays' building, on the west side of Fourth street, between J and K.

Daily Bee, Sacramento, Monday, March 23, 1863.

❖❖
Battalion

Farewell Ovation to California Cavalry. - The military comprising the First Regiment made a brilliant display on Monday, in conjunction with the three companies of the California Cavalry Battalion, which latter were about departing for the seat of war in the Eastern States. All of the thoroughfares along the line of march were crowded with people, who continually cheered, while ladies waved their kerchiefs to the brave lads bound to the battle-field. The superb music enhanced the imposing character of the display, which was as creditable to the Home Guards as complimentary to the departing troops. Arriving at Folsom Street Wharf, at an early hour, we find every nook and post which afforded even a glimpse of the steamer *Constitution* occupied. The decks of the *Sierra Nevada*, which lay alongside, and of the various sailing craft in the vicinity presented dense masses of spectators. Hundreds of row boats and sailing craft might also be seen flying up and down the Bay in the immediate neighborhood of the wharf. The adjoining piers and Market street outside of the pier gate, were blocked with persons of both sexes, some on foot, and many in vehicles. On no previous occasion have we seen so many live humans congregated at Folsom Street wharf. The military, with some delay and difficulty, forced a passage through the dense throng. The artillery, Capt. Bluxome, with two guns, moved to the northern end of the wharf, the escorting troops ranging themselves along the centre, whilst the passenger soldiers marched up the gang planks, and so to the decks of the steamer. Fully an hour and a half was consumed in final preparation for departure, during which period the battalion on board cheered their friends on shore, which were enthusiastically answered from the dock. Finally, at 11 1/4 o'clock, the paddle wheels of the leviathan craft began to revolve, and instantaneously with the movement, the cannon fired a salute. The American flag, and the guidons of the companies were conspicuously exhibited at the extreme stern of the ship. The troops ranged in long lines, with their officers at the head, represented a thrillingly interesting spectacle. The steamer backed down a few hundred yards, then returning, made a long and graceful sweep around several vessels in the harbor, and firing her farewell gun as she turned her prow seaward. On running down, she passed close alongside of the Federal sloop of war 'Cyane', and dipped her colors. The gallant tars of the latter, instantly sprang into the rigging, and gave rounds of hearty cheers which were responded to as lustily by the sea-bound soldiers. The manifold compliments paid the Cavalry Battalion on their appearance here will, we doubt not, be endorsed by our Atlantic neighbors. They are a stalwart soldier-like body, and fair representatives of California men. Although going hence to be incorporated into a Massachusetts Regiment, it will be seen by reference to the roster published in the Alta, that but twenty of the entire force originally hailed from the Old Bay State.

Alta California, San Francisco, Tuesday, March 24, 1863.

❖❖
Battalion

A Repentant Recruit. - Isaac Goslinsky is a Union soldier, 18 years of age: On the 22d he enlisted in the California Cavalry Battallion, which left yesterday for the Atlantic States. At the last moment he desired to back out; and accordingly, through his brother, applied for a writ of *habeas corpus* to Judge Sawyer, said Thompson, as he alledges, having him confined on board the steamer *Constitution.* We cannot learn that the young recruit got the benefit of the *habeas corpus* in time to save him from taking the long voyage.

Alta California, San Francisco, Tuesday, March 24, 1863.
[Research has not turned up the outcome of this matter.]

❖❖
Battalion

THE CALIFORNIA VOLUNTEERS (CAVALRY) EN ROUTE TO THE ATLANTIC

(From the Correspondent of the Alta, accompanying the Detachment)

At Sea, on board S.S. Constitution,
March 30th, 1863

Editors Alta:- Our arrival at Manzanillo yesterday, and our consequent approach to Acapulco, reminded me of my promise to you, and warns me that it is time to fulfill it, although I must confess to a lack of scarcely anything to write about.

Our Departure.

The 23rd day of March, 1863, will be a day long remembered, as well by those who on that day bade adieu to "the near and dear ones," and looked, perhaps, for the last time on the hospitable shores of our own loved California, as to those who, with streaming tears yet stout hearts, sent forth their loved ones to fight their country's battles, and thus aid in restoring our now distracted country to its former peace and prosperity, and to her proud position among the nations of the world; and while they mourned their absence, inspired by the true spirit of patriotism, they'd willingly give them to Death for the holy cause, in which so many others have fallen.

This command would here seize this opportunity to return thanks to their San Francisco friends, both civil and military, for their kindness and escort to the steamer. Californians my rest assured that, if ever this battalion meets the enemy in anything like its own numbers, it will give a good account of itself, and thus add lustre to the already bright fame of California. It may be some satisfaction for those who have friends in the battalion, to know that "the boys" are in the best of spirits, and "eager for the fray."

Quarters, Food, Etc.

Our quarters are pleasant, and, indeed, we have but one cause of complaint, and that is the Commissary Department, which is sadly deficient. Our fare is hard; indeed, it is miserable, and unfit for men many of whom left lucrative occupations and comfortable homes to fight for their country in its hour of need. But our officers are entirely exonerated from blame, the whole of which rests upon the Steamship Company, whose passengers we are. A spirited indignation meeting was held and a committee appointed from each company to confer with Major Thompson, but it was attended with little, if any, good results. At Manzanillo, yesterday, Major Thompson, Captains Eigenbrodt and Manning went on shore and ere long returned with several baskets full of eggs which were served to us this morning for breakfast, and you may well believe that "the boys" enjoyed the luxury.

The "Constitution Guards."

A company bearing the above name was formed on the second day out. It is composed of members of the several companies, who had previously been connected with other military organizations and knew the infantry drill. They are armed with the ship's muskets, and number about forty men. The ship's rifled cannon are also worked by an artillery company, who handle the guns scientifically. These precautions were deemed necessary, in view of some pirate that may be lurking on our track. But we are safe; and if any of Jeff. Davis & Co.'s pirates think they can capture *this* Constitution as easily as they violated the *other*-that of the Nation-let them try it and see.

A Sad Calamity

Happened on the evening of our second day out. About 10 o'clock P.M. the stillness of the night was broken by the startling cry of "man overboard;" it was soon ascertained that Hiram Townsend, of Company B, one of the guard, had fallen overboard. The alarm was given, a life-preserver was thrown over, and it is said to have struck the water within ten feet of the man. The steamer was stopped and a boat lowered, which however soon returned, reporting their search as fruitless. The sad accident happened thus: Townsend was on duty as a guard; feeling a little seasick he hurried to the ship's side and stepping up on the hawser-pipe, leaned over the rail to vomit; just then the ship rolled and, losing his balance, fell head foremost overboard. When we hurried to the spot his unsheathed sword still lay upon the deck, a fit emblem of a soldier's death. Being encumbered by a heavy army overcoat it was, doubtless, difficult for him to swim, but he was twice heard distinctly to cry out for help. Those in command of the ship are culpable in the highest degree and cannot be too much censured. They made but a trifling search for our comrade, and returned to the ship without even having found the life-preserver which was thrown overboard, and this, too, notwithstanding that the sea was smooth, almost a calm, and the moon shining. Yet, why complain? What is the life of one human being compared to the interest of this Steamship Company? It is another sin added to the already long catalogue, for which the Pacific Mail S. S. Company, and their employees will have to answer when they appear at the "Bar of Heaven's High Chancery." The deceased, Hiram Townsend, was a native of Michigan, from whence he emigrated to California in 1856, and whilst there was a resident of Walnut Grove, Sacramento County. He was a sober, steady and a good man; had for several years been connected with the Order of Sons of Temperance; his loss cast a gloom of sadness over the whole command, more so than had he died a soldier's legitimate death, on the field of battle, bravely fighting his country's foes.

Miscellaneous.

In spite of all that is going on, time drags along slowly; we have roll-call at 8 A.M. and at 6 P.M.; drill twice a day; the rest of the time is spent in reading, singing, sleeping and gazing on the vast expanse of waters around us.

The weather is delightful, and all are in good health, except Captain Adams, who had been indisposed, but is recovering under the influence of a more genial climate. But Acapulco is close by and I must close, My next will be from Aspinwall.

T. H. M.

Alta California, San Francisco, Monday, April 20, 1863
Evening Bulletin, San Francisco, Thursday, April 30, 1863
[Hiram Townsend, Company L, California Battalion. Thomas H. Merry, Company L, California Battalion; A native of New York, he came to California in 1850. A graduate of Santa Clara college shortly after the Civil War broke out. After the Civil War he returned to San Francisco where he practiced law, then moved to Ventura and finally to Santa Barbara where he died October 20, 1907.]

❖ ❖

LIGHT CAVALRY WANTED.

Fifty Men wanted For Companies C and D of the California Cavalry Battalion, for active service in the East.

The balance of the Battalion left for New York on the 21ˢᵗ of March, to be followed by the detachment on April 1ˢᵗ or 11ᵗʰ. All parties wishing to join this service can apply on FOURTH STREET, between J AND K, Sacramento, or on MARKET STREET, between Sansome and Montgomery, San Francisco, where all necessary information can be obtained.

Due notice will be given when the Battalion is full.

D. A. DeMERRITT.
Captain, Commanding Company D

The Daily Bee, Sacramento, Tuesday, March 31, 1863.

❖ ❖

APRIL, 1863

2 Bread riots in Richmond.
7 Federal Ironclads defeated in attack on Ft. Sumter.

❖ ❖

Battalion

A Cavalry Company Nearly Full. Lieut. McKendry's company for the 2d Cavalry, wants three men to meet the regulation standard as to numbers, and is in fine condition every way. So good a company should be put into the field as soon as possible. The recruiting office is at No. 2 City Hall avenue. *[Boston]*

Evening Transcript, Boston, Wednesday, April 1, 1863.

Reports of Mass. Regiments for March.

The battalion of the 2d cavalry regiment, Major Caspar Crowninshield commanding, at Gloucester Point, Va., had 13 officers and 190 men present on duty; on detached service 1 officer and 18 men; present sick 1 officer and 32 men; absent sick 9; died 2, viz.: Charles Leighton, March 26, and John D. Whitehill, March 30, both of Co. D.

Evening Transcript, Boston, Saturday, April 4, 1863.
[Roster shows a William Leighton, March 26 and a John Whitehall, March 31; both of Company K]

PITIFUL FALSEHOODS.-The Butte *Record*, in its last issue, speaking of Massachusetts and the emancipation proclamation, says: Behold, the long desired decree has been sent forth, and the pitiful echo to its broad proclaim reaches our Pacific coast, asking us, in our critical situation, to send her *[Massachusetts]* our best and bravest men, while she fails to fill her quota under the light draft of the Federal Government. There are two bald-headed lies in this. First, Massachusetts has never asked for a single man from the Pacific coast, and second, has more than filled her quota under every call of the Federal Government.

Solano County Herald, Suisun, Saturday, April 4, 1863

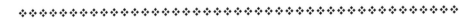

SECOND MASSACHUSETTS CAVALRY

Gloucester Point, Va., April 5, 1863

To the Editors of the Boston Journal:
We have good reason to rejoice on our Easter Sunday, and plenty of money to get eggs with. We have seen Uncle Sam's wallet, open too, and had the gratifying sensation of transferring its contents to our own. Of course all hands are happy. Not that we fight for money, by no means, but there are "the old folks at home," little ones too, and "the old women," who must not be forgotten.
Last Monday (Mar. 30) a most interesting event occurred. Fifteen men were out scouting, accompanied by Major Crowninshield and Captains Washburn and Holman. About three miles outside the lines, these officers were riding along the road a short distance in advance of their men, passing a dense piece of woods, when Capt. Holman hearing a noise, (some one speak-

ing) turned and discovered a narrow lane running into the woods to be filled with rebel cavalry. Our officers were fairly passed the head of the lane, which was very obscure, when the fortunate discovery was made. Seeing they were discovered, the rebs fired a volley and came charging out of the lane into the road. Our officers wheeled about and had barely room enough to pass the head of the rebel column, completely running the guantlet of a ceaseless fire. The enemy followed till within sight of our men, then halted and retired. We were not in sufficient force to follow, and therefore returned to camp.

It was a very narrow escape from capture; in fact they were cut off and got away again. The negros say there were twenty or thirty rebels armed with double barreled shot guns. How it was possible for our officers to escape without injury to either themselves or their horses is a wonder to all. An old barn on the side of the road opposite the lane, and in direct range, is filled with buck-shot so are the fences all along the road. The battalion has reason to be thankful that our Major is still with us, and companies D and K that their Captains are not in Richmond. All three of the officers have seen much service, but they all call this their narrowest escape.

We were out again on Thursday, foraging; went six miles to Abingdon Church (built in 1754) and Hickory York. We got a lot of grain, some good mules, cattle, sheep, etc.

Two deaths have occurred in our battalion; William Leighton of New Salem, died suddenly of heart disease March 25 and John D. Whitehill of Groton died in hospital of fever March 31. Both were members of Co. D, and were buried by their Company with military honors.

Cadet

Boston Journal, Tuesday, April 5, 1863.
[Roster shows as Co. K.]

Battalion

LETTERS FROM A CALIFORNIAN IN THE
MASSACHUSETTS CAVALRY- No. 2.

Aspinwall, N. G., April 6th, 1863.

Editors Alta:-   Here we are once more on the Atlantic side of the continent, and in one hour we shall leave here for New York. Since my last but little worthy of note has transpired; after leaving Acapulco, it was the same old routine, the same monotony, until we are glad once again to stand on *terra firma*, even though it be a foreign soil; but a few more days and we shall once more tread "our own native land."

A Heavy Gale

April came to us in a way that we shall remember for some time. When off the Gulf of Tehuantepec we experienced a very heavy gale. Some rich scenes were enacted, as usual in such cases. In the cabin, the ladies resorted to their *sine qua non,* and shed a vast amount of tears; the Chaplain offered long and fervent prayers; but nothing seemed to appease the wrath of old Boreas. Among the "soldier boys" there was also fun; many of them seasick, were paying the penalty for invading the domains of old Neptune; others, preparing for emergencies, buckled on life-preservers; while still others enjoyed the fun. Occasionally a wave would strike the ship and send its sparkling waters on board, and was greeted with a cheer. But all things must have an end, and this storm was no exception; the wind declined with the sun, and the next morning the sun, bathed in golden splendor, rose from a calm, smooth sea, and the *Constitution*, resumed her course, none the worse for the rough handling she had suffered. So may its namesake, the Constitution of our country, withstand the storm of civil war and come out of the conflict the stronger and more enduring for the ordeal through which it is now passing.

We arrived at Panama this morning, at 4 A. M., crossed the Isthmus in good time, and on arriving at Aspinwall we were all agreeably surprised to find the fine steamship *Ocean Queen* waiting for us, instead of the old *Champion*.

The command are in good health; James Sponegle, of Company B, a resident of Suisun City, is somewhat ill, but is fast recovering, and seems to endure his illness with good spirits.

A U. S. gunboat is here to convoy us on our trip; the pirate *Alabama* may be lying in wait for us, if so, she may get both a chase and a fight.

T. H. M.

Alta California, San Francisco, Thursday, April 30, 1863.
[Aspinwall, N.G. -Present day Colon- New Granada as Colombia was known.]

❖❖❖
Battalion Co's. D & G.

Mutiny At Camp Quincy-A Soldier Shot.

About 8 o'clock this morning, a revolt, resulting in fatal consequences, occurred in the 2d Massachusetts Cavalry Regiment, now recruiting at Camp Quincy, in the basement of Niles Block, on City Hall Avenue and School street. The circumstances, as we understand them from a hasty interview with recruiting officer George H. Quincy, were briefly these:

For an alleged sufficient military reason, Sergeant Burlingham attempted to put one of the men in irons, when the man resisted and knocked the Sergeant down, and several more of the company-now numbering 68 men-immediately fell upon and overpowered the fallen officer. Mr. Quincy, on hearing of the disturbance, called for the help of the police, and sent Lieutenants McKendry and Pinkham to the assistance of Sergeant Burlingham.

These officers, seeing the excited condition of the men, desisted for the time from any further attempt to iron the man, but called the troops into line and commenced a drill. Col. C. R. Lowell, Jr., now came into the camp, and ordered the man who was to be ironed to step forward. At this command the revolt broke out anew, and with increased fury-nearly the whole company drawing their sabres and rushing upon the officers, while the four policemen who were present took care to save themselves from all harm by a sudden retreat from the building.

During the melee, Col. Lowell, finding that no order whatever would be obeyed, with characteristic coolness selected the apparent ringleader of the mutineers, and with his revolver shot him in the region of the heart. He died on the spot in a very few moments, and the rebellion at once subsided. The officers all escaped with no serious injuries, but some of the men received sabre cuts.

The deceased was named William Pendergast. He belonged in this city, and was about 23 years of age. Coroner Sanborn took charge of the body, and will hold an inquest in the case tomorrow.

The name of the recruit, whose intoxication and disorderly conduct was the prime cause of the difficulty, and for which he was eventually put in irons, was William Lynch.

The company was mustered into the service of the United States about noon today, and will be sent into camp at Readville this afternoon.

Evening Transcript, Boston, Thursday, April 9, 1863.
Evening Bulletin, San Francisco, Tuesday, May 5, 1863
Saturday Evening Express, June 20, 1863
*[Lynch, of Co. G was executed at Fort Independence on Tuesday, June 16, 1863; William
Pendergast was from Co. D.]*

❖❖❖
Battalion

Second Massachusetts Cavalry
Soldier shot in Boston. - At the rooms occupied by recruits, under Niles' Block, Court
Square, a riotous manifestation was made Thursday morning, and in quelling it the military
officers, together with the police who were called in, were for a time overpowered, or likely to
be. In this condition of things Col. Lowell shot a private named Wm. Pendergast, with a pistol.
The wounded man died instantly having been shot through the heart. We saw inquiring people
crowding about the place a few hours later, but they were requested by a guard to "pass on."
Rum was the primary cause a venerable citizen said in our hearing, "Order must be maintained." So we say. But let it be through the enforcement of the liquor law; then life will be
safer by a considerable per cent.

Randolph Transcript and Norfolk Advertiser, Saturday, April 11, 1863.

❖❖❖
Battalion

FROM CHARLESTON.

Lieut. McKendry's Company of the 2d Cavalry, after the quelling of the mutiny, remained in perfect subordination. Just before 2 o'clock, five of the men, supposed to have been
the ringleaders, were given into the hands of the Police, and quietly taken to the lock-up to
await a trial by Court Martial. The company was then marched to the Providence Station in due
order, and took the cars for the camp at Readville.

Evening Transcript, Boston, Thursday, April 9, 1863.

❖❖❖
Battalion

Coroner's Inquest in the Camp Quincy Shooting Case. Yesterday afternoon, a jury
summoned by Coroner Sanborn held an inquest relative to the death of Wm. Pendergast, the
soldier shot at Camp Quincy on Thursday morning. The recruiting officer, George H. Quincy,
and Provost Marshall Scott of the military, and police officers Brooks and Nettleton, were
called as witnesses. Their evidence confirmed the general statements published, to the insubor-
dination of the men present in camp, and that the life of Lieutenant McKendry was endangered
by Pendergast, who was about to plunge his sabre into him when the shot of Col. Lowell took
effect. The result of the inquest was the following verdict:

"The jury say that Wm. Pendergast came to his death at about 8 1/2 o'clock on the morning of April 9, 1863, at Camp Quincy, basement of No. 2, City Hall avenue, from the effects of a pistol-shot wound, caused by a Minnie ball entering the upper part of the left breast, and passing through a portion of the lungs, said ball having been fired from a loaded Colt's revolver; and that said pistol was discharged by Col. Charles R. Lowell, Jr., commanding the 2d Massachusetts Cavalry, of which deceased was a member. And the jury further find that the said Col. Lowell shot the deceased in the discharge of his duty, and in defence of the life of one of his officers, the company being at the time in a state of revolt."

The jury was composed as follows: Dr. H.G. Barrows, foreman; Timothy R. Page, G.W. Allen, A.S. Drew, Josiah McClenathan, Ira Gibbs.

Evening Transcript, Boston, Saturday, April 11, 1863.

❖❖❖

Battalion

The Killing at Camp Quincy

Last Thursday morning, Col. Lowell killed a man, a soldier at Camp Quincy, who was insobordinate and who, it is alleged, was in the act of a deadly assault upon a sergeant. It is claimed that Col. Lowell, by killing the man as he did, prevented the man from killing the sergeant. An inquest was held over the body and the facts above stated appeared in evidence and the verdict of the jury was in accordance with the facts.

There is, however, a good deal of feeling on this subject. Many minds are not at all satisfied that justice has been done, or that all the facts in the case have been brought to light. It is alleged that no real examination has been held; and the jury was mostly constructed of persons who hang around Court Houses for any kind of a job; that nobody but the officers and police officers were examined; that no opportunity was given to any of the soldiers to testify to the facts as they understand them; that discredit has been thrown upon them as being incompetent to testify and that the verdict establishes nothing and shows nothing, inasmuch as it was rendered upon a partial and *ex-parte* view of the facts.

What makes the feeling more decided in this case is the reflection that officers have been increasing in arrogance and severity since the war began. They are presuming, many of them; they are filled with haughtiness and pride and they demand - Captains and Lieutenants - more homage that a Major General. Said one of them to us, when speaking of the shooting, "Col. Lowell was perfectly right, d—d 'em, I'd have shot a dozen of them." Now to those of us who have sons, brothers and friends in the army, voluntarily fighting for the Union, this sort of thing doesn't answer. It jars our feelings. It excites indignation. Especially when we know they who use this language and do these deeds are placed in command, not by merit, not by skill, not by bravery in the field, but by influence, and interest. They take a lion's share of pay, and can resign when they will, while the men who bear the heat and the burden of the day, who maintain the country by their sweat and blood and who - a majority of them - are fully equal in social position and intelligence to upstart officers - must remain for niggard pay and cannot resign however brutally brutal officers may treat them.

We don't know who this Col. Lowell is; we hear him spoken of as a brave man, a good man and a man of honor. If he be such a man he never will rest content with a pretended inquest on the death of Pendergast, nor sit down contented with what many of his fellow citizens consider a white-wash verdict of exoneration.

Roxbury City Gazette, Thursday, April 16, 1863.

❖❖❖
Battalion

Mutiny. In the late occurrence, the killing of the mutineer, Pendergast, the conduct of Colonel Lowell has been described, in some of the newspapers, as *"perfectly justifiable."* No doubt of it. But it was something more. It was an act of *unavoidable duty, the non-performance of which would have rendered Colonel Lowell liable to the punishment of death.*

Raw recruits, some of them certainly, appear to think that enlisting in the army is very much like getting ready for a frolic-a picnic- that they are to obey the orders of their superiors, just as long, as their orders are perfectly agreeable, and that combinations, to resist a command, are as justifiable, as to oppose an unpopular measure, in town-meeting.

Now it can do no harm to pour a little light upon this matter, from the highest source. It may be profitable for the recruit to "mark, learn and inwardly digest" these words from the articles of war:

"Art. 7. Any officer or soldier, who shall begin, excite, cause, or join in, any mutiny or sedition, in any troop or company, in the service of the United States, or in any party, post, detachment, or guard, shall suffer death, or such other punishment, as by a Court Martial shall be inflicted."

Article 8. Any officer, non-commissioned officer, or soldier, who, being present at any mutiny, or sedition, does not use his utmost endeavor to suppress the same, &c., shall be punished, by the sentence of a court martial, with death, or otherwise, according to the nature of his offence.

It appeared, upon the coroner's inquest, in the case of Pendergast, that the men not only refused obedience, and defied their superiors, but actually drew their sabres against them.

Article 9. Any officer or soldier, who shall strike his superior officer, or draw or lift up any weapon, or offer any violence against him, being in the execution of his office, on any pretense whatever, or shall disobey any lawful command of his superior officer, shall suffer death, or such other punishment, as shall, according to the nature of the offence, be inflicted upon him by the sentence of a court martial.

Sigma.

Evening Transcript, Boston, Friday, April 17, 1863.

❖❖❖
Battalion

Arrival of the California Cavalry Battalion for Massachusetts.

New York, 14th. The California cavalry battalion, commanded by Major Thompson, arrived in this city this afternoon, by the steamer Ocean Queen, from San Francisco via Aspinwall, after a very favorable and quick passage. The battalion was received at the pier by Colonel Howe, State Agent of Massachusetts, and escorted to the Park Barracks, which had been prepared expressly on short notice for their reception. The battalion comprises three companies, under command of the following officers: Major, DeWitt C. Thompson, Co. A-Captain, D.S. Eigenbrodt; 1st Lieutenant, R.W. Smith; 2d Lieutenant, H. Crocker. Co. B-Captain, Z.B. Adams; 1st Lieutenant, W.C. Manning; 2d Lieutenant, J.A. Baldwin. Co. C-Captain, G.A. Manning; 1st Lieutenant, A.W. Stone; 2d Lieutenant, J.C. Norcross.

Each company is composed of 100 men and three officers. Company D is already full at San Francisco, under command of Captain A. Demeritt, and were detained until the 18th of this month, to obtain uniforms. The late arrival of the Ocean Queen precluded their immediate transportation to the camp of the 2d Massachusetts cavalry regiment at Readville, and consequently they will not leave until Wednesday afternoon at 5 o'clock.

The men composing the battalion are all young, active and withy, and anxious for service. Many of them are farmers from all parts of California, and no inconsiderable number are miners. In point of intelligence they are inferior to none enlisted in the service-a sure guarantee that the *esprit du corps* which has always distinguished this favorite arm will be well preserved by them.

A meeting of Californians, sons of Massachusetts and New England, will be held at the Astor House on Wednesday, at 2 o'clock, to form an escort to the battalion on their departure.

A member of the battalion was lost overboard on the Pacific side from the steamer Constitution. There are no members under arrest, nor has there been any since leaving San Francisco, and there are but four on the sick list. The latter are at the New England Rooms. The battalion visited the New Bowery Theatre this evening.

Evening Transcript, Boston, Wednesday, April 15, 1863
New York Tribune, Wednesday, April 15, 1863
Alta California, San Francisco, Thursday, May 14, 1863.

❖❖
Battalion

The California Cavalry Battalion.

This fine body of men, commanded by Major Thompson, arrived in this city on Tuesday afternoon, by the steamer *Ocean Queen*, from San Francisco, *via* Aspinwall, after a favorable passage. The battalion was received at the pier by Col. Howe, State Agent of Massachusetts, and escorted to the Park Barracks, which had been prepared expressly, on short notice, for their reception. The battalion comprises three companies, under command of the following officers:

Major, DeWitt C. Thompson.

Company A - Captain, D. S. Eigenbrodt; First Lieutenant, R. W. Smith; Second Lieutenant, H. H. Crocker.

Company B - Captain, Z. B. Adams; First Lieutenant, W. C. Manning; Second Lieutenant, J. A. Baldwin.

Company C - Captain, G. A. Manning; First Lieutenant, A. W. Stone; Second Lieutenant, J. C. Norcross.

Each company is composed of 109 men and three officers. Company D is already full at San Francisco, under command of Capt. A. Demerritt, and were detained until the 13th of this month to obtain uniforms. Yesterday afternoon, the battalion was reviewed by the Mayor *[George Updyke]*, in the City Hall Park, after which they marched up Broadway to Union-square, and thence down to the Boston boat, where they embarked for Massachusetts at 5 P. M. They were escorted by a large deputation of Californians, with a portion of the Seventh regiment Band, and, on the route up Broadway, were greeted with various and enthusiastic demonstrations of welcome. One hundred girls, stationed at the lower windows of Haughwout's establishment, each holding in her hand a miniature flag, greeted the battalion with true feminine cordiality. Before leaving the Park Barracks, the battalion was drawn up in hollow-square, and listened to an eloquent and patriotic address from Gov. Nye, of Nevada Territory, in which he welcomed the soldiers of the Pacific to the shores of the Atlantic, and congratulated them that they were to join the sons of the old Commonwealth of Massachusetts in defence of this glorious Republic. The battalion is to be attached to the Second regiment Massachusetts cavalry.

New York Times, Thursday, April 16, 1863.
Evening Bulletin, San Francisco, Thursday, May 14, 1863

❖❖
Battalion

LETTER FROM NEW YORK
(FROM OUR SPECIAL CORRESPONDENT.)
New York, April 16th.
California Cavalry

The Ocean Queen brought us a fine battalion of cavalry from California, on their way to join their comrades in camp in Massachusetts. My doctor permitted me to jump into a stage and visit the New England rooms yesterday, and I found the boys in fine spirits and full of military ardor. They arrived on Tuesday evening, and tarried until five o'clock yesterday afternoon. The weather was fine, their reception was cordial, and even smacked of the enthusiasm with which we started out in the war, and they were much pleased with everything. Dinner, as usual, was served in the Park Barracks; and there Governor Nye of Nevada made an eloquent speech in eulogy of that patriotism which drew these hardy soldiers from auriferous mines into bloody and remote battle fields. At the hour of mail closing, yesterday, a procession of Sons of New England and New York, headed by the Seventh Regiment Band, escorted the Californians to the Washington Monument in Union Square, and thence down Broadway to the Boston boat, in which they embarked at five o'clock. Broadway was rainbow hued with bunting, and every window presented its bevy of girls or women waving handkerchiefs in welcome of the American soldiers from the Pacific. A salute was fired from the New England Rooms.
(Text Deleted)

Sacramento Daily Union, Tuesday, May 12, 1863

❖❖
Battalion

Arrival of the California Battalion at Readville. The three additional cavalry companies from California, consisting of 320 privates and ten officers, all fully uniformed and provided with sabres, arrived at Readville about ten o'clock this forenoon. They were placed in three barracks in Col. Lowell's camp, and immediately supplied with a good breakfast. The majority of the men are of New England origin. The acting Major, De Witt C. Thompson, went to California from Peru, Berkshire county.

Evening Transcript, Boston, Thursday, April 16, 1863.

❖❖

Battalion

The California Battalion at the East

(FROM OUR OWN CORRESPONDENT)

Camp Meigs, Near Boston, Mass.
April 19, 1863

Since my writing from Panama, I have nothing of special interest of which to write, further than of the good health and spirits of the Battalion generally, and of our safe arrival at Camp Meigs, Mass.

In justice to the Battalion, I should mention the marked difference in treatment experienced by the soldiers on the steamers of the Pacific and of the Atlantic. In the former the fare was good and our treatment by steamer officers gentlemanly. They were, apparently, loyal in feeling. All honor to the *Constitution*! Not so with the *Ocean Queen* on the Atlantic side. Salt junk and stale crackers constituted almost the entire fare, while growls and threats were the accompaniments. As to loyalty, I verily believe the vessel is destitute of its virtues entirely. Of the first-cabin steward, alone, I would speak with kind recollection. Nothing but mercenary and selfish motives, in my opinion, prevents the *Ocean Queen* from playing our country false.

Yesterday a new, though temporary reorganization of the battalion was made, by uniting the advanced fragment of Company D - about 35 men - with equal numbers from A, B and C, to complete a company of 80 men, and which is placed under the command of Lieut. Manning. The object, I believe, is to draw full company rations, and to make full battalion parade. The company will, probably, resume their original organization upon the arrival of Company D, under Capt. DeMerritt, and which the telegraph informs us, sailed from San Francisco on the 11th. It is now understood that the California battalion will form a portion of the 2d regiment of Massachusetts cavalry - the time of enlistment having expired in most of the original companies forming the regiment. It is the same in which the first California Hundred were quartered. From good information I learn that the 2d Massachusetts regiment will be officered, and lettered as follows:

Colonel of regiment, Charles R. Lowell, jr.
Lieut. Colonel, Henry D. Russell.
1st Major, C. Crowninshield.
2d Major, D.W.C. Thompson.
3d Major, (vacant)
Company A, Captain J. Sewell Read.
Company B, Captain Forbes.
Company G, Captain A. McKendry.
Company C, Captain Washburn.
Completing the First Battalion. The Second and Third Battalions will probably stand:
Company E, Capt. Charles Eigenbrodt.
Company F, Capt. F.D.A. DeMerritt.
Company L, Capt. Z.B. Adams.
Company M, Capt. G.A. Manning.
Company K, Capt. George Blagden.
Company I, Capt. George Holman.
Company H, Capt. Lewis Cobbett.
Company D, Capt. John Tibbets.

Recruiting is now going rapidly on, if not completed, for the fragmentary companies of the above regiment, raised in the State. Before this reaches you the Continental Telegraph will have informed the *Bulletin* as to our destination, which at present is said to be Fortress Monroe. Too much haste in bringing our boys into the field will be censurable, though they are "eager for the fray." My reasons for so asserting are, that though as brave as ever flashed a sabre, they are yet too inexperienced to pit against old cavalry men. But, let this go as it may, early or late, I firmly believe that death alone can vanquish them. From familiar acquaintance I know them to be men who understand what they have done and are doing, and who will be ready to triumph or die; and, not like Pillow, in a bloodless "ditch", but as brave and true men, who have long since "crossed the Rubicon" of early romance, and are now ready to take the result of the final "throw." California will not blush when the smoke arises from the battle-field in which her sons are engaged.

Quite a number of our boys have already obtained furloughs, not exceeding seven days, and have departed for a visit to the loved ones at home. I have already witnessed scenes that would almost bring tears from stones. Brave-hearted, glorious old New England! She meets her sons, and with loving accents, and a "God bless you!" bids them onward! at their country's call. I have never been in New England before, am not a Yankee, and am, therefore, an impartial judge; and I say it, her vitality is equal to a volcano, and her citizenship is eternal as her hills - and her vitality a good deal more productive. Give our Government that unity in execution which she has in real purpose, and her banner will soon wave triumphant without a star erased.

One thing is noticeable of the California boys, wherever they go, viz; good and gentlemanly behaviour. Singular as it may seem, it is nevertheless true, that our California Battalion will rank among the most sober and orderly - ay, and subordinate in the army. Submitting to discipline because it is right, our men quietly yield to submission to the officer, when they fail to recognize even equality in the man. Let it be understood that this is no fulsome flattery, but a credible fact. I wish that I might speak as commendably of the officers who command. But time will show. Of some of them, however, the highest hopes are entertained.

Before closing my letter I must speak of an evil which lies somewhere. Great coats issued to soldiers in San Francisco at $9 were here placed to their debit at $11.50; trowsers issued at $3 they have been obliged to pay $4.60 for; and miserable coarse undershirts, that you can buy on Commercial street for 6 bits apiece, are set down to them here at $1.40. Why this advance has been made on articles purchased a month ago in San Francisco I am at a loss to conjecture. Blankets and other necessary clothing are in ratio with the above fare! It is not a fault of the Government but of the Commissariat, and especially of the officers through whom they issue.

These are considerations that are patriotically overlooked by our men, who are resolved to do their whole duty, come what may. Good feeling and good health generally prevails.

Evening Bulletin, San Francisco, Tuesday, June 2, 1863
[Writer unknown]

❖❖

Gloucester Point April 19th/63

My dear Mammy

I have not written to you for sometime. I have been quite busy with Muster Rolls, Infantry Returns & other Battalion duties.

There is no news here, we hear the firing of heavy guns in the direction of Suffolk & suppose that they are doing some hard fighting down there. Gen Keyes & wife were over here yesterday & I rode round the picket line with them. That night there was an alarm the Infantry Pickets ran into the Fort. I took the California Company & went out there, but failed to see any Rebels, or any cause for an alarm.

Last night two of the Rebel Cavalry deserted to us. They report a small Cavalry force (100 men) some five miles from our lines. Today, by orders from Gen Keyes, I have sent two companies over to the Yorktown side of the River, they are to do picket duty near Williamsburg.

I am disgusted with our attack on Charleston, and the idea of giving it up because one gunboat (the weakest one) was destroyed. If we do not fight with anymore vigor than that we might as well give the thing up at once. We do not even seem to be threatening another attack & Beauregard will be able to release 30 or 40 thousand of his men, to reinforce Gen Lee or to pitch into us in North Carolina or at Suffolk. Hooker is our last chance if he does not thoroughly lick the Rebels at Fredericksburg we might as well shut up shop & go home. I confess that I am getting rather sick of the war, and utterly disgusted with the Administration.
[Last paragraph deleted-Editors]

Your affectionate son
Caspar

Caspar Crowninshield, Letters, Massachusetts Historical Society

Letter from C. P. Briggs.

We have a letter from our former townsman, Charley Briggs, dated at Gloucester Point, Va., April 20th. Charley was at that date on picket duty, scouting, foraging, etc. He says: "We have been several times at the neighboring rancho or plantation of Col. Hayes, but always treated them kindly. Although the women would abuse us and call us 'Gilt Letter Thieves', we paid no attention to them; till at last, the other day, Hayes' daughter must fire three or four shots at one of our vidette pickets as he was going past the house. We then had to take them prisoners, and burnt the house-a beautiful one-with all its contents, to the ground. The rebels harass our pickets every night-firing a few shots and then running. This of course, rouses the whole camp, and there is hardly a night passes but we are in our saddles as often as once at least.

We have what you may call splendid food most of the time. Roast pigs and oysters are abundant. I wish in my heart I could send you some of our York river oysters-the best in the world. They are of the most delicate flavor, and four of them will cover the bottom of the largest dinner plate. I have just bought half a gallon right out of the shell, for 10 cents. Indeed they are so plentiful that many of the boys have got sick of them.

The Californians can look the best or the most ridiculous of any military company you ever saw. On parade they outshine every company in the regiment, but when they are out foraging or scouting in bad weather, they are queer looking soldiers. Some will have Scotch caps, some dress caps; some dressed in ragged overalls, some in stable frocks-once white-and some in jackets. General Keyes, Col. Grimshaw and Major Crowninshield all seem to place entire confidence in us, and therefore we have to be first and foremost in everything. Two men of Co. C either deserted or were taken prisoners the other night.

You will recollect that Yorktown is the place where Lord Cornwallis surrendered to General Washington. I chipped a piece off the pillar that marks the place of surrender, as hundreds had done before me, and before this war is over, it will all be chipped away.

There has been very heavy cannonading all night over on James river at Suffolk-some 30 miles from here. The friends of Fred. Quant and Wm McNeal will be glad to hear that they are well."

The Napa County Reporter, Napa, Saturday, May 23, 1863.
[The surrender monument that stood at the beginning of the Civil War did not survive curious soldiers wishing a piece of it. First Confederate and then Union troops picked away at it until nothing remained.- Colonial National Historic Park, Yorktown, Va.]

❖❖❖

PACIFIC MAIL STEAMSHIP CO.

THE FOLLOWING

Steamships will be dispatched in the Month of APRIL, 1863:

April 23—SONORA, W. F. Lapidge, Com.

From Folsom street Wharf, at nine o'clock A. M., punctually,

FOR PANAMA.

Passengers will be conveyed from Panama to Aspinwall by the Panama Railroad Company, and from Aspinwall to New York by the Atlantic and Pacific Steamship Company.

A. B. FORBES,
Agent P. M. S. Co.,
ap3   Cor. Sacramento and Leidesdorff sts.

Alta California

❖❖❖
Battalion

BY TELEGRAPH TO THE UNION.

Steamer Sonora to-day carried over 300 passengers and treasure as follows: To England, $765,072.57; to New York, $102,016.83; to Panama, $27,600. Also, $19,000 worth of merchandise to Mexico and 232 bales wool for New York. Captain DeMerritt's Company-fifty men-of the Massachusetts contingent, were among the passengers.

Alta California, San Francisco, Thursday, April 23, 1863.
Evening Bulletin, San Francisco, Thursday, April 23, 1863
Sacramento Daily Union, Friday, April 24, 1863

Another Attack on Union Pickets at Williamsburg, Va. - Rebels Beaten Off.

A correspondent writing to the New York *Tribune* from Yorktown, Va., on the 30th ult. says: Early yesterday morning I was aroused by heavy firing in the direction of Fort Magruder. Upon repairing to the spot I learned that just at daylight our pickets were attacked at two different points by rebel cavalry, about 500 strong. At the same time a battalion of infantry made their way through the woods to the rear of our reserved pickets, and drew up in line in the main street of Williamsburg. Lieut. Wensel of the 5th Pennsylvania, who was in command of the pickets, 25 in all, perceiving this, and that his only chance of retreat was cut off, made a bold dash, charged upon the infantry, cutting his way out in gallant style, amid a perfect *sheet* of fire, not only from the rebel infantry, but *citizens*, who fired from their houses along the street.

Out of his little command he lost two men killed (who were immediately stripped of their boots by the "rebs,") and six wounded, including himself, he having received a ball through the shoulder. Three of his men were taken prisoners. Eight horses were killed, one receiving as many as thirteen balls. The rest of them reached Fort Magruder in safety. Capt. Baily of the 5th Pennsylvania cavalry, in command of the fort, then opened fire upon the town with shell from a 32 pounder, to which the "rebs" replied but once from a field piece, the shot falling short, doing no damage, and then commenced their favorite movement, "a skedaddle." A battalion of the 5th Pennsylvania cavalry gave chase, following them some miles beyond the town, capturing some four prisoners and re-establishing their pickets.

During the fight Colonel Lewis received information of a flag of truce being at the Queen's Creek Landing, which proved to be a party of rebel deserters which were undoubtedly sent as a ruse to attract our attention from Williamsburg. The party was brought into our lines, where they are now detained as prisoners. This raid was doubtless for the purpose of feeling our position, strength, etc., preparatory to an attack on Yorktown. To facilitate such a movement the rebels have repaired the railroad from White House to West Point, and are now able to run a train through from Richmond to West Point.

I understand that the gunboat *Commodore Morris*, which is blockading the York River, has gone up the Pamunkey River to destroy the railroad which the rebels have rebuilt.

Everything is quiet at Gloucester Point. Our pickets were fired on several times during last week, receiving no injury.

Alta California, San Francisco, Wednesday, May 6, 1863

Battalion

LETTER FROM THE FEDERAL ARMY IN VIRGINIA.
(From a Californian in the Massachusetts Cavalry)

CAMP WEST, NEAR FORT MAGRUDER, VA.
April 30th, 1863.
Camp Site at Gloucester.

EDITORS ALTA: When I wrote to you from Gloucester, we had been there some two weeks, and the weather was at that time very cold and disagreeable, but before we left, it had grown quite warm, and we were very comfortably situated when we left to what we were at the time I wrote, having stockaded our tents, floored them with lumber appropriated to our use from rebel owners, without their consent, and feeling good generally. While at Gloucester, we were out about twice a week, on an average, scouting through the country, and foraging, and I suppose that during our stay, we succeeded in capturing from rebel sympathizers, outside our lines, in the neighborhood of a hundred head of cattle, twelve mules, two wagons, six horses, about fifty head of sheep, and all the turkeys, geese, ducks, and chickens within five miles of the Point. Also, about one hundred bushels of wheat. Those of the feather tribe captured, went towards "comforting our inner man." A few of the cattle, ditto. The mules were turned over to the Quartermaster of the Battalion; likewise the wagons, and they now do good service in the Union cause, hauling our daily rations from Yorktown to our present place of encampment. The horses were awarded to those who captured them, and the balance was turned over to the Government. I never obtained a glimpse of an armed rebel, but some of the boys were fortunate enough to get a sight of the coat-tails of one occasionally, going at the rate of a mile in three minutes, but never got close enough to capture one. We were rather frequently alarmed at night by the vivid imagination of some of the pickets, creating regiments of rebel infantry out of tree stumps, and cavalry out of stray, harmless cows, at which they would fire, and send a report into camp that the enemy were right upon us in force, and in hot haste we would be compelled to crawl out from under the warm blankets, quickly saddle our horses, get into line, and advance to meet the foe, only, on making a reconnaisance, to find out that we had been sold; returning to camp greatly incensed at the sale, and invoking anything but blessings on the heads of highly imaginative pickets. We used to drill every day the weather permitted for the first month of our stay, and attained considerable proficiency, going through the different manouvres quickly, promptly, and all together, and we cannot be beaten very easily. The last month of our stay, as I have before stated, being taken up in foraging excursions, drilling was resorted to very seldom, and I expect that we enjoyed ourselves as well or better during our sojourn there than we ever will again during our continuance in "Uncle Sam's" service.

Camp West

We left Gloucester on the 20th of this month for this place, arriving here just before dark of the same day, and found that we would have to sleep on the cold, damp "sacred sod" for that night at any rate. We accordingly improvised the best shelter we could over us with our india rubber blankets, forming A tents on a small scale, under each one of which two men would creep, and throwing blankets and overcoats over us managed to pass the night pretty comfortably. The next day we received shelter tents, at least they are dignified by that title, the amount of cloth allowed each man is about five feet square, and by two joining stock and forming a partnership, enough is obtained to make a shelter for two men by driving stakes into the ground for the end, and making uprights of small trees with crotches in the end, using ridge poles of the same material, and stretching cloth over the ridge pole a small A tent is formed about five feet wide and the same height, in which two men can live pretty comfortably as long as it does not rain too hard. If it should rain hard, the cloth being very thin lets it through pretty fast, and then it is decidedly uncomfortable; and it is no rare occurrence for it to do so in this generally called "Sunny South." I think, judging from my experience so far, that it would be more appropriate to call it the Rainy South.

Our camp is now situated within half a mile of Fort Magruder, and about two miles in the rear of Williamsburg, on the very ground where nearly a year ago the desparate and hardly contested battle of Williamsburg was fought, and in which our troops were victorious; the picket line extends half a mile beyond Williamsburg now, but it was half a mile this side of Williamsburg and the rebels in small force holding the town, with their picket line just on the edge of it, but being a point of no importance, no steps were taken by the officer in command of the post, Colonel West, to get possession of it. And if the rebels had not chosen to evacuate the place it might still have been theirs, they only holding it by courtesy at any rate, for it could have been shelled very easily from Fort Magruder by the guns in position there. However, as the rebels left, the picket line was extended to where it is at present. While one of our company was standing on picket night, three rebels crawled upon him, and the cowardly scoundrels fired upon him, killing his horse at the first shot but not injuring him any. Finding they had not killed him they advanced upon him, and he broke for a fence, from behind which he delivered three shots at them from his revolver, when they stopped, one spunky man proving too much for three of the dastardly cowards. So much for their brag of one of them being equal to three of us.

It is the worst kind of murder to kill a man stationed on picket, and none but the most cowardly, pusilanimous rebels would attempt such a thing. The step from a traitor to a murderer seems to be easily taken, and quite natural; and all rebels caught lurking around picket stations, with arms upon them, ought to be hung to the nearest tree. Woe be to the one that should be caught by us!

The Cavalry's Position

We now form part of the advance brigade, Fourth Army Corps, the commander of which is Major General Keyes, formerly of California and whose headquarters are at Yorktown, which is situated some ten miles below here, and well fortified, and upon which we can fall back if driven from here; but I apprehend very little danger that we will be attacked here by any force large enough to drive us out. The number of troops here is about twenty five hundred; two thousand being infantry and the balance cavalry, the latter of which is composed of one battalion of the Fifth Pennsylvania and one hundred men from our battalion, comprising the whole of our company (which numbers seventy six men) and part of Company B, same battalion, enough to make one full company. Fort Magruder mounts seven large guns, and is garrisoned by three or four hundred infantry. The balance of the infantry are disposed in the redoubts which are thrown up around here, of which there are seven, and in all but one or two of which from one to two pieces of artillery is mounted. We cavalry are engaged in performing picket duty, and our turn comes twice a week. When we go out on picket we carry a day's rations with us, consisting of coffee enough to make two quart cupsfull, (one for supper and one for breakfast) sugar enough to sweeten the same, one loaf of bread and two large slices of bacon. Building a fire, there we cook the above mentioned rations, and eat them with a relish all the keener on account of doing our own cooking. We received Burnside's patent breechloading carbines a few days ago, and we are now thoroughly armed as cavalrymen. The carbines are very neatly made, light and serviceable, and capable, it is said, of throwing a ball five hundred yards with force enough to kill a man, and with great accuracy. When mounted, with all our arms on, we are pretty heavily loaded; and I expect we will all get round-shouldered, so much weight resting on our shoulders. My health, since leaving California, has been excellent, and I hope it may continue so. The climate here is said to be very sickly in the summer season, diarrhoea, dysentery, chills and fever being the prevailing complaints. It is now growing quite warm, and a person feels most comfortable in his shirt sleeves, and it will not be long before we are scorched by the heat of the sun.

T. D. B.

Alta California, San Francisco, Wednesday, June 10, 1863

MAY, 1863

1-4 Battle of Chancellorsville.
10 Death of "Stonewall" Jackson.
19 Union siege of Vicksburg.

Battalion

LETTER FROM THE CALIFORNIA VOLUNTEERS IN THE MASSACHUSETTS CONTINGENT.

(From the Correspondent of the ALTA CALIFORNIAN, Accompanying the Force.)

Camp Meigs. Readville, Mass.,
May 4th, 1863.

Editors Alta: Circumstances have combined to prevent me from sending you my regular correspondence, but at last an opportunity is offered, and I hasten to improve it.

From Aspinwall to New York

My last letter was written as we were about to leave Aspinwall, on the steamship *Ocean Queen*, from which the detail of events is continued. Shortly after leaving the wharf, we steamed past the British mail packet *Trent*, of Mason and Slidell notoriety; the "boys" of the California Battalion gave three loud and hearty cheers for Commodore Wilkes, U. S. N., and the John Bulls, misappropriating the cheers to themselves, felt elated by what they thought to be a compliment; but when they learned for whom the cheers were given, their faces became perceptibly elongated, and in a "double quick" they beat a hasty retreat from the quarter-deck.

From Aspinwall to the Island of Cuba we were convoyed by the U. S. gunboat *Connecticut*, a craft as beautiful in model as she is formidable in armament and warlike in appearance. Of our trip from Aspinwall to New York, suffice it to say that we were treated worse than dogs should be; crowded into a steerage, the atmosphere of which was enough to kill ordinary men: the food consisted of decayed "salt horse", salt pork ditto, and musty, hard bread. It was unfit for human beings to eat, and would have turned the stomach of a starved Digger Indian. You may form some idea of the feelings of our soldiers when I assure you that so driven to exasperation were they, that had the pirate *Alabama* hove in sight she would have been welcomed with cheers. But at last, half starved and emaciated, some sick, we reached New York, and with curses both loud and deep upon the *Ocean Queen*, her Captain, old Vanderbilt, and all connected with his steamship line, we once more walked on the soil of our native land.

Our Stay in New York City.

Our reception at the wharf was as follows: A delegation of a dozen hack drivers, two newspaper boys, a few old apple-women, whose pinched features and haggard looks plainly told that "the wheels of time" had not very lightly rolled o'er their heads— these, and a Deputy

Sheriff, with a writ of *habeas corpus*, which he served on Major Thompson, awaited our arrival. I will, however, do New York city but simple justice to say, that they knew nothing of the arrival of the Battalion, and therefore no preparations had been made to receive it. From the streamer the Battalion was marched to the Park Barracks, where it was hospitably received, and served with a good supper, which was relished with "gusto" by our half-starved fellows. In the evening, the entire Battalion went to the New Bowery Theatre, by invitation of its managers, and enjoyed the performance, the scenery of which was really magnificent. The New Bowery deserves success, not only for its merit, but also for the liberality and kindness of its managers. The day after our arrival in New York, the Battalion was formed in dress parade in the Park, and after having been addressed by Gov. J. W. Nye, of Nevada territory, marched up Broadway to Union Square, around the equestrian statue of Washington, and then down Broadway to the Battery, where it embarked on the Sound boat for this, our Camp, which we reached the next morning, by way of Stonington and Providence. Here we found barracks prepared for us, and we made haste to make ourselves comfortable in our new quarters.

The Prevailing Sentiment.

I must here remark that in one respect, we have, thus far, been sadly disappointed. When we left San Francisco many thought that our Battalion had been slighted, and not treated as men should have been who were going thousands of miles to battle-perhaps to die-for their country; and many remarked that we would find things very different when we reached the Eastern States. Well, *it is* very different, but the difference is in favor of California, for it is a fact which cannot be denied, that the war feeling, or general enthusiasm for the war and the Union is *much* greater in San Francisco and throughout California than it is here in Massachusetts or New York. The Massachusetts soldiers here in camp talk as our California Secessionists do. The people in the surrounding country, though mostly loyal, seem to be indifferent as to the result. When speaking of the condition of the country they sigh and say "it is no use; the war has lasted long enough." They denounce those at the head of the nation as either "corrupt" or "imbecile." Washington has been changed from the Capitol of the nation to the headquarters of the hordes of rascally army contractors and corrupt politicians that infest it. From what I have been able to observe, and my opportunities have not been limited, the masses of the people are tired of the way the war has been prosecuted, and would hail with delight any compromise that would bring it to an end. However, a few good victories by our troops in the field would cause things to wear a brighter aspect, and restore confidence as to the final termination of the pending issue.

Camp Meigs

Is situated nine miles from Boston on the line of the Providence Railroad. It is rather a pleasant place, surrounded by fine villages and country villas, but its boundaries are too limited for extensive cavalry drills. We are now fairly under way in learning the art of war; we have four hours each day of mounted drill, besides dress parade at eight o'clock in the morning and inspection of arms at six in the evening. The horses we have are very inferior, and not more than one in ten is really fit for the service required of them; many of them are wild and unmanageable, and some never were saddled before. We have had considerable sport in breaking these Massachusetts mustangs, as yet with few accidents. Serg't Gilbert R. Merritt, of Co. C, [M] had his leg broken by a kick while in the ranks, but is now doing well; Corporal Alfred A. McLean, of Co. B, [L] was thrown off of his horse, and had his ankle dislocated— also doing well; many others have been "piled," but none others seriously hurt.

An Excitement in Camp

For several days we have had considerable excitement in camp, caused by an order requiring every man in the battalion to sign an order on the State Treasurer for fifty dollars, this being the amount of State bounty paid to each volunteer on his enlistment. Now most of the men expected to be paid this bounty, but it seems that Major Thompson had pledged the bounty money to Amos A. Lawrence, of Boston, who thereupon advanced money to pay part of the transportation of the battalion from San Francisco to New York; hence, every man was directed to assign his bounty to Mr. Lawrence, by giving him an order on the Treasurer for it. This almost every man in the battalion refused to do. Then came threats of "guardhouse, on bread and water," etc., etc. After the excitement had subsided, seeing that it was no use to contend for their rights against so heavy odds, many of the men signed the order, at the same time denouncing the whole transaction as unfair and rascally in the extreme. In San Francisco, it was advertised and understood that the transportation of the battalion had been "provided for," and when we arrived here, we found the way it had been "provided for" was, that it should be paid with our State bounty. Not satisfied with us Californians coming here to fill up the Massachusetts quota, but that we should pay our own passages in the bargain. And now we have an order from the Commander of the Post, that no one shall have a furlough to go home, or even a pass to go beyond the lines of the camp, unless he signs the bounty orders.

A Camp of "Blackbirds."

Within half a mile from our camp is encamped the Fifty-fourth Regiment Massachusetts Volunteers. This is a regiment of negroes, "blackbirds", they are called here; they have flocked here to eat Uncle Sam's rations, wear his uniforms, and then leave when they get tired of it. A dress-parade of these fellows is a ludicrous sight—negroes of all shades, from the light mulatto to the blackest type of the African; and all sizes, too, from the swarthy plantation "hand" to the most diminutive bootblack. These negroes are recruited here from all parts of the country, and many of them are from Canada, having immigrated there by the "underground railroad." There are now six hundred and fifty of them in camp; they have been there several months, at an immense expense, and will have to be there a long while yet before the regiment is full, for they are running away about the same ratio that they are recruited. They enlist and lay around the camp a while, then get tired of the discipline and "skedaddle," although they have many more privileges than the white soldiers have.

This negro regiment is the special favorite of Governor Andrew, and receives many attentions from him. Four days ago the Governor, accompanied by Secretary S. P. Chase, came out to inspect the troops in camp; as usual, he visited the negroes *first*, made a speech to them, and then deigned to come over and see the California Battalion; but having spent most of his time with his "pets," he had only time to glance along the lines of the California boys, and remark to an officer that "they are a fine looking set of soldiers, but rather *green* yet." We confess to being somewhat "verdant," but not sufficiently so to again come all the way from California to help Massachusetts out of her scrape, have to pay our passages with our bounty, and when we arrive here, be put on a footing of equality, if not beneath, a negro. But it is a satisfaction to know and feel that we are not fighting for the State of Massachusetts, for if we were we would immediately ground our arms and leave; we are fighting for our country, its honor and its preservation, and for the good old flag we love so well, and we'll fight for it as long as there is an arm left to wield a sabre against the traitor hordes.

The California Quota.

California will be called upon to furnish more troops. Cannot she do this-take us from the Massachusetts quota, and put us in as a part of her own? It is the unanimous wish of the men composing the battalion, and petitions to this effect will soon be sent to our Governor. Massachusetts has treated us in a scandalous and shabby manner. We are under *no* obligations to her; we are citizens of California, and wish to represent our own State; and we are of opinion that if Gov. Stanford would take the matter in hand, that it could easily be done, and we would be under everlasting obligations to him. If this were done, we would take more pride in making our battalion an honor to California.

The Health of the Battalion.

The sudden change of climate has effected almost every man, but no serious illness exists. Captain Adams, of Company E, is down, sick with measles, but will soon be well.

As yet, we know not to what place South we will be ordered, nor when; but probably not before a month, for it will take three months before the men and horses will be well enough drilled to go into active service. But the sooner we leave the better, for we care not to stay another day in Massachusetts.

T. H. M.

Alta California, San Francisco, San Francisco, Saturday, May 30, 1863.

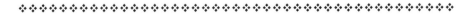

Chicago, May 13.-The N.Y. *Herald* has the following:

West Point, Va., May 9.-A portion of the Fourth Army Corps, Maj. Gen. Keyes commanding, reached this point shortly after 1 o'clock on Thursday night. These troops were conveyed hither in a large fleet of transports, convoyed by a fleet of gunboats. The landing was undisputed by the enemy. Immediately on landing, Gen. Keyes ordered a reconnaissance up York river road toward Whitehouse, the old base of operations of our army last summer. It was discovered that all the track on the York River Railroad, from West Point to Whitehouse, was recently repaired by the rebels, and that the railroad depot and bridge across the Pamunkey were destroyed. On the trip our cavalry rescued Lieut. Este, aid to Gen. Kilpatrick, and 15 men who were made prisoners near Fredericksburg, and were then in the charge of a rebel guard and being conveyed to Richmond. One lieutenant and 4 privates of the rebel army were captured. Our loss was Lieut. Croscer, killed by falling from his horse.

Evening Bulletin, Thursday, May 14, 1863.
[Includes Co. A]

LETTER FROM ST. LOUIS
(From the Resident Correspondent of the Alta California)
St. Louis, May 13, 1863.

Recent Bold Cavalry Raid in the South.

The importance of southern railroads being at last thoroughly appreciated, a system of bold cavalry raids in every direction seems to have been planned and put into effect with more than the average of success which usually attends such movements. Where so many good horsemen and bold fellows are wanted, it is a pity that the California Hundred and the California Battalion cannot have a share in these raids. Their time will come by and by. —————

Alta California, San Francisco, Tuesday, June 9, 1863

❖❖
Battalion
                                    Regimental Orders

                                        Head Quarters, Camp Capitol Hill,
                                        2nd Mass. Cavalry, Washington D.C.
                                        May 18, 1863
Genl Orders No. 4.
                        Hereafter no enlisted man shall be excused from dress parade, or daily drill, except those detailed on daily duty from Head Quarters, two company cooks, and such men as may be excused by the Surgeon or Commanding officer of the detachment.
                        Company Commanders will not excuse any others.
                                        By order of C.R. Lowell, Jr.
                                        Col. 2nd Mass. Cavalry.
                                        H.C. Pinkham, Lieut. Actg Adjut.

Regimental Record Books, National Archives, Washington D.C.

❖❖
Battalion

LETTER FROM THE CALIFORNIA VOLUNTEERS IN
THE MASSACHUSETTS CAVALRY.
————
(From the Correspondent of the ALTA Accompanying the Battalion.)
————

                                        Capitol Hill. Washington, D.C.,
                                        May 20th, 1863
Editors Alta: - On the 10th inst., while yet at Readville, Mass. we received orders to march, and accordingly on the 12th, in high spirits and with glad hearts, we left Massachusetts and turned our faces Southward, and now, here we are, at the Capital of the nation, and within a short distance of the enemy we all are so eager to meet, and from present indications we will soon have an opportunity of doing so.
    Our passage from Camp Meigs, in Massachusetts, to Washington was, indeed, very tedious, and we arrived here well nigh exhausted, having been up for three nights. We brought all our horses and equipments with us; the horses also suffered greatly, there being no opportunity to either feed or water them after leaving Jersey City, from which place we came entirely by railroad.

Leave Massachusetts Without Regret
    The men of the California Battalion left Massachusetts without regret, and so outrageously have they been treated by that State, or rather by its officials, that they disown being at all connected with it. When we arrived in Washington we were all hoarse from cheering so much. From the time we left Jersey City, passing through the States of New Jersey, Pennsylvania,

Delaware, and Maryland, we were everywhere greeted with cheers by the men, and fair ladies waived their handkerchiefs, and with their smiles bid us God speed.

We arrived in Philadelphia at 2 A. M., and found there a bountiful collation awaiting us, of which, by the by, we were all eager to partake. The "Volunteer Refreshment Room" is an institution of the "Quaker City." It is an immense room, beautifully decorated with flags, mottoes, and devices, brilliantly lighted. In this room are four tables, extending almost its entire length, and capable of seating upwards of one thousand persons. Here are fed all the Volunteers that pass through the city, either going to or coming from the war- free for all who fight for their country's cause- and here the Volunteer is welcomed by those in attendance, and if he is possessed of a spark of gratitude, he leaves it, as we did, thankful to the free-hearted, generous citizens of Philadelphia, at whose immense expense the "institution" is kept up and carried on.

An Incident.

An incident occurred here which is worthy of mention. When the men of the Battalion had finished breakfast, and were drawn up into line to leave the room, Major Thompson, who, by the by, is ever ready to give every thing and every body their just dues, proposed "Three cheers for the citizens of Philadelphia;" these, and a "tiger," too, were given with a hearty will; and then some one in the ranks proposed, "Three groans for Massachusetts," and these were given too. I record the incident as showing the feeling of the California Battalion towards the State of whose quota it forms a part.

At Baltimore the Battalion was likewise well received; it marched through it, and *did not go around it.* Here we saw what to us was a novel sight- a lot of rebel prisoners, who were captured during the recent battles of Hooker, and having been sent to this place were glad to take the oath of allegiance, and having done so, were sent North, there to breathe the air of freedom, and recover their lost patriotism. They were as rough looking as possible, dressed in all sorts of clothes, mostly grey, and though they looked rough, yet they were fine large men, whom, if engaged in a better cause, would do honor to any army.

Our Camp is in the suburbs of the city; it is a pleasant place; from it we can see the placid waters of the Potomac, and the many fortifications that skirt its banks. The "sacred soil" is within our sight, and we are eager to tread it, bloodstained as it is with the blood of heroes. I have not as yet had an opportunity to see the many sights around; when I do, I shall write again.

T. H. M.

Alta California, San Francisco, Wednesday, June 17, 1863.
["At Baltimore", a reference to the Baltimore Riots of April 1861.]

❖❖❖
Battalion

Letter From New York
(From Our Own Correspondent)
New York, May 23, 1863.

The Massachusetts Regiment, in which the California Volunteers Figure.
The second battalion of the Massachusetts 2d Cavalry, which left its camp near Boston one day last week, is now at Gloucester Point, York river, where the first battalion had already

been encamped for several weeks. The regiment now numbers 900 men in camp. Forty-nine, including the sick and the mutineers, were left behind, as were also Lieut. Col. Russell and Lieut. Papanti. The following is the roster of the regiment:

Colonel,, Charles R. Lowell Jr., Boston; Lieut. Col. Henry S. Russell, Boston; Majors, Caspar Crowninshield, Boston, and DeWitt C. Thompson, San Francisco, Cal.; Surgeon, Oscar DeWolfe, Chester; Assistant Surgeons, Harlow Gamwell, Huntington; and Eldridge M. Johnson, Agawan.

Captains-J.S. Reed, San Francisco, Cal.; William H. Forbes, Milton; George Blagden, Boston; F. Washburn, Lancaster; Charles E. Rice, Brighton; George F. Holman, Cambridge; A. McKendry, San Francisco; Charles S. Eigenbrodt, California; Zabdiel B. Adams, California; George A. Manning, California.

First Lieutenants-J.B. Brown, (Quartermaster,) Boston; Louis Cabot, Brookline; Charles B. Fox, Boston; William Rumery, Boston; L.S. Dabney, Cambridge; John Phillips, Boston; Goodwin A. Stone, Newburyport; Charles Payson, Boston; William O. Manning, California; Rufus W. Smith, California.

Second Lieutenants-J.W. Sim, San Francisco, Cal.; J.T. Richards, Campbridge; Henry E. Alvord, Greenfield; Warren J. Ball, Holden; Claud Schmidt, Newton, Worcester; Henry H. Crocker, California; Josiah A. Baldwin, California; John C. Norcross, California; William S. Wells, Northampton.

Evening Bulletin, San Francisco, Saturday, June 20, 1863.
[Second Battalion went to Washington D.C. not Gloucester]

Head Quarters 2d Mass. Cavalry
Camp East of Capitol, Wash. D.C.
May 23 1863.

General Order No. 8

1. Company commanders will see that there men wear on the forage Cap only the insignia of the corp, and the number and the letter all made by regulations all other letters must be removed before the next parade or inspection, and not again worn either in or out of camp.

2nd. All enlisted men going from, or, returning to camp, with leave must pass by the post of the Guard. The officer of the Guard will examine all passes and will see that the men leaving camp, are in full uniform without arms, and appear neat and clean. He will take up the passes of all men returning to camp and will send those expired passes to Head Quarters, with the Guard report Book. He will see that no intoxicating liquor is brought into Camp by men returning or by Teamsters He will arrest all men who return having overstayed their Furloughs or who return intoxicated. Reporting their names immediately to their Company Commanders.

By order C.R. Lowell, Jr.
Col. Comdg. 2d Mass. Cavalry
H.C. Pinkham, Lieut. Actg. Adjt

Regimental Record Books, National Archives, Washington. D.C.

Further of the Troubles of the California Hundred.
The following is from a private letter written by a soldier of the California Hundred to a friend in this city:

Gloucester Point, Near Yorktown,
May 25, 1863

Dear **** - You will perhaps be somewhat surprised at receiving another letter from me so soon, as I wrote you only a few days ago; but this letter will treat on a different subject altogether from what I have ever written before. I presume you have noticed that in my previous letters I have never mentioned anything concerning our officers, whether they were liked or disliked by the company. I have purposely avoided it, fearing that we might judge too hastily; hoping, too, that something might turn up in their favor to place them in a more favorable light before the company. I have waited and waited in vain; the hatred for our officers - our captain particularly - has been getting more and more intense every day, so that now there is not a private in the company but would shoot Capt. Reed at sight if they ever got a chance, and I think they would be justified in so doing. I hear you say this is strange talk; but when you hear the circumstances I believe you will not think hard of me. I will give you some items of events which have transpired since the company was first organized.

You will remember that there was a bounty offered by the State of Massachusetts of $200 to every man who would enlist for three years. The understanding with us was that the money we received should be made a company fund, to be used in paying our passage to New York, furnishing our uniforms and for any purpose the company might wish, and particularly in taking care of the sick. When we left San Francisco it was publicly announced in the papers that we were to have second cabin passage, and of course have second cabin fare.

We bade our friends good-bye who stood by hundreds on the wharf, amidst the soul-stirring airs played by the Presidio band, huzza after huzza going up until every man of us felt more proud than ever to be counted one of the "California Hundred."

Had I remained in your presence two minutes longer you would have thought me a poor specimen for a warrior. But to return to the subject. When we got outside the Golden Gate, we asked the Captain where we should find our bunks. He pointed to the deck, and said: "There is where you will sleep on this boat; just pick out the softest plank you can, and sleep on that." When dinner hour came we were all marched down in steerage, and there had a dinner of salt junk and hard bread. Very little was said on the Pacific side, from the fact that all hands were sea-sick. On this side, we came up on the *Ocean Queen*. We were all put down in the steerage, right in the bows of the ship, in a place about as large as your parlor. 100 of us slept there, 6 deep, with no air except what came through the hatchway. You can imagine what we suffered. We stood this without saying a word, until one day at dinner. The meal consisted of rice and hard bread, and such stuff you never saw; the rice was full of worms, and so was the bread. Flesh and blood could bear it no longer. The indignation of the men caused the tables to be turned bottoms-side up, as a slight expression of the appreciation of the fare. Capt. Reed came up on deck, called us all together, and said - (I give you the exact language used on the occasion, and you will please excuse me for writing such stuff to you): "Now I will see you all d—d and in h-ll before I will ever help a G-d d—n one of you again. "The result of this was, what little respect for him as Captain of the California Hundred was lost. I will not say that all lost their respect for him, for in the whole company there are sergeants *now* who would crawl around him and be offended at nothing, just for the sake of the offices they now hold. When we got to Reedville, he came to us one day and told us, (just to get the right side of us,) that he had been thinking of buying us our saddles, but the Colonel had advised him not to. "Now," said he, "boys, you can do just as you please; buy your own equipments, or not; the money is yours, and you can do as you see fit with it." We told him we would like to consider upon the matter, and so ended that.

About 2 weeks after that we got together and requested the captain to explain to us how much money there was in the Company Fund, and how much had been expended and for what. When we got through he said: "You seem to think that I am dishonest. This is the first time that my honesty was ever doubted. But, gentlemen, whenever one of you ever get a dollar of that Company Fund just let me know it." With these words he walked away. The matter was discussed some that night, but immediately after that we got our 10 day's furlough.

When we came back a good many of us were sent on recruiting service, and with the balls, parties, etc., the Company Fund was almost forgotten. Lieut. McKendrie refused to have anything to do with Capt. Reed, and resigned his position in the company, all on account of this fund question. He is a man, every inch of him. As soon as McKendrie resigned a man was put into his place, thereby passing the 2d Lieutenant who should have had the 1st Lieutenancy. This man's name is Rumery. The boys do not take very kindly to him, but he may come out all right. We will not judge too harshly.

McKendrie has raised a company of his own since we have been here. They are now, it is supposed, with the California Battalion at Washington.

We have written to headquarters to see if there is any way of getting our company funds, but no answer have we received, and in all probability we shall never receive any.

While at Williamsburg one of our boys was lucky in getting what was due him in a singular way, which I will recount. One day we were all at work in the woods, getting out timber for a stable, when one of the boys spoke up and said, "I should rather be in any other company in the regiment than this." The Captain was standing near, and replied, "You can be transferred to Company B, if you like, for no man in my company shall ask for a transfer more than once." The man accepted the offer, and that evening demanded his share of the company's fund. The Captain saw that the man had him, and he had to come out. As soon as this was known, the boys went by twenties for their *transfers.* Of course, they were not granted, for the Captain saw that he would soon be left without a company to command. This affair revived the Fund question again, so the boys went to work and wrote him a letter demanding an explanation of the Fund. The request was made in the most respectful terms in polite language. There was nothing in it that he could take offense at. Next day he wrote a letter in reply, stating that he intended to spend that money for arms whether we wanted them or not; that the money was his, and he was going to spend it as it best suited him.

You will easily see that with such things transpiring every little while, discord must prevail. The consequence is that there is a good deal of grumbling throughout the company, and we soon found out that nothing could be said but the captain would hear of it. We have for some time suspected a man in the company as the tale-bearer whose name is _____. Two or three of the boys got together and thought they would try him, to see if he was really the guilty party. So they went to work and made up a story to the effect that we had joined ourselves together as a guerilla band; that we were going to take our horses and everything we had some night this week, go across the lines and fight our way to Gen. Joe Hooker, then give ourselves up to Hooker and tell him that we have come here to fight; our officers were not competent to command us, and we wanted to be with some one who would give us a chance to show ourselves. The story was carried to _____by Corporal Crumpton and Sargeant Crum. They were to try to get _____ to join us; the bate took well. The boys had not left _____'s quarters ten minutes before he was seen wending his way to the captain's. About an hour after that the captain was seen on horseback going to the Fort. Nothing was thought of that until last night at 12 o'clock, when, the first thing I knew, I heard some one sing out, "Turn out." I awoke and saw a major and captain standing near us with drawn swords. At first I thought there was an attack on the picket line and they had come to wake us up. The first thing I said was, "Major, light that candle if you please, so that we can see to find our arms." The major says, "Oh, it's not necessary to take arms. You are under arrest." I asked, "What are we arrested for, Major?" He said he did not know. I went to the door of the tent and there stood four infantry men with fixed bayonets; just back of them, on the streets between the tents and the stable, a whole company were drawn up. We were ordered to fall out, with the exception of Sergt. Crum and Corp'l Crampton. They were ordered to go with the rest of the company. When we fell out (the non-commissioned) I went around to see if I could find out what was up. Down the river just at the foot of the camp lay a gunboat with ports open *ready to give us a dose* at a moment's warning. In the rear of the camp, so as to rake the whole line of tents, was a park of artillery. In the rear of the battery were two companies of infantry. Out to the right of this was a squadron of cavalry. So you see that to capture the gallant and noble California Hundred, while asleep, it took *400 infantry, 300 cavalry, 1 battery*, and a *gunboat*! If it takes this number to capture them *when asleep*, how many will it take to capture them while wide awake?

It seems that they expected to find us all under arms, ready to fight to the last. The Captain went over to the Fort and told the Colonel that the California Hundred were in a state of mutiny; that they were forming themselves into a guerilla band, and that he expected they would leave that night. Hence the arrest. The company were all put in the guard-house at the Fort.

Yesterday, May 27th, all the boys were brought over here and confined in the camp. The Colonel told the boys that he was heartily ashamed that he had anything to do with their arrest; that when he went over to the camp with his forces to arrest us, he expected to find us all under arms; but instead of that he found us asleep! He never was more surprised in his life. He gave the boys full run of the Fort and told them they need not stop in the guard-house at all; that he knew the California Hundred, and he could trust them anywhere.

Yesterday I went to Corporal Sterling and told him what I thought of him. About ten minutes after I was arrested. I don't know what the charge is, but suppose I shall find out soon, as the Captain is examining the boys one at a time. His only show is now to prove the company in mutiny, and have one or two of us shot. If he can't do this he will get himself into a scrape, as he has gone too far now to ever get out of it in any other way, and you can rest assured that he will do everything in his power to gain his case.

I expect this thing will be known all over the State through Capt. Reed, and I want the truth to be known in California, as we have friends there that we do not wish to be humbugged by anything that Capt. Reed might write. The California Hundred are just as patriotic to-day as they were the day we left San Francisco. All they ask is a good competent leader. As long as Capt. Reed is at our head we shall never be heard of in a fight, or in any other way except in trouble, if we have to depend on him to lead us on. I have seen him tremble so he could scarcely speak when there was nothing but a little firing in the picket line. He has never led us in any excursion yet, always stopping with the reserve and trusting to our lieutenants to lead us.

We expect to leave here for Washington soon. All I hope is that we will be put into active service to give us a chance to redeem the honor that (perhaps) we have lost. There is no knowing what will take place in the next month; but, come weal or come woe, I shall ever feel, that earnest love for my country that actuated me in leaving you all to take a hand in crushing this wicked rebellion.

Evening Bulletin, San Francisco, Wednesday, July 1, 1863
[The transferee was Joseph Nixon.]

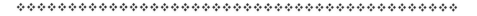

The California Hundred.

We have a letter from C.P. Briggs, formerly of this town, who enlisted some months ago in the famous "California Hundred," and who at the date of his letter, (May 25th,) was stationed at Camp Grimshaw, Gloucester Point, Va. It would appear that the "Hundred" have altogether disappointed the expectations of their friends, and that they are likely to prove of little service in the army of our country. We cannot presume to judge of the merits of the case, but let our correspondent tell his own story. He says:

"I address you a few lines to inform you that the grand career of the California Hundred is about to close. There has been considerable trouble lately among the men on account of the action of Capt. Reed, in keeping them out of the Company Fund Bounty money, making them do unnecessary work, etc. Eight of them were sent to Yorktown day before yesterday, for refusing to clean up around the officer's horse stables. But of all that we have seen yet, the trick of last night beats all. About midnight we were all surprised by being surrounded by four companies of Infantry, one of Cavalry and a section of Artillery of two batteries, headed by Col. Grimshaw, Lieut. Col. Trevis and Major Crowninshield. We were all disarmed, marched out into line, and with the exception of 8 of us, marched off to the fort. The affair is now undergoing investigation.

It appears that a Sergeant and a Corporal had taken it into their heads to ascertain how quick news would go to the Captain, and to find out who was the tale-bearer of all the yarns that had previously been reported, they adopted a plan by which they hit the right man the first time. They told a certain Corporal, whom they suspected, that about forty of the men had got disgusted and were going to form a guerrilla band and fight for the Government "on their own hook." They watched the man and saw him go to the Captain's tent. Nothing more was said that afternoon, and the affair had been forgotten until we were routed out at midnight, as already stated. The men will probably be released in a day or two, but the company will never be of any account again.

An examination has been going on all day, and the Captain says he has positive proof that some of our men have been in communication with the rebels, and that they have given them plans of our defences and information of all our movements.

Eight of our men were sent to Yorktown on Saturday, to await a Court Martial for refusing to do duty in cleaning around the officers' quarters. Among them were Fred Quant, and Jim Ackerman of Vallejo.

One Sergeant, one Corporal and 2 privates were singled out and sent to Yorktown to await a court martial for plotting treason, etc., while the balance of the company have been brought back to camp and are kept under guard. The examination is still going on. The boys take the thing easy-singing, etc. Billy McNeil and the Vallejo boys are amongst the rest. I am in hopes that they will be released to-morrow, but am afraid they will transfer us into different companies, for fear of a mutiny. The withholding of our Company Fund and too much "red tape" have caused all this difficulty. Could the boys once get into battle, they would make the biggest kind of a fight. In fact they don't care for five times their number. You can have no idea how valuable that Reporter was to us three, (Quant, McNeil and myself,) and even to the Vallejo boys. It seemed a Godsend-even more so than most letters-excepting of course, those from our sweethearts."

The Napa County Reporter, Napa, Saturday, June 27, 1863.

The First Colored Regiment Leaving Boston for the War-Cheers of the White Folks.

The pioneer colored regiment of the Northern States, as the 54th Massachusetts, left Boston one day last week for active service in the field. A gala day was made of the occasion of their departure, for everybody wanted to see what kind of a figure on parade these men of a despised race would make. The experiment seems to have been perfectly satisfactory, not only to the originators of the regiment, but to the infidels and the scoffers also, who had all along been predicting a ridiculous failure to Gov. Andrew's project.

It had been determined to have a parade on the Commons, previous to which the regiment was marched through many of the principal streets of the city, during which their grave demeanor and soldierly bearing were the theme of eulogium on all sides. "All along the route," says one account, "the sidewalks were crowded, and the windows and balconies were thronged. Men cheered and women waved their handkerchiefs, many of them more enthusiastically than ever they had done before. There was nowhere along the line a word of disapproval-not a sneer was heard, nor an unkind word expressed. In several places flags were thrown out by the occupants of stores or dwellings."

The regiment was subsequently reviewed by Gov. Andrews, in the presence of a vast throng of spectators who occupied every available spot overlooking the parade ground. Boston Common, where the review took place, never wore a gayer appearance, it is said, nor showed a greater throng of people, even on the most cherished holidays of the people. The review was by companies, the "soldiers marching in good time, and wheeling with a precision that showed that they had a clear idea of what was required of them, and that, with a little more practice, they would equal the best regiments that have left the State."

After the review the regiment marched to the Battery wharf, where they were embarked on board the steamer that was to take them to Port Royal. Along the route of the march, too, all the streets were "thronged with an approving multitude, who cheered the soldiers as they passed."

The Officers of the Regiment.

I have already, in a former letter, spoken very fully of the chief officers of this regiment-of the men of wealth and of high position who have volunteered to accept commands at which the miserable and besotted *habitues* of the rumshop and the brothel turn up their scarlet noses in affected disdain. It is not necessary to repeat here the eulogies that have been bestowed upon these self-sacrificing men. But, inasmuch as the departure from New England of this first regiment of colored men will mark the beginning of a new era in the conduct of the war for the Union, it is fitting that the brave men who lead it should be everywhere reknown. Here is a complete roster of the regiment:

Colonel - Robert C. Shaw.

Lieutenant-Colonel - Norwood P. Hallowell.

Major - Edward N. Hallowell.

Surgeon - Lincoln R. Stone.

Assistant Surgeon - C. B. Bridgham.

Captains- Alfred S. Hartwell, David A. Partridge. Samuel Willard, John M.W. Appleton, Watson W. Bridge, George Pope, William H. Simpkins, Cabot J. Russell, Edward L. Jones and Louis F. Enuho.

First Lieutenants - John Ritchie, Garth W. James, William H. Homans, Orin E. Smith, Erik Wulff, Walter H. Wild, Francis L. Higginson, James M. Walton, James M. Grace and H.K.I. Jewett.

Second Lieutenants - Thomas L. Appleton, Benjamin F. Dester, J. Albert Pratt, Charles F. Smith, Henry W. Littlefield, William Nutt, David Reid, Charles E. Tucker and William Howard.

Before leaving their camp at Readville, the 54th was honored with the presentation of several flags, there being present a large number of distinguished visitors, including his excellency Governor Andrew and staff, Surgeon-General Dole, Hon. Thomas Russell, Professor Agassiz, Professor William B. Rogers, Hon. Josiah Quincy, George S. Hale, Wendall Phillips, Rev. Mr. Grimes and others. The regiment was formed in a hollow square, and was addressed by Gov. Andrew at some length in making the presentations. He stated that it had been the desire of his heart that the regiment should succeed, and that his own personal honor was identified with theirs. The flags were four in number, one the gift of the mother, sisters and relatives of the late Lieut. Putnam; another from the ladies and gentlemen friends of the regiment; the National colors from the young colored ladies of Boston; and the State colors, a gift from the colored ladies of the Relief Society of this city. The flags, after hearty cheers by the men, were received by Lieut.-Col. Hallowell with appropriate remarks.

The second colored regiment of Massachusetts, which now occupies the camp just vacated by the first, has now nearly 600 men enlisted, and will be officered very soon.

The Rebel Vengeance against Negro Troops.

Almost simultaneously with the departure of the 54th, a despatch was sent over the wires from the Louisville *Journal*, announcing the capture at Helena, Ark., of a colored regiment, all of the soldiers of which, together with their officers, it is asserted were hung by the rebels. This may be set down as a weak invention of the enemy of the colored man, even without reference to the questionable source whence it comes. The negro-phobia of the Louisville *Journal* is quite as marked in one direction as is that of Garrison or Phillips in the other. The retaliatory measures threatened by the Union Generals will have the effect of making the rebels pause over the attempt to carry out the provisions of the inhuman measures adopted by their Congress.

Evening Bulletin, San Francisco, Tuesday, June 30, 1863
[The 54th left Boston Thursday, May 28, 1863.]

❖❖

CALIFORNIAN IN THE MASSACHUSETTS CONTINGENT

(From the Correspondent of the ALTA in the service.)

GLOUCESTER POINT, opposite
Yorktown, May 28th, 1863.

EDITORS ALTA:- We are now, as you will perceive from the heading, encamped again upon the same piece of sacred soil on which we first pitched our tents after our arrival in Virginia, having left Williamsburg two weeks ago for this place. The only part of the regiment that is here consists of our Company and Company B, numbering in all about one hundred men. The balance of this battalion are at West Point, near Richmond, having left here for that place on the day after our arrival here from Williamsburg. The California Battalion are encamped on Capitol Hill, near Washington, D.C., and it is rumored that the Major of this battalion has received orders to report there with his command as soon as possible, and I hope that Madam Rumor may be correct, for we should all like to see the whole regiment together, instead of being scattered around as at present in different parts of the South, so that if we ever should get into an engagement, there will be enough of the regiment present to make their mark.

In this Company considerable dissatisfaction exists, caused by the conduct of the Captain, J. S. Reed, towards us, and by his management of our bounty, commonly known as the Company Fund. You will recollect that when the authority was given him to raise this Company, that the State of Massachusetts agreed to furnish, and did furnish $20,000, which money it was supposed would be used to defray our expenses East, clothe us, and equip us with arms, so far as it would go. Well, out of that money we were clothed and furnished with blankets, besides having our passage paid to New York. Of arms none have been bought, Government furnishing us them, and consequently there still remains in the hands of the Captain between $8,000 and $10,000, which we consider belongs to us, and ought to be distributed amongst us, an equal amount to each man. The Captain refuses to do this, or even to render to us a statement or account of how much of this $20,000 has been expended, and how much there is remaining on hand. His refusal to render us a statement of account has led us to believe that he has not acted the part of an honest man in his management of the affair, and that he intends to appropriate the money to his own use, if he possibly can. Thinking thus, the privates have been severe in their strictures upon his conduct, and he has heard through spies circulating among us, (privates in the Company,) what a poor opinion is entertained of him, and also that we had taken steps to have the matter thoroughly investigated, and if he was wrongfully keeping this money from us, compel him to disgorge. Well, when he ascertained this, he took measures to create a false impression in the minds of the people regarding this Company, and to disgrace us. With this end in view, on last Sunday evening, the 24th, one of our Corporals, being in a joking humor, informed another Corporal, who tells everything he hears to the Captain, that this Company on that night intended to get outside the lines, and then form themselves into a guerilla band, and fight against that flag which we have solemnly swore to uphold and protect. Of course this was immediately communicated to the Captain, and the Captain (although I am certain he did not believe the story) immediately went up to the Fort on this side, and informed Colonel Grimshaw what he had heard, and more too, and requested him to arrest the whole Company on that charge. Colonel Grimshaw, not knowing anything about us, and the Captain representing to him that he would find us with our horses saddled, and ready to resist any force brought against us, called out his Regiment of Infantry, two sections of a Battery, and a Cavalry Company, came down to our Camp, surrounded it, and arrested all of us at 12 o'clock at night, finding us all in bed quietly sleeping. On being roused out, we were told to fall in line outside our tents, which we did without having any idea of what was up, and were marched to the Guard House, making no resistance at all, and having no idea of so doing, and we could have been arrested as easily by a Corporal's guard as by the force that did arrest us. It was not until the next morning, that we were made aware what we had been arrested for, and on hearing it, I was never more surprised in my whole life, for I do not believe there is actually one man in the Company that would be guilty of such a thing. The next day, all against whom the Captain could bring no charges, were released, and I am happy to say that five only were detained. They will soon be tried by Court-Martial and I think, acquitted. However, this act has brought upon Captain Reed the ill will of the whole Company, and there never will be peace in the Company until he leaves it, and that he has no idea of doing at present. So you see there is anything but a pleasant prospect before us.

A.B.

Alta California, San Francisco, Friday, July 3, 1863.
[A.B.-Unable to identify]

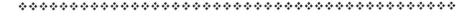

Hdqrs. 2 Mass. Cav.
Camp E. of Capitol
May 29, 1863

To
    Lt. O.S. Raymond,
        A.A.A.G. Provl. Brigade.

Sir:

In reply to your communication of date, I have the honor to state that, in case of urgent necessity, my companies could move from here at two hours notice. My men are mounted (nearly all the horses are well shod), and are armed as far as I care to have them at present; I have on hand new rations to June 5th, with exception of bread & fresh beef - & forage to May 31st; I am well supplied with waggons, & could probably get needful hard bread & forage to follow command at short notice. I should however be obliged to have a Lieutenant here to receive my tent, & some other supplies, Company property, which I should wish to turn in if ordered to the field so suddenly, but which I wish to retain if we are to remain here.

I would add that I was sent for by the Secy of War on Saturday last - & was told that my 1st battalion should be ordered up at once from Gloucester Point; in view of this, & the expected arrival of about 80 recruits from Massachusetts on June 10th to 15th, & also of the great inexperience of my men in the individual exercise of their pistols. I should consider it greatly for the good of the Regiment to remain here until at least June 20th - unless there be urgent occasion for taking the field.

        Respectfully Yr obdt servt
        C.R. Lowell, Jr., Col. 2 Mass.Cav.

Regimental Record Books, National Archives, Washington D.C.

The California Hundred and their Troubles.

The following is brought to us for publication by the father of one of those who sign it. We print it as of interest to the public. There are two sides to every story-this is one side. When the other side is told, we hope the facts will not prove as bad as they seem. As bearing on this subject, we direct attention to the statement by Mr. Ira P. Rankin, given in another column:

        Gloucester Point, Va., May 29, 1863

Editor Bulletin. - I venture to hope a communication as to the whereabouts and doings of the "California Hundred" will not be unacceptable to you.

We are now at our old camping ground, having just returned from picket duty at Williamsburg, where we had occasional intercourse with rebels through the medium of a flag of truce, and an amicable understanding between the very outer pickets of the rebels, resulting in the exchange of coffee and sugar for tobacco. All reports to the contrary, the rebels are not so badly off with the exception of such luxuries. As a general thing the Company are enjoying good health, being camped on a high bluff on York river.

There is a great discontent springing up in the company, owing to the conduct of Capt. J. Sewall Reed. You will recollect that the city of Boston gave the "California 100" $20,000 on the condition that said amount viz: $200 per man, should place the company in Boston, to be credited in the State quota. This $20,000 with donations, benefits, etc. swelled the amount to about $25,000. This money, after deducting the amount paid for passage, uniforms, etc., was put into Captain Reed's hands as a company fund, to be expended as the company saw fit. A short time since a committee appointed by the company applied to Capt. Reed, asking for a statement of expenditures, and other details. Capt. Reed not only refused to inform the company anything about the fund, but told them the company had nothing to do with it whatsoever. So, according to a statement we were bought for so much money to fill up the Massachusetts quota, and he pockets the proceeds. The point we make is, this amount of money ought not to be in the hands of one who denies all accountability incumbent on the charge, and claims, with a high hand, the right to dispose of this money without any regard to our wishes. This matter, however, is in process of investigation.

Capt. Reed's conduct to the men in other respects is no less reprehensible - it is really that of a supercilious tyrant. Instance the case of E. Henry Allen, who was ordered to groom the orderly sergeant's horse, which is clearly menial duty, and an article in the Regulations says "No non-commissioned officer or private shall do menial duty." Allen refused, and was immediately hung up by the thumbs. The company went in a body and told the captain if he would not take him down they would cut him down. He was taken down, sent over to Yorktown, and after being kept a prisoner two months, was tried by a general court martial and honorably discharged.

On the 23d instant, Ross, Hill, Campbell, Rowe, Quant, Ackerman and Powers were detailed for police duty. After all police duty was over they were ordered to clear away the manure and filth around and at the rear of the officer's quarters, which had been accumulating for weeks. The said officers had plenty of negro servants and hostlers lying around doing nothing. The men considering this menial duty, refused. They were arrested and sent to Yorktown, thrown into a slave pen, already overstocked with filth and vermin of all kinds, and our amiable Captain kindly suggested chains for them, the point of which bright idea their jailor failed to see. Charges were soon made out for "mutiny," "disobedience of orders," and "conduct unbecoming a soldier." The nights being chilly they sent for their blankets, but here again the Captain interposed, and for four nights they slept on the bare floor without any covering. They suffered more than our men in the Southern Capitol, and to add to their suffering, Reed communicated the intelligence that 3 years at the Rip Raps would be a light penalty for their heinous offenses.

On the night of the 24th inst. the camp of the "California 100" was surrounded at the hour of 12, by six companies of infantry, two companies of cavalry and two pieces of artillery, and the Company was successfully bagged. Out of the land of dreams they were roused to be told they were traitors and prisoners of war. They were then marched to the fort and to prison. Most of the men were released after thirty hours close confinement, though half of them do not know even now what they were arrested for. It has since transpired that the redoubtable captain had represented to Maj. Gen. Keyes that he was on the crater of a volcano just ready to hurl destruction upon all loyal representatives of the United States; that the company (the gallant "100") were in open insurrection, with their horses and arms all ready for a terrific dash through the picket lines, and then to form a guerilla band. Four of the men are now in the guardhouse, as ring leaders in this purely imaginary mutiny, to be tried for treason, without having been guilty of a disloyal thought even.

———

In behalf of the "California 100"
(For the sake of the two young men who sign the above documents we consider it best, at present, not to publish their names. - Ed. Bulletin.)

Evening Bulletin, San Francisco, Monday, June 29, 1863
[According to Official Records - E. Henry Allen was wounded in action at Rockville, Md. Died
of wounds through neglect of surgeon, in hospital at Washington, D.C., Aug. 16, 1864.]

❖❖❖
Battalion
    Statement of the Relations between Massachusetts and the California Volunteers.

————

Card from Ira. P. Rankin.

————

    Editor Bulletin. - Several letters have appeared in the paper, from members of Maj. Thompson's California Battalion, complaining generally that their treatment by the authorities of Massachusetts, and particularly in regard to bounty money claimed to be due them from that State. As many references have been made to these complaints, both by the city and the interior press, and as there appears to be much misapprehension about the whole matter, I deem it due, both to myself and to others, to give a brief statement of the real facts.

    At the time Captain Reed offered to raise a company, the city of Boston was paying a bounty of $200 to each soldier enlisting in her quota. After the acceptance of his offer, the sum of $20,000 in currency was paid into Bank in New York, subject to my order. Out of the money realized from this deposit, the company paid their recruiting and incidental expenses, bought their uniforms, and paid their fare by steamer to New York. The Pacific Mail Steamship Company very liberally carried them at half fare, so that on their arrival in New York they must have had, including some contributions made here for their benefit, a company fund of not less than about $8,000.

    After the departure of Reed's company, Major Thompson desired me to communicate to Governor Andrew his offer to raise a cavalry battalion of four companies on the same terms as had been made with Reed. The offer was made by telegraph, and the reply received from the Governor in the same manner. Several dispatches passed upon the subject, but the result of the correspondence was this: That they were then paying but $75 bounty, and the best they could do would be to pay the passage money of the troops to New York, and $20 each man for expenses of organization. The sum of $7,000 for the latter purpose was sent to me in greenbacks, mostly disbursed here, and the balance paid over to the company officers to meet incidental expenses of the voyage and upon arrival on the Atlantic side. For the fare I executed, as agent for the State of Massachusetts, a contract with the Agent of the Pacific Mail Steamship Company agreeing to pay $62.50 in New York for each private. And, I think, double that sum for each officer - payment to be made in gold coin. This, at then existing premium on gold at the East, was equivalent to about $10 to each man. Add the $20 each sent here, and the authorities of the State evinced their appreciation of California soldiers by getting them at a cost of $120 when they were paying at home a bounty of only $75.

    The complaint is, that the men were called upon to assign to Mr. Amos A. Lawrence their State bounty money. If such was the fact, the explanation I presume to be simply this: Mr. Lawrence and Mr. J.M. Forbes, two of the richest and most eminent merchants of Boston, both widely known by their charities, public spirit and patriotism, in order to relieve to some extent the Executive authorities of the State, have been during the past year acting as volunteer agents in the management of the recruiting service. From correspondence with those gentlemen, I know that the arrangements in regard to the transportation of the troops, etc., were made by them personally; and the simple truth in regard to the assignment of bounty money to Mr. Lawrence doubtless is, that he had advanced the passage money of the troops from his own pocket in the reasonable expectation of being partially reimbursed by the bounty money to which they were entitled under the laws of the State. And in this there was no hardship or injustice. No bounty was furnished or expected from the State. Major Thompson and his officers understood distinctly that she only assumed the expenses of transportation and organization in the manner I have described, I have reason to believe, and do not believe that the privates had any different impression. I repeatedly heard reference made in conversation to the $100 bounty paid by the United States, but never a word about any State bounty. If there was in the minds of any of the men a misapprehension on the subject, they must have been mislead by their officers when recruiting, which I am unwilling to believe without evidence.

It may be proper to avail myself of this opportunity to refer to numerous unkind and unjust attacks upon my native State, including one from the Governor of California, in regard to the enlistment of men here to count a part of the Massachusetts quota, as if unable or unwilling to respond to the calls of the Government from her own population. No defense of Massachusetts in regard to the present war is necessary. If there is any fact known and read of all men throughout the whole country, it is the exhuberant loyalty, liberality and patriotism with which that State has poured forth her treasures of men and money, and sacrificed her best blood in defense of the Union against foul treason, from the first shot at Fort Sumter to this day. She did not send to California for aid, although, if she had done so, I see no harm in it; she simply accepted the offer of loyal and earnest men who wanted to be engaged in active service for the suppression of the rebellion. They had not the means necessary to place themselves in the field; she furnished them. The result is an addition from California of some 500 good and brave men to the cavalry arm of the service in Virginia, where if their friends are not deceived in them they will do gallant service for their country, and do credit both to Massachusetts and California.

Ira P. Rankin.

Evening Bulletin, San Francisco, Monday, June 29, 1863
Napa Valley Register, Napa, Saturday, November 14, 1863

❖❖❖❖❖❖❖❖❖❖❖❖❖❖❖❖❖❖❖❖❖❖❖❖❖❖❖❖❖❖❖❖❖❖❖❖❖❖❖

JUNE, 1863

9   Battle of Brandy Station.
14 Battle of Second Winchester, Virginia
20 West Virginia becomes the thirty-fifth state.
27 Major General Meade replaces Hooker as the commander of the Federal Army of the Potomac.

❖❖❖❖❖❖❖❖❖❖❖❖❖❖❖❖❖❖❖❖❖❖❖❖❖❖❖❖❖❖❖❖❖❖❖❖❖❖❖

Died. - A letter to Wm F. Halsey, from his son, at Camp Brightwood, near Washington, announces that Hiram Chrisler died in hospital, of fever, about the 1st of June. He was one of those who left here to fill up the ranks of the Massachusetts Volunteers.

The Solano Herald, Suisun, Saturday, July 11, 1863.

[William F. Halsey, Co. L; Hiram C. Christler, Co. E, died of disease June 3, at Lincoln Hospital Washington D.C.]

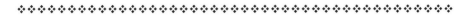

Hd Qrs 2d Mass Cavly
Camp Brightwood June 3d, 1863

General Orders
No. 12
The discharging of fire arms in and about this camp or on marches is strictly forbidden unless in the discharge of duty or by permission of the Comdg officer.
By order of
C.R. Lowell, Jr. Col.
H.C. Pinkham, Lt. Actg Adjt

Hd Qrs 2d Mass Cavly
Camp Brightwood, June 3d, 1863

General Order
No. 13
In order to reduce the severity of Guard duty of this command the number of posts of Camp Guard have been diminished but camp lines are the same as before, beginning at Major Thompson's quarters from thence following the road around to the post of the Guard, thence to a point near the well thence following the picket fence around to the Major Thompson's Quarters and any enlisted man found outside of the lines with out a pass or proper authority will be punished same as though he had run Guard.
But the commdg officer hopes that no occasion will be given.
By order of
C.R. Lowell, Jr. Col.
H.C. Pinkham Lt
Actg Adjt
Regimental Records Books, National Archives Washington, D.C.

Battalion

LETTER FROM THE CALIFORNIANS IN THE MASSACHUSETTS CAVALRY

Headquarters 2d Mass. Cavalry
Camp Brightwood,
Near Washington, D.C., June 22, 1863

Editors Alta:- A two weeks' furlough to go North, press of business, and other circumstances, have all combined to prevent me from sending you my regular letter. Acting on the principle that "tis better late then never," I avail myself of a spare hour, this Sunday morning, to give you an account of our doings hereabout.

Routines of Camp Duty, Etc.
My last was written from East Capitol Hill, where we first encamped on our arrival in the District of Columbia. After staying there nearly three weeks, doing little or nothing, we were

ordered to this post, to do picket and patrol duty. Some of your readers would doubtless like to know how we put in the time. At 5:30 A.M. the bugle awakens us from our slumbers and breaks the spell of our pleasant dreams of loved ones far away, and calls us to arise and resume the daily duty of soldiers. In a moment we are up and dressed, blankets are rolled up, tents put in order, and we sally forth to answer at roll call. This over, the horses are led to water, fed, cleaned, and inspected. The bugle now sounds the breakfast call; the "boys" give vent to their delight as they rush off after their tin cup and plate, and to go the company kitchen to receive their scanty breakfast— scanty because Uncle Sam has to fatten so many army contractors at the expense of his soldiers that his rations have become rather short. At 8 A.M., mounted and fully armed, we go to dress parade, and thence to drill, until 10:30, when we are recalled to camp. One hour of rest intervenes, and then the horses are again watered and fed. At noon the dinner call is sounded, and, with appetites sharpened by the morning's exercise, we rush to our dinner. Here allow me to remark, en passant, that our surgeon has "shut down" on beans for us; says that they are not healthy, and our California "boys" are wrathy thereat, for being deprived of one of their staples of food. We drill again at 2 P.M. till 4 P.M., return to camp, clean and feed our horses, get supper, answer to our names at "retreat" and then our day's work is done. Two hours follow, and we are again called up to roll call at "tattoo;" at 9 P.M. "taps" are sounded, the lights put out all over the camp, and we stretch ourselves on the ground, with a rubber and saddle blanket under us and our bed blanket over us, and sleep as soundly till morning as if we were reposing on the softest and most luxurious couch.

Picket and Scout Duty

Having given briefly the routine of camp life, I will give an insight to scout and picket duty. Each day about forty men are detailed for this duty; they are under the command of a Lieutenant, and leave camp at guard mount. Dividing the command into squads, they scour the country for ten or fifteen miles around, picking up stragglers of other regiments, and keeping a sharp lookout for any of the "Rebs" that may be prowling around in search of information or spoils. The "boys" much prefer this kind of duty to that of camp, for they have more liberties, enjoy themselves well, and like the excitement of being on the move, with the possibility of a skirmish. They are out one or two days, then return to camp, and others take their place.

The Californians are fast adapting themselves to the duties, pleasures, and perquisites, etc., of soldiers; they perform their duties promptly, willingly, and faithfully; do their share of growling, and exercise all the other prerogatives appertaining to the profession. They are becoming quite skilled in "foraging;" chickens must not venture too near camp, and woe to the cow that dares to enter its lines; she is soon caught and stripped- of her milk. Withal, time passes rapidly by, but we are tired of this monotonous camp life, and are eager to go into active service in the field.

Active Duties.

The Californians made a raid into Virginia. On Wednesday, of last week, our camp was thrown into a state of great excitement by the arrival of a courier, who came rushing into camp with despatches to our Colonel. The contents were soon known; we had orders to march with all haste to Edward's Ferry, on the Potomac, where Moseby's Rebel Cavalry had crossed, and burned the Camp of the Sixth Michigan Cavalry. It was not long ere we were in motion, carrying with us three days' rations. Our forces consisted of the California Battalion, four Companies; three Companies of "Scott's 900," *[11th New York Cav.]* and two of the Second Massachusetts Cavalry, all under the command of Col. C. R. Lowell, Jr. After traveling some sixteen miles, we came to the Camp of the Sixth Michigan Cavalry, the scene of the morning's conflict-it lay a mass of smouldering ruins. It appears that Moseby's Rebel Cavalry, disguised in the uniforms worn by U.S. troops, crossed the Potomac, and took the Camp by surprise; a skirmish ensued, which resulted in several killed and wounded on both sides. But they left in a hurry, leaving their dead on the field, and taking with them fifteen horses. Finding that the Rebels had fled, we pushed on in pursuit of them, rode to Poolesville, Md. and camped for the night. After feeding our horses, and taking a little rest, at two o'clock in the morning, we were in our saddles, and once more on the march. At dawn we crossed the Potomac at White's Ford, and most of us then, for the first time, stood upon the sacred soil of Virginia. We were now in the enemy's country; flankers and skirmishers were thrown out to prevent the possibility of a surprise. One of these parties arrested and sent in a man belonging to the Tenth Vermont Volunteers, who had been taken prisoner on the day before by Moseby's cavalry and paroled. He told us that he had left the rebel cavalry at Leesburg that morning, that they knew we were coming, but were not afraid, for we could not take the place. Taking the Vermontor with us, we made haste to overtake the rebels, but the poor fellow could not keep up on foot, and seeing a man plowing near the road we confiscated one of his horses and put our man on him. We quickened our pace and were soon in sight of Leesburg. The advance guards fixed their saddles and then charged into the town, but alas! the rebels had fled; not one could be seen. The place looked desolate, stores and shops were closed, and only a few old men, some women and "contrabands" could be seen. Passing along the street, in some of the houses the women would rush to the windows, and when to their disgust they saw the Union cavalry marching proudly along, they'd slam the shutters to and retire beyond the vulgar gaze of us "abolitionists."

We stopped to rest both men and horses in the outskirts of the town. Our men were much disgusted; though repeatedly insulted in passing through the streets, they were not allowed to touch a single thing, not a house was searched; had they been we would have captured a lot of rebels, for we afterwards ascertained that a number of them were at that very time hid in cellars, and not being strong enough, did not venture out to attack us. So much for dealing glove-handed with the rebels. Our Colonel, I suppose, learned this when he was a member of McClellan's staff. But let me assure you that that policy is getting "played out;" the rebels march through our country, steal or destroy all they can lay hands on, sack and burn our towns, and if we hope for success in putting down this hellish rebellion we must get over our nice points of etiquette and treat them as rebels, enemies of our common country, and deal with their property accordingly. Our boys had rode sixty miles, were hungry—having had only a few hard crackers and water to eat—yet the cattle and swine of rebel owners fed in safety by the roadside, for to kill them and satisfy our hunger would not be pursuing a "conciliatory policy." But it will not be so another time, our men are determined on that.

But I have digressed. Leaving Leesburg we started for Middleburg, some sixteen miles distant; we traveled through a country naturally fertile, but now laid waste by the opposing armies. It is a deplorable sight to see fine plantations, orchards and fields without fences, large mansions deserted or burned to the ground; these, as you approach the Federal lines, you find occupied by runaway negroes. In one place particularly, I saw a large and beautiful mansion, doubtless once the dwelling of some wealthy F. F. V., where, not long since, luxury and indolence reigned; and now, how changed! The former masters were gone, and as our column marched by, a hundred wooly-heads were stuck out of the windows, and numberless half-nude youthful "contrabands" rushed to the roadside to see us. These once were "chattels," but are so no longer, being freed by the emancipation proclamation. A careful observer will notice this fact, that the negroes always appear glad to see our troops, and are ever ready to assist them to the extent of their power. At Leesburg they would take off their hats to our men and exclaim, "De Lord bless you, massas," and in a low tone, warned us "dat de Secesh am close by," showing that their hearts were in our cause, if they only dared to assert it.

At Little River Turnpike we met several companies of our cavalry. They reported no rebels around, and so we turned our horses' heads campward. This night we encamped on the farm of Mrs. Lee, mother of the rebel General of that name. We picketed our horses in her fine orchard and made ourselves generally at home.

We had an early start the next morning, and reached camp the same day by way of Chain Bridge and Washington City. During our raid we traveled about 150 miles, and then returned to camp, having accomplished nothing save tiring out both men and horses. We are now expecting marching orders every hour, for the rebels are near, and our services may be needed. Our men are ready and eager for the fray, and though a great deal of dissatisfaction exists among the Californians, on account of the bad treatment they have and are now receiving, yet they do not allow this to interfere with their duty to their country, and California need have no fears-her honor is safe in their keeping; they will *never* disgrace the State they love so well.

Accident
A sad accident occurred a few days since. Capt. D. A. DeMerritt, of Sacramento, commanding Company F, had his leg broken by a fall from his horse. He is now doing well, but it will be some time ere he can resume his command. Hiram Chrystler, of Capt. Eigenbrodt's Company, and Dan'l K. Chaffee, of Capt. Adams', died recently, at the Lincoln Hospital, Washington. There is considerable sickness among our men now, ten per cent of them being on the "sick report."

We have this day heard of the Union nominations in California, and heartily approve of them; the Judicial part of the ticket could not be bettered. May they prove successful at the coming election.

T. H. M.

Alta California, San Francisco, Friday, July 17, 1863
[F.F.V. - First Families of Virginia. H. Chrystler Co. E; D. Chaffee Co. L; of typhoid.]

❖❖

JULY, 1863
- 1-3 Battle of Gettysburg.
- 4 Vicksburg surrenders to the Union Army.
- 13-16 New York Draft Riots.
- 18 Assault on Fort Wagner by the Fifty-fourth Colored Infantry.

❖❖

Gloucester Pt. Va. July 2d/63

My dear Mammy

I have not had time to write to you for some time & the news is that I have been engaged in making raids for the last ten days. 1st raid was made from this point, we went up to King & Queen Court House & took 7 Rebel Cavalry men prisoners, all of Capt Littleton's Company - many horses mules & contrabands - Gone three days & did some hard & rapid marching.
2d Raid
All the Cavalry on this point consisting of my Bat. & parts of the 12th Ill & 2N.Y. all under the command of Col Davis of the 12th Ill Cav. were ordered to report to Col Spear of the 11th Pen. Cav. We did so & took transports for the White House on the Pamunkey. We left here one

afternoon & got to the White House at an early hour in the morning. One Company of Reb. Cav. flying at our approach. At White House we formed in lines of battle after disembarking & prepared to advance one of my Companies taking the advance. At Tunstals Station the advance saw a train of cars which however escaped us. We marched to within 16 miles of Richmond & halted for the night. Resumed our march early in the morning. Marched northward til we came to Nelson's Farm here I was ordered to leave one squadron to guard a bridge. I did so & on we went to Hanover Court House here we captured a Rebel baggage train of 35 wagons & on we went to a place called South Anna bridge over which the railroad runs & the object of the expedition was to destroy this bridge, here we found the Rebels a force of Infantry intrenched behind breast works my men were dismounted & ordered to charge the works on foot, while a squadron of Pen Cav. charged them in the flank. After some preliminary fighting we all charged & carried the works. I lost one man killed & one wounded, my men were the first in the works & behaved first rate. We killed 13 Rebs dead & wound many & took 8 Officers & 100 men all of the 44th North Carolina prisoners. We burned the bridge & returned to Hanover Court House there we found Gen W. H. F. Lee (a former Classmate of Ben C & a son of Maj. Gen. Robert Lee) Who had been wounded in some Cavalry fight with Hookers men. Col Spear put him in a Carriage & took him along with us. I went up & spoke to him, he remembered me well. I offered to do & did all I could for him. I had a long talk with him he asked all about his old friends. We slept that night at Nelson's farm & marched the next day for the White house had several little skirmishes with Bushwackers & took a few of them prisoners. We got into White house late that evening after a very hard march. The next day I got leave to go down to Gloucester Point to get some things & I have as yet been prevented from going back by a bad case of diarhea. I shall however go back tomorrow or the next day. I forget to say that Gen Dix & 20 thousand infantry are now at the White house. I am also disgusted to find that Col Spear now gives almost all the credit of the affair to his own Regt. It is natural enough however but not the less disgusting. Some of the New York papers which mention it as a very brilliant affair do not even mention that we were there. Our men & officers are very angry about it.
[Last paragraph deleted-Editors]

Caspar Crowninshield, Letters, Massachusetts Historical Society

Battalion

LETTER FROM THE CALIFORNIANS IN THE MASSACHUSETTS CONTIN- GENT

(From Correspondent of the ALTA CALIFORNIA, Accompanying the Battalion.)

CAMP OF THE CALIFORNIA BATTALION,
SENECA CREEK, Md., July 4th, 1863.

EDITORS ALTA:- I know not how, under the present circumstances, I can better cel- ebrate the ever glorious Fourth than by devoting a portion thereof to the columns of the ALTA. Here we are, encamped on Seneca Creek, twenty-five miles from Washington City. It is a beautiful location for a cavalry camp. The scenery is lovely: grass, water and wood are plenty; by saying that wood is plenty, I mean that there are several fences of oak rails, which are appropriated to our use and comfort- for soldiers never cut wood when fences are near.

The Fourth of July.

While our friends in California, and elsewhere, are this day making themselves joyful in celebrating our great anniversary, we trust that in their joy they are not so forgetful of us, as not to wonder where we are and how we are spending the Fourth. It is thus: We arrived at this camping place last evening from Poolesville, Maryland, and this morning were busy in pitch- ing tents, fixing lines for our horses, and arranging the camp: this done and we are lying around camp taking it easy, for we have had fatigue enough of late and both men and horses stand much in need of rest, having been four days without unsaddling. This is a miserable day: dark, heavy clouds overhang the sky, the atmosphere is hot and sultry, and heavy showers keep falling every hour. For us there is no celebration, no joyful demonstrations, except on this morning when some of our "boys" brought into camp a butchered steer they had "foraged."

The "Artillery of Heaven" alone is busy overhead, rolling its loud thunders along, as if a great battle was being fought by the contending elements above. Part of our forces are out on picket duty, keeping a sharp lookout for "rebs" they being quite plenty in this neighborhood.

Change of Camp to Poolesville, Maryland.

My last letter was written from Brightwood, D. C. On the day following we were ordered to Poolesville, to do scout and picket duty. But we did not stay there long, for the day after our arrival we had the pleasure of seeing no less personage than General Joseph Hooker: he has now been superseded, but with the army he is "Fighting Joe Hooker" still. His army was then making forced marches in three columns, to reach the upper part of Maryland and Pennsylva- nia, where the rebels, in great force, were making a raid on rather an extensive scale.

A Stirring Scene.

I take it for granted that few, if any, of your readers have ever seen an army of upwards of one hundred thousand men under march. I will not attempt to do it justice, for it would require a pen more graphic than mine to do so: but let me assure you that it surely is an imposing spectacle. I stood by the roadside and gazed at it for hours without tiring: there was no mo- notony about it. The Second Army Corps passed first. At the head of each Brigade composing it, marched the Commanding General and his Staff and body-guard: then follows the fine Brigade band, occasionally playing patriotic airs to encourage the weary soldiers along: then one by one the regiments go by, their colors and banners flying: some of these are stained with the blood of those who proudly and bravely bore them on the field of battle: they are pierced by bullets and rent by fragments of shell, and bear other proofs of having been in many a gallant fight. The men, too, looked rough, with faces tanned by the hot sun of Virginia. Their uniform showed signs of hard service, but the men are rugged and enthusiastic: and, animated by knowing that they are engaged in a good cause, they march boldly forth to do their duty. There you may see regiments from New York, Pennsylvania, and other States, forming Brigades and Divisions. There are no dissensions between them: they feel that they are engaged in a common cause, and with one object in view- to put down the rebellion-and to this end they devote their energies and their lives, without a murmur of complaint. As they march along, they laugh and joke and seem happy enough, as they plod along the muddy roads, occasionally resting, and eating their rations of "hard tack and salt pork" with as much gusto as an epicurean would sit over his oysters and veal cutlets. Long marches with knapsack and arms to carry sharpens a man's appetite, and if your readers do not believe it, let them try it.

For an hour we stand by the roadside seeing such and such a brigade pass by, followed by their ambulances carrying the sick and wounded. Five thousand Infantry have now passed, and here comes a body of Cavalry. The gallant Gen. Stahl rides at its head. It is his brigade, five thousand strong, composed of New York, Pennsylvania and Michigan Cavalry. They have done good service in Virginia, and have become a terror to the rebels, having whipped them in every encounter. For another hour we stand gazing at this great sight. Five thousand men and as many horses are marching by fours past us. It is an animated scene. They are hurriedly pressing forward after the enemy, and the horses also seem to enter into the spirit of it. A number of batteries now follow. These are light artillery. The pieces, some iron and some brass, are mostly twelve-pounders, each drawn by six horses, as is also its caisson. Thus, I stood transfixed to this spot, until I had seen thirty-five thousand Infantry, five thousand Cavalry and about one hundred pieces of artillery pass by me, and left only when driven away be approaching darkness. During the whole night troops kept passing our camp, all bound in the same direction. You may form some idea of the amount of transportation necessary for such a number of men when I assure you that the wagon train of these two corps, Second and Third, was fifteen miles long.

An Honor to the California Battalion.

General Hooker and Staff stayed all that day and the next night at Poolesville, during which time Major Thompson paid the distinguished Californian a visit, and asked him to take the California Cavalry Battalion as his body guard: this the General hesitated to do, as we had been stationed at Poolesville by orders of the War Department, but he granted us the privilege of escorting him on the road to Harper's Ferry. So the next morning we mounted our horses, and headed to Harper's Ferry, in the best of spirits.

General Hooker went to Frederick, at which place he was concentrating his army, and we encamped near Harper's Ferry. We all felt glad now, for we were likely to witness and participate in the great battles about to be fought in Pennsylvania, and which may prove the decisive ones of the war: but again we were doomed to disappointment, for we were that night ordered to Poolesville, to look after Stuart's rebel cavalry, which was then crossing the Potomac into Maryland.

The Return to Poolesville and Pursuit of the Rebels.

According to orders, the next morning we started from Harper's Ferry, marching on the tow path of the Chesapeake canal for some distance, and then across the country to the ford on the Monocacy River. Here we heard that 2,000 rebel cavalry were at Poolesville, so we prepared for battle, and hurried on. Arriving at camp, we found everything safe, and no rebels near, but Stuart in command of three Brigades of Cavalry, and several pieces of artillery had crossed the Potomac at Seneca, and were then making for Hagerstown, and thence to join Ewell in Pennsylvania. Without making any stay at Poolesville we hurried on in pursuit of Stuart's rebel cavalry. You may laugh and think it preposterous for one Battalion, three hundred strong, chasing three Brigades of the renowned cavalry, twelve thousand in number: yet such is the fact, and we followed them up so close that at times our advance guard was not more than three quarters of a mile from the rebel column. We arrived at Rockville at 10 P.M. and saw a number of army wagons yet burning, having been set on fire by rebels. We had now been on the march from early morning, and halted to rest both men and horses, and at 2 in the morning were again in our saddles, and hard after the rebels to watch their movements.

Our First Rebel Prisoners.

Our advance guard was under the command of First Lieut. W. C. Manning, formerly of Company F, Second Cavalry, and who, I may here remark, is as brave, dashing and gallant a young officer as can be found in the Union army, and a clever fellow besides. Both him and his brother, Capt Geo. A. Manning, are much loved and respected by all with whom they come in contact. The advance guard (your correspondent was one of the number) hurried along the road to Brookville, meeting many prisoners who had been captured and paroled by the rebels. At this town, we heard that Stuart's cavalry was only three miles ahead, and that some stragglers were on the road, close by, we pushed on, and soon had the satisfaction of seeing three "greybacks;" we put spurs to our horses, and soon captured two, and the horse of a third who took to the brush. Part of the advance guard was detailed to take the prisoners back to the column, and the balance still kept on after the rebels, and soon we saw two coming from a house by the roadside, and hardly were they aware of our presence before we had our pistols cocked and within ten feet of their breasts and ordered them to surrender. A rebel lieutenant fell to the lot of your correspondent, who ordered him to deliver up his arms. This he did with rather a bad grace, and "forked over" three revolvers and his sword, and was then marched to the rest of the command, where the "California boys" received them joyfully. That morning we captured nine rebels, several horses and mules. These were all sent to Washington as an addition to the stock on hand. We followed the rebels until we turned them over to the care and attention of Gen. Pleasanton who will see that they do not want for anything in the shape of lead and cold steel. We know that the gallant Pleasanton took such good care of the rebel cavalry that he whipped them the next day. Having accomplished our mission, we returned to Poolesville, and, the day after came here to Seneca, and now here we are, doing picket and scout duty.

The Glorious News.

These have been received here, and we feel joyful over the victories of our brave companions in arms. Lee's army defeated, routed and demoralized: Vicksburg fallen and in our possession. Everything is now working finely: keep the ball rolling, and soon we shall have the rebels whipped, the rebellion crushed, and then peace and prosperity will again be with us, and then, hurrah! back to California again. But, hold on- I must not anticipate too much. The horizon is not yet clear-a few clouds are yet visible, but may they soon be dispersed.

Miscellaneous.

The health of the men is good, and they are all in fine spirits, doing their duty faithfully, and with honor to themselves and the cause. There is still much ill feeling between the Californian officers and men, and those belonging to Massachusetts. It may yet culminate in serious trouble: but more of this in my next.

Lieutenant J. A. Baldwin has gone to the "Blockhouse" with a detachment of men. He is proving himself a fine officer, and very justly stands high with the men. His undoubted bravery, gentlemanly and unassuming manners, are passports to the hearts of those with whom he comes in contact.

Wm. F. Welsh, of Captain DeMerritt's company, was captured and paroled by the rebels. He was carrying the mail and despatches from Washington when he was ordered to halt: but instead of doing so, he put spurs to his horse and tried to escape. The rebels fired a number of shots, and Welsh only surrendered when his horse was shot from under him: but he destroyed the despatches. The rebels abused him, calling him a Californian Yankee, a nigger-stealing thief, and other vile epithets, for resisting and trying to escape. As the rebels were taking him through Rockville, Md., some of the citizens grossly insulted him. We have them "spotted," and will square accounts with them some day. The mail carrier is waiting and I must close.

T. H. M.

Alta California, San Francisco, Sunday, August 2, 1863.
[General Hooker & Major Thompson held adjoining properties in Sonoma County, & in 1852 had jointly purchased 2500 acres of the Santa Rosa Ranch.]

❖❖❖❖❖❖❖❖❖❖❖❖❖❖❖❖❖❖❖❖❖❖❖❖❖❖❖❖❖❖❖❖❖❖❖

The California Hundred.-We have just received from Charley Briggs, of the California Hundred, a copy of the "Cavalier," published at Yorktown, Va., July 7th, in which we find the following paragraph:

The Second Massachusetts Cavalry. In the recent skirmish at North Anna Station, the 2d Massachusetts Cavalry bore a prominent part with the 11th Pennsylvania, and displayed throughout the greatest coolness and valor. The "California Hundred," which composes part of this command, is particularly well spoken of. The 2d Massachusetts lost one killed and two wounded.

The Napa County Reporter, Napa, Saturday, August 22, 1863.

❖❖❖❖❖❖❖❖❖❖❖❖❖❖❖❖❖❖❖❖❖❖❖❖❖❖❖❖❖❖❖❖❖❖❖

Ashby's Gap.-By a private letter from James M. Hawkins, a volunteer in the Massachusetts 2d Cavalry, (California contingent,) we learn that two days before that battle he had been appointed chief bugler to the regiment; that he was shot in the head in that battle, and his horse shot under him and fell on him, breaking his left arm and two of his ribs; that he was taken prisoner, but the boys, under the lead of Ben. Hoxie, made a dash and rescued him. He is in fine spirits, and determined to fight it out.

Solano Herald, Suisun, Saturday, August 22, 1863.
Solano Herald, Suisun, Saturday, September 12, 1863.
[Battle of Ashby's Gap, July 12, 1863; Hawkins, Co. L; Hoxie, Co.L.]

❖❖❖❖❖❖❖❖❖❖❖❖❖❖❖❖❖❖❖❖❖❖❖❖❖❖❖❖❖❖❖❖❖❖❖

Gloucester Pt. Va. July 14th/63

My dear Mammy

I have been so very busy lately that I have been unable to write to you. for the last 20 days we have been continually at work and hard work it has been. We have had only one fight and I wrote you a short account of that - it only lasted a short time. My men did most all of it, the bullets flew round liberly but I only had one man killed & one badly wounded.

My men fought first rate. We took the Rebel rifle pits killed 13 & wounded 8 & took 100 prisoners. the fighting was mostly hand to hand & our men ran the Rebels through with their sabres. My command got a great deal of credit for it down here but the newspapers have not mentioned us at all; however that is to be expected. We took among the prisoners a Lt. Col. a Major two Captains & 4 Lieutenants all of the 44th North Carolina - Afterwards we took Gen. W.H.F. Lee (a Classmate of Ben C) prisoner, I used to know him well in College, and I had a long and pleasant talk with him. We also captured a wagon train of 40 wagons. This was captured by our advance guard which was part of this 1st Squadron of my command. The expedition was very pleasant & highly successful. One day we went by the Church where George Washington was married & near there I fell in with an old man by the name of Reeves who said he was a distant relative of W.C. Reeves. We had one or two little skirmishes with Bushwhackers but it did not amount to much. When we got back to the White House I was not very well & so I went back to Gloucester Pt for a day or two and got well & returned. I wrote you a short note from the Point which I suppose you received in due time. We are now on a River at Gloucester Point anxiously waiting orders to go to Washington, but we do not get them yet & perhaps may not get them, in the mean while we are very comfortable here. Gettysburg victory was a costly one for us. Poor Charley Mudge *[?]* & the rest of the fellows. I see no mention in the papers of the 1st Mass Cav but suppose that they have been doing some fighting & hope Charles is all right. I have not had a letter from him for a long time. I sent you 200 dols some time ago which you have never acknowledged I hope you have it. How is the Draft going on in Massachusetts.

   Love to all
    your son Caspar

Caspar Crowninshield, Letters, Massachusetts Historical Society

LETTER FROM THE CALIFORNIANS IN THE
ARMY OF THE POTOMAC.

Operations in Virginia.

GLOUCESTER POINT, July 14th, 1863

Eds. Alta:- For over two weeks, from the 24th of June to the 10th of July, we were kept very busy making raids on the Peninsula and harassing the rebels. On the 20th of June our battalion and a detachment of the Twelfth Illinois, under command of a Lieutenant Colonel Davis, left this Point on the steamer *City of Albany*, for the White House. At the same time, on six other steamers, the Eleventh Pennsylvania Cavalry embarked at Yorktown for the same place, which we arrived at the next morning, about seven o'clock, having laid at anchor at West

Point the preceding night. On our arrival at the White House a small force of rebel cavalry was discovered, but they rapidly made themselves scarce, leaving for us about two tons of hay which they did not have time to destroy. The steamer on which we were first made the landing, and half of our Company were deployed as skirmishers on foot, advancing into the country a mile from the landing, but did not succeed in getting within shooting distance of the rebels. In a short time they were recalled, and in the meantime the troops were landed as fast as possible, forming in line of battle as fast as landed. It was 11 o'clock before the last man had reached *terra firma*, and it was not until 3 o'clock P. M., that we left White House for a march up the Peninsula, under command of Colonel Spear, of the Eleventh Pennsylvania, the intention being to burn a railroad bridge over the South Anna river, thereby destroying railroad communication between Richmond and Gordonsville. We marched that afternoon about twelve miles, encamping at night in a large field by the roadside, and notwithstanding it rained heavily, were, soon after tying our horses, fast locked in the embrace of Morpheus - forgetful of rebels, "or any other man." At day light the next morning we were aroused from our slumbers, and hastily partaking of our breakfast- consisting of coffee and hard tack- were again in the saddle and "marching on," one-half of our Company being honored with the advance.

Nothing worthy of note transpired until we reached the Old Church Hotel, where we captured a Surgeon of the rebel army, a Captain, and five privates, also half a dozen twenty-pound boxes of tobacco, which was quickly divided among the soldiers and heartily appreciated by them. About 12 o'clock we came in sight of a large rebel wagon train drawn up on the top of a hill within half a mile of Hanover Court House, the mules unhitched and feeding, and the drivers (mostly negroes) reposing in fancied security. We had heard, a short distance back, that there was quite a force of rebel cavalry at the Court House, or, as the darkey from whom the information was obtained expressed himself, "a right smart of 'em."

When we came in sight of the train, "draw sabre," was the order, and we were instructed to leave the wagon train to be disposed of by those in the rear, while we should charge right on into the town. When within five hundred yards of the Court House, the order to "Charge" was given, and away we went at full speed, into the place, and through it, but only saw some half a dozen rebels, whom we easily captured. Some of the men were then dispatched to cut the telegraph wire, and others to intercept a train of cars which was discovered going towards Richmond, but they arrived at the track just too late, and the train went on its way rejoicing. The wagon train was attended to by those in the rear, the prize consisting of fifty wagons, two hundred mules, and some commissary stores, which Jeff could ill afford to lose. The bridge we were to burn was some three miles from the Court House, and we soon arrived there, and saw that there were some rebels guarding it. Col. Spear immediately ordered the half of our Company that were in the advance, and armed with carbines, to dismount and deploy as skirmishers through a corn field, towards the bridge where the rebels were concealed behind the thick growth of trees and bushes which lined the stream over which the bridge was. It was accordingly done, our First Lieutenant taking charge of us, and as soon as we got within range of the rebels' rifles, they commenced popping at us, the bullets flying in rather too close proximity to our heads to cause a feeling of safety. We however, sent them our complements whenever we could obtain a sight of them, and advanced to within one hundred yards of the bridge, where we found a small breastwork thrown up, running parallel with the stream, and ensconced ourselves behind that, loading and firing as opportunity offered, and toppled over more than one of them.

The Engagement.

In the meantime, two squadrons of cavalry, (the Eleventh Pennsylvania) had forded the stream about half a mile above the bridge, and charged down upon the rebels, but could not do any good, and went back again out of range. Two mountain howitzers belonging to the Eleventh had been positioned behind us, and also commenced throwing shot and shell at the rebels, but not very accurately, and therefore did but little good. By this time we were reinforced by the balance of our Company, on foot, and about fifty of the Pennsylvania, ditto, and we effected a crossing of the stream on a foot log, about one hundred yards above the bridge, unknown to the rebels, and concealed ourselves in the bushes, from which the rebels had retreated to a log house and breastworks commanding the passage of the bridge. It was now understood that the cavalry and dismounted men were to charge together- the cavalry charge to be made as a feint, for the purpose of drawing their fire, and the real charge to be made by us from another direction. Accordingly, the charge was made, the ruse succeeding admirably. Their fire was directed at the cavalry, and before they had time to reload their pieces we were upon them, and in three minutes had control of the approaches to the bridge. Those who could, skedaddled for an earthwork below the bridge, but finding it would be useless to resist longer, they ran the muzzles of their guns into the ground, threw up their hands and surrendered, after a loss on their side of ten killed and twenty wounded. The loss on our side, three killed and six wounded including, from our Company, J. B. Burdick, killed, and Richard Ellet seriously wounded. The number of prisoners captured by us during that trip was 111, including Brigadier General Lee, a son of the rebel Commander, 10 officers, from a Colonel to a Lieutenant, and 110 privates. As soon as the skirmish was over, the bridge was fired, and was "growing small by degrees and beautifully less," very fast when I last saw it. The number of rebels engaged in the fight was 125, and belonged to the Forty-fourth North Carolina Conscripts, and they fought well against such heavy odds. I asked one of them if he knew what he was fighting for, and he said he did not; that he was a poor, uneducated white man, had been forced into the army, and fought because he was compelled.

The Return.

After burning the bridge, we immediately started back for the White House by a different route from what we had come, and on the 28th, at dusk, reached it, finding that during our absence some 30,000 of our troops had been concentrated there, under command of General Dix and Keyes. We here encamped until the 1st of July, when we again started out- this time accompanied by 10,000 infantry and six batteries of artillery, 12-pounders- with the intention of destroying a railroad bridge at Hanover Junction, over the Pamunkey River, which would destroy railroad communication between Richmond and Fredericksburg, and also inducing the rebels to believe that a movement was contemplated on Richmond, and therefore preventing them from sending any of their troops congregated around Richmond, to reinforce their armies at other points where they were greatly needed. The last named object was accomplished, but the first was not, as General Getty, who was in command, found that the rebels had the bridge too strongly defended for him to take it, except at the sacrifice of a large number of lives, and we were accordingly marched back again to the White House, which place we reached after an absence of just one week. This bridge is situated five miles nearer Richmond than the one Colonel Spear's expedition burned, and if it could have been destroyed, would have been a heavy loss to the rebels.

At White House.

On arriving at White House this time we found the place nearly deserted. The troops that were here having all been ordered to Washington, to reinforce the Army of Gen. Meade and aid him in annihilating Lee's rebel army, which he has already so well commenced. The troops we were with also found orders awaiting them to the same effect; and on the morning of the 8th they, with the exception of one brigade of infantry and the cavalry, were embarked on transports. There not being sufficient transports for all, the infantry and cavalry, took the land route for Yorktown the same day, where we arrived on the 10th, and all, with the exception of our battalion, went from there to Washington. We are on our old stamping place at Gloucester, and, as there is no infantry here, are performing infantry picket duty in conjunction with about two hundred dismounted men belonging to the Harris light cavalry. A battery of artillery and five hundred cavalry is now the only force stationed here to guard the place. Yorktown is pretty well deserted also, only a sufficient number of soldiers having been left there actually necessary to perform garrison duty. All the negro men in this vicinity, and there were some three hundred of them, have also been taken away to Fortress Monroe for the purpose of shoveling dirt for their kind and indulgent father "Uncle Sam." It is very dull indeed here, at present, and I hope we may soon have more active duty to perform than garrisoning this place. The weather is very warm and sultry, but very little sickness prevails, this being about as healthy a place as there is in the South.

T. D. B.

Alta California, San Francisco, Monday, August 10, 1863.

❖❖

Battalion

LETTER FROM THE CALIFORNIANS IN THE ARMY IN VIRGINIA.

(From the Correspondent of the ALTA CALIFORNIA accompanying the Battalion)

IN CAMP NEAR ALEXANDRIA, VA.,
JULY 17, 1863.

\EDITORS ALTA: I hasten to seize a brief opportunity to give you an account of the late stirring events in our battalion which have transpired since I sent you my last letter.

A Second Raid and Scout into Virginia.

While we were encamped on Seneca Creek, Maryland, doing picket duty in that vicinity, and enjoying the luxury of a little rest and quiet, we were suddenly ordered on a reconnaissance into Virginia, to ascertain if Ashby's and Snicker's Gaps, in the Blue Ridge, were fortified or held by the rebels; and soon the whole camp was astir, drawing rations and making other preparations for marching. Leaving Seneca about dark, we traveled ten miles to Rockville, and before daybreak the next morning we were again on the road to Washington City, passing through it, and crossing into Virginia over Long Bridge. Here we made the necessary preparation for a hasty march-left the wagons behind, taking only the ambulance; at dawn we were in our saddles and on the turnpike leading south. This road is the one in which our great armies passed when going to Centreville and Bull's Run. Everything on either side of it is in ruins-no fences, no fields of grain. Houses once beautiful and grand, are now either deserted and gutted of their contents, or torn down entirely, to furnish wood for the soldiers; and as we march on nothing but desolation meets the eye. We reached Fairfax Court House-the only importance attached to this place now is historical. The houses are old and dilapidated, the "Court House" is used for a stable by the cavalry, and, altogether, the place might well be called a "one-horse town."

Leaving the main road leading to Centreville, we proceeded to Aldie, where our troops fought the rebels three weeks ago. We saw evidence of the battle: fresh made graves showed where slumbered the brave dead; dead horses lay scattered here and there over the field and in the road, filling the atmosphere with the effluvia of putrifying flesh, the inhabitants being too lazy to bury or remove them. A red flag hoisted over a barn showed that it was used as a hospital. Riding up to it, I found a number of our wounded lying there; they appeared to be as comfortable as possible under the circumstances; their pale, emaciated faces told plainly of the pain and suffering they had so heroically endured for their country's sake.

We encamped a mile beyond the town, and the next morning, bright and early, we took the road to Ashby's Gap. Our scouts, occasionally, would see and capture a straggling rebel, or one of their pickets. We were now passing over a beautiful country; nature seems to have been lavish of her gifts, and bestowed, even too freely, upon this part of Virginia; for though the country is indeed lovely in appearance, and fertile in soil, yet the inhabitants thereof are *intensely Secesh,* and cast withering looks upon us as we passed by them. At 2 P. M., we reached the town of Paris, at the entrance of Ashby's Gap. Here our advance guard was fired on by the rebels, and here our first blood was shed.

Our Fight at Ashby's Gap.

The advance guard was composed mainly of men from Captain Eigenbrodt's company, and commanded by Lieut. John C. Norcross, as gallant and brave an officer as ever drew a sabre. The fire of the rebel pickets did no injury, they having shot too high, as the bullets whistled over the heads of our men. At the top of the hill, in the Gap, the rebels were drawn up in platoons across the road. On seeing them, Lieut. Norcross ordered the men to charge on them, leading the charge himself, ahead of his command. They had proceeded but a short way when they were fired on by the rebels, behind a stone wall by the roadside, and from behind bushes. This unexpected fire, from an invisible enemy, for one moment threw the handful of men composing the advance guard into consternation; but they quickly rallied, and, being reinforced again, charged on the rebels. They had now left the road, and were firing on our men from behind the stone wall, and apparently fighting Indian fashion. The rebels having been scattered, the second platoon of Company L. charged through the Gap, as did also parts of companies E. and M-and down the hill they went to the Shenandoah river, in the valley of the same name. The rebels had crossed the river, and now the fight was carried on by our men on our side of the river, and the rebels on the other, firing with carbines, at a distance of about two hundred yards. Here our men killed six rebels, and ere long not one could be seen, and the fight was over. But a small portion of the battalion was engaged, the rebels being only about seventy in number. But few were needed to "clean them out," and these done it most effectually and thoroughly, killing nine, wounding several who were carried off, and taking thirteen prisoners. Our loss was two killed, four wounded, and six taken prisoners.

The Killed, Wounded and Prisoners.

Harry P. Irving, of Half Moon Bay, San Mateo county, was killed. He was shot in the breast, and as he lay wounded a rebel came to take his arms from him; though almost dead, yet he tried to use his pistol, when the rebel shot him as he lay on the ground and there killed him. Irving was buried by us in the town of Paris, near the battlefield.

Walter J. Barnes, of San Francisco, was killed by a bullet, which entered one shoulder and passed through the body. He lived for about four hours, and died in the ambulance. He was perfectly conscious to the last. He was buried with the honors of a soldier at the town of Upperville, Va.

While the relations and friends of our fellow comrades may mourn the loss of those who were "near and dear" to them, we extend to them our heartfelt sympathy, for we, too, mourn their loss. Yet it may be some consolation for them to know that both acted with distinguished bravery, and died like gallant soldiers, as they were, faithfully performing their duty to themselves and to their country, and in a good cause.

Wounded.

Sergeant William F. De Forrest, of Marysville, in the head, (wound serious, but not necessarily mortal,) is now in the hospital, doing well; Bugler J. M. Hawkins, of Suisun City, Solano county, slightly wounded in the head, and injured by a fall from his horse, will soon be well; Morris Jay, flesh wound in the shoulder, was taken prisoner and afterwards re-captured; Wm. H. Moore, flesh wound in the leg.

Prisoners.

Lieut. John C. Norcross, of Iowa Hill, Placer county, was taken prisoner while commanding the advance guard. This officer acted with great bravery during the engagement, and for his gallant conduct is worthy of special mention. He has endeared himself to us all by his gentlemanly deportment and social qualities. We hope soon to see him exchanged and returned to his command. Richard T. Brickley, Thomas W. Cobbey, Hiram Venum, and Thos. Garrity, of Company E; Roswell R. Smith, Company L, were also taken prisoners. Sylvanus Shaw, Company E, was taken prisoner and afterwards recaptured.

Our Return to Camp.

Having accomplished our mission, we started on our return to Washington. Nothing worthy of mention occurred, until the following day, when it was understood that we were to make a dash into Leesburg and capture any rebels that might be there. On nearing the place we divided into three parties and entered the town by as many ways. It was beautifully done, and quite exciting, as our boys, flushed by their recent victory over the rebels, with drawn pistols charged into the town, much to the terror of its rebel inhabitants. We searched several hotels and private houses, broke open a store and captured a lot of tobacco; this proved a rich prize, as our boys had for some time been rather short of the "weed." We also captured two rebel officers and several horses.

Five miles from Leesburg we captured Albert Leigh, a noted rebel spy and guerrilla, for whom the Government had long been searching; twice has he taken the oath of allegiance, and has violated it without regard to its sanctity or value. The detective who accompanied us, had orders to take him "dead or alive." He was surprised and captured alive, at his house, and is now safely mured inside of a prison in Washington; report says that he will, ere long, be hung as a spy. We took him from his house amid the tears of the women and their abuse of the Yankees. The scene was decidedly rich, but I have neither time nor space to detail it.

As we passed a humble, but neat looking, cottage by the road side, a lady-God bless her! - stood in the door, smiling and waving her white handkerchief to us. It presented such a contrast to the frowning looks of the women, and cowardly, sneaking looks of the men we had met with in Virginia, that we felt inclined to stop and thank her; but not being able to do this, we contented ourselves by thanking God that, at least, there was one Union woman in Virginia. We reached our camp at Brightwood, D. C., well nigh exhausted, both men and horses-the latter having been saddled for five days and nights.

The expedition was entirely successful. Of the conduct of both officers and men, it can well be said that they all acted nobly and bravely. They vied with each other in doing their duty most faithfully; and we are now all eager to meet the enemy and avenge our brave comrades. We are likely soon to have an opportunity to do this, for we are now on our way into the enemy's country, and we leave here to-day as soon as some fresh horses come for us, most of the old ones being worn out by our recent long marches and hard work.

The readers of the ALTA must excuse this poor letter. I am sitting on a bale of hay-writing on a piece of board on my knee for a desk, and keeping an eye to my dinner, which consists of some coffee, fried bacon and hard bread. We only have luxuries when in the enemy's country, when we "forage," (in California you'd call it stealing,) and make pigs, chickens and calves suffer, and seize all the milk and butter we can lay our hands on.

But I am admonished it is time to close. On our return from our present expedition I will give your readers its details. For the present, *adios!*

T. H. M.

Alta California, San Francisco, Thursday, August 13, 1863.
Solano Press, Suisun, Monday, August 2, 1863.

❖ ❖

Head-Quarters of the Army,
Adjutant General's Office,
Washington, July 20th, 1863.

Special Orders,
  No. 322

Extract,

2......The Battalion of the 2nd Mass Cavalry now serving in the Department of Virginia will be immediately ordered to join the regiment in the Department of Washington. By command of Major General Halleck.

E.D. Townsend
Asst. Adjt. General

United States Military Telegraph

By Telegraph from <u>Yorktown</u>
Dated <u>July 25th 1863.</u>
To <u>Col H. Pelonze</u>

Battalion 2nd Mass Cavalry has not Left for
Washington Do you wish it to Leave. No
such order has been received here. It is
now twenty 20 miles distant with infantry
after three companies of Rebel Bushwackers.
Will return in the night. Have you any
orders for it. Dont send it away if you can
keep it. I have no other cavalry for
Gloucester County to spare.

I.J. Wistar
Brig. Genl.

Hd Qrs Fort Yorktown
    July 27 1863
Special Orders
No 46
        In compliance with Special order No 322 from the Adjutant Generals office Washington D.C. dated July 20th 1863 the Battalion of the 2nd Mass Cav now serving at Gloucester Pt will embark immediately on the Steamers, Express and Juniata and proceed to Washington to join their Regiment without further orders

                                By Command of
                                    Brig. Gen. Wistar
                                    Stephan W. Reynolds
                                    A.A.G.
Capt. Reed
        2d Mass Cav

Regimental Record Book, National Archives, Washington D.C.

❖❖

                        Hd Qrs 2d Mass Cavly Centreville, Va.
                                July 29th,1863
General Order
    No 28
                In accordance with the provisions named in the forgoing General Order No. 27, the Court convened at the precise hour named therin and proceeded at once to an investigation of the "charges and specifications" prepared against Capt. Z.B. Adams, 2d Mass Cav.

            Present Maj. W.H. Forbes, 2d Mass Cavly President
                "   Capt Chls S. Eigenbrodt "   "
                "   Lieut Rufus A. Smith   "   "

Charge and Specifications prepared against Capt Z.B. Adams 2d Mass. Cav.

            Charge - Habitual violation of the third paragraph of Army Regulations.
                    Specification in this that, the Captain Z.B. Adams, of the 2nd Mass Cavalry, Vols., did on or about the 19th day of July, 1863, while a portion of the regiment was at a halt, on line of march near Centreville, Va., in a threatening & insulting manner, say to the non-commissioned officers and privates of Co. "F" 2d Mass. Cav. "Keep your horses in line God damn you, or I will chop your heads off." and that he Capt. Z.B. Adams, frequently uses insulting and abusive language toward the enlisted men belonging to Co. "F" 2d Mass. Cav. Vols.

                                C.R. Lowell Jr., Col.
Approved C.R. Lowell, Jr.,   2d Mass. Cavly
        Col. 2d Mass. Cavalry

Witness: Abraham Lafhirty }
        Charles Harkin   }Corporals
        George Thayer   }

Jules Fieldman,   }
Dennis Seymour, and } Privates
James McDonald   }

The accused, Capt. Z.B. Adams, 2d Mass Cavalry was brought before the Court and the foregoing Specifications and Charge was then read to him, when he was asked, "do you plead guilty or not guilty? he replied as follows:

To the Specification Not guilty

To the Charge   Not guilty

Whereupon Corporal Abraham Lafhirty, of Co. "F" 2d Mass. Cavly. was summoned to appear before the Court, and upon being first duly sworn, deposed as follows: 1st Ques. "Was he a Corporal in Co. "F" 2d Mass. Cav."? ans. Yes. 2d. Ques. "Were you present with Co. "F" 2d Mass. Cav. on or about the 19th of July 1863, while on a march near Centreville, Va.?" Ans. Yes.

3d. - "Did you hear Capt. Adams, 2d Mass. Cav. say to the non-commissioned officers and men of Co. "F", 2d Mass. Cav. in a threatening and insulting manner, "Keep yourselves in line God Damn you, or, I will chop your heads off"? Answer - I do not recollect as to his saying or using the words "God damn you" but did hear him say, "Keep your horses in line or I will chop your heads off."

4th Question - "Have you frequently heard Capt. Adams use insulting and abusive language towards the men belonging to said company?" Ans. Yes.

Corporal Charles Harkins, of Co. "F" 2d Mass. Cavalry, was now called and upon being first duly sworn, testified as follows:

I am a Corporal in Co. "F" 2d Mass. Cav. was present with the Company on or about the 19th day of July, 1863, while on a march near Centreville, Va., Heard Capt. Adams, 2d Mass. Cav. say to the non-commissioned officers and privates "Keep your horses in line, or God damn you I will cut your heads off." Had heard Capt. Adams, on previous occasions, use insulting and abusive language toward the men belonging to said company.

Corporal Geo. Thayer, of Co. "F" 2d Mass. Cav. sworn, testified as follows: I am a corporal in Co. "F" 2d Mass. Cav. was present with said company on or about 19th July, 1863, at or near Centreville, Va., Heard Captain Z.B. Adams say to the members of Co. "F", while at a halt at said place, "If they did not hurry and dress up, that he (Capt. Adams.) would do either cut their damned ears or heads off." Could not say positively whether Capt. Adams used the words ears or "heads". Had frequently heard Captain Adams use insulting and abusive language towards the men belonging to said Co. "F" 2d Mass. Cavalry.

Private Jules Fieldman, of said Co. "F" called before the Court, and upon being first duly sworn, deposed as follows:

That he was a private of Co. "F" 2d Mass. Cav. was present with said Co. on the 19th day of July, 1863, near Centreville, Va., Heard the accused Capt. Z.B. Adams 2d Mass. Cav. say to the non-commissioned officers and privates of said Co. "F" "Keep yourselves in line, or God damn you, I will cut your heads off."

Never heard Capt. Adams, use insulting or abusive language toward the men belonging to said Company, on any previous occasion, nor since.

James McDonald, private of Co. "F" 2d Mass. Cav. was now called before the court, and upon being first duly sworn, testified as follows:

I am a private in Co. "F". 2d Mass. Cav. I was present with the Co. aforesaid at or near Centreville, Va., on or about July 19, 1863. Heard Capt. Adams, 2d Mass. Cav. say in a threatening manner to the men when at a halt, "Fall in the ranks there, or I'll cut your heads off." It was the only occasion wherein he had ever heard the accused use insulting or abusive language toward the men of said Co.

Counter evidence

At the instance of the accused Capt. Geo. Blagden, 2d Mass. Cavalry, was summoned before the Court, and being first duly sworn, said that he never heard Captain Adams, at any time use any language towards Co. "F", that he considered abusive or insulting, and that his (Capt. Adams) treatment of said Co. had never to his knowledge been abusive.

There being no further witnesses the court was closed, and after mature deliberation and examination of the evidence adduced, find the accused, Capt. Z.B. Adams, as follows:

Specification - Not guilty

Charge   - Not guilty

W.H. Forbes

Maj. 2d Mass. Cavalry

Charles S. Eigenbrodt, Capt. 2d Mass. Cav.

Lieut. R. W. Smith, 2d Mass. Cavly.

Head Qrs. 2d Mass. Cav.

July 30th, 1863.

The proceeding of the Court of Inquiry in the case of Capt. Z.B. Adams are not valid, as the record omits to show that the court was duly sworn in presence of the accused.

After a careful review however of the testimony and finding, the Col. Comdg. has decided that the ends of justice would be served by allowing the finding to be made public, Capt. Adams, is of course released from arrest.

The Colonel takes this opportunity of enjoining upon officers a strict observance of the 3rd paragraph Army Regulations. The discipline of the regiment cannot be obtained without this. The men should be fully instructed as to what is required of them, and their immediate obedience to officers and non-commissioned officers should be enforced, without recourse to strong or injurious language.

The Colonel calls the attention of both officers and men to the growing habit of profanity - it is ungentlemanly and unsoldierly - It not checked, the penalties authorized by the 3rd and 4th, Articles of War must and will be enforced.

By command

C.R. Lowell., Jr.

Col. 2d Mass. Cavalry.

Regimental Record Books, National Archives, Washington D.C.

AUGUST, 1863

8   Lee offers his resignation, which Davis rejects.
17 Major bombardment on Fort Sumter.
21 Quantrill raids Lawrence, Kansas.

The California Hundred
The Other side of the Case of Capt. J. Sewall Reed.
Camp Wyndman, (opposite Washington, D.C.)
August 3, 1863.

Editor Bulletin. - Although one's imagination is often very fertile, I never saw it so plainly evinced as in two letters I lately read in your paper, published about July 1st, relating to certain matters pertaining to the condition of the "California Hundred," as a body, and which places our captain, J. Sewall Reed in no enviable light. Smaller matters, resulting only in talk naturally incident to a soldier's life, never could have obtained my attention; but when this company and its commander is assailed and abused by the writings of men in confinement for wrong-doing at the time, they knowing full well that anything they might write to a friend and get published in California could not be gainsayed for months at least, and their statements could have full sway for the time being, it is a fit opportunity for all who have any respect for themselves or the honor of our country, to deny any and all such statements as are therein mentioned.

I cannot proceed to enumerate each one of the various "counts" that Capt. Reed has been found guilty upon by this constituted judge and jury, but when assertions are made, on no authority, to the effect that there is no man in the company but would shoot Capt. Reed, and others of a similar stature, I assert openly and plainly that there is not the least shadow of truth in them; and let those writers ask any of the men as to our officers' bravery, and but one reply will be made; "We are more than satisfied, we are *proud* of their daring; we have been with them before the enemy and *know* them."

The origin of these Munchanson stories is found in the fertile brain of one or two persons we have among us, who do not feel satisfied unless at the head of some defiant few, called about them by windy word; and who when their efforts are nipped in the bud, loudly prate of "Company Fund," tyranny and cowardice. Not one of the sentences purporting to be from Capt. Reed are truthfully penned, in regard to any of the points mentioned, and most of them are mere fabrications, the fallacy of which can be plainly seen by the circumlocution and hyperbole manifest in the issue of words composing them; and in every case what has been said and done by Capt. Reed, has been entirely excusable from the actions of just such men as are above mentioned.

As to the Company Fund, Capt. Reed has always done what was best for the company, and just what was expected would be done with it by those of the company who have taken pains to inform themselves of the matter from the first, how it was organized, its object, etc. And even for the good of the company, not for himself, when we moved to Gloucester Point, Va., that there would be no difficulty in case of his death, he transferred the whole thing into the hands of our then Lieut. McKendry, now captain of Company G, where the fund now rests and is drawn upon when the company expresses a desire for anything it may need. Instead of his taking or desiring to take any advantage of the money being in his hands, to convert it to his own use, Capt. Reed has, in my belief, acted strictly honest from the outset, and I believe will continue so to do.

Capt. Reed did not have the company arrested, and so stated to his men; but he laid the information he had received before the superior officer, Maj. Crowninshield, and he, not being able to make any exceptions where a few had excited many to talk of mutiny and desertion, did his duty and had all arrested. Capt. Reed took immediate measures to have all to whom no suspicion could be attached released and returned to their quarters, and then made an example of those who would not be taught by any but harsh means what a soldier's duty was.

But I have said enough to convince any honorable person that the stories of men under arrest and smarting from some fancied wrong are not to be believed till at least both sides of the matter are heard. I am not ashamed to request my name to be published, as I desire this to be, and can, without fear, refer you to prominent men in San Francisco, who, I have no doubt, will vouch for my general truth and veracity.

Hoping this will have its intended effect, that of convincing you all that the *morale* of this company still exists, and that an honorable name may be relieved from so foul an opprobrium as has been cast upon it, I am, yours for the Union and Justice,

Chas. M. Kinne,
1st Duty Serg't, Co. A, 2d
Mass. Cavalry.

We fully concur in the above:

Henry Armstrong, Orderly Sergeant,
G.C. Doane, 2d Duty Sergeant,
R.S. Ellet,
Jas. L. Wheat, Quartermaster Sergt.,
Chas. E. Allan, 3d Duty Sergt.,
Isaac R. McIntosh, 4th Duty Sergt.,
Benj. Locke, 5th Duty Sergt.,
William Chase, Member,
John Sharp, San Andreas,
William N. Percy, 6th Duty Sergt.,
John A. Hill, 1st Corporal,
E.R. Sterling, 2d Corporal,
H.F. Woodman, 3d Corporal,
George F. Davis, 4th Corporal,
J.W. Ihren, 7th Corporal,
Henry C. Sherman, 8th Corporal.

Fairfax Court House, Va., August 5, 1863.

Messrs. Editors. - I have seen several letters published in the *Bulletin* in regard to Capt. Reed and the California Hundred. I pronounce so much of said letters as relates to the Company Fund and the treatment of his men on the passage to New York, as false; and who ever would write such statements must be utterly devoid of all honor or truth. The money is in my hands, and is drawn upon by Capt. Reed, as he may require for the use of the company.

In regard to the other statements made, I know nothing about them, as I have not been with the company since leaving Readville, Mass.

Hoping you will publish this, in justice to Capt. Reed, I have the honor to remain, your obdt. servant,

Archd. McKendry,
Captain, comdg. Co. G, 2d Mass. Cavalry

In Camp near Centerville, Va., August 15, 1863

Editor Bulletin. - In your paper, I lately read two letters from the "California Hundred." The first, written to a friend, is a mess of misstatements; the second (the two signers) contains some truths in relation to the company, but is untrue as regards Capt. Reed. In justice to Capt. Reed and for the satisfaction of many in San Francisco who contributed to the company fund, I propose to state a few facts concerning Capt. Reed, the company and the fund.

In the first place, every man was told before he enlisted that the only bounty he would receive would be the United States bounty of $100. Many said they did not want even that; if anyone had asked for more, he would have been booted out of the company. It was understood by all that the whole fund was to be used to uniform and equip the company. When we arrived at Readville, Mass., Capt. Reed stated to the Colonel his intention of buying saddles, arms, etc., for the company, but the Colonel persuaded him not to do so, as the saddles would be worn out and many of the arms lost or useless long before the three years would expire, and that he would then have to draw from the United States; that he might as well draw first as last, and save the fund. Capt. Reed finally concluded to keep the money as a company fund, to be used for the benefit of the sick and wounded, and also to purchase whatever might be necessary for the use of the company - the balance to be divided among the men at the end of the war. Capt. Reed stated this to the company, and it met with their approval.

When we arrived in Readville, the snow had been thawing and the mud was ankle deep. Many of our men had thin boots, worn out; they would have suffered greatly if they had been compelled to wait to draw from the Government. Capt. Reed immediately went to Boston and purchased 100 pairs of the best cavalry boots, which cost between $600 and $700. As it was, many of the men were sick for two or three weeks. In lounging around on the steamer, their caps had become soiled - so much so, that they were only fit for stable use. 100 caps were bought.

Whenever the men have wanted money they have drawn on the fund money for private use, to be paid in when pay day rolled around. On our trip down from Readville to Gloucester Point, everything that could be had was bought for the men's comfort. At Gloucester Point overalls were bought to keep their uniforms clean. (This was the second lot.) They are now wearing hats that arrived a few days ago, "made expressly for the California 100." In fact, the fund has been used in every way for the men's comfort - so much so, that it caused considerable trouble among the Massachusetts troops, until they learned that we had a company fund, and they still envy the men of the One Hundred their comforts. A strict account of every cent expended has been kept, and the balance is on hand. If Capt. Reed should be called away from the command to-morrow, I believe he would give an accurate account of everything, and turn the balance over to the company; but as long as he is in command of the company he will keep the fund, and use it as he has heretofore. All the excitement has been got up by a few, who no doubt think that they could use it to better advantage than Capt. Reed or any one else. There are many other instances that I could cite, where the company has received and enjoyed the benefits of the fund, but they would occupy too much space. If the fund had been divided when we arrived in Readville, I do not believe there are 20 men in the company who would have had a cent when we left.

The "two signers" say that "Capt. Reed's conduct to the men is that of a supercilious tyrant, " and they instance the case of E. Henry Allen, who was ordered to clean the Orderly Sergeant's horse. Allen was ordered to groom the horse by Lieut. Rumery. He refused, and the Lieutenant then ordered him to be tied up by the thumbs. Capt. Reed was absent at the time this occurred. When he returned he had him taken down, thereby incurring the displeasure of the commanding officer, for interfering with another officer when punishing a private for disobedience. The company never "waited on the captain and told him they would cut him down if he was not taken down."

The case of Ross and others, who were detailed for police duty, was more of the work of these mischief makers, (a mild term,) who spread the idea that it was menial duty, and to prove that they were right, quoted an article in the Army Regulations, which says that no non-commissioned officer or private shall do menial duty. If these men had read further there would have been no trouble, but they closed the book at that passage, and did not open it again until after the trouble. Those same men now do the work they refused to do then, and do it willingly, because they are satisfied that it is their duty, and that it is not menial.

The writer to a friend says that he has seen Capt. Reed "tremble" when there was an alarm at the picket lines. We have seen Capt. Reed *stand firm* when the enemy was before him and real work was to be done, and he was the first to enter into it. The officers and men of the company do not doubt his courage - they have seen it tried, and are satisfied. The same writer says that Capt. McKendry left the company on account of the fund. When we left Readville, Capt. Reed placed the fund in Capt. McKendry's hands, and has only been able to draw on it since then through him. He still has it in his possession.

To close, I would say of the men, (with the exception of the few mischief makers,) that I cannot speak too highly of them. They are always spoken of, wherever they go, as the best behaved and most quiet men in the army. Their courage is not questioned by friends or foes. I am proud to be connected with them.

Lieut. John W. Sim,
Company A, Cal. 100, 2d Mass. Cavalry

Evening Bulletin, San Francisco, Wednesday, September 16, 1863

Battalion

LETTERS FROM A CALIFORNIAN IN THE MASSACHUSETTS CONTINGENT

The following are copies of letters from a young man in the California Company E, of Second Massachusetts Cavalry, now stationed at Centreville, to his mother in this city, from which we are permitted to make extracts:

Camp Second Massachusetts Cavalry,
Centreville, Va., 45 miles from
Washington, August 5th, 1863.

Editors ALTA: Again having a few spare moments, and feeling pretty well and my wounded leg being considerably better, I will improve the present opportunity to write you. Our boys went out again last night, after some of Moseby's guerrillas, who have been committing depredations around here, such as tearing up the Alexandria and Ohio railroad. We have met Moseby's force three times; once at Ashby's Gap, where I was wounded, and again at Gum Springs, at the foot of Bull Run mountains, and captured prisoners, wagons, ammunition, and military stores, &c. Altogether, in both actions, we have had some ten men killed and fifteen or twenty wounded, and among the latter myself, and I consider it a very lucky escape for me, for I was not wounded in the back. Nine of us were mounted as a squad to intercept runaways, and coming upon eight or ten guerrillas they fired upon us, and I had the extreme satisfaction of settling the accounts with this world of the rebel who wounded me. That one thing has given me more satisfaction than all the doctor's stuff I have taken. My friend, Stephen Estelle, the young man you met me with on Second street, just after we had called at your house, was among the killed. My poor horse has also gone. I had formed quite an attachment for him. "Poor Burnside" was his name. He had already carried me safely through one fight, and behaved with more than ordinary common sense. We all think that one year will end the war. I hope so, and that the Government will pay our passage back to California. Please send me postage stamps. Note paper, here in Virginia, costs three cents a sheet, and as we have not been paid for a long time, of course have no money to buy with.

Your affectionate son,
(signed) Willie

[There is a Stephen H. Esten on the roster, however he survived the war and is interred in Evergreen Cemetery, Santa Cruz.]

Headquarters Cavalry Brigade,
Centreville, Va.,
Sunday, Aug. 9, 1863

I am again in the company, on duty, and will send you a few items on this occasion in answer to your welcome letter received a few days since. We are now in a brigade of cavalry encamped here. Our colonel now has the command of all the detachments of cavalry in this department. We are all in Gen. Heintzelman's department for the defence of Washington. There are encamped here part of the 14th New York, 6th Michigan and 1st Rhode Island cavalry, and our regiment. We have also been joined by the California Hundred and companies A, B, C, D, K of the First Battalion- altogether about 1200 efficient cavalrymen. We are encamped near Gen. King's headquarters. He has also here about 3,000 infantry and 300 or 400 cavalry, belonging to the Army of the Potomac. It was expected Lee or Stuart would try to turn our left flank at this place; hence a large force is kept here. Our duty and orders are for Col. Lowell to camp here at this post for the protection of Government property and trains from Moseby's attacks, as this road by the way of Alexandria and Fairfax Court House, is the only one between our Army of the Potomac and Washington.

We go out on a tour of fifty or sixty miles around Fairfax Court House every three days-that is, one company. Some one of the companies are out every day, and we have, almost every day, a brush with some of Moseby's cavalry.

Two days ago we captured forty wagons, which he had taken only the day before, within four miles of Alexandria, and our boys have had plenty of everything good. Some of the wagons were sutlers', and we have had lots of can fruit, boots, etc. I captured some five cans condensed milk, four cans turkey, two of peaches and four of strawberries; these are all worth $2.50 per can out in the front-so you see, for these few days, we have pretty good living, and our boys enjoy themselves and are contented as long as their appetites are satisfied.

Present my respects to all inquiring friends, and tell them I am well and not sorry that I ever entered the service of my country; and that although, through incapable and incompetent officers, we are subjected to very many petty annoyances and troubles, still, the cause is the same, and for our country's sake, we will strive to bear up to the end. This war cannot possibly outlive another year. In this hope we have much consolation. A letter at any time will be very acceptable; and don't forget to send a few stamps.

Very respectfully,

———

Alta California, San Francisco, Wednesday, September 9, 1863.
[William H. Moore, Co. E]

❖❖

OUR LETTER FROM ST. LOUIS.

———

{From the Resident Correspondent of the Alta California.}

———

St. Louis, August 11th, 1863.

THE CALIFORNIA BATTALION AFTER MOSEBY'S GUERRILLAS.

The California Battalion, in the Second Massachusetts Cavalry, is at work. Referring to a recent chase after Moseby's guerrillas, near Washington the correspondent of the *St. Louis Republican* writing August 4th, says:

Moseby was too closely followed by the Second Massachusetts Cavalry, under Col. Lowell, to escape with all his plunder. Col. Lowell's advance reached the neighborhood of Aldie late on the night after the raid, and finding itself close on the heels of the enemy, camped in the woods and threw out pickets. Before daybreak these pickets discovered other pickets within one hundred yards of them. A mutual hail was exchanged, but each party was too wary to tell the other which side it represented, and several hours were spent in a confab in which each side tried to pump the other, until just as day broke, when the Federal pickets cut the matter short by informing the enemy of their true character, This was followed by an attack from the rebel pickets, in which a Federal was killed. Lieut. Manning, commanding the advance, gathered up his men, 18 in all, and pushed the enemy's pickets back to their main encampment, a mile distant, when the captured plunder was discovered in charge of about 80 men, under Moseby himself. Lieutenant Manning charged them with such impetuosity and daring as to drive them away from the train, but Moseby rallied his men, came back on him and drove him in turn about a half mile, killing one and wounding two of the eighteen. He then went back and began setting the train in motion; but, Manning was not at all disposed to give it up so, and charging on him again, compelled him to turn his attention from the train and see to his self-protection. Again Mosby ran his annoying enemy back about a mile, sending oaths as well as bullets after them in lively style. But at this juncture Colonel Lowell appeared with the main force, and the rebels concluded that it was time to make tracks. They drove off a few wagons, cut the mules out of others, and attempted to burn everything they left behind; but our cavalry dashed into them, capturing many of the wagons and some prisoners. The last seen of Moseby he was disappearing over a hill, driving his troops before him and fanning himself with his broadbrim white hat.

During the skirmish with Col. Lowell's advance some of his men captured a Union trooper, and tried to kill him, after he had surrendered, by shooting him, the ball striking a memorandum book in his breast pocket, smashing a heavy gold pen, and spending its force in an ugly bruise. Mosby came up soon afterwards, and getting an inkling of what was going on, demanded to know who shot the prisoner. All of the scoundrels swore off, and Moseby applied to the prisoner himself, who informed him several fired on him, and he could not tell which one hit him. The chieftain had drawn his revolver when he first arrived, and shaking the weapon at the guilty squad, swore he would like to shoot the man who did it, shamed them for their conduct, and threatened, if another case of the kind happened, to kill all concerned. This is the kind of man he is-queer too, for a guerilla. This tale is told by the prisoner himself. The Second Massachusetts cavalry is composed entirely of Californians, and is a match for Moseby or any other guerrilla.

Alta California, San Francisco, Thursday, September 3, 1863.

❖❖❖

From The Seat of War. - Our old neighbor Charley Briggs, writes us a long letter, dated at Centreville, Va., in which he gives us a graphic picture of the events of the campaign in Virginia. We have not space to publish his letter at length, although it is quite interesting. The friends of Billy McNeil and Fred Quant, both Napa boys, will be glad to learn that they are all well. "Long Williams," who formerly kept a fruit store in Napa, has been in the hospital at Washington for seven months, and at the date of our correspondent's letter, (Aug. 17th,) was going to join his regiment. He belongs to the Missouri Sharpshooters. The writer says: "he isn't any shorter than when he was in Napa." Charley's present address is, Washington, D.C., California 100, Company A., Mass. Cavalry.

The Napa County Reporter, Napa, Saturday, September 19, 1863.

❖❖❖

Hd Qrs Cav Forces Dept Wash
Centerville Aug 20th 1863

Col L.C. Baker
  Washington;

Colonel

I see by the papers that there has been some secession troubles in California, and it is reported here that a force of regular troops are being sent there. If this is the case it would be against the interest of California to try to raise troops there to come here, on the contrary the five companies which I have helped raise, now here, should be sent there first, as they intend to return there when discharged, and are ardently devoted to the interest and safety of that State. They were all enlisted there, and are entitled by army regulations to be discharged there, and transportation provided to San Francisco, so the Government would gain by sending them in preference to other troops. A large proportion of these companies are composed of the most intelligent, and patriotic young men in California and would make good officers and non-commissioned officers for new regiments if more should be raised. They have now been in the service about seven months, and came on here intending to do their best for the cause of the country, but if California which they all love so well, is in any danger from rebels within or foreign foes without they would much prefer to go back and fight there, one half of the efficiency of the California Companies has been destroyed by being attached to the 2d Ms Cavalry which is controlled by a small clique of young Boston aristocracy, who to advance their own personal interests have already broken the agreement, pledges, good faith and honorable obligations of the State of Massachusetts made to us before coming here. The

Governor accepted the Battalion as a representative force from California in the war at the East, to remain intact, and be officered and filled by Californians. This Battalion has been broken up by order of Col Lowell, against the protest and wishes of all, two companies remaining with me, and one assigned to each of the other Battalions, whose commanders are personal friends of his, for the purpose of giving them a respectable command, which they had not, and could not get otherwise. There are about four hundred and fifty of our Californians with fourteen officers in the Regiment, while there are but about one hundred and fifty Massachusetts soldiers, with some thirty officers including all the Field and Staff but myself, and the officers of seven skeleton companies. All the fighting and important service has been done by the Californians, but Col Lowell and the 2d Ms Cavalry have all the public and official credit given the regiment. As we are doing our country service we do not mind this, but we do not wish to be used and treated by the officers, and in a regiment, of another State, like hirelings for the purpose of making promotions and reputations for officers which we have all become to hate, and despise. It is very hard for the officers and men of these fine companies, who came from California with such high hopes of doing good service for the cause of the Union, and at the same time making a reputation for themselves and their State, to be used as machines to accomplish the agrandizement of a few officers who do nothing or care nothing for them, or their State, and who have tried to order out and crush out every thing Californian about them. If the War Department would detach these Companies from the 2d Ms Cavalry and send them to California where they are anxious to go if there is war in that State, or let them act here as a California Cavalry Battalion which they were raised for I know they would do much more and better service than as they are now, and at the same time an act of justice, and I might say humanity, would be done to as fine and brave a body of men and soldiers as ever formed under our Flag. If troops should not be wanted in California seven new companies could be raised there and join these five and make a splendid regiment here, or they could go there and help form one. The California Companies are designated in the 2d Ms Cavalry as Cos. A, E, F, L and M, and any change should include all officers, and men enrolled, and mustered in California. Please submit these matters to the Secretary of War and try and do something for us. Every man in California would be glad to see us out of our unfortunate position. I am Colonel Most Respt Yours

D.W.C. Thompson
Maj. Cal Cav Batt
2Ms Cav

Record Group 393. entry 5818, National Archives, Washington, D.C.

In Camp Centreville,
Aug. 22/63

Maj. Genl. H. W. Halleck,
> Genl. in Chief

General,
  I have the honor to enclose copies of letters referred to me by Gov. Andrews of Massachusetts, with endorsements. It is evident that there has been an entire misapprehension as to Major Thompson's wishes - he nowhere suggests the detachment of his present Battalion from the 2nd Mass. Cavalry - nothing was further from his mind at time of writing. He wishes permission to raise in Cala for service in the East a new Regiment (three new Battalions) to be

called the 3rd Cala Vol. - to be officered partly by promotions from 2nd Mass. Cavl, partly by selections from the Cala Cavalry - the regiment to be raised in California under the same conditions and with the same assistance as the Govt. offers to new Volunteer regiments in Massachusetts or New York, except that the selection of officers is to be approved not by the Gov. of the State but by the War Dept. or Genl. Wright, the intention being to avoid all political appointments - the regiment to be accepted by the U.S. Govt. in Cala & to be brought to the East at U.S. expense. In forwarding Major Thompson's proposition again, I take the liberty of giving you my opinion upon three points:

1st - From Major Thompson's success in raising my 2nd Battalion and from frequent conversation on the subject with the officers from Cala, I am convinced that no one could undertake the recruiting of such a regiment with better chance of success than he - & that his estimate of dates when the several Battalions are likely to be ready, is probably not far out of the way.

2nd - From the excellent judgement displayed in the choice of officers for his present Battalion, I am convinced that the War Dept. would have no reason to disapprove of any officers whom Major Thompson might select for a new regiment raised in a similar manner.

3rd - The men composing my present Cala Battalion are of the class of which our first Eastern regiments were made up - all young, vigorous and zealous - all hating a rebel - too good for hunting horse thieves (as Major Thompson suggests for them), but on that or any other duty worth three of the ordinary recruits now picked up in our Eastern Cities. This is my deliberate opinion, after experience.

I think it but right to state my opinion in the above points; with other reasons for or against Major Thompson's plan I have nothing to do.

Respectfully your Obdservt

C.R. Lowell, Jr.

Col. 2 Mass. Cavl.

Regimental Record Books, National Archives, Washington, D.C.

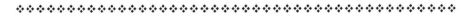

OUR LETTER FROM WASHINGTON, D.C.

_____

{From the Resident Correspondent of the Alta California.}

_____

Washington, Aug. 22, 1863.

The California Cavalry.

On Sunday evening the officers in command of the corps of the defences of the Potomac, embracing Chain Bridge, hearing of depredations committed by Moseby's gang a few miles back of the bridge on the road to Fairfax Court House, ordered out a skirmishing party of twenty-four men, under Captain C.S. Eigenbrodt, of the Massachusetts Second Cavalry, (Californians) who, traveling all night overtook them early in the morning, and, though Moseby had between thirty and forty men, Captain Eigenbrodt gallantly gave chase. The "bushwhackers" prudently flew, pursued by our men so hotly that they were obliged to lighten themselves of plunder as they went along, literally strewing the road for over seven miles in the direction of Fairfax Court House. Captain Eigenbrodt's horses being much jaded by the previous night's reconnoitering he was reluctantly forced to give up further pursuit, which he did, bringing off two men - our own recaptured - five horses fully equipped, and a considerable amount of plunder. Captain E. and his brave little company deserve much credit for the fearless and gallant manner in which they discharged their duty on this occasion.

Alta California, San Francisco, Wednesday, September 16, 1863.

Centerville Augst 25th 1863

My dear Mammy

I have just returned from an other long tramp after Mosby. We had 100 horse coming out to us from Washington 30 men leading them out, & having contrary to orders started without the Regular Guard which comes out every day, & which they were ordered to join. Mosby with 80 men attacked them suddenly in front & from behind, & a short but sharp fight ensued. The Sergt in command of my men & 5 others were killed several wounded & 10 taken prisoner. The Rebel loss was 1 Capt killed 1 Lieut badly wounded & 4 men killed. We don't know how many wounded. Mosby was badly wounded in the chest & in the groin & is concealed somewhere in the woods now. We did not get word of this until 4 hours after it had taken place. We saddled up & gave chase but his men divided up into small parties & took to the woods. We captured a few of them & recaptured 19 horses had a very hard ride & got back at 12 o'clk last night. I have today sent out two parties to comb the woods & examine all the farm houses near where the fight took place & hope to take Mosby. However it is almost like hunting for a needle in a hay stack. On our way back to Camp one of my Capts. suddenly became crazy, & thought that we were going to hang him. All of a sudden he darted into the woods & got away from us. We hunted two hours for him but could not find him. This morning he returned to Camp of his own account & is still as crazy as a coot. *[Capt. D.A. DeMerritt, see T.H.M. letter of September 6, 1863]*

Everything goes on well here although I wish we were not worked quite as hard. The Regt needs drill & discipline and if I could have one month of leasure I could make a splendid Regt of it, but as it is we are on the raid almost all the time.

By the by several of the Officers came to me the other day & said that if Col Lowell was made Brig. Gen. that all the officers had determined to send in a petition to Gov. Andrews asking to have me made Colonel. I was very much pleased to find that they liked me as an officer, for Comdg Officers are not apt to be liked, particularly if he happens to be younger than most of his officers, as is my case. However I thanked them, but said that I should prefer to have things take their own course.

The Colonel & I get on very well together. He is a very brilliant man, but is to hasty in his judgement of men & things, and is so very ambitious, that he sacrifices everything for advancement. Major Forbes is, as I have always said, one of the finest fellows I have ever met with. I had a pleasant letter from Charles the other day.

Well I must close this note - give my love to all -

I hope Cora likes her wagon - Fanny I hope is getting on well now. Your affectionate son
        Caspar

P.S.
My man John has not turned up yet. I don't care though as I have a good man from one of the companies.

Caspar Crowninshield, Letters, Massachusetts Historical Society
["I have a good man" the muster rolls for this period show Henry Mazy, Co. A., as officer's servant.]

MOSBY'S OPERATIONS IN VIRGINIA

Another Large Haul of Sutlers' Wagons.

Mosby Dangerously Wounded.

New York, Aug. 27. The *Times'* special Washington dispatch states that Mosby's operations in our immediate front are assuming rather gigantic proportions. From a band of 60 desperados his force has grown to 800 able-bodied guerillas, who prey upon everything that passes between Fairfax and Warrenton. Early yesterday morning with his whole force, he attacked a sutlers' train between Centreville and Bull Run, captured 41 wagons with their teams, a number of Government horses and much other property on its way to the army.

A Washington dispatch in the *Herald* states that it is generally believed that Mosby was fatally wounded on Monday. It says: "On Monday Mosby led a force toward Annandale, while a portion of White's command scoured the neighborhood of Falls Church and Bailey's Cross Roads. Upon that day a large drove of cattle and horses had been sent out to the front from Alexandria, and the horses falling behind the cattle and having a small escort, were attacked near Annandale by Mosby, who succeeded in capturing a number of animals and escaping without loss.

A short time after, the 8th Pennsylvania cavalry came up, overtook the guerillas, and after a sharp fight recaptured most of the horses. The guerillas scattered and fled as far as Mills' Cross Roads, where they collected, and sent back a small wagon for a wounded officer who had been left near the scene of the engagement. Securing the wounded man, the rebels passed up the Leesburg pike through Drainsville, to which point they were pursued by our cavalry without success.

All of the inhabitants along the route taken by the guerillas state that the wounded man was Mosby, and that his injuries are regarded by his men as being of a very dangerous character, the ball entering his back below the shoulder blade. The wound bled profusely, and in many places on the route the vehicle could be traced by the drops of blood in the road. As the party were careful to carry the wounded man to Leesburg before he could receive medical attention, it is very probable that death has now ensued.

White is now in the Bull Run mountains near Goose Creek, from which point he can at any time dash down upon us without a moment's warning.

The 2d Massachusetts cavalry has done good service in chasing up the guerillas and preventing depredations, but until a larger force is sent in pursuit of White we shall continue to hear of his operations in this vicinity. He has been driven beyond the mountains several times during the last month, only to follow back upon the heels of our returning cavalry, capture men and horses and again escape. It is to be hoped hereafter that the rebel cavalry will, at least, be kept outside our fortifications."

Boston Journal, Boston, Thursday, August 27, 1863.
Evening Transcript, Boston, Thursday, August 27, 1863.
Alta California, San Francisco, Friday, August 28, 1863

Guerilla Warfare on the Upper Potomac. *Washington, 29th..* Some of Scott's 900 men have recently been making reconnaissances on the line of the Ohio and Chesapeake Canal. There was no appearance of the enemy on Thursday, but at one o'clock yesterday morning, two pickets belonging to a force of 64 men who were stationed at Edward's Ferry, when about two miles above, were fired upon, one shot striking Alonzo Picket of Co. D, going through his jaw, and inflicting a dangerous wound. They were both captured, and after being deprived of their horses and arms, were permitted to return to camp. Capt. Halleck, with 16 men, set out on a reconnoiter; four of his advance were captured, and found the camp in possession of 300 or 400 men, supposed to be Moseby's or White's. The reserve which had been left here was attacked and retired to the pits in the rear, where they were when last heard from.

Our forces at Muddy Branch, yesterday, captured two men, one of whom admits he piloted Stuart into Maryland previous to the battle of Gettysburg.

Official information was received today at Gen. Heintzelman's headquarters of a skirmish on Monday last, between a detachment of the 2d Massachusetts cavalry regiment and California regiment, and Moseby's men. The attack by Moseby was made at Carlyle's tavern, on Little River turnpike, a few miles this side of Fairfax, at 2 P.M. Our men, numbering only twenty-five, were attacked in front and rear at the same time, but fought manfully. Our loss was two killed, three wounded and nine taken prisoners, together with all the horses our men had in charge, fifteen of which, however, were afterward recaptured, leaving eighty-five still in the hands of the rebels. The loss of the enemy was one captain and lieutenant killed, and one lieutenant and three privates wounded. Moseby himself was wounded in two places, in the side and thigh. His wounds are regarded as mortal. Col. Lowell pursued the enemy as far as Snicker's Gap, but they succeeded in making their escape by reason of having constant relays of fresh horses.

Evening Transcript, Boston, Monday, August 31, 1863.
Boston Saturday Evening Gazette; Saturday, August 29, 1863
New York Tribune, Tuesday, September 1, 1863.
[Scott's 900- 11th New York Cavalry, Col. James B. Swain]

Col. Lowell's Cavalry. The National Intelligencer states that it was Col. Lowell's command of cavalry consisting of three regiments, which inflicted the repulse upon Mosby's guerillas, already reported, on Monday, after a severe engagement.

Evening Transcript, Boston, Saturday, August 29, 1863.

Warrenton Junction, August 30.-We have just received a despatch from Fairfax, saying that five guerrillas were captured at that place this morning who state that Moseby was shot twice, in the bowels and breast, and had been taken to Richmond.

The cavalry that brought in the prisoners state that they were informed by citizens of Drainsville, yesterday, that Moseby died near that place on Friday. Prisoners do not doubt the report, as he was pronounced mortally wounded. White is now in command of the Confederate forces north of the railroad.

Alta California, San Francisco, Wednesday, September 2, 1863.
New York Tribune, Tuesday, September 1, 1863.

❖❖❖

When Mosby's Saddle was Emptied.

To the Editor National Tribune:

In a late issue of The Tribune I noticed a letter from R. P. McRay, of the Eleventh Pennsylvania cavalry, in reference to the fight at South Anna Bridge and the charge of the California One Hundred. This reminds me of the bravest little fight, either on or off record, which was participated in by the said California One Hundred and battalion. August 24, 1863, a detail of twenty-four men from the California One Hundred and battalion, while bringing from Washington 104 horses, and bound for Centerville, Va., were attacked by eighty Confederates under Mosby. The attack was made from the woods, upon both rear and front, Moseby leading the charge in front. At the first fire four of our men were killed and seven wounded. As quickly as possible the boys dismounted (as to each one of their saddles three led horses were fastened, and fought the guerillas on foot, with the result that they killed seven and wounded a like number among the latter being Mosby himself, and saved twenty-five horses. Our loss was four killed, seven wounded, and seven taken prisoners out of twenty-four men engaged.

If anyone can show a braver fight than that with as good results, let him write it up, and we of the One Hundred and battalion will give him the palm. Moseby's wounds were very serious, and for six months we heard nothing from him or his guerillas. To Carlos M. Jenkins, of the battalion, now of Los Angeles, Cal., belongs the credit of wounding Mosby, and under very trying circumstances, as at the first fire he and his horse were wounded, the horse being killed instantly, and falling upon Jenkins' wounded ankle, pinning him to the ground. In that position, lying on the ground, he opened, however, upon the rebel advance with his two six-shooters, lifting Moseby out of the saddle, and making it warm for the rest while his shots lasted. He was taken prisoner, and was fifteen months in Andersonville.

S. G. Corbett,
California One Hundred,
No. 311 Taylor St., San Francisco, Cal.

The National Tribune, Washington, D.C., Thursday, October 4, 1883.
[Samuel J. Corbett, Co. A; Carlos M. Jenkins, Co. E: Battle of Gooding's Tavern]

❖❖❖

Where Mosby's Saddle Was Emptied.

To the Editor National Tribune:
  In a recent issue of The Tribune I noticed a letter from S. G. Corbett, of the California One Hundredth, describing a fight in which I took part and in which the details were not fully correct, and I now wish more fully to describe. On August 24, 1863, parts of companies A, F and L, of the Second Massachusetts cavalry, under command of Sergeants Barnum and Short, were detailed to take 100 horses to Washington, D.C., and there turn them over to the proper authorities, and again draw 104, and return with them to Centreville, Va., a distance of twenty-seven miles. While enroute we were met by some eighty or one hundred Confederates, under command of Mosby, all mounted. Just before meeting Mosby, however, we had passed the Eleventh Pennsylvania, who were going home on furlough, and they had gone but a short distance when we were attacked by Mosby in front. I was in the advance in line and saw the guerrillas as they came out of the brush in single file and formed in fours as they got out in the road. Someone in front exclaimed, "There they are now, boys!" and at this moment the firing began. As quickly as possible some of our boys commenced dismounting (as each one of us was leading horses fastened to our saddles), and we commenced fighting, our men in front firing first. They returned the same immediately, killing four of our men and wounding seven, while seven more were taken prisoners out of a detachment of twenty-seven men. We had nothing but our side-arms - revolvers and sabers - and we had no cartridges but what were in our revolvers, and there was no escort with us. Six of us escaped, and had not the Eleventh Pennsylvania heard our firing and returned, we would have all been captured. The writer was among the number that escaped, and I left on foot, as my horse was killed. This all occurred within our lines. If any of the boys can throw any further light upon this subject, I would be pleased to hear from them.

Benj. F. Beeth,
Private of Co. F, 2d Mass. Cav.

Warren, Maron Co., Mo.

The National Tribune, Washington, D.C., Thursday, November 8, 1883.
[Benjamin F. Beeth, Co. F; William H. Short, Co. F; Sgt. Barnum should read Varnum, Joseph B., Co. M]

Centervil Aug 30th, 1863

  I recived your letter of the 25th and was glad to here from you and to here that you are all wel I am in first rate helth and thare is not much sicknes in eny of the camps about here, the nites are geting quite cool and we begin to want our blankets witch we left in Washington. We have spent the pased weak in hunting Moesby as usual without much suckses. Last saduday twentyfive men of this ridg went to Washington with 100 condemned horses and started back on monday with as menny new ones when about half way through they wer atacked by Moesby with 60 men they wer taken by serprise but forte as wel as they could under the circumstances each man had three horses hitched to his saddle and when the rebs charged in among them nearly all were dismounted by thare horses geting tangeld and thrown, but som of the boys got together at an old house clos by and emted thare pistols among them and then made thear escape as best they cold the rebs got most of the horses and seven or eight prisners and left fore of thare number dead and one wounded in the road the wounded one was brot in to camp but has since died. Of our men two wer kiled and one wounded throw the stomack he is not expected to recover. 10 of the men belonged to this Co and the rest to the Cal. Bat. One of the kiled and the wounded one belong to this Co. As soon as the news got to camp the hole ridg started in presute and we chased them for three days but only got a few prisners but they say that Moesby was severly wounded in the scrape and we have hered since that he is not ex-pected to live but we cannot find whare he is I hope he has got his dose. I recive my paper reguly evry weak I wish you wold send me som more stamps as I am most out give my love to all hands.

Sam Hanscom

Courtesy of Bruce MacAlpine, Concord, MA.

LETTER FROM A CALIFORNIAN IN THE MASSACHUSETTS CAVALRY, IN SERVICE IN VIRGINIA

CAMP NEAR CENTREVILLE, VIRGINIA,
August 30, 1863.

Join the Regiment

Editors Alta: This morning, having no guard duty to perform, I concluded that my time could not be more pleasantly or profitably employed than in giving you some account of our doings for the last month, and acting upon that conclusion I will now proceed to do so. About the 26th of July, orders were received at Gloucester Point for our battalion of cavalry to report, as soon as possible, to our regiment, then at Camp Wyndham, opposite Washington City. With great alacrity preparations were accordingly made to so as it had long been our wish to get with the regiment, and to see our friends in the California battalion; therefore, but a few days elapsed, after the reception of the order, before we were in Washington, making the trip to that place by water, in a small, slow coach of a steamboat. On our arrival at Washington we marched through Pennsylvania Avenue, and then down to the Long Bridge, crossed it, and were soon at Camp Wyndham, at which place we did not find any more of the regiment than those who were on the sick list. Those few, however, welcomed us with three cheers and a tiger, and we returned the compliment by doing likewise for the California battalion. At this camp we remained for five days, and we were heartily glad when ordered away from there, as it was the most unhealthy camp we had been in during our life as soldiers.

Picket Duty- After Guerrillas

From there our Company proceeded to Fort Ethan Allen, defences of Washington, and camped in its vicinity on a high bluff, on the south side of the Potomac, overlooking the Chain Bridge, and it proved to be the most pleasant camp we had yet been in, and we flattered our-selves with the hope that we might remain there a long time, but were sadly disappointed. Our duty at this place consisted of standing picket at night only, at a place called Langley, outside of the defences of Washington. We were on duty every night, but still we were satisfied to remain there. We had been there but just one week, however, when we were relieved by another company from our regiment, and ordered to report at Centreville, which was accordingly done, but on our way up we met two sutlers whom Moseby and his gang had robbed but a short time before we met them, and having a guide with us who knew every foot of the country, we started after the guerrillas, hoping to overtake them, and pursued them rapidly as far as Gum Springs, (hearing of them all along the route as being but a short distance ahead,) when the guide declared it would be useless to pursue them further, and we had to return as we went, empty-handed, beside losing two horses, killed by the severity of the ride. The next day we came across four or five sutler's wagons, in a ravine a hundred yards from the road, and helped ourselves to such eatables as we found, which the guerrillas in their hurry had been compelled to leave behind, and we felt very thankful to Moseby for leaving us so much. A soldier has no pity at all for the misfortunes of a sutler, as they are in the habit of charging soldiers an extortionate price for everything they sell to them, and when a chance offers to make up this extortion, it is gladly taken advantage of. On the third day after leaving the Fort, we arrived at this camp, and it is probable we shall remain here all winter, unless the rebels drive us out.

The business we are engaged in here is hunting up guerrillas, and trying to keep the country between this place and the Blue Ridge clear of them; but, thus far, we have not been very successful. We have chased them and hunted for them, it is true, but they are just as thick as ever in the country it is our business to keep them out of. Whenever we find them, they always have us at a disadvantage. They are kept well informed of our movements, and with the small force which Colonel Lowell has to operate against them with, it is impossible to keep the country clear of them. They remain in this section for the purpose of plunder, and I am sorry to say, that as thieves, they are very successful. As for fighting, it is something they will not do, unless they greatly outnumber us and there can be no doubt of a certainty of success.

Moseby after the Horses

On the 24th inst., as a Sergeant and twenty-four men were bringing out to this camp ninety-nine good horses, in place of the same number of condemned ones, which they had taken in to Washington, each man leading three and riding the fourth, they were attacked by Moseby and seventy of his gang on the turnpike road, about half-way between this camp and Alexandria, at 3 o'clock P.M., and they succeeded in taking seventy-five of the horses, making ten of the men prisoners, and killing Sergeant Varnum, of California, Company M; Private J. D. McCarty, of the Hundred, and seriously wounding Private Vierick, also of the Hundred. Our men were attacked at a place in the road where it was not much wider than to admit of the passage of four horses abreast, which was the order they were marching in, and the first knowledge they had of the guerrillas was hearing the report of their pistols, and a shower of bullets whistling around them. Many of the horses were wounded, and commenced rearing and plunging, throwing many of the men from their horses and all into confusion. About ten of the men succeeded in getting into a place where they could show fight, and did so until they had emptied their pistols, killing five guerrillas, and, it is reported, seriously wounding Moseby, when that better part of valor, discretion, prevailed, and jumping from the road over a fence, they hid themselves in the high weeds until the guerrillas left, which they did in five minutes after the attack was made. When the news reached this camp of what had occurred, the regiment was started out after them, but after a two days search, returned, as usual, unsuccessful. An investigation is now being made in Washington, with the view of ascertaining on whom the responsibility rests for the smallness of the escort with the horses, and I sincerely hope that whoever it may be, will be made to suffer the greatest punishment allowed.

Promotions, etc.

The Captain of our Company (Reed) has been promoted to the position of Major within the last two weeks, and he now promises, as he has left the Company, to distribute the money amongst us which is in his hands of the Company Fund, and steps have been taken to have the distribution come off as quick as possible. Our First Lieutenant (Rumery) has been promoted to a Captaincy and our Second Lieutenant J. W. Sim, has been promoted to the First Lieutenancy of our Company, and a few days after his promotion he was presented by the Company with an elegant sabre, belt and pistol holster, the whole costing $125. Captain Washburn, a Massachusetts man, is now our Captain, and, so far, is liked very well; and as for the Second Lieutenant, we have none. The weather here is very pleasant during the day, but the nights are nearly cold enough for frost. Fruit is plentiful in this vicinity, but the quality is the poorest I ever saw. It is all seedling fruit, and that accounts for its worthlessness. Those who have lived here a long time say that grafted fruit does not do well in this climate, so they are for ever barred from one of the greatest accessories to the enjoyment of a country life- in not having good fruit.

I have now given you about all the news that would be interesting, and the bugle is sounding the call for hungry soldiers to walk up and get their beans, and I must therefore come to a halt.

T. D. B.

Alta California, San Francisco, Monday, September 28, 1863.

❖❖❖

The 2d Cavalry. George W. Veirick, Co. A, 2d Mass. Cavalry, died of gunshot wounds, August 31st. During the month of August 24 men from this regiment were sent to the general hospital, and 54 remain sick in the regimental hospital.

Evening Transcript, Boston, Friday, September 18, 1863.
[George W. Vierick was wounded at Gooding's Tavern, Fairfax, Va.]

❖❖❖

SEPTEMBER, 1863
7   Confederates evacuate Battery Wagner and Morris Island
19-20 Battle of Chickamauga

❖❖❖

The Cavalry Fight Near Centreville.

Camp Cavalry Forces,
Near Centreville, Sept. 1st, 1863.

To the Editor of The Boston Journal:

In your issue of August 27th I notice an article headed "Mosby and his operations in Virginia," giving the honor of the little fight that occurred on the 24th, between our men and

Mosby's, to the Pennsylvania Eighth Regiment. Wishing to give honor to whom honor is due, I will simply state the facts as they occurred. On Saturday, August 22d, a detail was made from Company A, and from every Company in the California Battalion-in all 25 men, from the Second Massachusetts Cavalry, to take some condemned horses to Washington. They went through to their destination without accident or trouble of any kind. On their return from Washington on the 24th, with 102 good horses for the regiment, almost three miles this side of Fairfax they were attacked by Mosby, and his gang of guerillas, in all about one hundred men. Our boys were taken entirely by surprise, being attacked both in front and rear at the same time. At the first fire from the guerillas the horses that the men were leading (each one having four) commenced to rear and plunge furiously, thereby dismounting several of the men, throwing them under the horses' feet, causing to some of them severe injuries. As soon as the boys got clear of the horses, they commenced firing on the guerillas, causing three to bite the dust immediately, and wounding three others, two of whom have since died. The other one who was wounded but got away, has since proved to be Mosby himself. He was wounded in two places. It was reported in camp, yesterday, that he had died of his wounds. Our loss is two killed, two wounded, and nine taken prisoners-one killed, one wounded, and one taken prisoner out of the California 100, Mosby making off with seventy-five of the horses. If we had had twenty-five more men with the detail, acting as guard, I think Mosby and his gang would have got what they so richly deserve-a good, sound thrashing. As for the Pennsylvania Eighth, the first we ever heard of them was when we read the article in your paper in reference to the fight.

S. J. C.

The Boston Journal, Friday, September 4, 1863.
[Samuel J. Corbett, Co. A]

Centervile, Sep 6th, 1863

Dear parents

        I have not recived eny letter from you this last weak and supose that it hase ben delayde on the road. We have ben dooing the same old round of duty as usual onley we have not ben out on a scout this weak. We have not heard enything of Moesby latley onley that he is dead but that needs conferming thare is no doaut that he was badley wounded the other day and may be dead. Our man that was wounded died three days ago that makes five men that have gonin since we have ben in the war and som have ben discharged and others transferd to other companys so that we dont muster more than seventyfive now and not more than fifty for dooty. Cap Read is to be permoted to major and Cap Washben is to have comand of this company. Our horses are in bad conditon and with the hundred that Moesby got from us leavs nearly half of the ridg dismounted. I am in good helth and so are most of the ridg the wether is geting quite cool and comfertbale but the flies are so thick here in the tent that I cant rite enymore, give my love to all hands

Sam Hanscom

Courtesy of Bruce MacAlpine, Concord, MA.

OUR LETTER FROM THE CALIFORNIANS
IN THE MASSACHUSETTS CAVALRY, IN
SERVICE IN VIRGINIA.

(From the Correspondent of the ALTA CALIFORNIA accompanying the Battalion.)

In Camp, Near Centreville, Virginia,
September 6th, 1863.

Editors ALTA:- We have been going from one place to another in search of guerrillas until we have brought up at this place, which is intended for our headquarters, until we again "change our base" of operations, and go somewhere else. Truly the maxim that "one knows not what to-morrow will bring forth," is verified here every day, almost every hour, for one moment we may be sleeping soundly, and the next be awakened by the bugle and called on to saddle and be off. At Alexandria we had a beautiful camp on the banks of the Potomac; our Sibley tents were nicely pitched, the Company streets clean; indeed everything was arranged with a view to the health, comfort and efficiency of the men, under the orders and personal supervision of Major Thompson, who never loses an opportunity to add to the comfort and pleasure of his "California boys," for which he daily wins a stronger hold upon their affections, and he is entitled to the grateful thanks of the men composing the California Battalion, for the interest he has ever manifested in their welfare. Finding that the camp at Alexandria was too far from where the Regiment was operating, it was moved here to Centreville, and now here we are encamped on the very spot occupied by the rebels two years ago. On the west of our camp, on the top of a ridge commanding the valley, are still standing the earth-works and fortifications erected by the rebels under Beauregarde. These, though dismantled, could with little labor be made available, but "the powers that be" seem to think that they will never again come into requisition, for they take no pains to keep them from going to ruins. Yet many are of the opinion that another great battle will yet be fought on the old field of Bull Run. I was astonished the other day when I saw how near the rebel troops had been to Washington. Traveling through the woods, I came to an old camp of a South Carolina Regiment within seven miles of that city; on the trees, over the letters "7th S. C. V." were cut the names or initials of rebel soldiers who had encamped there. But one thing is certain, they will never again pollute the "sacred soil" by their armed presence.

Centreville and Vicinity.

If there is any locality that has more than another suffered from the ravages of war, it is this. The sin of secession certainly was great, but the punishment which has justly been meted out to the inhabitants of the border counties of Virginia is well nigh commensurate with their deserts. Nearly every house in Centreville has been either burned or torn down, and the whole country around it has been devastated. Fairfax Court House, the county seat, has also suffered to a great extent, but it ought to be razed to the ground, for it has ever been, and is now, the hiding place and resort for the guerrillas that infest the country around it. The citizens too, have suffered a great deal, and many of them are driven to awful straits-fallen from wealth and luxury to poverty and want; their slaves have left them, compelling the masters to labor for their bread. I have seen ladies who, before the war broke out considered themselves "F. F. V.'s," and altogether too good to work, but who are now to be seen peddling pies, cakes, and such things, to Union soldiers-not because they have any sympathy for our cause, but because they are driven to it by straits of necessity, with starvation staring them in the face. But they have brought this state of things upon themselves, and now must suffer the just consequences of their treason; yet in many cases it seems hard. I have learned that to be a *good* cavalry soldier here, one is required to have a heart as hard as adamant, and a determination which nothing can change, Picture in your "minds eye" a scene like this, and tell what you would do under the circumstances: A lot of our men go out on a horse-capturing expedition; a squad of them ride up to a house; a search ensues, and a horse is found, just as you are about leading the horse away, out comes the old lady and the girls; a beautiful girl throws herself on her knees before you, and, with uplifted eyes, begs you not to take away poor old "Tobe;" she tells you how they have raised him from a colt, and is now the only horse they have left; another girl throws her arms around the old horse's neck and kisses his honest cheek, while tears flow in torrents down her own. Reader, I know not what *you* would do, but I felt like saying: "Young ladies, keep your poor old horse, and if that does not satisfy you, take mine, too." But orders are orders, and must be obeyed; a halter is put on the horse, and he is led away, leaving the entire household in tears.

A Visit to the Battle-field of Bull Run.

On Sunday last I availed myself of an opportunity to visit the celebrated battle-field of Bull Run. Passing through the dilapidated town of Centreville, we took a road running nearly South. A gallop of four miles over this road and we could perceive that we were approaching the battle-field, broken-down or burnt gun-carriages, caissons and other ordnance could be seen on every hand, There they are, evidences of the awful panic that brought defeat to our brave but inexperienced soldiers. Having crossed Bull Run, which is quite a creek, over a shaky bridge, we came to a large stone house by the roadside; this is known as the "Stone Hospital," having been used as such during both battles. An old man lives there; he was present and witnessed both the sanguinary conflicts; he kindly volunteered to show us the "sights"- awful "sights" they are, indeed. Around the house, in the yard and under the trees are the graves of those who fell there. Leaving the road we pass over a field, scattered over which may yet be seen knapsacks, broken muskets and other soldier accouterments, while here and there are seen solid shot and shell in large quantities. Some of the latter have exploded, but most of them have not and are still charged; also broken ordinance and other implements of war. After scouring some relics we pass on and soon reach the spot where the battle raged most fiercely, and here we saw "sights" that will long dwell in our memories: the skeletons of the brave ones who fell in that bloody conflict lay on the top of the ground, uncovered and exposed to view- not one or two, but hundreds. Some of these had never been buried at all, only a little earth had been thrown over them, and this has been washed away by the rains, leaving the remains entirely uncovered; again, where the dead had been buried in shallow trenches, the earth settled and the water had washed it away, leaving rows of skeletons exposed to view. We noticed particularly the skeleton of a Union soldier (we could tell by the blue clothes) lying by the root of a tree, with his musket lying across his body; he had never been buried; doubtless was wounded, crawled to this tree, and there died. It is a burning shame that the Government allows these remains of humanity to thus remain unburied. Sickened by the horrid sights around us, we turned our horses' heads campward, gave them a loose rein, and were ere long, inside the lines of our camp.

Doings of the California Battalion.

Since my last, which was written at Alexandria, our Battalion has been engaged in the most active service. When General Meade's great Army of the Potomac moved on to the Rappahannock, it left the country between it and the Potomac entirely unprotected, except along the line of the railroad; the consequence was, that Moseby and White, with their bands of guerrillas, kept continually prowling on the highways, capturing small detachments of Union troops; but their chief line of business was capturing trains of sutlers' wagons, on their way from Washington to Meade's army.

These guerrillas were turned over to the tender mercies of the Californians, and they have now well nigh rid the country of their presence. These scoundrels are not regular rebel soldiers; you may see them in the day time at the farm-houses, protesting their loyalty, and with a long, sober face, ready to swear that they are "Union men." As soon as night comes, then they arm themselves, assemble at some *rendezvous*, and from there sally out to rob and plunder on the highway. These arrant cowards will not fight, but will run on the approach of any force, even though inferior in numbers to themselves.

We have had several chases and fights with Moseby's guerrillas: the first was by a detachment of Capt. Adams' Company, under the command of Lieut. W. C. Manning; Moseby had captured a train of thirty-two wagons, laden with sutler's goods and fifteen prisoners. The rebels were quarreling as to how they should divide their plunder, when two of their rear-guard came rushing up to the train, yelling "the Yankees are coming," and soon our brave boys came charging on the guerrilla band, which numbered sixty, while our men were only twenty-nine strong; yet, despite this great odds, the rebels were completely routed, leaving all the plunder and their prisoners in our possession. But our victory was not without loss, for we had two killed and two wounded. The following is our loss at this fight:

Killed- Peter Raymond, of San Francisco, pierced by six bullets; Hazen D. Little.

Wounded- Chauncey A. Hull was severely wounded, but is now doing well, at the Hospital in Alexandria; James Bard was slightly wounded and taken prisoner, but was afterwards recaptured by our men.

This fight took place near Aldie, just at daybreak; our "boys" fought with great bravery, and did themselves credit. Raymond and Little were buried in the door yard of a large brick house near the scene of conflict, and there may they in peace "sleep the sleep that knows no waking."

Not long after this Capt. Eigenbrodt, who was with his Company doing picket duty near the Chain-bridge, heard of some depredations having been committed by the guerrillas, and started out in pursuit of them. After riding all night, he caught up with the "rebs," but they preferred running to fighting; then followed a lively chase; the rebels had their horses loaded with plunder, which, in their flight, they threw away, literally strewing the road with it. The gallant Captain and his brave Company chased the rebels for about seven miles, when he was forced to give up further chase owing to the jaded condition of his horse; he succeeded in taking five prisoners and all the plunder.

It now becomes my painful duty to record a blunder, which resulted disastrously to us, but the responsibility of it rests on the Massachusetts officers.

Lieut. H. C. Pinkham, Acting Quarter-Master of the Regiment, went to Washington with a detachment of men, leading in used up horses, to be exchanged for fresh ones. Having procured these, he sent the twenty-six men, in charge of Sergeant J. B. Varnum, leading out one hundred and two fine horses. Each man had four.

They got along well enough until within four miles of the Fairfax Court House, when one of the men at the head of the column suddenly exclaimed, "There's some rebs," and just at that moment about sixty of them left their ambush and charged on our men. You may well imagine the confusion that ensued; the horses, green and untrained, became frightened at the pistol shots, and also unmanageable, and stampeded down the road; but another party of rebels attacked our men from the rear. The confusion that followed may better be imagined than described. Some of the men had three horses tied to their saddles, were dragged off and dismounted; but our "boys," though laboring under great disadvantages, fought like heroes. It can truly be said that never did men fight more bravely than did ours on this occasion. Sergeant Varnum, having discharged all the loads from his revolver, caught a rebel by the throat and was beating him over the head with his empty pistol, when another rebel came up, and putting a pistol to his head killed him instantly. John A. Cain and L. W. Turner got over a fence, and were shooting, when a rebel Captain and another officer rode up and with an oath ordered them to "Come out!" but our "boys," instead of obeying the order, sent out some bullets, killing the rebel Captain and wounding the other "reb." John W. McKinney, of Suisun City, also distinguished himself, and was slightly wounded in the head. But it is useless to make distinctions, they all did well. Corporal J. W. Owen, of the California Hundred, was taken prisoner, but afterwards escaped from his captors. Our loss was two killed and two wounded; Sergeant Jos. B. Varnum, killed, (shot in the head,) of Iowa Hill, Placer county; privates John McCarty, of the California Hundred, killed; G. W. Viereck, of the California Hundred, wounded, has since died, and J. W. McKinney, of Suisun City, wounded, now nearly well. Beside this, we lost eighty-seven horses, a lot of horse equipments, arm, etc.

As soon as the news of this disaster reached our camp, Col. C. R. Lowell, Jr. took every available man and started out in pursuit of the guerrillas, but as usual, he failed; he succeeded, however, in using up both men and horses to his satisfaction. [The incidents above narrated, less full particulars, appeared in our columns a few days since.-EDITORS ALTA.]

The War Department has detailed us for the special purpose of clearing the surrounding country of the rebel guerrillas that infest it: if they expect us to accomplish this, by no means an easy task, they must let us fight the guerrillas our own way, either as we hunt Indians or at their own game of bushwhacking; but we never can catch them by traveling over the turnpikes, while perhaps at the very time the guerrillas are hid in the woods by the roadside, laughing at our folly. Let Major Thompson have absolute command of his Californian battalion, and of the California Hundred, who, by the by, are now here with us, and they will soon make short work of the guerrillas; but Col. Lowell will never do it, for all the knowledge that he possesses of fighting Indians or guerrillas has been acquired by reading Sylvanus Cobb's stories in the *New York Ledger*, while burning the "midnight oil" at Harvard, but what he is deficient in this, he more than makes up in his knowledge of dress parades and policeing camps.

Gen. Stoneman, Chief of Cavalry, ordered a Court of Inquiry, to ascertain on whom rests the blame of this disaster. The evidence has been taken, but we have not, as yet, heard the conclusions at which the Court has arrived, but we do know that it was a gross piece of negligence to send over one hundred horses with only men enough to lead them, without an escort of any kind, over a road infested by guerrillas, just waiting for opportunities to rob and plunder.

The Relations between Massachusetts and the Californians.

These are no less complicated or unpleasant then they have been heretofore, notwithstanding the letter of Ira P. Rankin Esq., published in the *Bulletin*, and reprinted in Boston, and sent here for our edification, but which, after being read, left us as much in the dark as ever. We complain not of Massachusetts as a State, for we know that she has done nobly for the cause of the Union, but we do complain of her officers, who have treated us in a most niggardly and contemptible manner. We have just reason to complain of the Colonel that the State chose to command this regiment. Col. Lowell has done all in his power to spite us, both officers and men; he has divided and broken up our battalion, putting one Massachusetts and one California company to form a squadron, when it was specially agreed that our battalion should remain intact, under the command of our own Major. He has chosen Massachusetts men to command the Californian companies, when we have Lieutenants worthy of promotion, and in whom we have confidence. But it is useless to enumerate our list of grievances.

Thanks to Major Thompson and the friends of the battalion in Washington, it is possible that our connection with Massachusetts may ere long be severed, and be turned over where we properly belong, to the California Quota, and then we'll redouble our exertions to add to the already bright fame of our loved State. If General Hooker had remained in command of the Army of the Potomac, he would have long since, taken us out of this detested regiment. But if all other means fail, we can get out of it by joining the "Veteran Corps" soon to be organized.

Miscellaneous.

Captain D. A. DeMerritt, formerly of the "Sacramento Rangers," has met with another misfortune. You will remember that some time ago he broke his leg while at Brightwood, D. C.; he has been suffering from this, but he had so far recovered the use of his leg as to be able to ride, and had gone with command on a raid, when he was attacked with a fit of insanity, and twice he left the column, but was brought back; a third time he put spurs to his horse and dashed madly into the woods; a large number of men went in pursuit of him, but the search was fruitless, owing to the darkness of the night. The command returned to camp, and the next day, just as an expedition was about starting out in search of him, Captain De Merritt rode into camp, alone and insane; he received medical attendance here, but getting worse, he was sent to the Asylum in Washington, where now he is, worse, it is said, than when sent there. His many friends in California will learn this intelligence with sorrow, for Captain De Merritt is a gentleman highly esteemed wherever known.

Lieut. J. W. Sim, of San Francisco, was the recipient of a beautiful sword and belt, presented to him on the occasion of his promotion to First Lieutenant. This was intended as a testimonial of the high esteem in which Lieut. Sim is held by the Company, the "California Hundred," the members of which, having been in the field with him nine months, know well his merits as an officer and a gentleman.

Lieutenant J. A. Baldwin, is now the Acting Adjutant of the regiment, and discharges the duties of the office with honor to himself and to the entire satisfaction of every one. No officer is more highly esteemed here than is Lieutenant Baldwin, and I am sure that his many friends in San Francisco will hear of his promotion with pleasure.

Sergeant Kinne, formerly of the California Guard, has been promoted to Sergeant-Major of the regiment, which position he now very ably fills.

The health of the Californians is excellent, notwithstanding this is the sickly season, and the exposure to which they have been subjected, not one of them has of late died of disease.

Our election for California State officers came off here on Sunday last, much to our gratification. Of course the Union votes preponderated, nearly three hundred votes being cast, out of which Downey received *three*, and Low the balance. There are not many Copperheads among those that are in arms for the defence of the Government. By telegraph we have learned the result of the election at home; our boys gave hearty cheers and are in high spirits, and send greeting to their friends at home.

T. H. M.

Alta California, San Francisco, Sunday, October 4, 1863.
The Daily Bee, Sacramento, Tuesday, October 6, 1863
[See TDB letter of Aug. 30, 1863. All from Companies A, E, L & M.]]

California Battalion. - A correspondent of the *Alta* writing from a camp near Centerville, Va., September 6th, says, that in a skirmish near Fairfax Court House, John W. McKinney, of

Suisan City, distinguished himself. He was slightly wounded, but, at the time of the writing of the letter, was nearly well.

Solono Press, Suisan, Saturday, October 10, 1863

> Hdqrs. 2d Mass. Cavalry
> Centerville, September 7, 1863

To
> Brig. Gel. L. Thomas,
> > Adj. Gel. U.S.A.

General,

In justice to the Captains of the California Battalion of my Regiment, I have the honor to call your attention to the following facts.

The recruiting for my California Battalion was begun January 26th, 1863. No advantage was taken of General Order #75, 1862, & no 2nd Lieuts were mustered in at Commencement of organization - no officers at all were mustered in most cases until the Companies were filled to a maximum. In Massachusetts, on the contrary we mustered in 2nd Lieuts at once under Genl. Order #75, 1862 - & generally mustered in Captains & 1st Lieuts when the Companies reached a minimum. Thus on the roster of officers the California Captains now rank unduly low - & it is to correct this injustice that I apply to the Dept. for an order to the following effect:

That the muster in date of Capt. Chas. S. Eigenbrodt be changed from March 18/63 to March 3/63 the day when he had a minimum (83 accepted men) recruited & enrolled - of Capt. Zabdiel B. Adams from March 18/63 to March 6/63 - of Capt. David A. DeMerritt from May 19/63 to April 23/63.

So far as backpay is concerned the difference is very slight - but the change will in some cases give to a deserving officer the Command of a squadron to which I am unable on the present roster consistently to assign him.

> > Respectfully
> > Your odbt. servt.
> > C.R. Lowell, Jr.
> > Col. 2 Mass. Cavl.

Regimental Record Books, National Archives, Washington D.C.

> Letter From A Soldier
> _____

> > Camp near Centreville,}
> > September 7, 1863. }

Editor Herald:-In the few lines which I have with pleasure undertaken to write to you, I shall attempt to tell my experience of the war since I have been a soldier in the army.

When we enlisted in the Massachusetts Battalion at San Francisco, we were disappointed about getting off when we expected but said nothing. We were told that transportation was provided for us, and that we would get $100 United States bounty, and $50 State bounty; and on our arrival in Boston we would get the State bounty and $25 of the United States bounty. That would be $75 for each; but we got only $25 of that-though we still said nothing, thinking that Uncle Sam's machine for making greenbacks had broken down and he must be behind hand, and that when he got his machine again in operation he would pay up. But in about a week we were drawn up in a line, and Capt. Adams told us that the funds expended in getting up the Battalion had been borrowed from Amos A. Lawrence, and that he wanted us to assign that State bounty over to him; one by one the men were called out and told that he wished them to sign the document. Some of the boys signed it, and some refused to do so. When my turn came, I walked out and refused to sign it, and was ordered by the captain to stand to the right and report myself under arrest to the corporal who had charge of the others in my fix. When he was done, the captain told them who had acceded to his demand to go to supper, and then told us that "boys' play was done with; that those papers had to be signed, and that he would give us until reveille in the morning to make up our minds;" and, "if we did not sign then, that he would put us in the guardhouse and feed us on bread and water for eight days" - winding up with the pleasing assurance that we would be drummed out of the service!

We have had several hard fights, in which the boys of the Battalion and "Hundred" showed their valor and won a proud name. Several of our boys have been killed or wounded. I was shot in the head by a rebel at Ashby's Gap, and was a prisoner for a while; but my company made a charge and routed the rebels, recapturing me and three other boys. I was laid up for about three weeks, but am now all right again; and I have a scar on my head that I am proud to say I received while fighting for my country.

If we had officers that we could trust, we could challenge the world in a fight; we have four or five officers on whom we place reliance-among whom are Lieuts. Baldwin, Mannings, and Smith, Capts. Manning, and Rumsey, and First Sergeant Anderson, in Company L, (to which I belong,) - and they are the best men in the world; they don't pretend to be any better than well-behaved privates, who would follow them if they knew it was to certain death. But the other officers all work against them. My friends Morris and Owen assured me that Captain Adams was a good and fine man, but I have not as yet perceived the point. I think he is the meanest man that breathes, and am sure that, while no man in the company would raise a hand to save his life, many would lift both hands to see him die or disgraced, such is the feeling of hatred he has inspired.

The boys in the Battalion from Suisun are all well but J. McKinne, who was wounded and Billy Halsey, who has been sick most of the time; he is willing and tries to do all he can, but he is not the man for this business. We have the name of being the best battalion now in the field; Hooker tried to get us along with him, and would have succeeded had he remained in command. We are satisfied to be put anywhere where there is fighting to be done, for that is what we enlisted for-not to lay around a city and be Starr King soldiers, for that will not save the country; to do that, we have to go after the rebels like men-show them that they are fooled whenever they think they have a good thing on us, for we can't be whipped-make them think we are "iron-clad, clipper-built" California boys!

The general supposition now is that peace will be declared in three months, for all things appear to be in our favor now. If Meade jumps Lee once more, there will be an end to it, we think; for thousands of the rebels have found that they are upon the wrong as well as the weak side, and are giving themselves up daily. I sincerely hope that my relatives in the Golden State-my father especially-have come to the conclusion that they have taken a wrong stand in this great struggle between our Country and her Enemies.

James M. Hawkins.

Solano Herald, Suisun, Saturday, October 10, 1863.
[James M. Hawkins, Company L]

Headquarters Second Regiment Mass. Cavalry
California Battalion Camp at Centerville, Va.
September 8, 1863.

We are continually hunting guerillas. We see them occasionally but at a distance, when our horses are beat out after marching from 24 to 48 hours, and theirs are fresh.

The difficulty we have in coming to more frequent encounters is due to the fact that every man and woman in this country is a spy for them and keep them advised of our movements. But the Californians have the credit of being the first to head off Mosby and his death wounds were caused by their pistol shots.

He attacked twenty-five of us with one hundred of his robbers. We each had three led-horses attached to our saddle horse and, being hampered, besides being somewhat green, we were compelled to dismount and fight them on foot.

When Mosby commenced the attack, he passed the word to his men, "Boys, if they are New York or Michigan Cavalry, don't fire on them." But when he found out whom he had to contend against, he shouted, "Go in boys! fight like demons; they are Californians."

He had hardly said this before he got three shots, for luck- one in the breast, one in the side and the other in the thigh. Of these, it is reported, he has since died.

The robbers had one captain and one lieutenant killed, and four privates wounded. We had one sergeant and one private killed and nine taken prisoners.

We have traveled all over this country, from the Point of Rocks to Warrenton, along the Blue Ridge and all through the Bull Run Mountains. But the Rebs don't want to fight us.

I am writing under difficulties for I have to make a desk of a tin plate and hold it on my knee.

F. F. M

Daily Call, San Francisco, Sunday, October 11, 1863.
[F.F.M.-Unable to identify. Skirmish at Goodings Tavern]

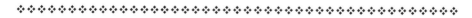

Rebel Guerilla Hunting. *Washington,* 21st. Reliable information has reached here that at noon on Friday last, Col. Lowell, in command of the 2d Massachusetts cavalry, and detachments of the 13th and 16th New York cavalry, started out in pursuit of the guerilla White. Col. Lowell found that White had crossed Goose Creek at Cockrell's ford, and crossed the country in nearly a straight line toward Mount Gilead and Hughesville, passing near Ball's Mills at 11 o'clock on that day. The trail of White's men was discovered early on the morning of Saturday, and was followed to a point near Mount Gilead.

Satisfactory evidence then appearing that White was back on the Snickersville road, Colonel Lowell returned to Dover and Aldie to camp. As the result of the expedition three of White's men were captured and killed. Four citizens on horseback were also arrested under suspicious circumstances. In some of the places visited by Colonel Lowell he was informed that White had notified the people that they had been conscripted, but no steps it appears, had been taken to force them into the rebel service. It was currently reported at Aldie that both White and Mosby had received orders to leave Loudon county, and move nearer to the main body of Lee's army. All the guerillas that have been recently at home have gone west within a day or two.

Evening Transcript, Boston, Tuesday, September 22, 1863.

War Department
Adjutant General's Office
Washington, Sept. 22, 1863

Colonel C. R. Lowell,
    2d Mass. Cavalry,

Sir:

By direction of the Secretary of War, I enclose herewith an extract from the proceedings of a Court of Inquiry convened in this city by virtue of Special Orders, No. 380, War Department, Adjutant Genl's Office, August 25, 1863, and to say that you will be careful to prevent the recurrence of similar omissions and neglects on your part in future.

I am , Sir,
Very Respectfully,
Your obt. Servt.
(sd) C. A. Nichols
Asst. Adjt. General

Through the Major General Commanding Dept. of Washington.

War Department
Adjutant General's Office,
Washington, Sept. 22, 1863

Lieut. H. O. Pinkham,
    2d Mass. Cavalry,

Sir:

By direction of the Secretary of War, I enclose herewith an extract from the proceedings of a Court of Inquiry convened in this city by virtue of Special Orders, No. 380, War Dept. Adjt. Gen'ls. Office, August 25th, 1863, and to say that you will be careful to prevent the recurrence of similar omissions and neglects on your part in future.

I am, Sir,
Very Respectfully,
Your obt. Servant,
(sd) C. A. Nichols,
Asst. Adj. Genl.

Official:
  C.A. Nichols
Asst. Adj. Genl.

Thro Genl Heintzelman,
Comdg Dept Washington

Extract from Proceedings of a Court of Inquiry which convened at Washington, D.C., by virtue of Special Order No. 380, dated War Dept., Adjutant General's Office, Washington, August 25, 1863.

x   x   x   x   x

The horses captured were under the charge of Sergeant Varnum and twenty two enlisted men of the 2d Mass Cavalry (Volunteers), that the Sergeant was acting under the instructions of Lieutenant H.C. Pinkham, Actg. Regt'l. Qrm. 2d Mass Volunteer Cavalry, with no specific instructions as to what he should do, except that he should push through without an escort unless he should chance to meet one on the road, that by some change in arrangements, there was not on the day specified the usual escort sent from Colonel Lowells Command, of which Lieut. Pinkham was not informed - as he should have been - the evening previous.

It seems that at the time of the attack the horses were four miles from Fairfax Court house (where there was a guard), in a small clearing with fences on both sides of the road, and that the attack was made from front and rear almost simultaneously by a force of about eighty men, mounted, and in Rebel uniform, and that Sergt. Varnum and one enlisted man were killed, and nine enlisted men and sixty nine (69) horses captured. This about 3:30 P.M., August 24, 1863.

(sd) George Stoneman,
Maj. General,
President

(sd) H.L. Abbot,
Col. Ist Conn. Arty.
Recording

Official:
C.A. Nichols
Asst. Adjt. Genl.

Extract from the Proceedings of a Court of Inquiry - convened at Washington D.C. by virtue of Special Order No. 380, from Adjutant Generals Office, dated August 25th 1863, are in the opinion of the Court,

1st Col. C. R. Lowell, 2d Mass Cavalry, for not having telegraphed on the evening of August 23d 1863, as he intended and should have done - to Lieut. H.C. Pinkham Actg. Regt. Quartermaster 2d Mass Cavalry the officer sent for the horses, informing him of the change in the arrangements in regard to escorts from Washington to Centreville; and for not giving Lieut. Pinkham specific instructions how to act and what to do.

2nd Lieut. H.C. Pinkham, Actg. Regtl. Quartermaster, 2d Mass. Cavalry who was blamable in sending the horses with no other instructions except to push them through, and in not having taken pains to find out what escort could be made available; and in not having given specific directions to the Sergeant in charge of the horses to avail himself of some competent escort.

(signed) Henry L. Abbott	(signed)	George Stoneman
Col. 1st Conn. Arty.		Maj. Gen'l. Vols.
Recorder		President

War Dept, A.G. Office
Washington, Sept. 22d 1863
Official:
 C.A. Nichols
Asst. Adjt. General

Regimental Record Books, National Archives, Washington D.C.

❖❖❖

News of September 30th.
A Harper's Ferry letter, dated the 28th, says Maj. Cole's cavalry had a skirmish with 150 of Moseby's gang, on Friday last. Our forces charged upon the rebels, who fled in every direction. A number of prisoners were taken, and seventy-five horses and mules recovered.

Alta California, San Francisco, Saturday, October 3, 1863.

❖❖❖

Latest Despatches
Washington, September 30, 1863
Moseby's cavalry are reported as still slashing around. On Monday they passed within a mile of the half detached camp of the Second Massachusetts regiment, whose headquarters is at Centerville. He seems to have no fears of capture, and finds but little trouble in penetrating our lines.

Alta California, San Francisco, Saturday, October 3, 1863.

❖❖❖

Head Quarters
Fort Norfolk Va
Sept 30th 1863

Major
        I have the honor to report that the terms of imprisonment in the Cases of Joshua C Ross and George Anderson Privates Co "A" 2d Mass Cavalry expires today.
They were both charged with conduct prejudicial to Military discipline. Sentenced to 3 months hard labor. Sentence approved June 30th 1863
I am Major
Very Respectfully
Your Obt. Servant.
T. Kobes
1st Lieut actg Post Adj

Major A.E. Bovey
Provost Marshal
Norfolk "Va"

Regimental Record Books, National Archives Washington D.C.

OCTOBER, 1863

  5   Confederate torpedo boat *David* attacks the *New Ironsides*
 16   Grant named head of the new Military Division of the Mississippi

FAIRFAX STATION, VA.,
Oct. 5th, 1863.

EDITORS REGISTER.- Sirs, all quiet on the Potomac. Every one looking up Winter quarters. To-day all the Command of Gen. King, consisting of Larrell's Brigade, Corcoran's Irish Legion, and the Cavalry forces in and around Centreville commenced moving into Fairfax Court House and this place for Winter quarters. There is no one here now but the 4th Delaware Brigade, which is on duty, principally as guards, on the cars between Alexandria and Culpepper. The rebels are thick as bees around here, but in no great force. I have been here eleven days and eight nights; of the eleven there has been some depredations done by them on the road. Last week they set fire to a R.R. bridge, three miles from Alexandria, and next night to one on the Bull Run, two miles from here, but was seen too soon by our pickets to do much damage. They also took up two rails near by. They are continually chasing in soldiers that go outside to buy eggs and butter, and it is next to impossibility to catch them.

The California 100 have been out on foot the past week, with pistol and carbine, hunting them Indian fashion, and they have succeeded in getting one of the worst rebel captains, of Mosby's gang, and three privates. His name is Wilson, and has been making it a practice when he killed any of our soldiers to cut their throats and otherwise mutilate their bodies after they were dead. The proofs are positive against him and he is safe in the old Capital prison. Fred Quant, H. Fillebrown and Sargt. Doane are the ones that took them. The captain said that had he known that they were Massachusetts men he would have died then and there in his trenches, and would have saved one or more of our boys before he was taken or killed himself. But all's well that ends well.

This is what they call the Sunny South and the sacred soil of Va. Well it is, I reckon, but give me California yet. In our travels through this country, as yet, we have not seen anything but waste. Buildings burnt, fencing destroyed, orchards cut, hacked and bark stripped off by horses. For cattle, horses, sheep or hogs to be seen, in fact, it looks desolate enough. The fruit is very poor indeed, this year, by the trees being so mutilated, and they are very bitter.

My duty here is to receive all cars freighted to our Brigade; compare it with the manifest and deliver it to our wagon master; also forward all stores and ordnance stores to Head Quarters. Very pretty clean work, and only about three hours work per day.

There has been quite a string of promotions in our company. Capt. Reed is Major.

I will in some future day give you in detail the amount of work of importance done by the Hundred. It amounts to considerable, although they have made no big strikes at any one time. McNeil and Quant send respects to all their friends.

Respectfully your Obt. Servant,
C. P. BRIGGS.

The Napa Valley Register, Napa, Saturday, November 7, 1863.

WASHINGTON ITEMS.

New York, 6th. The Herald's Washington despatch says that Col. Lowell of the 2d Mass. cavalry, commanding the cavalry brigade in front of the defences of Washington, has removed his headquarters to Fairfax Court House. The instructions of his scouts and squadrons actively engaged in the pursuit of Mosby's men, are to burn every house where a rebel is found. This course has been adopted by Col. Lowell as the only means to rid Fairfax and Loudon counties of the daring marauding bands, who have caused annoyances and committed depredations that have been tolerated too long.

Last night the guerillas entered Fairfax Court House and seized a considerable quantity of goods, the property of sutlers doing business in that place.

Evening Transcript, Boston, Tuesday, October 6, 1863.

WASHINGTON ITEMS.

A party of the 13th N.Y. Cavalry came up with Moseby and 10 men at Aldie. Moseby was reading a newspaper as his horse walked along. On the approach of our party the guerillas galloped off.

It was stated some time ago, that the citizens of Loudon and Fairfax counties had petitioned Jeff. Davis to have Moseby removed from the region as the horses which he captured did not compensate for the horses taken and damage done by the Union troops in their pursuit of him.

To this Jeff. Davis and Gen. Stuart responded that the people could not see the good done by Moseby with his men, which was keeping a large force of the enemy employed around Washington, which might otherwise be employed elsewhere.

Evening Transcript, Boston, Wednesday, October 7, 1863.

Oct. 16th, 1863
Camp near Edwards Ferry, Md.

Dear Parents

You will see by the heading that we have moved quarters since I wrote you last. We are now in Maryland doing Pickett Duty on the Potomac. It was at this point where the main body of the Rebels crossed when they made their last raid into Md. & Penn.

Our Co. is the only Cal. Co. here but there are three Mass. Co's. here. The four together form what is called a Battalion we are commanded by our Cal. Major (Thompson). There is also several Co's. of Scotts' Nine Hundred Cavalry.

I have been acting as Sergt. Major of this Battalion since we have been detached from our Regiment. In my new capacity I have to do some different duty from what I did with the company.

I am now what is called one of the non-commissioned Staff. That is I am acting in that Place.

There has been a very heavy battle fought for the past few days.

For three days there has been the most fearful cannonading that I ever heard.

But I must close for I have just received an Order to inform the Officers of this Battalion that every company is to Pack up all their company property for there is a large force of Lee's Army within a short distance of this Place.

The news here is not very favorable from the Army of the Potomac. I am afraid they are whipped by Lee (confound the Army of the Potomac) (I am down on it don't amount to Grass) it never has!

I do not know when I will have a chance to write again.

I hope I will have a chance to write good news when I write again. I am well, I have received two or three letters from you since I wrote last. Good Bye for the Present.

John Passage sends his respect to all.

He received a letter from Eva last night.

From Your son

Robert H. Williams

(Direct as usual)

Manuscript Collection, Huntington Library, San Marino, California - Miscellaneous letters of Robert Henry Williams, Co. F. 2nd Mass. Cav. Regiment; [John Passage, Co. E.]

Headquarters Department of Washington.
October 18th, 1863.

Colonel,

In obedience to orders from Hdqrs Dept Washington, dated Oct. 15, '63, I have inspected the pickets of Major Thompson, 2 Mass. Cav'y. Comd'g Cavalry Detachment, and have the honor to report as follows.

The line of river picketed by this officer extends from Muddy Branch to the Mouth of the Monocacy, while his patrols extend from Great Falls to Chick's Ford.

His posts are distributed as follows -

	Comd Officer	noncomd.	privates
Muddy Branch	1 }	4	18
Seneca Ford.	}	3	9
Young's Island "	}	3	9
Conrads "		3	9
White's "	1	4	24
Mouth of Monocacy		1	4

The Aqueduct at Mouth of Monocacy as well as the Fords of the Potomac above have been guarded by Infantry of the Middle Dept. These were however withdrawn on Friday afternoon, without notice to Maj. Thompson, leaving Chick's Ford (now the best on the river) the ford at Nolan's Ferry & the Aqueduct entirely unprotected.

I directed Maj. Thompson to establish a small post of observation at Mouth of Monocacy, detached from the picket at White's Ford - and, until otherwise ordered, to send frequent patrols to Chick's Ford. During the day this ford can be watched from the block house at Monocacy.

The bank of the river is thoroughly patrolled each post being visited every two hours. They are also visited by the Comdg. officer & by two officers specially detailed. At least three patrols will be sent in the night to Chick's Ford the last remaining out til after daylight, and it will be visited at least once during the day.

I found both officers & men at the pickets well instructed & vigilant. The patrols duty I believe to be well performed.

In accordance with orders I directed Maj. Thompson to use extraordinary vigilance in his observation of the country above Poolesville and to patrol it thoroughly & also to report promptly any information he may acquire.

The force at the disposal of Maj. Thompson is small for the duty required. Many of his horses are partially disabled from want of shoeing. He reports that the only blacksmiths of his command are on duty at Head-Quarters of Lowell's Cavalry Brigade and requests that two may be sent him - He is provided with forge & tools.

The camp of the detachment is situated on the Seneca Road, about one mile from Edward's Ferry. He has sent in his sick, hospital & superfluous baggage, and requests orders as to the disposition of his tents, of which he has 28 Sibly & 12 wall. His command is well supplied with shelter tents.

From 5 PM 16th inst to 12 M. 17th inst. the river rose between 8 & 9 inches and was rising very slowly at the hour. The fords are all easily passable.

I am, Colonel.

Very respectfully Your obd Servt

Chas. R. Horton

Capt. & ADC

Regimental Record Books, National Archives, Washington, D.C.

GUERILLA RAIDING.

Washington 19th. Yesterday, White's and Mosby's guerillas, numbering 1000 men, came down from Aldie, near Chantilly, and taking the Frying Pan road, succeeded in getting between the army and the defences of Washington. One gang came down within a mile of the Chain Bridge and fired into the rifle pits of one of the forts. Several officers were captured; together with six men of the 13th N.Y. cavalry, and a number of wagons, horses, &c. Our cavalry was sent in pursuit, and overtaking them, a brisk fight ensued, in which the rebels were defeated and driven with considerable loss.

It was reported today that 700 horses had been captured by Mosby's guerillas between here and Fairfax Court House. It turns out, however, that a lot of about 1000 horses, sent to the army, were stampeded through the carelessness of the guard. About 700 of them scattered, but they are being rapidly recovered by our cavalry and Quartermaster's men detailed for the purpose.

New York, 20th. The Times despatch says: Yesterday afternoon a captain of the 2d N.J. cavalry and six men were captured by Mosby's guerillas, a short distance beyond Fall's church. A number of horses were also captured.

Evening Transcript, Boston, Tuesday, October 20, 1863.

'He is a Marked Man."

Two writers from the army have used the above expression in reference to soldiers who saw fit to cast their votes for John G. Downey for Governor at the recent election. One of these correspondents wrote from Fort Craig in New Mexico, and the other from the California Hundred in Virginia. From the similarity of the expressions used, it is perfectly plain to any man of common sense that there is a concerted plan to annoy and persecute the volunteer who saw fit to exercise the right of suffrage as he chose, and cast his vote for a Democrat for office. Yes, reader, out of two hundred men at Fort Craig, and one hundred from California in Virginia, but one in each command had the hardihood to march up and vote for a Democrat! There must have been more, but the poor, miserable devils dared not vote their sentiments, for they knew they would be "marked men" as long as they remained in the service.

Semi-Weekly Beacon, Red Bluff, Saturday, October 24, 1863.

Our letter from Washington, D.C. Washington, October 25, 1863 - Moseby Still in Field.- Yesterday morning a squad of capturing pillagers who were out for the purpose of capturing sutler's wagons and Government horse, were met by a detachment composed of Baker's Rangers and the California Battalion, who charged upon the rebels and killed one and took three prisoners. Charles Mason was shot in the head, and Jack Barnes, who has been released three times upon his oath of allegiance, and Ed Stratton and Bill Harrover were made prisoners.

Alta California, San Francisco, Monday, November 23, 1863
[October 22, 1863 Col. Lafayette C. Baker-First District of Columbia Cavalry]

The California Hundred in the Field.

Hardships of Campaigning in Virginia.

The following are extracts from a letter written by a soldier in the "California Hundred" to his father in San Francisco:

Vienna, Va., October 25, 1863

Dear Father. - * * * * I said that I had not time to write to you of late. The reason you may infer from the lively times we have had for some time back. Our regiment (the 2d Massachusetts Cavalry) I will warrant has had harder times for two months past than almost any other in this field of service, although of a different nature than some. Our duty has been to keep the communications open to Gen. Meade's army and look after Mosby and White, and other guerillas that infest this part of Virginia, which keeps us going about all the time. Often have I been in the saddle ten hours at a stretch without dismounting for anything, and for six days (when out scouting) the saddles were not allowed to be taken off the horses. I tell you it is pretty hard, in the cold and wet weather that we are having now, to have to travel often all night without rest, and all next day, with the exception of a few minutes to cook grub, and all the time raining so that you can with difficulty get fire enough to make coffee, and so have to make a meal on "raw pork and hardtack." And one is in luck to have the hard tack, for it most always gets spoiled with the rain soaking through the haversack; and when not raining it is so cold at night, and we get so chilled, that one does not feel as though he could do *everything*. Some nights when we stop to camp we have to hold our horses in line of battle all the time, (it is mighty seldom that we are allowed to tie them to the trees,) and make ourselves as comfortable as we can. You can imagine how comfortable we feel after traveling all day through the rain and wet to the skin. We just lay ourselves down in the mud and wet, holding our horses by the bridle and try to snatch a few moments of sleep - running the risk of our animals (which are always hungry on a scout, for we cannot carry much feed, as we must go as light as possible,) stepping upon us, which they sometimes do in their restiveness for want of feed. Cold as it has been we are not allowed to build fires at night, and our cooking must be done in the daytime.

But do not think I complain - I am only giving you my experience - for I stand it all as well as any of them; in fact, I grow fat. We have to do all this to keep from being taken by surprise by the rebs, who are always ready to take advantage of any chance that presents itself to pounce upon us. We are always ready, if we see or hear any rebs, to give them a fight. Lately we have had a good many fights with them, in all of which we have whipped them badly. I think that we have crippled the gang of Moseby more than any other troops ever did before.

I have been in two more fights since I wrote to you last, one of which was in the nighttime, but like all night fights was badly managed. I was on picket at the time. It was 12 o'clock when the rebs came. The one on picket with me was Corporal Washburne *[Luman P. Washburn, died Nov. 14, 1864]* of my company. He was shot through and through, and is not expected to live. I must say that I came near getting shot myself, for I had no less than five shots fired at me before I reached the rest of the boys, who were stationed about 200 yards to the rear. The balls flew mighty wicked - one rebel was killed. How many were wounded I do not know, as in the darkness they got off, aided by the thick brush and woods in the vicinity. You can bet I gave them all the shots I had, and then out came the sabre, but I did not have occasion to use it, as the rebs left us so soon as they found our camp was aroused and ready. I have since learned that they were a portion of Moseby's men, in command of Lieut. Williamson, next in rank to Moseby, and a man of desperate character. This took place about three miles from this place, near Bailey's Cross Roads.

I don't think I am destined to be taken off by any reb bullet. It is a sure thing that I am alive and hearty yet and getting stronger and healthier every day - in fact, I never was in such good health in my life. I am on duty all the time, I am one of the few duty men that the company has left, for we can muster but 40 men for duty any day, and we left San Francisco with 100 men. I cannot speak well of the men, who, after costing the Government so much money and trouble to get them here, desert the "Stars and Stripes" or else shirk their duty by playing sick, (for some of them do play it,) so as to get transferred to the "invalid corps," being too big cowards, after seeing the danger to face the music. I scorn such soldiering and hope that a rebel bullet may find its way to my heart, if ever I neglect to do my duty when able, or fear to fight when the time comes. I think that the Ruler of all things controls my destiny, and when the time comes to die I must go whether on the field of battle or at home. Talking about battle, although as yet I have not been in any of the big ones, I must say that there is something charming in the whistle of a bullet and in the charge. You feel all *heroed* as if you could whip any rebel that came in reach - and who *would* not feel so when he sees before him traitors firing on the Old Flag and its defenders - men fighting against the best Government on earth! But I must hasten.

You will see we are stopping at Vienna, a small town about 8 miles from Centreville, and it is expected that we will winter here, though nothing is certain as to winter quarters. We form part of a line of troops maintained between Washington and Meade's army, to keep communications open; and in the spring we will probably join his army. At present we belong to the Twenty-second Army Corps, and are brigaded with the 16th and 13th New York Cavalry, under command of acting Brig. Gen. C.R. Lowell, our Colonel.

It is so difficult writing on my knee and on the ground that you must make allowance for my writing. But I will have to get through with this pretty soon to go on duty. It comes so often that I scarcely have time to write even this, and have to snatch time by piecemeal.

Before closing, I must not forget to mention the part that our regiment has taken in the late "raid" of Lee up to this part of the country. We were the first troops to make a scout through Snicker's and Ashby's gaps into the Shenandoah Valley, to find out whether Lee was advancing by that route, or not, and after he had advanced we were kept busy scouting and on picket down as far towards Lee's lines as possible or safe. To take the Washington and other papers for authority, we have done good service, for they give us a great deal of credit. It is true that we have lost some good men, but the rebels, whenever we saw them, were sure to run, or if they showed fight *always* got the worst of it. We have in the last two weeks killed and captured and wounded many a rebel. About twelve or fifteen of our regiment are at present in the prisons of Richmond.

Duty calls and I must close. A kiss to the dear little sisters and love to all.

S.W.B.

Evening Bulletin, San Francisco, Tuesday, December 1, 1863
The Napa County Reporter, Napa, Saturday, December 12, 1863.
[Samuel W. Backus, Company L]

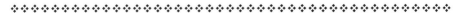

Camp at Fairfax County, Va.
Oct. 29/63

Dear Father, haveing waited patiently and anxiously four weeks for a letter from some one of you in answer to these which I have written and which remain unanswered as yet, I thought I would write once more and see if I can found out where & how you are. When I wrote last we were at Centerville a few after I wrote we moved Camp to Fairfax Court House we remained there five days just long enough to get our winter quarters nicely furnished then we were ordered to this place where we have been ever since and from appearances shall remain here this winter doing Picket duty. this Picket duty is the worst Business that ever I had anything to do with. we get one night in Bed out of seven. While on Picket we have to hold our horse by the Bridle so that it is next to impossible for a man to get any sleep. There is three men at a post one mounted all the time. it is useing up the men mighty fast. there is more men on Sick report than there is for duty. it is Just Killing men and accomplishing nothing for Rebels are so scarse about here as $20.00 gold pieces. We the Californians have been signing a petition today addressed to the Secretary of War to give us active service. there is more men Dieing from hard and useless work in Camp than ever were or will be in Battle. our Hospital is full. the Diseases are generally Rheumatism, Diarrhea & Fevers all brought on from exposure, want of Sleep &c. One of our Majors, a Gentleman & a Soldier (Major Crowninshield), told Col Lowell that he was working his men too much. The Col. said the men did nothing. never mind every Dog has his Day and ours will come some time and then a private will be as good a man as those that wear straps upon their shoulders. to give you some idea of what an Officer of the great American Army is I will give you one instance of their Consequences. yesterday one of the Teamsters of the 16th N.Y. was driving along with his team. a Major Came Rideing along and told the Teamster to get out of the way. he answered al right Sir. the Major wheeled his horse around and said that is no way to speak to an officer, then drew his Sabre and struck the man twice atop of the Head and twice on the side inflicting very severe wounds so that he was taken senseless to the hospital. and what do you suppose will be done to the officer. probably be reported slightly by the Colonel nothing more even if the man should die. there is thousands of such cases in the Army every day. nothing of the kind has even occurred in our Battalion yet nothing but fear keeps our officers from doing something of the kind in fear of the Men. I know nothing more to write now and I will Close with the request that you will answer this upon Rec'pt. Remember me to all and direct your letters to Washington, D.C. and oblige your

Ever Affectionate Son
James B. Randall

From Mother's Certificate, Civil War Pension Records, National Archives, Washington, D.C.
[Randall was a private in Co. L. Captured by Mosby's guerillas Dec. 10, 1863, and sent to
Andersonville Prison. There he became ill and died July 15, 1864]

NOVEMBER, 1863

19 Lincoln's Gettysburg Address
23 Battle of Chattanooga
24 Battle of Lookout Mountain, Tennessee
25 Battle of Missionary Ridge

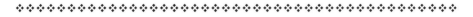

Hd. Qrs. 2nd Mass. Cavalry
Vienna Va Nov 2nd 1863

Special Orders
____No. 5

In accordance with orders received from Hd. Qrs Dept of Washington, Capt. J. Sewall Reed, is hereby directed to take companies E, L and M, of this regiment, and proceed to Poolsville, Md., where he will report to Major D.W.C. Thompson, commanding detachment of 2nd Mass. Cavalry, for special duty. The duty performed, Capt. Reed will return to this camp.

By Command of
C. Crowninshield
Major Commanding
2nd Mass Cavalry

Regimental Record Books, National Archives Washington, D.C.

Vienna Nov. 9th 1863

My dear Mammy

I have not written to you for a very long time I believe. The box containing the boots arrived here three days ago. I am happy to say that the boots were as near what I wanted as could be possibly expected. I should however advise Rice to devote a little of his spare time to the study of the anatomy of the human leg and more particularly of the male calf. If he could get a cast of Appollo's leg & try one of his top boots on it, it might amuse him. The cigars you sent me were very good indeed & all the other things were all right. No particular news here. Moseby has been very quiet of late & I hope he will continue so as it is very cold sleeping out with only an overcoat on now. Colonel Lowell has returned & brought his wife with him he is very unpopular with the Regt. & every prays that he may be made a Brigadier Gen. so that we may get rid of him. I get on with him very well I think he likes me & as a companion he is very pleasant but I don't consider him much of a soldier although I do consider him the most talented young man I have ever met with and he is as brave a little fellow as ever lived, but is hasty inconsiderate and has not very good judgement. He has however a most unbounded confidence in his own ability. All this is you know said to you "sub rosa".

[Last two paragraphs deleted-Editors]

Your son
Caspar

Caspar Crowninshield, Letters, Massachusetts Historical Society

MOVEMENTS IN VIRGINIA.

The gallant Mosby is again in the saddle. On Tuesday last he made a foray on the Yankees within a mile of Gen. Meade's headquarters, near Warrenton, Killed three, wounded several, and captured thirty-six white Yankees, some eighteen or twenty black ones, and 130 mules and horses.

(Richmond Examiner.)

Evening Transcript, Boston, Thursday, November 5, 1863.

OUR ARMY CORRESPONDENCE

Letter from Second Massachusetts Cavalry

Cavalry Camp, Vienna, Va. Nov. 25, 1863.

To the Editor of The Boston Journal:

This camp is composed of the 2d Massachusetts and 13th and 16th New York cavalry regiments-they being the cavalry force, Department of Washington under command of Col. Chas. R. Lowell.

The brigade was at Centreville at the time my last letter was written- that was three months ago. For two months we remained there constantly busy, picketing, patrolling, scouting. The enemy in our vicinity during our sojourn there were the guerrilla bands under the noted chiefs, Majors Mosby and White. During the summer their raids upon sutlers' and army supply trains were frequent and successful, but although we generally retook most of the property, the rebels through their perfect knowledge of the country and the sympathy of the inhabitants who aided in covering their movements, were nearly always able to escape. Sometimes we took a few prisoners, sometimes wounded or killed one or two, but usually they knew of our coming and "skedaddled" without resistance.

On one occasion only did Mosby show fight. August 24, he, with about sixty men, actually attacked twenty-five armed men. But the latter were all mounted on green horses and each had three to lead-they were a hundred fresh horses just coming form Washington. Mosby got the horses and one or two prisoners, but not without a sharp fight with our men, who had to dismount and take to the bush. Sergeant Joseph B. Varnam of "M" Co. was in command of our men and was killed; one or two others were wounded. We killed two of Mosby's officers on the spot, and several of his men were wounded. Major Mosby himself was wounded at this time. Washington, New York and Boston papers gave accounts of the wounding of the noted guerrilla-some of his death-but I saw no correct statement. Let me state here distinctly that the whole credit of this little brilliant affair is due to men of the 2d Massachusetts Cavalry-not an officer nor a man of any other regiment had anything whatever to do with it, "Ariel" to the contrary notwithstanding.

For about five weeks Mosby was *hors de combat* and all was quiet. Then he again made his appearance and has since occasionally captured a picket or a patrol, run off with a citizen who declared his loyalty, or some other equally small operation.

October 5th we moved from Centreville to Fairfax Court House, five miles nearer Alexandria. We remained there but four days, then came over here. Vienna is a station on the Loudon and Hampshire Railroad, fifteen miles from Alexandria, The railroad has been repaired so that trains run daily between our camps and the latter place. By way of Chain Bridge and Georgetown it is but two hours ride to Washington. Our location, therefore is good, and as we have by considerable labor made our quarters in camp quite comfortable, we hope to remain here through the winter. Col. Lowell has recently been North upon important private business, and judging from appearances at brigade headquarters since his return we think he expects to remain here some time.

No orders to go into winter quarters have yet been received, however, nor will there be while the fine weather which we have lately been having continues. Taking advantage of it Col. Lowell sent out an expedition a week ago which returned day before yesterday, having had great success.

The force consisted of one hundred men, from our regiment only, under command of Captain W. M. Rumery of Co. H, and Lieut. J. W. Sim of Co. A. Capt. R. was fortunate in having for a guide a deserter from Mosby's gang [Charley Binns]. Gum Springs, Aldie, Middleburg, Upperville and Paris were visited and guerrillas were found quite plenty. Twenty-eight prisoners were brought in, including one officer, all belonging to Mosby's permanent band. About fifty horses and thirty head of cattle belonging to persons on whose premises rebels were found, were confiscated. The prisoners all agree that this capture leaves Mosby but about twenty of his old men, and it will be impossible for him to get recruits enough to make up another effective gang. So it appears that the 2nd Massachusetts have again, for a time at least, quieted that troublesome individual.

Weekly-almost daily-the dispatches from "the front" tell of captures by "Mosby's guerrillas." Doubtless there are guerrillas enough down there; the mountains are full of roving bands of marauders, but it is humbug calling them all *Mosby's* men. We have been dealing with him for four months constantly, and all have become perfectly satisfied that Maj. John S. Mosby's command is generally about fifty men, often less, seldom more, and only on great occasions when something very special is on the *tapis* can he raise a hundred. His principal field of operations is and has been in this vicinity, rarely south of Centreville and Fairfax Court House, or south of Leesburg-never west of the Blue Ridge. We have weakened him much of late, and will endeavor to keep him quiet until spring, if not longer.

Captain Cabot, with Lieutenants Parker, Welch and Clark, and one hundred recruits, arrived from Readville October 26, and we were glad to have our number thus augmented.

Companies C, F, G and I are on detached service near Seneca Falls, Md. Major Thompson is there in command. Capt. George F. Holman is Acting Assistant Inspector General on Col. Lowell's staff. Sergeant Major Charles M. Kinne has been promoted to Second Lieutenant, and is Acting Adjutant, and First Sergeant D. R. Irwin of Company K takes his place as Sergeant Major.

We have recently enjoyed a short visit from John M. Forbes, Esq. Any one having friends in the regiment, and who may visit Washington, should come out to our camp, either by cars from Alexandria or direct from town. It is but a short ride.

CADET.

Boston Journal, Saturday, November 28, 1863.
[John Forbes, father of Major William H. Forbes]

While we were at Vienna one of Mosebey's lieutenants deserted, came into our camp and offered to act as our guide in capturing the men of Mosebey's command in their individual lodgings. Mosebey had no regular camp, maintained no continuous military organization. On the contrary his men were quartered among the residents of a territory in the neighborhood of Aldie and bordering the Blue Ridge on the East and would be brought together by prearranged signals whenever their services were required. To capture them, scouting expeditions of 60 or a 100 men were sent out, all but ten or twelve of whom would go dismounted. The dismounted men would travel through by-roads and timber and at night so as to conceal their movements. The mounted men would keep to the highway near. When they reached a neighborhood where it was expected that Mosebey's men were to be found they at night would raid the farm houses and if fortunate take two or three or more of Mosebey's men prisoners. These expeditions usually consumed three or four days. The first scouting expedition for which Mosebey's lieutenant acted as guide left camp one Sunday afternoon, and after proceeding some distance up the railroad track the command was halted and the 1st lieutenant of our Company Rumery, in command undertook to get the lieutenant drunk to see how he would talk and act when in that condition, there being some doubt as to his good faith; the result was that our lieutenant was very much more affected by the whiskey than was the other. On leaving camp a special detail of two men was made whose duty it was to always keep near Mosebey's lieutenant and if they found him treacherous to shoot him. There was however never any sign of treachery on his part.

Towle Recollections, Bancroft Library, University of California at Berkeley
[Lieutenant Charley Binns-Mosby's 43rd Battalion Virginia Cavalry.]

❖ ❖

LETTER FROM A CALIFORNIAN IN THE
ARMY OF THE POTOMAC.

ON PICKET, NEAR VIENNA,
November 28, 1863.

EDITORS ALTA: More than a week has elapsed since I wrote to you last, but picket duty and scouting expeditions have so occupied my time for the last ten days that I have not had time enough in camp to enable me to compose a letter, and even now, as you will perceive by the heading of this, I have to write to you while on duty. I am writing this in the only school-house there is within ten miles of Vienna, or at least the only one where at the present time the young ideas of Virginia are taught to shoot. The place is known as Tyson's Corner, taking its name from the owner of the land. Tyson is a sound Union man, and has been so from the beginning. He voted against the secession of this State, and has always acted in accordance with that vote. For doing so he has been much prosecuted, and much of his property destroyed; but he still has his dwelling house and barn left, although they have been fired once or twice by the rebels, and only saved from destruction by the greatest exertions, He has a large family here, and they are fearing all the time that the guerrilla band of Mosebey's will make a raid this way, and capture the old gentleman, as they have sworn to do. Fearing this, Mr. Tyson hardly ever passes the night under his own roof, having to seek shelter as night comes on at some place less exposed to guerrilla depredations. I suppose you are astonished that such a state of things should exist within fifteen miles of the Capital of the Union, and in the rear of the Army of the Potomac; but it is even so, notwithstanding the skill and strategy exhausted for its prevention.

After Moseby.

A little over a week since, a Lieutenant of Moseby's guerrilla band came within our lines and gave himself up, and at the same time expressed a desire to guide a party of our men to the haunts of the guerrillas. Accordingly, he was sent out with a detachment from our regiment, consisting of one hundred men, twenty-five of whom were mounted and the rest dismounted and armed with carbines and revolvers. Two days after this party started out, another detachment of one hundred and fifty men were sent out, fifty of whom were from the Thirteenth and Sixteenth N. Y. Cavalry, the whole under the command of Col. Lowell. This last party took with them three days' rations. The first party took four. It was raining at the time of starting, and continued to rain until the "wee sma' hours" of the next morning; not one of your big-drop California rains, but a drizzling, insinuating Virginia rain, that thoroughly saturated your clothing before being hardly aware of its raining at all; one of those miserable, depressing-spirit rains that makes one feel as though there was nothing in this world worth living for-in fact, the very worst rain that ever brought into requisition India-rubber overcoats and boots. But I am digressing. We marched, or rather the horses did, until 3 o'clock, P. M., when a halt was ordered, and building fires in the woods by the roadside, made ourselves some coffee and dried our clothes. Here we stopped until it ceased drizzling, and then started again, soon striking the Aldie Pike, on which we kept, passing through Aldie and Middleburgh, which latter place we reached just as the morning stars were visible above the horizon. Here we remained until daylight, and again pressed on, meeting three miles beyond Middleburgh the party of one hundred men that had started two days before us. On coming up with them, it was ascertained that they had been very successful in their guerrilla search, having captured twenty-one of Moseby's gang without firing a shot. The guide had taken them to places where he knew the guerrillas were in the habit of spending their nights, and every one of them, to use a vulgar phrase, were "caught napping," as they were all enjoying.

"Tired nature's sweet restorer, balmy sleep."
However, the application to their heads of a loaded revolver, caused them to deliver up their firearms and themselves without making any disturbance. With them were taken their horses also. The Colonel was so much pleased at their success, that after cooking our breakfast, our horses' heads were pointed for camp, towards which place we went as far as Mount Zion Church, two miles this side of Aldie, and there camped, waiting the return of two small scouting parties that had been sent out from where we met the hundred. In about three hours one of the parties returned, bringing with them four more of Mosby's men, that they had overhauled after a long chase. There were five in the party they chased, but one of them refusing to surrender, after repeated demands had been made for him to do so, they were compelled to shoot him, which they did, inflicting a mortal wound. Upon the return of this party, the Colonel, having a newly-wedded wife at camp, concluded to see her that night, and taking the advance guard as an escort, started at a hard-gallop, and kept it up the whole distance, some thirty miles, making it in three and a half hours. The next night the main body arrived in camp, with the prisoners all safe, and the following day they (the prisoners) were sent into Washington, and took up their quarters at the Old Capitol.

A sad accident happened to one of the men detailed to guard the prisoners, the night they remained at our camp. Wilson was his name, and he was a member of Company L. California Battalion. Standing in the doorway of the log-house in which the prisoners were confined, resting the butt of his carbine on the door sill, (a log a foot through,) and leaning his breast upon the muzzle, the carbine suddenly slipped from the sill, striking the hammer as it went, which exploded the cap, and the charge entered his breast, just over the heart, coming out under the shoulder blade, on the back, causing his death in a few minutes. He was sincerely regretted by all who knew him, as of him it could truly be said, that
"None knew him but to love,
None named him but to praise."
Affairs remain about the same as usual at Vienna. The cars come and go once a day, bringing out provisions and forage, and carrying in cord wood, of which there is any quantity

piled up on the line of the road. Glorious news is every day received from the army of Grant, at Chattanooga. They are repulsing the rebels at all points, capturing prisoners by thousands and artillery batteries by dozens, and causing a general demoralization among the soldiers of the Southern Confederacy. Meade is also preparing to do something in the vicinity of Fredericksburg, and in and out of the army a feeling of cheerfulness prevails, which is the natural consequence of success.

T. D. B.

Alta California, San Francisco, Tuesday, December 29, 1863.
[Frederick Wilson]

❖❖❖

War Department
Adjutant Genl's Office
Washington, D.C.

Special Orders Nov. 28th 1863
  No. 528

(extract)

      The Superintendant of the Government Hospital for the Insane having reported that Captain D.A. DeMerritt, of Co. F 2nd Massachusetts Cavalry, has entirely recovered his health he will be discharged from the Hospital, and will join his Regiment without delay.

By order of the Secretary of War

Official E. D. Townsend
  Samuel Greek Asst. Adjt. Genl.
   Asst. Adjt. Genl.

Regimental Record Books, National Archives, Washington, D.C.

❖❖❖

DECEMBER, 1863

8 Lincoln's Proclamation of Amnesty and Reconstruction

❖❖❖

Headquarters Cav. Forces Nr. Potomac
Muddy Branch Dec 3rd 1863

Col. C. R. Lowell, Jr.
  2d Ms Cavalry
     Colonel
          In compliance with your request that I should furnish you a statement in writing of what information I had in relation to certain petitions from the men in the five Cal companies in 2 Ms Cavalry to be transferred to Col Bakers Rangers I have the honor to report that the first I heard of them was on the 27 of Nov when I was in Washington by order of Maj. Gen Auger to make arrangements in relation to the Maryland election. On that day I met Sergt

Williams of Co. E on the side walk. He was on his way to Baltimore to vote. I asked him what the Cavalry forces at Vienna were doing and how the Cal companies were. He told me generally and informed me that the Cal companies had sent petitions to the Secretary of War to be transferred to Col Bakers Rangers. I asked him if the officers had signed them and he told me no that it was intended that they should not join the men in the matter, and had not been consulted about the petition or words to that effect. On the 5th Nov after Capt Eigenbrodt had returned from the election at Clarksburg with his company he informed me that the Cal men had sent petitions to the Secretary of War to be transferred to Col Bakers Rangers and I think he said that the officers had not taken any part in the matter.

About the same time my orderly private White Co. E informed me that some of the men had told him that the Californians had petitioned the Secretary of War to be transferred to Col Bakers Rangers. This was told him when he was in Washington with me on the 2 Nov or at my camp by men who came over from your camp during election about the 4th or 5th of Nov. I dont know which. One of the Cal companies (Co "F") is attached to my command but I did not see or hear of any such petition being signed in my camp and did not know of any such having been signed or sent to the Secretary of War until Capt Washburn came to my camp to investigate the matter unless I inferred it from the general information I had received that the Cal companies had sent such petitions. I was not informed or consulted in relation to the petitions and gave them but little thought as I was constantly engaged with my military duties and supposed as they had been sent to the Secretary of War he would either approve or reject them and that would end the matter.

I am Colonel
Most Respt Yours
D.W.C. Thompson
Maj. 2 Ms Cav
Comdg Post

Regimental Record Books, National Archives, Washington, D.C.
[Col. Lafeyette C. Baker, 1st District of Columbia Cavalry]

❖❖

WASHINGTON NEWS AND GOSSIP.
MOSBY'S GUERILLAS.

Almost every day we hear that some supply train or sutler's wagon has been captured by the force of that apparently ubiquitous "raider," Major John S. Mosby. It is, however, well known that Mosby has not a hundred men under his command, and that most of the depredations have been committed by the residents, "farmers by day-soldiers by night;" while some of the sutlers have purposely gone over with their goods, to be returned paroled and with large profits. To put a stop to this, a cavalry force has been organized, under the command of Col. C. R. Lowell, of the Second Massachusetts Cavalry. It consists of that regiment, the Thirteenth and Sixteenth New York: and they are fast learning the haunts, not only of Mosby's guerillas, but of the disaffected residents. Col. Lowell is a Massachusetts man, who was commissioned in the Sixth United States Cavalry soon after the rebellion broke out.

Daily National Intelligencer, Washington, D.C., Thursday, December 3, 1863

❖❖

Cavalry Camp
Muddy Branch
Dec 5th 1863

Col J. H. Taylor
Chief of Staff
Colonel
I returned to Camp on the 3rd inst. Everything in my command continues in good order. My officers and mens quarters are now in good condition for winter. As soon as the lumber comes up for my stables I shall have them completed so that the horses will be well taken care of. My general arrangements on the river continue as heretofore.
I am Colonel
Most Respt Yours
D.W.C. Thompson
Maj 2 Ms Cav
Comdg.
Regimental Record Books, National Archives, Washington, D.C.

❖❖❖❖❖❖❖❖❖❖❖❖❖❖❖❖❖❖❖❖❖❖❖❖❖❖❖❖❖❖❖❖❖❖❖❖❖❖❖

Recovery of Captain De Merritt. - The readers of the Alta were informed some time since, of the insanity of Captain D.A. DeMerritt, formerly Captain of the Sacramento Rangers, and since Captain of Company F, Second California-Massachusetts Cavalry, originating in the pain and fever produced by the breaking of his leg, by his horse rearing and falling with him. After his insanity became so marked that he escaped from camp, in Virginia, and took to the road in the night, disuniteing the partially reknit fractured bones, he was taken to Elizabeth's Hospital, at Alexandria, and his many friends will be glad to learn that he is not only recovering the use of his injured limb, but has so completely recovered the use of his reasoning faculties, that he has been offered the command of his company again, and will soon be restored to active service in the field.

Alta California, San Francisco, Monday, December 14, 1863

❖❖❖❖❖❖❖❖❖❖❖❖❖❖❖❖❖❖❖❖❖❖❖❖❖❖❖❖❖❖❖❖❖❖❖❖❖❖❖

LETTER FROM THE CALIFORNIA COLUMN WITH THE ARMY OF THE POTOMAC.

———

(From the Correspondent of the ALTA Accompanying the Same.)

———

CAMP OF CAVALRY, BRIGADE,
VIENNA, VA. Dec. 7th, 1863.
EDITORS ALTA:- I have just returned to this command, having, for upwards of two months, been absent from it on detached service in Maryland, and avail myself of a hurried opportunity to communicate to you our doings and whereabouts.
My last letter was written at Centreville, where our regiment was at that time stationed, from there it was ordered into winter quarters at Fairfax Court House, and began making the necessary preparations, such as stockading tents; but their stay there was short, for when Gen. Meade's great Army of the Potomac fell back to Centreville, this brigade which is composed of

the Second Massachusetts Cavalry, Sixteenth and Thirteenth New York Cavalry, was ordered to this post, and for one night it can be said to have been at the "front," it being stationed between the Sixth Corps, on the left of Meade's Army, and the rebels. Since then the "boys" have divided their time between hunting guerrillas and preparing their winter quarters, which, by-the-by are now well nigh completed. But your readers must not think that because we have gone into winter quarters that we are to remain passive and idle; quite the contrary; there is more guard and picket duty to be done now than before; patrols scour the country for miles around the camp, and occasionally a raid is made beyond our lines into rebeldom.

A Rebel Guerrilla Turns Over a New Leaf.

About two week's ago Charley Binns, of Moseby's guerrillas, came riding into camp, and expressed his desire to leave the rebel service and become a Union man-that he was tired of it, and was moreover, convinced that he had been on the wrong side. He was taken to headquarters, and there he told the Colonel that, if he would promise him pardon for his bad conduct in the past, he would make amends for it in the future, and would lead a party to a place where a lot of Moseby's guerrillas could be captured. Of course, at first we all doubted his sincerity and good faith; for we thought that a man who would betray his companions in arms, (rebels, though they were,) would not hesitate to betray his former enemies. But "Charley" has not only satisfactorily proved his sincerity, but proved to be a brave and gallant soldier, a skillful and expert guide, knowing every road and cow-path in Virginia, and is altogether a most valuable acquisition to our cause-so much so, that Moseby had offered a reward of ten thousand dollars for his capture.

A "Dough-Boy" Raid After the Guerrillas.

Having become satisfied of Charley Binns' good faith, an expedition was gotten up to go after Moseby and his guerrilla band. It consisted of seventy-five dismounted men, armed with Sharp's carbines and Colt's revolvers, and twenty-five others mounted, all under the command of Capt. Rumery, who, though a Massachusetts officer, has won the esteem and respect of every man in our battalion by his daring and bravery, and the uniform kindness he has ever shown to our California boys, treating them as men should be treated. The expedition was gone six days, during which time they killed one rebel guerrilla, captured twenty-five more, besides a number of horses, a quantity of arms, to say nothing of the many chickens, turkeys, and other fowl, foraged, confiscated and appropriated to the comfort of our boy's "inner man." A similar expedition went out a few days since, consisting of one hundred and four mounted men, under the command of Capt. Adams, and accompanied by Charley Binns, who is now our regular guide. He has cast off his suit of rebel grey and donned the true Union blue, and receives for his services three dollars per diem. We were out three days, captured four of Moseby's guerrillas and several notorious rebel citizens. Another "dough-boy" expedition is now contemplated. It will leave here to-night or to-morrow. Your correspondent will accompany it, and furnish the details thereof to the ALTA.

An Excitement in Camp.

About two weeks ago the monotony of camp life was broken by the report that, at last, the Californians had broken the chains that bound them to this accursed Massachusetts regiment, and were to be transferred to Colonel Baker's "Mounted Rangers," petitions to that effect having been signed by them and sent to the Secretary of War. But, unfortunately, Colonel Baker's office of Provost-Marshal of the War Department was just then discontinued, and the thing fell through, much to our regret. However, we are still in hopes of getting out of this regiment, and being accredited to the quota of California where we properly belong. I think that if the California Legislature would pass an act appropriating a sum sufficient to reimburse Massachusetts for her outlay in recruiting our battalion, that there would be no difficulty in obtaining our transfer to the quota of our loved State, and be accredited to her, when called on for more troops.

Major Thompson and his Command.

Major Thompson is now in Maryland, in command of the cavalry forces within the defences of Washington, consisting of the Third Battalion of Second Massachusetts Cavalry and seven companies of "Scott's 900." They have a fine camp at Seneca Falls. Md.; the Major, with his usual solicitude for the welfare and health of his men, has obtained everything that will conduce to their comfort and health, and has besides been very successful; since he went over there the rebels have not dared to cross the river, in search of spoils and plunder, as they were want to do.

At the Maryland general election, which was held last month, all the voters were required to take and subscribe to an Oath of allegiance to the Federal Government. Many of the citizens gladly availed themselves of the opportunity and to declare their loyalty but others took it as one does a dose of medicine; while others still finding it too bitter a pill for them to swallow, left the polls without voting, and talked loudly of this infringement on their "Constitutional rights." Those latter were of the species known as the Copperheads, and flourish in some parts of California as well as here. The following is the General Order issued by Major Thompson on election day, and a company of Californians was sent to each voting district of Montgomery County to enforce-some of the Copperheads having boasted that Union men should not be allowed to vote. This order will be read with interest by Californians; it has the ring of true metal in its every line:

Headquarters Cavalry Forces
Near Potomac,
Edwards Ferry. Md., Nov. 3, 1863.

General Orders No. 5-In compliance with orders from Major General Auger, commanding Department of Washington, a military force will be stationed in each Election District of Montgomery county, during the election on the 4th instant.

Such force will maintain order and protect the ballot boxes from the commencement of said election until the returns are completed.

The United States Flag will be raised over each building where the polls are held and every Judge of Election before he acts, and every citizen before he votes, must swear and subscribe to the oath of allegiance prescribed by Act of Congress, approved July 2, 1862.

Any person who shall, during said election, or hereafter, say or do anything against the Government of the United States, its flag or its officers, or who shall say or do anything to encourage or support any pretended Government or force in opposition thereto will be promptly arrested and brought to these headquarters. And any person who commits any depredation on the ballot box of any District, or who shall violently resist the military force in the discharge of their duty will be shot on the spot.

All persons are ordered during said election and hereafter not to sell or give any intoxicating liquors or spirits to any soldier of this command, and every place where the same is sold or kept within one mile of each voting place will be closed during said election, and all persons who disobey this instruction will be arrested and punished, and their property confiscated according to military law.

A commissioned officer will be present at the polls during the voting and making the returns and see that these regulations are strictly complied with, and commanding officers are charged with the prompt execution of these orders.

Captain McCallam, with seven companies of "Scott's Nine Hundred," will have charge of the guards and pickets on the Potomac, and the patrols on the canal and roads.

Captain Reed, commanding Second Massachusetts Cavalry, will have charge of this camp. Captain Rice, with Companies C, G and I, Second Massachusetts Cavalry, will be stationed at Medley's Hill, near Poolesville; Captain Eigenbrodt, with Company E, at Clarksburg; Captain Adams, with Company L, at Leytonsville; Captain Manning, with Company M, at Coleville, and Lieutenant Smith, with Company F, at Rockville. The headquarters of this command will be at Rockville, on the 4th instant.

By order of Major D. W. C. Thompson, Second Mass. Cavalry, Commanding Forces.

Aug. B. Heselton
Lieutenant and Acting Adjutant.

Miscellaneous.

Many of the Sergeants and others have, of late, been affected with a disease known here as "Nigger regiment on the brain." It seems that Massachusetts is going to raise a regiment of negro cavalry, to be the 4th Massachusetts, and thirty of the commissioned officers will be taken from this regiment; some have been offered commissions and declined them, while others, with less scruples, seek such positions and would gladly accept them if offered. Capt. Adams, of the California Battalion, is spoken of as candidate for the position of first Major of the "Blackbirds," and for the sake of his company it is hoped that he may get it; but it is somewhat doubtful, he having applied for a commission as Lieut. Colonel of another negro regiment, and when brought before the Examining Board failed to pass the necessary examination.

The friends of Capt. D. A. DeMerritt will learn with pleasure that he has entirely recovered from his insanity; has been pronounced fit for duty by his physicians, and will ere long resume the command of his company.

Corporal Luman P. Washington, of our battalion, was mortally wounded, and has since died. He was shot one night by a band of guerrillas while on picket. He was a resident of Iowa Hill, Placer County, a true and noble soldier, loved and respected by every one with whom he came in contact, and his loss is severely felt by us; He was the second man from Iowa Hill that has been killed in our battalion. Chauncey H. Hall, of Co. L, who was wounded near Aldie, some three months ago, has lost the entire use of his arm, and will be discharged as no longer fit for service. Thus, one by one, are dropping off the true and loyal hearts that prompted by patriotism, left the genial shores of California, and, alas! will return thither no more.

The health of the Californians is excellent; most of them look ragged and hearty, but we all somewhat dread the coming winter. We hail with cheers every victory gained over the rebels, for each one brings us so much nearer to our loved California and the loved ones there; and may the time soon come when we shall be with them again, and when peace and prosperity may once more reign over our distracted country.

T. H. M.

Alta California, San Francisco, Tuesday, January 5, 1864.
["Scott's 900", 11th N.Y. Cavalry, Col. James B. Swain]
[Lumen Washington -Lumen P. Washburn, Company L]

❖❖❖

Headquarters Cavalry Camp
Muddy Branch Dec 10th 1863

Col. C.R. Lowell Jr
Comdg Cavalry Camp
Vienna, Va
Colonel

I have the honor to inform you that on Friday last I was informed that Mr Trundles House between Conrads Ferry and Leesburg had been robbed of Silverware, Clothing, Cookery and light articles to the value of one thousand dollars, by four soldiers believed to be from the picket at Conrads Ferry. I immediately sent Capt. McKendrie my Provost Marshall to investigate the matter. He found most of the property, hid under the hay in a barn near the picket station, and returned it to Mr Trundle. Afterwards he learned that four of the men belonging to the picket there, went over the river in a boat on the night of the robbery. Soon after Capt. McKendrie went up there four men deserted namely privates Lynch *[Thomas B. Leach],* Pendell *[Martin M. Pendall]* and DeWald *[Frederick DeWald]* of Co F and private Howe *[there is a Joseph Howe but no record of a Dec. desertion]* of Co G. DeWald and Howe going together and a short time afterwards the other two. They left after 12 o'clock at night and before Capt McKendrie had had time to fix the crime on any one. Since then I have received information that Lynch and Pendell got across the river, when and how I cannot find out and have gone to join Mosbys men. They are very smart and dangerous men and if they get with Mosbys gang they will - if they are disposed - be very troublsome. They told on the other side that they had deserted from the picket at Conrads Ferry and were going to Moseby. They were last seen about six miles from Leesburg on the road towards Middleburg. I enclose their descriptive list for your information.

I am Colonel
Most Respt Yours
D.W.C. Thompson
Maj 2 Ms Cav
Comdg

Hd Qrs Cavalry Camp
Muddy Branch Dec 11th 1863

Col J.H. Taylor
Chief of Staff
Colonel

I have the honor to report to day that military affairs in my command continue in good condition. The rebels do not trouble this side of the river in the least and the disloyal element of this section of country has been very quiet since the State election. I regret to have to report to you that on the afternoon of the 4th inst Mr Trundle who has a very large farm and lives near Leesburg came to my camp and informed me that four soldiers had been to his house during his absence and robbed it of silver ware and other higher valuable property to the amount of about one thousand dollars and he had strong suspicions that they were from my pickets guards at Conrads Ferry. This was done in the evening in the presence of his help who could no resist them. I informed him that I would immediately investigate the matter and early the next morning I sent Capt. McKendrie with a few men to find the property if possible and arrest the robbers. He could not find any of the property in the camp at Conrads

Ferry or get any information then in relation to it but on further search in a barn nearby under the hay he found nearly all the articles taken from Mr. Trundle and has returned them to him. After this discovery but before he could trace out the men who committed the robbery four men deserted from that post and soon after he positively ascertained that the deserters were the men who crossed the river and took the property. I shall try to find them if within reach of my command. I enclose descriptive lists of the men which please forward to the proper officer to aid in their arrest.

In the matter referred to me a few days ago in relation to horse thieves in uniform near Rockville I have the honor to report that one of the parties referred to has been arrested and is now in camp and I hope to take the others soon. Three government horses, and saddles, and some arms were found with this man.

The greatest trouble I have had with this command has been to prevent robbing and stealing from Citizens and prevent drunkeness among some of the officers. I have made the most stringent regulations to prevent such and have enforced them firmly with Citizens and soldiers who caused trouble and injured the public service.

I am Colonel

D.W.C. Thompson

Maj 2 Ms Cav

Comdg

Hd Qrs Cavalry Camp

Muddy Branch Dec 14th 1863

Col J. H. Taylor
    Chief of Staff
        Colonel

I have the honor to again report that everything continues in good condition in my command. Mosby and Underwood one of his Captains were near the river at Young Island ford Thursday evening, making inquiries of a citizen who has sent me the information, as to the location and strength of my picket guards and camp. I have also been informed that he has been ranging with from sixty to eighty men from Leesburg down, between the river and Drainsville pike.

Enclosed I send for the information of the General Commanding a Statement of the present strength of my command. Of the 37 men at Whites ford it takes 12 to picket at the mouth of the Monocacy. I should have 22 men at Conrads ford and the same number at Youngs Island and Seneca Locks and 12 men at Muddy Branch ford and if possible the same number at Edwards Ferry for Camp guard, prisoners, and quartermasters and commissaries property. I require 21 men and 3 non-commissioned officers. This takes 157 men detailed for guard duty. These Companies require more or less for their own work and fatigue parties for various purposes take a larger number of men. For a patrol from here to the Monocacy and back every 2 hours (some 30 miles) of 2 men each requires 24 men daily, I regret to say that I am obliged to reduce my guards and patrols less than they should be and I cannot get men enough to do the necessary company and fatigue work.

When I first took command here there were 210 of the Scott 900, Col. Swain has made some changes in the companies and detachments here which I supposed were for the good of his Regiment but he has retained so much percent each time that the number of his Regiment here now is less than 150, from the character of the officers and men sent here I would have judged that this command was considered a place of banishment from his more

217

elegant quarters. The men I can manage but I regret to say that I have been obliged to send to Regimental Headquarters under arrest or orders five of his officers who were useless to this command. I am informed that Col Swain has 36 buglers and full corps of saddlers, farriers, blacksmiths, at least one officer for each company, and a good battalion commander. I am anxious that no trouble shall occur while I have charge of this line and I shall do the best possible with what men I have, but there are not enough here now to do the work as I commenced, or as it should be done. I hope I shall have as many as I started with and more if possible.

I am Colonel Respt Yours
D.W.C. Thompson
Maj 2 Ms Cav Comdg

Hd Qrs Cavalry Forces
Camp near Muddy Branch Dec 14th 1863

Major D.W.C. Thompson
     Comdg Cav Forces

Major, The following is a statement of the distribution of Enlisted Men belonging to this command.

"Scott's 900" Cav.

	For Duty	Sick	Absent With leave	Retd to regt	
Company "B"	28	5	5	2	
" "D"	12				
" "F"	37	Stationed	at Whites	Ford	
" "G"	39	4	1	8	
" "H"	18	2	"	12	
" "K"	11	Stationed	at Seneca	Lock	Part of each Co on patrol Duty at the various fords.
Total	145	11	7	40	

2d Mass. Cav.

	For Duty	Sick	Absent With leave	Retd to regt	
Company "C"	18	"	1	"	
" "L"	46	6	8	"	
" "G"	25	3	2	"	
" "I"	26	4	2	"	
Total.	115	13	13		
Grand Total	145	24	20	40	

G. D. Denison
Lt. and Act. Adjt.

Part of each Co on picket duty at the various fords.

Hd Qrs Cavalry Camp
Muddy Branch Dec 21st 1863

Col J.H. Taylor
   Chief of Staff
      Colonel
         I have the honor to report that I returned to camp from Washington last Friday. Everything in my command on the line of the river is in good order. The boards &c for my shed stables have arrived and I am finishing them as fast as possible. I send in today two prisoners Thos Warfield and Columbus Crocket taken by my provost guard near Laytonsville. They are bad characters and have the reputation of aiding deserters to escape, annoying union men by shooting their stock &c and are known to have robbed citizens in the vicinity.

Very Respt Yours
D.W.C. Thompson
Maj 2 Ms Cav Comdg.

Regimental Record Books, National Archives, Washington, D.C.

CAVALRY.

General Halleck's statement of the number of cavalry horses destroyed by our army will strike every body with astonishment. A remount for the whole service once in two months is the rate at which our horses are used up by want of skill and often culpable neglect of the animals. Four hundred and thirty-five thousand horses will be needed for the coming year if the evil remains unchecked. The enormous waste of horses was one of the points which was urged quite early, we believe, by those who wished to see the volunteer cavalry force kept within narrow limits. The admirable service done by this force will outweigh its immense and needless expense in the opinion of the country. The immense consumption of horses, however, is an evil which is felt outside the army or the Treasury. The stock-breeders declare that if it goes on it will permanently injure the breed of horses in the country. The horses of mature age are being taken up by the Government so fast that young horses are put to work too early, the result of which will ultimately be seen in the diminution of the average size. - *Boston Advertiser.*

Daily National Intelligencer, Washington, D.C., Saturday, December 19, 1863.

LETTER FROM THE CALIFORNIANS IN
THE ARMY OF THE POTOMAC.

———

(From the Correspondent of the ALTA in the Battalion.)

———

{In Camp, at Vienna, Va.
December 22d, 1863.}

EDITORS ALTA:- In my last letter I mentioned an expedition which was to start that day on a raid beyond the Bull Run Mountains, and now, in order to give your readers an insight to the *modus operandi* of guerrilla hunting, I will give you the details thereof.

The Expedition Leaves.

We left our camp at this place about 9 A. M., eighty as jolly Californians as can be scared up anywhere, in about equal numbers from each company of our Battalion, well mounted and armed, all under the command of Captain Adams, and accompanied by Charley Binns, our rebel guide; and here I will remark *en passant*, that our boys "go their whole pile" on Charley, for he has shown himself to be a brave and dashing fellow-qualities which ever win the admiration of a soldier, and, besides, he is true to our cause, and enthusiastic in its service. We marched along through fields and by-roads, avoiding the turnpikes, so as to keep our approach from being known to the rebels and their sympathizers. It was an exceedingly cold day, and we rode facing a cutting northwest wind, which chilled us through, in spite of our overcoats, and gave our faces a purple glow. At 4 P.M., we reached the foot of the mountains, and halted at the house of a notorious rebel, named Hutchison, who has five sons in the rebel army, and two pretty daughters at home, one of whom boasted that she had helped to hoist the first rebel flag raised in Loudon county, in this State. We searched the house, but found nothing we wanted, except a good supper, which was spread on a table. However, we captured two good horses; but one of the aforesaid pretty girls pleaded so hard and eloquently with Captain Adams, that his gallantry got the best of him, and one of the horses was left. Our guide, Charley Binns, helped to search the house, but the folks did not recognize him, though he stated to us that these same girls, had often hidden him away when our men had been searching for guerrillas; such was the change wrought in him by true Union clothes.

The Bivouac.

From this house our guide took us to a deep ravine near by, where we fed our horses and built good fires, and by them we made our cup of coffee and roasted a piece of bacon, which, together with a couple of "hard tack," were relished with as much gusto as a good dinner at a first class San Francisco restaurant. We sat by our bivouac fires, telling stories and relating adventures in our own dear California, waiting for the moon to rise and the rebels to go to bed.

At 11 P.M. we sallied forth, and soon began the ascent of the mountains before us. It was a rough ride, over rocks and tangled woods, but we were in good spirits, and felt elated at the prospect of fun ahead, and so we pushed on, regardless of the cold night-the coldest I ever experienced-but for that very reason-a good one for our purpose-it being very cold, the "rebs" would not be likely to sleep in the woods, and would be "at home" when we honored them with a little visit.

Across the Mountain.

We arrived at the summit of the mountain at 1 A. M. and surrounded and searched a log shanty, where a poor Virginian ekes out a miserable existence. Finding no "rebs," we descended the mountain on the west side, and soon came to a large house, which was duly surrounded. A loud knock summoned the inmates to open the door; but no answer was made, and your correspondent, pistol in hand, jumped through a window, into a room where a crazy boy lay sleeping, and from there to another room, where the mother and daughter of "sweet sixteen' stood shivering *en dishabille*. Leaving them to finish dressing, I hastened to open the door, and in rushed the searching party, which consisted of our advance guard. We searched the house, but found no rebels. We did, however, find the pantry, and therein a large head-cheese, which, together with other eatables, were duly appropriated and divided around. The lady of the house acknowledged that her husband was in the rebel service, in White's guerrillas, but claimed that she had not seen him in several months, which we knew to be false, as our guide had been there with him not more than three weeks before.

Searching Process Continued.

We left them, and from there went half a mile across a field, and halted at a log farmhouse, which was duly invested, and a loud knock at the door was answered by a female voice, and it was opened by a portly female, who inquired what we wanted. Without stopping to answer we rushed in, and for a few moments stood warming ourselves before a blazing hickory fire, while the aforesaid female stood looking at us in amazement, and suddenly exclaimed; "Well, if you's aint Yankees!" to which we replied that we most assuredly were some of the venerable Sam's nephews.

"Where's your husband?" said Charley Binns. "There's the dear little fellow" answered the Amazon, pointing to a bed in the corner of the room, and just then a head was lifted from where it lay hid under the bed cover.

The wife was evidently the better man of the two-and a most rabid rebel she is too, taking advantage of her sex to give vent to her treason. We searched the house, but without success, and left it and its occupants in disgust.

Thus far we had had poor luck, and again we mounted our horses. A gallop of half a mile brought us to the house of a Mr. Hixon; we were surprised to see lights burning, and soon surrounded the premises and entered the house. In the lower room the old man, wife, and four girls, were sleeping-all of them were much frightened and stood looking in amazement at each other. We searched the lower part of the house, but found nothing we wanted, except a handsome bed quilt with the United States coat of arms in each corner, which was captured and now adorns the bed of your correspondent. Candles in hand we rushed up stairs, and there hid in a large feather-bed, we found a full-blown, genuine rebel.

"Get up, get up," says Ben. Brown *[L]*, at the same time punching him with his pistol, by way of emphasis.

The reb reluctantly obeyed, and when brought down stairs, proved to be Dave Hixon-one of the worst desperadoes of Moseby's guerrillas. As soon as we reached the lower room with our prisoner, the whole family burst into tears and vented their grief in loud lamentation.

"They are going to take Cousin Dave away, and we won't see him any more," cried the poor girls.

We told "Cousin Dave" to make haste and prepare himself for a little trip to the "Old Capitol," where his comforts would be attended to by mine host of that pleasant resort for Southern gentlemen, who think that Uncle Sam's Government is not good for them.

How the Negroes Acted.

The plantation negroes, as soon as they learned that we had captured Cousin Dave began clapping their hands and jumping for very joy, and begged us "to take old massa too." They surrounded and besought us to take their master, exclaiming "Oh, please, do take old massa along wid you; he am de biggest rebel of de whole." We asked them what they were doing up so early (it was about 4 A.M.), and they told us that their master often made them get up at that hour and go to work in the field. So we concluded to take "old massa" along, and now both him and his promising nephew are safely lodged in the "Old Capitol."

Further Incidents.

While this was transpiring at the house, some of the boys went to the barn, and there found a fine mare, which we concluded to take along. As soon as the old lady heard this, she jumped our of bed and in the accent peculiar to Virginians exclaimed; "Oh, gentlemen, don't take my *marr*-please don't take my *marr*." But we heeded her not. She followed us to the gate in her night-clothes, begging all the while, and when she found her entreates in vain, she madly told us to take the *marr* and go to h—! with her, which latter command we'd rather be excused from obeying, as no horses are admitted within Pluto's domains.

From this place we went by a side-road to a large tannery. We searched all the premises, but only found a fine lot of apples, which were to be sent to the rebel army the next day. We freely helped ourselves, as we did also to some good butter and corn cake. It is astonishing how riding in the cold night air will sharpen a man's appetite-it is equal to Hostetter's Bitters.

It was now nearly daylight, and after searching a few more houses we crossed over to the Little River Turnpike, and then passed through the town of Aldie before its rebel inhabitants were up. We rode a couple of miles further and halted alongside of a good rail-fence, which we used to build us good fires; and there we cooked our breakfast. Chickens had now taken the place of bacon, and good bread or corn cake that of "hard tack," making us a sumptuous meal. This over, we were again on our horses, and our guide took us across several fields to a deep ravine, in a secluded spot, where we lay hid all day, resting ourselves and horses.

On The Road to Leesburg.

At eight P. M. we again sallied forth and took the road towards Leesburg. The first house we searched we had the good fortune to capture two of Moseby's men and their arms; they were very impudent and indignant that we should thus have gobbled them up, and were opposed to that mode of warfare. We did not stop to argue the point with them, but made them walk at a lively pace to keep up with our horses. The next house we searched was that of Mr. Ellsworth, a wealthy planter, himself a Union man, but whose family are most intensely Secesh; on this occasion we had particular business with his son "Bill," also one of Moseby's gang. On entering the house, the ladies were, appeared or pretended to be very much frightened-one fainted for fright. They assured us that there was no one in the house whom we wanted, and they had a great horror of soldiers, and asked the Lieutenant not to allow them to come in. But we did go in, and searched the house without success, and were about leaving the house, when a negro woman, for the bribe of a promised calico dress, told us that Bill was in the house. We again searched it, and Charley Binns crept up from the garret and found our game stretched our between the plastering and the roof, and brought him out, If ever a rebel did look sheepish, it was this one. As soon as we reached the parlor, and the ladies saw that we had the object of our search, they gave the most terrific screams-indeed I never heard such screaming. Whilst the mother was making preparations for Bill's trip to Washington, the young ladies, four in number made themselves busy in alluring us Yankees; the youngest, a beautiful girl of sixteen, would grind her teeth, look as "savage as a meataxe," and kept saying, "Oh! if hate could only kill," and other expressions of hatred. The father looked on these proceedings quite unconcerned, and just as we were leaving the house, gave his son some wholesome advice, and said; "I told you to keep out of the rebel service, but you would not mind me; now, you are going to prison, and I don't want you to return till the war is over."

We searched a number more houses with varied success, and then went to Leesburg, but found no rebel force there, and then went towards Drainsville, searching the houses on the way. Shortly after sunrise we halted to cook our breakfast and feed our horses from rebel corn, and here we did some tall foraging, and had a meal such as only hungry soldiers can appreciate. From this place we started on our way back to camp, and arrived there before sundown, bringing with us our prisoners, captured horses, and other spoils.

This brief sketch is sufficient to let your readers see what kind of duty we are doing here, but it does not consist entirely of trips like this; our men have a great deal of picket duty to do, besides work around the camp, so that it is quite a relief to go on a raid.

Picket Duty.

Is getting to be quite dangerous here, of late. An attack upon one of our picket posts is almost an every night occurrence. About a week ago, our pickets at the cross roads two miles from camp, were attacked by a party of about fifty rebels, taking one of our men prisoner, and capturing six horses fully equipped. The prisoner taken was James B. Randall, Company L, California Battalion. He resided in San Francisco, and held an office under Major Solomon, when he was U. S. Marshal. Randall is a good soldier, and a good Union man every way. The poor fellow is, here this, in the Libby Prison at Richmond. And here mark the contrast; this Randall has a brother who edits a contemptible, dirty rebel sheet published in Sonora, Tuolumne county; it is called *The Dixie*. One brother is doing his utmost to destroy the very Government for which the other is now suffering the horrors of a Richmond prison.

Another Attack.

Since writing the above another of our picket posts has been attacked. Last night, about nine o'clock, our pickets at Hunter's Mill, were attacked by guerrillas and two of our battalion shot. Oscar Burnap, of Company E, shot through the breast, and mortally wounded; he formerly resided at American Valley, Plumas county; and Seth H. Cooper, of Iowa Hill, Placer county, shot in the head; a bad wound, but not necessarily mortal. The blame of this sad affair rests solely upon Col. C. R. Lowell, of our regiment, who now commands the cavalry brigade. He appears to have no regard for the lives and liberties of our men; sending five men to stand picket three and four miles from camp, where no assistance can reach them until it is too late. When the news of the disaster reaches camp he sends out a party of men and marches them around over the turnpikes and returns to camp. In a few days more the same is repeated-the pickets attacked, several horses and arms captured, and some of our men either shot or taken prisoners. Colonel Lowell has shown himself entirely incompetent and unfit to command even a corporal's guard, and ought to have the eagle shoulder-straps torn from his shoulder, and made to serve in the ranks; and but for the corrupt political influence that procured his appointment, this would be done. Every day he sacrifices the lives of better men than he ever dare be, and it is to be hoped that there will be an end to it sometime.

Miscellaneous.

Captain D. A. De Merritt has resumed the command of his Company; he is now entirely well, and has been so pronounced by the Surgeons. He is over in Maryland, under Major Thompson's command.

Lieut. Baldwin has just returned from a furlough, looking well and hearty. He is now attached to Company M. This Company is indeed to be envied; they have one of the best Captains in the regiment, and now they have Lieutenant Baldwin. Would that all the officers in the Union army where such as Captain George A. Manning; we'd hear of more victories and fewer defeats; it would be a pleasure then, rather than a burden, to serve in the army. California may well be proud of him.

Captain Z. B. Adams is now absent on a furlough to his home in Massachusetts. By his conduct he has won the ill-will of nearly every man in our battalion. In a future letter I will give you some account of his doings here.

Sergeant-Major Kinne, of San Francisco, has been promoted to Second Lieutenant, and is now Acting Adjutant.

William B. Clarke, formerly a clerk in the San Francisco Post Office, and a member of Captain Eigenbrodt's Company, has been promoted out of this regiment to the Second Lieutenant in the Fourteenth Kansas, and is now at Fort Scott, Kansas; he is a fine soldier and a clever gentleman, and we rejoice at his promotion.

Our boys are in good health and spirits; they have so discharged their duties that they have won an enviable reputation in this Department, and are complimented wherever they go; and California may well be proud of her battalion.

T. H. M.

Alta California, San Francisco, Sunday, January 31, 1864.
[James P. Randall died July 15, 1864 at Andersonville of starvation]

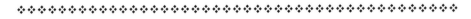

California Battalion. - B.F. Hoxie, of Company L, Second Massachusetts Cavalry, writing from Vienna, Va., under date of December 22d, to a friend in this place, says: "All of the boys from Suisun are in good health. Four of our pickets were shot last night by the bushwhackers. Two were shot after they surrendered - one through the breast, and the other through the head. Two of the pickets were from California, and two from New York. We have just returned from an expedition in the Shenandoah Valley. The rebels made a raid on the Orange and Alexandria Railroad, and we were sent to cut them off, but were to late by four hours. It would have been pretty hot for us - the rebels had two thousand, and we only five hundred. We have had a good many men shot in skirmishes. The first time we went to Ashby'\s Gap I got a shot so close to my nose that I thought it was gone. The rebels were concealed in the bushes, and they fired in good order. But we managed to kill twelve of them and took sixteen prisoners."

Solano Press, Suisun, Saturday, February 6, 1864
[Benjamin F. Hoxie, Company L]

1864

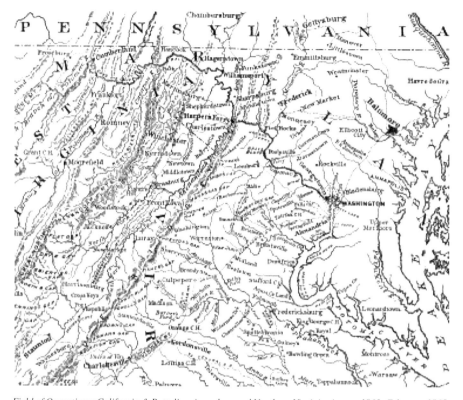

Field of Operations: California & Battalion, in and around Northern Virginia. August 1863- February 1865.

The year opened with the Californians spread out in winter camps, with some encamped near Seneca, Maryland, guarding the fords of the Potomac, and others encamped at Vienna, Va. February saw the loss of Capt. Reed at Dranesville as well as a number of men killed or taken prisoner which was a major blow to the California troops.

Early July brought them to the defence of Washington against the siege of The Capitol by Jubal Early.

In August, Sheridan was given command of the Middle Military Division and the 2d Mass. Cavalry Regiment became a part of the Reserve Brigade in Sheridan's Army of the Shenandoah. They entered upon a long and arduous campaign, suffering many losses, including the loss of Colonel Lowell at Cedar Creek, October 19. Colonel Crowninshield then took command of the Reserve Brigade.

Also about this time, the California Hundred and Battalion, because of their diminished numbers, became lost in the larger units to which they were attached. Consequently, news coverage seemed to cease, and it's only by reading the news coverage of those larger units that we're able to account for the balance of the year 1864. The end of the year was spent clearing the Shenandoah of the rebel forces. Here took place the battles at Winchester, Fisher's Hill, Cedar Creek, Woodstock Races, etc.

❖❖

JANUARY, 1864

2 Federal troops occupied Santa Catalina Island, California, removing possible smugglers.

22 Major Gen. Rosecrans named commander of the Federal Department of the Missouri.

❖❖

Native Californian Cavalry for the North.-Capt. Ramon Pico's Company of native California Cavalry, numbering some seventy-five men, rank and file, came in from the Presidio yesterday afternoon, and embarked on board the steamer *Panama* for Humboldt Bay. They are to be stationed in the Humboldt country, and employed in the work of hunting out the hostile Indians, who have, as a general rule, been too nimblefooted for our infantry soldiers, and have given the people of the northern part of the State a great deal of annoyance.

Alta California, San Francisco, Sunday, January 3, 1864.
[See Alta California of March 11, 1863]

❖❖

New York, January 16. - The *Herald's* Army of the Potomac despatch says; Col. Lowell's cavalry brigade have returned to Fairfax from a reconnaissance to Snickersville, Berryville and Leesburg. No traces were found of Stuart's cavalry.

Evening Bulletin, San Francisco, Tuesday, January 19, 1864

California Battalion. - Wm. F. Halsey has received from his son a very handsome colored print, containing the names of the officers and privates of Company L, 2d Massachusetts Cavalry. We recognize several familiar names of former residents of Suisun among the number. The print is ornamented by patriotic designs and portraits of Hooker, Butler, Rosecrans, Buford, Burnside and Segal. Over all is the motto: "Inflexible in faith, invincible in arms." It is quite an ornament, and Mr. Halsey intends having it neatly framed.

Solano Press, Suisun, Saturday, January 30, 1864
[William F. Halsey, Co. L]

                                                        Camp Cav Forces Vienna Va.
                                                              Jan. 31st 1864

Dear Parents

I received your letter of the 24th yesterday but could not get time to answer it before I have been so very busy in my new office. You see by the heading of my letter that I am in Virginia at Regimental Hd. Qrs. it will be one week tomorrow since I arrived here; the last letter I wrote you was a day or two before I left Muddy Branch, Md. I am regularly appointed Sergt. Major of this Regiment now. My appointment dates from Jan. 25th as that is the day the Old Sergt. Major was promoted to Lieut.

I was jumped over the heads of two or three sergeants who outranked me, so that at present I stand No. 1 in the line of Promotions. I have more work to do here than I had at my old place but that is nothing. I am better posted than I used to be, so that I can make my work easier.

Ma wished to know about the Pudding etc. I am glad you spoke of it for I thought I had written about it before.

Thompson was nearly crazy when he saw what I had brought & he thought more of the Pudding than all the rest he said it was the best he ever tasted of in America. He thought that jell cake was splendid he said it was the best he ever saw also the mince Pies. What John & I took together lasted us about a week & almost all the boys in the Company had a piece of either one or the other. I would like it if you could send me a small box by express with a little Butter as butter is worth 50c per lb. here, if you should send butter put it in tin do not send fruit cake for that is too rich food, send an account of what you have to pay out & I will send you the money as soon as we are paid off, if you should send anything in that way Direct By Express it to

                                                   Sergt. Major Robt. H. Williams,
                                                   2nd Reg. Mass. Cavalry Vols.,
                                                              Washington, D.C.

You wished to know if Capt. DeMerritt was Promoted so as to leave a vacancy, he is not. He is only acting Asst. Inspector General. Our Col. expects to be a Brigadier Gen. soon; & when he is promoted our Capt. will be Asst. Inspector Gen. on Lowell's staff which will make him a Major.

I must close for it is almost midnight. The Adjutant has just left the office.
Tell Irene I will write as soon as I can. Love to all Kiss Little Annie for me.

My Respects to Sate, & all other inquiring friends, write soon & direct to your son

Sergt. Major R. H. Williams
2nd Mass. Cav. Vienna, Va.
via Washington, D.C.

Manuscript Collection, Huntington Library, San Marino, California
[Robert H. Williams, Co. F; Edward Thompson; John Passage.]

❖❖

FEBRUARY, 1864

5   Colt pistol factory destroyed.
9   Mass escape of Federal Officers from Libby Prison.
17   Confederate submarine *H. L. Hunley* sinks the *U.S.S. Housatonic.*
20   Battle of Olustee, Florida.
27   Federal prisoners of war begin arriving at Camp Sumter (Andersonville).

❖❖

LETTER FROM THE CALIFORNIAN BATTALION,
SERVING WITH THE ARMY OF
THE POTOMAC.

(From the Correspondent of the ALTA, with the Column.)

Camp of Californian Battalion,
Vienna, Va. February 7th, 1864.}

EDITORS ALTA: Pressure of duties has broken in upon my good intentions of writing more often than I have of late; but I will "seize time by the forelock," and avail myself of this Sunday evening in camp to write you and give a brief account of our doings since my last letter from this place.

Picket Duty.

This is the most arduous, as well as the most dangerous, duty we have to perform; and not a little unpleasant, too, in this the middle of winter, when the nights are bitter cold, and the days raw and chilly. Every day thirty of our men are detailed, and, with as many more from the Massachusetts companies, leave camp at 1:30 P. M., to go and relieve the outer pickets. The first three posts are at the Blacksmith Shop, Tyson's Cross Roads, and at the Lowensville Church, all of them on the road between this place and the "Chain Bridge" across the Potomac. Five men and a corporal are left at each of these posts; the rest go half a mile beyond Lowensville and camp in the pine woods; these constitute the reserve. The pickets pass the time from daybreak till dark, sitting by the fire reading, sleeping and chatting, while one man stands sentinel, and, he, in turn, is relieved every two hours. As soon as it is dark, the picket is moved to some place in the thick pine woods, near by, in order to deceive the rebels, and to prevent being shot by some lurking bushwhacker, a species of the *genus homo* abounding in this vicinity. Of course it will not do to have a fire, for that would be equivalent to informing the rebels of the picket's place of concealment. The night is passed sitting or laying on the damp, cold ground, with arms in hand, and ready for use at a moment's notice. As you may well imagine, it passes slowly away, and the weary soldier watches with eager gaze to catch the first gleam of light that appears on the eastern horizon to announce the approach of the coming day. Slowly it comes at first, but increasing as each minute goes by, until, bathed in golden splendors, old Sol himself appears, illuming the mountain tops, and with his genial rays gladdening the heart of the faithful sentinel, who for twelve long hours has been wrapped in darkness. The picket is now moved to the road where it was stationed before, and stays there until relieved in the afternoon.

Attacks upon Pickets.

In civilized warfare these are of rare occurrence, but of late they have ceased to create much excitement. There are many rebels infesting the country around here, concealed in the woods and in the houses of their sympathisers. These scoundrels are dismounted, and in order to procure or steal horses, have done deeds of daring worthy of a better cause, such as coming into this camp and stealing from the Massachusetts companies eighteen horses at one time and six at another.

A reserve of twenty men and one lieutenant go out every evening, and when night comes conceal themselves in the thick pines, where even an owl would fail to find them, and remain there until morning. If a picket post is attacked during the night, this reserve, instead of going to their assistance, by orders from headquarters, conceals itself, if possible, more effectually. Some of the boldest of our number have dared to ask "what good does this reserve do?" None in the world. It is only a part of Lowell's strategy. He is trying to outdo that of the redoubtable general of the "Mackerel Brigade," who surrounded an army of "Southern Confederacies" with *one* man, while himself, mounted on his "architectural steed" Pegassus, witnessed the difficult performance which his rare strategy alone could have accomplished. Where could he have learned all this strategy? Certainly not within the classic halls of old Harvard; not from reading the campaigns of Ceasar; by, aye I have it!-on the staff of General McClellan, the would be Copperhead President of the United States. Pickets are attacked, horses and arms captured, and still the eagle is perched upon his shoulders, from whence it ought to have taken its flight long ago.

Arduous and dangerous as picket duty may seem, most of our men prefer to go out and do it rather than stay in camp and be subjected to dress parades, reviews, inspections, and other annoyances.

A Raid to the Blue Ridge.

Hearing that a lot of rebel cavalrymen were rusticating around Middleburg, and the adjacent towns, on furloughs, and to steal horses, we started out to pay them a visit. Col. Lowell was in command of the expedition, which consisted of the four California companies, some of the Massachusetts, and detachments from the Thirteenth and Sixteenth New York Cavalry. They marched by the Little River turnpike to Mount Zion Church, Col. Lowell's favorite halting place. From this place, Captain Adams, with his company and a few New Yorkers, were ordered to take a side road and go to Upperville. Shortly afterwards, Captain Eigenbrodt was ordered to take his company, and a few others, and go to meet Captain Adams at Middleburg; but on approaching this town he saw rebels here and there in squads; a courier was sent to Colonel Lowell to inform him of this, but he was captured by the rebels. Captain Eigenbrodt found it imprudent to go further, for the rebels largely outnumbered him, and was reluctantly forced to return to the main column. The gallant Captain wanted to charge through the town at the head of his brave company, (E), but the guide would not listen to it. When Colonel Lowell was informed of all this, he, instead of taking his whole command and going up there to fight the rebels, and also reinforce Captain Adams, got his column in line, and, after considering a moment, remarked, "*I guess I'll let Adams sweat*," acting on the maxim, "He who fights and runs away," &c., he made for camp with all speed, leaving our noble "boys" to their fate; but they were equal to the task, met the rebels, chased them, capturing and killing several, and returned to camp the following day. All our boys done nobly on this raid, as indeed they always do. Thomas McFarlane, a resident of the Mount Diablo Coal Mines, was wounded in a hand-to-hand encounter with a guerrilla. The rebel fired ten shots at Mc, two of which took effect on his horse, and one pierced his thigh; but, after this, still undaunted, he drew his sabre, having fired all the shots in his pistol, and ran the rebel through the body, and hit him a cut on the head, which finished him. A spring wagon was captured, and our wounded comrade brought to camp, and he has now well nigh recovered from his wound.

A Noted Guerrilla Killed.

Hearing that several noted guerrillas had been seen lurking in the vicinity of our camp, a small party of dismounted men were sent out one dark night to search some suspicious houses. At 2 A. M. they surrounded one of these, and a rebel within, hearing the noise, caught up his boots in one hand and pistol in the other, and tried to escape by the front door; but finding our men there he fired several shots, and then ran for the back door; but there he found one of the boys who fears no living rebel!-Pringle of "L" Company-and he put a carbine ball through the body of "Johnny Reb.," wounding him so that he died a few hours after. He turned out to be a notorious guerrilla named Meade, formerly a resident of Maryland; he confessed having attacked the pickets on several occasions, and before he died expressed his opinion that it was "very wicked for men to shoot at each other."

I am sorry to have to acknowledge a serious loss on this occasion. George L. Barnes, of Capt. Manning's Company, a resident of Marysville, was mortally wounded, shot in the abdomen, and has since died. He was a good man and a brave soldier, and his death is much deplored by his comrades, and by all who knew him. It may be some satisfaction to his friends in California to know that his last hours were attended with peace and comfort. The members of his Company bestowed every attention upon him and did all that a most loving mother could do. When death had released the noble soul from within the mortal clay, and it had taken its flight to regions of bliss above, I saw tears of sorrow trickling down the cheeks of his brave comrades, as they vowed vengeance on the accursed traitors who had thus brought to an untimely end God's noblest work-an honest and brave man.

Our Prisoners in Richmond.

In my previous letters I have informed you of the capture of several members of our battalion, and their confinement in Richmond. We have lately learned that they have fared rather badly during their imprisonment at the rebel capital. Lieutenant John C. Norcross, of Placer County, who was captured last July at the battle of Ashby's Gap, is still living, and in apparent good spirits, but has suffered much for want of proper food and clothing. I am pained to have to chronicle the death of several of our California boys at the Libby Prison. Roswell R. Smith, of Eureka, Sierra county, died December 14th, from sheer starvation and want; Hiram Vennum also died at the Libby. Both these men were much esteemed by their respective companies, and I can truthfully say that better or braver men never took up arms for the cause of their country. Thomas W. Cobby, of Company E, was also a prisoner there, but being very sick, and when death was near at hand, he was paroled, sent to the Parole Camp at Annapolis, and there died.

Major Thompson and His Command.

Major Thompson has moved his camp from Edward's Ferry to Muddy Branch, Maryland, where he commands the cavalry forces north of the Potomac, in the defences of Washington, where he is now in winter quarters. I paid a visit to his camp a week or two ago, and was much pleased with the admirable arrangement of everything. Major Thompson, with that regard to the wants of his men which is so characteristic of him, has left nothing undone which would in any way promote their comfort and safety. He is much esteemed by both men and officers, and very justly stands high in the estimation of General Augur, commanding this Department. His amiable wife is now at his camp, and like a good, sensible woman, prefers to share her husband's campaign life on the "tented field," rather than the routine of fashion and pleasure at the North.

Promotions.
Quite a number of promotions have taken place in our Battalion since my last letter. Sergeant Walter Morrison, of Co. E, has been promoted to be First Lieutenant in the 9th Ohio Cavalry. He resided in Sacramento and Yolo counties, and is well known there. Sergeant John Anderson, of Princeton, Mariposa county and Sergeant Samuel F. Tucker, of L Co.; Sergeant Edgar Blanche and Sergeant Mallory of E Co.; Sergeant Allen and Wheat, of the California Hundred, and Sergeant George F. Wilson, have been made Lieutenants in the 5th Massachusetts Cavalry, a regiment now being raised in Boston. Sergeant Wm. F. Short, formerly a Captain in the California Volunteers, has been made First Lieutenant in a U. S. colored regiment. Negro Troops are all the go now, and I willingly confess that my prejudices against these troops have been removed, by knowing how well and bravely they have fought against the rebels. I am now in favor of arming every negro capable of bearing arms, and let them aid us in putting down this hellish rebellion. Every rebel they kill is so much clear profit. Sergeants Armstrong, Meader and Wilson, *alias* Poe, have been made Second Lieutenants in this regiment.

Miscellaneous.
The health of our Californians is much better than we expected; the cold weather has not affected them as much as we all thought it would. While on this subject allow me to pay a tribute to the merit of our California blankets. They were made to order for us at the woollen mills in San Francisco, and in quality surpass any to be had here. We prize them very highly, and would not take double their cost for them. When one of us loses his "California blanket" he feels as if he had lost his best friend.

Oscar Burnap and Seth H. Cooper, who were wounded while on picket duty some time ago, are slowly recovering from their serious and painful wounds.

The spring campaign will soon open, and then lookout for lively times. We are in hopes of being sent to the "front," and if we are you'll hear a good account of the "California boys."

Since writing the above, we are called upon to mourn the loss of another of our number. Cyrus B. Jones, of Captain Adams' Company, breathed his last this morning, at two o'clock, in the hospital at this place. Jones was a native of Texas, his family having emigrated to California in the early days, and settled in the San Jose Valley, where they now reside. When the rebellion broke out, instead of following the example of his deluded Southern brothers, he launched boldly forth in the cause of the Union, and when our Battalion was being organized in San Francisco, he joined its ranks. When we took the field and began active operations, he was always among the foremost in doing his duty, always ready, always willing. About six weeks ago while on picket duty at Lowensville, he was attacked by rebel guerrillas; he fired at them, killing one, and then tried to escape by running to the woods; but the rebels cut off his retreat, and his horse ran up against those of the rebels, and he was thrown heavily to the ground. In the fall he was seriously injured, and has never recovered from those injuries. After a month of suffering he was taken to the hospital, and there died this morning. He was much esteemed by all his Company (L), and out of it. We extend to his sorrowing parents our heartfelt sympathy for the loss of their loved son, who is mourned by us all. He will be buried with military honors this afternoon, and with grief-laden hearts we will follow the body of our fallen comrade to his last resting place, and may Virginia's flowery soil rest lightly upon him.

T. H. M.

Alta California, San Francisco, Tuesday, March 8, 1864.

❖❖

Head Quarters 2d Massachusetts Cavalry
Vienna, Va. February 7th 1864

General Order}
   No. 10   }
                    1. Before a Drum head Court Martial convened at Hd. Qrs. Cavalry Camp, Vienna, Va. at 8 o'clock, P.M., February 6th 1864, W.H. Forbes 2d Mass. Cavalry is President; was arraigned and tried Private Wm. E. Ormsby, Company E, 2d Mass. Cavalry, on the following Charge and Specification.
Charge Desertion to the Enemy
                    Specification In this - that the Private Wm. E. Ormsby, Co. "E" 2d Mass. Cavalry, a duly enlisted Soldier in the Service of the United States did on or about the 24th day of January 1864, while on Picket guard at Lewinsville, Va., desert from said Service and go over to the Enemy, taking with him his arms and equipments and horse, and did remain absent until taken on the Fifth (5) February 1864, dressed in Rebel Uniform, armed and in the act of using his arms against the United States. This at Lewinsville, Va., on or about the 24th day of January 1864, and at Aldie, Va., on or about February 5th 1864.
To which Charge and Specification the Prisoner pleaded as follows
To the Specification of the Charge Not Guilty
                    "   "   Charge   Not Guilty

          The Court having Maturely considered the evidence adduced and the Statement of the Prisoner in his own behalf, find the accused Private Wm. E. Ormsby, Co. "E", 2d Mass. Cavalry as follows.
To the Specification of Charge Guilty
     "   "   Charge   Guilty

          And do therefore Sentence him, Private Wm. E. Ormsby, Co. E, 2d Mass. Cav. to be shot to death at such time and place as the Commanding Officer may direct in the presence of the Brigade.

          II The proceedings findings and Sentence in the above case of Private Wm. E. Ormsby, Co. "E". 2d Mass. Cavalry are hereby approved and the prisoner will be shot to death this day at 11 O'clock A.M. in the presence of the Brigade.
          III For such an offense Death is the only punishment and the Commanding Officer hopes and believes that the Summary Execution today will prevent forever the necessity of its repitition in this Command.
          IV The Drum head Court Martial of which Major Wm. H. Forbes, 2d Mass. Cavalry is President is hereby disolved.

By Order
Col. C.R. Lowell, Jr.
Col. 2d Mass. Cavalry

Comdg. Caly. Comp.
Officers
G.A. Stone
1st Lieut. and A.A.A.G.

Regimental Record Books, National Archives, Washington, D.C.

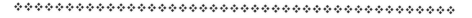

LETTER FROM THE CALIFORNIA HUNDRED.

Vienna, Virginia, Feb. 8th, 1864.

Eds. Reporter: It has been some time since I have heard from anyone from California. I do not write now for the purpose of giving you any news, for all news that would interest you is received by you before my letter could reach Washington. There was quite a time here yesterday, caused by the execution of one of our California Battalion boys. William E. Ormsby, of Co. E., Cal. Batt., 2d Massachusetts Cavalry, deserted on the 24th of January, taking with him two horses and five pistols. He was captured February 6th, by Captain Reed's squadron, was tried by drumhead court martial, and shot on Sunday, 7th, at 12 o'clock M. He met his fate without flinching, and while marching he kept step with the music and smiled at every one of his acquaintances as he passed them. He was called "Pony", from his being formerly one of the Pony Express riders. When our men attempted to capture him he fought hard, and charged on our men (four of them) twice, and fired twelve shots before he ran. Our men headed him into a corral and thus captured him. Two of our men were wounded by him.

Our regiment is filling up quite fast from recruits from Boston, and now numbers some 930 men, and 50 more are to be here this week.

You can be assured that the seven hundred bounty men catch it. They are made to build the abatte around the camp, guard the wood trains, do camp guard duty, etc. Our command are getting furloughs (two out of each company) four from 10 to 20 days. I have just returned from one of 25 days. [See marriage notice in another column. "That's what's the matter."-ed.]

Three of the sergeants of the California Hundred have received commissions in the 5th Massachusetts Cavalry (negros), a new regiment now getting up in Boston, and several others have declined accepting. Wm. McNeil is expecting a commission through the influence of his cousin, Maj. Forbes. Billy is a very good soldier. Fred Quant is a member of the band. Our band will be as good a one as there is in the U.S. service, in six months. Their instruments were made to order (new pattern) of the best German silver. The drums cannot be had yet as there is no material either in New York or Boston to make them of. They are to be made of German silver also. These instruments are purchased by moneys from the regiment fund, which fund, if reports be true, amounts to about $30,000, and is in the hands of Amos Lawrence, Boston.

We have had two cases of small pox in camp, neither of which proved fatal, and at present there are no indications of its appearance. Our command has captured about 200 of Moseby's guerrillas, and about 120 citizens, prisoners, during the past three months. We have lost some 75 all told-nabbed while on picket duty, shot by rebels in ambush, and by desertion.

The Vallejo boys all went to Washington to see Capt. Frisbie on his arrival, and dined with him. Conness, Shannon and Higbie are doing all they can for the California boys, by helping them get furloughs and leaves of absence, commissions, etc.

The probability is that we will go to Texas next spring. The boys all send respects, while I remain the same old

Charley Briggs.

The Napa County Reporter, Napa, Saturday, March 12, 1864.
["That's what's the matter" - Briggs-Gardner - In Boston, Dec. 29th., by Rev. Mr. Edmunds, Mr. Charles P. Briggs, formerly of Napa City, Assistant Quartermaster of the Cal. Hundred, to Miss Mary Ann Gardner, daughter of the late George R. Gardner, of Nantucket.]

❖❖

UNITED STATES MILITARY TELEGRAPH
By Telegraph from <u>Washington</u>
Dated <u>February 8th 1864.</u>
To <u>Brig. Gen. Tyler</u>

Maj. Gen. Auger directs that the order from Col. Lowell relieving Cos F & G by Cos K & M 2d Mass Cavy be countermanded & that here after Maj. Thompsons command is not to be interfered with except through these Hd Qrs.

Respy
C.H. Raymond
ADC

Regimental Record Books, National Archives, Washington, D.C.

❖❖

LETTER FROM THE CALIFORNIAN BATTALION, SERVING WITH THE ARMY OF THE POTOMAC.
———
(From the Correspondent of the ALTA, with the Column.)
———

Camp of Californian Battalion,
Vienna, Va. February 14th, 1864.}
EDS. ALTA: One week ago today we were called upon to witness the most painful scene enacted since we have been soldiers-one of our number was shot for deserting to the enemy.
The Desertion.
About three weeks ago, we were astonished to hear that William E. Ormsby, (sic) of Captain Eigenbrodt's Company E, had deserted to the enemy, taking with him two of the best and fleetest horses in the regiment, fully equipped, and several Colt's revolvers. Being thus well armed and mounted, he hastened to Aldie, where he had contracted an intimacy with a young lady of the rebel persuasion. Ormsby was at the time on duty as one of a patrol from Lowensville to camp, made one round and returned to the Reserve; being in possession of the countersign, he had no difficulty in getting through the lines. Soon after the news reached the camp, a detachment of about sixty men started in pursuit, but returned after a fruitless search of two days. About two days after this, another scout left camp and proceeded to Aldie, and while resting in the town, the advance guard of twenty men were charged on by nine guerrillas, with Ormsby at their head. They thought our Californians were New Yorkers, and could easily be

captured; but they counted without their host, for the advance guard was composed of men from Captain Eigenbrodt's company-boys who have never yet turned their backs to the enemy. The charge was gallantly met by our men, and the rebels were soon compelled to beat a hasty retreat. Ormsby acted with great bravery; he was foremost in the charge and the last to retreat, but, finding that he could not escape on his horse, he left him and tried to get away on foot, but was soon surrounded and made a prisoner. Two of our men were slightly wounded in the skirmish.

The scouting party returned to camp late in the afternoon with the prisoners, and the rumor soon spread all over the camp that Ormsby was to be immediately shot. That same evening a Drum Head Court Marshal was organized, and Ormsby brought before it, and pleaded "Not Guilty" to the charges and specifications; but the evidence was of such a nature that the Court could not do otherwise than return a verdict of "Guilty;" but it was not made known until morning. Early on Sunday morning, the prisoner was informed of his fate, and he had but little time to prepare himself for the awful ordeal through which he was so soon to pass. He spent the morning in writing and in religious exercises, being attended by the regimental chaplain.

The Execution.

At 11 P.M. the doomed man was led from the Guard-house and joined in the procession, in the following order: First came the brigades band, playing a solemn dirge; then the shooting party, composed of twelve Californians armed with Sharp's carbines; after them followed the coffin, borne by four men and behind it, walking with firm and steady step, came Ormsby, attended by the Chaplain. He was perfectly composed, and seemed determined to meet his fate like a brave man as he was. The procession marched from the office of the Provost Marshal to the place of execution, where the whole brigade was drawn up in a hollow square. On reaching the fatal spot the procession halted, and Ormsby asked permission to address his company, which was granted to him by Major Crowninshield. Marching up to where they were drawn up in line, he spoke to his comrades briefly, asked Captain Eigenbrodt to forgive him, told his friends to take warning by him, and concluded by saying that he hoped our cause would suc-ceed, for it was the right one, and hoped that the Stars and Stripes would, ere long, float in triumph over the whole Union, and then bade them goodbye. He was then marched back to the spot where he was to be shot. Passing by Maj. Crowninshield, he saluted him and told him that he hoped his regiment would be an honor to him.

After kneeling in prayer, he rose up calm and collected, the Provost-Sergeant then stepped up and tied his wrists before him, Ormsby then pulled open his blouse and shirt, baring his breast, he said in a firm voice, pointing to his heart, "Boys, do your duty; aim right here." A black handkerchief was then tied over his eyes, to which he objected. The Sergeant then stepped back, and Lieut. Alvord, Provost Marshal, gave the command "Ready-aim-fire!" Simultaneously with the last command twelve carbines were discharged, and Ormsby fell backward on his coffin-dead. Thus sadly ended the career of a gallant soldier, a jovial companion, a brave but misguided man.

While none of us can justify the conduct of Ormsby in deserting to the guerrillas, still there are mitigating circumstances in this case. Some time previous to the desertion of Ormsby, while out on a scout, he single-handed captured two rebels, but one of them managed to escape and Ormsby took the other to the command. On reaching camp, he was charged with having been bribed to allow the prisoner to escape, and on this charge, unfounded as we know it to be, he was put under arrest in the Guard house, and was kept there a month without charges being preferred against him and without officially knowing the cause of his arrest. Naturally sensi-tive, smarting under the sense of his wrongs, he was galled by this bad and unjust treatment, and took the first opportunity to leave the scene of his wrongs. Then again he was influenced by the subtle power which that rebel girl possessed over him, which he had not the moral courage to resist, though he could face death unappalled.

More Promotions.

The many friends of Lieutenant J. A. Baldwin in San Francisco will be rejoiced to hear of his promotion. He is now First Lieutenant, and in command of Company K. I think I do not detract the others, when I say that no officer in this regiment is so universally esteemed as is Lieutenant Baldwin. His known bravery, his zeal for our cause, combined with his uniform kindness and affable manners, are a ready passport to the hearts of all with whom he comes in contact. May he continue to rise in the scale of promotion until covered with glory, he shall return to the midst of his friends in California.

Sergeant Henry Kuhls, of Company L, a resident of Howland Flat, Sierra county, has been promoted to be Second Lieutenant of Company K. He is a gallant soldier, a clever gentleman and well worthy of promotion. Sergeant McIntosh, of the "California Hundred," has also been promoted to be Second Lieutenant.

Captain Z. B. Adams has, we are sorry to say, failed to get a commission as Major of the Massachusetts Negro Cavalry. When our Battalion left San Francisco, Company B was proud in thinking that they had a good Captain; but alas! how sadly they have been disappointed. Before we had taken the field he began to show his true colors, and since then has been daily growing worse, until he has now well nigh reached the climax of meanness and disgrace. By his tyrannical conduct he has lost the esteem and incurred the hatred of his men; by his habitual intemperance, he has lost their respect and forfeited every claim to decency; his bad conduct has several times caused him to be placed under arrest. Altogether, he is a disgrace to California, a disgrace to the service and to the brave Company, than which a better one cannot be found in the army. I have abstained from mentioning these facts for the reason that I dislike to write anything derogatory to either men of officers or the California Battalion; but proper regard for the truth forbids me from any longer remaining silent about it.

The California Delegation.

We, while on a visit to Washington, last week, paid a visit to our California Delegation in Congress; these gentlemen have been ever courteous to the members of our battalion. California may well be proud of her Delegation. With one exception, and for the first time, she is properly represented in Congress.

In the popular branch of Congress Hon. Thomas B. Shannon is the *man*, and appears the same Tom Shannon of the California Legislature; ready to debate, enthusiastic in whatever he undertakes and with a determination that nothing can appal, he generally manages to carry his point; add to these qualities his jovial disposition and cleverness, and it is not to be wondered that he is so popular. Messrs. Higby and Cole are also worthy members of Congress, but do most of their work in the Committee Rooms.

The General Prospects.

At no time since the outbreak of the rebellion, have the affairs of the nation worn a brighter aspect than at the present time. The president's call for "three hundred thousand more," is being answered with an enthusiasm equal to the first call for volunteers to defend the capital from the threatened attack of the insurgents. From every State comes the cheering news that all the young men, awaking to sense of duty, are enlisting *en masse* for the last blow at the rebellion. This enthusiasm is brought on by several causes; the almost unanimous reenlistment of the veteran volunteers has set an example to those who have heretofore stayed at home, and showed that they at least have confidence in the overthrow of the rebellion; then, again, the prospects of a speedy peace, together with the inducements of large bounties, and the advantages secured in the future by having served the Government in its hour of need, all operate to bring men into the army. By the time that the spring campaign is fairly open, our Government will be prepared to strike blows at the rebellion that nothing will be able to withstand. Our resources and means of carrying on the war are no more exhausted now than they were in the beginning. How is it with the enemy? with their ports blockaded, so that they cannot resort to importation from foreign sources, and have to depend on the natural resources of their own territory, and this being daily abridged; with an army kept intact only by fear, and entirely demoralized, and from which hundreds are daily coming over to our side, as we have often seen them; thrown off by their pretended friends abroad; altogether, is it to be wondered at that the prospects of the South are so gloomy? The sooner they lay down their arms and return to their allegiance, the better it will be for them; many of them already realize this fact, and are taking advantage of the President's Amnesty Proclamation.

We were much pleased to read the patriotic resolutions passed by the California Legislature, and particularly so the last one, which in eloquent terms endorses the Administration of Mr. Lincoln, and recommends him for reelection.

The Soldier's Vote.

We learn by a telegram that the Supreme Court of California has pronounced as unconstitutional the law allowing her soldiers to vote. We know not the points on which this decision is based, but certainly it cannot be as to the general features of the law or the abstract principle. Now, in our Battalion, a majority of its members have left property in California, on which they pay taxes, and therefore should have a voice in the selection of officers that are to administer to the Government of the State or County. But take the other case; even if they had no property there, no one will deny that they are citizens of the State of California, and as such they are entitled to certain rights. Now, are they to forfeit these rights of citizenship because the General Government called for their assistance, and they, actuated by patriotism and love of country, responded to that call? Such cannot be the case; the principle of allowing soldiers to vote *is right*; if the old law needs any amendments, let these be passed by the Legislature now in session. So, Messrs. Solens, pass the law, and let the California Boys in Uncle Sam's army cast their votes for their favorite-*Good, Honest Old Abe.*

Miscellaneous.

We are now enjoying one of those delightful spells, denominated here "a cold snap," when one is almost frozen by sticking his head out of our stockaded tents. There is no "Sunny South" around here-at least we've not seen it.

A large number of our men are suffering from severe colds and influenza, but otherwise their health is good. They are in good spirits, anxiously looking forward for the war to come to a close, so that they may return to their loved California again.

Those having friends in the Battalion cannot please them better than by writing to them often, and by sending them California papers containing local and other news; these are eagerly sought after, and read, advertisements and all.

T.H.M.

Alta California, San Francisco, Tuesday, March 22, 1864.

Second Massachusetts Cavalry.

Cavalry Camp, Vienna, Va., February 14, 1864

To the Editor of the Boston Herald:

You have already had an account of the execution of one of our men for desertion. He went over to the enemy and was recaptured with arms in his hands. Before he was shot he addressed his old association as follows: "Friends and comrades, I have a few words to say before I bid you farewell. Believe me, I never fully realized the enormity of my crime. I did not intend to remain with the enemy. I meant to sell them my horse and arms and get home with the money. I want you all to take warning from me. Never leave the cause in which you are engaged; you are on the right side. Stick to the old flag until it is everywhere triumphant and I hope you will all come out alive. I have no fear of death. I believe that even now I die gloriously, that the severity of the punishment is an atonement for my crime, and that my death is for the good of my country. Good-bye."

The conduct of the prisoner throughout was noble. There could never be a braver death. When he bade Col. Lowell adieu, a few hours before his death, he told him that he blamed no one but himself; that the sentence was but just, and required for the good of the service. He had considerable property in the west, which he left to a widowed mother in New England.

It is impossible to concieve of a more impressive scene and occasion of greater solemnity. The event seemed to throw a general gloom over the whole camp, and made the day more of a Sabbath than I have ever seen in the army before.

Since my last letter there have been several changes in the regiment, especially among the officers. Squads of recruits are constantly arriving from Massachusetts, and the companies are being fast filled to the maximum. The regiment will be 1200 strong by the end of the month.

Capt. Holman has been relieved from duty on Col. Lowell's staff, and is now at Camp Meigs, Readville. Capt. D.A. DeMerritt succeeds him as Acting Assistant Inspector General. Second Lieutenant Henry E. Alvord has been promoted to First Lieutenant, and appointed Provost Marshal of the brigade. Second Lieut. Chas. M. Kinne and Sergeant Major P.R. Irwin have been promoted to First Lieutenants and Regimental Adjutant and Commissary, respectively. First Sergeants Armstrong, Meader and Wilson have been promoted Second Lieutenants. These changes all took place about January 1.

Captains Washburn and Cabot have left us to be respectively Lieut. Col. and Major in the 4th Massachusetts Cavalry, and Lieutenants Emery and Welch to be senior captains in the 5th. Besides these, other vacancies of a higher rank will soon occur in the regiment, and to fill these quite a number of promotions will be made.

To-day, in compliance with a special order from the War Department, Col. Charles R. Lowell turns over the command of our brigade to Col. H.M. Lazelle, 16th New York cavalry, and reports to Washington for detached service in the Cavalry Bureau.

Cadet

Boston Journal, Friday, February 19, 1864.

Execution of Ormesby.

Editor National Tribune: - Wm. E. Ormesby lived at Colesburg, Iowa, in 1861. Ormesby and I left Omaha, Neb. on May 9 to cross the plains with a train of about 300 horses and mules, about 150 men and about 25 women. We got thru all right in August, 1861, and I didn't see

Ormesby again till I had enlisted in Co. E, California cavalry Battalion, to fill up the 2d Mass. Cav. I met him at San Francisco, and he enlisted in Co. E with me.

When the 2d Mass. Cav. went into camp at Vienna there was a call for a man to volunteer to carry the mail to and from Alexandria every other day, and Ormesby volunteered to do it. He carried it for about six weeks or more, and was chased by Mosby and his men many times. One day the horse was so used up that he was afraid to start out. A citizen there had a horse, and Ormesby traded with him by paying $15 to boot.

When the Colonel saw it he ordered Ormesby's arrest. He lay in the guard house for three weeks, and then they tried him, and the verdict was three months' pay stopped and one month extra duty. That made him mad, and he deserted the next morning after he got out. He stole two horses, two carbines and two revolvers, and went over to Mosby.

Soon after Capt. Russell, of Co. E, captured him and brought him in, and a drumhead court-martial followed. He was sentenced to be shot the next day at 10 o'clock. He told me that he had done wrong, and asked me to write to his folks at Colesburg, Iowa, and I told him I would. Then he shook hands with the boys and said good-by, and walked to his place with the Chaplain. When the Chaplain pulled down the black cap Ormesby told him to please raise it up, that he wanted to talk to the guard. It was raised, and he placed his hand on his heart, and told the guard to put their bullets right there, and they did. I am much pleased with Comrade Chas. H. Flourney, of the 2d Mass. Cav., in standing by Ormesby, I would like to hear from him and my other old comrades. - E.O. Enos, Elgin, Iowa.

National Tribune, Washington, D.C., Thursday, December 28, 1911.
[Charles H. Flourney, Erastus O. Enos, Company E]

❖❖

THE ARMY OF THE POTOMAC

An Affair Between Cavalry and Guerillas

A Detachment of the Second Massachusetts Surprised by Mosby's Men

Our Losses Eight Killed, Seven Wounded and from 50 to 75 Made Prisoners.

Washington, Tuesday, Feb.22.

It is stated that yesterday morning about 11 o'clock, as a detachment of the Second Massachusetts Cavalry, under command of Capt. J.S. Reed, who had been out on a scouting expedition, were returning toward Dranesville, Va., on the way to Vienna, they were attacked on the Dranesville Pike, about ten miles from the latter place by a gang of rebel guerillas, supposed to be under the notorious Mosby, concealed in the pines. In the detachment of Massachusetts Cavalry there were 150 men, while Mosby, it is supposed, had at least between 200 and 300 men. The Second Massachusetts were fired upon from the dense pine woods near Dranesville, and retreated. Afterward eight of our men were found dead and seven wounded, while, it is supposed, from fifty to seventy-five were taken prisoners. At least, that number is missing; but as scattering ones are coming in from time to time, the number will doubtless be considerably reduced. Among the prisoners is Capt. Manning, of Maine. Capt. J.S. Reed, the Commander of the detachment, was shot through the left lung, and died in a few minutes after being wounded.

Capt. Reed's corpse has been brought to this city, and will be embalmed by Drs. Brown and Alexander, and thence be sent North to his wife, who lives in Dorchester, Mass.

Mosby beat a precipitate retreat. Troops were at once sent in pursuit of the guerillas, but the pursuing party has not yet been heard from.

SPECIAL DISPATCH TO THE N. Y. TIMES
Washington, Tuesday, Feb. 23.
Escape of Some of the Cavalry

Lieut. Dabney, of the Second Massachusetts Cavalry, and twenty-five men who were captured by Mosbey's guerillas at Drainsville, succeeded in effecting their escape. They crossed the Potomac at Muddy Branch. Not more than twenty prisoners in all are still in the hands of the rebels.

New York Times, Wednesday, February 24, 1864
The Boston Journal, Boston, February 24, 1864.
Daily National Intelligencer, Washington, D.C., Wednesday, February 24, 1864.
Evening Transcript, Boston, Wednesday, February 24, 1864.
[The battle took place near what was then Ankers blacksmith shop.]

❖ ❖

CAPTAIN REID. The intelligence of the death of this officer of the Second Massachusetts Cavalry will be felt here and on the Pacific as among the very sad sacrifices of worthy life caused by the war. He was known formerly in this vicinity as an estimable citizen; and the circumstances under which he left his new and distant home to enter the army, were such as increased the regard in which he was before held, and to win for him the respect of the public. All will remember the fine appearance of the California Hundred at their reception in this city, and their manly deportment whilst they remained with us. They enlisted in San Francisco from the highest motives, and came from the other side of the continent to fight for the nation and its republican institutions. Captain Reid was active in raising this excellent command, and always zealous for its welfare. He has fallen in defence of the righteous cause to which he devoted himself, and in the discharge of his duty. He will be mourned as a kinsman and friend. His memory will be honored as the memory of a faithful and loyal soldier should be.

Evening Transcript, Boston, Wednesday, February 24, 1864

❖ ❖

The Second Mass. Cavalry. *List of Killed and Wounded at Drainsville, Va., on Feb. 22.*

We have a letter from Chaplain C.A. Humphreys, of the 2d Mass. Cavalry, dated Vienna, Va., Feb. 24, in which he states that while a detachment of that regiment were marching along the Drainsville turnpike on Feb. 22, at 11 o'clock, they were fired upon by the enemy, concealed in some thick pines at the side of the road, and being thrown into confusion were then charged upon by an overwhelming force of cavalry and scattered. The following is a list of the killed and wounded already brought to camp.

Killed. Capt. J. Sewall Reed, commanding 2d Battalion; privates James Miles, Stephen Spoone, Richard Powers, Co. B; James S.W. McCammon, Henry H. Dexter, George W. Ferrie, Co. M; Abraham Waters, Co. K.

Wounded. Corporals James O'Halloran, Co. B, and Henry Wyatt, Co. C; privates John B. Hayden, Co. B; Charles M. Thomas, Co. M James Seccin, Co. M; Jos. Spofford, Co. H.

A party was to start on Wednesday morning to see if more could be found in the vicinity of the fight. Capt. Geo. A. Manning was taken prisoner (not wounded); and Lieut. Wm. C. Manning is missing. It is reported that he is a prisoner and that he is slightly wounded. The attacking party was led by Mosby. They stripped our dead of their hats, boots and spurs, and Capt. Reed of every thing but his under-clothes.

The Boston Journal, Friday, February 26, 1864.
Evening Bulletin, San Francisco, Thursday, February 25, 1864

❖ ❖

February 22d, in Virginia, Captain J. Sewall Reed, of the "California One Hundred" Killed in action.

Death of Capt. Reed, of the "California Hundred." A telegraphic despatch from late Lieutenant now Captain Archibald McKinney, to George Reed of this city, dated Washington 23d, announces the death of Captain Sewall Reed of the "California One Hundred" - killed in action on Washington's Birthday, the 22d of February. Tiger Engine Company, of which Capt. Reed was one of the founders, shows the flag at half-mast, in token of mourning.

Evening Bulletin, San Francisco, Thursday, February 25, 1864
Alta California, San Francisco, Friday, February 26, 1864.
[Captain Archibald McKendry; George Reed, brother. Tiger Engine Company was a volunteer fire company in San Francisco]

❖ ❖

Starting After the Enemy

On the morning of Feb. 20, 1864, a detachment of the 2d Mass. Cav. and a small detail from the 16th N.Y. Cav. started from camp with a roving commission after the enemy. Maj. J.S. Reed was in command of the column, which comprised Co. M, commanded by myself, with 41 men; a detail of 21 men from Co. E, commanded by my brother, Lieut. W.C. Manning; a detail of 17 men from the 16th N.Y. Cav., in command of Lieut. Cannon, and Co. B, 2d Mass. Cav. numbering 45 men, under Lieut. Dabney; making a total of 127, including officers, 51 of whom were Californians.

On the night of the 21st we went into camp at a farm house about 10 miles above Dranesville. A detachment of the 13th N.Y. Cav. camped there with us, and the next morning the two detachments started for headquarters, taking separate routes. Our column took the Dranesville pike. I noticed that the rear of the column was straggling badly, and I rode back to the head of Co. B, urging the officers to keep the men closed up. I stopped a few minutes to talk to Lieut. Dabney and light a cigar, and as I left him I took out my watch and noticed that it was 10:50 o'clock. When I again reached the head of the column Maj. Reed was riding about 40 yards in advance with Charley Binn, a supposed deserter from Mosby's Rangers, who was acting as guide. At that place there was a thicket of small pines on our right, and on our left a rail fence inclosing an open field. I had hardly time to take in the situation before I heard a single shot, followed almost at once by a volley coming from the thicket on the right just in advance of the place where Maj. Reed was riding. Thinking that the advance guard had been attacked, I gave the command; "Forward!" The words had scarcely left my lips before a volley reached us from the thicket, and my command faced to the right to receive an expected charge from the enemy. With carbine and pistol they fired an occasional shot. Thinking that the enemy would charge thru the thicket, I cautioned them to reserve their fire and be ready to receive them. When the firing commenced in front Maj. Reed rode back thru the column to the rear, and that was the last I ever saw of him. He was killed. Where Binn went the Lord only knows. There was a short lull in the heavy firing, and I rode back to the rear of my company, and, calling Lieut. Manning, directed him to take down the fence and form his command in the field; that I would hold the enemy in check until he got ready and fall back on him. As I was about to turn my horse to ride back to the head of the column, I felt a sharp stinging pain in my leg, and my horse made a jump that nearly unseated me. As I rode back the firing from the thicket commenced in volleys again, but no foe was in sight all this time. It seemed to be the tactics of the enemy to charge us thru the thicket almost to the edge of the road and deliver a volley or two, then fall back to repeat the same tactics over and over again. They had the bulge on us, and meant to keep it.

A duel in the Road.

At about the fourth charge one of the Rangers either having a little more "sand" than the rest or being unable to control his horse, broke from the brush, coming out into the road almost directly in front of me, firing two shots in quick succession, the first one going wild, the second one striking my horse in the neck just forward of the right shoulder. Almost simultaneously with his last shot my pistol went off, and he fell from his horse onto the hard pike. Whether it was a bullet from my pistol that struck him or one from the pistol of one of my men I never knew or wanted to know. All of this happened in a few seconds, but as I raised my pistol to fire I got a good look at his features, which so impressed me that I can recall them vividly to-day. He was the only one of the enemy that I saw during the fight. At that time several of my men were killed and wounded, and the Partisan Rangers were getting in their deadly work from ambush, just like a lot of Missouri guerrillas.

My command was standing in line. Not a man had broken from the ranks. They were watching every opportunity to get in a shot by locating the enemy by the sound of the crack of their revolvers, while I was waiting for movements of Lieut. Manning in getting his men thru the fence and forming in the field, which he succeeded in doing; but, alas! too late.

I turned to speak to Gosson, one of my men, who was wounded in the arm. My horse went down on the hard pike, falling on my leg, which caused me such excruciating pain that I nearly fainted. My horse arose to his feet again, made a lunge sidewise, and we both rolled into the ditch by the side of the pike, and I was lost to the world for awhile. When I returned to consciousness I was a captive in the field about 20 yards from the fence, supported in the arms of Simonton, one of my men, who was wounded, and another wounded man from Co. E was dousing me with cold water.

I could not tell the time of day, as I had been separated from my watch as well as other loose personal property, probably by those who had despoiled the body of Maj. Reed. My cavalry boots were in the possession of one of the Rangers, who was standing near, and a boy about 14 or 15 years of age named Hutchinson, was trying to shoot me. I learned that one of the Rangers, who had some knowledge of surgery, had removed my left boot to get at my wounded leg, from which he cut out about 22 No. 4 shot. (I can count about that number of scars whenever I want a reminder of the fight.) The boot was then taken by one of the other Rangers, who, knowing that boots always came in pairs, removed the other one. About a month before that date I was ordered out on a scout around the Blue Springs country, with instructions to arrest every male member of the numerous Hutchinson family old enough to shoot. In making my raid among the lot captured was this boy and father. Owing to the pleadings of his mother and sister, I was induced to release the boy, who then wanted to shoot me, because, as he said, I had taken his father prisoner.

As I lay on my back minus watch, purse, hat, boots, etc., and unable to move, a Ranger officer with a detail of men came up, and ordered the men to take the prisoners down to the pike near a house, and, turning to me, very kindly inquired about my injuries, and wanted to know what had become of my hat, boots, etc. I told him that he would probably find them among his men. He called a man named Stewart, and had him take charge of me and to see that every article taken from me was returned. First came my hat, but minus the cord, which was afterward returned, then watch, purse, and, last of all, but very reluctantly, my boots.

The Good "Union" Men.

I noticed many familiar faces of the good, honest, "Union" men that I had many times seen at their homes in the surrounding country, who were mixed in with the Rangers that day. The fact is that nearly every man living in Virginia within the field of Mosby's operations was aiding him or fighting in his ranks. Mosby had at all times a perfect knowledge of the movements of our troops, and while these "good, honest" farmers were professing their Unionism to us they were gathering information, and sending it by members of their family thru lanes and byways to him.

I was so thoroly helpless from my injuries that there was quite a debate as to the advisability; of taking me with them, but finally they concluded that an officer of my rank was too good a thing to leave. As all the carriages they could procure were filled with their own dead and wounded, they decided to put me on a horse and carry me that way until they could find another carriage, which they assured me would be in a very short time. During the hours of daylight my friend Stewart divided his time in supporting me on my horse and keeping the guerrillas from stealing my boots that hung on my saddle; but as the day began to wane they dropped off, singly and in pairs, to their homes to resume the role of good Union men. At dark we halted at a house, and Stewart tried to get some kind of a vehicle, but did not succeed, as the man told him that he had none at home. When he was told by Stewart that he wanted it for a wounded Union officer, he answered; "Shoot the————Yankee; that's the best way to get rid of him." I had passed this man's house several times before, and had talked with him as a Union man, but it was so dark he did not recognize me. After the most fearful ride of my life, we arrived at the house in the mountains some time after midnight, where I was laid on a lounge in a room where there were several people. On another lounge was a young man and a doctor was dressing his wound. After the doctor had got thru with him he came over to me, I told him I was afraid my whole leg was dislocated. After pulling and twisting for awhile he had my leg carefully bathed and bandaged, which gave me so much relief that I dropped asleep.

My Wounded Roommate.

When I awoke my wounded roommate, who I recognized as the youth who fell on the pike in front of me in the fight that day. He recognized me and said that I was the man who shot him. I understood afterward that he died that morning.

The first and only time I ever saw Col. Mosby was that morning when the prisoners were mustered in on the lawn ready for the march to Richmond. I was packed out of the house and laid on the grass, and when the prisoners were lined up by their mounted guard they found out that I could not march, so the officer in command sent a man to report the fact to Col. Mosby, who shortly appeared. Mosby asked me if I could ride a horse if they fixed a mattress on him, so I could recline on it. I told him that perhaps I could, but I preferred boarding there awhile if it was agreeable to the landlord. He smilingly replied that no doubt the rest of the prisoners would prefer to do so too, as our friends were liable to come that way any time. After they had lashed the bedtick on the horse I was lifted in place, and so commenced our six days' march to Richmond and Libbey. - George A. Manning, Lewiston, Idaho.

National Tribune, Washington, D.C., Excerpts from an article of Thursday, August 18, 1910. [George Manning and his brother William were imprisoned at Libby until War's end. Herman Gozzens died at Andersonville, September 1864; Anthony Simonson died at Andersonville, August 26, 1864 - both men were of Company M; No record of a Stewart in either Company E or M]

Muddy Branch
Feby 23rd 1864

Dear Minnie

Having some leisure time this evening and concluding there was no more pleasant way of amusing myself and at the same time thinking you had as soon hear from me as not, made up my mind to write you a short letter. It may be my writing so often will be considered a bother by you more than anything else, but for me to receive letters is a pleasure anytime and judging you rightiously, will think they please you. This makes the second one since I have heard from you, but am in hopes you answered my other some time ago. We have been having a little excitement in Camp lately. Some of our Regt had a fight with Mosbys Guerillas yesterday and got the worst of it considerbly. One hundred & twenty five of our men were drawn in an ambush & surrounded by about Four Hundred Rebs. They were pretty badly cut up. We dont know for certain how many we have lost, there has only 40 returned to Camp yet. We lost one Major killed, that was worth more to us than nearly all the other Officers & have heard of there being nine of our men killed and thirteen badly wounded. The rumor was that the Rebs intended to attack our Camp last night but I have seen nothing of them yet. We are prepared for the Johnys anytime. Are expecting finaly to be ordered out to follow them up at any moment and I think the most of us are anxious to go, for its the first time Moseby ever made our Regt run, even if He did out number us. Such is a soldiers Life sometimes all excitement then again, the dulest of all from here to Tennesee and spring. And I am in hopes we will, for being on the Potomac is getting to be stale. Something new for me once in a year certain or I should be wishing I never was a soldier. My friend Thompson is still here in the tent with me is well and says if we both have the luck to get out of the Army alive we will see Delavan soon after the close. He is sure to make a visit - there with me for I have told him so much about the place that He says He feels as though he was as well acquainted there as any one!

Minnie think of Me as safe & well for I will assure you I am feeling perfectly safe, nor do I fear any harm coming to me from a stray bullet even if we are attacked. Am a believer in presentiments to a certain extent, and mine is that I shall see you again before I die. Give my love to Our Mother in particular and the rest in General, for my especial benefit Minnie, write very often, take pattern by me and write without receiving a letter

From yours forever J Passage

Courtesy of Mary Paynter, Madison, Wisconsin

[John Passage, 1st Sergeant, Company F; Miss Minorca (Minnie) Peets whom John would wed 2 February 1865 in Delavan, Wisconsin; Edward Thompson, Company F, commissioned 2d Lieutenant, March 25, 1864.]

LETTER FROM THE CALIFORNIAN BATTALION, SERVING WITH THE ARMY OF THE POTOMAC.

(From the Correspondent of the ALTA, with the Column.)

In Camp, Vienna, Va. February 24th, 1864.

EDITORS ALTA:- Our camp is wrapt in gloom; today we followed to their last resting place the remains of the noble and brave men who two days ago met a glorious death, fighting for their country.

The Raid.

On Saturday last, the 20th instant, a scouting party composed of one hundred and twenty-five men from the Sixteenth New York Cavalry, fifty from the Thirteenth New York Cavalry, and one hundred and thirteen of the Second Massachusetts Cavalry, of which latter about fifty were Californians, left camp to scout through the enemy's country. At first everything went well enough; on the second day out they met a party of rebels, attacked them, killing and wounding several and taking some prisoners. This took place in the vicinity of Middleburg. From there the party proceeded in the direction of Leesburg, camping near the latter place on the second night out. In the morning the party divided up into two lots, the New Yorkers returning to camp by way of Gum Springs, and our boys by way of Drainsville, and were going along the turnpike in the best of spirits, laughing and joking. When within four miles of Drainsville, the advance guard, all of whom were Californians, saw a few rebels ahead and kept following them up, and were within three miles of Drainsville when the attack commenced.

The Fight.

The rebels were hid in the thick pine woods, and the first fire was poured on the advance guard, and this was the signal for a general attack. The rebel cavalry came rushing from a side road, and when the advance guard turned to go to the main column, they found themselves cut off. They then tried to make a flank movement and join them in that way, but were again disappointed; the rebels were now on every side of them, and two parties of them charged on our boys, but they gallantly cut their way out and managed to reach the pine woods, five of their number being taken prisoners, by their horses being shot from under them, and being otherwise dismounted. Those that reached the woods were compelled to leave their horses, and sought safety in the thick woods where the rebel cavalry could not follow them.

Let us now notice the doings of the main column. As soon as the advance guard was fired on, the rebels opened an awful fire on the main column and threw it into confusion. Captain J. Sewall Reed, who was in command, gave the order to form platoons, but he was soon dismounted, and was shot in the arm and also in the eye, which killed him instantly. In this moment of danger, Captain George A. Manning, as brave and gallant a soldier as ever drew a sabre, seeing that delay was ruin, immediately assumed command, and by his example of bravery and coolness tried to rally the men; his own Company rallied around him, as did also the brave boys of Company "E" (Captain Eigenbrodt's), and for a time they stood and fought gallantly against the awful odds of the rebel hordes. The very air resounded with the reports of the pistols and carbines; thick as hail flew the leaden messengers of death, but still undaunted stood this gallant band, fighting like heroes for their country and for the honor of California. They could have escaped by an inglorious flight, but they had not come all the way from California to turn their backs to an insolent and base foe and heroically stood their ground until the rebels, seeing that bullets could not drive them, charged down on them in awful numbers, and the brave Captain together with his gallant boys were compelled to surrender as prisoners of war, and are now on their way to Richmond, which is but little better than death.

There were also about sixty men from the Massachusetts companies; most of these were raw recruits, poorly armed, and, with a few exceptions, acted shamefully, but not more so than some of their officers. In order to understand the situation they were in, I will explain it. The main fighting was done on the turnpike, on both sides of which there was a rail fence and woods, and in these the rebels were concealed at first; many of them were dismounted. Some of these Massachusetts recruits being poor riders, their horses green and unmanageable, were running up and down the fence, holding on to the pummel of the saddles, and the rebels shooting into them, as one would into a flock of frightened sheep. Most of them were taken prisoners; their officers jumped their horses over the fence and ingloriously fled. I blush to own that one of these officers was Californian. In justice to the other California officers I will give his name. He enlisted in our battalion in San Francisco under the name of William E. Poe; was made a Sergeant by Captain Manning and some weeks ago was promoted to Second Lieutenant, which position he now so unworthily and dishonorably fills. When he was promoted he gave William L. Wilson as his right name, and bears it now. When the attack was made he was among the first to run, leaving his Company to its fate, and thus proved himself what we always took him to be, a bass coward, unworthy to wear the uniform of a Union officer, which he has twice disgraced. He is besides, a Copperhead of the rankest kind; as such he defended Morgan, the guerrilla, horse thief and robber, and said that he was a "perfect gentleman."

This Wilson, *alias* Poe, is one of the loudmouthed Southern braggarts, who are ever boasting of their blood and their chivalry, but who are always found wanting when they come to be tried. We hope soon to see this valiant (?) Copperhead shorn of his uniform, and either sent South among his friends, the rebels; or, like the other rebels, be sent to the Old Capitol, to sojourn there for a time.

February 25th- 2 o'clock,. A.M.
The Killed, Wounded and Missing.

The scouting party that left camp yesterday morning, to go to the scene of the late battle, has returned. It could not reach its destination owing to a force of rebel cavalry being there, and now, we are going out after them, every available man, with three day's rations and plenty of ammunition. We leave in two hours, and I must hasten to finish this. In relation to the late fight, suffice it to say, that our men were surprised, ambushed and attacked by a force at least three times its own number. They fought bravely, and did the best they could under the circumstances. The following is the list of Californians killed, wounded, and missing;

Killed- Captain J. Sewall Reed, Acting Major, and in command. James S. W. McCammon, Henry H. Dexter, George W. Ferrier- all of Captain Manning's Company.

Wounded- J. W. Locke (slightly), Joseph Seccin both of Captain Manning's Company.

Missing- (Most of whom are known to have been taken prisoners): Captain George A. Manning, First Lieutenant William C. Manning (is reported slightly wounded). William H. Lawrence, J. W. Halstead, P. J. Hackett, Joseph Burke, William Bell, H. Gozzen. David Knapp, George W. Lee, James Munroe, Ed. Price, A. Simonson, Archibald Taylor, Henry Goodrich, Thomas Z. Stevens-all of Captain Manning's Company. Levi W. Turner, Josiah B. Crawford, Arthur J. Wooster, George Wilcox, Frank Paris, Jackson Fisher, Byron H. Grover, John A. Cain, Judson A. Mosmer, John Spaulding, William W. Millican-all of Captain Eigenbrodts Company. News has just reached us that six of our men managed to escape from the rebels, and had reached Point of Rocks in safety; the despatch does not give their names.

Incidents, etc., etc.

The accounts of the fight abound with incidents of individual bravery and gallantry. James S. W. McCammon, in the thickest of the fray, was heard to call out; "Rally, rally, Californians, and don't give way;" but the next moment he was lying dead, a bullet striking him over the right eye, and thus ended the career of as brave a man as there was in our Battalion. Hamilton, of Company E, was attacked by about eight rebels, and when ordered to surrender, he turned on them, fired several shots, and killed two "rebs." Rodgers, of the same Company, was told to surrender, but replied that he "couldn't see it;" his coat was pierced by three bullets, and to use his own expression, the air was hot with bullets; he got dismounted and escaped by taking to the woods. John W. Howe, of Company L. volunteered to go on this raid, "just for fun," and got enough of it such as it was. He fought bravely, took one rebel prisoner, and also a small rebel flag; when he looked around, they were coming at him from two sides; his horse was shot under him, and he was compelled to let his prisoner go, and seek safety in the woods. He is now in Camp, all right, and ready for the rebels again. It is useless to draw invidious distinctions; the men of Companies E and M, all of them, acted with the greatest bravery on this occasion, as, indeed, they do always. But it is enough to make one weep to see our own thinned ranks; but it is to be hoped that they may ere long be exchanged, and once again returned to us.

Mrs. J. Sewall Reed has been in Camp for nearly two months, and her grief at seeing her husband thus brought back to her, cold in death, may better be imagined than described. The rebels stripped Captain Reed of all his clothes, except shirt drawers and stockings; they also stole the boots from our dead and wounded.

But I must close, as I hear the bugles blowing "Boots and Saddles;" my own gallant horse is sadly died, and I must be off. All the Californians are going, and be it victory or death, I'll share their fate.

T. H. M.

Alta California, San Francisco, Friday, March 25, 1864.

Head Qrs. 2nd Mass Cavalry
Vienna Va. Feb 25th/64

Dear Mother

I will answer your welcome letter now. It is now midnight almost & I was up all last night but that is nothing once you are used to it. Since I wrote home last there has been a very great change in this Regiment.

The twenty first of this month Capt. Reed of the Cal. hundred left camp with three Companies altogether numbering (125) men & 6 Officers, the next day as they were returning to camp they were fired upon by Rebels who were concealed in the bushes on both sides of the road.

Capt. Reed was killed trying to encourage the men to fight. Capt. Manning & his Brother, a first Lieut. were both taken Prisoners by the Rebs, besides 55 men.

Our boys killed 9 Rebs, so we were told by the citizens.

It is lucky for me I think that I was not in camp when they went for I should have gone with them I think.

We heard from them last night & that was what kept me up all night was making Details to go out after them this morning before daylight; nearly all of the regiment have gone out, the Adjutant went out so that I could not go for we can not both leave at the same time.

I must close for I am so very tired & sleepy.

I have not used one fourth of my Butter yet.I tell you that is beautiful butter.

I wrote to Irene a few days ago and gave her all the Particulars.

I will try & write more next time kiss Annie for me also the little Boys tell Walter that means him & his Pets.

Love to all,

Send your own & Pas Pictures
From your
Soldier Boy
Robert H.

Manuscript Collection, Huntington Library, San Marino, California
[Sgt. Major Robert H. Williams, Co. F]

❖❖❖

LETTER FROM THE CALIFORNIA HUNDRED.

Vienna, Va., Feb. 26, 1864.

Eds. Reporter: I am sorry to inform you that we have been licked like the d—l for the first time by Moseby's guerrillas, assisted by the Eight Virginia Cavalry. The particulars are these: being informed that Moseby was hovering around in this vicinity, Maj. J. Sewell Reed, with Companies E and M (California boys) and Company B (Massachusetts men), one hundred strong, went out to find them, and found them at Snickers Gap, had a skirmish with them, routing and killing three of them. Seeing it would be dangerous to follow them, he retraced his steps back, and while camped the rebels-700 or 800 strong-passed around him and stationed themselves in ambush at some cross roads two and one-half miles from Drainsville, and ten miles from our camp. When our forces came up they kept still until our advance guard had passed, and then poured volley after volley into the head of the column, and at the same time charging upon the rear. It was a complete surprise, and would have confused the best organized soldiers in the world. Our forces scattered as best they could, but many were taken prisoners, who, as yet, we cannot tell. We have found 12 killed and 15 wounded, and 60 missing. Captain Manning, of Company M, has sent us word that he is a prisoner with 25 of his men. His brother, Lieutenant Manning, was wounded in the knee, and is also a prisoner. Our old Captain J. Sewell Reed, of the California Hundred was killed while trying to rally a few men that were trying to stand by him.

It is thought that six or seven of our men will die of their wounds.

The rebels made quite a haul-60 horses, saddles and equipments. The fight occurred on Washington's birthday. Mrs. Reed has been in camp all winter, and mourns the loss of her husband deeply. She regrets that he did not have his favorite Hundred with him. It so happened they were on picket duty that day. Major Reed's body was embalmed in Washington and sent to Boston.

248

The Second Massachusetts Cavalry and the Sixteenth and Thirteenth New York Cavalry have gone out to-day, and the Fourth Delaware have gone in a different direction, to take possession of Snickers and Ashby's Gaps, and they think they can corral Moseby's men, and with hopes of giving them Hail Columbia with variations.

We don't pull off either hats, caps or boots when we "turn in" at night-bet you.

I'll drop you another line soon.

Charley Briggs.

The Napa County Reporter, Napa, Saturday, April 2, 1864.

THE REMAINS of Capt. J. Sewall Reed, Second Massachusetts cavalry, have been brought home by the Chaplain of the regiment, and will be buried with military honors from Rev. Joseph H. Mean's church, in Dorchester, on Thursday, March 2d, at 11 o'clock. The National Lancers have kindly tendered their services as escort.

Evening Transcript, Boston, Saturday, February 27, 1864
[Chaplain Charles Humphreys]

Hd. Qrs. 2d Mass Cav. Vienna Va. Feb 27th/64

My dear Mammy

I have been very busy for the last week and have been unable write. Last week Capt Reed out on a scout with 100 of our Regt. was ambuscaded by Mosby with 3 or 4 hundred men. It happened in this way. Capt Reed was marching on the Drainsville pike about 5 miles beyond that place. The Capt. had out as a advance guard first 4 men & 100 paces behind them a Sergt & 14 men 300 paces behind them came the rest of the Column. He was marching his men as we always march & his defeat was not owing to any carelessness on his part. The Rebs attacked in front in the rear & along the whole flank of our column. Our men were entirely outnumbered & surrounded they fought well but had no chance.

As soon as I heard the news I took 250 men & went up there as fast as possible, but as it was some way from our Camp, by the time I arrived there the Rebels had been gone 12 hours, so I could only pick up our dead & wounded & bring them into Camp, which I did. Poor Capt Reed was found dead in the road striped to his shirt & draws. We also found about 12 dead men & 7 or 8 badly wounded. Two days afterwards we sent up a scout to Drainsville to see whether the Rebels had come back there & they came back & reported that there were 700 men under Moseby in that part of the country. The Brigade was ordered out & I was put in command & ordered up there to attack the enemy. Two pieces of artilery were sent to me, but I concluded not to take them. I went out & went all through the country up as far as Leesburg but could not find any force of the enemy & after marching 55 miles, I returned to Camp. I miss poor Capt. Reed very much (he was acting as Major of the 2d Bat.) he was honest & brave & a great friend of mine, his wife was in camp at the time & a brave woman she proved herself to be. Capt Reed died possessed of no property & I understand that Mrs. Reed's family are not well off. If you should ever meet her say a kind word to her for my sake.

Feb. 29ᵗʰ 1864

The only news today is that Gen. Kilpatrick has gone down to try & take Richmond. Butler is also to send up a Cooperating force. I hope it may be done but it is a very doubtful thing to say the least.

Gen. Sedgewick's Corps is also on the move somewhere. Well I cant think of anything more to tell you. Give my love to Grandfather & Grandmother tell Cora to write soon & tell me what she has been doing lately, love to Fanny & John.

> Write soon to your son
> Caspar

Caspar Crowninshield, Letters, Massachusetts Historical Society

❖ ❖

I note what you say in reference to the general officer, it must be the Baron von Massow who was with me in the winter of 1863-4, and was severely wounded in a fight with the California Cavalry Battalion near Dranesville in Fairfax County Feb. 22 1864. Captain Reid commanding officer shot Massow. Col. Wm Chapman saw him shoot Massow, and instantly shot Reid. I rode up a few seconds later, Massow and Reid were lying within a few yards of each other Reid dead. We carried Massow to George Carters place in Loudon——Oatlands——where he stayed until he got well enough to return to Germany. I remember that I gave him a very complimentary letter when he left. A few years ago I saw in a newspaper that he commanded a German army corps. You can see his picture in Scotts Partisan Life, and an account of his being wounded page 203. Massow and Col Chapman were friends and allways rode together. If you see Chapman or Beattie, tell them that you have heard from him. I would like to hear from Massow. He was a splendid soldier and gentleman.

705 Post Street, San Francisco, Cal.
Virginia Historical Society
[Although unsigned, the above partial note is assumed to be from Mosby, written some time between 1885 - 1901, when he was an attorney for the Southern Pacific Company in San Francisco.]

❖ ❖

MARCH, 1864

9   Grant promoted to the rank of Lieutenant General.
10 Grant named General in Chief of Federal armies.
12 Federals begin Red River campaign in Louisiana.
17 Fighting on Red Mountain, California.
18 Major General William T. Sherman takes command of the
    Federal armies in the West.

❖ ❖

Second Massachusetts Cavalry. - From a private letter, dated March 1st, from B.F. Hoxie, formerly of this place and a member of the Second Massachusetts Cavalry, we are permitted to take the following items of interest. The writer says: "All of the boys from Suisun are well, except John Taylor, who is lying at the hospital, sick with the measles, but is rapidly getting better. You will see in the papers an account of the disaster that happened to our regiment. We had twenty-five killed and wounded and fifty missing. Most of the men were recruits. Company E lost thirteen men, and their Captain and Lieutenant. Our company was not in the fight. About a week ago, I came near getting shot in a skirmish, while chasing two rebels. My messmate was shot through the leg, but he killed the rebel with his sabre. Most folks think that soldiers have a good time while in winter quarters, but the reverse is the case. We have been scouting all winter, and have drawn four different sets of horses this winter. The men are so different in the Atlantic States from the men in California. I would not live in the Atlantic States for anything. Bill Halsey is one of the bravest in the company. When we start on a scouting expedition, he has his mind made up to die, if necessary. Jim Hawkins, also, shows good pluck. We are all in hopes that the war will end this summer."

Solano Press, Suisun, Saturday, April 2, 1864

Second Mass. Cavalry. The following members of the 2d Mass. cavalry regiment have been missing since the recent fight with Mosby, and are supposed to be prisoners:
Sergt. Ephraim H. Phinney of Stafford, Ct., Corp. George Z. Robbins of Ware, Mass., Corp. George B. Sanborn of Boston, David Dennison of Canton, Mass., John Carroll of Boston, Cushman Stevenson of Lowell, Charles T. Rich of Amesbury, Mass., Joseph Kemp of Jamaica Plain, Phillip McDonald of Boston, William R. Jackson of Brooklyn, N.Y., Thomas Rice of Boston, Arthur L. Hyde of Boston, Thomas Kelly of South Boston, George F. Duley of Ashland.
Wm. Downey and John B. Hayden, both of Boston, have died of wounds.

Evening Transcript, Boston, Thursday, March 3, 1864.

The Funeral of Capt. Reed. The National Lancers, Capt. Slade, turned out this morning over 100 men, to pay a tribute of respect to the memory of Capt. Reed. The Lancers, accompanied by the Chelsea Brass Band, left their armory shortly after 9 o'clock, and passed through Tremont and School streets, received the officers of the various cavalry regiments now at home, these being in carriages. The column then resumed the march for Dorchester, where the funeral services took place at Rev. Mr. Means's church, at 11 o'clock.

Evening Transcript, Boston, Thursday, March 3, 1864.

SECOND MASSACHUSETTS CAVALRY.
Funeral of the Late Capt Reed. The funeral services over the remains of the late Capt. J. Sewall Reed of the "California Hundred," Second Massachusetts Cavalry, took place in Rev. Mr. Means' Church, in Dorchester. The attendance was very large and included quite a number of officers of the regiment, and also Ex-Mayor Teschmaker of San Francisco, and other Californians who chanced to be in Boston or vicinity. The services were conducted by Rev. Mr. Means, assisted by Rev. Dr. Morrison of Milton, and Chaplain Hennessey, of the 2d Cavalry,

who accompanied the remains from Drainsville. The remains were conveyed to Mount Hope Cemetery for Interment, and the national lancers, Capt. Lucius Slade, performed escort duty.

Boston Herald, Friday, March 4, 1864.
[Paper is in error. The Chaplain was Charles A. Humphreys]

❖❖

Head Qrs Tyler Division
Fairfax Court House, Va
March 5, 1864

Colonel,
   In compliance with order recd from Hd Qrs Department of Washington Genl Tyler desires you to relieve the 3d Battalion 2nd Mass. Cavl now at Muddy Branch by the 1st Battalion of the same regiment. Major Thompson will be retained in command at Muddy Branch.

Very respectfully
Your obt Servt
W.A. Lacliotti
Capt & AAG

Col HM Lazelle
 Cmg
Cavl. Brigade, Vienna

Lieut E. Y. Lansing
 A.A.A.G. Cav. Brigade.
Sir

   On Tuesday March 8th pursuant to order from Maj. Gen, Auger's Hd. Qrs. I sent the 1st Batt. of this Regiment to Muddy Branch, Md. to relieve, so the order stated, the 3d Batt. of the Regiment at that place. The 1st Batt. arrived at Muddy Branch at 2 P.M. Wednesday the 9th inst. Major D.W.C. Thompson, who's in command their has failed as yet to relieve the 3d Batt., although he has had ample time to do so. I understand he declines to send the 3d Batt. back as he says that he has received no order to do so. I would respectfully inquire whether two Battalions of this Regiment are to be kept under Major Thompson at Muddy Branch, Md.

   I would also respectfully state that the detail from my Regiment is so large that the men have scarcely every other night in bed and some of them have been on duty two nights in succession.

Very Respectfully
Your Obt Servt.
C. Crowninshield
Maj. Comdg. Regt.

Hd Qrs. 2d Mass. Cavalry
Vienna Va. Mar 12, 1864

E. Y. Lansing
1st Lt. & A.A.A.G. Cav. Brigade
Sir

I received on Monday March 8th an order to send the 1st Batt of this Regiment to Muddy Branch Md, to relieve the 3d Batt. of the Regt. at that place. I obeyed the order at once, but was much surprised to have a particular Battalion designated, as I have always supposed that the Comdg Officer of a Regt. would be allowed to designate the Batt or companies with which other portions of his Regiment should be relieved. It can certainly make no difference to the Commanding General of the Department what particular companies are sent to Md. while it makes a great difference to the Regiment. It is well known here that Major Thompson has openly stated his intention of getting certain companies away from the Regiment, in defiance of the wishes of the Commanding Officer. It is respectfully submitted at least that the Comdg. Officer of a Regiment rather than a subordinate should guide the selection of detachments of his command. Unless this is the case it seems to me that a subordinate officer could by intriguing and false representations obtain the order for details which would greatly impare the efficiency of a Regt. and the Authority of the Commanding Officer. I was very unwilling to send four good companies over to serve under Major D.W.C. Thompson, an officer of this Regt, who is continually endeavoring to create dissatisfaction among the enlisted men of the Regiment and who is totally lax in matters of discipline and drill and entirely ignorant of nearly all the other duties of a Cavalry Officer. I believe that the efficiency of any companies sent to him will be materially lessened, as I hear that of those so long with him have already been. For confirmation of this I would respectfully refer to Col. C.R. Lowell who formerly commanded this Regiment and under whom Major Thompson served for some time, and to Capt. D.A. DeMerritt who lately inspected Major Thompson's command, by Col. Lowell's order. I would also respectfully submit that if Major Thompson is to be allowed to interfere with the details of this Regiment, the authority of the Comdg Officer - and the Esprit du Corps of the Regiment will be very much impared. It does not seem to me to be improper to make this remonstrance, and respectfully to request that any future interferance by Major Thompson in the details or affairs of this Regiment be promptly discountenansced.

I have the honor to be
Very Respectfully
Your Obt. Servant
C. Crowninshield
Major, Comdg. Regt.

OFFICE U.S. MILITARY TELEGRAPH.
WAR DEPARTMENT
The following Telegram received at Washington, 10:40 A.M. March 13, 1864,
From Fairfax C.H.
Dated, March 13, 1864.

Lt. Col. J.H. Taylor.
Chf. of Staff.

In compliance with your order March 9th 1864 the first Batt 2d Mass Cavalry was sent from here to relieve the Batt at Muddy Branch, but up to this time the 3d Batt has not reported to the Regimental Commander making us accordingly short of Cavalry. Please have the 3d Battalion returned to us as soon as possible.

R.O. Taylor,

B.G. Comdg.

Regimental Record Books, National Archives, Washington, D.C.

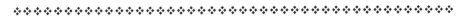

The following biography of Captain J. Sewall Reed was taken from a sketch written by Mrs. Reed at the request of John H. Morison, to be used by him at the Memorial Services held for J. Sewall Reed at the First Congregational Church in Milton, Massachusetts on March 13, 1864.

James Sewall Reed was born in Milton, Mass., April 3, 1832. Of his early life, his schoolboy- days, you know probably as much as I can tell you. My personal knowledge of him relates more to his California life; though, as a child, I remember having a mortal dread of him, as I always saw him with a *gun* in his hand. He was naturally of an impulsive, ardent, enthusiastic character; and in 1849, during the rage of the "gold fever," became much interested in California. With him, to think was to do; and he became so desirous to try his fortune in that distant land, that his parents reluctantly gave their consent, though he was a boy but little more than seventeen years old. An extract from his journal says, "On the 30th of October, 1849, we set sail from Boston in the good ship 'Argonaut,' bound to San Francisco; making up our minds for a 'life on the ocean-wave.'" Here, at the outset, he shows himself possessed of the characteristics of a good traveler; being always cheerful, making the best of every event, never discouraged, and always finding something pleasant amid the darkest scenes. They sailed round the Cape Horn, and made a quick and prosperous voyage; going on shore at Valparaiso, eighty-nine days out from Boston. On the 13th of March, 1850, they dropped anchor in the Bay of San Francisco. Here commenced his first experience of "camp-life:" for, on landing, he pitched his tent, and commenced house-keeping washing, cooking, &c., for himself. He immediately found plenty of work; and, that he might lose no time, he commenced building a flat-boat for river-travel. Finishing this, he next tried his hand at painting; at which he continued for some weeks. His brother having arrived in California, as soon as they could get ready, they started for the mines. They worked at mining, and were quite successful, some six or eight months; when, thinking their claim entirely worked out, and becoming a little tired of the life, they concluded to return to San Francisco. While mining, they had enjoyed camp-life in perfection, with sometimes a scarcity of provisions, which were very poor, even when abundant; but the life was not distasteful, and many pleasant hours were spent there. They thought they had completely exhausted the wealth of their mine; but Sewall has since told me that the same dirt had been worked over several times since, and each time had paid better than the first, so little was mining understood in those days. Returning to San Francisco, he soon obtained a situation with Macondray & Co., one of the leading firms of the city. At first, he was employed in the lumber-yard, taking account of the delivery and buying of the article; but soon entered the store as salesman, where he continued, winning the respect and love of his employers, until 1854.

At this time, all who are acquainted with California history will remember that the moral dangers to which a young man was exposed were neither few nor small; and older, stronger men often fell victims. But, from the first, Sewall had absolutely set his face against these things; and such was the natural purity of his character, his innate love of goodness and truth, that what to many was enticing, to him was disgusting; and few passed through the ordeal of those early California days more free and uncontaminated than he. His good mother's teachings here proved their value: he reverenced that mother, and did not forget her while away.

His military life commenced as early as 1852; and I think he served in every position, except first lieutenant, from a corporal up to captain, first in the Eureka Light Horse-Guards, and afterwards the First Light Dragoons. In 1854, he returned to his New England home on a visit; and had so changed during the five years' absence, that even his mother did not know him. He came home *viâ* Nicaragua; and though the route was in bad condition, and detentions were frequent, he always found something to enjoy, while many were only annoyed.

He returned to California in November, 1854; and, soon after his arrival there, he went with a friend into the tea-business, which was quite successful, and in which he continued to show his abilities as a business-man.

1856 was a year famous in California history; and he acted a conspicuous part in that Vigilance Committee which accomplished so much for the State. At this time, he was captain of the First Light Dragoons. I copy from his letter the account of his connection with the beginning of difficulties. He says, "On Sunday, I went to Gov. Johnson, and tendered my resignation as captain of the Dragoons, telling him that I was going to join the Vigilance Committee. He refused to accept it; but I joined them, and, at eleven o'clock, was sworn in by special request, although they did not take any members that day; and I am a member of the Citizens' Guard, a company of a hundred and twenty-five men, used for duty at the court-rooms." At this time, the Committee did not themselves know the arduous duties that lay before them; and, after the first difficulty was settled, they thought all would be quiet again; but they were mistaken. When Sewall resigned his commission as captain of the Dragoons (most of the company having left also, and joined the Vigilance Committee), he joined the Citizens' Guard as a private. In three days, he was promoted to the position of captain of one of the companies,- the Guard having been increased and divided into four companies. Here he remained for a time, till he was elected captain of a company of Dragoons. There was quite a strife for a little time as to which company should keep him; and it was finally settled by Col. Olney himself, who said, that, for the good of the cause, Capt. Reed must go with the Dragoons; for there were good infantry officers in plenty, but few that understood cavalry as well as Capt. Reed. So he became captain of Company B, Citizens' Dragoons, V.C.; and continued to act in this capacity while he was needed. His company numbered a hundred and sixty men. They met for drill every evening, and oftener if circumstances required. Business was almost entirely suspended during this excitement, and all were interested in learning "the art of war." Men of every rank and position shouldered the musket, and stood in the ranks; and Sewall often said that he had men in his command old enough to be his father, yet all earnest and enthusiastic, ready to sacrifice life and fortune in the support of justice and right. I copy the account of the taking of "Judge Terry" as an example of the state of excitement there: "I was sitting in my office, about two, P.M., when I saw crowds of people rushing down the street. Supposing it was a fire, I thought but little of it; when, in a minute, I heard the tap of the Committee-bell, and I knew then there was trouble somewhere. I closed my store immediately, as all my neighbors were doing, and started for the stable. Men were rushing through the streets as if wild; and I soon heard the cry, 'Judge Terry has killed one of the Vigilants!' I had my horse saddled, and started for headquarters, where I found my company present and in line. I reported to the general, and, in less than half an hour after the bell rang, was on the ground among some two thousand men, who had surrounded the building whither Judge Terry had fled. Judge Terry was taken prisoner, though not a gun was fired or a man hurt; and in another hour the city was quiet again." Sewall was also sent more than once on expeditions that required courage and ability, such as searching houses, making arrests, &c.; and always succeeded to the satisfaction of the Committee.

Business in the city was now very dull, and Sewall became interested in some mining speculations in Lower California. Some friends were going down to that country to locate grants, mines, &c.; and, having had an excellent offer made to him, he concluded to accompany them, thinking to increase his store of worldly goods, and enjoy a trip through Lower California at the same time. It was a wild, almost unknown country; but his love of adventure led him to look upon the journey as one of pleasure rather than toil. He left San Francisco in May, 1857; going by water to Santa Barbara,-one of the southern ports of California. From here he went to Los Angelos, San Pedro, San Diego, and other towns in that vicinity; riding on horseback hundreds of miles, spreading his blankets in the open air, yet always happy, always cheerful; often obliged to shoot his supper before he ate it; writing his letters on his saddle-cloth, the top of his hat, a tin plate, or a milk-pan; visiting mines; locating grants; riding sometimes sixty-five miles a day; traveling among the Mexicans and native Californians, -himself nearly as brown as they. He speaks of them as treating him very kindly, and being very hospitable towards the "Americanos;" and goes into raptures over the beautiful scenery that is constantly attracting his attention. I copy one remark that will show his love for the "old flag:" "I shall spend the glorious Fourth on Mexican territory, and not under the 'stars and stripes;' but the American flag shall float over me that day; if I can find the cloth to make one." He remained in this country some nine months, and then returned to San Francisco again. This trip was a failure in a pecuniary point of view; for he could not get the salary promised, as one of the parties had died; and he returned rather discouraged, his hopes of success had been so sanguine.

He had been in the city but a short time when the "Frazer River excitement" turned the heads of the Californians. Gold had been discovered in large quantities in British territory, and it was thought it would prove a second California. The excitement in San Francisco was intense; and, with the hope of gaining what he had lost in Lower California, Sewall determined to join the multitude that were hurrying northward to the new El Dorado. In company with one friend, who was to share the hardships and the success of the trip, he left San Francisco, in June, 1858, in a steamer bound to Victoria, Vancouver's Island. At Victoria they purchased an Indian canoe; and, with three other men, -making five in all, - they commenced the journey up the river. It was a hundred miles to Fort Langley, their first landing-place; and they intended to go a hundred miles beyond this. Their canoe was heavily laden, and the river-currents were very strong. In speaking of the journey, Sewall says, "I think it is the hardest work I have ever done;" and he had done a *little* of that during his life.

He spent the 4th of July, 1858, at Fort Langley; and, as they were on British ground, he determined that an American flag should float over *their* tent, on that day at least. So, the previous day, he set himself to work to make a flag that should be a reminder of his home; and that flag is now in my possession. An old red flannel shirt furnished the material of that color, an old white-shirt was torn up for the white, while a blue blanket furnished the field for the stars. He could not make the stars to suit him; and so he cut the figures '76 out of some white, and sewed it upon the blue; and this flag floated over his tent on that day, on that British soil. Here, too, he had only his tent to live in, his blankets for a bed, and was obliged to do his own cooking, washing, &c.

They went up the river as far as Fort Yale; and, not being able to go any farther in their boats, they landed, and proceeded by land some twenty miles over the mountains on foot, and heavily laden, as there were neither horses nor mules in that country. About twenty miles above Fort Yale, he and his friends staked out a claim, and again commenced mining, as sanguine of success as though disappointment had never crossed his path. Until the gold excitement, no one had traveled this country but Indians. The Hudson-Bay Company had a few men at the different forts or trading-posts; but they did not travel about the country.

The Indians called them "King George's men," and the Americans they called "Boston." The same qualities which gained him friends among the Mexicans in California won the friendship of the Indians of this northern land; and many were the presents of fish, berries, &c., that he received from them. But *all* were not so well disposed, as one event in this history will prove. Sewall was one day sitting in his tent, when suddenly there came in an Indian chief with some four or five of his tribe. At first Sewall, thinking no evil, took little notice of them; but they soon commenced looking about them, and gathering up such articles as they could see, intending to take them away. Sewall was alone; but, seizing his revolver, he stepped forward, bidding them not to lay a finger on an article, or he would shoot them all. His resolute daring cowed the chief; and he fell on his knees, and begged for life. Sewall bade him get up; which he did, saying, "Boston good Indian, Boston no coward!" His partner soon returned and has since told me that he had no doubt Sewall's courage saved both their lives; for those Indians were very unfriendly to the whites. From this time, the chief, with all his tribe, were Sewall's warmest friends, -constantly bringing him little presents of such as they had; and it was not long before it was in his power to do them a kindness. The various tribes of the upper country had troubled the miners so much, that, at last, the miners determined to exterminate the whole number. Sewall heard of the organization, though he did not join them. He was some distance from the white settlements which had been annoyed,- they being some forty miles farther up the river; but, feeling that his Indian friends were in danger, he determined to save them if possible. I copy his words: "Three of us started for the Indian ranch just before dark, on the same evening that the company of miners were to perform their work of extermination. As I was the only one who could speak the *Chinook tongue*, I told the chief that he must pack up and leave for the mountains immediately, or the whites would kill them. In less time than I could tell them, they were packed, and ready to leave, bag and baggage." The old chief shook hands with them, and gratefully thanked them, saying they would not forget it. That very night, their houses were burned; and they would have shared the fate of the rest, had it not been for the timely warning. Very early the next morning, Sewall was awakened by a visit from the old chief, with a present for him; and, while he remained in the country, they were his constant friends.

The Frazer-River gold mines proving somewhat of a humbug, they left the country in November, returning to San Francisco not much richer in worldly goods than when they left, but with a larger experience, and many pleasing recollections of hours spent there. Sewall, through all this time, never once alludes to the hardships and discomforts, except to mention the facts; and always was cheerful, and sanguine of success. He engaged with his whole heart and mind and strength in every scheme which interested him, and never gave up till he was convinced that he had exhausted the whole. He was very expert in the use of tools; very quick and active; and I have heard it said of him, that few men could accomplish so much in a given time as he could. In speaking of his travels, he says, "I have traveled about some in my life. I have been south as far as latitude fifty-six degrees, and here I am at fifty degrees north. I have lived under Chilian, Mexican, and English governments; and the only way a man can truly prize our own glorious Republic is to see and travel in foreign lands. I am a thorough American, and I glory in it."

Early in the spring of 1859, Sewall again came East; and we were married the 25th of May, 1859; and, in September of the same year, we returned to California. Sewall now determined to settle down, and enjoy the pleasures of domestic life, which possessed an especial charm for one who had been so long a wanderer. He purchased a ranch some sixty miles from

San Francisco; and there, in quiet happiness, he devoted his time to the cultivation of his ranch. We had lived there about a year, when, even in our distant home, we heard the nation's cry of alarm at the fall of Sumter; and when he heard of the mustering of armies, and knew that danger was threatening that land he loved so well, he would often say to me, "If I were only a single man, I should certainly go East, and join the army." Even as early as this, he began again the study of military science, and interested himself in all pertaining to it; and, in the summer of 1861, he joined a company of men, as private, who met for drill and instruction in military matters; but, knowing full as much as any of them, he was frequently the instructor. During this time; his mind was unsettled; his thoughts were often dwelling on the danger that was threatening that land he loved; and I have often heard him say, "that if this, the best government the sun shone on, was destroyed he should not wish to live." He would have joined the army at this time, had it not been for me; but I *could not* give him up. In November, 1861, we again returned to San Francisco,- an excellent situation being offered him there, together with a better opportunity to serve his State as a military man; for at that time it was seriously thought that there would be trouble there. A new zeal had been given to the different military organizations; and he was soon re-elected captain of his old company,- the First Light Dragoons,-having resigned that position when in Lower California. Here I hoped he would be content, and gratify his love of military life as captain of that splendid company; but his heart was with those noble men who were sacrificing their all for their country, and again and again was the unwelcome subject discussed between us. I *had* felt that there were plenty of men here, that there was no lack of material, and that his services were not needed; but when I heard that men were less willing than formerly to volunteer, and that drafting even must be resorted to in Massachusetts, I felt that it was my duty to give up my precious husband to the cause. I saw that *good* men were needed, and I knew how admirably adapted he was for the life; and I, too, loved my country too well to see her destroyed without doing my all to save her. I had no sooner given my consent than he proceeded to act; and, with other Massachusetts men, formed a plan, the result of which you know. A finer body of men than the California Hundred, as they were called, was scarcely to be found in any State; and they left San Francisco, Dec. 11, 1862, for Boston; arriving in New York the 2d of January, and in Readville the next morning. They formed Company A, Second Massachusetts Cavalry. They remained in camp a little more that a month; when they were ordered to Gloucester Point, Va. Here they were chiefly engaged in picketing, scouting, &c.; in all of which they performed the various duties assigned them so as to win the respect of their commanding officers. In April, the rebels came down upon Fort Magruder and Williamsburg; and Capt. Reed was ordered there in command of a squadron. Our force there was not large; yet, contrary to their expectations, they were not attacked; and, after a stay of about a month, the command returned to Gloucester Point. They remained here about a month longer; when they received orders to join Col. Spear's command in his raid up the Peninsula, and here they saw their first severe fighting. I send you a letter from one of the members of the company describing the taking of the South Anna Bridge; which was done by Sewall's command. It is not for me to speak of his coolness and bravery; but I can say that his actions at that time but increased the respect and confidence of his men. They approached quite near Richmond at that time, and were successful as to the object of the expedition. Soon after their return, they were ordered to join the army in the defence of Washington; and were finally camped at Vienna, Va. For the last four or five months of his life, Sewall had commanded a battalion, though not commissioned as major; and no officer in the whole regiment was more popular or more respected. Of the closing scenes of his life, I presume you are informed. It seems so sad, he was so young, and just upon the verge of military life,- so promising, so beloved; but 'tis well. He gave his life to that country he loved so much, and fell as a brave soldier wishes to die. Had he remained in San Francisco, he would have attained distinction in civil life; but he cared not for it.

[The Sermon, in its' entirety, was entitled "Dying For Our Country" A Sermon on the Death of Capt. J. Sewall Reed and Rev. Thomas Starr King and was printed by John Wilson and Son, Boston, 1864.]

Life in the Libby Prison

The Trinity Journal publishes a letter from Wm. Norris, a California soldier in the Massachusetts Contingent from California, to his brother, which we append.He writes from the National Hospital, Annapolis, after having been exchanged from the rebel prison at Richmond.

"You desired me to give you a description of my capture and imprisonment. I will endeavor to do so in as brief a manner as I can. On the 22d of August I was detailed to go to Washington in company with twenty-five other men to exchange worn-out horses for the same number of good ones. We got in Saturday evening and remained over Sabbath in the city. On Monday at 11 A.M. we left for camp, having four horses a piece. We went until 3 P.M., when, as we were passing through a short lane in the pine woods, we discovered a platoon formed in front of us. We instantly formed in line. They shot several of our horses at the first fire. We replied, and our horses soon became unmanageable. I got my horses untied from the saddle, but could not manage the horse I was on. We continued firing several moments, when we were charged in the rear by another platoon, when it came to a hand and hand fight. I could have got away if I had made use of the time, but I thought it would not do to leave the boys in trouble, so I continued to fight, until five men stepped out of the smoke and demanded my surrender. I found it was no use to say no, as I would be shot if I did. They ordered me to mount my horse, and be off. We rode forty miles that night, and when we stopped we were nearly parched for water. We asked them to allow us to go and get a drink, or that they would get us some in our canteens. But they only cursed us as d—d Yankees, and said that if they had the power they would hang us. In the fight Moseby himself was wounded in two places. In the morning we had to start afoot for Richmond. We walked to within fifteen miles of Culpepper, when we gave out. Our feet were so swollen that we had to cut our boots off. Here fourteen of us, (as others were added to the number on the way,) had to pay $75 to get a man to haul us to Culpepper, from whence we went by way of the cars to Richmond, where we arrived 29th of August, and were locked up for the night in an apartment 50 by 100 feet. It was kept wet all the time to prevent the graybacks from driving the prisoners out. They could be seen at all times crawling over the floor.

We were allowed no fire, and I had to lay on the floor, without any blankets, and after the rebels had taken their share as they called it, all the clothes I had left was a thin blouse, a cotton shirt, one pair of pants and no drawers. I had $10.50 left of my money. I took cold. In the morning we were marched to Belle Island, where we were allowed two acres and a half for six thousand men, and less than one half of them had tents to sleep in, and no blankets at all. Our rations consisted of one-half ration of bread, and soup made of one ounce of beef, to one spoonful of beans, boiled in a pint of water. One ounce of beef per day was all allowed. The beans were full of worms; they would rise in the kettle until you could scarcely see the water. The water we had to use was from holes sunk between the tents six feet deep in the earth. Graybacks were to be seen at all times of the day crawling over the sand, and floating on the water. The small space of ground we occupied was ditched around and the guards stood on the outside. At sundown the gates were shut that led to the rear, and were not opened until sunrise the next morning. It took until noon every day to carry off the filth of the night. I remained here one week and saw men die off in piles, like hogs in the Winter in the Western States. After I had been there about a week I took sick with the measles; remained a week longer and was unable to walk, when two of our boys carried me into the hospital as it is called. I gave them all the money I had left as they were starved until they did not look natural, and I did not suppose I should ever want any more. The hospital was a long tent with no floor. The sick were laid in rows so close that is was almost impossible to turn over unless all turned. None were allowed in the tent but the sick, and no lights at night. I was lying one night between two men who were very sick. About midnight one of them seemed to be worse. As I turned to him he gave a struggle. I felt his brow, it was cold and damp. He was dead. The other one was in much pain. I lay a few moments and heard him catch his breath as if in great pain, and then turned back to him. But he too was dead. About six feet from where I laid another was groaning. In a moment it stopped. A comrade lying by his side said he was dead and then all was silent.

I was given over for as good as dead by the doctor, and did not expect to live from one hour to another; nor did I desire to live, for I felt that I had seen enough. Here I remained a week longer, and never had a dose of medicine. But I was favored of the Lord with violent fever, which reacted to my benefit. They then removed me to Libby Prison hospital, where I had a straw bed and one blanket. At this place the doctor pronounced me beyond hope, so I got no medicine. After remaining a week, the rebels were arranging to send a boat load away, and took my name, and they said I would die on the oars before I reached City Point. But the Lord kept life in me, so that their expectations were thwarted. I arrived at City Point on the 29th of September, and came to this hospital the 30th. Where I am well taken care of, and am slowly but steadily regaining my wonted health of body and mind."

The Daily Bee, Sacramento, Thursday, March 17, 1864.
Mariposa Weekly Gazette, Saturday, March 26, 1864
[William Morris - Co. E]

❖❖❖❖❖❖❖❖❖❖❖❖❖❖❖❖❖❖❖❖❖❖❖❖❖❖❖❖❖❖❖❖❖❖❖❖❖❖

LETTER FROM THE CALIFORNIANS
WITH THE ARMY OF THE POTOMAC.

(From the Correspondent of the ALTA, in the Battalion.)

Camp of Cal. Cavalry Battalion,
Vienna, Va. March 25th, 1864.}

-Editors ALTA:- Since my last letter from this place, written shortly after the disaster at Drainsville, little has transpired with us worthy of record. Our total loss at the Drainsville fight, including Massachusetts recruits and twenty-two New Yorkers, stands as follows: killed, 14; wounded, 12; taken prisoners, 76-which must be acknowledged to be rather a severe loss out of 138 men.

News from Richmond.

A few days ago we had the pleasure of receiving a letter from Captain Geo. A. Manning, of our battalion, who was taken prisoner by the rebels in the late fight. He writes that himself, his brother, (Lieut. M.,) and twenty-four of his own men, had safely arrived in the rebel capital, and were as "comfortable as circumstances would admit" in Libby Prison. The Captain writes in good spirits, and expresses a hope that he may soon be exchanged, and once again leading his brave company in his country's battles. A better officer, a braver man, a kinder gentleman or truer friend than Captain George A. Manning does not exist in the army or out of it. California may well feel proud of being represented in the Army of the Potomac by such men as him. We all hope that his deliverance from bondage may be speedy, and that he may soon be returned to us.

Major Thompson's Command.

Some days ago an order came to the commanding officer here for the first battalion of this regiment, composed of three California companies and one Massachusetts, but the commanding officer had no idea of parting with the Californians, and to evade the order he changed the companies composing the first battalion, substituting Massachusetts men for Californians, and thus sent them over to Maryland. Companies E and M (A and C of the battalion) or at least the few that are left of them, are now with Major Thompson. The Major has been very successful with his command in guarding the fords on the Potomac, and stands deservedly very high in the estimation of Major-General Auger, commanding the Department of Washington.

Promotions in the Regiment.

The promotions in the Second Massachusetts cavalry have been quite numerous of late. Major Crowninshield has been promoted to be Lieutenant-Colonel, and commands the regiment. He is a fine officer, having been in the service since the outbreak of the rebellion, and is one of the very few Massachusetts officers who have treated the Californians as men and patriots should be treated; he has shown them many acts of kindness and indulgence; for this and his acknowledged bravery and military experience he has won a strong hold on their affection. Captain Z. B. Adams, of San Francisco, at last succeeded in obtaining a commission in the Fifth Massachusetts cavalry, (negroes,) and has gone to Boston to join his command. He presented to his old company the beautiful Guidon presented to him by D. Norcross, of San Francisco. It is now safe in their keeping, and they hope to take it back to the city from whence it came, unstained by dishonor, though rent by rebel bullets. Captain Adams' company (L) is now commanded by Lieutenant Stone, in the absence of Captain Wm. C. Manning who is a prisoner in Richmond. Gus. A. Doane, of the California Hundred, a resident of Santa Clara, has been promoted out of this regiment, having received a commission in the Marine Brigade of the Mississippi flotilla. Doane is a good soldier and a clever gentleman, and this promotion could scarcely fall on more worthy shoulders. Lieutenant Henry Kuhls, of whose promotion I wrote some time ago, has been assigned to Company K, he is succeeding beyond our expectations in the discharge of his duties as an officer, and is very highly esteemed.

The Spring Campaign.

Is likely to open lively. Grant-"old U. S."-has now the command of the army, and for once we have the "right man in the right place," he is going to work in the reorganization of this army in a manner that will insure success. The Army of the Potomac will in a few weeks be numerically one hundred and seventy-five thousand strong, and will be commanded by Grant in person on the field. He will not allow himself to be dictated to by corrupt politicians in Washington. He has the love and confidence of his soldiers, and of the masses of the people, and these will stand by him in whatever he may do.

Large bodies of troops are now passing out to the front, the new levies of recruits are taking the place of the veterans in and around Washington, and these latter are going to the Army of the Potomac, which is being reorganized under the personal supervision of General

Grant. To accomplish this, requires time, but I am much mistaken if the first day of May does not see this army in a state of splendid efficiency, and marching against the host of traitors in their front. I am of opinion that a new era is being inaugurated in the history of the Army of the Potomac. Grant will not advance until he is sure that he is ready, all the "On to Richmond" cries of fanatics to the contrary; but when he does, there will be less retreats and fall backs than has hereto fore been it's lot. But while this is going on in the Army of the Potomac, the other armies are by no means idle. The blow will be struck simultaneously by land and by sea, and if we are then successful, then indeed must the rebels give up their cause as hopeless.

The Movements of our Battalion.

What we are to do, or where we are to go, during the approaching spring and summer campaign, is with us as yet a matter of conjecture. We are in hopes of being sent to the front to join the cavalry force of the brave and gallant Kilpatrick, whose dashing exploits have written his name high on the scroll of fame. It is possible that we may be kept here hunting and fighting guerrillas until the end of the war; but, deliver us from such service-it is harder work and accomplishes less than any other that we could do. The health of our boys is generally good. Some have been troubled with rheumatism and colds, but stormy March is now well nigh over, and, with the approach of warm weather, they will all be right and hearty again.

The Coleman brothers, from Grass Valley, Cal. paid us a visit a short time. Californians visiting us will always meet with a hearty welcome.

T. H. M.

Alta California, San Francisco, Thursday, April 28, 1864.

❖❖❖

APRIL, 1864

3 Maj. Gen. Philip Sheridan becomes the Army of the Potomac Cavalry Commander.
12 Confederates capture Fort Pillow, Tennessee.
17 Grant ceases further exchange of prisoners.
30 Jefferson Davis' son dies from a fall.

❖❖❖

[Here, Valorus Dearborn of Company A, tells of the disposition of the "Company Funds"]

April 1, Friday
Serg't Hussey departed after noon.
Benjamin left on furlough.
Weather cloudy and commenced to rain soon
after dinner.
Have been to work on log hut for the
S..... etc.
Lieut. Davis returned to Camp Shining like a
gold dollar. He is authorized by Mrs. Reed to

settle the Comp. fund. The Comp. was called together at 8 o'clock in the evening to take such measures as they deemed necessary. The Comp. voted to accept Mrs. Reed's statements as being as near correct as circumstances will admit. After this they voted that a paper be drawn up and each member appropriate as much as he saw fit to on Walter Reed, Capt. Reed's son, he being a cripple and bids fair to remain one through life. Looking upon this as being a noble tribute I placed opposite my name $10.00.

Valorus Dearborn Diary - Bancroft Library, University of California at Berkeley
[Walter Sewall Reed died at Dorchester, Mass., March 24, 1886 of Nephritis, age 25. He is buried, as is his father, at Mt. Hope Cemetery, Mattapan, Mass.]

The members of Company A Second Massachusetts Cavalry, (California Hundred) have given to Walter Sewell Reed, the son of their late commander, Capt. J. Sewell Reed, the sum of $1,000, in token of the respect and love they bore that lamented officer.

The Napa Register, Saturday, June 11, 1864.

DIED.

==

LEE-At Vienna, Virginia, April 7, 1864, after a short illness of two days, Alfred Foster Lee, (aged about 23 years,) a native of Amesbury, Mass., and recently of Vallejo, California.

Alfred F. Lee was one of the eight members of the Vallejo Rifle Co. who responded to their country's call and enlisted in the California Hundred and went to the seat of war to fight the battles of the Union. At a special meeting of the Vallejo Rifle Co., held on Tuesday evening, May 10th, 1864, the following preamble and resolutions were unanimously adopted, as expressive of the feeling of the Company in view of the death of their late comrade:

Whereas, God in His providence has seen fit to remove by death patriot and soldier, our former companion and brother, Alfred F. Lee of the California Hundred; and,

Whereas, our fondest hopes have been blighted and our friend taken away, therefore,

Resolved, That, as a faint testimonial of our appreciation and regard, we hereby express our common regrets at his decease, and deep sympathy with those who, holding a nearer friendship, have so much more cause to mourn his early death.

Resolved, That in Alfred F. Lee we have ever found a true patriot, a good soldier, and a sincere and genial friend; and in his decease the country has lost a most devoted and brave soldier, and an intelligent and promising citizen.

Resolved, That a copy of these resolutions be sent to his parents, and also published in the Solano Herald, Press, and Cal. Spirit of the Times.

Committee   { Lieut. A.S. Campbell,
on   { Corp. H.H. White,
Resolutions,   { " , D.W. Helms.
Vallejo, May 12, 1864

Solano Herald, Suisun, Saturday, May 14, 1864.

WASHINGTON, MONDAY. MAY 2.
FROM THE ARMY
A Fight With Mosby's Guerillas

The *Star* says: "The cavalry expedition sent out from Vienna last Thursday, under command of Col. Lowell, returned to that place yesterday, after having visited Leesburgh, Rectortown and Upperville. Near Upperville a portion of Mosby's guerila band was encountered, when a sharp fight ensued, which resulted in the loss to the rebels of two killed and four wounded, and twenty-three taken prisoners.

Col. Lowell lost three men killed and four wounded. Col. Lowell returned safely to Vienna with the twenty-three prisoners captured from Mosby, and also three blockade-runners, twenty-five horses, and a large quantity of wool, tobacco and other contraband picked up on the route.

New York Times, Tuesday, May 3, 1864.
[Thursday, 29 April 1864]

Ben Hoxie writing from Vienna, Va., under date of April 29th says: "There are stirring times here now. This is to be the hardest fight on the soil of Virginia. I am satisfied as to the result - this summer will close the war. The weather is fine, and we are in good spirits. We had a good chase on last Sunday. We traveled twenty-one miles in two hours and a half. I had the good fortune to capture the only prisoner - Lieutenant Hunter - and wounded one other."

Solano Press, Suisun, Saturday, June 4, 1864
[Lt. W.L. Hunter, Co. A, 43rd Battalion Virginia Cavalry, captured April 22, near Hunter's Mill, Fairfax Co., Va.]

Killed. - Sergeant Clark, formerly of Downieville, Sierra county, was killed in the latter part of April, while engaged with the California Battalion, in a fight with Moseby's guerrillas, near Leesburg, Va.

The Napa Valley Register, Saturday, June 4, 1864.
[Charles A. Clark, Co. L, April 30, Rectortown, Virginia]

MAY, 1864

5-7   Battle of the Wilderness
8-21 Battle of Spotsylvania Court House
 15   Battle of New Market, Shenandoah Valley

Hd. Qrs. 2d Mass Cav. Vienna Va. May 2d 1864

My dear Mammy

We have just returned from a long scout and I am rather too tired to write a long letter today. This is only to let you know that I am all right. We had several skirmishes with the Rebs with the following result. We lost 2 killed 3 wounded & 2 prisoners. The Rebs lost 3 killed 2 wounded & 26 prisoners who fell into our hands, wether they lost any more killed or wounded whom we did not get I can't say. After our little skirmish Capt DeMerritt of F Company in returning his pistol to his holster shot himself badly through the foot.

I enclose Mosby's signature & a ring made out of a Yankee bone, taken from one of the Rebs. Everything in the box you sent me was first rate except the Soups & the Patte. I wish you would ask Dr Warner whether this ring is made of human bone or not.

> Your son
> Caspar

Caspar Crowninshield, Letters, Massachusetts Historical Society

Condition of Capt. De Merritt. - The many friends of Capt. J.H. *[D.A.]* DeMerritt, late of the Sacramento Rangers, (Company F, Second Cavalry, C.V.) and more recently Assistant Inspector General of Cavalry, in the command of General Ashley, in the Army of the Potomac, will be glad to learn that he is recovering from the painful wound in his leg and foot, received on the 2d inst., in a skirmish preceding the general advance of our forces, and is likely to emerge from the hospital at Washington, for the third time, a sound man. The news comes in the shape of a telegraphic despatch dictated by his wife, at Sacramento. The gallant Captain had resigned his position as Inspector of Cavalry, in order to resume his old position in the California Massachusetts Battalion, and was on his way to the front when the skirmish occurred in which he was last wounded.

Alta California, San Francisco, Friday, May 20, 1864.

An Incident of the Battle Field. - Some weeks since, the fact of Capt. J.H. *[D.A.]* DeMerritt having been again wounded in a skirmish with the rebels of Virginia and sent to the Hospital at

Washington, was published in the Alta. We learned yesterday the particulars of the affair, which are somewhat singular. It seems that the Captain was on horseback and was drawing his revolver to fire, holding it at the moment in his right hand, immediately in front, and on a level with his breast, with the muzzle pointing downwards. A ball from the enemy, which would have struck him full in the breast but for the revolver, struck one of the chambers of the pistol and discharged it, the bullet from the chamber striking him in the leg and inflicting a very severe and painful, but not dangerous wound. Had the pistol not been in that position his leg would have been uninjured, but the musket ball would have killed him on the spot.

Alta California, San Francisco, Friday, June 24, 1864.
[Wounded May, 2]

❖❖❖

[Here Valorus Dearborn tells of the change over from Sharps to Spencer Carbines]

> May 23, Monday
> Spent   .25
> Reviewed by Lieut. Col. Crowningshield at
> 7 A.M.
> Privates Pelham and Copeland ordered to report
> to their camp this day for duty.
> Changed Sharpes Carbine for Spencer seven
> shooter.
> Rail Road Bridge near Falls Church 1 P.M.
> Towle, Porter and Dearborn to guard this
> Bridge for the next 24 hours.

Valorous Dearborn Diary - Bancroft Library, University of California at Berkeley

❖❖❖

OUR ARMY CORRESPONDENCE.

Letter from the 2d Massachusetts Cavalry.

Cavalry Camp. Falls Church, Va.,
May 26, 1864.

To the Editor of The Boston Journal:

The 2d Mass. Cavalry is now in this camp. Lieut. Col. Crowninshield commands the regiment. Colonel Lowell was absent on duty in the Cavalry Bureau from the date of my last letter, Feb. 18, until April 4, when he resumed command of the brigade to which our regiment is attached. During his absence, Col. H.M. Lazelle, of the 16th New York Cavalry, commanded the brigade, and the disaster on the 22d of February, near Drainsville, was the only important event.

Since Col. Lowell has resumed command, reconnoisances and scouting parties have been the order of the day, and in all these our regiment has had its full proportion of men engaged, and does nearly all the real work. The result of the recent expedition has been the capture of between fifty and sixty of Mosby's guerillas, including two officers and many of their best men, the killing and wounding of a dozen more, with one officer, and the capture of about a hundred horses, with arms, equipments, uniforms, and much valuable contraband property. The losses of the regiment have been: Sergt. Clark and Private Hatch of Co. L, and Corporal Charles Goodwin of Co. H, killed, several wounded and three or four prisoners.

The most successful of the late raids was the last day of April, under command of Col. Lowell. On this, parts of Fairfax, Fauquiar and Loudon counties were well scouted, and we had constant skirmishes with Mosby's men, although they nowhere appeared in any force. Twenty-one prisoners were taken, over forty horses and a large amount of wool, cotton, tobacco, and other valuable contraband goods. A private apartment in a house near Middleburg, frequented by Mosby, was discovered by the Provost Marshall, and the private papers of the guerilla chieftain taken, including his commissions and other important documents.

Maj. Gen. Auger, commanding the Department of Washington, has sent many of his troops to General Grant, but still retains our brigade. The rest of our division, consisting of infantry and artillery, was ordered away a fortnight ago, together with its commanding officer, Brig. Gen. R.O. Tyler. This leaves Col. Lowell the command of all the troops in this Department outside of the fortifications.

On the twenty-third inst. The Orange and Alexandria Railroad was abandoned by the Government to Springfield Station, and orders were received for the lines of the cavalry brigade to be correspondingly drawn in to Annandale, Falls Church, and Lewinsville. This was done the next day, and we are yet scarcely settled in the new camp.

Our present location is very pleasant and apparently healthy. The village of Falls Church, which is within rifle shot, is on the Alexandria and Leesburg turnpike, nine miles from the former place and six miles from Georgetown, via Ball's Cross Roads and the Aqueduct Bridge. The regiment is in shelter tents. All mail should still be addressed to Washington, D.C., and express matter to Alexandria, Va. A train runs daily between the latter place and camp.

Lieut. Col. Crowninshield and Maj. Forbes are the only field officers on duty here. Maj. Thompson, with Co. B, D, E and M, is still on detached service in Maryland. Maj. Blagden is on duty at the War Department, Inspector General's office. Capt. Manning and Lieuts Manning and Norcross are still prisoners in rebeldom. Capt. Holman is in Massachusetts yet. Lieut. Payson is on Gen. Devons' staff. Capt. Demerrit is temporarily disabled by a wound in the ankle, caused by the accidental discharge of a pistol. Dr. DeWolf and Lieut. Alvord are on duty at Brigade headquarters. Asst. Surg. Gamweee has been promoted to Surgeon of the 5th cavalry. Lieut. J.W. Sim has resigned on account of ill health and returned to California. All our other officers are on duty with the regiment.

A band of fifteen pieces, the members taken from the ranks, has been organized and drilled during the winter, and now discourses on all appropriate occasions. It is very popular and deservedly so, being one of the most pleasing features of the camp.

Cadet.

The Boston Journal, Boston, Monday, May 30, 1864

❖❖

Hd. Qrs. Cavalry Camp
Muddy Branch May 30, 1864

Col. J. H. Taylor:
Chief of Staff,

Colonel:

I have the honor to report that on Saturday afternoon three men appeared at the usual landing place on the Md. side at Edward's Ferry and hailed the picket on this side stating that they were refugees, and wanted to come over and at the same time holding up a handkerchief the usual signal. Two of my soldiers went over in a boat after them. When they arrived near the landing the white signal was dropped and these three with five others, which had been secreted nearby, commenced firing at the men in the boat, which soon struck the land, and they were taken prisoners. They were taken back and robbed of their pistols, watches and part of their clothing, and were then taken to Leesburg and paraded through the streets to the gratification of the robbers and citizens. One of the men was wounded in the thigh.

> I am Colonel,
> Most Respectfully Yours,
> (sgd) D.W.C. Thompson
> Maj. 2d Mass. Cavalry
> Comdg. Post

Hd. Qrs. Dept. of Washington
2d Army Corps. June 4, 1864
Official:
>   C. C. Auger,
>   Maj. Genl. Comdg.

Regimental Record Books, National Archives, Washington, D.C.

❖❖❖

JUNE, 1864

1-3 Battle of Cold Harbor.
  8 Lincoln nominated for President.
 18 Siege of Petersburg begins.
 19 Confederate ship C.S.S. *Alabama* sunk by U.S.S.
     Kearsarge.
 27 Battle of Kennesaw Mountain, Georgia.

❖❖❖

> Where is John Burbank if he is in
> Washington I will go in and see him

> Hd. Qrs. 2nd Mass Cav.
> Falls Church, Va., June 2nd/64

Dear Sister & Brother

I received your very welcome letter to night.

I have been very uneasy about Dick & am glad to hear that he is all right & doing well.

You see by the heading of this that we are in a new camp at a place called Falls Church; nearer to Washington than Vienna by about ten (10) miles; so that at present we are but about six (6) miles from the Capitol Building.

I suppose you will ask what we moved in for? I will tell you nearly all of the old Regiments have been sent away from the Defences of Washington to aid Gen. Grant; & new

(100) day men put in the Fortifications to Guard the City & Moseby is of course aware of this; so in consequence he has collected all the men in this part of the state that he can & makes frequent raids in toward the city for he does not fear those (100) day men chasing him, in fact he would like to have then come out after him for he would (Gobble) them all sooner or later for they do not understand his mode of fighting besides they are not acquainted with the country.

Nearly all of our Regiment is out after one of his Parties I wanted to go very much but could not as it is the first week in the month & we have a great many Reports to make out which takes (3) three of us (3) or (4) Days to do.

I have been out on two raids since I wrote last we have lost two (2) Prisoners & (2) two killed & (3) wounded. We killed four (4) wounded six (6) & Captured 42. I think that is doing very well.

I must close for I am tired & it is near midnight. My love to all who may think enough of me to inquire about me.

I send a Picture of our men of Co. F. Sergt. John Passage is Orderly Sergt. of Co. F now. he is doing well. he went out on the raid today.

Tell Ma not to worry about that ten dollars. I will make it a Present to you (Irena) & Ma.

Good night & Pleasant Dreams
From your Brother
Robert

Sergt Major

2nd Mass. Cav
Falls Church Va.

Irena }
Walter} write soon & every time you here from Dick

Manuscript Collection, Huntington Library, San Marino, California
[Robert H. Williams, Co. F]

❖❖❖

A CARD FROM THE OFFICERS OF THE FIFTH MASSACHUSETTS CAVALRY IN REFERENCE TO MAJ. Z. B. ADAMS.

Headquarters. Fourth Regiment
Massachusetts Cavalry,
City Point, Virginia, June 5, 1864.

Editors Alta: - The undersigned, formerly of the Second Massachusetts Cavalry, having noticed, with much surprise, an article in the Alta California, (over the signature "T.H.M.") in which the private and official character of Major Z. B. Adams, Fifth Massachusetts Cavalry, late Captain Second Massachusetts Cavalry, is seriously attacked, desire to state -
First - That in the estimation of the superior officers of the Second Massachusetts Cavalry, and in our estimation, Capt. Adams was one of the best and most highly esteemed officers in the regiment, and is an officer whom we are, and ever have been, proud to serve with!
Second - At the date of the communication referred to, it was known throughout the regiment that Capt. Adams had received the appointment of Major in the Fifth Massachusetts Cavalry, a fact of which "T. H. M." could not have been ignorant!

Third - Capt. Adams was *once* placed under arrest, certain charges having been preferred against him which appeared to require formal investigation. A court was ordered, composed of Major Forbes, Captain Eigenbrodt and Lieut. Smith, the last two being members of the California Battalion. Capt. Adams was at once restored to duty without censure!

We cannot, however, in justice to a thorough soldier and a brave and gallant officer, refrain from noticing so slanderous and injurious an attack.

Major Adams, as an officer, does honor to California, the State of his adoption, as to Massachusetts, the State of his birth.

Frances Washburn, Lieut. Colonel Commanding Fourth Mass. Cav., late Captain Second Mass. Cav.

Louis Caboz, [Cabot] Major Fourth Mass. Vol. Cav., late Captain Co. B, Second Mass. Cav.

W. N. Percy. Second Lieutenant, Fourth Mass. Cav., late Sergeant Co. A, Second Mass. Cav.

H. B. Welch, Captain Fifth Mass. Cav., late Lieut. Co. F, Second Mass. Cav. Cal. Battalion.

H. E. W. Clark, Captain Fifth Mass. Cav., late Lieutenant Second Mass. Cav. Co. E, Cal. Battalion.

John Anderson, First Lieutenant Fifth Mass. Cav., late First Sergeant Co. L, Second Mass. Cav., Cal. Battalion.

J. L. Wheat, Captain Fifth Mass. Cav., late Q. M. Sergeant Co. A, "Cal 100," Second Mass. Cav.

A. T. Mallory, First Lieutenant Fifth Mass. Cav., late Q.M. Sergeant, Co. E, Cal. Battalion, Second Mass. Cav.

Edgar M. Blanche, First Lieutenant Fifth Mass. Vol. Cav., late First Sergeant Co. E, Cal. Battalion, Second Mass. Cav.

R. M. Parker, Second Lieutenant Fifth Mass. Vol. Cav., late Corporal of Co. A. "Cal 100."

Chas. E. Allan, First Lieutenant Co. B, Fifth Mass. Cav., and Assistant Provost Marshall Hink's Division, late Sergeant Co. A, Second Mass. Cav., "Cal 100."

Alta California, San Francisco, Thursday, July 7, 1864.

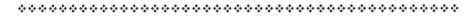

Decimated. - Most of our readers doubtless remember the departure of the "California Hundred," the first California soldiers to proffer their services to aid the Government in crushing the rebellion. Well do they remember how proudly these choice spirits marched through our streets, and, with elastic step, walked aboard the vessel which bore them hence. Alas! of that gallant band of one hundred, but twenty-five remain in the land of the living. All the rest, including Capt. Reed, have fallen in battle, or perished in the privations and hardships of the campaign. The above facts are obtained from John Sim, Second Lieutenant of the Company, who returned on the steamer *Constitution* yesterday. He would not have left his brave compatriots in arms, but that a severe and protracted sickness prevented him from doing a soldier's duty.

Alta California, San Francisco, Thursday, June 9, 1864.
The Napa County Reporter, Napa, Saturday, June 11, 1864.
[According to" Massachusetts Soldiers, Sailors & Marines in the Civil War", at the time of Sim's resignation: 10 had transferred; 8 deserted; 4 discharged for disability; 4 killed in action; 3 died of wounds. A total of 29, leaving 71 still on active duty.]

LETTER FROM A SAN FRANCISCAN WITH
THE ARMY OF THE POTOMAC.

We are permitted to give publicity to the following letter from a young resident of this city, now serving in the Army of the Potomac, addressed to his relatives here:

FALLS CHURCH, Va., June 14th 1864.

Last Wednesday morning, the 8th inst., orders came rather hurriedly that all of our regiment in camp should get three days' rations and be prepared to move in an hour. Such was accordingly done, and at the appointed time all was in readiness. Three days' rations were also packed in wagons and taken along with us. Our destination was supposed to be the Army of the Potomac, but in this, as the sequel proved, we were mistaken. The first day we marched to Brentsville, and there bivouacked. The next morning, early, we were joined by fifty ambulances, and it then leaked out that we were bound for the vicinity of Fredericksburg to gather up our wounded remaining there in rebel hands. After the ambulances joined us a move was again made, and that night we bivouacked at Independent Hill, having crossed the Occoquan during the day. On the evening of the third day the Rappahannock was reached, and our bivouac for that night was on its banks. The next morning the stream was forded at United States Ford, some five or six miles above Fredericksburg, and in a few hours we entered the Wilderness, wherin such terrible fighting occurred during the first two or three days of Grant's "on to Richmond" movement. We had not entered it far before the signs of the struggle that had taken place there became apparent. On both sides of the plank-road upon which we were traveling, the woods were filled with newly made graves, and the entire Wilderness, ten miles long and four wide, was one vast graveyard. In many places the dead still remained unburied, the bodies lying where they had fallen, both Union and rebel soldiers. In some places the road, for three or four hundred yards, was strewed with corpses in the last stage of decomposition, and it was a terrible sight to be compelled to witness. Most of the bodies had been stripped of their outer garments, and all had been robbed. Where the pants still remained on the body, the pockets were turned inside out. Boots or shoes I did not observe on any of the bodies. With one exception, the bodies of those I saw were instantly killed. In the exceptional case, the head of the body was lying upon a blanket, the poor fellow having crawled to the side of the road and laid himself down there, probably, with an idea that he would be noticed and taken care of, but had soon died.

The Wilderness.

Is covered with a small growth of trees from ten to twenty feet high, principally oak and pine, and the growth is very thick-in some places almost impassable. To render it still more impregnable, the rebels had constructed earthworks through its entire length, from an eighth to a quarter of a mile apart, and it seemed to me almost impossible that they should have been driven out of such a place. The wonder to me is not that so many lives were lost in the battles of the Wilderness, but that so many went through it unscathed. A wounded Union soldier and participant in the fight informed me that both sides would form in lines half a mile in length and distant apart not more than twelve yards, and keep one continued sheet of flame between them for hours at a time without any advantage being gained by either. As one man fell another would step up and fill his place, and another and another. Each man of our side seemed to possess the energy and determination of their indomitable commander. Nothing but death could turn them aside from their purpose to whip the rebels, and, actuated by such a high motive as "love of country" they did it. In some places along the line no firing was heard at all, but terrific fighting was done with bayonet-a regular hand to hand conflict, in which the most active won. The trees all through the Wilderness from the ground up to the height of a man's head are riddled with bullets, and it is astonishing how anything larger than a mouse could have lived where bullets were flying so thickly. I ascertained from a negro woman who was over the battle ground two days after the fighting and before many had been buried that with the exception of one place where a formidable breastwork was charged by our men, that dead rebels were thicker than dead patriots. Before getting through the Wilderness we came to a hospital in which were fifteen wounded Union soldiers, and quite a number of wounded rebels. Only two of our men were pronounced fit to stand being removed, the rest were left behind in the hands of rebel doctors and nurses. They say, however, that they are well treated, not as well as they would be in our hospitals but as well as the facilities of the rebels will admit of.

Beyond the Wilderness.

At Locust Grove, near Orange Court-house, we came to another hospital in charge of rebel attendants, and there we found over forty of our men wounded, many of them with one of their legs amputated. Forty-one of them were placed in the ambulances and two left behind; their time on earth being but for a few days it would only have been an aggravation to have moved them. They were delighted upon finding out we had come to take them into Alexandria, where so much better treatment would be secured, and actually hurrahed, although at the expense of considerable pain. One of them upon being told he was hardly fit to move, burst out crying, and said it was just his luck to be always left behind; declared that he would go anyhow; that he would rather die going towards Alexandria than at the place he was then in. He entreated the doctor so earnestly to take him along that he was finally taken, and when we left the ambulance train at Fairfax Court-house was in good spirits, and had stood the ride that far very well.

The Rebel Sentiments.

Many of the rebel attendants upon our men also entreated to be taken along with us, and all that conveniently could be taken were. They said "the Confederacy is nearly played out. We are tired of this fighting, and wish to get away from it." They say it is the common belief among the rebel enlisted men that if any of them escape to our lines and take the oath of allegiance to the United States Government they will be compelled to fight for us. Were it not for that belief thousands of them would desert to the right side. This is told to them by rebels of position and influence, and having no way of arriving at the truth, must perforce believe it is even so. Nothing but actual experience in the matter will convince them the contrary is the case.

It is further represented to them that the North is drained of men to the same extent as the South, and that the only recruits we are now getting are emigrants from Europe, enlisted immediately on their arrival on our shores. All this is believed by them. If the truth of the matter could only be made apparent to the rank and file, that our resources and power are as great now as at the commencement of the war, the effect upon the rebel armies would be more demoralizing than a dozen Wilderness defeats.

Our Return.

Having taken from Locust Grove all our wounded able to be removed, the object of our mission was accomplished, and our steps were retraced to the Rappahannock, near which we bivouacked for the night, or rather half of it, as we did not reach there until about 12 o'clock, midnight. The next morning we recrossed the Rappahannock, and made the best of our way in the direction of Alexandria. That night one of the wounded, whose leg had been amputated five days previous, died and was buried in the field in which we tarried for the night. The chaplain of our regiment being present, consigned the body to the grave, with a brief prayer and in a few impressive words. The deceased was a member of the One Hundred and Forty-ninth Regiment

Pennsylvania Volunteers, and leaves a wife and two children in Philadelphia, to mourn his loss. Nothing further worthy of note happened during the remainder of the trip, and the camp at Falls Church was reached at midnight of the 13th. The trip was easier on men and horses than any expedition we have yet made in this portion of Virginia. Both came in good order and condition.
T. D. B.

Alta California, San Francisco, Friday, July 15, 1864.

Va
Camp Falls Church
June 14th 1864

Dear Minnie

Your last letter was here in Camp probably two or three Days before I had a chance to read it, for when I returned last evening at 12 oclock I found it here. Have been on a six Day Raid this time and went farther down in Virginia than we ever did before & will try to give you a slight discription of the trip. In the first place we went prepared to have a fight & expected one when we left. There was about 800, (Eight Hundred) of us with a train of Sixty Ambulances. The news came to Washington that the Rebels were taking our wounded that were left at the Wilderness and carrying them to Richmond as Prisoners, & we were sent to bring them away, but our Luck was to be a little to late for some of the Rebel Cavelry had got there about 24 hours ahead of us & taken away over two hundred of our poor fellows. Still we done some good for they left about 50 & we brought them back with us. I am now satisfied with the Front have never seen anything in my Life that looked half so horrible as the Battle Field at the Wilderness. The woods & Roads even for 8 or 10 miles around are strewn with the Dead and not one in a Thousand hardly have been touched since they fell. Lay there & Decayg on the Ground like so many Cattle. Riding along the Road a distance of not more than fifty-Rods we counted 125 (one hundred & twenty five) Dead Soldiers & that was not a comparison with what we see back from the Road a short distance in the woods. The Citizens living there have buried some few of theirs the Rebel Dead near the Road, but all of our Soldiers nearly lay just as they fell with the Exception of being stripped of Every thing of any value. I have seen some pretty hard sights before but never wish to look on another like the Battle Field in the Wilderness, the wounded were pleased nearly to Death to think we had come after them, they were all expecting to go to Richmond as fast as the Rebs could get them away. We had no fight for they were to quick on foot for us & left when they heard of our coming, but we took some 30 or 40 Prisoners by coming on them unawares. The most Exciting part of our scout was after getting in to Camp, the news came soon after getting here that Moseby had followed us in here with 8 or 9 hundred men & One Battery. We had just got unsaddled & ready to take a sleep after our Riding night & Day for six Days when Boots & Saddles sounded & we all had to Saddle up again. Turned in as soon as we were through & slept about two hours when we were waked up very sudenly by the screaming of Shells & Noise of firing Carbines & Pistols. We have been kept in readiness from One Oclock last Night till about two hours ago, & its now 3 in the Afternoon to give Mr. Moseby a thrashing in case He sees fit to stand & give us a chance to fight Him, but for the last 2 or three Hours I have not heard any firing & dont believe we shall have any show to get at him, still he may be trying even now to get his Battery in position to give us a few shells I saw one Burst about a half mile

from Camp this morning but have seen none since. There was some excitement though for a while around here, however its very quiet now and I dont think we will have much of a fight after all & finaly am not very anxious about it Myself, for I would much rather be certain of seeing you again than taking the chances of being left as many of our Soldiers have been on the Soil of Virginia. But Minnie you must not wory about Me a great deal for I am in the fighting business & will take my chances with the rest of Uncle Sams Men without murmering for the time Im in the Service. At the same time wishing for the close very soon, you are certainly no more anxious for my return than I am to get there once more, but at present fate is against me and I am obliged to stay away from all that is Dear to me at Home for some time yet, and Minnie you do not doubt My honesty now Im sure, that is being honest when I tell you that to lose the love I am positive you now feel for me would be more than a trifle for my mind is perfectly clear when I tell you that you are Dearer to me than the world. I would be willing to lose (no not willing) but had if it were necessary rather lose every friend in the world than my Minnie. It is easy for you to see by the foregoing I would much sooner be with you isnt it. You wished to know if I heard from California often. I have not heard from them but once since leaving last Jany. Em was not married then nor do I think she will marry Mr. G. am expecting a letter from there soon & will give you all the News when I do. Here are a few Postage Stamps that were taken from a Reb on the Chancelorsville Battle Ground I send them as a memento of my trip ———————————————. Will finish here By Sending love to our Mother & Remaining as ever your devoted Friend & promised (well you may guess the rest can you) John Passage
I have not looked this over to see how many mistakes there is but will read it for you when I get home.

Courtesy of Mary Paynter, Madison, Wisconsin

Hd. Qrs. 2nd Mass. Cav.
Camp near Falls Church Va.
June 14th/64

Dear Parents
    I received Irenas & Dick's letter & two papers this morning about 2 O'C AM. I was very glad to hear from you for I have not been in camp since the morning of the 8th when we were ordered to hold ourselves in readiness to march at 15 minutes notice with six days rations. We left camp about noon not knowing where we were going; all we knew was that we traveled southward. We camped about nine O'C P.M. on the Alexandria & Brentsville Turnpike near Brentsville to wait for a train of Ambulances from Washington which arrived at daylight it was then we found out where we were going as soon as we got ourselves a cup of coffee to drink we moved on, Our entire force consisted of (100) of the 13th N.Y. Cav. Mounted & (50) Dismounted, also a similar force of the 16th N. Y. Cav. & (250) Mounted & (100) Dismounted of Our Regiment all of this regiment were armed with Spencers Patent Carbines (seven shooter) the train consisted of (44) four horse) & (10) two horse) Ambulances besides 6 Army wagons with Forage, rations, & Medical stores.

We crossed the Occoquan River at Wolf Run shoals, after nearly two days travel we reached & crossed the Rappahannoch River at United States Ford, this was the morning of the Eleventh. after crossing the River we moved toward Chancellorsville where we arrived at nearly noon this place is noted for one of the hard Fought Battles of this war here we would see human skulls & Bones lying above ground in some Parts passing through this place; we marched over one road which runs through the Wilderness Battle Field it was the Plank road where Gen. Sedgwick marched his column to (Locust Grove or Robertsons Tavern) in & beside this road were a large number of the dead of both Armies lying on top of the ground. You would also find a great many graves where some Friend had performed the last act of Human Friendship toward the fallen Hero. We soon came to Parkers store where you will remember there was some very heavy fighting at this point the Rebs suffered most. We found Hospital Tents erected & filled with wounded but the Rebs had been there a few days before & moved away all who were able to ride in an Ambulance, so that we did not get but two of the wounded at this Place; That was the object of our Trip as we heard the Rebs were moving them away as fast as they were able to stand the ride From Parkers Store we proceeded to Locust Grove (Robertsons Tavern) where we found (43) of our wounded who were able to ride but could not walk besides twelve who were able to walk. They all went with us as a mass of course there were about (25) wounded Rebs at this place all of whom were unable to move The Hospital at these places were in charge of one of our surgeons who had a wounded Reb surgeon to assist him Our surgeon came with us. On our way from this place we passed over that portion of the Battle Ground between Robertsons Tavern & Wilderness Tavern where the heaviest part of the Fighting was done some parts of this ground was taken & retaken five & six times I saw in one small nook near the woods bodys lying on top of the ground so thickly that my curiosity led me to count them & there were (125) men killed and not buried on a piece of ground not as large as your garden from the well down to the lower end. What do you think of that? We recrossed the Rappahannoch that next morning at daylight & came home by the way of Brentsville Manassas Junction, & Centreville.

Excuse Haste for I am

Tired & Sleepy

From Your Affct son

Robert H.W.

Manuscript Collection, Huntington Library, San Marino, California

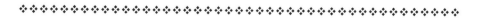

June 15th 1864 Falls Church Va.

My dear Mammy

I have been out on a scout for the last week and that is the reason why I have not written to you. We were sent down to the Wilderness, where Grant fought for two days, to recapture some of our wounded men who were taken by the Rebs & who were said to be still down there under a small Guard. We took ambulances with us & succeeded in finding 42 of our wounded whom we were able to remove we also took a few Rebels. We passed over a large part of the two days battle & I never saw anything like it in my life the woods are so dense (we halted in the road & I walked into the woods for some distance to see the enemies brestworks) that you can hardly get through. Many dead bodies are still lying unburied Union & Rebels just where they fell. In front of one Rebel brest work one of my officers counted 145 Union soldiers besides numerous graves or pits where they had been buried.

[Last of paragraph deleted-Editors]

Your son
Caspar
Caspar Crowninshield, Letters, Massachusetts Historical Society

Falls Church june 18ᵗʰ 1864

Dear Parents
      I recived your letter of the 8ᵗʰ two or three days ago and thort I wold not answer it til today. We have ben out to the battlefield of the Wildernes and have ben gon seven days the place is riteley named for it is a wildernes of all kinds of timber for miles around. We crossed the Raphanock at the U.S. ford and went to Chanservile and from thare we tooock the plank road into the wildernes and now we cold see som sines of the battle the trees wer spotted with bulets and we saw menny placeses whare the ded had ben berred when we had gon a mile we came to whare the fite was the hottes the rebs had rifle pits on both sides of the road and thare must have ben hard fiteing to have taken them and here the ded lay unbered thikley on both sides of the road blew and gray about equel the trees wer spect with bulets and none above eight feet from the ground so they must have shot wel. Here we found three or four teems belonging to citersons, they wer loded with stuf they had picked up on the battle ground the men sed they lived fifteen miles away. I presom they belong to the FFV they wer in good buisness with the Buzards robing the dead thare wer six of us in advance and we went through them for thare diner it was boiled han and buisquet and butter and made us a good meal and we needed it. Our buisnes was to recapture a lot of our wounded that the rebs had taken. About five miles into the wildernes we came to a number of tents with the red flag flying over them but thare was onley thirtey or fortey rebel wounded thare to bad to be moved our wounded had ben taken away the day before and wer on the way to som rebel prisen. From this place we turned to the rite and went across onto the pike a distence of five miles to a place called Locus grove here we found a little patch of cler ground and a lot more of hospittle tents thare wer fortey two of our wounded here and about fortey more had died most of the wounded had a leg off onley two or three hit in the bodey thare was one of our sergents and two reb sergents in charge of the hospittles both the reb doctor wer drunk when we got thare and had quite a lot of rifle whiskey on hand stil. The boys wer glad to see us and wer glader stil when we told them we wer going to take them away we loded them into the amberlances and came back to chancervile on the pike this road is whare the hard fiteing was don, on the 6ᵗʰ of may, and the ded wer laying in the road and on both sides of it. We camped that night betwen chancervile and the river and started for home the next morning. The journel has stoped coming and I dont want it eny more give my love to all

Sam Hanscom

Courtesy of Bruce MacAlpine, Concord, MA.

❖ ❖

A San Joaquin Soldier in Grant's Army.

The Stockton *Independent* has the following interesting particulars from the Army of the Potomac:

"L.H. Manchester, formerly of French Camp, in this county, now an officer in Taylor's division (cavalry) of the Twenty-Second Army Corps, on the Potomac, writes to his friend, Assemblyman Allen, under date of June 23d, some interesting matters connected with Grant's army. He says the blows inflicted on the rebel army by Grant for the thirty proceeding days were fearful, and that the universal conviction of the army is that the rebellion cannot survive the present Summer and Autumn. Grant, he says, is a favorite with all - officers and men reposing in his earnestness, courage and ability, the utmost confidence. Given the men needful for so great an enterprise, they have not a doubt that he will take Richmond and destroy Lee and his army. To use his own language, "Grant knows all about fighting; give him any number of men in his army and he will manage to fight them all; he piles them in (as he says himself) whenever he means to hold any important point." Manchester avers that Lincoln is omnipotent with the soldiers. They are almost to a man in favor of his re-election to the Presidency, and this is because they think he has done well in the past, considering the obstacles which he had to overcome. We quote from this soldier's letter as to camp life and duty on the Potomac. He says: "Our business is on post and picket duty; chasing after horse thieves and bushwhackers, nipping blockade runners and deserters, and picking up all sorts of refugees of all colors. We are scattered all over the country in small squads, sometimes mounted, at othertimes afoot, sometimes in rebel gray and again in Uncle Sam's blue. This is what you may call the true Cossack life. We live on beans, fresh beef, butter, eggs, wild cherries, coffee and tea. For amusement, in daytime we sometimes go on a scout and raise the d—l with some old reb's butter establishment. There is no falling out here; when an alarm is given, night or day, we do not stop to see whether it is true or not, but fall right into line at the bugle's sound. Five minutes too late would lose the camp, should it prove to be rebs. Three of our boys have just been discharged for disability - two of them caused by pistol shots and the other by dislocation of the knee joint. One of them, Oscar Burnap, was shot after he had given up his arms, last Winter while on picket duty near Vienna. The shot passed through his lungs, leaving him a broken down man for life. R.T. Brickley was shot through the hand by accident. S.W. Shaw had his knee dislocated while on picket duty". Of the cruel treatment our prisoners experience at the hands of the Richmond authorities the reader may judge from the pictures which accompany the official report upon the Fort Pillow massacre and upon rebel treatment of prisoners generally should they ever see the document with the photographs of some of the poor starved victims which accompany it. These photographs, it appears, have very properly been distributed through the army, and it is to them which Manchester alludes in the following lines; "You ask for my picture. I will send it; but cannot imagine what you want with it unless it be to frighten rats and squirrels, or to go into the vinegar business. I send you some other pictures of a different sort. From a glance at them you can see the cause of the sour looks of your humble servant. They are only four out of some one thousand. One of our poor fellows now in camp came back to us in the same condition - his hip bones and shoulder blades worn through the skin when he reached Annapolis. His name is William Morris, of Trinity county, California. Thomas J. Colby died soon after he was landed. When the rebels captured him at Ashby's Gap, July 12th, 1863, he weighed one hundred and seventy pounds; when he died his weight was one hundred and eight! Starved to death. Morris says he saw H. Venum, of Company F, while on Belle Island, pick up old bones, set down, scrape them, and eat the scraping. Others pounded up old bones with a hammer and eat them. Vennum starved to death on Belle Island. Oscar Blanchard, of Company E, starved to death in the same place. I could write more on the same subject, but I will not. It is too horrible to put on paper. I send you four photographs. show them to all the Copperheads in the county and then leave them at the *Independent* office (we have them) so that the whole public can see. If after this they can vote the Copperhead ticket, nothing under heaven would reform them."

Mariposa Weekly Gazette, Saturday, July 30, 1864.
[Luman A. Manchester, Co E, taken prisoner July 13, 1864 at Rockville, Md., escaped August 20, 1864. Mustered out as Sergeant; All from Co. E; Colby shown on roster as Cobbey; Annapolis, Md. had been established as a parole camp to tend to paroled Union prisoners. A search for the photos has been unsuccessful to date.]

❖❖❖

JULY, 1864

3 Siege of Washington
6 Lieutenant General Jubal Early invades Maryland.
9 Battle of the Monocacy, Maryland.
11 Confederates reach the outskirts of Washington.
17 General John B. Hood replaces General Joseph E. Johnston.
20 Battle of Peachtree Creek, Georgia.
22 Battle of Atlanta, Georgia.
28 Battle of Ezra Church, Georgia.
30 Battle of the Crater, Petersburg.

❖❖❖

July 6th

100 of our boys that were out on a raid were attacked by Mosby and whipped near Aldie. Mosby had 300 Cavalry and one piece of Artillery. our loss is 30 killed and wounded and about the same number taken prisoner. Our men were under the command of Major Forbes and he is to blame for the whole affair.

July 7th

Major Forbes, Lieut. Amory and our Chaplain were taken prisoners and Capt. Stone of Co. L. mortally wounded in yesterday's fight.

July 8th

Three of the captured men came in to camp this P.M. they succeeded in getting away from the Rebs. they report the Rebel loss as 23 killed. they do not know how many were wounded as they were

taken away in wagons. Co. A. lost 2 killed, 2
wounded and five missing. Corporals Bumgardner
and Hanscomb killed and Sergts Plummer and
Hilliard seriously wounded. A. Loane and four
Recruits missing.

Samuel J. Corbett Diary - Bancroft Library, University of California at Berkeley
[Battle of Mt. Zion Church.]

❖❖❖

July 7th 1864

My dear Mammy

Major Forbes & 100 of our Regt. out on a scout were surrounded by Mosby who had
artilery & 400 men. Our men were defeated - Major Forbes & Ned Amory are missing. Some
of the men who have just come in say that Ned was taken prisoner, probably not wounded his
horse threw him. I shall telegraph to Mr Amory as soon as I hear anything reliable. What we
hear now is unreliable. A strong party of our men has just gone out to find out the facts. I should
have gone but I am on a General Court Martial & the Col wished me to stay here. Use your own
judgement about saying anything about this, though before this reaches you I shall probably
have telegraphed to Mr Amory. Some of the men say that they saw him fall off his horse in
jumping a fence. Whether he fell off or was shot off is at present doubtfull. I am inclined to
think that he is a prisoner but not wounded. No one knows what has become of Major Forbes.
I pray God he is safe - he is a man who would fight to the last & I fear he is killed - this last you
must mention to no one.
       Your son
        Caspar
I will write again soon.

Caspar Crowninshield, Letters, Massachusetts Historical Society

❖❖❖

The Second Massachusetts Cavalry.

The following extracts from a letter from the Second Massachusetts Cavalry contain the latest
authentic details of the late skirmish of a portion of that command. Under date of the 8th, the
writer says:

"Major Forbes was sent out on a scouting party on the 4th of July, before anything was
known of the big raid, his force consisting of about a hundred men of the 2d Mass. cavalry, and
fifty men of the 13th N.Y. cavalry. They heard of Mosby passing through Leesburg with the
plunder taken at Point of Rocks, escorted by fifty or sixty men, and tried to intercept him.
Meantime Mosby had increased his force to two hundred or more, and became the assailant, on
the 6th, near Aldie Gap, having a field-piece with him.

Our forces chose their position and were in line of battle, but were overpowered after a
sharp fight in which about 12 were killed, 35 escaped, and 87 were recovered wounded, 40 to
50 are known to be prisoners, including Lieut. Amory of the 2d Mass. Cavalry, Lieut. Barns,
13th New York (both unhurt). This leaves 30 to 40 unaccounted for who may come in. Lieut.

Kuhls, 13th New York, escaped dismounted, and is the only officer saved thus far.

The Major had his horse killed while rallying his men, was pinned to the ground, and taken unwounded.

The chaplain, Mr. Humphreys, after showing much spirit, and doing his best to encourage the men, was taken. Captain Stone of Newburyport, while trying to rally the men, was severly wounded. Sergeant Hilliard, A, distinguished himself in trying to rally the men, and was wounded. Lieut. Schuyler, 13th New York, was badly wounded. A message was left by Major Forbes at a farm house that they were well treated. Mosby took his prisoners toward Upperville, and with the large raid on our hands and he well ahead it was manifestly impossible for Colonel Lowell to pursue him. No names are mentioned beyond that above given."

Evening Transcript, Boston, Monday, July 11, 1864.

❖❖❖

Capture of Some of Second Massachusetts Cavalry.-*Washington, 9th.* A letter from Avondale, *[Annandale]* Va., eight miles west of Alexandria, says a scout of 150 men from the 2d Massachusetts and 13th New York cavalry, under Major Forbes, went to the vicinity of Aldie, where they met Mosby with a large force and one piece of artillery. Mosby charged on them, killed 10 or 15, and captured the whole party, horses and accoutrements. On the receipt of the news, Colonel Lowell started off at midnight, with 200 men of the 2d and 13th, and Captain McPherson of the 16th New York cavalry joined him at Fairfax, when they proceeded to Aldie, where they found 25 wounded men and 11 dead, whom they buried. They scoured the country about that region, but found that it was of no use to pursue Mosby, as he had twelve hours' start toward Upperville, where he had taken his booty. Our party returned last evening with the wounded.

Captain Stone of the 2d Massachusetts cavalry of Newburyport, Mass., is lying dangerously wounded at Centreville. Thirty rebels were at Fairfax Court House yesterday.

Evening Transcript, Boston, Monday, July 11, 1864
New York Tribune, Monday, July 11, 1864.
[Goodwin A Stone Co. L, died July 18, 1864]

❖❖❖

Falls Church, July 9th, 1864

Since I last wrote you we have had a tremendous fight with Mosby on Alda *[Aldie]* Pike. Out of 150 men that went out only 30 of us came back whole. Alda is twenty miles from here; we started from Falls church July 5th, it was a splendid day, and little did we think that for a good many of us it would be the last time we should see camp. We arrived at Leesburg that night where we shot one reb, he would not surrender, so we shot him. We stopped there all night and started for Alda the next morning and arrived at Alda Pike at five o'clock in the afternoon. It was a beautiful day, the sun shone with unusual warmth.

Major Forbes, who was in command, ordered us to feed our horses; the way we do it is one half of us feed, the rest remain bridled until we get fed, then they feed. We had fed our horses and were just putting our bridles on when Mosby fired on us, he emptied some of the saddles, the rest of us jumped on our horses and the third platoon was ordered to fire. There was a large piece of woods alongside, Mosby was in that when he fired; as soon as he fired about 200 of them charged on us, bursting into our midst and causing death and destruction wherever the pieces went, that excited the horses and away they scampered, some without and some with riders. It seemed as though a kind Providence watched over me - the balls whistled around me like hail. Our commanding officer must have got excited for he did not give any orders what to do, and so every man went on his own hook, he was soon taken prisoner with a lieutenant, and we fought with desperation for we knew it was death or Richmond with us, but we could not stand it long. Our officers were all killed or taken prisoners, so we were broken and scattered, my brave horse was shot from under me, the ball grasing my leg. I jumped up and mounted another horse that was passing by, when a reb came riding up and told me to surrender, (I was just pulling out another revolver) I told him I could not see it. He put his pistol to my head and fired, just as he fired my horse sprung to one side and spoilt the shot, the ball just went by my ear inflicting a slight wound on my temple, that was tall work and I started but not before he bit the dust. Then two rebs started after me, it was a race for life, and as their horses were better than mine they soon came up with me. One of them, who was ahead, had the point of his sabre within four inches of my back, when our Chaplain rode up and shot him through the back; if ever I thanked God it was for that. The other reb made a slash at my head with his sabre, I put my head down on the horse's neck and down came the sabre taking me on the head and shoulder, he meant to cut my head off, but the horse caught the blow, and slightly wounded me on the head and shoulder. The wound is not much so don't be uneasy, I am doing well. I nearly fell from my horse but the fellow paid for it with his life, for as he rode by I had just strength enough to raise my revolver and get sight on him and fired, he fell from his horse like lead, I am sorry for it but could not help it. I got in camp last night pretty well exhausted, when I write again I will tell you how I got away from them.

Yours truly,
Nathan C. Huestis

Courtesy of Wynne Saffer, Leesburg, Virginia
[On roster of Co. H as Heustis, a carpenter, originally from Yarmouth, Nova Scotia]

❖❖❖

OUR LETTER FROM ST. LOUIS.

{From the resident correspondent of the ALTA CALIFORNIA}

St. Louis, July 14th, 1864.
The California Cavalry Boys After the Guerrillas.
On the 5th instant, according to a Washington corespondent, Colonel Lowell, commanding a brigade of cavalry, consisting of the 2d Massachusetts, 16th New York and 13th New York, and having its headquarters at Falls Church, sent out a detail of two hundred and fifty picked men on a scout to Leesburg and Aldie, for the purpose of ascertaining if any considerable rebel force was in Loudon county, threatening the passage of the lower fords of the Potomac into Maryland. The troops were commanded by Major Forbes, of the 2d Massachusetts. They advanced to Leesburg, and thence to Aldie, without meeting any rebels, and from the latter place had started on their return on Wednesday, by the road to Fairfax Court House, when Moseby's band, nearly four hundred strong, with two pieces of light artillery, intercepted them at a point near Mount Zion Church. The rebels were drawn up in the road, barring the further progress of our cavalry, when first seen, and immediately opened with shell from their cannon,

and brisk fire from carbines and small arms, before which our cavalry could not stand, although they made a gallant resistance. The superior numbers of the enemy and their artillery, afforded them every advantage, and they succeeded in killing, wounding and capturing nearly all the command. Maj. Forbes is known to have been wounded and captured, and nearly all the other officers are reported prisoners. Up to twelve o'clock last night, more than thirty-six hours after the fight, less than a dozen of the command had returned to Fairfax, but it is supposed many of them are straggling and will yet come in. Yesterday Moseby made his appearance between Centreville and Fairfax when Col. Lowell immediately started after him with three hundred picked men, and at last accounts was fighting him.

Alta California, San Francisco, Monday, August 8, 1864

Telegraphic Despatches.

Upwards of 2000 rebel cavalry bivouacked in Rockville on the night of the 10th. Monday morning they engaged Col. Lowell's cavalry, but the result had not been received in Washington.

Mosby has 242 men in his command, and expects to have his force increased. In the fight at Aldie Mosby captured 81 cavalry men, killed 20 and captured a Major and one piece of artillery, a 12 pounder.

No casualties have been reported on our side in the fight this morning between Lowell and the rebel cavalry

Evening Transcript, Boston, Tuesday, July 12, 1864.

OPERATIONS NEAR WASHINGTON.

On Sunday evening a body of rebels, variously stated from eight hundred to two thousand, entered Rockville and dashed through to a point a few miles this side of that village. Halting there for a brief while they retraced their steps to the town, where they bivouacked for the night.

Yesterday morning they assailed a cavalry force under Col. Lowell, thrown out to ascertain their strength. The point of this skirmish was in the vicinity of Rabbit's creek post office, between Tennalleytown and Rockville. Subsequently we heard of their skirmishing about noon, on and around the Seventh street turnpike, near the Clagett farm and the residence of Francis P. Blair, Esq. We also had reports of their appearance at other points. There was no serious fighting during the day. On our side there were in all twenty or thirty casualties, occuring from the pickets and sharpshooters of the enemy.

Daily National Intelligencer, Washington, D.C., Tuesday, July 12, 1864.

OPERATIONS NEAR WASHINGTON.

We regret to state that before decamping from the city the "raiders" burnt the country seat of the Hon. Montgomery Blair, the Postmaster General, and rifled the mansion of his father, Mr. Francis P. Blair, abstracting, it is supposed the papers and correspondence of this gentleman, covering a period of forty years.

CASUALTIES.

The following, who were wounded within a day or two in front of Washington, are at Carver Hospital: Geo. O. Wise, Wm. Nichols, Jas. H. Orten, Thos. Cox, Michael Grimes, Robert Powell, Geo. F. Parlow, N.J. Welcome, Charles H. Fuller, Wm. Price, Wm. Hazard, Paul Farnham, Eastman Dulin, Orton Cole, A.F. Barrenson, John Gillespie, and Frank Hill, all of 2d Massachusetts cavalry.

Daily National Intelligencer, Washington, D.C., Thursday, July 14, 1864
[From Co's. B, D & M]

OUR LETTER FROM THE CALIFORNIANS IN VIRGINIA.

———

(From the Correspondent of the ALTA CALIFORNIA.)

———

On the Field, Near Blue Ridge, Va.
July 17, 1864.}

EDITORS ALTA: A despatch bearer leaves here for Washington, and I hasten to send you a brief account of our doings. For five consecutive days we have been fighting the rebels. Starting in front of Washington, where we first fought them, we have been following them up, and now no rebel remains in Maryland except those who sleep beneath her flowery soil, and these are by no means few; in one place I saw four hundred negroes burying the dead. The heavy guns of the forts around Washington mowed them down like grass, and not being able to stand such force they withdrew, and have ever since kept on retreating back to Richmond. I hasten to relieve the anxiety of those who have friends in this battalion by informing you that in these late fights no Californians have been killed; but quite a number of them are wounded, and some of them severely, and some have been taken prisoners. I will soon furnish you with a detailed account of our doings, together with the names of our killed, wounded and prisoners. We have driven the rebels entirely out of Maryland, and they are now trying their best to reach Richmond with their immense quantity of spoils, but I am much mistaken if they are not intercepted and routed.

It is impossible to give even an estimate of the damage the rebels have done in Maryland; but what is the best, is that the greatest part of the injury was done to rebel sympathizers, for the Union men, aware of the approach of the rebels, removed all their valuables, horses and cattle, to places of security, while the Copperheads took no such precaution, relying on their sympathy for the rebs as a safeguard against their depredations.

Parts of the Sixth and Nineteenth Corps are with us, making a force of twenty thousand men in equal proportion; besides these, General Hunter's command is to meet us today five miles from here, and then, with a strong column; we will push on after the rebels and follow them to Richmond.

We are playing the same game on the rebels that they played on us in Maryland. Our track is marked by devastation and ruin. We wish to show them that we can play as high a hand as they can. It is amusing to see the doings of the twenty thousand Infantry with us. They have no scruples about helping themselves to everything that suits their tastes.

I must close. My excuse for this poor letter is haste, and that I am writing it on the cover of a box of hard tack, with confusion and noise on every side. The Californians have, as they ever do, acted with great gallantry and bravery, and have been very highly complimented. They fill the post of honor, as advance guard of the whole column.

T. H. M.

Alta California, San Francisco, Friday, August 19, 1864.

❖❖❖

PURSUIT OF THE RAIDERS.

LOSSES OF SECOND MASS. CAVALRY.

Death of Capt. Stone, of Newburyport.

OFFICERS CAPTURED.

New York, 19th. The Tribune's Washington despatch says:

Our forces were, at last accounts, seven miles beyond Leesburg, in pursuit of the rebels. It is believed that Gen. Evans was left behind, wounded severely. There was heavy firing yesterday, near Edwards Ferry, supposed to have been an attack on the rebel rear.

On Saturday, the rebels were in strong force half way between Drainsville and Leesburg. The rebel killed and wounded before Washington will exceed 2000. They represent 6 regiments and three divisions.

The 2d Mass. cavalry lost in the fight at Aldie, 6th inst., over 80 killed, wounded and missing. Capt. Stone of Newburyport died this morning. Major Forbes, Lieut. Amory, and Chaplain Humphrey were captured.

Evening Transcript, Boston, Tuesday, July 19, 1864.

❖❖❖

SOME OF THE DEAD.

One of the city reporters who has visited the fortifications out Seventh street refers to an interesting spot in the immediate vicinity of Fort Stevens which forms the burial ground of twenty-nine Union soldiers who were killed in the conflict of the 12th instant. One of the lost appears to have been unknown. The graves of the remainder are labelled with their names and regiments as follows: ......J. Dolan, 2d Mass.

Daily National Intelligencer, Washington, D.C., Tuesday, July 19, 1864.
[James Dolan, Co. D]

❖❖❖

New York, July 23. - The *Post's* special says a part of Mosby's cavalry, between 200 and 300 men, have entered West Maryland, but it is not known whether there are more behind.

Alta California, San Francisco, Friday, July 29, 1864.

LOCAL MATTERS.

Capt. Goodwin Atkins Stone, of the 2d Mass. Cavalry, died at Falls Church, Va., on the 18th inst., of a wound received in a recent encounter with Mosby's men. He graduated from Harvard College in 1862. He was a native of Newburyport, and as the Herald of that city very truly says, "he was a noble-hearted young man who has offered his life for his country-one of that heroic army of martyrs, whom patriotism led to the field of strife and death. Among all the young men of our city, there was perhaps not one of greater promise. Healthy, hopeful, generous by nature, pure of life, educated with care, he was beloved by his immediate acquaintences and all felt proud of him."

Evening Transcript, Boston, Wednesday, July 20, 1864.

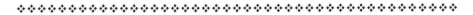

Camp Falls Church Va
July 25th 1864

Dear Minnie

You must not scold me for being so long silent for I have been since the 7th of this month up to the present time every Day in the Saddle & sometimes a large portion of the night am even now so much worn out tis almost impossible to hold my pen steady enough to scribble even this, but I am sure you will wish to know something about me. {hence this} since the 10th of this month I have seen fighting enough to suit the most fastidious & shall not wish to be in another engagement for some time to come. Our Regiment have been under fire for 3 Days at a time during this last Raid on Washington by the Rebs. I have Escaped injury in some manner but would be impossible to say how, for in the heaviest fight we had, I was in advance of nearly all my Platoon, & had the Bullets fly around me thicker than hail, was fired at by about 50 Infantry Men while getting over a fence & afterwards looked at the place & saw more than 20 Bullet holes in the rails. Am very lucky I think and am more of the oppinion then ever I shall eventualy get out all right. It would please me to give you a full acount of our marches for the last two weeks but I am at present to tired to try. Will send you this short note now & write again soon at more length. In the last letters I received from you, you said I would have to get back there this Fall if possible in order to protect you from the thieves. Dont let them steal you Minnie for if there is the least chance in the world for my coming I certainly shall & claim you as my own. If we remain here any length of time I shall write you again in a few Days. My Love to our Mother & more than love to Minnie. Yours J.P.

My Co has lost in killed wounded & prisoners the last two weeks 26 men & our whole Regiment 268 thinning us off pretty fast isnt it for two weeks time.

Courtesy of Mary Paynter, Madison, Wisconsin

Washington July 25th 1864

Respected Lady

I trust you will pardon a stranger for addressing you a few lines when you learn the painful duty that I have to perform which is to announce to you the death of your noble and patriotic Son who was shot in a Guerrilla fight on the 6th inst near Aldea, Va. I had hoped that an abler pen than mine had informed you of his fate ear this, but learning today that it had been neglected I opened your letter to learn the address. Ah little did you think when you pened those words of hope and council for his comfort and benafit that ear it reached him his Eyes would be dim in death. But he died like a true patriot and hero. He lived but a few hours after receiving the fatal shot but was concious of his approaching end and expressed a willingness to die for his country. We who had come with him from the peacefull shoars of California to help our country in her hour of trial and nead and had served beside him for a year and a half wer much grieved at his loss for our prolonged acquaintance had taught us to love and respect him. For Saml was a noble boy. But a fatal rebel bulet took him from us and we can only respect and honor his memory and emulate his example. Pleas excuse this hasty scroll I would write you more of the particulars but for want of time. So adieu for the present from   John Winship

To Mrs. Elizabeth Hanscom   Co A 2nd Mass Cav

Courtesy of Bruce MacAlpine, Concord, MA.
[Battle at Mt. Zion Church, July 6, 1864]

AUGUST, 1864

3   Battle of Mobile Bay - Admiral Farragut
7   Maj. Gen. Sheridan given command of the Middle Military Division.
23   Fort Morgan, Mobile Bay, falls to the Federals.
31   General McClellan nominated for president.

Camp near Frederic Md
Aug 3rd 1864

Dear Minnie

Having time for the first time in nearly two weeks to write will improve it with pleasure by penning a few lines to My own Dear Minnie. After writing my last letter & telling you I would soon write again at more length my time was all taken up till now, without having the first opportunity of writing again. We were at our old Camp, Falls Church but part of two nights & one Day before we were ordered to Harpers Ferry, & have been kept on the move constantly till now and will not very likely remain here more than to Day. I have been seeing Soldiering in all its different phases for the last Month, and am candid enough to say without prevaricating in the least that Citizens life is by far the most pleasant & let me once more be free from the duties of a Soldier and my thirst after glory will never run away with my better judgement again. Shall be perfectly satisfied to become an easy going Citizen without ever even as much as wishing to hear the clash of Arms

& roar of Battle more. No a quiet life with the one I love will suit me by far the best. Am probably doing no more than my duty by being as I am a Soldier but am saying as far as pleasure is concerned a Citizens life is by far the most preferable. We are occasionly or rather have been having considerable fighting to do. Our Regt are kept as advance Guard & scouts and we run against the Johneys frequently having a skirmish lasting only a short time generaly, but long enough to lose a number of Good Men every time. Our loss alone in the 2d Mass Cav, has been since the 7th of July up to the present time in Killed wounded & Prisoners two hundred & sixty eight. My Co has lost in Killed wounded & Prisoners 26, besides twenty-one missing. The missing ones are no doubt better away for they never take any part in a fight & are what might be properly termed a nuisance to any Co. our Co has the praise from the Col of being a fighting lot. He says they are the only ones in the Regiment who are willing to take more than even chances with the Rebs. He may well feel a little proud of us for had it not been for Co F's dismounting the time we had the fight in Rockville our Col would have been taken Prisoner certain, but after our Boys dismounted & commenced shooting with their seven shooting carbines, the Johneys concluded twere time to turn & run the other way, we Killed 20 in the street in less than a minutes time. we lost 11 there in the fight, but not one killed they were all wounded & will probably all get well in time. I am still among the favored, have not been touched by either shot or shell and have been in every skirmish or fight the Regiment has had, am very lucky indeed, for Im positive the Bullets have some of them been aimed towards me. One place where I stood by a pair of Bars I looked at afterwards & found in the Boards over twenty Bullet holes, & am confident by the whistling around my head I was there. We shall probably not remain here for any length of time & I am not able to say where we are going, & finaly have not much interest in our movements, can see no difference in the managements of affairs now to one year ago. Dont think our commanding Generals are trying very hard to close the Rebellion. Am willing to stay my time out & let them use me as fast as they can but would Rarely be willing to try it for another 3 years. Write often Minnie & Direct as usual, my Love to My own Dear Minnie. J.P.

Where I shall next write you from is more than I can tell, but will continue to write every opportunity. I have not heard from you in over two weeks, and am some what anxious to get a letter. I will get them once in a while by your directing the same as usual. Excuse the writing I am siting on the ground & have nothing to write on except mother earth.

Courtesy of M. Paynter, Madison, Wisconsin.

Cavalry Camp near
Halltown, Va. Aug. 9th 1864

Lt. Col. Caspar Crowninshield
Comdg 2d Ms Cav

       Colonel
           I have the honor to tender my resignation as Major in the 2d Ms Cavalry and request that it be honorably accepted. I respectfully submit the following reasons for the same. Some eighteen months since I raised in the State of California a Battalion of four companies of cavalry and came east with them with the expectation that it would be an independent command and a representative force from my state in the war. The State of Massachusetts paid

the transportation of this Battalion from California for which the number of men in it were credited to her quota, but it was not the wish or intention of those who raised the Battalion to have it lose it's state identity or be merged in any other organization. On the arrival of the Battalion east it was assigned to the 2d Ms Cavalry and has been with it since, and has to a great extent lost it's identity as a representative force from California, much to my disapointment and regret. This unfortunate arrangement has produced such an unpleasant state of feeling between myself and the superior officers of the Regiment that it is not my wish, and I do not think it is my duty to remain in it longer. I believe that I can render much better and more satisfactory service to my Government and the cause of the Union in some other position. I have been constantly in the service for more than eighteen months without any loss of time from leave of absence or sickness, and on this account I respectfully request that this resignation be accepted to take place on the 31st of this month so as to give me time to settle my accounts with the Government which I am prepared to do and turn over all property in my charge.

> I am Colonel Most Respt Yours
> D.W.C. Thompson
> Maj 2d Ms Cav

Hd Qrs 2d Mass Cav
Aug 9th 1864

Approved and respectfully forwarded to
Col. C.R. Lowell Comdg Brigade.
C. Crowninshield
Lt. Col. Comd Regt

Hdqrs 3d Brig 1st Div
Halltown, Aug 6

The resignation approved & earnestly recommended, as being for the good of the Regt. & the service. Major Thompson's service in organizing the batt entitles him to an honorable discharge.
> Respectfully forwarded to Division Hdqrs.
> C.R. Lowell, Jr.
> Col. 2 Mass. &
> Comd Brigade

Hdqtrs 1st Cav Div
Aug 9 1864
Approved & respectfully forwarded.
> W. Merritt
> Brig. Gen.
> Comdg

Head Qrs. Cavalry
Middle Military Division
Harpers Ferry, Va. Aug 9th 1864

Approved & respectfully forwarded.

BGen
Chief of Cavalry

Headquarters
Middle Military Division
August 9 1864

Respectfully forwarded to the Adjutant General U.S. Army.
This officers resignation was accepted by special Orders No. 3
para 12 from these Headquarters August 9, 1864.

P.H. Sheridan
Major General
Comdg

Regimental Record Books, National Archives, Washington, D.C.

❖❖

Head Quarters Middle Mil. Division
August 9, 1864

Special Orders
No. 3
Extract,
Major D.W.C. Thompson 2d Mass. Cavalry having tendered his resignation for satisfactory reasons is hereby honorably discharged from the Military Service of the United States
with condition that he shall receive no final statement until he has satisfied the Pay Dept. that
he is not indebted to the Government.

By Command
Major Gen'l Sheridan
(sgd) E.B. Parsons
A.A.G.

Regimental Record Books, National Archives, Washington, D.C

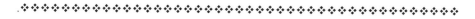

From the Shenandoah

Maj. Thompson, of the Battalion, refuses to serve under Col. Lowell, and has resigned. Only
one hundred and twenty men and officers are left in the Battalion.

Alta California, San Francisco, Tuesday, September 20, 1864.

On the March from
Charlestown, Va Aug.9/64

Elizabeth Hanscom

I recd your Letter of July 21ˢᵗ some days since but have had no opportunity to answer untill now. I am very sorry for I know your anxiety. Your Son was killed near Aldie, Va by Mosby's Men, along with several of his companions. he was shot through the head he lived but a few hours & had every care that the circumstances would allow he was buried near Little River Church, Va near where he fell. I know of no way you could obtain his body as he lies within the Enemies lines. he recd the usual burial of those who fall in the field. I do not think his grave is in anyway designated, such things however worthy the Soldier or gratifying to his friends - at times is impossible - I have his Bible, a likeness & some few of his keepsakes that I gathered up after writing you at Falls Church but we were ordered away so sudden that I placed them with the Co. property which is now stowed in Washington. I will send them to you the first oppertunity. I am very sorry I could not answer before, but I have been in the Saddle 30 days steady. The Regt has lost heavily this Summer - but we in common must bear our loss - and for our great personal & National sacrafice hope for a sure reward. Hoping & trusting we may all meet again, I remain

Your Friend
H.G. Burlingham
2d Lt Co A 2d Mass. Cav.

Courtesy of Bruce MacAlpine, Concord, MA.

Aug. 9th

We are camped in a beautiful Oak grove and are waiting for the ballance of the troops to get together. four days rations were issued this forenoon, Major Thompson of the California Cavalry Battalion started for home this P.M., having resigned his commission.

Samuel Corbett Diary - Bancroft Library, University of California at Berkeley

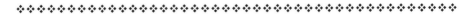

Captain Goodwin Atkins Stone. The manly humility of this officer would, whilst he was living, have shrunk almost with pain from words of praise, however deserved, for obedience to conscientious convictions,-the doing of what those convictions enjoined as duty. He aspired to be true. Human applause and outward success were not what he first desired or sought. So certain are we of this that we can almost see his reproachful look as we turn to write ever so briefly of what he was and what he did.

But we may not heed that look. Now that he has died, it becomes us for a higher purpose than that of eulogy to speak of his worth. In these times it is needful to keep in remembrance such an example of early and consistent fidelity, to be moved by the inspiration of its truth. It rises above all low interests, all sordid and narrow views, in the clearness and beauty of its unsoiled sincerity; whilst it gains in the touching impressiveness of its unobtrusive admonition, by having its moral purity revealed amidst the physical horrors of war and the shadows of the tomb. Men like Captain Stone do not go to the battle field, and do not fall in scenes of

carnage, without a providential purpose-without teaching in their noble careers a divinely appointed lesson. This we must believe, if we believe that one of the agencies of the highest
instruction is the gift and unfolding of souls of rare endowment and rich fruitage. The message
quickened memory and loving meditation hears whispered, from the embowered grave of the
young soldier, is as a message from heaven. Surely the most careless will say it should be
reverently heeded.

Capt. Stone was born in Newburyport, Mass. He fitted for college at Dummer Academy,
in the parish of Byfield, near that city, and graduated at Harvard University in 1862. He left the
school he was teaching at Concord, N.H., in the Spring of 1863, and came to Boston to apply
for a commission in the Second Cavalry, under Colonel Lowell. He was successful and entered
at once upon his duties as a Lieutenant; efficient as a recruiting officer, and making rapid
progress in his new profession of arms-a profession for which he had no special taste, and
which he assumed only for the purpose of serving what he regarded as the sacred cause of
right. Those who saw and knew him at that time will remember his modesty and his energy, his
gentleness and his decision, his entire freedom from all pretensions, and his calm, profound
earnestness. He had counted the whole cost of the step he had taken; and no rashness or reck-
lessness, no sudden, inconsiderate impulse, left out of view the hardships and the dangers
which the taking of that step involved. He was prepared to encounter them all, and, if need
should be, to yield up his life in the struggle to save the nation to freedom. As he started in his
course as a soldier, so he continued until it ended at the grave. His bravery, his fine intellect, his
scholarly acquisitions, his genial disposition, his gentleness, and the truthfulness of his whole
character, won from all who served with him or under him the respect and the love which had
before been felt for him by his classmates and friends at home.

No one could be jealous of him; he carried himself with such simple and modest dignity.
No one could doubt him; he was so transparent in the thorough honesty and attractive sweet-
ness of his bearing. His clear, open, bright face, his quietly assured movements, his unstudied
straightforwardness of speech and act, disclosed at a glance as it were, the healthfulness of his
inner nature and the strength and grace that were harmonized in the symmetry of his soul.
Since his death his fellow students and his comrades have been eager to express the affectionate esteem in which they all held him for his abilities and his virtues. He was a soldier, a
scholar and a gentleman; and in all these he was also a Christian. Filial in spirit toward the
Father in heaven, fraternal in spirit toward his fellow men, the central motive forces of his
being were strong religious faith and unflinching religious principle. He was, however, in his
early piety, intelligent, bright and happy, without the slightest taint of self-righteousness, the
faintest approach to austerity, or the least shadow of gloom. His consecrated life was manly
and joyous and in its crystal brightness.

As a skilful and efficient officer, his record was a proud one. His men bear tearful testimony to his bravery and his goodness; and his influence was felt not only in his own regiment,
but throughout the brigade to which it belonged. It was a sad hour to the whole command
when he was stricken down. This happened on the 6th of July, whilst he was acting as junior
officer of a detachment on a reconnoissance. Toward the evening of that day, encountering a
superior force of Mosby's cavalry, they were taken at a disadvantage and scattered. Capt. Stone
rallied a few of the men twice; but the number was too small to make a stand, and they had to
save themselves as they best could to avoid being captured and sharing the fate, as prisoners, of
some of their companions. Whilst cutting his way out Capt. Stone was wounded mortally in the
spinal column. He kept his saddle, however, rode thirteen or fourteen miles, pursued half the
distance by the enemy, arrived at Centreville about 9 o'clock, and found refuge in the house of
a Union citizen. He was removed the next day to Falls Church, where he lingered for nearly a
fortnight. He died quietly on the 18th of July, at the age of only twenty three years.

Thus closed another of the young lives of which so many have been ended in the hospital and on the battlefield. Some have said these terrible sacrifices are too great a price to pay, even for the triumph of such a cause as that which has demanded and still demands them. But those who made the sacrifice did not think so. Those yet in the field and who are ready to accept a soldier's grave, if God wills it, do not think so. And no one, when as unselfish and as prepared to fight or fall or suffer as our young heroes have been and still are, will reproach the dead or the living by thinking so. As we learn from the examples of the intelligent, single-hearted, high-principled and earnest New England youth who have addressed themselves to the terrible work of war, to overthrow the treason that would rob the republic of its greatness and its liberty, in what consists the truest living for ourselves and our race-we shall not in a crisis like the present be, in thought, word or deed, recreant to freedom and humanity, or to this Government and the Union instituted and formed to promote the interest of both.

Evening Transcript, Boston, Tuesday, August 16, 1864

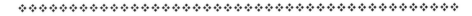

THE LATE CAPTAIN STONE.

Editors Alta: The Alta, a few days since, quoted from the Rev. Dr. Bellows' remarks before the Pioneers, an affecting account of the death of the gallant "Captain Goodwin Stone, of the California Hundred." Now, as Captain Stone has some friends here, I deem it worth the while to correct the wrong impression unwittingly given by the Reverend Doctor. Captain Stone was not of the California Hundred, nor ever saw California. He was of the Second Massachusetts Cavalry, and Assistant Adjutant General of Volunteers, and without spinning out a statement of perhaps not general interest, I would merely add, that Captain Stone was a native of Newburyport, Massachusetts; fitted for college at Dummer Academy, Byfield, Massachusetts; graduated at Harvard College in 1862; entered the Army in 1863, and in a gallant action with Mosby's cavalry received his death wound, lingering two weeks, and dying at the house of a Union citizen at Centreville.
Byfield.

Alta California, San Francisco, Sunday, September 18, 1864.
[Stone died July 18, 1864, after being wounded at Aldie/Mt. Zion July 6. He was Captain of Co. L, and prior to that Co. K.]

MOSBY'S EXPLOIT NEAR BERRYVILLE.
The Richmond Sentinel of the 17th instant has the following notice of an official dispatch received at Richmond on Tuesday from Col. Mosby:
"Col. Mosby reports that he attacked the enemy's supply train, near Berryville, on the 13th instant; captured and destroyed seventy-five loaded wagons, and secured over two hundred prisoners, including several officers; between five and six hundred horses and mules; upwards of two hundred beef cattle, and many valuable stores. A considerable number of the enemy were killed and wounded. His loss two killed and three wounded."

Daily National Intelligencer, Washington, D.C., Monday, August 22, 1864

GOOD NEWS FROM THE UPPER POTOMAC

Major Gen. Sheridan has been assigned temporarily to the command of the forces in the Middle Military Division, consisting of the Departments of Washington, the Middle Department, and the Departments of the Susquehanna and Northwest Virginia.

The news received yesterday confirms previous reports that the rebel forces have been withdrawn from Maryland to the south side of the Potomac. The Baltimore American says:

"Hagerstown was reoccupied by our forces on Saturday. The rebel retreat is said to have been made in great haste, the movement of our forces on the south side of the Potomac threatening their rear. Gen. Wright's command, composed of the Sixth and Ninth Corps, and Gen. Crook's troops, crossed into Virginia on Saturday, and the prospect of a battle is therefore regarded as imminent. The main rebel force under Gen. Early is reported to be retreating on Winchester.

"Gen. Sheridan has been temporarily placed in command of the defences of Washington, the Middle Department, including Maryland, and of the Department of the Shenandoah. This places him in command of all the section of the country menaced by the rebel invasion. He has doubtless been selected for his command by Gen. Grant, who has tested and knows his qualifications. We have confidence that he will bring order and system out of the confusion that has lately ruled, and infuse such energy into the direction of military movements in his department as will put an end to the raiding of the rebels into Maryland and Pennsylvania."

Daily National Intelligencer, Washington, D.C., Wednesday, August 10, 1864

> Hd. Qrs. 2nd Mass. Cav.
> Skirmish Line Near Berryville
> Shenandoah Valley Va Aug 20/64

Dear Mother

I have just received a letter from you written Aug. 8th it is the first time we have read any mail for 7 days. When I received one from Irena. I have not received my shirt but the mail carrier says it is safe with the teams in the rear we are the advance line of skirmishers we have been skirmishing nearly every day for 15 days with but small loss, we have had two sharp fights with them over at Winchester & one at Cedar Run.

We left Falls Church July 26th/64 have been Marching & Fighting all the time. I am very well. Never better since I have been out this time I have seen Generals, <u>Sheridan</u>, Hunter, Wright, <u>Custer</u>, Wilson, & Merritt besides several more. We belong to Gen Merritts Division it is 1st Cav. Division 3 Brigade Middle Department. Our Col is Comndg the Brigade & Skirmish line for 3 miles. John is well so is Lieut Thompson both send their regards to all.

I must close write often & Direct as usual. I am Sergt. Major yet, & expect to be for some time. At present I am Acting Adjutant of the Regiment Our Adjutant is Acting Asst. Adjutant Gen. to Col. Lowell who is Act. Brig. Gen.

I have plenty to keep me busy
From your Affct son
Robert H. Williams

I wish Pa would order me a Pair of Boots of the same size & style as the Pair Levi made for Capt Kellam, that is, Grain Leather tops seam behind but Calf uppers not too light but Medium Pegged the Best he can make for twelve (12) dollars I will have the money for him next month I am certain.

Robert H

Manuscript Collection, Huntington Library, San Marino, California
[Robert H. Williams, Co. F]

FROM SHERIDAN

Washington, August 24. - Mosby's men appeared in the vicinity of Fall's Church last night. This morning, at five o'clock, the garrison at the stockade at Annadale, consisting of two hundred and seventy-five men of the Sixth Cavalry, were attacked by the enemy under Mosby, who had two pieces of artillery and two or three hundred men. On taking his position Mosby demanded the surrender of the garrison, which was refused. He then opened fire with the guns. The cannonading lasted for three-quarters of an hour. The garrison is still holding out. Mosby withdrew. Annadale is about ten miles from Alexandria.

Alta California, San Francisco, Wednesday, August 31, 1864.

FROM THE UPPER POTOMAC.

Correspondence of the Baltimore American.
Headquarters Middle Department,
In the Field, August 25-8 A.M.
The usual quiet of the past few days was disturbed yesterday by a movement on our part, which consisted in a reconnoissance being made by a detachment from Crook's command and the Nineteenth Army Corps, to ascertain the strength and position of the enemy in our front.
The force from Crook's command consisted of the Ninth and Fourteenth Virginia and the Thirty fourth and Ninety first Ohio infantry, of Johnson's brigade, Duval's division, together with a regiment of cavalry, under Col. Lowell, which consisted of two squadrons of the Twenty-second Pennsylvania, commanded by Major Meyers, and two squadrons of the Second Massachusetts. This force was instructed to move quickly on the right flank of the enemy's skirmish line, and if possible get in their rear, whilst another force, consisting of the Tenth, Eleventh, and Fifteenth Virginia infantry, of Thoburn's division, moved out to attract their attention in front. It was intended that the force thus deployed should capture the whole or a greater portion of the enemy's skirmish line.
At precisely twelve o'clock Duval moved his force to the front, and advanced in two battalion lines, keeping his men as much as possible under cover, to prevent the enemy from ascertaining his strength or probable intentions. He had not proceeded far when he encountered the advance of the enemy's skirmish line, who were under cover of "rail pens" hastily

thrown up, and affording shelter for five or six men. These "rail pens" were situated about eight hundred yards in advance of our skirmish line in an open field, with a belt of woods on the right and left, and a large corn field in rear. As soon as the enemy's advanced line discovered the approach of our force they hastily retired to the corn field in rear, where a portion of their reserve was stationed, and who were immediately drawn up to resist our further advance.

Col. Duval continued to move forward his force, a portion of which was completely hid from the enemy's observation until he got nearly four hundred yards in their rear, when suddenly discovering him they wheeled into line and opened a heavy fire on his flank, compelling him to change front and face one line to the right. This move had the desired effect, for they were shortly driven to retire, when our cavalry were ordered to advance and charge them, which they did in fine style, killing and wounding quite a number, and capturing six prisoners. In this charge Major Myers, of the 22d Pennsylvania cavalry, was wounded by a splinter of a shell in the leg.

As soon as the enemy became convinced we meditated an attack on his skirmish line they brought reinforcements rapidly forward from the direction of Charlestown, and moved one battery of artillery to a commanding position in a piece of woods, the fire from which enfiladed our advance. As soon as the enemy's battery commenced firing, Battery B, Fifth United States Artillery, commanded by Captain Dupont, and Battery D, First Pennsylvania, commanded by Captain Rosney, opened on them with marked effect, and an artillery duel was commenced which lasted for about twenty minutes, when the enemy's battery was withdrawn.

Our forces fell back, having accomplished all that was intended, with the exception of the capture of the enemy's entire skirmish line. We however took about thirty prisoners. It was no part of the General's plan that they should bring on a general engagement; on the contrary, they received strict orders to avoid fighting as much as possible. The result of the reconnoissance established the fact that the enemy were still in our front in considerable force. The prisoners captured state that Rhodes and Ramseur's divisions are detailed for picket duty in our immediate front, and the rest of the Confederate forces under Early are at Charlestown. They differ in their statements with respect to Longstreet. Some of them positively assert that he is here in person, whilst others are equally confident that he is not here, but that two of his divisions have crossed, under command of Gen. Picketts. Our total loss in Crook's command will not exceed forty-three wounded and six killed.

After we fell back yesterday the enemy resumed his old position, and picket skirmishing was kept up until dark.

Daily National Intelligencer, Washington, D.C., Saturday, August 27, 1864

Head Qrs. 2nd Mass. Cav.
Near HalltownVa

August 26th/64

Dear Parents

The shirt is all right & a better fit if possible than the other. I think I shall remember it for a long time, the day I received that shirt. I had just finished the last letter I wrote you when I received the shirt, but no sooner had that arrived than Our Skirmish line was driven in & the Rebs opened on us with shot & shell from a Battery of three Guns but their triumph was short, for we rallied & drove them back to their old position after a sharp fight we had one man killed,

& 10 wounded, the next day we moved toward Harpers Ferry via Charlestown. They allowed us to go but a short distance when they advanced on us & charged us with Cavalry supported by Infantry & Artillery. At Berryville we Halted & fought them for about two hours when Our Battery opened on them & we charged them & drove them nearly a mile when we moved forward again they did not trouble us again that day.

There were two Shells burst within six feet of my Horses heels but both escaped uninjured. I was of course obliged to be where there was the most danger for I must keep with the Colonel & He was always in the front when we were moving toward the enemy & in the rear when moving from them there were several solid shot & shell passed between us when not more than 20ft. apart, but we were lucky. Yesterday a part of our Regiment went out on a reconnaissance & succeeded in Capturing several Picket Posts we had a Captain killed. We have lost in Killed & wounded within the past month 10 killed & 50 Wounded about.

We are expecting an attack on Harpers Ferry (hourly) I can hear heavy cannonading up the Potomac towards Martinsburg I wish Our Generals would allow the Rebs to go to Canada.

I must close, John Passage is well he is out on the advance skirmish Line has been there for three days He was on Our advance skirmish line twice When the Johnnies attacked us in Force But as yet they have failed to touch him. My Kind Regards to Eva & all inquiring Friends.

From Your Affct son
Robert H. Williams

Manuscript Collection, Huntington Library, San Marino, California

FROM SHERIDAN'S ARMY

A charge was made at 4 o'clock yesterday afternoon by Col. Lowell, with a small detachment of cavalry, on the enemy's skirmish line to the left of Halltown, which resulted in the capture of some prisoners, from whom we received some important information, which leaves no doubt that the enemy are in force and prepared to take advantage of any weakness in our lines. In the charge we lost Capt. Idenbock *[Charles S. Eigenbrodt]* of the 2d Massachusetts, killed, and some three or four were wounded.

Evening Transcript, Boston, Saturday, August 27, 1864.
Alta California, San Francisco, Tuesday, September 20, 1864.

Another Patriot Gone.

Capt. C.S. Eigenbrodt of the California Cavalry, was killed instantly in the action of September 2d, while leading a charge in the Shendoah Valley.

Capt. Eigenbrodt was at one time Supervisor from Washington Township, in this County, where he owned a ranch. When he raised his company, he recruited part of his men here. He was an esteemed citizen, a good, a brave man.

Alameda County Gazette, Saturday, September 24, 1864.
(Paper in error, Eigenbrodt was killed August 25 near Halltown, VA.)

CAPT. CHARLES S. EIGENBRODT.

Editors Alta: As some errors have been made by the press in regard to the life and death of the gallant soldier whose name stands at the head of this article, I have thought it my duty to make public what I may know of one who, for all the traits of character which makes the true gentleman and soldier, was not surpassed by any officer in the service of the United States.

Capt. Eigenbrodt was born at Jamaica, Long Island, in 1825, and was therefore thirty-nine years of age at the time of his death. His ancestors were old Knickerbockers of New York, so well known in the early history of that state.

Capt. Eigenbrodt came to California in 1849, and was engaged for some time in exploring the coast from San Francisco to the mouth of the Columbia. He was with a party of daring adventurers who met with many hair-breadth escapes from the Indians and other perils, but finally reached San Francisco in the fall of 1850. Soon after this, Capt. Eigenbrodt settled in Stockton and became a partner of John M. Horner, in that city. He then became an active member of Charity Lodge, No. 6, I.O.O.F., an institution that did much for relieving the sick and distressed among the early pioneers of that section of California.

In 1854 he removed to San Francisco, continuing in business here until 1858, when he removed to Alvarado, where he had purchased one of the best ranches in Alameda County. Early in the spring of 1863, he raised a cavalry company, principally among his friends and neighbors, and being placed in command, went with them to the theatre of war in Virginia, where he and his company fought through many a well contested fight. He fell on the 25th of August, at the very front of Sheridan's army, as he was commencing his march South. In the first charge, Captain Eigenbrodt was shot through the breast, fell from his horse, and died instantly. His regiment (for he was then in command) then fell back. The rebel prisoners, who were captured the next day, spoke highly of the gallantry of the brave Captain, and said that they themselves had carefully buried the body in a soldier's grave. We understand that Dr. Eigenbrodt, of New York City, has gone to Virginia to recover, if possible, the body, and to deposit it in the family vault at Jamaica.

Thus perished one of California's bravest and best men, and when the final roll shall be made up of the gallant sons of the Pacific, the name of Eigenbrodt will occupy a place beside those of Baker, Mathewson, and a host of patriots, who shed their heart's blood for the honor and glory of our common country.

At the time Captain Eigenbrodt enlisted he was one of the Supervisors of Alameda County, and in this as well as in all the relations of life he commanded the respect of his friends and neighbors.

He was a leading and active Odd Fellow, a member of the Grand Lodge, and did much for the diffusion of the benevolent operations of that Order. Long will his many virtues be remembered by that fraternity.

The old California Guard of this city remember him as one of its most efficient officers and members.

An old friend does not expect to look upon his like again.

Templar.

Alta California, San Francisco, Sunday, October 2, 1864

LOCAL MATTERS

Chaplain Humphreys. The friends of Chaplain Charles A. Humphreys, of the 2d Mass. Cavalry, who was taken prisoner in Virginia some time since, have heard from him at Charlestown, S.C. He had been taken to various places in Georgia and elsewhere, and had been deprived of all of his effects, so that he was quite destitute. His health was good. Having reached Charlestown, there is a chance for his receiving decent treatment, we suppose; and it may possibly be his good fortune to be early exchanged.

Evening Transcript, Boston, Monday, August 29, 1864.
[Taken prisoner at Mt. Zion Church, July 7, 1864]

❖❖❖

Va

Camp near Smithfield
Aug 31st 1864

Dear Minnie

It is My misfortune not fault in not writing to you sooner. Our Regiment have been on the move all the time for about 30 Days & I have not seen spare time enough to write till now, nor am I entirely certain of being able to finish this. Have just been called in from the skirmish line where our Co has been kept for 8 Days without being relieved. We have been moving backwards & forwards through the Shenandoah Vally over a month, fighting more or less every day. Yesterday my Co made a sabre charge at the Johneys about two miles from where Im writing, our loss was two killed & 5 wounded. We ran the Rebs over 3 miles, have not learned how many they lost in killed, but saw several fall from their Horses myself & am confident they must have had quite a number more wounded then we did. I was near enough to cut with my sabre yesterday than first time, dont know as I have any inclination of being quite as close again for some time to come, still my luck carried me through safe, with nothing more than a few scratches received not from the Johneys but an unfriendly Apple tree that my awkward steed ran against with me. I am getting tolerable well satisfied with Soldiering by this time, especially the kind we are doing now. First the Rebs retreat down the Vally as far as Strasburg. Our Forces folowing them up. Then we turn back & the Rebs follow us up as far as Hall Town about 4 miles from Harpers Ferry. The Cavelry has nearly all the fighting to do for our Infantry have been marched up & down so often they are nearly tired out & do not get to where we are soon enough to take much part in any engagements we have had. Where I am writing this letter now yesterday would have been rather unpleasant business for the Rebs were throwing shells at some of our Cavelry stationed here then & it is no trouble to pick up some pieces close to where Im sitting and Company is geting smaller every Day or two. All it numbered for Duty this morning was 22 & we left Falls Church in july with 86 Men. There is quite a number who have probably got the shell fever & do not like to get very close to the enemy, but the most of our Co that are missing are either killed wounded or prisoners. I am in hopes my turn will not come for at least another year as Im somewhat anxious to see & be with My friends again by that time but it is hard to tell when my luck will be from this time forward for I am at varience slightly with our Co officer & do not hesitate to let him know that I think him the meanest man in the Army, & for spite He gives me a chance to be shot at every opertunity that He possibly can. if He will go as far as I would like to go with Him, I will rid the Co of a big Nuisance certain but He is one of the kind that is willing to be as near the war as possible. I am not certain He can do me much harm but if there is any chance to get me captured I think would suit Him to send me on any scout where I would be likely to be taken. I will write to you Minnie as often as possible & wish you to not wait for me but write often as our mail carrier comes where we are nearly evry week & I could get news from you evry time in case you would take the trouble to write so often Minnie I dont mean trouble exactly for I dont imagine its any great bother for you to write, still I do not wish you to wait for me but write often & receive the grateful thanks of yours truly J.P.

Give my regards to all the folks & keep any amount of love for my Minnie yours truly JP.

This is poor writing and not very clean paper but it is the best I can do under the circumstances.

Courtesy of M. Paynter, Madison, Wisconsin.

❖❖

SEPTEMBER, 1864

 1 Confederates evacuate Atlanta, Georgia.
 2 Federal Army occupies Atlanta.
 4 John Morgan Hunt killed
19 Third Battle of Winchester, Virginia.
22 Battle of Fisher's Hill, Virginia.

❖❖

The Soldiers for Uncle Abe.-The following is an extract from a private letter from John W. McKinney to a gentleman in this valley. It is dated "Harpers Ferry, Va., September 5th, 1864," and shows the estimation in which the soldiers hold both the Administration and its enemies:

"What do you think of "little mac" for President? And how is the State going? Old Abe suits me, with U.S. Grant to command the Armies of the Union. "Tis ever our delight the Johnnies bold to fight, but we don't like the copperheads who stay at home and cry, 'Put down the rebellion!' while at the same time they are doing all they can to keep it going, and every chance they get they send the rebels arms and ammunition and grub and clothing."

Semi-Weekly Solano Herald, Suisun, Saturday, October 22, 1864.
[John W. McKinney, Co. L]

❖❖

Hd. Qrs. 2d Mass Cav. Summit Point Va. Sept 8th 1864

My dear Mammy

I have just received your letter of Augst 31st.

The day after I wrote to you from Halltown Va. we, that is my Regt., charged the Enemies Picket line again. We captured one Lt. Col. 3 Capts. 3 Lieuts & 75 privates of a South Carolina

Regt. We took about as many prisoners as we had men engaged & every one said the Regt did splendidly, we have no reporters with us & so you will probably see no mention of it in the papers. We have a very good reputation in this army & have to do a great deal of hard work. In this fight we had one of our best officers killed (W. Meader) & several men. The next day we advanced & my Regt had the advance. We charged the Enemy just beyond Charlestown Va. but were driven back after a sharp fight in which we lost some first rate men killed. The next day we had a rest & the day after that we fought the Rebels at this place & killed two Lts. & 3 privates of the 5th Va Cav & took 5 prisoners. The next day we advanced & fought their infantry (all this is my Regt alone) & were driven back two miles with only a slight loss (Capt Rumery shot through the head, not badly) & so on.

Yesterday afternoon my Regt & the 1st & 2d Regular Cavalry drove the Enemy over the Opequan Creek, sharp fight while it lasted. We lost 4 men killed & the Regulars had one Capt killed, we fought their infantry. The Regt is getting pretty well used up, in one fight at Berryville about ten days ago we lost a great many men. Well I won't tire you with an account of all our fights. I have escaped so far unhurt. I am very dirty & covered with fleas & have not felt very smart for the last week but am all right now. As I write our infantry is just coming up - that is a good thing - I hope we may have a little rest for a day or two now. Gen. Sheridan's plan, I think, is to keep Early in the Valley as long as he can & prevent him from going into Maryland or Pennsylvania & not to fight a battle unless he is pretty certain to win it. So far the Cavalry has done all the work.

[Last paragraph deleted-Editors]
                    Write Soon
                           Your son, Caspar
Caspar Crowninshield, Letters, Massachusetts Historical Society

❖❖

To His Wife
Ripon, Sept. 12, 1864.

I'm expecting to start a new colour for the Brigade this afternoon. The old one, red, white, and blue, with cross sabres in the white, is entirely worn out. I shall run up, for the present, a white triangle with dark blue border, and cross sabres in the middle, this is furnished by Government; but in a week or so I expect from Baltimore a new one of the old pattern. My colour for the old Brigade (3d) was the L Company, Second Massachusetts guidon, red and white silk, with a wreath and a star with the L in the centre, very ambitious forsooth, but the prettiest colour in the army. The others are all of bunting, except General Sheridan's and perhaps others I have not seen. You'll wonder at me, being willing to carry anything so "gaudy," but my well-known modesty enabled me to do it.

Life and Letters of Charles Russell Lowell, pg. 346, Edward W. Emerson, Kennikat Press, Port Washington, N.Y.

❖❖

NEW ENGLAND OFFICERS IN CHARLESTOWN PRISON.
Among those exchanged were......; Chaplain C. Humphreys, 2d Mass. Cavalry.

Evening Transcript, Boston, Monday, September 12, 1864.

From the Shenandoah NEW YORK. September 11.-A Berryville despatch of the 10th to the <u>Herald</u> says Colonel Lowell, with the Twentieth Massachusetts and two other cavalry regiments, yesterday destroyed four flour mills, several smaller mills on Opequan Creek, and captured several prisoners.

 A Harpers Ferry despatch of the 10th, states that the rebels are still in force near Winchester and Bunker Hill. All was quiet at the front.

Alta California, San Francisco, Thursday, September 15, 1864.

FROM THE SHENANDOAH VALLEY.
The following official despatch from Gen. Sheridan, received at the War department yesterday morning, informs us of a successful encounter on Tuesday between a portion of his command and Kershaw's division of the enemy:

NEAR BERRYVILLE, September 13 - 7 P.M.

This morning I sent Gen. Getty's division, of the Sixth Corps, with two brigades of cavalry, to the crossing of the Summit Point and Winchester road, over the Opequan creek. Rhodes', Ramseur's, Gordon's, and Wharton's divisions were found on the west bank. At the same time Gens. Wilson and Mackintosh's brigade of cavalry dashed up the Winchester pike, drove the rebel cavalry at a run, came in contact with Kershaw's division, charged it, and captured the Eighth South Carolina regiment, sixteen officers and one hundred and forty-five men, and its battle-flag, and Col. Hennegan, commanding brigade, with a loss of only two men killed and two wounded. Great credit is due to Gens. Wilson and Mackintosh, Third New Jersey and Second Ohio. The charge was a gallant one.

A portion of the Second Massachusetts Reserve brigade made a charge on the right of line, and captured an officer and eleven men of Gordon's division of infantry.

Our loss in the reconnoisance is very light.

P.H. Sheridan, Maj. Gen.

Daily National Intelligencer, Washington, D.C., Thursday, September 15, 1864.

[Samuel Corbett, Co. A, gives some details of the charge in his diary]

Sept. 13th

This Brigade went out on a reconnaissance this morning. Our skirmish line ran in to the Rebels line and were captured. the 2nd Mass Cav. charged recapturing our men and taking their captors prisoner and captured their first line of

rifle Pitts. After some cannonading we retired
the Rebels being too strong for us. Our loss is
22 killed and wounded Dearborn of Co. A.
seriously wounded.

Sept. 14th

Cold and stormy the 2nd Mass moved camp to the
rear of Brigade Hd. Qrs. drew rations this P.M.
Mail arrived everything quiet in front. General
Custer complimented the 2nd Mass Cav. on the
splendid charge they made yesterday by saying that
it was the best Cavalry charge he ever seen made.
Yesterday Wilson's division captured an entire
S.C. Regt. 350 men.

Samuel Corbett Diary - Bancroft Library, University of California at Berkeley

Second Mass. Cavalry. At the reconnoisance at Lock's Ford, on the Opequan, in the
Shenandoah Valley, on the 13th inst., which was shared in by two small detachments of the
Second Mass. Cavalry, commanded by Lieuts. Thompson and Crocker, after having got in the
flank and rear of the enemy's pickets, who were very numerous, the rebels threw down their
arms; but finding the cavalry, who were dismounted, to be so few in number, they picked up
their muskets again and began to fire. Lieut. Thompson thereupon charged them with the sabre, captured a Lieutenant and ten men and put the rest to flight. The casualties in the Second
Mass. on this occasion were as follows:

Wm. Johnson, D; George W. Morse, D; Edward McKnight, D; Alexander Logan, D;
Wm. Colegan, C; John Riley, G; John McLaughlin, G; Corp. John F. Shiffer, F; Valorous
Dearborn, A; Jos. McGleason, I; Winfield S. Wilbur, I; Richard Fleet, C; Francis Donahue, H;
Chas. H. Granville, K; Wm. Kelley, B.

Evening Transcript, Boston, Saturday, September 17, 1864.

Camp near Summit Point
Sept 15th 1864

Dear Minnie

Once more after a
long time I will try to take time enough to write you a short note. I received a letter from you
written Sept 7th last evening and to tell the plain truth there was more pleasure derived from
reading it than has fallen to my lot for some time past. You should certainly hear from me once
a week if it were possible for me to get the opportunity of writing that often, but our work here
in the Shenandoah Vally has been very hard for .... all the time we have been here, and I have
scarcely had time enough to make a report of our Companys losses. We were for about 15 days
in the saddle, nearly the whole time night and day, and since then we have not remained in one
place without being on duty for more than 8 or 10 hours at a time. I have commenced at least as

many as five letters within the past week, but have succeeded in sending not one. Am expecting to be obliged to leave here before finishing this, as there was a deserter come in to our lines last evening with the report that Early was going to attack our forces today. I am in hopes he will, for the chances are then this campaign will end before long, as it has been heretofore we were fighting with a small force every day and the Cavalry has had nearly all of it to do, but if there is a regular engagement, bring it on. It will certainly either give us a chance to rest a little after it's over or send a good many to where they will need none.

I may write somewhat discouragingly Minnie or might have done so in my last still I'm far from being so. Am perfectly willing to remain a soldier during my term of enlistment and do my duty as one. I was telling you what kind of Officers we had. I have no better opinion of them at present either. Only the day before yesterday we were ordered out under the command of Gen Custar to make a recognisance of the enemies lines. Our Regiment was put in the advance and after getting to where the Rebel pickets were posted, my Co. and Co. D were ordered to make a charge on an Infantry force of 88. We numbered from when we started from the Column to charge 40 men but when we got within close shooting distance our number was reduced to about 20 men & one officer as the rest had what they termed slow horses & could not keep up. Our Co commander went till the Bullets commenced whistling around our heads pretty freely fast enough, but was suddenly taken with the slow horse fever & I saw nothing more of him until we had got through the fight & were on our way back to the rear with 18 Prisoners we had captured. I told Him then that if we wanted to find a lieut during a fight all we had to do was to send back to the rear & they were sure to be found. I dont mean to say they are all that kind, but its our luck to be blessed with such a one at present. You say you are fearful he will do me some harm by not being friendly with me, do not fear it in the least My Dear Girl for a hundred such men as He is could neither make my life shorter nor longer a day. The only way He has of showing his spite against me is to give me all the Extra Duty He can, and Im perfectly healthy & tolerable strong, consequently am able to do all He can find for me to do with perfect ease. At the time of our charge I spoke about Sgt. Roberts & myself had fast horses & succeeded in getting some ways ahead of the rest of our Boys. We help capture the 13 & then started after more. If it had not been for an order coming from Custar for us to turn back just as it did I would not have been here to write this for Roberts & myself were within twenty rods of their Reserve numbering 3? Men. They did not dare to shoot at us much on account of their own men which we had cut off. Still they gave us a few shots. Neither of us were touched but my horse was hit twice. Our loss was 2 killed & 8 wounded besides losing 15 horses. The Rebs lost 13 Prisoners 34 wounded that we saw & several killed. My Co has lost a good many men since I last wrote you & there has never been one lost when I was not with them. Have had 3 men shot right beside me & have never even received a scratch yet. Am positive Minnie Your Prayers for my safety are answered & am in hopes you will still continue to offer them up in my behalf. I have written now more than I thought I should have time to & will close by sending My Love to my own Dear Minnie. Yours truly J.P.

It has been some 3 hours since I commenced this and there is no more from the enemy yet. I am of the oppinion that the Deserter I spoke of did not tell the truth dont think we shall have any regular engagement to day certain. Will write you as soon as possible. Give my regards to all enquiring friends & believe me to remain as ever Yours only J.P.

Courtesy of M. Paynter, Madison, Wisconsin.

THE CAVALRY CHARGE AT WINCHESTER

On the 19th of September, at two A.M., the Second U.S. Cavalry, Captain T.F. Rodenbough in command, moved with the Reserve Brigade of the First Cavalry Division to the Opequon, reaching Seever's Ford before daylight. The enemy's cavalry pickets retreated across the creek after exchanging a few shots in the darkness. The regiment was deployed, mounted, in the fields to the right and left of the ford, with a small picket in the road dismounted, the reserve occupying the out buildings of a farm house in close proximity to the ford. At daylight the enemy's infantry pickets could be distinctly seen in force on the opposite side of the creek, making preparations to resist any attempt on our part to effect a crossing. The opposite bank of the creek was steep and thickly wooded; and to the right of the ford a deep cut, through which the Winchester and Potomac Railroad passed. The bridge, the roadway of which had been destroyed, crossed the creek diagonally. The stone abutments and piers were intact. The abutment and the adjoining pier on the enemy's side were at an angle with the wooded bluff, making the arch directly in the line of the deep cut.

A short time before sunrise, General Merritt, commanding the First Cavalry Division, ordered Colonel Lowell, in command of the Reserve Brigade, to carry the ford and effect a lodgement on the opposite bank. General Merritt, in his official report, writes as follows:

"This was done in fine style by Colonel Lowell, who threw over dismounted men, closely supported by the Fifth U.S. Cavalry and part of the Second Massachusetts Cavalry, mounted. In making this lodgment on the left bank Captain Rodenbough, of the Second United States Cavalry, with his gallant regiment, was particularly conspicuous in charging down the hill, across the creek, and up the opposite incline, in the face of a galling fire from the enemy's infantry, who had taken possession of the railroad cut, and were completely covered from our fire. The Second advanced (a heroic little band), almost without firing a shot, until it had gained the crest of the cut. Here a number of prisoners were taken, with but small loss."

For a time the fire of the enemy's infantry from the cut was simply terrific. The writer and Lieutenant Wells, and two orderlies, mounted, were unfortunately imprisoned in the arch way between the abutment and adjacent pier on the enemy's side; the bullets, hot from the muzzles of their guns, striking the abutment pier and water like leaden hail. We were face to face with the enemy, yet powerless to harm him. Our only salvation was to hug the abutment until that portion of the regiment immediately on our left had gained the crest of the cut. Minutes were long drawn out; and, in a fit of impatience, Lieutenant Wells rashly attempted to take a peep beyond the corner of the abutment, thus exposing his horse, which instantly received a serious wound in the shoulder. The writer, with equal rashness, attempted to recross the creek, and, when in the middle of it, heartily wished himself under the protection of his good friend, the abutment; the bullets being so neighborly and so fresh from the musket as to have that peculiar sound incident to dropping water on a very hot stove. Suddenly the cheers of our men apprised us that the crest of the cut had been gained and a portion of the enemy's infantry captured.

By sunrise the Reserve Brigade was in position across the Opequon, connecting with Custer's brigade on the left, which had gallantly carried Locke's Ford, three-quarters of a mile below. General Merritt, in his official report, writes as follows:

"After the junction of the lines on the other side of the Opequon, both brigades were ordered to advance and press the enemy vigorously, keeping him engaged; the object being to prevent Breckinridge, who was known to be in our front, from sending his corps to join the rest of Early's forces near Winchester, or at least, if he did send it, to follow closely in his rear and get on the enemy's flank."

As we advanced, the roll of musketry and booming of cannon on our left apprised us that our main infantry line, under General Sheridan, was in action. We seemed to catch fresh inspiration from the sound; horses quickened their pace, while the faces of officers and men betokened that cheerful confidence and determination which are the earnest of brave and heroic deeds.

About eleven o'clock a line of the enemy's infantry was seen in the edge of a thick belt of woods, protected by rail barricades, directly in front. They waved their battle flags defiantly, and by their actions plainly said, "Take them if you dare!" It seemed rash-yes, almost foolhardy- to charge a line of infantry so well posted and protected. But the command was no sooner given to charge than the First Brigade and Second United States Cavalry rushed upon them, and, in the face of a fearful musketry fire, actually reached the barricades. We failed to break their line, and were obliged to retire hastily in some disorder. Nor did we secure their battle flags, but rode so boldly for them and so close to them that the color bearers hurriedly carried them to the rear of their line.

This was a desparate charge, lasting but a few minutes, and, though unsuccessful, its moral effect on the enemy was plainly visible in the subsequent events of the day.

In this charge Captain Rodenbough's horse was killed within a few yards of the barricades, and Orderly-Sergeant Schmidt, of Company K, succeeded in mounting the captain behind him on his own horse, the powerful gray thus saving both their lives.

About two o'clock the entire First Cavalry Division moved in a general advance. The Second Brigade and artillery, which had remained on the right bank of the Opequon, crossed, moving in column on the road from Seever's Ford to Winchester. The First and Reserve Brigades advanced across fields and through woods, uniting with the Second Brigade at the junction of the Seever's Ford road and Winchester and Martinsburg pike, four miles from Winchester.

Breckinridge's Corps had fallen back on Winchester, leaving Early's flank protected by his cavalry, which was routed by General Devin's Second Brigade, and driven in confusion beyond the junction of the roads well towards Winchester.

But little time was consumed in placing the three brigades in easy supporting distance of each other, the First Brigade on the right, the Second in the centre, and the Reserve Brigade on the left, looking well to the protection of that flank and communication with our infantry. In this order the division moved forward, meeting with no opposiition until the open fields near Winchester were reached, when the First and Second Brigades charged a strong force of the enemy's cavalry, and drove them in confusion and disorder into the town. As soon as our line was re-established, the Reserve Brigade formed in column of squadrons and awaited developments. In this position we were exposed, without any cover whatever, to the severe fire of a battery on our left front. The range was short and aim accurate, each shell bursting directly over the brigade, and one tearing away the two front and rear files on the left of the first squadron of the Second United States Cavalry. For a few minutes we dismounted and lay on the ground at the heads of our horses. As the order was received to capture the battery, "To horse!" and "Forward!" were sounded in quick succession; but the battery withdrew at the moment we were formed to charge it.

While awaiting in suspense our next movement, the enemy's infantry was distinctly seen attempting to change front to meet our anticipated charge. Instantly, and while in the confusion incident to their manoeuvre, the Second Brigade burst upon them, the enemy's infantry breaking into complete rout, and falling back a confused and broken mass. General Merritt, in his official report, writes: "The brigade emerged from the fray with three stands of colors and over three hundred prisoners." "This blow, struck by General Devin, was at the angle of the line caused by the enemy refusing his left to meet our attack." "Soon Colonel Lowell (Reserve Brigade, which formed to the left of the old position from which Devin charged) entered the lists. His heroic brigade - now reduced to about six hundred men - rode out fearlessly within five hundred yards of the enemy's line of battle, on the left of which, resting on an old earthwork, was a two-gun battery. The order was given to charge the line and get the guns."

It was well towards four o'clock, and, though the sun was warm, the air was cool and bracing. The ground to our front was open and level, in some places as smooth as a well-cut lawn. Not an obstacle intervened between us and the enemy's line, which was distinctly seen nervously awaiting our attack. The brigade was in column of squadrons, the Second United States Cavalry in front.

At the sound of the bugle we took the trot, the gallop, and then the charge. As we neared their line we were welcomed by a fearful musketry fire, which temporarily confused the leading squadron, and caused the entire brigade to oblique slightly to the right. Instantly officers cried out, "Forward! Forward!" The men raised their sabres, and responded to the command with deafening cheers. Within a hundred yards of the enemy's line we struck a blind ditch, but crossed it without breaking our front. In a moment we were face to face with the enemy. They stood as if awed by the heroism of the brigade, and in an instant broke in complete rout, our men sabring them as they vainly sought safety in flight. In this charge the battery and many prisoners were captured. Our own loss was severe, and of the officers of the Second Captain Rodenbough lost an arm and Lieutenant Harrison was taken prisoner.

It was the writer's misfortune to be captured, but not until six hundred yards beyond where the enemy was first struck, and when dismounted in front of their second line by his horse falling. Nor did he suffer the humiliation of a surrender of his sabre; for as he fell to the ground with stunning force, its point entered the sod several inches, well nigh doubling the blade, which, in its recoil, tore the knot from his wrist, flying many feet through the air.

Instantly a crowd of cavalry and infantry officers and men surrounded him, vindictive and threatening in their actions, but unable to repress such expressions as these: "Great God! what a fearful charge! How grandly you sailed in! What Brigade? What regiment?" As the reply proudly came, "Reserve Brigade, Second United States Cavalry," they fairly tore his clothing off, taking his gold watch and chain, pocket-book, cap, and even spurs, and then turned him over to four infantrymen. What a translation-yea, transformation! The confusion, disorder, and actual rout produced by the successive charges of Merritt's First Cavalry Division would appear incredible, did not the writer actually witness them. To the right a battery, with guns disabled and caissons shattered, was trying to make to the rear, the men and horses impeded by broken regiments of cavalry and infantry. To the left, the dead and wounded, in confused masses, around their field hospitals - many of the wounded, in great excitement, seeking shelter in Winchester. Directly in front, an ambulance, the driver nervously clutching the reins, while six men, in great alarm, were carrying to it the body of General Rhodes. Not being able to account for the bullets which kept whizzing past, the writer turned and faced our own lines to discover the cause and, if possible, catch a last sight of the Stars and Stripes.

The sun was well down in the west, mellowing everything with that peculiar golden hue which is the charm of our autumn days. To the left, our cavalry were hurriedly forming for another and final charge. To the right front, our infantry, in unbroken line, in the face of the enemy's deadly musketry, with banners unfurled, now enveloped in smoke, now bathed in the golden glory of the setting sun, were seen slowly but steadily pressing forward. Suddenly, above the almost deafening din and tumult of the conflict, an exultant shout broke forth, and simultaneously our cavalry and infantry line charged. As he stood on tiptoe to see the lines crash together, himself and guards were suddenly caught in the confused tide of a thoroughly beaten army - cavalry, artillery, and infantry - broken, demoralized, and routed, hurrying through Winchester.

Army and Navy Journal, Vol.13, P202. November 6, 1875.

THE SHENANDOAH VALLEY.

The plans of the Rebels in the Shenandoah Valley have not yet developed themselves, and we have a conflict of statements and opinions as to their intentions. At one time during the week they were officially reported to have disappeared from our front, and the inference was drawn that the success of General Grant upon the Weldon road, had compelled Early's return to Richmond. Later advices, however, represent the enemy as still in force before General Sheridan, and apparently preparing to resume the offensive. On Thursday, the 25th, and Friday, the 26th, reconnoissances were made by our cavalry to discover the enemy's position. On the former day General Torbert advanced on our right up the Winchester Pike, coming in contact with the enemy in force, near Leetown, a portion of his force narrowly escaping capture, being flanked by the Rebel infantry. A running fight was maintained until night, our troops falling back to a safe position between Shepherdstown and Harper's Ferry, with a loss estimated at between one and two hundred. On the following day, Friday, the 26th, General Crook on the left, ordered out Wells' brigade of Thoburn's division. Here the enemy developed little strength, giving way before our forces with the loss of a hundred prisoners, most of whom were captured by Colonel Lowell, of the Second Massachusetts cavalry. Our loss is reported at one hundred.

As the result of this reconnoissance, the enemy were discovered to have left our front, and on the morning of Sunday, the 28th, General Sheridan was on the march, with his cavalry in advance, carefully reconnoitering in various directions. The enemy were found, however, near Smithfield, five or six miles to the Southwest, by General Merritt, who attacked the Rebel cavalry vigorously, driving them through the town and beyond Opequon Creek where he came in contact with infantry. General Custar's brigade of cavalry with Ransom's battery were moved across the creek for the purpose of making a reconnoissance towards Bunker Hill. But after an encounter with the enemy's skirmish line, they retired across the stream, followed by infantry, who attempted to outflank them. Our cavalry accordingly fell back upon Smithfield, in season to escape the movement. Here they were met by General Rickett's division of infantry before whose advance the enemy found it prudent rapidly to withdraw. Our loss in this affair was less than one hundred, including Dr. Rulison, Medical Director on General Torberts's staff. Lieutenant Hoyer of the First Regular cavalry was also killed. Some prisoners were captured by our cavalry. The results of this encounter have set at rest for a season the reports that the Rebels are leaving the Valley, though we are obliged to close our account this week before his position and force are clearly ascertained. It is evidently General Sheridan's plan for the present to securely hold his position in the Valley, attempting no venturesome expedition, but keeping his force in hand to checkmate any movement of Early looking to an advance northward. With our Armies once more in process of reinforcement we have the most to gain from delay.

Army and Navy Journal, Vol. 2, pg. 19. September 3, 1864

Another Californian Wounded. - A letter from J.A. Baldwin, now a Captain in the California Battalion, forming part of the Second Massachusetts Cavalry, dated at Gilbert's Ford, Va., November 20th, has been received in this city. From this letter we take the following: "On September 19th, as I was leading a charge of my squadron, in the battle of Winchester, I was shot in the knee joint, producing a compound fracture, and in a moment after my horse was shot under me and down I came; I laid on the field about half an hour, when I was carried off an laid on this bed, and here I have been laying ever since. My surgeon says I shall probably be here for six weeks to come. I suffered greatly, and it was feared, for a number of days that my leg must be amputated, I shall have a stiff knee, but that is far better than no leg. As soon as I am better I shall go home on a six weeks' leave of absense." Captain Baldwin is well known as an old San Franciscan.

Alta California, San Francisco, Saturday, December 10, 1864.
Alta California, San Francisco, Saturday, January 7, 1865.
[Josiah A. Baldwin, Co. L]

❖ ❖

[Here, again, Corbett briefly notes the progress of the Shenandoah campaign]

Sept. 22nd

Camped two miles to the south of Front Royal last night. broke camp this morning at 5 O'clock. Some cannonading on the right last evening. Met the Rebels eight miles from Front Royal and have been fighting all day. they have a very strong position known as Fisher's Hill the fighting is mostly with artillery shot and shell are flying around loose and we are all hungry and ugly, no rations yet.

Sept. 23rd

Fell back five miles last night. this morning when near Front Royal on a flank movement, Mosby's Guerrillas charged in to our advance guard. We pitched in to them driving them to the mountains killing seventeen and taking four prisoners, two of whom we shot and the other two we hung in retaliation for shooting two of our men that they had captured. I had the pleasure of capturing one of them myself. We passed through the town then came back. We camp to night inside the Rebel works that they occupied yesterday, they having evacuated them last night. the Rebels have lost very heavy in killed, wounded, and Prisoners in this fight.

Samuel Corbett Diary - Bancroft Library, University of California at Berkeley

❖ ❖

OCTOBER, 1864

5 Battle of Allatoona, Georgia.
19 Battle of Cedar Creek, Virginia.
23 Battle of Westport, Missouri.
31 Nevada becomes the thirty-sixth state

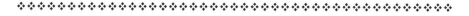

Mount Crawford Va. Oct 2d 1864

My dear Mammy
I wrote you last from Summit Point Sept 8th. Since that time I have not had an opportunity to write, & if I had there has been no chance to send a letter. From the 8th until the 19th we had almost dayly skirmishing on the Opequan. The 19th was the Winchester fight, we commenced the fight at daylight by crossing the Opequan & we fought from that time until dark. At about two o'clk all the Cavalry had come together on the Martinsburg & Winchester pike; the whole force of the Enemies Cavalry was just in front of us. The country was very open & a splendid place for a Cavalry fight. Averill was on the right of the road with Custar just behind him, Merritt was on the left of the road. I had two squadrons of my Regt deployed as skirmishers in front of Merritt, & I was supporting them with two more. Soon the Rebel Cavalry charged & drove back our skirmishers on the right & left of the road; I had posted my reserve just on the edge of a wood & I managed to check the Rebels on the left of the road. In the mean while our Cavalry was formed in line ready to charge, soon the buglar blew, on they came 6 or 7 thousand men with sabres drawn & shouting like demons. It was a splendid fight, I never shall forget it. We rode completely over the Rebel Cavalry, the natives say the Rebel Cavalry have not stopped running yet. We charged the Infantry & routed them taking over 900 prisoners, 9 battle flags & 2 guns & three Caissons. If night had not closed in so soon we should have destroyed Early's Army. Every one says that this was the most splendid Cavalry fight of the war. I had two officers mortally wounded & lost some very good men. The next day we rushed in & found the Rebels entrenched in a very strong place called Fisher's Hill, just beyond Strasburg. The Cavalry, Wilson's division & Merritt's were sent round through Front Royal to go down through Lauray; at a place called Snake Hill we found the Rebel Cav. strongly entrenched, we attacked but could not carry their position. We fell back to Front Royal; we then had a fight with Mosby & killed & hung 14 of his men. I am glad to say that my Regt had nothing to do with this.

The next day we again advance & had a splendid Cavalry fight at Lauray; we utterly routed the Rebel Cavalry. I charged with two Squadrons of my Regt & took the Battle flag of the 5th Va. Cav. During the next four days we followed the Rebels through Stanton down to Waynesboro, here we were attacked by there Cavalry & Infantry & were forced to fall back. My horse "Old Jim" was killed by a shell here, my right leg had a narrow escape. Poor Jim, I was very sorry to lose him, I shall never get a horse like him again. This was on the 28th, we got to this place on the 30th & have been here since. It is about 7 miles below Harrisonburg. I don't know when I shall have an opportunity to send this letter but I hope soon. I hope that our mail man will be up tomorrow, & then I shall be able to send it. I think I get all your letters in time. Give my love to all - Write when you can, (I know you do) tell Cora to write also.
            Your son
            Caspar
Caspar Crowninshield, Letters, Massachusetts Historical Society

                                          Near Mt. Crawford, October 5, 1864
        I was sorry enough the other day that my Brigade should have had a part in the hanging and shooting of some of Mosby's men who were taken, I believe that some punish-

ment was deserved, but I hardly think we were within the laws of war, any violation of them opens the door for all sorts of barbarity, it was all by order of the Division Command, however.

Excerpt from Life and Letters of Charles R. Lowell.

Shooting Mosby's Men.

Editor National Tribune: I have noticed quite a number of articles in The National Tribune about the capture and shooting of Mosby's men. We had been up in the Luray Valley, and were coming down with Lowell's Brigade in advance, with a company of Regulars as advance guard. Near Front Royal Mosby's men fired on this advance guard from the brush at the side of the road. That company got out of there in quick time. Then Col. Lowell's orderly came back full speed, shouting at the top of his voice: "Col. Lowell wants a California company."

The first was Co. L, and we were at the head in less time than it takes to tell it, nor did we stop for five or six miles. Mosby's men scattered in small squads to get away. When we got together near Front Royal we found we had nine prisoners.

Our command had gone on, but soon after going thru the town we overtook Custer's Brigade, which was in the rear of the column, and had halted for dinner. We called to them, and asked if they did not want some prisoners to guard. Some one at Custer's headquarters said: "Yes, if you do not want them, turn them over to us and we will take care of them."

We marched them (only nine) to the side of the road, and went on our way rejoicing. The next day we went back by the same road, and those same men lay by the roadside, with a paper pinned on one, stating that they were shot by order of Gen. Custer in retaliation for men shot by Mosby, giving time and place. The credit of the capture belongs to Co. L, 2d Mass. Cav. One who was there and in the chase - F.E. Barron, Co. L, Cal. Battalion, 2d Mass. Cav..

National Tribune, Washington, D.C., Thursday, May 18, 1911.

[Here, Corbett tells of the "burning of the Shenandoah"]

Oct. 4th

Came back to our old camping ground last night.
the Infantry is four miles to the rear of us.
Near Harrisonburg an order was issued this A.M.
for all Citizens to pack up and leave this valley.
either go North or South. Men are now riding
through the country issuing this Order. this
evening we commence burning all the barns and
store houses in this vicinity.

Oct. 5th

Last night the heavens were lit up for miles with
the glare of burning buildings, houses and barns
are alike destroyed. the intention is to clean out
the valley completely this afternoon We moved
back to the right of our Infantry near

Harrisonburg. No fighting to day. the Johnies
keep out of sight. the town of Dayton was
destroyed this P.M. by Gen Wilson.
[Gen. Thomas F. Wildes]

Oct. 6th

Broke camp this morning at 7. passed through
Harrisonburg at 9. Matches were issued to the
Regt. with orders to burn everything in the shape
of forage that could be found, as I write,
hundreds of barns and store houses can be seen
burning. Transportation furnished all Citizens
wishing to go North free.

Samuel Corbett Diary - Bancroft Library, University of California at Berkeley

❖❖

[The following letter tells the rest of the story on Dayton's fate.]

Clarington, Ohio, March 16, 1912.

My Dear Sir:

Yours of the 11th recd. In reply will say that I was a main partici-
pant in that stirring and heart-rending event of Oct. 5th, 1864, at the town of Dayton, Va.,
where, at 5 0'clock P.M., by an order issued by our commander, Genl. P.H. Sheridan (order No.
890, I was ordered to take my regiment, the 116th O.V.I. and set the torch of destruction to
every building in that beautiful town, for what some foolhardy citizen had done, or was supposed to have done - the killing of Major Meigs of Sheridan's Staff.

Now the reason why the order of Genl. Sheridan was not carried out is, Genl. Thomas F. Wildes of my brigade, at one time colonel of the 116th O.V.I. (my regiment, who was a
particularly ideal officer under Sheridan, and suited Sheridan on account of his bravery and
fighting qualities, begged and prayed Sheridan to revoke the order, as my regiment, the 116th
O.V.I., formerly Genl. T.F. Wildes' regiment, was the regiment detailed by Sheridan to carry
out his heart-rending order. Gen. Wildes prevailed on Sheridan to revoke the order, and I got
the order 5 minutes before we were to apply the torch to that beautiful and peaceful town.

When I announced the revoking of the order, there was louder cheering than there
ever was when we made a bayonet charge.

I know every foot of ground in that country. I was only 17 years old then, and my
heart fairly leaped for joy when the order was rescinded. Brigadier-Genl. Thomas F. Wildes,
together with the regimental officers, are the ones who saved those towns, Dayton, Harrisonburg,
and Mt. Crawford, from being burned down.

Yours very truly,

Col. S. Tschappat.

A History of Rockingham County, Virginia, John W. Wayland, Ph.D.
*[At the time this letter was written, S. Tschappat was serving as Mayor of Clarington, Monroe
County, Ohio]*

❖❖

MOSEBEY'S RAID.

New York, October 15. - The *Herald's* correspondent, writing from Martinsburg on the 14th, says: "Mosby made a most audacious and successful attack upon the westward bound express train, ten miles east of this place, at a place known as Quincy Siding. The engine was thrown from the track. Two paymasters and several other officers were captured, with over $200,000 of Government funds. The passengers were robbed of money and valuables. The cars were set on fire, burning all the property. The engineers and fireman were badly scalded, and their recovery is doubtful.

Alta California, San Francisco, Monday, October 17, 1864.

❖❖

[Here Corbett gives a brief description of the Battle of Cedar Creek]

Oct. 19th

Reveille sounded this morning at half past three. this was only for our Brigade. While we were getting breakfast a heavy musketry firing was heard in the direction of the 8th Corps. as soon as possible we saddled up and got in to line. by this time portions of the 8th Corps began to pass by us going to the rear. We moved out to the front. When the Rebels opened on us with thirty pieces of artillery. All the Cavalry with the 6th Corps of Infantry behaved splendidly the 8th Corps were completely demoralized. the 19th not quite so bad, but in not very good fighting humor. the Rebels at the first onset drove us about half a mile but we formed our line of Battle and by good stubborn fighting held them check. the fighting continued so for four hours. When Gen Sheridan came on to the ground, as soon as it was known that he was with us everything wore a more cheerful aspect. the boys began to cheer as he rode down the line and new courage seemed to be inspired all through the army. We now began to drive the Rebels very slowly, at three O'clock the order came for us to charge the Rebel line with Cavalry by Brigade to see if we could break the line. We all tried it but it was no use. they were to strong for us. in this charge Col. Lowell was slightly wounded and Capt. Smith killed. at 2 O'clock orders were issued for the whole Cavalry Corps to charge together. Supported by the 6th Corps, the Bugle at Hd. Qrs sounded the charge. When the whole Cavalry Corps burst upon the Rebel line with a "yell" it was too much for them. they could not stand it. at first they wavered then broke, then ran, and the day for them was lost.

Oct. 20th

The Rebels made a grand skedadelle last night. We captured every thing they had on wheels. at the first onset yesterday morning, the Rebels captured 21 pieces of artillery from us. they used these guns on us all day, but we recaptured our guns and came back to camp with 56 of theirs. The loss in the 2nd Mass. Cav. is 35 killed and wounded of Officers we lost Col. Lowell and Capt. Smith Killed. Lieuts. Crocker, Hussey, and Kuhls, wounded. We drove the Rebels as far as Mt. Jackson then fell back to Woodstock. darkness having set in so that it was impossible to pursue them farther. details from the different Regts. have been at work all day burying the dead. We have 3000 prisoners, ten Battle flags, and all the Rebel wounded.

Samuel Corbett Diary - Bancroft Library, University of California at Berkeley

Near Strasburg Va. Oct 21st/1864

My dear Mammy,

I was delighted to receive your letter of the 10th this morning. You probably have seen by the papers all about our great victory of the 19th. I will not go into particulars. It was the most desparate fight I have ever saw. Up to 3 o'clk P.M. we were beaten & had lost 21 pieces of Artillry. Sheridan was not in the field in the morning but when he did get up, he found our men badly beaten, he got them rallied & pitched in & won a Splendid Victory, taking 43 pieces of Artillry & 2,500 prisoners. Our Cavalry had desparate fighting to do & behaved very splendidly. Col. Lowell was mortally wounded & died the next morning. I had one officer killed & 3 wounded in this battle, & many men killed & wounded. The charge in which Col. Lowell was killed was a very desparate one. We charged over an open field —— the Enemies Infantry posted behind a stone wall and with 4 or 5 pieces of Artilery. We charged all most up to the wall but we could not carry it. Their fire was <u>perfectly fearful</u> Grape & Cannister & Musket balls came into us in perfect showers, we were driven back with considerable loss. How any of us escaped I don't see, but thank God who spared me. When the Colonel was shot I took command of the Brigade & am in command of it at present. I suppose that some Colonel or General will soon relieve me. Colonel Lowell died like a hero & he certainly was one of the bravest of the brave, he is universally regreted & is a great loss to this <u>Army & to the Country</u>. Before he died he told Dr. DeWolf what he wish to have done with his things, he said "give my pistol to Caspar I was very fond of him". I wish some of the young men at home could have seen him leading his brigade in that terrible charge & then have seen him on his death bed & have heard him say "my only regret is that I cannot do something more for our cause". No hero of old was more fearless than he. It makes me very sad to think of his poor wife, she is to be confined in a month. You say in your letter that you hear I have been sick. I was unwell for two days but that was all, McKendry was in command of the Regt for those two days. I am very well now & only rather tired from hard work. We did whip the Rebels dreadfully - the Reb prisoners say that they think our Cavalry is the best in the world. I think we shall have a rest now for some time. Early's Army is utterly routed & unless he is very heavily reinforced by Lee he will never dare to come anywhere near us. I will try to write again soon - love to all - your last letter was a first rate one.

> Your son
> Caspar

Caspar Crowninshield, Letters, Massachusetts Historical Society

❖❖

Death of Capt. Smith. - Geo. H. Quincy, recruiting agent of the 2d Mass. Cavalry, has received a telegraphic despatch, stating that Capt. R.W. Smith, of San Francisco, California, of the same regiment, was killed in the battle of Cedar Creek.

Evening Transcript, Boston, Tuesday, October 25, 1864.
[Rufus W. Smith, Company F, killed in action October 19, 1864]

❖❖

ANOTHER CALIFORNIAN HERO GONE. - By the telegraphic despatches received yesterday, we learn of the death of Captain R. W. Smith, of the Second Massachusetts Cavalry, who was killed in the battle of Cedar Creek on the 19th instant. Captain Smith was well known here as the Captain of the "Light Guard" of this city, a position which he resigned to become the First Lieutenant in Captain Eigenbrodt's Company, Californian Battalion, for service in the East. Upon the death of Captain J. Sewall Reed, Lieutenant Smith was promoted to the Captaincy of the California Hundred. Captain Smith was a native of Maine, and at the time of his death was about thirty years of age. He had resided in this city for a number of years, and was much respected. No member of the battalion had a higher reputation for courage, gallantry and daring. He was ambitious of distinction, and would have been promoted to the Colonelcy of the regiment but for his untimely death. To a friend, a gentleman of this city, who visited him "at the front," a few months ago, he remarked that "he would either wear the eagle on his shoulder or perish on the battle-field."

Alta California, San Francisco, Sunday, October 30, 1864.

❖❖

Amongst the many promising officers who fell at Cedar Creek, was the gallant and accomplished Colonel Charles Russell Lowell. He was born in Boston in 1835, of a very distinguished ancestry. He was graduated successively from the Boston Latin School and from Harvard College, first in his class, in 1854.

His purpose was to be a master machinist, and in following out that plan he was connected, first with the Ames Works at Chicopee, and afterwards with the rolling mills at Trenton, N.J.. His health failing, he spent nearly two years in Europe.

He was the elder and only brother of Lieut. James Jackson Lowell, and the cousin of Lieut. Wm. Lowell Putnam; both young men of the finest promise, who fell early in the war. Col. Lowell was married about a year since to a sister of Col. Shaw, the martyr hero of the attack on Fort Wagner.

At the outbreak of the war, he was a superintendent of iron-works in Cumberland Valley, Maryland. He hastened to Washington, and tendered his services to the country. He was assigned to a Captaincy in the Sixth cavalry; went through the Peninsula campaign with Stoneman, and subsequently served upon McClellan's staff. In the winter of 1862-63, he was detached to raise and command the Second Massachusettts Cavalry, and proceeding to Washington, was soon after assigned to the charge of a brigade. For a year he made himself of great value in protecting the environs of Washington from Mosby's cavalry. When Sheridan took charge of the Middle Department, Lowell's brigade was assigned to him. Through all Sheridan's campaign, Colonel Lowell performed conspicuous and brilliant military service.

It was in the very height of the victory of the 19th, that Colonel Lowell was mortally wounded, on the *thirteenth* horse shot under him in Sheridan's campaign of the Shenandoah. His first wound was received about one o'clock on the day of the battle of Cedar Creek, from a spent ball which struck him in the breast. The concussion of the lungs was so great as to cause anxiety. General Torbert urged that he should be carried from the field; but this he refused. Though his voice could only be raised to a whisper, he hoped to lead the final charge; and so he did. He was carried to the rear, and a little parapet of earth thrown up to shield him; he lay there motionless for two hours, having exacted a promise that he should be told when the charge was ordered. This came at 3 o'clock. He was then raised up and placed upon his horse, and for a time appeared to receive new life. He rode to the front, amid the cheers of his men, and took the command which had devolved on Lieutenant-Colonel Crowninshield. His clear voice was gone, but all saw by the waving of his sword, and by his eye, what he meant. He whispered the orders to his officers, and they were passed along the lines.

It was half an hour before the bugle sounded the grand charge. Then his strength rose with the occasion; he threw into it his whole life; it was for him the final charge as for many other brave men. A ball pierced him from shoulder to shoulder, and laid on a shelter tent he was carried from the field. Though paralyzed, he remained conscious, and gave minute directions about the business of his command. He dictated letters and sent loving messages to his young wife, his parents and friends. Col. Lowell was married about a year since to a sister of Col. Shaw hero of the attack on Fort Wagner. His intellect remained clear till the time of his death the next day. *[21st Oct.]*

He was buried at Mount Auburn Cemetery, Cambridge, Ma., with the honors of a Brigadier General, his commission having been issued before his death. General Sheridan had recommended him for this promotion as early as the 9th. On that day his brigade had beaten in a fair fight more than twice their number of the best of Early's cavalry.

How well General Sheridan said to the aide of Lowell, who brought the news of his death; "My God! is Lowell dead? how many of us might better have been spared."

[This is a composite of reports published in The Boston Evening Transcript from Saturday, October 22, 1864 thru Thursday, October 27, 1864.]

❖ ❖

Of the Battle of Cedar Creek and the Gallantry of All the Troops Engaged.

Editor National Tribune: I have read with a great deal of interest the conflicting accounts of the doings of the Nineteenth Corps at the battle of Cedar Creek, on Oct. 19, 1864, and deprecate the feeling manifested. It wont do at this late day to charge such a large body of men with cowardice. Cowards there were in every organization, but they were seldom found at the front. The Nineteenth Corps was composed of excellent troops. Their bravery was proved on many a battlefield, and at Cedar Creek, in the latter part of the day, they retrieved the ill fortunes of the morning with their usual gallantry. Having served in the cavalry - one of "Sheridan's Rough Riders," brave Lowell's Brigade, Merritts Division - and having taken an active part in the battle of Cedar Creek, and being impartial as to the Sixth and Nineteenth Corps, I propose to give a brief account of that affair from my standpoint, and in doing so will not be guilty of injustice to any of our brave boys in blue who so gallantly routed Jubal Early on that day.

THE POSITIONS
of the several corps were as has been stated by other correspondents. The Sixth Corps had the right and occupied the fields to the right of the main Valley pike, between Kernstown and Strasburg. The Nineteenth and part of the Eighth Corps occupied the left, beginning near Front Royal and extending toward the pike road, and a little back from the Shenandoah River, which at this point makes a bend nearly at a right angle toward the center of the Valley. The cavalry were scattered along this line. Our brigade was on the left of the Sixth Corps, and not far from the Valley pike. Writing from memory only, I don't pretend to be entirely accurate as to locations.

On that day before the battle orders were received that our Cavalry Brigade, starting at early dawn, should make a reconnoissance in force of the enemy's position. At about 3 o'clock on the morning of the 19th the headquarters Buglar sounded

"BOOTS AND SADDLES"
and the call was reechoed through our camp. As we had been campaigning all Summer in the lightest possible marching order, without over-coats or blankets, it did not take long to make our toilets, and in a few minutes we were in line. Being yet dark, we were told that we could make coffee. God bless the army coffee, chickory and all; for what would we have done without it?

At daylight we left our camp, first marching toward the front, past some of the Sixth Corps camps, and afterward changed our course across the Valley toward Front Royal. We had gone but a few miles in this direction when we met demoralized infantrymen of the Nineteenth Corps making for the rear as fast as they could run. Meantime we had heard the firing toward our left and kept on in that direction until about 8 a.m., when we struck the enemy. From that time until nearly dark, we were fighting most of the time, and lost heavily in both officers and men. It was here that our brave Colonel (Charles R. Lowell), commanding the brigade, was shot while gallantly leading a charge, and died soon after. Time and Time again we

CHARGED THE REBEL INFANTRY,

while our Spencer carbines rang out the death of many a Johnny; so that it is hardly modest for the Sixth Corps to claim the entire credit of that victory. But I here wish to give the praise to which that gallant Sixth Corps is so justly entitled. That they bore the brunt of that battle there is no doubt; that they checked the advance of the exultant rebels is also true. They stood their ground like a wall of fire. Such firing of musketry I never heard; it was one continued roar like the heaviest thunder, only 10 times louder. In the meantime the gallant Phil Sheridan had come upon the scene, assumed command, and turned the tide of battle, with his usual result. What promised to be a defeat became a glorious victory.

So sure was Early of victory that he made no provisions for a retreat, and when they began to waver and our boys charged, they became panic-stricken and fled in utter confusion; then our cavalry charged after them, and, to state it briefly, captured everything they had on wheels, including the 18 guns which they had taken from the Nineteenth Corps at early morning.

THE "SURPRISE'.

It appears that Kershaw had asked and obtained from Early the privilege of leading the attack on the Nineteenth Corps. He surprised and captured the pickets and then boldly charged into their camp. Eighteen guns were captured where they were parked. Many officers were captured as they issued, undressed, from their tents, and thus the men became panic-stricken, and did the best they could to get out of a bad scrape, and no blame can be attached to them. I may incur the wrath of some of said officers, but regardless of that will state the bottom facts of the case. Whiskey was the cause of the defeat. A big sutler train passed us the day before the battle, and went to the camp of the Nineteenth Corps. Does anyone remember that? I think it was that day that the sutlers opened up in camp, and what followed was a grand carousal and drunken spree, and many of the officers were captured ere they had aroused from their drunken sleep. And thus it was that the men, seeing how things were going, soon became demoralized and fled for safety; and rightly, too. Now hold your wrath, ye officers of the gallant Nineteenth Corps. I don't make the wholesale charge that all the officers were drunk - far from it; but that very many of them were in that condition is true, and many comrades will bear me out in this charge. The rebels then took to

PLUNDERING THE SUTLER WAGONS,

and in so doing so neglected to follow up the temporary advantage they had gained; but they were busy going through the sutlers, and cleaned out that train. I remember seeing a dead rebel on the field that had on seven new sutler shirts, one slipped over the other. So, comrades of the Sixth Corps, deal kindly with our comrades of the Nineteenth. Remember how the boys of the 2d Mass. Cav. used to supply you with tobacco on some of our Virginia raids. Should this be read by any of my dear old comrades who remember me, let them write to me; and be assured that as long as life lasts they will be held in affectionate remembrance.

T.H. Merry, Sergeant, Co. L, 2d Mass. Cav.,
California Battalion, Hueneme, Ventura Co., Cal.

The National Tribune, Washington, D.C., Thursday, May 12, 1887

❖❖

CAVALRY AT CEDAR CREEK.

Lowell's Brigade the First to Oppose Early in the Morning.

Editor National Tribune: Comrade John P. Beach, Trenton, N.J. in a recent issue, asks some comrade to name the regiments that were the first to oppose Early's troops on the morning of Oct. 19, 1864, at Cedar Creek.

Col. Chas. R. Lowell, with his brigade (Reserve Brigade) - consisting of the 2d Mass. Cav., 6th Pa. Cav., 6th U.S. Cav., and a New York regiment of cavalry (5th, I think,) - was the first to oppose the advancing forces of Early on that memorable morning, covering the retreat of the Sixth Corps, under Gen. Wright, after Early had captured the camps of the Nineteenth Corps and his men stopped to plunder it.

Col. Lowell's Brigade had been much with the Sixth Corps theretofore, and fought with them until there was a pretty good understanding and confidence between them; and when Gen. Wright, with his corps, commenced the retreat, after the demoralization of the Nineteenth Corps, it was Lowell's Brigade which covered that retreat until Sheridan arrived.

The Nineteenth Corps cannot be said to have opposed the enemy, as their camps were surprised in the early morning, those escaping going pell-mell down the Valley toward Winchester.

The Sixth Corps was orderly in its retreat, moving slowly, the cavalry not falling back, but shifting position occasionally, while the artillery of both sides played havoc with what was in sight. When Gen. Sheridan came the Sixth Corps was face about, and after slight manuvering for position the Sixth Corps, on the right of the Middletown pike, facing the town, made a charge that started the enemy to running, and at a previously-agreed-upon cannon-shot from a certain point Col. Lowell led the cavalry charge through the town of Middletown that utterly routed Early's army, and forever expelled him from the Valley.

Lowell, in this charge, far ahead of his men, was killed, being shot from the upper story of a house in Middletown. Col. Lowell, with his brigade of cavalry, was among the first - as he always was when there was fighting to do - if not the very first, who opposed Early's advance after the rout of the Nineteenth Corps, as mentioned.

Chas. H. Flournoy, Co. E, 2d Mass. Cav., Knoxville, Tenn.

The National Tribune, Washington, D.C. Thursday, October 21, 1897.

❖ ❖

Camp near Cedar Creek
Oct 24th 1864

Dear Minnie

I wrote to you only a few Days ago but since my last there has been a very heavy Battle fought & presuming you might wish to know how I fared through the fight will say I am all right, have received not even a scratch so far. Our Regiment was under a very heavy Artillery Fire all Day. We were only 150 strong in the morning, out of that number we lost 2 officers killed & 3 wounded. 6 enlisted men killed & 23 wounded & 47 horses killed. I had two horses shot during the day 1 killed & the other so badly wounded I had to leave him still I managed to keep Mounted through the fight there were plenty horses running around in every direction without riders. It was a hard fought Battle and a horrible scene to witness the Dead and Wounded were scatered over the Field promiscously. The Rebs early in the morning had taken the 8th Army Corps by surprise & captured 23 pieces of our Artillery & 1700 Prisoners. Our Infantry were all falling back & had it not been for the Cavelry, Gen Sheridans Army would have been badly whipped. The Rebs had turned our own Artillery on us besides what they had of their own & the way they shelled our Cavelry for about 3 hours was awful. The Regt I belong to made three different charges on one Battery & were repulsed each time. We charged against Infantry & Artillery both. When my horse was shot we were within two hundred feet of their Battery. Our Colonel was killed in the same charge & as soon as He fell our men fell back only a short distance enough & formed again. By this time Gen Sheridan had got the Infantry formed in line of Battle & were advancing on the double quick. The order was given for the whole line to charge cavelry and all. The Johnys could not stand this but broke & ran for Dear life. Our cavelry close on their heels. We captured as near as I can learn now 47 Pieces of Artillery 3500 Prisoners 400 waggons & ambulances and a good many of our own men back again. Whipped them so badly I dont think they will care about trying us for at least a week. My Co lost pretty heavy for the numbers of men we had. There were only 10 of us in the morning & at night we numbered six, two killed & two wounded. Sgt. Roberts, my particular friend, was wounded not very seriously however, will probably be around again soon. I have no time to write more as the mail is just going to start. Give my Respects to all Enquiring Friends & receive the best wished for your future hapiness of one that thinks often of his absent Minnie

> With Love, I remain
> As ever Yours
> J.P.

Courtesy of M . Paynter, Madison, Wisconsin.

❖❖❖❖❖❖❖❖❖❖❖❖❖❖❖❖❖❖❖❖❖❖❖❖❖❖❖❖❖❖❖❖❖❖❖❖❖❖

NOVEMBER, 1864

8 Lincoln reelected President.
16 Sherman begins the March to the Sea
21 Confederates advance toward Tennessee.
29 Sand Creek Massacre, Colorado Territory.
30 Battle of Franklin, Tennessee.

❖❖❖❖❖❖❖❖❖❖❖❖❖❖❖❖❖❖❖❖❖❖❖❖❖❖❖❖❖❖❖❖❖❖❖❖❖❖

Nov. 1st

Four men from the 1st N.Y. Cav, were captured and hung by guerrillas yesterday, with a note on each which read, "This is the fate of all foragers." I hope that we shall have a chance to get even with them soon.

Samuel Corbett Diary - Bancroft Library, University of California at Berkeley

❖❖❖❖❖❖❖❖❖❖❖❖❖❖❖❖❖❖❖❖❖❖❖❖❖❖❖❖❖❖❖❖❖❖❖❖❖❖

FROM THE SHENANDOAH VALLEY.

A letter dated at Gen. Sheridan's headquarters on the 5th instant says;
Gen. Early and his rebel army are at Newmarket, where every thing is life and activity in reorganizing and preparing for a late fall campaign. Early swears he will give Gen. Sheridan's

army another trial before snow falls in the valley, and that he will either sweep our army from *terra firma* or die in the attempt. The army now under direct control of Early consists of about ten thousand men of all arms, some of whom are only partially equipped.

The rebels have already commenced to show themselves in small parties on the flanks and front of our position. They have just organized a system or cordon of flag signals from points on the North Mountain, overlooking our position, and leading to points beyond Fisher's Hill, and possibly to Newmarket. With a good field glass the rebel signal flags are seen in full operation, and at night the flags are replaced with torch-lights - blue, white, and red flashes.

Mosby is still operating on our line of communication between here and Martinsburg. Mosby in person, with a portion of his command, is between Winchester and Cedar Creek. Yesterday afternoon an army wagon, escorted by ten cavalry soldiers, was attacked by guerrillas between Newton and this place. After a brief affair seven of our troops were captured, one was killed, and two escaped. Our men were deceived from the fact that the rebels were clad in United States cavalry coats and pants. The real character of the rebels was not known until the rebel officer politely requested our men to "surrender or die."

Daily National Intelligencer, Washington, D.C., Saturday, November 12, 1864.

❖❖❖

Nov. 10th

Broke camp this morning at 7. Moved up the Rail Road about three miles and camped. drew five days rations this P.M. Lieut. Col. Crowninshield and Capt. McKendry received their commissions one, as Colonel, the other as Major, in the 2nd Mass Cav.

Samuel Corbett Diary - Bancroft Library, University of California at Berkeley,

❖❖❖

NEW YORK, November 19. - The *Herald's* Shenandoah despatch, of the 16th, says that all is quiet since Early fell back to Fisher's Hill. Deserters say that Early has but fifteen thousand men under his command. All the reinforcements received since the battle of Cedar Creek consists of returned convalescents and small squads of soldiers who were away on detached service. When Early recrossed his army over Cedar Creek on Friday night last, and after his cavalry were so handsomely whipped by Merritt, the infantry refused to stop any longer, and Early was obliged to order them back to the works at Fisher's Hill. The *Herald's* despatch of the 17th says: everything is quiet. A Cavalry reconnaisance as far as Mount Jackson failed to discover the presence of the rebel army, except a few stragglers. The residents of the country say they were told by rebel officers that the army is to go into winter quarters at Staunton, and no further attempt will be made to recover possession of the Valley this winter. The rebel rank and file are said to be wretchedly provided with provisions and clothing.

The Washington *Republican* says: Information has been received that Ewell's and Early's forces had retreated up the Valley, hotly pursued by Sheridan. The opinion of officers is that Sheridan will leave a force at Lynchburg to hold it, and send his main force in aid of the anticipated advance of Sherman on Charleston.

Alta California, San Francisco, November 21, 1864.

Nov. 24th

This is Thanksgiving day. had a magnificient
dinner of Hard Tack and Pork. I was bound to have
something a little extra, so I soaked my Hard Tack
and put sugar on it, and you bet it was gay! this
afternoon we had Dress Parade and services. it
was pretty hard work, walking through the mud up
and down the line.

Samuel Corbett Diary - Bancroft Library, University of California at Berkeley

OUR LETTER FROM ST. LOUIS.

(From the Resident Correspondent of the Alta California.)

St. Louis, Nov. 25, 1864.

Escape from Mosby's Guerrillas.

Captain Brewster, Commissary of the First Brigade of the First Cavalry Division, lately
captured by Mosby's men, has returned, having escaped both death and imprisonment. He and
four others were captured while on their way from Winchester to army headquarters. As they
were passing along the turnpike in the vicinity of numerous others, who were bound in other
directions, they were accosted by a party about ten in number, which they met dressed in light
blue overcoats, and whom they supposed to be our men, and ordered to surrender. The order
being accompanied with presented revolvers, they thought it prudent to comply with it. This
occurred about midday, in the vicinity of Newtown, from whence they marched in the direction
of Ashby's Gap, and before night met the "Colonel," as Mosby is styled by his men. They
crossed the Shenandoah and passed through the gap to Paris, where they spent the night, and
remained the whole of the next day and night.

On the next day (Sunday) they marched to Rectortown, on the line of the Manassas Gap
Railroad, where Mosby, finding he had some of Custer's men, kindly informed them that he
had an account to adjust with Custer, and that they must draw lots to see who the seven were
out of the whole number (twenty-nine) who should be hanged in retaliation for seven of his
men who had been hanged a short time previously by Custer's orders. The ballots were prepared, seven having numbers on them, and the rest blanks. Five of the numbers were drawn on
the first trial, but one was drawn by a drummer boy, who was released because he was not a
bearer of arms. One or two more trials were made, the captain each time escaping with a blank.
Lieutenant Bisosway, of the Fifth New York heavy artillery, drew a number, but was released
and one of Custer's men substituted for him. This was the last seen of the victims by their
comrades, who were marched under a light guard to Sperryville, where the captain contrived to
make his escape, and under various disguises not proper to mention here, returned to General
Sheridan's headquarters in safety. The account of the execution, or attempted execution, of the
seven victims has already been made public. Four were killed and three escaped, one of the
latter being Captain Brewster's orderly.

On Sunday there was an assembly of Mosby's command at Rectortown. They were a fine looking set of fellows, well dressed, and most of them commssioned officers in the rebel army, who prefer the romantic life of marauders to that of civilized warfare in the field. Some of them were well mounted, well dressed, and a majority of them provided with Union overcoats. They were nearly all of them highly intelligent and well educated men, armed with sabres and revolvers, very few having carbines. They seemed well disciplined, and exhibited the utmost confidence in the Colonel. The Captain was informed that it was decided at the assembly to go down and pitch into the Eighth Illinois.

Alta California, San Francisco, Monday, December 26, 1864.

❖❖❖

DECEMBER, 1864

13 Sherman reaches the sea after capturing Fort McAllister, Georgia.
15 Battle of Nashville, Tennessee.
20 Confederates evacuate Savannah, Georgia.
26 Sherman captures Savannah, Georgia.

❖❖❖

FROM THE SHENANDOAH.

NEW YORK, December 6. - The *Tribune* special correspondent with the Army of the Shenandoah of the 4th says: the cavalry expedition under Gen. Merritt, which has been absent a week in Loudon Valley, has returned. They brought away about 2,000 head of cattle, sheep and hogs, and have left the whole region over which they pass without hay or forage of any kind. Barns containing hay were burned, and the haunts of Mosby and his gang have been thoroughly cleaned out. A few rebel prisoners were taken. The party was followed and attacked by bushwhackers at various points, but met with no serious opposition. The results of this raid in renovating the valley, which has been the lurking place of Mosby's and other guerillas, is most important, and will greatly increase their difficulties in subsisting in that part of the country.

Alta California, San Francisco, December 10, 1864.

❖❖❖

Dec. 7th

Dress parade and a new formation of the 2nd Mass Cav Regt. Weather very pleasant. the first Rhode Island Cavalry reported to this Brigade this P.M. The Brigade is now composed of the 2nd Mass, 1st R.I., 2nd and 6th Regular Cavalry, commanded by Colonel Crowninshield of the 2nd Mass.

Samuel Corbett Diary - Bancroft Library, University of California at Berkeley

❖❖❖

The Gallant California Hundred - We are indebted to Mr. John W. Crosley for the following letter and muster-roll of the gallant "California Hundred", which will be read with interest by the numerous friends of those brave men throughout the Pacific States. The list of those who have given their lives for their country and the Union is fearfully large, but there is consolation in the thought that for a holier, nobler cause, men never died, and the memory of the fallen will long be cherished in the hearts of a grateful and patriotic people.

"I suppose you have kept posted regarding our battles here in the Valley, and throughout the Army generally, and so I can add nothing like new in that line. I can say, however, that while you have read of battles and cavalry charges, I have been realizing them, and I can truly say that I have seen enough of the Johnnies and their shot and shell for one campaign. Ever since the 10th of July last, the Second Massachusetts Cavalry have been on the go and have generally had their fingers in the pie whenever our Colonel (and Brigade Commander) could get us within shooting or charging distance. After Sheridan took command of the Army, for twenty one consecutive days, the regiment, or portions of it were under fire, and I can say from experience that reb bullets neither sound nor feel remarkably well. I was slightly wounded in the hip at Waynesboro, below Staunton, but which did not keep me from duty but for a few days. Our regiment (and the California companies particularly) has won a splendid name for fighting qualities. At Winchester and the late battle at Cedar Creek and Middletown, we had our hands full, as also in the cavalry fight with Reaser, October 9th. There is something exciting in a cavalry fight, especially after you get the rebs running, and are after them, capturing cannon, men and horses. On the 9th of October, the Second Massachusetts Cavalry took four cannon, three caissons, five wagons, and some thirty prisoners. It was a dead run for over fifteen miles, and if you had seen me, with cap off, sabre in hand, and covered with dust that day, you would hardly have recognized the quiet youth you first met at 33 Sacramento Street.

"The California Hundred has had its share to do in the regiment, and still has the name of being the best command in the regiment. Of one hundred and one who left California with it, but fifty remain on its company rolls, nine of whom are in southern prisons. It has also, lost two Captains and one First Lieutenant killed; and A. McKendry, who came out with us as a First Lieutenant is now Major in the regiment. Lieutenant Sim was discharged for disability, and returned to California some months since.

"I will enclose a list of the Hundred, with their present rank, and remarks, which perhaps you will be glad to look at, and then if you will hand it to the editors of the Alta for them to make an item of, I will thank you. I have been requested by many of the Hundred to send it to some paper, but thought perhaps it would be better to send it to some one known in San Francisco, who would hand it to them. It may give some information to our friends there that they would be glad to hear.

"Send a paper if they conclude to publish anything regarding the Hundred.

"I remain, as ever, your friend,
        "C. Mason Kinne
     "Adjutant Second Massachusetts Cavalry"

1. Hugh Armstrong. First Lieutenant Second Massachusetts Cavalry.
2. C. H. Ackerman. Corporal.
3. J. B. Ackerman. Killed in action at Halltown, Va. Aug. 20, 1864.

4. H. W. Allen. Transferred to Veteran Reserve Corps.

5. C. E. Allan. Captain Fifth Massachusetts (Colored).

6. Henry E. Allen. Died of wounds at Rockville, Md., July 13, 1864.

7. George Anderson. Deserted.

8. W. G. Anthony. Sergeant. Prisoner, August 13, 1864.

9. J. B. Burdick. Killed in action, South Anna R.R. Bridge, June 26, 1864.

10. C. E. Benjamin. Regimental Commissary Sergeant.

11. T. D. Barnstead.

12. D. O. Balcom. Second Lieutenant Second Massachusetts Cavalry. Prisoner September 19, 1864. Paroled from Libby Prison.

13. H. G. Burlingham. Second Lieutenant Second Massachusetts Cavalry.

14. W. H. H. Bumgardner. Corporal. Died of wounds received July 6, 1864 near Aldie, Va.

15. C. Balke. Deserted and apprehended.

16. A. F. Baker. Deserted, apprehended, and deserted again.

17. N. A. Beach. Deserted.

18. C. P. Briggs.

19. J. Blake. Discharged for disability.

20. E. B. Campbell.

21. J. Carey.

22. W. W. Collins. First Lieutenant Tenth New York Cavalry.

23. S. J. Corbett. Regimental Band.

24. W. Cunningham.

25. J. M. Chalmers.

26. S. Chandler.

27. Henry Crum.

28. W. R. Crumpton. Company Quartermaster's Sergeant.

29. George F. Davis. Lieutenant Fourth Massachusetts Cavalry.

30. C. S. Dewey. Deserted.

31. Valorous Dearborn. Corporal. Died of wounds received at Opequan Creek, Va., September 13, 1864.

32. C. F. Dempsey. Prisoner, August 24, 1863.

33. G. C. Doane. First Lieutenant in the Western Army.

34. R. S. Ellet. Second Lieutenant in the Western Army, Miss. Marion Brigade.

35. A. C. Forbes. Killed-shot himself accidentally at Harper's Ferry, Va., August 8, 1864.

36. J. Freeman. Deserted.

37. H. H. Fillebrown.

38. J. Fletcher. Sergeant. Wounded and prisoner, August 10, 1864, near Winchester, Va.

39. B. D. Gibbs.

40. G. W. Goulding. Prisoner, Rockville, Md. July 3, 1864.

41. Fred Hall.

42. S. Hanscom. Corporal. Killed in action near Aldie, Va., July 6, 1864.

43. W. Hammerburg. Deserted.

44. C. W. Hill. Returned to his original regiment as a deserter.

45. J. A. Hill. Discharged for disability.

46. W. H. J. Hillard. Sergeant. Wounded near Aldie, Va., July 6, 1864.

47. George Holt.

48. J. A. Hunt. Discharged for disability.
49. J. L. Hunter.
50. W. H. H. Hussey. Second Lieutenant Second Massachusetts Cavalry. Wounded, Cedar Creek, Va., October 19, 1864.
51. A. Magary. Deserted.
52. G. M. Johnson.
53. C. Mason Kinne. First Lieutenant and Adjutant Second Massachusetts Cavalry. Wounded (slightly), Waynesboro, Va., September 28, 1864.
54. F. Knowles. Deserted.
55. A. Laighton. Died of disease, Washington, D.C., July 8, 1863.
56. A. Lee. Buglar. Died of disease, Vienna, Va., April 7, 1864.
57. C. Legler.
58. A. Loane. Prisoner, near Aldie, Va., July 6, 1864.
59. F. O. Libby. Corporal.
60. Benj. Locke. Sergeant.
61. H. Mazy.
62. J. Merriam. Prisoner, Rockville, Md., July 13, 1864.
63. J. McCarty. Killed in action near Fairfax Court House, Va., August 24, 1864.
64. J. D. McCarthy. Hospital Steward Second Massachusetts Cavalry.
65. J. R. McIntosh. First Lieutenant Second Massachusetts Cavalry.
66. W. H. McNeil.
67. E. Nellis. Deserted.
68. H. Nelson. Deserted.
69. J. Nixon. Killed by guerillas near King and Queen Court House, Va., June , 1863.
70. J. W. Owen. Second Lieutenant Second Massachusetts Cavalry. Prisoner, August 24, 1863, and escaped.
71. J. W. Pelham.
72. W. N. Percy. Lieutenant Fourth Massachusetts Cavalry.
73. M. G. Pool.
74. C. H. Powers.
75. Geo. Plummer. Sergeant. Wounded near Aldie, Va., July 6, 1864.
76. R. M. Parker. Lieutenant Fifth Massachusetts Cavalry (colored).
77. F. J. Quant. Regimental Band.
78. H. Rice. Deserted, apprehended, and discharged for disability.
79. W. A. Robinson. Sergeant-Major Second Massachusetts Cavalry.
80. J. C. Ross.
81. Calie Rone.
82. R. C. Samuel.
83. H. Schrow. Corporal. Wounded at Halltown, Va., and Fisher's Hill, Va., October 9, 1864.
84. H. C. Sherwin. Sergeant.
85. B. Siralls.
86. S. Smith. Corporal.
87. C. L. S. Speight. Prisoner, near Berryville, Va., August 13, 1864.
88. W. Starr.
89. E. R. Sterling. Lieutenant Fourth Massachusetts Cavalry.
90. Geo. M. Towle. Corporal.
91. H. S. C. Tubbs. Prisoner, Rockville, Md., July 13, 1864.

92. G. M. Thompson. Lieutenant Eighty-sixth United States volunteers.
93. G. W. Verick. Died of wounds received near Fairfax Court House, Va., August 14, 1864.
94. W. W. West.
95. J. L. Wheat. Captain Fifth Massachusetts Cavalry (colored).
96. P. E. White. Buglar.
97. J. H. Williams. Discharged for disability.
98. J. Winship.
99. H. F. Woodman. First Lieutenant Second Massachusetts Cavalry. Wounded and prisoner, September 24, 1864, Waynesboro, Va.
100. E. W. Woodward. Captain Twenty-fifth United States Cavalry.
101. James Watson.

SUMMARY.

Promoted to Officer:...................................19
Killed in action.. 9
Shot accidentally..1
Died of disease... 2
Transferred... 2
Deserted...................................….................12
Discharged for disability.............................4
Promoted to N. Com'd Staff........................ 3
_____

Total dropped from Company Roll......................50

Prisoners of War... 9
Detached in various duties from the Company............16
Still in Company..25

Total carried on Company Roll.............................50

OFFICERS.

Capt. J. Sewall Reed. Killed in action, February 24, 1864.
First Lieutenant A. McKendry. Major of Second Massachusetts Cavalry.
Second Lieutenant J. W. Sim. Promoted to First Lieutenant and discharged for disability.

Alta California, San Francisco, Friday, December 16, 1864.
Sacramento Daily Union, Monday, December 19, 1864
Solano Herald, Suisun, Friday, December 30, 1864

A Regiment of Veteran Californians For The East.

Nearly all our California volunteers enlisted originally with the expectation of being called to take an active part in the war on the Atlantic coast, and a very large number of the veterans now being mustered out of service are extremly anxious even now to go home and do battle for the

Union. Some hundreds of the discharged veterans have already gone home more would do the same if they were able to do so. We are credibly informed that the hint conveyed in the recent despatches from the East regarding the formation of a veteran corps under command of General Hancock, has already been acted upon, and General Mason has telegraphed to the War Department for permission to raise a regiment of veteran Californians under veteran officers, immediately, and that there is little doubt that a favorable reply will be received, in which case the required number of men will be forthcoming within sixty, and possibly thirty days. This regiment would be the first to really represent California in the East - the *companies* first raised here being credited to another state - and its members would take that pride in their character which would be the surest guarantee of their earning distinction on the battlefields of the Union.

Alta California, San Francisco, Friday, December 16 ,1864

A Reconnaisance by the Cavalry to Gordonsville - Two Guns Captured - The Rumored
Death of Mosby.
From Our Own Correspondent.
Winchester, Va., Wednesday, Dec. 28, 1864.

The Second Cavalry Division, commanded by Gen. Powell, after a nine days' tramp, during the most inclement weather of the season, returned to camp yesterday evening. No one can imagine the hardships and privations of a cavalry campaign at this season of the year, especially in such weather as we have had in this latitude during the present month, without a little experience. It is bad enough in the best of weather to travel without a commissary train and only such rations as each man carries tied to his saddle, but when this occurs in alternate cold and wet weather, every man sleeping upon the cold ground when opportunity occurs to sleep at all, without tent or any other covering save a blanket, the suffering of the men is sometimes next to intolerable; indeed, men not infrequently sink under the hardships they endure under such circumstances. The poor dumb brutes of horses suffer equally as bad as their riders. The First Division, Gen. Devin commanding, which left at the same time as the Second Division, it is expected will return to-day. The whole command under Gen. Torbert left on Monday, 19th, and, passing through Chester Gap, moved upon Gordonsville. At the Rapidan River, Lomax's cavalry was encountered, but they were forced to retire, leaving two guns behind. In the gap between that point and Gordonsville, Kershaw's division of infantry was met. A sufficient demonstration was made to compel the enemy to expose his whole force, when our cavalry, in obedience to instructions, retired, not having artillery to contend with such a force, even if it had been within the scope of instructions received.

RUMORED DEATH OF MOSBY.

Several of Mosby's men captured on this expedition, assert that Mosby was shot and mortally wounded a few days ago at Rector's Cross-roads by a trooper from the Department of Washington. He was eating dinner at the time the shot was fired, the ball passing through his heart. Running into the yard he was shot again through the bowels; and the man who fired this shot pulled off Mosby's boots-he wore a very nice pair-but the man did not know who he was at the time. This report is confirmed by citizens and negroes, so the officers say, in the vicinity of where the transaction occurred, and simultaneously comes a published report from Washington, that the notorious guerilla chief has at last met the fate he so richly deserved. I state the facts and circumstances as reported to me, without giving any opinion in relation to the matter, only that the officers of the different brigades make the same reports, and they believe that Mosby is really dead.

Alta California, San Francisco, Friday, December 30, 1864
New York Times, Sunday, January 1, 1865

THE CALIFORNIA HUNDRED

From a private letter, received from a young man formerly employed as a compositor in this office, who went to the East with the "California Hundred," we make the following extract, which is of interest to many, both here and in California:

"The Second Massachusetts Cavalry has had plenty of good hard fighting during the last five months. As a proof of this I would state that no less than twenty-one commissioned officers have been killed, wounded or taken prisoners since July 1st, 1864. the fields of Halltown, Rockville, Berryville, Smithfield, Charlestown, Opequan, Winchester, Luray, Waynesboro, Drainsville, Fisher's Hill, Middletown and Cedar Creek are stained with the blood of that little band of five companies which left the Golden State a little more than one year and a half ago. Some of these had their homes among the silver-bound mountains of Nevada, among whom were Sergeant Wakefield and Lieutenant Henry F. Woodman, of Gold Hill. The regiment was under fire nineteen days during the month of August, and in one of those days, in a charge on the enemy's breastworks the noble and brave Charlie E. Meader, of Dutch Flat, California, fell, pierced through the brain by a minie ball. The day before, Captain Eigenbrodt, of San Francisco, fell upon nearly the same spot—two of the bravest men I have ever seen. Their loss cast a gloom over the regiment, but since then it has been deepened by the loss of Captain Rufus Smith., also of San Francisco, who fell on the memorable 19th of October, in the battle of Cedar Creek. That day Colonel Lowell was also killed, and H. H. Crocker, Henry Kuhls and W. H. Hussey, from California, felt rebel lead, being wounded. Lieutenants Baldwin and Thompson, of San Francisco, were wounded just one month before, at the battle of Winchester. Only a few of those who came from the Western Slope are now left. Some have been discharged; some commissioned, but many are in their graves. As yet I have not received a scratch-am one of the very few who have not been wounded. " The writer of the above is now First Lieutenant in the old company with which he left California. He says he hopes to "stand it through and again to see the silver hills of Washoe." May he!—

Virginia Enterprises

Alta California, San Francisco, Friday, January 13, 1865
Napa Valley Register, Saturday, January 21, 1865
[The writer is most likely Hugh Armstrong, Co. A, a printer prior to enlistment. Commissioned 1st Lt., May 3, 1864. Captain H. H. Crocker received the Medal of Honor for "galantry at Cedar Creek, Va., Oct. 19, 1864" by mail 30 years later, Jan 13, 1896!]

1865

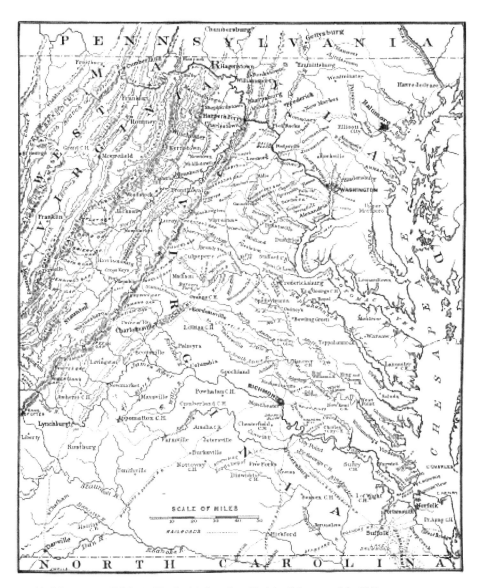

Field of Operations: California Hundred & Battalion, Virginia. February – July, 1865.

The Californians were a part of Sheridan's long march from the Shenandoah to the out-skirts of Richmond, they were actively engaged in some of the war's final battles: Dinwiddie C.H., Five Forks, Sayler's Creek; and they witnessed the surrender of the Army of Virginia at Appomattox C.H.

At mustering out there were 182 of the original 500. But this is not to imply that the balance were lost. Thruout the war, many were promoted to commands of other units; many were prisoners yet to be released; some had deserted early in the war.

❖❖

JANUARY, 1865

13 Hood resigns command of the Army of Tennessee.
15 Federals capture Fort Fisher.
19 Sherman reaches South Carolina.
31 Thirteenth Amendment submitted for ratification

❖❖

Jan. 1st 1865

Nothing of interest for the last three days. We went on a serenade last evening to the 6th regulars, had a fine time.

Jan. 3rd

Went on a serenade last evening to the 2nd Regulars, had splendid time, champagne flowed freely, and some of the boys got dizzy.

Jan. 31st

Grand Corps Review by Gen. Sheridan there is some talk of his leaving us for the Army of the Potomac. Miss Major Pauline Cushman was present at the review.

Samuel Corbett Diary, Bancroft Library, University of California at Berkeley

❖❖

FEBRUARY, 1865

3 Hampton Roads Conference
6 General Lee becomes General-in-Chief of the Armies of the Confederate States.
12 Lincoln officially elected president.
17 Federals capture Columbia, S.C., Charleston evacuated .

❖❖

A California Pioneer in the War.-Archibald McKendry, who left here in the California Hun-dred as First Lieutenant, was first promoted to Captain of Company G, 2d Massachusetts Cav-alry, which Company he recruited himself at Boston, then promoted to the rank of Major in August, 1864. After the battle of Cedar Creek he had command of the regiment, and is now in command of the Second Massachusetts Cavalry, First Rhode Island Cavalry, First, Second,

Fifth, and Sixth Regular Cavalry and "E," and "M" Batteries, attached to the First Division, and known as the Reserve Brigade. He was with Sheridan in all his battles, and, although he has never received a wound, he has had three horses shot under him in action.

Alta California, San Francisco, Sunday, February 19, 1865.

[Corbett here describes the start of the long march from Winchester to Petersburg]

Feb 27th

Drew five days rations last night. Reveille sounded this morning at 3 O'clock, broke camp at 5, camped this evening near Woodstock. killed one Rebel and captured three this P.M. I have no idea where we are going.

Feb 28th

Resumed the march this morning at 6 O'clock. We are going towards Staunton.

Feb 29th

Marched until 3 o'clock this morning then camped twelve miles south of New Market. We are now waiting for the Pontoon train, as they were stuck in the mud the last we saw of them.

Samuel Corbett Diary, Bancroft Library, University of California at Berkeley

MARCH, 1865
4 Lincoln's Inauguration.
11 Federal troops occupy Fayetteville, N.C.
13 Confederacy approves use of Negro soldiers.
19-21 Battle of Bentonville, N.C.
29 Appomattox Campaign opens.

A Disabled Soldier. - Mr. John A. Hill was one of the "California Hundred." In 1862, while a resident of San Francisco, he enlisted, went East with the Company, and served with it for fifteen months, at the end of which period, while engaged in making a charge on the enemy, his horse fell, and he was severly bruised in the breast. He went into the hospital, but his lungs continued to bleed, and he was so weak that he was honorably discharged from the service. He returned to this city and went to work in the Miners' Foundry, but took cold and his lungs are now affected. His physician advises him to go to the foot-hills of the Sierra Nevada. He has no means, and he has for some time been depending on the charity of his friends. Some of them now wish to call on the general public to contribute something to his sustenance, and they desire us to state the facts so that the matter may not be entirely new to those upon whom they may call. Mr. Hill has a copy of his honorable discharge, and a letter from Capt. J. Sewall Reed, both of which we have examined and found satisfactory.

Alta California, San Francisco, Thursday, March 2, 1865.

[*The long march continues*]

March 1st

Reveille sounded this morning at 3 o'clock. Broke camp at 5. had a little fight near Staunton. Whipped the Rebels capturing thirty. one Col. one Major and a Capt. We forded the North branch of the Shenandoa and moved to the South. Camped five miles North of Staunton.

March 2nd

This has been a cold rainy day. broke camp this morning at 5 0'clock. Passed through Staunton at 12 noon. General Custer's Division is in the advance. Met the Remnant of Early's army near Waynesboro of 1500 men had a little fight. Whipped them, capturing 1,150 men, nine pieces of artillery, and 150 wagons. Early with part of his staff got away on the cars, and this is the end of Early's splendid army of 50,000 that he had last summer. We also captured thirteen battle flags. Went in to camp four miles from Waynesboro. the mud very deep. it is impossible to take a piece of artillery out of the road. We have lost 2500 horses through fatigue since leaving Winchester. The dismounted men will go back to Winchester as guard for our Prisoners.

March 3rd

Broke camp this morning at 5 o'clock. Moving through Waynesboro at 1 P.M. the roads are in terrible condition. dead Rebels are lying around loose in the mud. We crossed South River and halted have been at work all day burning wagons and destroying the Iron R.R. bridge at Waynesboro. Resumed our march at 7 P.M. it has been raining all day.

March 4th

Ploughed through the mud until half past twelve last night then went in to camp. We are now through the gap. I believe it is called Rockfish

Gap. We made but eight miles yesterday. Broke
camp this morning at 7 O'clock. We are guarding
the wagon train as it is our turn to be in the
Rear to day. We had to abandon one of our Bass
Drums as it was impossible to carry it all day.
The rain has been pouring down upon us everybody
wet through.

March 5th

Marched until twelve O'clock last night then
camped at Joy Hill (anything but joy for us.)
resumed our march this morning at day light. Moved
to Charlottesville and drew two days Rations of
coffee and sugar. We now have to live on the
country. We destroyed our empty wagons and went in
to camp 3 P.M. and still it rains.

March 6th

Broke camp at daylight and marched to Scottsville
where we went in to camp. the Troops have been at
work all day destroying Confederate Government
Stores.

March 7th

Resumed our march at daylight. We are now on the
James River Canal. have been at work all along
the line of march destroying the Canal and Government Stores. Went in to camp at 11 P.M. near New
Market. *[Now Norwood]*

March 8th

Broke camp at daylight and moved to Bend
[Bent] Creek.
We expected to cross the River here but found that
the Rebels had burned the bridge and as we have
not got Pontoons enough to span the River we have
to fall back to New Market.

March 9th

Went in to camp last night at 12 O'clock and such
marching never was done before. It rained all day
yesterday and all last night. It was intensely
dark and the mud so deep that we would have to
dismount and pull our horses through it. We Head
Quarter fellows got in to a stable. We found it
occupied by about 500 Negroes, Men, Women, and
Children, all thrown in promiscuously. We made
them take one side of the building while we
camped at the other. I was very sick all night,

having a severe head ache. Reveille sounded this
morning at 4 O'clock. Mud is every where knee
deep and still it rains. No breakfast this morning,
have been on the march all day down the canal.

March 10th

Last night we passed through Howardsville and
marched all night. passed through Scottsville
this noon. Moved in to the woods and unsaddled
remained here one hour then saddled up and moved
on towards Columbia.

March 11th

Marched until 1 O'clock this morning then went
in to camp near Columbia. did not break camp until 3 O'clock this P.M. then moved through the
town and camped in the woods. drew seven days rations
of Sugar and Coffee. Moved about a mile
then camped for the night. It still rains.

M'ch 13th

Marched all last night. crossed the North Anna
River and went in to camp on the Virginia Central
R.R. at 2 O'clock this morning. Broke camp at 6
and went to work destroying the Rail Road. Worked
until 6 O'clock this afternoon then took up our
line of march again.

M'ch 14th

Went in to camp last night at 12 O'clock near
Fishers Hill Station. burned the Station this
morning. Crossed the Pamunkey River and a little
brush with the Rebels. the 2nd Mass. Cav. captured
three cannon here at the bridge. We lost one of
our scouts killed. Went in to camp at Little
River Bridge. 7 p.m. This place is known as
Talorsville.*[Taylorsville]*

M'ch 15th

Broke camp at daylight. Crossed the Little River
and burned the Bridge and Depot at this place.
been skirmishing all day. our advance is checked
in this direction.

M'ch 16th

Left the Rebels to take care of themselves last
night. We quietly left the line, forded the North
Anna at Ox ford at 12 O'clock. River very swift and

deep. We had seven men drowned while crossing.
Went in to camp on Banks of the river.

M'ch 16

Broke camp at daylight. Came up with the wagon
train this P.M. and went in to camp near
Monkohick 10 P.M. *[Mongohick]*

M'ch 17th

Broke camp at daylight. Passed through Ayletts
and camp at King Williams Court House. This is
the same ground that the Cal. 100 passed over two
years ago.

M'ch 18th

Broke camp at 9 this morning. Marched to the
White House Landing and camped there is one
Brigade of Infantry here and several Gun Boats.
Moved camp again about two miles, I think we
shall stop here sometime. Drew five days Marching
Rations, and forage. the first that we have drawn
since leaving Winchester. about one third of our
men are dismounted.

M'ch 20th

Drew clothing this P.M. turned in our poor horses
and received Mules in exchange. The dismounted
men are all going to City Point. None of the Band
are allowed to be dismounted. We have nine mules
in the Band with a good prospect for more. We
have not had a mail for 21 days. I hope it will
come soon.

M'ch 24

Drew five days rations. this evening we played
for Gen Sheridan at his Head Quarters on board the
steamer Metamara.

M 25th

Reveille at daylight. Broke camp at 7 O'clock. We
are bound for City Point. We camp to night near
King Charles Court House. *[Charles City Court House]*

March 26th

Broke camp at daylight, crossed the James River at
Deep Bottom Bridge. We crossed on Pontoons.
President Lincoln passed up the River on the boat
"Ocean Queen" as we were getting ready to cross.
We played him several Patriotic Airs, which he

acknowledged by waving his hat. We marched about
two miles then camped in the woods.

M'ch 27th

We vacated our camp at 7 this morning, crossed the
"Appomattox River" at "Broadway landing" and
camped within three miles of Petersburg. They are
shelling the City from one of our forts, in answer
to a few shell they threw at us as we passed.

March 29th

Drew five days rations last night and broke camp
at daylight this morning, bound for the South
Side Rail Road. crossed the South Weldon R.R. and
Hatchers Run. have been marching all day through
mud and swamp.

[Here Corbett notes the beginning of the Battle of Dinwiddie Court House]

March 30th

Went in to camp last night at 11 O'clock. Broke
camp this morning at daylight. passed through
Dinwiddie Court House. here we met the Rebels and
have been fighting all day. the firing ceased at
dark. Went in to camp near Stony Creek.

March 31st

The Ball opened at daylight. The fighting has
been very obstinate all day. the Rebels are going
to keep us from the Rail Road if they can, while
we are as fully determined to tear it up. The
country here is thickly wooded so that cavalry
have to fight dismounted. It has been about an
even thing. Neither side gaining any advantage,
although we have captured a large number of
Prisoners, mostly from A.P. Hill's Corps. While
out on a foraging expedition this afternoon I was
captured and taken into an Earth Work. I was on
my horse and was led in by a Rebel Sergt. as soon
as they got me inside the works, they let go the
horse. I at once made a break for liberty. My
horse jumped up over the breastwork and then
across the ditch outside, but the worst part of
the ride was down a fearfully steep hill. Just as
I was about half way down it, my right stirrup
strap tore out from the saddle. This threw me,
but being a good rider I hung on with my left

foot and succeeded in getting back into the
saddle, but wrenched my side terribly. this gave
me great pain, but as there were six mounted Rebs
after me, I had no time to waste on small matters.
I succeeded in eluding my pursuers by getting into
the woods and so got hack to camp. Upon
examination I found that two of my ribs were
dislocated. I strapped them up with a carbine
strap and took my place in the Band, as being in
command everything depends on my being on duty.
upon my return I took the Band to the right of the
line. While playing on this skirmish line this
P.M. The whole Band came near being captured. We
beat a hasty retreat.

Samuel Corbett Diary - Bancroft Library, University of California at Berkeley

SOME MUD MARCHING

Dead Horses Made a Trail to White House Landing and Dismounted Men Left in Rebeldom

Editor National Tribune: In December, 1864, after the campaign in the Shenandoah Valley, everything went along quietly until the night of Dec. 18, when we of the 2d Mass. Cav. were ordered to have our horses shod. The anvils were ringing all night long.

Early in the morning we were ordered to saddle up and be ready to march. We were given three days' rations of pork and hardtack, and oats enough to last the horses two days, and started on what was called the Gordonsville raid.

It was a cold, disagreeable march, and men and horses suffered much from exposure.

We were obliged to sleep on the snow without shelter and our march thru snow, rain, slush and mud and fording streams played us out. We returned to our camp at Winchester, Va., after 10 days with many men sick and horses played out.

On Feb. 27 (65), we again broke camp and about 10,000 cavalry started down the valley headed for Richmond under Phil Sheridan, with Merritt heading the First Division and Custer the Third.

Down thru the valley again, thru Harrisonburg and Staunton to Waynesboro. The place was fortified, but in a few hours it was captured, with about 1,500 prisoners.

At the time of the battle the trees were coated with sleet and ice. Our command swept on thru to Rock Fish Gap, thru Charlottesville, down to Scottsville, on the James River, and up the river towards Lynchburg, returning again to Scottsville, destroying the locks in the canals, railroads, etc., until, on March 18, we arrived at White House Landing, on the Pamunkey River - 20 days in the mud, lying every night on the wet ground without shelter.

The mud everywhere was awful. Many of the men dismounted were not able to keep up and were left behind at the mercy of the rebels. Hundreds of horses, thru the constant suction of the mud, would have their hoofs to loosen and come off. They were shot, leaving a trail all the way to White House Landing. A third of the horses in my company went down and out on that trip.

Samuel A. Smith,
Corporal, Co. F, 2d Mass. Cav., Hopkinkton, Mass.

National Tribune, Washington, D.C., Thursday, February 1, 1923.
[Samuel Smith enlisted February 22, 1864.]

I sent several Photographs some time ago; did you receive them.

Prospect Hill Pleasant Valley
March 8th, 65

Dear Father
I wrote to Irena the 3rd & sent ($20) twenty dollars for you on the (1st) first of the month I sent a bundle containing two California Blankets (which would have been thrown away had I not sent them home.) I also sent my box of trinkets.

Mother will know what to do with the things.

I wish as soon as you receive either, or all, you would let me know.

Naughty Little Phill. is raising the Duce with Gen. Jubal Early, very early in the Spring.

Gen. Early is expected to appear in Harpers Ferry tomorrow with (1000) one thousand of His men; they will be accompanied by a large number of U.S. boys, the U.S. Boys will carry the Muskets; as they have a very great regard for Jubal & his friends & do not wish to fatigue them.

Sheridan is still on the move & in all probability join Sherman soon.

I close; be sure & write as soon as you receive any of those things.

Love to all; Respects to all enquiring friends

From Your Affet. son
Robert H. Williams

Prospect Hill Pleasant
Valley Md. Mar. 9th/65

My Dear Intended Wife
I think you must have more time to write than I, or, else you have more energy for I have received three letters from you, all written within one week that is better than I could expect & more than I deserve although I try & improve every opportunity.

I told you Gen. Sheridan was out on an expedition up the Valley; He has succeeded in capturing Gen. Early & over one thousand men; the Prisoners are expected to arrive at Harpers Ferry tomorrow.

I shall go over & see them if nothing happens. I am well & have a very good place to stay, I sleep in a house by the kitchen stove.

I am very grateful to you Dearest for your Kindness in writing to me so often.

From <u>One</u> Who <u>Loves</u> <u>You</u> Dearly,
Robert H. Williams

Manuscript Collection, Huntington Library, San Marino, California

❖❖

On Board steamer

W. Whilldin Chesepeake Bay
Mar. 25th 1865

Dear Parents

I wrote to Irena on the cars between Harpers Ferry & Baltimore the 20th inst.

We arrived at Baltimore at 6 OC A.M., 21st, Left Baltimore at 4 1/2 OC P.M. Arrived at Fortress Monroe at 9 1/2 A.M. the 22nd left Fortress Monroe at 7 1/2 P.M. arrived at Yorktown & Anchored at 12 M. left Yorktown at 6 O C A.M. 23rd arrived at White House at 1 1/2 O C P.M. distributed the Mail & started back yesterday at 2 O C P.M. anchored at Yorktown last eve at 7 O C left Yorktown this morning at 6 O C. We are now on Chesepeake Bay it is rather cool on the water today.

I will send you some money in a few days to pay Mr Larnard.

I sent a small package to Mother some time ago it contained a gold chain & ten dollars in Green Backs. The chain was taken from a Reb who brought it together with several others & ten watches taken from the citizens in Pennsylvania during the last Raid up there.

One of our men got them from a reb on that Gordonsville raid while I was home.

Our Command were to leave White House today on their way to City Point where we expect to meet them next Tuesday.

I have sent Irena a piece of Music Composed by Our Band Leader. We are on our way to Washington after the Mail which accumulated since Tuesday (When I say we I mean the Mail Agent of the Cavalry Corps)

We expect to reach there tonight or tomorrow morning.

I will try to see John Burbank & Mary before I return to City Point. Love to the Children

Direct as usual
From Your son
Robert Henry

Manuscript Collection, Huntington Library, San Marino, California

APRIL, 1865

1　Battle of Five Forks, Virginia.
2　Confederate Government leaves Richmond.
3　Federal troops occupy Richmond.
4　Lincoln visits Richmond.
6　Battle of Sayler's Creek
9　Surrender of The Army of Northern Virginia at Appomattox
　　Court House.
14　Lincoln assassination.
15　Lincoln dies.
26　Surrender of Joseph Johnston near Durham Station, N.C..
27　*Sultana* explodes and sinks.

April 2d 1865
Near Dinwiddie Court house Va.

My dear Mammy

I have just time to write a few lines to let you know that I am all right so far. We have been fighting for three days & yesterday we were very successful we fought on foot & with the 5th Corps & captured a long line of brestworks & took many guns & several thousand prisoners. I have lost one officer taken prisoner 4 wounded & many men. The infantry are on our right & are fighting desparately but with what success I can't yet say but I think everything is going on well. Lt. Thompson of my Regt whom you saw last summer is very badly wounded but I hope not fatally. Ned Amory is not with us & I am very glad of it, he is with dismounted men at Citypoint.

I will write when ever I can - give my love to all
　　　　　Your son
　　　　　　Cas

Caspar Crowninshield, Letters, Massachusetts Historical Society
[Edward Thompson survived wounds received at Dinwiddie Court House, March 31,1865]

　　　　　　　　　　　　　　　City Point Va.
　　　　　　　　　　　　　　　April 3d 65

Dear Parents
　　　　"How are the mighty fallen" Oh no! guess not! I knew Little Phill Sheridan would have to come down here with his Cavalry before we could get Richmond, night before last He cut the South Side Railroad; & last night the Rebs evacuated Petersburg, today they left Richmond "how are You Least Ditch!"*[?]*; night before last Sheridan captured (6,400) six thousand

four hundred Prisoners & (17) seventeen pieces of Artillery. What do you think about what I said when I was home about Peace being Proclaimed before the Fourth of July.

I do not know whether you can read this or not. I feel so good that I can hardly content myself to sit still long enough to write. I have been as Petersburg as from the Deaf & Dumb Asylum to Delavan today, but was obliged to return to attend to my Mail; I shall start for their again tomorrow morning at 6 OC.

Sheridan cut loose from the left of the Army took the fifth Army Corps with Him, with ten days rations & forage no one knows where he will turn up next with the exception of Old Abe & Lt. Gen. Grant. Old Abe is here yet he went into Petersburg two hours after our forces entered the place. Since night before last there have arrived at this place (15,000) fifteen thousand Prisoners Rebs. What do you think of that? I received a letter from Mother & Mills. I must close it is so dark that I cannot see the lines

From Your son
Robert H.

Manuscript Collection, Huntington Library, San Marino, California

City Point Va.
April 5th/65

Dear Mother

I returned from Petersburg late last eve. I was over there several hours. Our shells have never done any harm of any account to the Main part of the City but it was not because they could not throw them there but because Our men tried to avoid injuring the Churches which are in the most central portion of the city.

The people appeared glad to see us, not because they were Union from principle, but because they were Union by being whipped & tired out by the war.

Everything was perfectly quiet there some of the Johnies when they were skedadling through the city went into the cellars & hid until Our men came into the city & then they came out & gave themselves up. I have sent my old Blouse home by express. I will try to go to Richmond tomorrow.

Good Night Mother
From Your
Son

Robert

Irena has not asked me to wear that
chain but I guess she will be careful of
it let her wear it on State occasions if
she wishes.
Robert.

Manuscript Collection, Huntington Library, San Marino, California

[The Battle of Five Forks]

April 2nd

The fighting lasted until 8 O'clock last evening.
When the 1st Division flanked the Rebels and
captured their last line of works. We camped
right on the ground pretty well tired out. this
is the Battle of the "Five Forks". The fighting
commenced this morning at daylight but did not
last long. We cut the South Side Rail Road at 9
A.M. Our Brigade was the first on the Road.
Petersburg fell in to our hands this morning. The
Infantry and Artillery were fighting all of last
night. heaviest cannonading I ever heard.

April 3rd

Met the Rebels at dark last night and fought them
until 11 O'clock. We drove them five miles and
camped in line of Battle. A Rebel Battery got a
good range on the Band and made us vacate with the
loss of two horses killed and one man slightly
wounded. Broke camp at 11 O'clock A.M. Marched
very fast until 7 O'clock this afternoon then went
in to camp. the Rebels are right ahead and doing
their best to get out of the way.

April 4th

Broke camp this morning at daylight, received the
news of the fall of Richmond, the Boys are all in
good spirits, and the Rebels are doing the tallest
kind of skedadeling, the Road is full of abandoned
wagons, caissons, forges, and guns. We
burried some of the latter and marked the spot
with head boards. Crossed a branch of the Appomattox near Amelia Courthouse. found the Rebels behind Earth Works and in a strong position. fell
back and went into camp, got supper When Boots
and Saddles sounded and we are again on the move.

April 5th

Marched all night to the right, flanking the
Rebels, took breakfast in an Orchard on the road
to Berksville *[Burkeville]*. Crossed the Danville Rail Road
near the above place and found the Infantry
intrenched in line of Battle. Stopped here three
hours then moved back 2 miles and camped this P.M.
Gen. Custer captured 200 wagons and burned them.
the whole of Lees army is now in front. raining
all day.

April 6th

Drew five days rations of Coffee and Sugar last
night. Broke camp this morning at 7. Met the
Rebels and opened the Ball at 10. We have been
fighting all day and are whipping them badly.
Gen. Ewell surrendered his Corps this P.M. We have
captured 30 guns, 27 Battle Flags, and more
prisoners than we know what to do with. four Major
Generals and several Brigadiers. This is the
Battle of "Harpers Farm". Went in to camp this
evening at 8 O'clock.

April 7th

Reveille at 4 O'clock. the fighting commenced at
8. it seems the Rebels did not get enough of it
yesterday, but want to try us on again. The Battle
lasted three hours firing very heavy, both musketry and cannon. We have captured quite a large
number of Prisoners and the Rebs are again on the
run. We have followed them very closely and went
in to camp at 10 O'clock this evening five miles
from Prince Edwards Court House.

April 8th

Broke camp this morning at 7 O'clock Custer has
been ahead all day pushing the Rebels, no
fighting of consequence until 3 P.M. when we
struck the "Lynchburg and Richmond Rail Road",
here Custer went in capturing five locomotives and
trains loaded with rations for Lees army and more
Prisoners than he had men to guard them. The
Rebels seam to be demoralized and do not fight
with their usual vigor and well they may be for we
have kept them going for the last two weeks.

[Appomattox]

April 9th

We marched all night and until 2 O'clock this
morning, and how much longer we would have
traveled there is no knowing if we had not run
slap in to the Rebel line of Battle and received
their fire. We then concluded to stop and lay down
and hold our horses. the first streak of daylight
lighting up the horizon was the signal for the
Ball to open and it did open with a will. We had
nothing to oppose Lee but cavalry and nobly did
they do their work. We fought them dismounted.

they tried hard to break our line and poured in
the shot and shell with their musketry until the
air seemed full of it. at half past eight the
fifth Corps came up. the fighting lasted but an
hour longer, when at 9:30 A.M. Lee sent in a Flag
of Truce. We have him completely surrounded with
all trains in our hands. the Flag came first to
Gen. Sheridan, he gave Lee five minutes to lay
down his arms. Lee then wished to see Gen. Grant.
Grant came up and agreed to a four hours armistis
to last until 2 P.M. When the time was up nothing
had been done and another armistis granted until
9 O'clock tomorrow morning. This place is called
Appomattox Court House. We camp here tonight. We
were playing at Sheridans Hd. Qrs. while the
negotiations were going on. Saw Grant, Sheridan,
Mead and Lee and in fact all the big Generals at
Head Quarters this afternoon.

April 10th

The Rebel Army of Virginia under command
of Gen. Robert E. Lee lay down their arms this
A.M. at 9 O'clock. the Officers were allowed to
wear their side arms. the number of men Rank and
file is 15,000 they were all Paroled on the
spot. We high Privates don't like the idea of
giving the Rebels any conditions whatever, but we
are willing to trust Gen. Grant and will try to
think it is all right. The Cavalry broke camp
this morning at 7 O'clock and are on the road back
to Berksville. Marched until 6 P.M. then went
into camp.

[Death of Lincoln]

April 16th

A dispatch came to these Head Quarters anouncing
the death of President Lincoln this morning. We
did not believe it at first, but it was confirmed
this afternoon. he was assassinated while in the
Theatre at Washington by J. Wilkes Booth, an
actor. every man in the army feels as though he
had lost a Friend. the men feel worse than though
they had lost every Battle in the campaign. the
camp wears a very sorrowful aspect. it seems so
hard that just as the war ended he should be
killed but perhaps it is all for the best. We will

hope that Mr. Johnstin will be his avenger and
treat these Rebels as they deserve.

Samuel Corbett Diary, Bancroft Library, University of California at Berkeley

Mosby Surrenders On The Same Terms As Lee.

From Virginia

New York, April 20th. -The *Herald's* advices from Winchester, the 18th, say that Mosby surrendered his forces to General Chapman, at Perryville *[Berryville]* on the 17th, on terms similar to those granted to Lee. It is understood that Gen. Resser *[Rosser]* has also asked that his command be included in the cartel. Mosby's men number, probably seven hundred. Great numbers of Lee's soldiers are arriving within our lines. They scout the idea that any portion of their army had gone to Johnston, and say when the case is fairly understood by Johnston's men that they can go to their homes, and they will go.

Alta California, San Francisco, Friday, April 21, 1865.

28th
Broke camp at 4:30 this morning crossed the
"Roanoke" River on a Rebel Pontoon bridge crossed
the Danville *[Richmond and Danville]* R.R. at Scotsburg,
here we received the news of the surrender of the Rebel Gen
Johnson. The members of the Band who went out for
horses returned this evening they brought in seven
mules, 2 horses and 6 Negroes, they met a large
 number of "Lee's" soldiers, but were not molested.

Samuel Corbett Diary, Bancroft Library, University of California at Berkeley

Moseby's Surrender.

All His Men and Officers Give Up, but He Runs Away - A Reward Offered for His Capture.
[OFFICIAL.]
To Maj.- Gen. Dix:
War Department, Washington,
Saturday, April 22, 1865.

Maj. Gen. Hancock reports that nearly all of Moseby's command have surrendered, including nearly or quite all of the officers, except Moseby himself. Some of Moseby's own men are hunting for a reward of two thousand dollars, offered for him by Gen. Hancock, who has been directed to establish his headquarters at Washington.

EDWIN M. STANTON, Secretary of War.

New York Times, Sunday, April 23, 1865.

❖❖

The Terms of Mosby's Surrender.
———————

From Virginia.
———————

New York, April 24th. - The Times' special Washington despatch says that Mosby has secured a basis of agreement similar to that obtained by Johnston. A person present at the consultation informs the correspondent that the memorandum, or basis of agreement was drawn up by General Chapman, in presence of twenty-two Federal and twenty rebel officers, and it provided that Mosby should surrender upon the same terms as Johnston, if the latter should surrender. That two days' armistice should be allowed, to submit the agreement to General Hancock for his approval, and that if Hancock approved, then ten days were to be allowed Mosby to get a reply from Johnston, and in the meantime no skirmishing should take place in Farquar and Loudon counties. That if Johnson failed to surrender, or got whipped, Mosby should surrender on the terms upon which Lee surrendered.

Alta California, San Francisco, Tuesday, April 25, 1865.

❖❖

New York, May 3 - The Richmond *Whig* of April 25th states that Mosby took leave of his men at Salem, Fauquier county, telling them to disband and return home. He was bound for Texas, and did not want them to accompany him, as they might put their necks in a halter. He then rode off with a small number of old companions.

Evening Bulletin, San Francisco, Monday, May 8, 1865
The Daily American Flag, San Francisco, Monday, May 8, 1865

❖❖

City Point Va
Apr. 29th/65

Dear Parents

I recd a letter from Mother a few days since & yesterday recd one from Father with one enclosed from Thurber. I scarcely know what to write about. Great events crowd one after another in such rapid succession that it is almost impossible for one to comprehend the vast magnitude of the least, beginning with the fall of Charlestown, Wilmington, Goldsboro, Raleigh, Kniston, Richmond, Petersburg, Grensboro, Gen. Lee's Army, Our own loss of Our noble President & lastly Gen. Shermans almost fatal blunder which has been recalled & Johnston has finally surrendered to Grant unconditionally at least we have such a report here now.

Gen. Phill. left Petersburg last Monday Morning with all the Cavalry having ten days rations, to join the 6th Sixth Corps which left Burks junction on their way to help Sherman. We heard from them two days ago & then they were only ten miles this side of the North Carolina line still moving on toward Johnston's Army.

We have Orders to stay here until sent for to bring the mail, but now that Johnston has surrendered I think the Cavalry will return to this Point before long, (at least I hope so).

I have been thinking what I should do when I get out of the Army.

I have about made up my mind that I will come back there & content myself with that portion of the World & work at my trade. (that is if there is plenty to do.) <u>What do you think of that</u>?

Has Dick ever said anything about what he intends to pursue when out of the Army. Write soon & tell me what you think of my resolves.

From Your son
Robert H.

Manuscript Collection, Huntington Library, San Marino, California

City Point Va
April 29th/65

Dear Friends
    Carrie & Dave

I have not much time to write but I will try & do better than you did so far as time is concerned, although I may not interest you, for I have so much to write about that I can not make up my mind where to begin. Well, in the first place we will, Hurrah! Hurrah! Hurrah! & Tigers: for, it we have not whipped the world, we can do it: that of course is just the same as though we had already done so.

Poor Sherman: what a terrible Blunder He made. I am sorry for Him & sorry for myself for it will keep us in the service at least one month longer than it would have otherwise done.

The death of Father Abraham did not make any difference in the duration of the war that I can see, for the Machinery of Government did not halt for even one moment, everything moves on just as though nothing had happened, still you can discover in the looks of even the soldiers that some great Calamity has befallen them & theirs: there is scarcely an Officer or soldier in the army but what wears some token of affection or mourning for Our Lamented Chief, even if Washington had lived in this day of strife & commotion I doubt if even he would have become loved, mourned & I would almost say Worshipped as Abraham Lincoln Our late President was. It seems almost sacrilegious to say that I do not think His superior or even His equal has lived on earth since the Ascension from the Mount of Olives, but I must say that I do honestly & Firmly believe it, & I wish you to remember that I am not now nor never was a man worshiper: but I have seen so much of this Great & Good Man that I can but admire & applaud; but his life will speak out for itself & does not require my feeble pen & mind to applaud.

I expect to be home to help you Celebrate the Fourth of July, that is if Sherman does not hold any more peace conferences with Joe Johnston or some other Joe.

Your Friend Robert H. W.

In Great Haste

Manuscript Collection, Huntington Library, San Marino, California

❖❖

MAY, 1865

10   Jefferson Davis captured by Federal troops.
23   Grand Review of the Army of the Potomac.

❖❖

Disposition of Booth's Remains.

Washington, May 3d.-Booth's heart and head have been deposited in the Army Medical Museum in this city. The corpse was placed in charge of two men who, after various movements calculated to baffle curiosity, dug a grave in the ground close to the Penitentiary, where for some years felons have been buried. The earth over it is smoothed carefully, and sodded over. A strong guard is now in charge of the spot, and will continue to keep it undisturbed until the grass is grown so thickly that no one will ever be able to distinguish the place where the assassin's corpse is interred.

New York, May 4.-A Jacksonville (Florida) letter says that fifteen hundred Union soldiers formerly imprisoned at Andersonville were transported down the Florida Central Rail on the 28th to within 10 miles of Jacksonville, and conditionally released. Several hundred entered our lines the same night, who presented a very pitiable appearance, many barely able to walk.

The Daily American Flag, San Francisco, Monday, May 8, 1865.

❖❖

5th

The "Feminine Gender" of Petersburg are turning their whole attention to making Pies & Cakes for the Soldiers. I should judge by the taste of them that they were made from the flesh of our abandoned horses! Peanuts are also plenty.

May 6th

We are still in camp awaiting the arrival of Sherman's troops. his Cav. commenced crossing the River this A.M. Sheridan occupies the same house for his Hd. Qrs. that he occupied before the evacuation of this City. We play there this evening.

Sunday May 7th

All quiet on the Potomac to day. nary cracking of
Peanut, or munching of horse pie breaks the
stillness of this beautiful Sabath morning.
The people of Petersburg are obliged to Remember
the Sabath day and keep it holy hence the
scarcity of the above mentioned articles in camp.

8th

The 15th & 17th Corps of Sherman's Army passed
through Petersburg yesterday and camped near the
town. Drew five days Rations and received orders
to clean up our instruments preparatory to going
through "Richmond".

[Return to Washington]

May 16

Last night we played at Army Corps and Division
Hd. Qrs. Broke camp this A.M. at 9, passed
through Falls Church at noon all of the people
here came out to welcome their old friends of the
2nd Mass. Cav. Went into camp at Camp Windham.

17

This is a very pleasantly situated camp being
right opposite the city of Washington with the
beautiful Potomac between. In all probability
we will remain here some time. We drew five days
rations this P.M.

May 21

It has been raining for the last three days and we
have had a very wet time in our pleasantly
situated camp fortunately or unfortunately we
cannot control the weather U.C. Fordham, Grant,
Chandler, and Silver reported to the Band from
Dismounted camp at Chappel Point Md. This is also
a pleasant place to camp, being in the woods and
near the R.R. There is to be a grand Review in
Washington tommorrow of the Army of the Potomac
and Sheridan's Cavalry and we have to be ready to
move at 7 tomorrow morning.

[The Grand Review]

May 23rd

Reveille at 4 this A.M. Moved out of camp at 7.
All of the boys looking their very best, all of

our mules were exchanged for horses & we all have
on new clothes. This does not suit the army as
they wanted to turn out just as they came from the
front, but we have to obey orders. We passed
thro Washington at 9. The city is full of people
from all over the U.S. as a scene like this will
never be witnessed here again. 150,000 men are in
line. We were in Company front, the line extending from curbstone to curbstone. The sight is
magnificient beyond description. We were reviewed
by President Johnson, Genls. Grant, Sherman,
Sheridan etc. We all feel badly about President
Lincoln. It is too bad that he could not have
lived to see this grand culmination of his good
work

May 24th

It being simply impossible for the whole Army
to be reviewed yesterday, as after 7 hours of
continous marching only half of it had passed the
stand, it was decided to review Sherman's Army
today, so at 9 A.M. it commenced its march. I went
from our camp to get a look at the "Bummers".
They are a splendid looking lot of men, everything
moved along in Military order, and the cheering
all along the line was immense. This ends the
inspection of the Grandest Army that ever fought
for human rights. our work is done. The country
is again united and human Slavery, that has cursed
the country for a hundred years is a thing of the
past.

Samuel Corbett Diary, Bancroft Library, University of California at Berkeley

Promotions Among The California Battalion.
Following is a copy of an official order awarding promotions for gallantry to members of the
California Battalion who have fought through Sheridan's campaigns, and whose names are
those of old neighbors to many in San Francisco. The battalion was at Washington when the
order was issued;

Headquarters 2d Massachusetts Cavalry

May 27, 1865

General Orders No. 6.}

The following officers and non-commissioned officers, for meritorious conduct during the
last year have been recommended for promotion as follows, and will be obeyed and respected
accordingly:

1st Lieut. H. Armstrong to be Captain, vice Baldwin, deceased.
2d Lieut. Wesley C. Howe, to be 1st Lieutenant, vice Armstrong, promoted.

1865

Sergt. Maj. W. A. Robinson to be 2d Lieutenant, vice Howe, promoted.
1st Lieut. J. R. McIntosh to be Captain, vice Phillips, discharge.
2d Lieut. John Passage to be 1st Lieutenant, vice McIntosh, promoted.
1st Sergt. John Finny to be 2d Lieutenant, vice Passage, promoted.
1st Lieut. H. G. Burlingham to be Captain, vice Norcross, discharged.
2d Lieut. W. H. Hussey to be 1st Lieutenant, vice Burlingham, promoted.
Sergt. G. E. Baldwin to be 2d Lieutenant, vice Hussey, promoted.
1st Lieut. Edward Thompson to be Captain, vice Manning, discharged.
2d Lieut. D. O. Balcom to be 1st Lieutenant vice Thompson, promoted.
Sergt. W. H. Hilliard to be 2d Lieutenant vice Balcom, promoted.
By order of
C. Crowninshield,
Colonel Commanding Regiment
H. G. Burlingham, Lieut. and Adjt.

Evening Bulletin, San Francisco, Monday, July 3, 1865

❖❖

JUNE, 1865
6   Guerilla leader Quantrill dies in Louisville, Ky.
23   Federal blockade of Southern states ends.

❖❖

SECOND MASSACHUSETTS CAVALRY.
Died, on the 10th inst., at his home near Boston, of camp fever, Huntington Frothington Wolcott, Second Lieutenant Second Massachusetts cavalry and A. D. C., aged 19, eldest son of J. Huntington Wolcott, and great grandson of Oliver Wolcott, one of the Signers of the Declaration of Independence.

Among the thousands who have fallen in battle or by disease during the war, no one has laid down a purer life with nobler devotion than the young officer whose death is here recorded. Possessed of all that renders life desirable, with every inducement to ease and indulgence in the pleasures of youth, a simple sense of duty caused him to take part in the great struggle of his country. Under all the temptations of Army life, he retained unsoiled the purity of his character. His gentleness won the affection of his fellow-soldiers, as his courage did his respect. Having participated with honor in the glories of Sheridan's last campaign, he accompanied the triumphant return of the Army, escaping the dangers of the field, only, alas! To die from disease contracted while in the service.

Army and Navy Journal vol. 2; pg. 718.

❖❖

United States Sanitary Commission. *[crossed out]*
Sir
While laying at Falls Church, Va. your son & myself camped to gether, when he went out on that unfortunate raid, he left in my charge, his effects. At the time of his death, his watch, money etc the rebels took from his person. I should have sent his other effects to you, but the invasion of Washington by Early than taking place, we were ordered to

351

the front and as all Company baggage had to be stored, I sent his personal property with the rest. After the campaign in the Vly we went into winter quarters - at Camp Russell - Shendh Vly - our blankets were then sent to us. I procured Sam's & sent it to you - also his jacket - via Adam's Express 3 days ago, we recd the rest of the Co. baggage, and I hasten to send to you, the rest viz - a daguerotype, his bible, sewing kit etc. on receipt of which I wish you would wright, and inform me. You can direct - Co A, 2nd Mass. Cav., Washington, D.C. We expect to be mustered out of the service soon and on our arrival in Mass, any information that I can give you in regard to your son - will be with pleasure.

I remain Your
Most Abdt Servt
Chas H Powers

Co A, 2nd Reg Mass Cav.
Camp near Clouds Mill, Va June 8 *[1865]*

Courtesy of Bruce MacAlpine, Concord, MA.
[Samuel Hanscom, Company A]

Sword Presentation

The sword the citizens of this place intend presenting to Lt. Hepburn in recognition of his services in the Army of the Potomac has been received and is now on exhibition at the office of Wells Fargo & Company. The subscribers to the testimonial are requested to meet this evening at the Court House to make the necessary arrangements for the presentation.

Calaveras Chronicle, Mokelumne Hill, Saturday, June 10, 1865.
[James W. Hepburn, Company E; discharged March 22, 1865 for promotion as 2d Lieut. Company A, 2d California Cavalry; mustered out April 7, 1866]

June 19th, 1865
There is a strong rumor in camp that the 2nd Mass Cav. is to be immediately mustered out of the Service. I am very much in hopes that this will prove to be true. The knowing ones say that we will be home on the 4th of July.

20
This evening we played for Col. Crowninshield of the 2nd Mass as he has resigned and will leave us tommorow. We hate to lose him as he is the best liked officer in the Regt. But it will not be long until we shall need no Officers but every man will be his own.

June 21
Col Crowninshield left us this A.M. He wrote us a very nice farewell letter which I succeeded in

getting into my possession just after it was read
to the Regt. Major McKendry takes command of the
Regt.

Samuel Corbett Diary, Bancroft Library, University of California at Berkeley

Head Qrs. 2nd Mass. Cav. Vol's
June 20, 1865
Soldiers of the 2nd Mass. Cavalry my resignation having been accepted I must bid you Farewell. We have served together for over 2 years and the trials of those years will never be forgotten. The friends we have lost and the Glorious Victories in which we have participated will live in our memories forever. For the high reputation which this Regiment has obtained both for Gallantry in the Field and Soldiers conduct in Camp, I thank you. I feel justly proud of our Regiment. There is no stain upon our record and hereafter we can proudly boast that we belonged to the 2nd Mass. Cavalry and fought under Sheridan.

By Order of
C. Crowninshield
Col. 2nd Mass. Cav.

Regimental Record Books, National Archives, Washington, D.C.

About Moseby.

New York, June 23d.-The Lynchburg Republican says a brother of the guerrilla leader, Moseby, recently appeared at the Provost Marshal's office in Lynchburg, and inquired if the partisan Chief would be paroled if he surrendered himself, to which an affirmative answer was given. A few days afterwards Moseby made his appearance, but in the meantime orders had been received from Richmond not to parole him, and as he had come in under a promise of safe guard, the Provost Marshal felt bound in honor not to take advantage of his position, and ordered him to leave Lynchburg, which the soldiers were directed to see he did without molestation.

Alta California, San Francisco, Sunday, July 9, 1865.

29
We have been kept on short rations now for several
days and this morning the Regt. turned out en mass
and demanded of McKendry that more and better
rations be furnished. He immediately ordered a
day's rations issued and promised to do all he
could to help us.

June 30

Five days rations were issued to day about one
half of the stuff was condemned at once and
returned to Washington. I suppose some contractor
is trying to work off his old stock on the Soldier
- We played at Genl. Wells Hd. Qrs. this evening.

Samuel Corbett Diary, Bancroft Library, University of California at Berkeley

❖❖❖

JULY, 1865

7   Execution of Lincoln conspirators.

❖❖❖

The Fourth at Mokelumne Hill.

The eighty-ninth anniversary of our National Independence was celebrated at Mokelumne Hill in a manner highly creditable to the town.————At the close of the orations, Captain Hopkins, who during the early years of the war served in the army of the Potomac, presented to Lieutenant James W. Hepburn, late a soldier in the cavalry under the gallant Sheridan, with a beautiful sword purchased by the citizens of Mokelumne Hill and vicinity as a token of their appreciation of the service rendered the country by one of their former townsmen.

Lieutenant Hepburn thanked them "for their noble gift" and said that " whatever may be the sum of the services I have rendered to our country in the war which has just closed, and whatever the peril incurred, thousands and hundred of thousands of others have freely done the same."

At the conclusion of Lieut. Hepburn's speech, three rousing cheers and a tiger were given by the crowd, which had closely gathered around the stand to witness the interesting ceremonies.

Calaveras Chronicle, Mokelumne Hill, Saturday, July 8, 1865.

Massachusetts Troops to be Mustered Out. A despatch has been received by Major F. N. Clarke, from the War Department, stating that under the order to muster out surplus troops the following named Massachusetts regiments will be disharged. Department of Washington- 2d, 56th, 58th, infantry, 2d cavalry; Department of North Carolina- 117th, 28th, infantry.

Evening Transcript, Boston, Tuesday, July 11, 1865.

❖❖❖

Wednesday, July 12, 1865
    In camp at Fairfax, Va. Had a dress Parade Colonel Crowninshield Flag Presented to the Californians of the 2ⁿᵈ Mass.

Frederick Quant Diary, Bancroft Library, University of California at Berkeley

❖❖

[Mustered Out at Fairfax Court House and Return to Readville]

July 19, 1865
There were a large number of honorary promotions
to day of, the 100, Sergts Crompton and Fletcher
were made 2 Lieuts. We were mustered out of the
U.S. Service this P.M. We are now Brevet Citizens
and will remain so until we doff this blue uniform.

21st
The General sounded for the last time in this
Regt. this A.M. We turned in our tents at 9
A.M. Left camp at 6 P.M. Walked to Vienna and
went into camp. The Band took up their quarters
in the old Hospital.

July 22nd 1865
Embarked on the train at 6 A.M. Took breakfast at
the Soldiers Rest in Washington then marched to
the Baltimore and Ohio R.R. depot, where we took
cars for Baltimore where we took dinner. then
went on board the cars for Philadelphia.

23rd
Arrived in Philadelphia this A.M. at 2. took
breakfast at the Union Vol. rooms, and we had a
splendid meal, from there we crossed the Delaware
River on the Ferry and took the train for N.Y.
City -at 2 P.M. took dinner and went on board of
the Steamer for Providence R.I.

July 24 1865
Arrived in Providence at 9 A.M. We had our
breakfast on the boat. Took cars for Readville
Mass, which place we reached at 12 M. We are
quartered in Barracks and will remain here until
we are discharged

.Samuel Corbett Diary, Bancroft Library, University of California at Berkeley

❖❖

Co. "A". California Hundred, 2nd Mass Cavalry were mustered out of the United States Service this the 19th day of July 1865, at Fairfax Court House, Va.

<u>We have ever tried to do our duty faithfully</u>

W. R. Crompton
1st Sergeant

Regimental Record Books, National Archives, Washington, D.C.
[Wesley R. Crompton enlisted in Co. A, Dec. 1862 in San Francisco]

❖❖

Hd. Qrs. 1st — Brigade
Fairfax Ct. House, Va.
July 20, 1865

Col. J.H. Taylor,
Chief of Staff & A.A.G.
Col:

I have the honor to report that the 2nd Mass Cavalry were mustered out of Service yesterday, the 19th inst by Lieut. Lee A.C.M. and are now ready for transportation home.

I am Col.
Very Respectfully
William Wells
Brig. Gen.
Comdg.

Regimental Record Books, National Archives, Washington, D.C.

❖❖

CAVALRY MUSTERED OUT.

New York, 21st, The Herald's special Washington despatch says all the cavalry corps attached to Department of Washington have been mustered out, the last regiment leaving yesterday.

Evening Transcript, Boston, Friday, July 21, 1865.

❖❖

Camp Meigs
Readville, Mass.
July 24th, 1865

Sir:

I have the honor to report the arrival at this post of the 2nd Regt. Mass. Cav. Aggregate strength, 883.

Very respectfully
Your obdt. servt.
Robert Davis

1st Lt. & Bvt. Capt. 2nd U.S. Inf.
Mustering Officer

Bvt. Capt. F.N. Clark
Chief M. Officer
  State of Mass.

Camp Meigs Readville Mass
July 24th 1865.

Col. F.N. Clark
Chief Mustering Off.
  Boston, Mass.
      Col.

        I respectfully request that the Ordinance Dept receive the Arms to be turned over by the 2d Cav Mass Vols at the earliest possible day.

I Am Sir
Very Respectfully
Your Obt. Svt.
(sgd) —Kro————
Capt. 2d U.S. Inf.
M Off.

Head Quarters Chief Mustering Officer
and Military Commander
Boston Mass. July 25th 1865

Col. John Hendrickson
  13th Regt., V.R.C.
    Galloup's Island B.H.
Sir

        I am directed by Brvt Col. F.N. Clark U.S.A. Chief Mustering Officer to inform you of the arrival in this state of the 2nd Mass. Vol. Cavalry which is now at Readville Mass.

Very Respectfully
Your Obdt Servant
Alfred Townsend
1st Lieut U.S.A.
Post Adjutant

Camp 2d Mass. Cavalry
Readville Mass.
July 27th 1865

Friend Benj:

        Yours of the 10th inst to Lieut Passage has been placed in my hands for reply. The Regiment was mustered out of service at Fairfax Court House on the 20th inst and arrived here on the 24th inst and are awaiting our pay & final discharge which we shall probably get in 3 or 4 days all papers are made and all property turned in. You and every other

357

absentee are included in the Muster Out but all absentees must receive their discharge & pay from the Hd. Qrs. of the Department where they are located.

Furguson was discharged from Hospital on the 13th of June. I saw him in his citizens suit the day we arrived here. He is looking finely although his wound still troubles him some. McKendry came home Col of the Regt., Rumery Lt. Col., Wm Manning, Richards and Alvord Majors, and promotions in the line too numerous to mention. Robinson the Sergt Major when you left the Regt is 1st Lt & Adjutant. You would have worn home the Straps also if you had stuck by the Regiment. I expressed my opinion & contempt of the institution quite too freely after my return to the Regt to be reinstated although I was told that I probably would be. I told a Staff Officer they might shove it up all I wanted was my Buzzard.

B.F. Partridge is Capt of H. Co., Sergt Foster of M Co. came home 1st Lieut of H & Sergt Varnem of M Co 2d Lieut of H. "Johnny come lately" Capt of E Co. But mind you the beauty of all these late promotions is they were never mustered into the U.S. Service as such and never will be and while McKendry made a great spread coming home with the Eagles on his Shoulders he only gets a Majors discharge the most of the Captains get a Lieutenants Discharge and almost every Lieut gets a Sergeants Discharge the same as you and I do "Vive La Humbug".

This damned concern commenced in Fraud and ended in Humbug.

Mulligan & Cross both deserted. I recd a letter from Cross today he is at home. I may go out and see him next week.

Write to me on receipt my address for the present will be Care of Cleaveland & Co corner of Tree & Cross Sts Portland Maine.

I intend to go to Mobile Ala about the 1st Sept. My brother Ed whom you saw at Falls Church is Editor & Proprietor of the "Mobile Daily News" call and see him if you go there.

I shall look for a letter from you certain.

Yours truly

H. W. Hale
QrMr Sergeant Co. H
2d Mass Cavy
soon
Mr. H. W. Hale
Citizen of the U. States of
America

P.S. The Regt came home with 833 men in the ranks.

Regimental Record Books, National Archives, Washington, D.C.

Return of New England Troops. *New York, 23d.* The 2d Massachusetts Cavalry, Col. McHenry, arrived here at noon today and quartered at the Battery Barracks. After partaking of a collation prepared by Gov. Howe, they marched up Broadway, paying an enthusiastic marching salute to Gen. Hooker at the Astor House. They left at 5 o'clock, P.M., for Readville.

The 5th Connecticut regiment left last night for Hartford.

Evening Transcript, Boston, Monday, July 24, 1865.
[Colonel Archibald McKendry]

Arrival of the Second Cavalry Regiment At Readville. The 2d Mass. Cavalry Regiment, Col. Archibald McKendry, of San Francisco, Cal., numbering 884 men, arrived at the Readville camp this morning, from New York. The first detachment of the regiment left the State *[Mass.]* on the 12th of February, 1863, and the main body of it on the 11th of May, following. The 2d has been attached to the Army of the Potomac. The regiment will remain at Readville to be paid off.

Evening Transcript, Boston, Monday, July 24, 1865.

31st
Orders have been received to pay us off tomorrow.
We Californians are in considerable of a worry as
to our transportation back to California. All
kinds of rumors are aflote especially the one that
we will not get a cent. Well, lots of us must
stay here if we don't.

.Samuel Corbett Diary, Bancroft Library, University of California at Berkeley

AUGUST, 1865

[Paid Off at Readville and Return to a "Citizen's Suit of clothes"]

Aug. 1st 1865
No pay to day - The Paymaster says that he has no
orders to pay us our transportation money. The
Californians are all feeling very blue, those who
want to return to that State. There are a number
of our boys who intend to remain on this Coast,
consequently transportation money does not affect
them much.

2nd
A telegram from Washington was received in this
camp this P.M. stating that the Californians
would not receive transportation from the
Goverment. This makes the boys sick.

Aug 3rd 1865
Capt. Burlingham went to Boston this A.M. to find
out if possible who owes us this transportation,
whether it is the Gov. or the State -He sent a
dispatch to Washington to ascertain this.

4th
We received a dispatch from Washington stating
that it does not belong to the Gov. to pay
it -consequently it falls to the State of Mass.
We have decided to receipt for what pay is due us
when we are paid off and leave the transportation
business in the hands of a lawyer.

Aug 5th 1865
We were all paid off to day. There was a slight
mistake of six months in my account, and I would
not sign the PayRoll. The cause was this -When
we were paid off the last time it was at City
Point. I did not need the money so did not answer
to the roll, but the Orderly Sergt of Co. A signed
all the names of the Co and mine amongst the
rest. I did not know this so I have to straighten
this out. I will attend to this Monday. The Cal
100 gave Capt. Burlingham power of Atty to act for
us in the transportation matter.

Aug 6th 1865
I left camp for good yesterday P.M. and arrived at
Sister Lizzie's last evening —I have once more
put on a Citizen's Suit of clothes and feel like a
free man -No more reveille turning out at 3
A.M. in the cold and wet and cooking a breakfast
of Pork Hardtack and coffee, No more standing
picket to be shot at by Rebel guerrillas. No more
rolling up in wet blankets, to take a roll in the
mud to sleep -No more standing in line of Battle
with Bullets and Shells Singing their sweet Songs
in our ears, putting many of us to Sleep with
their gentle lullaby, the Soundest Sleep ere known
to Mortal Man -No more shall my ears listen to
the loud roar of the Artillery or the pop-pop of
the Musketry. In all probability I shall never
live to see another Army fighting in this
country -I am glad that I have had this
experience. I am glad that was so fortunate as
to be one of the defenders of this Grand Republic.

7th
Went to Boston this A.M. and received my pay in
full, Capt. Armstrong testifying to the facts in
my case. This does not include my transportation.

Aug. 8th 1865
I find that I am a very badly used up man now

that the excitement of the War is over, I find
that I am completely let down from nervous
prostration. I cannot sleep in the house, the air
seems so close, and the beds are too soft. I find
myself lying on the floor every morning with no
knowledge of how I got there. My broken ribs
hurt -in fact I am one mass of hurt. During the
last campaign in six weeks I lost 40 pounds of
flesh, and had it lasted 2 weeks longer I should
have left it all on the Sacred Soil of Va.

Aug. 13th 1865
For the last few days I have been visiting my
relatives at Newten Corner and Upper Falls-
this P.M. I went to Church with Sister Lizzie
in Cambridgeport, right in the middle of the
sermon things commenced looking black to me & I
started for the Isle, just as I reached it, I
fainted dead away. Some of the congregation
carried me to the vestry and it took an hour to
bring me to. It created quite an excitement for
the time. This proves to me that I am a badly used
up Soldier -and that I must get back to the
Pacific Slope as soon as possible.

Samuel Corbett Diary, Bancroft Library, University of California at Berkeley

U.S. MILITARY TELEGRAPH

WAR DEPARTMENT
(Telegram) Adjutant General's Office,
Washington, August 4th, 1865

Adjutant General W. Schouler,
Boston, Massachusetts,
Your request by telegraph of yesterday to the Secretary of War, that the California members of the Second (2d) Cavalry be furnished transportation to California is not favorably considered.
Any transportation heretofore furnished individual members was without the sanction of the War Department.
Please see the correspondence relative to the organization and acceptance of the said troops into the United States service.
(signed) Thomas M. Vincent
Asst. Adjt. General

Official copy respectfully furnished for the information of Colonel F.N. Clark, Chief Mustering Officer, Boston, Mass.

Thomas M. Vincent
Asst. Adjt. General.

3:50 PM Aug 7 1865
By telegraph from <u>Washington Aug 5th 1865</u>
To <u>Maj Gen Sheridan</u>
The Second Mass. Cav. has been mustered out.
Thos M Vincent
A.A.G.

Regimental Record Books, National Archives, Washington, D.C.

❖ ❖

SEPTEMBER, 1865

❖ ❖

The California Cavalry Battalion, which was mustered out July 18th, took part in 46 engagements......Fifteen returned to California on the last steamer - among them is McKinley, of Suisun.

Solano Herald, Suisun, Friday, September 15, 1865.
[John W. McKinney, Co. L.]

❖ ❖

OCTOBER, 1865

❖ ❖

[Return to San Francisco]

Oct. 2, 1865
For the last three weeks I have been visiting my
relatives in Mass., Conn., & New York -I have
bidden them all good bye, and took the Steamer New
York for Aspinwall this noon. We left the wharf
at 2 P.M. with 700 Passengers -Fred Quant and
wife and Jack Fletcher are on board, so I have
company.

10
Arrived at Aspinwall this A.M. took breakfast in
town and took cars for Panama at 1 P.M. which
place we reached at 5, and went on board the
Steamer Colorado.

Oct. 16 1865

Arrived at Acapulco this A.M. We took on coal
and water and left at 6. This place is now held
by the French, it is almost depopulated by the
Natives no fruit could be obtained.

24

Arrived at San Francisco at 12:30 M. after an
absence of nearly 3 years -Went to Cousin
Mary Staple -found the family all well and
expecting me.

Samuel Corbett Diary, Bancroft Library, University of California at Berkeley

History of the California Hundred in Brief.

The friends of the gallant California Hundred, will read with interest the original
muster roll of that now famous Company, with the remarks by their commander, giving the
history of the Company in brief, which has been handed us for publication:

Captain J. Sewall Reed-Promoted Major. Killed in action with Mosby's guerrillas at Drainsville,
Virginia, February 22d, 1864.
First Lieutenant Archibald McKendry-Promoted Captain of Company G, subsequently pro-
moted Major, and mustered out as Colonel Commanding regiment.
Second Lieutenant John W. Sim-Discharged by Special Order of the War Department, at Vienna,
Va.., May 4th, 1864.
Armstrong, Hugh-Promoted to First Sergeant, subsequently to Lieutenant, and subsequently
Captain, and mustered out as Captain of California Hundred.
Ackerman, Charles H.-Promoted Corporal, subsequently Sergeant, subsequently First Sergeant
California Hundred.
Ackerman, James B.-Killed in charge at Halltown, Va., August 20th, 1864.
Allen, Henry W.-Transferred to Invalid Corps from Camp Windham, Va., July 20th, 1863.
Allen, E. Henry-Wounded in action at Rockville, Md. Died of wounds through neglect of Sur-
geon, in hospital at Washington, D.C., August 16th, 1864.
Allan, Charles-Promoted Sergeant, subsequently First Lieutenant of Fifth Mass. (Colored)
Cavalry.
Anderson, George-Deserted August 2d, 1864; returned under President's Proclamation Act,
April 4th, 1865.
Anthony, William G.-Promoted to Corporal, subsequently to Sergeant Company C.
Burdick, Joseph B.-Killed in action at South Anna Bridge, Va., June 26th, 1863.
Benjamin, Charles E.-Promoted Sergeant Company A, subsequently transferred to Non. Com.
Staff, as Commissary Sergeant.
Barnstead, Thomas D.-Promoted to Sergeant Major, July 21st, 1865.
Balcom, Darnly O.-Transferred to Company G, promoted to Sergeant, subsequently to Second
Lieutenant, and subsequently to First Lieutenant.
Burlingham, Henry G.-Promoted First Sergeant, subsequently Second Lieutenant, then to First
Lieutenant and Adjutant, and mustered out as Captain of Company G.

Bumgardner, William H.H.-Promoted to Corporal. Died at farmhouse of wounds received in action with Mosby's guerrillas at Mount Zion Church, July 6th, 1864.

Balke, Charles-Promoted Corporal July 21st, 1865.

Baker, A. Frank-Deserted from Readville, Mass., subsequently returned, was restored to duty, deserted again from Falls Church, Va.

Beach, Nathan A.-Went home to Canada on furlough from Headquarters, Washington, D.C. , and failed to return.

Briggs, Charles P.-Mustered out July 30th, 1865.

Blake, Josephus-Discharged in Boston, Mass., on account of bad eyesight, Sept. 1st, 1863.

Campbell, Edward B.-Promoted Corporal July 21st, 1865.

Carey, Jeremiah J.-Promoted Corporal July 1st, 1865.

Collins, Wm. W.-Promoted Second Lieutenant, Tenth New York Cavalry.

Corbett, Samuel J.-Promoted Corporal, subsequently reduced to the ranks, subsequently promoted Sergeant of Regimental Band-reduced to the ranks July 18th, 1865.

Cunningham, William-Mustered out July 20th, 1865, as Saddler.

Chalmers, John M.-Mustered out July 20th, 1865.

Chandler, William S.-Discharged from hospital at Washington, D.C., July 1865.

Crum, Henry-Promoted Sergeant, subsequently reduced to the ranks, subsequently promoted Corporal, then Sergeant.

Crumpton, Wesley R.-Promoted Corporal, reduced to the ranks, subsequently promoted Corporal, then Sergeant. First Sergeant of Company, promoted Second Lieutenant July 9th, 1865.

Davis, George F.-Promoted corporal, then sergeant, subsequently Second Lieutenant Fourth Massachusetts Cavalry.

Dewey, Charles S.-Deserted from Readville, Mass., February 27th, 1863.

Dearborn, Valorus-Promoted Corporal February, 1864. Killed in action at Opequan Creek, Shenandoah Valley, Va., September 13th, 1864.

Demsey, Cyrus F.-Taken prisoner by Mosby at Coyle's Tavern, Va., August 24th, 1864, subsequently exchanged and returned to Company, May 19th, 1865.

Doane, Gustavus C.-Promoted to Sergeant, subsequently reduced to ranks, subsequently promoted to First Lieutenant Mississippi Marine Brigade.

Ellett, Richard S.-Wounded in action at South Anna Bridge, Va., promoted from Hospital at Gloucester Point, Va., to Lieutenant Mississippi Marine Brigade.

Forbes, Alexander C.-Killed by accidental discharge of pistol, at Halltown, Va., August 9th, 1864.

Freeman, James-Deserted from Camp Windham, Va., August 1st, 1863.

Fillebrown, Henry H.-Mustered out July 20th, 1865.

Fletcher, John-Promoted to Corporal, subsequently to Sergeant, captured in action on Opequan Creek, Va., August 10th, 1864, subsequently exchanged and returned to Company, May 21st, 1864, promoted Lieutenant July, 1865.

Gibbs, Byron D.-Promoted Corporal March 23d, 1865.

Goulding, George W.-Captured in action at Rockville, Md., July 13th, 1864, subsequently exchanged and returned to Company May 2d, 1865, promoted Corporal March 23d, 1865.

Hall, Frederick-Promoted Corporal November 1st, 1864, promoted Sergeant July 18th, 1865.

Hanscom, Samuel C.-Promoted Corporal. Killed in action near Mount Zion Church, Va., July 6th, 1864.

Hammerburg, William-Deserted from Readville, Md., January 26th, 1863.

Hill, Charles W.-Promoted at Gloucester Point, Va., to his old command, First Lieutenant First Missouri Cavalry.

Hill, John A.-Discharged for disability from Vienna, Va., April 1864.

Hilliard, William H.I.-Promoted Corporal, subsequently Sergeant, subsequently Second Lieutenant Company B.

Holt, George I.-Discharged from Hospital at Annapolis Junction, Md., June 10th, 1865.

Hunt, James A.-Discharged for disability, at Gloucester Point, Va., May 10th, 1863.

Hunter, John L.-Mustered out July 20th, 1865.

Hussey, William H.H.-Promoted to Corporal, subsequently to Sergeant, subsequently to Second Lieutenant Company C., mustered out as Captain.

Johnson, George M.-Mustered out July 20th, 1865.

Knowles, Frank-Deserted from Readville, Mass., January 26th, 1864.

Kinnie, Charles M.-Promoted Sergeant, subsequently to Lieutenant, subsequently to Captain and A.A.G. Reserve Brigade, First Division Cavalry.

Leighton, Alfred L.-Died of fever in Hospital, Washington, D.C., July 25th, 1863.

Lee, Alfred-Company Bugler. Died in Hospital at Vienna, Va., of brain fever, May 1st, 1864.

Legler, Charles-Mustered out July 20th, 1865.

Loane, Abraham-Captured in action with Mosby's Guerrillas at Mount Zion Church, Va., July 6th, 1864, subsequently exchanged, and discharged from Hospital at Readville, Mass., June, 1865.

Libby, Frank O.-Promoted Corporal, subsequently reduced to the ranks.

Locke, Benjamin-Promoted Corporal, and subsequently Sergeant.

Mazy, Henry-Mustered out July 20th, 1865.

Merriam, Jonathan-Captured at Rockville, Md., July 13th, 1864, subsequently exchanged, and discharged from Hospital at Readville, Mass., June, 1865.

McCarty, John-Killed in action at Coyles' Tavern, Va., August 24th, 1863.

McCarthy, John D.-Promoted Hospital Steward.

McIntosh, Isaac R.-Promoted Corporal, subsequently Sergeant, subsequently Lieutenant, then to Captain Company F.

McNeil, William H.-Promoted Corporal. Discharged by Special Orders A.G.O., June 20th, 1865.

Magary, Albert-Deserted from Readville, Mass., January 26th, 1863.

Nellis, E.-Deserted from Readville, Mass., Jan. 26th, 1863.

Nelson, H.-Deserted from Readville, Mass., Jan. 26th, 1863.

Nixon, John-Transferred to Company B. Killed by bushwhackers, while at a house near King and Queen's Court House, Va.

Owen, John W.-Promoted Corporal, subsequently Sergeant, subsequently Second Lieutenant, accidentally shot himself through the foot, and was discharged from Hospital, May, 1865.

Pelham, James W.-Discharged for disability from Hospital at Frederick, Md., June 4th, 1865.

Percy, William-Promoted Corporal, subsequently Sergeant, subsequently Lieutenant Fourth Mass. Cavalry, afterwards Captain.

Pool, Melbourne Z.-Mustered out July 20th, 1865 as Wagoner.

Parker, R.M.-Promoted Corporal, subsequently Lieutenant Fifth Mass. (Colored) Cavalry.

Powers, Charles H.-Promoted Sergeant, subsequently reduced to the ranks. Promoted Corporal July 21st, 1865.

Plummer, George-Promoted Corporal, subsequently Second Lieutenant. Mustered out as First Lieutenant California Hundred.

Quant, Frederick J.-Promoted Corporal, subsequently reduced to the ranks.

Rice, Hamilton-Deserted from Readville, Mass., subsequently arrested and discharged from Hospital, Washington, D.C.

Robinson, Wm. A-Promoted Sergeant-Major, subsequently Lieutenant and Adjutant.

Ross, Joshua C.-Mustered out July 20th, 1865.

Rone, Carlos-Transferred to Invalid Corps, subsequently discharged from Hospital at Philadelphia, Penn., for disability.

Samuels, Richard C.-Mustered out July 20th, 1865.

Schrow, Henry-Promoted Corporal, discharged from Hospital at Washington, June 20th, 1865.

Sherwin, Henry C.-Promoted Corporal, subsequently Sergeant and Q.M. Sergeant of the Company.

Sivalls, Benson-Discharged for disability from the Hospital at Alexandria, Va., June, 1865.

Smith, Samuel, Jr.-Promoted Corporal and subsequently Sergeant.

Speaight, Charles L.-Captured by Mosby's guerrillas near Berryville, Va., August, 1865. Died in Prison at Danville, Va., February 25th, 1865.

Starr, William E.-Mustered out July 20th, 1865.

Sterling, Edward R.-Promoted Corporal, subsequently Sergeant, subsequently Lieutenant of the Fourth Mass. Cavalry.

Towle, George W.-Promoted Corporal, October, 1864. Promoted Sergeant July 18th, 1865.

Tubbs, Henry S.C.-Captured in action at Rockville, Md., July 13th, 1864, subsequently exchanged and returned to Company, May 21st, 1865. Promoted Corporal July 1st, 1865.

Thompson, George-Promoted Second Lieutenant Ninety-Sixth Regiment New York Infantry.

Verick, George W.-Died of wounds received in action at Coyles' Tavern, August 24th, 1863.

West, Wells W.-Mustered out July 20th, 1865.

Wheat, Jas. L.-Promoted Sergeant, subsequently Second Lieutenant Fifth Mass. (Colored) Cavalry, subsequently Captain.

White, Peter E.-Promoted Sergeant and Chief Bugler.

Williams, J.H.-Discharged for disability at Boston, Mass., October, 1863.

Winship, John-Mustered out July 20th, 1865.

Woodman, H.F.-Promoted to Corporal, subsequently to Sergeant, Company G., subsequently to Lieutenant, wounded in action at Waynesboro, Va., September 28th, 1864. Died of his wounds at Mount Jackson, Va

Woodward, E.W.-Promoted Second Lieutenant, Twenty-Fifth New York Cavalry, subsequently Captain.

Watson, James-Promoted Corporal November 1st, 1864, promoted Sergeant July 18th, 1865.

Alta California, San Francisco, Thursday, October 5, 1865

Lieutenant Sim. - In the roll of the California Hundred (Company A, Second Massachusetts Cavalry,) published in yesterday's Alta, the name of First Lieutenant John W. Sim appears with the remark, "Discharged by special order of the War Department, at Vienna, Va., May 4th, 1864." In justice to Lieutenant Sim, we should state that he entered the service as a Second Lieutenant, was promoted to the First Lieutenancy for honorable service, and was in command of the Company when dismissed upon a Surgeon's certificate of physical disability which incapacitated him from rendering further service, and not, as might possibly been inferred by strangers, from any negligence of duty or infraction of rules.

Alta California, San Francisco, Friday, October 6, 1865

NOVEMBER, 1865

6 Confederate ship *Shenandoah* surrenders to British.
10 Capt. Henry Wirz, commander of Andersonville Prison,
executed.

THE FLAGS OF THE CALIFORNIA HUNDRED.- Mr. Geo. W. Towle, Jr., of Santa Clara, one of the survivors of the gallant "California Hundred," who left here in December, 1862, to serve in the Army of the Potomac as a portion of the Second Massachusetts Cavalry, was in town to-day on his way to Sacramento, with the original company flag, or guidon, carried by the company through their whole campaign, and now donated by the survivors to the State of California. On the staff is a silver plate bearing the following inscription: "Presented to the California Hundred by Daniel Norcross, of San Francisco, December 1st, 1862. Presented to the State of California by the remaining members of the California Hundred, July 24th, 1865." The colors of the guidon are faded and the silk worn and torn to shreds and patches by long service on the field, and it was found necessary to attach a large blue satin pennant to the staff on which to inscribe the list of battles in which the company participated. This list, which is printed in gold, is as follows:

"South Anna, Drainsville, Aldie, Fort Reno, Rockville, Poolsville, Summit Point, Berryville, Berryville Pike, Charlestown, Hall Town (four days,) Opequan, (six days,) Winchester, Luray, Waynesboro, Tom's Brook, Cedar Creek, South Anna, White Oak Road, Dinwiddie Court House, Five Forks, Sailors Creek, Appomattox Court House."

Accompanying the flag is a letter, neatly engrossed on parchment, addressed to the Adjutant General of the State of California, and signed by each individual of the company now remaining alive. The letter reads as follows.

Camp of Cavalry Forces,
Fairfax Court House, Va.
July 20th, 1865.

"To the Adjutant General of the State of California:
Sir-   "The California Hundred, the first Company organized on the Pacific Coast for the war in the East, and the suppression of armed rebellion, prior to their departure from San Francisco, California, December 11th, 1862, were presented by Daniel Norcross, Esq., of San Francisco, with the Bear Flag which this letter accompanies. This flag has been carried by the Company through nearly three years of active service, including twenty-three general engagements, (as denoted upon the pennant,) and under which three of our Company Commanders and many of our comrades have fallen. And now, at the final muster-out and discharge of the Company, the remaining members, whose names appear in this letter, respectfully present it, through you, to our adopted State, California.

"The accompanying American Flag was presented to the Hundred upon their arrival in Massachusetts, by Miss Abbie A. Lord, a patriotic young lady of Charlestown, Massachusetts, but has never been carried upon the field of battle as it was too large for the cavalry service. (It has never been unfurled by the Company except in one instance— to enshroud the remains of our original Company Commander, Captain J. S. Reed.) It is the wish of the Company that the same disposition be made of this as of the Bear Flag.

Wesley R. Crumpton,	Charles H. Ackerman,
Chas. E. Benjamin,	Chas. Blake,
Chas. H. Powers,	Chas. Legler,
Thos. D. Barnstead,	Benj. Locke,
John L. Hunter,	Wm. E. Starr,
J. Carey Ross,	Cyrus F. Demsey,
Geo. Anderson,	Geo. W. Towle, Jr.,
Wells W. West,	Wm. Cunningham,
Geo. M. Johnson,	Henry Mazy,
Ed. B. Campbell,	Peter E. White,
Frederick Hall,	M. Z. Poole,
Wm. G. Anthony,	John Fletcher,
Geo. W. Goulding,	Byron D. Gibbs,
Samuel Smith, Jr.,	C. P. Briggs,
Richard C. Samuel,	Henry Schrow,
H. H. Fillebrown,	Jerimiah J. Carey,
Henry S. E. Tubbs,	John D. McCarthey,
Geo. I. Holt,	James Watson,
Henry S. Sherwin,	Wm. H. McNeil,
Isaac R. McIntosh,	Darnley O. Balcom."

Only a portion of the Company have yet arrived from the East, the remainder being unable to pay the rates of fare demanded, and the State of Massachusetts having declined to forward them, on the ground that as they were mustered into the service of the United States in San Francisco, it was the business of the General Government to return them to the place from whence they were received into the service. The War Department has now consented to furnish transportation for those still at the East, and all who desire will, therefore, be returned here within a short time. They have deserved well of their country and our State, and their services will, we trust, not soon be forgotten by their fellow-citizens.

Alta California, San Francisco, Thursday, November 2, 1865
The Daily Bee, Sacramento, Friday, November 3, 1865.
Daily Union, Sacramento, Friday, November 3, 1865.

LOCAL NEWS.

California Hundred.-Geo. W. Towle, Jr. of Santa Clara county, and one of the survivors of the "California Hundred," arrived here this morning and deposited in the office of Adjutant General Evans the war worn guidon of the company. The California Hundred, under Captain J.S. Reed, left here in December, 1862, and in the Army of the Potomac did good service. About forty of the California Hundred survive. The guidon shows the marks of battle. It is made of silk - two pieces of equal width - one red and the other white. On the red are the letters "U.S.," and on the white the California bear. In letters of gold is the list of the battles in which the California Hundred were engaged. The list is: South Anna, Dranesvillle, Aldie, Fort Reno, Rockville, Poolsville, Summit Point, Berryville, Berryville Pike, Charlestown, Hall Town, (four days), Opequan (six days), Winchester, Luray, Waynesboro, Tom's Brook, Cedar Creek, South

Anna, White Oak Road, Dinwiddie Court House, Five Forks, Sailor's Creek, Appomattox Court House. On the staff is a silver plate, which bears this inscription: "Presented to the California Hundred by Daniel Norcross, of San Francisco, December 1, 1862. Presented to the State of California by the remaining members of the California Hundred, July 24, 1865." The guidon is tattered and torn from service, but will be carefully preserved as a memento of a hundred Californians who exhibited their patriotism nobly on the battlefield. In a day or two the flag will be formally presented to the State, and will be deposited in the office of the Secretary of State. Accompanying the guidon is the letter of presentation, signed by the forty survivors.

The Daily Bee, Sacramento, Thursday, November 2, 1865.

❖❖❖

DECEMBER, 1865

18 Thirteenth Amendment abolishing slavery in effect after ratification by the twenty-seventh state.

❖❖❖

Epilogue
1866-1937

In subsequent years, the California Hundred and Battalion would appear in the news as a part of a special event or a patriotic holiday; or sadly, in the obituary notices. But their fame followed them right up to the death of the last veteran, William Morris, December 10, 1937.

1866

Relics of the War.-At the mass meeting, at Platt's Hall this evening, where Colonel Hawkins will lecture on the war, there will be exhibited several battle-flags which saw service in the late rebellion. Two of them have been kindly loaned by Maj. D.W.C. Thompson, of the California Cavalry Battalion, and one which was recently brought from the East, to be presented to this State. It was brought out by Col. McKendry, who left this State as First Lieutenant of the California Hundred, and was Colonel of the California regiment, when it was mustered out of service, to the survivors of which the flag was presented by their former Colonel-Caspar Crowninshield. It bears the names of twenty-five of their victorious fields. The Euterpians will be present at the meeting and sing several of their patriotic songs.

Alta California, San Francisco, Thursday, February 22, 1866.

Presentation of Flag to the State.-We publish the following interesting correspondence, which will explain itself:

Sacramento, March 7, 1866.

To his Excellency, F.F. Low, Governor of the State of California-Governor: In behalf of five hundred Californians who were mustered into the United States service in 1862, and left this State by order of the War Department to join the Second Regiment of Massachusetts Cavalry, I have the honor of presenting to the State of California the accompanying flag, on which are inscribed the names of twenty-five victorious battles in which the regiment participated.

The Second Massachusetts Cavalry served in the Regular Brigade, First Division, Armies of the Shenandoah and Potomac, and under the gallant Sheridan took an active and honorable part in all the battles of the valley, and the last battles of the war around Richmond, up to the final surrender, and were mustered out of the service in August, 1865. The following list of battles were inscribed on our flag by order:

South Anna Bridge,	Opequan (6 days),
Ashby's Gap,	Winchester,
Drainsville,	Laurau,
Aldie,	Waynesboro,
Fort Stevens,	Tom's Brook,
Fort Reno,	Cedar Creek,
Rockville,	South Anna,
Poolsville,	White Oak Road,
Summit Point,	Dinwiddie Court house,
Berryville,	Five Forks,
Berryville Pike,	Sailor's Creek,
Charlestown,	Appomattox Court house.
Halltown (4 days),	

The inscription on the plate shows that this flag was presented to the Californians of this regiment by Colonel Casper Crowninshield, who succeeded to the command after the death of General Lowell, who was killed at Cedar Creek.

I Have the honor to remain your obedient servant,

ARCHA. McKENDRY,
Late Colonel Second Massachusetts Cavalry.

State of California, Executive Department,

Sacramento, April 5, 1866.

Sir: The great pressure of business incident to the closing of the session of the Legislature must be my excuse for not sooner replying to yours of March 7th.

To welcome returning soldiers bearing victorious banners is among the most pleasant duties of a patriot at any time; but to receive such a band as yours, with such a flag, is a privilege that has been enjoyed by the Executive of no State. The history of the organization and subsequent services of your gallant band is full of interest which can scarcely be equalled in the annals of the war. To have traveled six thousand miles by sea and through foreign countries to assist in putting down a rebellion against liberty in our own, and to return from a victory so complete, make a record of which the whole State should feel proud. And though many of your number have fallen, their deeds will live and their valor bless their country for all time.

On behalf of the people of the State I return you and your companions most hearty thanks and lasting gratitude for your gallant services.

Your flag shall rest among our most cherished treasures,

I am, dear sir, your obedient servant,

FREDERICK F. LOW, Governor.
Archa. McKendry, late Colonel Second Massachusetts Cavalry, San Francisco.

The Daily Union, Sacramento, Friday, April 6, 1866.

❖❖
Survivors of Andersonville.

Of the men who suffered in the prison pen at Andersonville there are said to be only five on this coast. These are desirous of meeting any comrades from the East who were prisoners at Andersonville on Thursday evening next at 8 o'clock at 37 Sutter Street. The occasion should be a memorable one and no survivors now in the city should fail to attend.

Alta California, San Francisco, Monday, April 2, 1866.
❖❖

Head Quarters Post of Leesburg
Leesburg, Va. April 9, 1866

Captain E. W. H. Reed
A.A.A.G. Dist of Shenandoah

Captain:
I have the honor to report that one, John S. Moseby late Colonel and Guerilla in the Army of the so called Confederate States did appear and parade the streets of Leesburg Va. about 9 o'clock A.M. today wearing Rebel uniform with Military buttons, in

direct violation of General Orders Published in June, 1865, and republished here about February 1, 1866. I immediately sent a guard for the purpose of arresting him and causing to be removed said buttons, which fact was evidently soon made known to him, as he immediately went in a store and changed his apparel for that of a citizen in which dress he was found by the guard.

Upon appearance of said guard, he, said Moseby, did use insulting language and did repeatedly remark that "If an attempt was made to arrest him he would soon create a force that would massacre every damned Yankee in the town."

As he did not have on the buttons, no further notice of him was taken until about 11 o'clock A.M. when he reappeared with said uniform and buttons and after walking up very near the barracks occupied by the troops, and in which I have an office, he retraced his steps and posted himself on a street corner as conspicuously as possible. This fact being reported to me, I immediately proceeded to said corner and found said Moseby and said to him, "Mr. Moseby you cannot wear those buttons in the town," to which he replied "You have not got enough men to make me take them off."

About fifteen minutes thereafter Mr. Moseby was making a north-easterly course across the fields, fences etc., at an extremely rapid rate pursued by some skirmishers who fired several shots, but without effect, consequently he escaped.

I therefore respectfully and most earnestly request, as an act of justice to the few loyal people of this community, to my command and the undersigned, that a detachment of Cavalry be sent here or that some other means be adopted to insure his arrest (Mr. M.)

> I am Captain
> Very Respectfully
> Your Obedient Servant
> John T. Macauley, Capt. 7th U.S. V.V.
> Commanding Post

Regimental Record Books, National Archives, Washington, D.C.

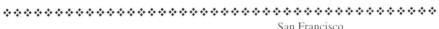

> San Francisco
> June 29, 1866

His Excellency
Governor Low
  Sacramento,

  Governor

The members of the California Hundred and California Cavalry Battalion who served in the 2d Ms Cavalry will parade in this city on the coming 4th of July.

I have the honor to request on their behalf that your Excellency will loan them the colors which they have deposited with the state, consisting of the Guidon of the Cala 100 with the Bear painted on it, the Cavalry standard 2d Ms Cav with battle names inscribed on it, and the silk flag presented to the Cala 100 by the Ladies of Charlestown, Ms.

If you do not think it advisable to send all these flags I wish particularly that you would let us have the Guidon referred to use with others of the Battalion.

If you will order these flags sent to me by Wells Fargo & Co Express I will see that they are properly used, and promptly returned to you as before!

Most Respt
Your Excellencies
Obt Sevt
D.W.C. Thompson
Late Maj. Cal Cavl Bt
No 408 Montg St

California State Archives, Sacramento, California

CITY ITEMS.
THE CELEBRATION TO-DAY.

The veterans of the California Hundred and California Cavalry Battalion will parade to-day, and will carry their splendid flag inscribed with names of their fields of operations, campaigns they were in, armies they belonged to, and fifty battles in which they were engaged. They will also carry their war-worn and battle stained guidons, which have been in some of the most memorable engagements of the war. They will parade in connection with the California Volunteer's Union of this State, thus uniting the brave Californians who have fought for the country at the East, and over the rough mountains of the Pacific slope. These two Associations will meet at Dashaway Hall, at 9 0'clock this morning, and will be escorted to their position in the procession by the First Regiment of Infantry, C.M., with the Second U.S. Artillery Band. This escort has been kindly tendered by Col. Joseph Wood, as a compliment to these brave and patriotic Californian veterans.

FOURTH OF JULY PROGRAMME.

The following is the programme for the regular exercises to-day, as arranged by the Executive Committee and the Grand Marshal:

A Federal salute will be fired by the First California Guard at sunrise.

The Divisions comprising the procession will form under the direction of their respective Marshals, as follows:

That portion of the First Division composed of Stevenson's Regiment, California Hundred, California Battalion and California Volunteers Union, will form on Filbert street, west of Powell, right resting on Powell.

FIRST DIVISION.
CALIFORNIA VOLUNTEER BAND.

Stevenson's Regiment.
California Volunteer Band
Veterans of Mexican War.
California Hundred and Battalion.
California Volunteer Union.

[Excerpted from the full article]

California Volunteer Union.-A large and enthusiastic meeting of this association met at the Police Court room last evening. A large number of discharged soldiers were added to the rolls. Communications were received from the California Hundred and Battalion, expressing their gratification of the honor conferred upon them by the Union, in requesting them to act as escort, and stating that Major D.W.C. Thompson had been appointed Marshal, and that the Union, Hundred and Battalion would be escorted to their position in line from Dashaway Hall by the First Regiment of Infantry, C.M., Colonel Wood, with the Second Artillery Band. A vote of thanks was given to the ALTA and other papers, for numerous favors extended to the association. The meeting adjourned with three cheers and a tiger for the Hundred and Battalion and Grand Marshal Badger, and they were given with hearty goodwill. All members and soldiers desiring to take part in the parade are requested to meet at Dashaway Hall, at 9 o'clock A.M. sharp.

Alta California, San Francisco, Wednesday, July 4, 1866.

❖ ❖

FOURTH OF JULY CELEBRATION.
THE GRAND PROCESSION.

This was, as had been intended, the grand feature of the day's celebration, and was such a success as would make up for many shortcomings in other particulars.——— The procession moved from Washington Square promptly at the hour named in the programme, and the advance wheeled into Montgomery street from Washington, moving southward, at 11:30 A.M., precisely. The rear did not reach the same point until 7 minutes to 1 P.M., so that the time occupied in passing a given point would be one hour and twenty-three minutes.

When it is remembered that the military, which formed a leading feature of the procession, marched by Companies in double ranks, occupying the entire width of the street from sidewalk to sidewalk, it will be seen that the numbers in line must have been immense. ——— In the advance, after the Marshal and his Aides, came Company A, Second U.S. Artillery, and Company M, Second U.S. Artillery. ——— Stevenson's Regiment, the Veterans of the Mexican War, the California Hundred and Battalion, and the California Volunteer Union, followed, with war worn and faded guidons and banners torn with bullets and fretted to mere rags by the winds of many a bloody day. Conspicuous were the veterans of the California Hundred and California Cavalry Battalion, in the First Division. They were organized in this city in the fall of 1862. The California Hundred with one hundred men, under Captain J. Sewall Reed, since killed in battle, and the California Cavalry Battalion-four companies-four hundred men, under Major D.W.C. Thompson. These companies served together through the war and mustered out only one hundred and eighty-two men, many of those severely wounded, and some so bad that they have not been able to return to this State. These veterans carried three flags; a war worn tattered and battle scarred guidon-this belonged to Captain Horace B. Welch's Company and was carried in the first regiment that entered Richmond on the 3d of April, 1865; a camp flag used by the Californians in Maryland and Virginia the sight of which has often gladdened the hearts of our brave soldiers, and floated over their camp in defiance of rebel arms; and a third-the finest and most memorable flag that connects and associates California with the war. This flag is an honorable history of the Hundred and Battalion, and had the following inscriptions: "Dep't. of Washington," "Army of the Potomac," "Sheridan's Cavalry," representing the armies they served in; "Potomac River," "Orange and Alexandria Railroad," "Shenandoah Valley," "James River," "Petersburg," "Appomattox River," representing their field of operations; "Gettysburg Campaign," "Mosby's Guerillas," "Early's Defeats," "Capture of Richmond," "Surrender of Lee," "Grand Review," representing the important operations they were actors in. On the fourth and fifth red stripes, in letters of gold, are "California Hundred," and "California Cavalry Battalion," connected with a laurel wreath, and between them are "Organized Oct. 1862-500 mustered in; Discharged August, 1865-182 mustered out." On the white stripes are printed, in beautiful letters of red and blue, the names of fifty battles in which these Californians were engaged, as follows: South Anna Bridge, Brookville, Ashby's Gap, Coyle's Tavern, Little River Pike, Drainsville, Rectortown, Point of Rocks, Aldie, Frederick Pike, Tenallytown, Fort Reno, Fort Stevens, Rockville, Poolsville, Leesburg, Snicker's Gap, Nolan's Ford, Shepardstown, White Post, Middletown, Cedar Creek, Kearnstown, Winchester, Berryville Pike, Charlestown, Summit Point, Halltown, Berryville, Smithfield, Opequan Creek, Knox Ford, Front Royal, Smoke Mountain, Wray Court House, Mill's Ford, Waynesboro, Mount Crawford, Tom's Brook, Strasburg, Madison Court House, Gordonsville, South Anna, White Oak Road, Dinwiddie Court House, Five Forks, South Side Railroad, Devil's Ford, Sailor's Creek, Appomattox Court House. During the ceremonies at the Metropolitan theatre, the colors were displayed from the right of the Stage, and the battle scarred veterans who had borne themselves so bravely and victoriously were seated on the stage, with the officers and honored of the day.

Alta California, San Francisco, Friday, July 6, 1866.
[Excerpted from the full article. The flag described is known as the Thompson Flag, now in the Capitol Museum, Sacramento, Ca.; 2ⁿᵈ Lt. Horace B. Welch,Co. F, disch. Feb. 3, 1864 for promotion as 2ⁿᵈ Lt., Co. C, 5ᵗʰ Mass. Cav.]

CITY ITEMS.

The Dead of the California Hundred.-At a meeting of the veterans of the California Hundred and California Cavalry Battalion, held on Wednesday evening, the following resolutions, which will meet with a hearty response from all loyal Californians, were unanimously adopted:

Whereas, A large number of the officers, non-commissioned officers and privates belonging to the "California Hundred" and "California Cavalry Battalion," lost their lives while serving in the Union army and are buried on the battle-field; by the line of march; in hospital cemeteries and in rebel prison grounds, many of their graves unmarked and unknown; therefore,

Resolved, That it is the duty of this Association, consisting of the surviving members of the "Hundred and Battalion" to erect, or assist in erecting a monument to the honor and memory of our fallen friends and fellow soldiers, and that we will, as an Association and individually, work for this noble purpose until such monument is completed.

Resolved, That this Association is desirous of uniting with all veterans and loyal residents of California in erecting a monument alike honorable to the State and worthy of her heroic dead, wherein shall be inscribed the name of every citizen of California whose life was lost in the military or naval service of the United States during the late war.

Resolved, That the Association request the following named gentlemen, who have been identified with the Volunteers from California, to act as a Committee to collect funds, fix the location and superintend the building of such a monument; His Excellency F. F. Low, Governor of California; Hon. Leland Stanford, ex-Governor of California; Maj. Gen. H.W. Halleck, U.S.A.; Brevet Maj. Gen. Irwin McDowell, U.S.A.; Brevet Maj. Gen. J.F. Miller, late U.S.V.; Brevet Maj. Gen. P.E. Connor, late U.S.V.; Brig. Gen. G.S. Evans, Adj't. Gen. Cal.; Col. R.C. Drum, Ass't. Adj't. Gen. U.S.A.; Col. O.M. Brown, late First Cal. Cav.; Col. Ed McGarry, late Second Cal. Cav.; Col. D.W.C. Thompson, late Cal. Cav. Bat.; Col. A. McKendry, late Cal. Hundred; Col. E.A. Rigg, late First Cal. Inf.; Col. T.F. Wright, late Second Cal. Inf.; Col. R. Pollock, late

Third Cal. Inf.; Col. J.F. Curtis, late Fourth Cal. Inf.; Col. G.W. Bowie, late Fifth Cal. Inf.; Col. A.E. Hooker, late Sixth Cal. Inf.; Col. C.W. Lewis, late Seventh Cal. Inf.; Col. A.L. Henderson, late Eighth Cal. Inf.; Surgeon J.M. McNulty, late U.S.V.; Surgeon S.F. Elliott, late U.S.V.; Capt. C. Mason Kinne, late A.A.G., U.S.V.; Capt. L.C.H. Baldwin, U.S.N.; Capt. S.E. Woodworth, late U.S.N.

Resolved, That the President of this Association send a copy of these resolutions to each gentleman named for said Committee, with the request that they will meet for organization at 8 o'clock P.M., on the 2d of October next, at the Occidental Hotel, San Francisco.

Alta California, San Francisco, Friday, September 21, 1866.

THE MONUMENT TO OUR FALLEN HEROES.

The Committee requested to act for the purpose of erecting a monument to the memory of the fallen heroes of California, by the "Veterans of the California Hundred and Battalion," met on Tuesday evening at the Occidental Hotel, and perfected their organization, and are determined to use all endeavors to prove the project not only theoretically feasible, but, with the aid of loyal Californians, financially practicable. The following is the plan of organization:

NAME.
California Union Soldiers' and Sailors Monument Association.

OBJECT.
The object of this Association shall be to erect in the name of the loyal people of California, a monument to the honor and memory of all United States soldiers and sailors from this State, who lost their lives during the late war.

OFFICERS.
President-Governor of the State of California, *ex officio*.
Vice President-Major General of the California National Guard, *ex officio*.
Treasurer-D.O. Mills, Esq., President Bank of California.
Secretary-Captain C. Mason Kinne, late U.S.A.
Executive Committee-Maj. Gen. H.W. Halleck, U.S.A.; Maj. Gen. J.F. Miller, late U.S.V.; Brig. Gen. G.S. Evans, Adj't. Gen. Cal.; Col. D.W.C. Thompson, late U.S.V.; Capt. S.E. Woodworth, late U.S.N.

The following resolutions, which were framed and embodied, as a part of the programme, will explain the manner in which the Association intend to act:

Resolved, That this Association request the following citizens of California to collect and remit subscriptions for the "Union Soldiers' and Sailors' Monument" to the Treasurer of this Association, viz.: All State officers, Judges of the Supreme Court, District Court Judges, County Judges, Sheriffs, County Clerks, General, Field and Staff Officers of the California Guard, local express agents, and all Postmasters in the State.

Resolved, That it is the opinion of this Association that the monument proposed to be erected in honor of the deceased Federal soldiers and sailors from California be placed on Union Square, in the city and county of San Francisco, and that the President of this Association request the Honorable Board of Supervisors of said city and county to grant permission for that purpose.

Resolved, That all military officers and architects in this State be invited and requested to furnish to this Association, designs for a monument, to be constructed of California granite, marble or other California material, and to cost $50,000.

Resolved, That every member shall use his influence for the successful and immediate accomplishment of the object of this Association, but no member shall receive any pay for services rendered for such purpose. After the transaction of some other general business, the meeting adjourned, with instructions for its officers and Executive Committee, to act in furtherance of the object in view, without delay.

Alta California, San Francisco, Thursday, October 4, 1866.

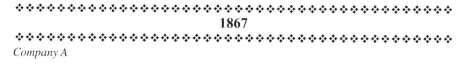

1867

Company A

Death of One of The California Hundred.-Mr. **Henry Fillebrown**, one of the California Hundred, died in this city on Saturday, a few minutes before two o'clock. Mr. Fillebrown had been unwell for a number of months, but did not take to his bed until Thursday last, and only then at the urgent request of his family and physician. He was a brave young man, and served his country faithfully, saying the day before his death, that he "should rather have died on the field of battle." All honor to his name, His funeral will take place to-day, at two o'clock, from his residence on Tehama street, between Fifth and Sixth.

Alta California San Francisco, Monday, January 28, 1867.
[Interred at Cypress Lawn Cemetery, Colma - Laurel Hill Mound; Henry Fillabrown will be remembered as the first man to enlist in the California Hundred.]

1869

Local Matters.

Floral Tribute to the Patriot Dead-The Ceremonies Yesterday.

The second annual floral decoration of the graves of those who sacrificed life in the struggle to preserve the nation's honor untarnished, by the Grand Army of the Republic, occurred yesterday. About 12:40 o'clock, 300 members of the G.A.R. were drawn up in line on Market street, opposite their headquarters, each member bearing a bouquet or wreath. At the head of the line were borne three battle flags, viz; the flag of the California Hundred and Battalion, that of the Second Infantry California Volunteers, and the headquarters flag of Gen. John F. Miller. Shortly after 1 o'clock the National Guard, under the command of Lieut. Vaughn, accompanied by the band of the Twenty-first U.S. Infantry, marched down the street and took their place at the head of the line. The procession then started on its way to the cemetery, the sidewalks of the streets through which it passed being densely crowded with spectators. As the veterans passed along Bush street bouquets, wreaths and baskets of flowers were frequently presented to them. Little girls came tripping out from gardens with their aprons full of nosegays, and in many instances appeared fully conscious of the sacred cause they were assisting.

Upon arriving at the cemetery the escort halted, and the Grand Army and citizens proceeded to the grave of Gen. E.D. Baker. The Grand Marshal, Maj. Z.B. Adams, read the order of Gen. Logan designating the observance of the day, and alluded, in a few brief remarks, to the solemn duties of the occasion. Rev. A.L. Stone, Grand Chaplain of the Order, then delivered an eloquent and impressive prayer, during which every head was uncovered and every heart seemed touched. The band played a solemn dirge, after which the Grand Marshal introduced Col. Olney, who delivered a speech.

Evening Bulletin, San Francisco, Monday, May 31, 1869.
[Laurel Hill Cemetery was vacated and in May of 1940. Col. Baker and his wife were reinterred in the Officer's section of the National Cemetery, Presidio of San Francisco.]

❖❖

Company A

HILL-In this city, December 1st, of consumption, John A. Hill, aged 37 years, who served during the late war in the "California Hundred."
  The funeral will take place to-day at 1:30 P.M., from the Powell street M.E. Church. Comrades of the G. A. R. and friends of the deceased are respectfully requested to attend.

The Chronicle, San Francisco, December 2, 1869.
[Interred at the National Cemetery, Presidio of San Francisco]

❖❖

1874
❖❖

CALIFORNIA HUNDRED.

Annual Reunion of the Members of this Veterans Organization.

On Tuesday evening the veteran California Hundred Battalion held their annual reunion at G.A.R. Hall, New Montgomery street, it being the eighth anniversary of their organization as a society, and also the commemoration of the Battle of Appomattox (Lee's surrender), in which the veterans participated as a portion of Sheridan's Cavalry. There were present a large number of the society with their wives and lady friends. Letters were read from distant comrades, and the President announced the death of a comrade, Charles H. Powers, California Hundred, who was killed at Antelope Station, U.P.R.R. The following resolutions were adopted by the society.
  Whereas, in the Providence of God our late comrade and friend, Serg't. Chas. H. Powers, of "A" Company (California Hundred), has been summoned hence to answer to the great and final roll call of mankind; therefore be it
  Resolved, That in his sudden death we recognize the loss of one who was an honorable man, a warm and genial friend, and a true soldier - one that has stood beside us on so many trying occasions in the dark days of our country's trials.
  Resolved, That it is with sorrow we learn that our late comrade has passed away, and that we deeply sympathise with his bereaved mother and relatives.
  Resolved, That so far as it is possible, we unite as an organization or otherwise, with those who are making suitable arrangements in paying the last sad rites to his memory.

The election of officers followed, with this result: President, Henry Mattox, Company "M"; Vice-President, J.B. McIntosh, Co. "A"; C.P. Kelly, Co. "E"; J. Cassel, Co. "F"; J.F. Tucker, Co. "L"; W.H. Jennings, Co. "M"; Secretary, C. Mason Kinne; Treasurer, D.W.C. Thompson.

An eloquent address was delivered by the President and an original poem was read by the Secretary.

After the transaction of necessary business was completed, the Veterans with their ladies assembled in Sanders' Hall where, after doing full justice to the supply of rations furnished by the Commissary Department, they enjoyed themselves in dancing until one o'clock, when the command was dispersed, and the different detachments ordered to their respective quarters. The reunion was a very pleasant gathering of old comrades, some of whom had not met since the end of the war.

Alta California, San Francisco, Saturday, April 11, 1874.

1879

COLONEL MOSBY.

Arrival of the Famous Guerrilla Chieftain in this City.

Colonel John S. Mosby, the Confederate cavalry commander, who is famous as the great guerrilla chieftain of the rebellion, arrived overland last evening and is stopping at the Palace Hotel. Colonel Mosby was recently appointed by the President, Consul at Hongkong, for which place he departs by the City of Peking on Saturday. Colonel Mosby is anything but the great, muscular, ferocious looking man which the popular imagination supposes the guerrilla chief to be. He is below the average height, is of slim build, with small, clear cut features, and close-cropped, light brown hair sprinkled with gray. Colonel Mosby's appearance is that of a man of great nerve and determination. Colonel Mosby admits that he has been given no instructions by the authorities at Washington in relation to the Chinese question which would be of interest to the people of this coast. His views on the national political outlook may be briefly summed in two things which he regards as inevitable; Grant's nomination as the Republican candidate and his election. Colonel Mosby says that the South will not be near so "solid" against Grant as people generally think, and he sustains the conviction that Grant will carry two or three of the Southern States.

The Daily Evening Post, San Francisco, Thursday, January 2, 1879.

MILITARY ITEMS.

Col. C. Mason Kinne, Major Z.B. Adams, Major S.W. Backus, Lieut. C.P. Kelly, Lieut. George W. Towle, Lieut, Robinson, Lieut. Mortimer - all of the California Hundred and Battalion - called on Col. Mosby, at the Palace Hotel, yesterday. Having fought on opposite sides during the war, and being pitted against each other for some two years, the reminiscences were very interesting.

Alta California, San Francisco, Saturday, January 4, 1879

1883

Company L
Death of A Well Known Citizen

    The death of **Benjamin Wate Case Brown**, a well and favorably known citizen of Santa Barbara was announced this morning. He died after a long and painful sickness and might be said to have gradually passed away. The deceased was a native of Rhode Island and at the time of his death was forty-eight years of age and a marinero by avocation. He came to Santa Barbara about sixteen years ago since which time he has made this his home. He was a man of sanguine, impulsive temperament, brave as a lion, generous to a fault and positive in character. His devotion to his country was exceeded by none. When the cannonading at Fort Sumter had scarcely ceased to echo over the waters of Charleston Harbor the name of B.W.C. Brown was enrolled as a volunteer for the Union. He was one of the patriotic one hundred who went first to the "front" from California, the advance guard of those who followed after. Brown was wounded and his constitution some what injured in the war. When he came to Santa Barbara he became an active participant in every public enterprise, and was the organizer of the first fire company in this city. He had hosts of friends and no enemies. His only enemy was himself, he neglected his health. His funeral will take place this afternoon at 2 o'clock to which his friends are invited to pay their last tribute to a brave man and a good citizen.

The Daily Press, Santa Barbara, Monday, July 9, 1883
[Interred at Santa Barbara Cemetery]

1884

Company L
Suisun Items.

    Ben. F. Hoxie, who was sent from here to the Napa Insane Asylum, is not improving any. Poor fellow, he went through unscathed many of the battles of the rebellion, and then returned home to end his days in a mad-house.

The Vacaville Reporter, Saturday, January 5, 1884.
[Hoxie died December 9, 1884 and is interred at the Suisun-Fairfield Cemetery]

THE "CALIFORNIA HUNDRED."

    Be good enough to state how many, if any, returned to this state at the close of the war, and if any are now living in this city, and their name, of the "California Hundred," who went East to participate in the war of the rebellion? C.H.

    [We have been shown the original roll of the "California Hundred," and from it we find that the following-named members of that company returned to this coast since the close of the war, and the remarks will show their whereabouts as near as we can ascertain: Lieutenant

Archibald McKendry, San Jose; Lieutenant John W. Sim, dead; Charles H. Ackerman, Ukiah; Charles E. Allan, Washington Territory; Charles E. Benjamin, San Francisco; Charles P. Briggs, Napa City; Ed. B. Campbell, Prescot, Arizona; Samuel J. Corbett, San Francisco; H.H. Fillebrown, dead; John Fletcher, Antioch; Byron D. Gibbs, Pacheco; John A. Hill, dead; George I. Holt, Santa Cruz; W.H.H. Hussey, San Francisco; George M. Johnson, Washington Territory; C. Mason Kinne, San Francisco; Abraham Loane, San Francisco; Jonathan Merriam, San Francisco; Isaac R. McIntosh, San Francisco; Fred J. Quant, Antioch; William A. Robinson, San Francisco; E.R. Sterling, Woodland; George W. Towle, San Rafael; E.W. Woodward, San Francisco; James Watson, San Rafael. We may note in this connection that Robert O'Meara, now confined in San Quentin prison, was never a member of the "famous California Hundred." as he claimed in an interview with the reporter of a contemporary.]

The Morning Call, San Francisco, Sunday, January 6, 1884.

❖❖

1885

❖❖

Company A

Death of Charles Phelps Briggs.

He breathed his last, January 3rd, at 11:15 o'clock. For four weeks he had been confined to his bed from which he was fully conscious he could never arise. Still he was resigned calmly, patiently and heroically bearing his suffering with the spirit of one who had laid hold on the Christian's faith. Deceased was born in Springfield, Mass., in 1825, and came to California, settling in this county, in 1843, when he was but 18 years old. He married the second time, his first wife having died, in 1863. He leaves besides a wife, seven children and nine grand-children. During early times in this county, he served as Deputy Sheriff for nine years. When the Mexican War broke out he entered the army and did gallant service in the ranks for his country. Again when the nation was plunged in the throes of civil strife, he shouldered his musket and fought for peace and his country's honor. It was while enduring the hardships and privations of army life that he contracted a pulmonary disease that finally took on the fatal form of consumption. After the war was over he settled in the East, but in July, 1882, returned to Napa.

He was an honorable and upright man, possessed of many warm and sympathetic qualities that earned him more than the esteem of all who knew him. His funeral took place Monday afternoon at 2 o'clock, from the Presbyterian Church, Rev. Richard Wylie officiating. The following gentlemen acted as pall bearers: Messrs. G.M. Francis, W.A. Smith, Phillip Plass and D.W. Nelson of Napa; A.B. Stuartvat and James Lawson of St. Helena; J.D. Flynn of Yountville, and John Whitney from the Veterans Home. A number of ex-soldiers and veterans from up the valley were present at the funeral. At the cemetery the Kilpatrick Post, G.A.R., of St. Helena, took charge of the remains and performed their ritual at the grave.

The Napa Reporter, Friday, January 9, 1885
The Napa Register, Napa, Friday, January 9, 1885.
[Interred at Tulocay Cemetery, Napa]

Company K

COBB-Near this city, February 25th, Charles S. Cobb, beloved husband of Isabel M. Cobb, a native of Massachusetts, aged 43 years.

(The funeral will take place on Friday next, February 27th, at 2 P.M., from the family residence, Clowse lane, near this city. Friends and acquaintenances are invited to attend.)

The Stockton Evening Mail, Stockton, February 25, 1885.
[Interred at Stockton Rural Cemetery]

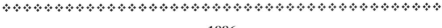

Company A

Col. McKendry's Death.

The Santa Cruz *Sentinel* says: "Col. Archibald McKendry of San Jose died at Camp Alhambra Monday evening at 10 o'clock. He was a resident of San Jose, and came to Camp Alhambra a few weeks ago for the benefit of his health. Before his death he requested that an autopsy be made to ascertain the character of his trouble, as there had been conflicting opinions among his medical advisers in regard to his disease. On Tuesday morning Drs. Fagen, Bailey and Morgan made the autopsy and found the immediate cause of death to be perforation of the bowels and extravisation of their contents in the cavity from cancer of the stomach and consequent ulceration. Col. McKendry was a pioneer of this State, and left this State during the war as one of the officers of the "California Hundred."

Daily Mercury, San Jose, June 11, 1885.
[Interred at Oak Hill Memorial Park, San Jose]

1886

The California Hundred.-What is known as the California Hundred and Battalion will meet at the Occidental Hotel at 7:30 Sunday evening next, to greet 25 or 30 Eastern comrades. There will probably be a total of about 50 to sit down to an elaborate dinner which is a part of the programme. The original "California Hundred" was commanded by Capt. Reed, who was killed at Drainsville. His widow is now here as a member of the Women's Relief Corps from Massachusetts.

Evening Bulletin, San Francisco, Friday, August 6, 1886

1890

Company L

MAJOR Z. B. ADAMS DEAD

Close of the Career of an Active War Veteran..

Major Zabdiel Boylston Adams died at his residence, 1309 1/2 Golden Gate avenue, last evening after an illness of several months. Major Adams was well known in the community, having lived in California since April, 1853. He was born in Massachusetts September 9, 1834. He had a record of many years in the National Guard of California, having enlisted September 15, 1856. He was promoted to the position of corporal in 1857, sergeant in 1858, lieutenant in 1859 and was captain of the "Nationals," now C Company, in 1862.

Early in 1863 he raised a company of California Cavalry Battalion in this city and was mustered as Captain of Company L, Second Massachusetts Cavalry, March 19, 1863, and served with that regiment till he was promoted to the rank of Major of the Fifth Massachusetts Cavalry on March 2, 1864. He was severely wounded in the battle of Baylor's Farm, near Petersburg, Va., June 15, 1864, and the bullet he there received in his lung was the ultimate cause of his death and will be buried with him on Wednesday next. After a tedious illness he recovered and rejoined his regiment in September, 1864, and was in the Texas expedition after Kirbey Smith and was mustered out October 31, 1865.

Major Adams was one of the first to join in organizing the Grand Army on this coast, in 1867, and was a charter member of Post No. 1. He was post commander three times, and a member of Thomas Post at the time of his death, as well as a companion of the California Commandery of the Military Order of the Loyal Legion since January, 1878.

In his civil and military life Major Adams was always earnest and active, quick to think and to act, and had many warm friends.

His funeral will take place under the auspices of George H. Thomas Post, at 320 Post street, on Wednesday next at 2 P.M.

The Chronicle, San Francisco, Sunday, August 10, 1890.
[Interred at the National Cemetery, Presidio of San Francisco]

Company E

McEWEN - In this city, December 12, of congestion of the brain and heart failure, W.L. McEwen, a native of New York, aged 52 years. [Sacramento (Cal.) and Rochester (N.Y.) papers please copy.]

The Chronicle, San Francisco, Saturday, December 13, 1890.
The Oakland Tribune, Oakland, Saturday, December 13, 1890.
[Interred at the Mountain View Cemetery, Oakland]

❖❖❖

1891

❖❖❖

Company A

GEO. I. HOLT.

Death of a Member of the One Hundred Regiment.

Geo. I. Holt, a well known citizen of Santa Cruz, died yesterday at his home in this city.

He was born January 3, 1831, in Melrose Massachusetts. Came to San Francisco in 1854. He spent several years in the mines. He was a member of the first California One Hundred Regiment that left San Francisco in 1862, under the command of Capt. Reed, for the war of the Rebellion. He served through the war without receiving a wound. The following is a copy of his honorable discharge from service:

GENERAL HEADQUARTERS,
STATE OF CALIFORNIA,
ADJUTANTS GENERAL'S OFFICE.
Sacramento, January 25, 1885.

To all whom it may concern: This is to certify that George I. Holt, private of Captain J.S. Reed's Company California Hundred Regiment of California Volunteers, who was duly mustered into the service on the 25th day of November, A.D. 1862, to serve three years, was honorably discharged from the service of the United States on the 10th day of June, A.D. 1865, at Annapolis Junction, Md., by reason of expiration of term of service as appears on record in this office.

Witness my hand and seal of my office, the day and year first above written.

(SEAL.)   GEO. B. COSBY,
           Adjutant-General California.

Official: J.J. Tobin,
           Assistant Adjutant-General California.

He came to San Francisco twenty-three years ago in company with Otis A. Longley, where he has lived ever since.

He was a prominent member of Branciforte Lodge, No. 96, I.O.O.F., which he had joined within six months after coming to Santa Cruz. About a year ago the lodge presented him with a handsome watch and a lot in the cemetery. He was also a member of the Wallace Post, G. A. R.

The funeral services will be conducted Sunday at 2 P.M. by the I.O.O.F. and G. A.. R. Post.

Santa Cruz Daily Surf, Santa Cruz, January 31, 1891.
[Interred at Santa Cruz Memorial Park, Santa Cruz]

❖❖❖

The funeral of the late Geo. I. Holt Sunday afternoon was largely attended, the I.O.O.F. and G.A.R. turning out strong. The remains were interred in the I.O.O.F. Cemetery. Among the floral pieces was one from survivors of the California Hundred. Before the casket was lowered Abram Loane, of San Francisco, who fought side by side with the old veteran, took his Grand Army badge from his coat and placed it on the casket as a tribute from a comrade.

California Hundred.
A Talk With Colonel Kinne Who Was Their Captain
Col. C. Mason Kinne and Abram Loane came down from San Francisco Sunday to attend the funeral of their late comrade, Geo. I. Holt. Mr. Loane was captured by the Confederates in Virginia and was ten months in Andersonville. Colonel Kinne went from California as a private with the Hundred, and when the war closed was adjutant of the Second Massachusetts Cavalry Brigade. ....Speaking of Geo. I. Holt, Colonel Kinne said: "There might have been more brilliant fighters, but none better or braver. In Virginia his company was ordered out on a scouting expedition, but through some oversight George, who was on picket duty, was forgotten, and when the company returned two days later he was found still on duty.".........

Santa Cruz Sentinel, Tuesday, February 3, 1891.

California "100."
Among the many enjoyable features of the Grand Army gathering this week, we are glad to note a little social reunion of a few survivors of the well known California Hundred. Comrade McNeil, the infant of Company A, Second Massachusetts Cavalry noticed that there was at least five of them left and arranged a quiet dinner on Thursday evening at the Sea Beach Hotel, at which were present the following comrades, and very properly and fortunately each had their own wife with them at the table, which was beautifully decorated with profuse floral gatherings from our Santa Cruz gardens:
W.H. McNeil escorted Mrs. C. Mason Kinne, W.H. Hussey walked in with Mrs. E.W. Woodward, Mrs. Hussey took the arm of W.A. Robinson, E.W. Woodward followed with Mrs. Robinson and Col. C. Mason Kinne devoted his attention to Mrs. McNeil. Thus honors were easy and no one complained that an exchange of parties for an hour at the table was anything but conducive to a pleasant interchange of social greetings and the party retired from the dining room with the full intention of meeting in Fresno next year with such additions to their numbers as can be recruited from the few survivors of that well-known body of men who left our State, at their own expense, in 1862 to help fight the battles of the Union.

Santa Cruz Daily Sentinel, Saturday, April 25, 1891.

Company L

BALDWIN-In this city, July 5, Captain Josiah A. Baldwin, a native of Boston, Mass., born December 29, 1827, aged 63 years, 6 months and 6 days.

Friends and acquaintances are respectfully invited to attend the funeral this day (Tuesday) at 1 o'clock, from the family residence, 722 1/2 Capp street. Interment, Laurel Hill Cemetery.

The Chronicle, San Francisco, Tuesday, July 7, 1891.
[Reinterred at Cypress Lawn Cemetery - Laurel Hill Mound]

❖❖
Company A

DR. SAMUEL J. CORBETT.
Dr. Samuel J. Corbett died unexpectedly of heart disease about 1 o'clock yesterday morning at his residence, 402 O'Farrell street. He had been out spending the evening with his wife at the house of a friend, and when he retired at 11 o'clock seemed in good health and spirits.

The deceased was a well known physician in this city, having been in practice for many years. He was also a prominent member of the G.A.R., having been one of the "California Hundred," which left this State early in the war to join a company of the Second Massachusetts Cavalry. He served through the campaign of the Army of the Potomac and Shenandoah.

Dr. Corbett was born at Rome, N.Y., in 1836. The funeral will be under the direction of the Grand Army.

The Chronicle, San Francisco, Thursday, November 12, 1891
The Morning Call, San Francisco, Friday, November 13, 1891.
[Interred at the National Cemetery, Presidio of San Francisco]

❖❖
Company F

Death of a Veteran.

An aged veteran named **J. A. Read** died at the Yountville Home on Saturday. Deceased formerly lived at Hollister in this State. He enlisted April 22nd, 1863, and served in the 2nd Mass. Cavalry over 2 years. His death was the result of gradual decay of the physical powers, he being 84 years old. The funeral took place at the Home Sunday afternoon.

The Napa Register, Napa, Friday, December 25, 1891.
[Interred at the Veteran's Cemetery, Yountville]

1893

Company F

COLEMAN-In this city, August 5, James M. Coleman, a native of Massachusetts, aged 46 years.

The Chronicle, San Francisco, August 8, 1893.
[Interred at the National Cemetery, Presidio of San Francisco]

1894

CAPTAIN W. H. H. HUSSEY.
An Honorable Record Won in the Defense of His Country.
CAPTAIN W.H.H. Hussey of Oakland has been an active member of the Grand Army of the Republic for a quarter of a century, having been mustered into Lincoln Post of San Francisco in 1869 and transferred to Lyon Post No. 8 in 1875, of which post he is a past commander. His record as a veteran of the war of the rebellion is one of which he can justly feel proud, as several of his comrades who served with him will testify to his bravery on many hotly contested battle fields.

Captain Hussey enlisted as a private of the California Hundred in the fall of 1862, which company went East and joined the Second Regiment of Massachusetts Volunteer Cavalry, commanded by the late General C.R. Lowell. Early in the spring of 1863 four more companies, under command of Major D.W.C. Thompson, joined the regiment in Virginia, making five companies of California troops in the regiment.

The service of the organization was most trying for the first year, being opposed by the dashing Colonel John Mosby with his splendidly mounted command, ever ready to take advantage of a midnight dash. It was in one of those hand to hand engagements at night that many of the regiment were killed or taken prisoners, among whom was the late Captain J. Sewell Reed, who recruited the California Hundred in San Francisco and who was shot through the head at Dranesville, Va.

Captain Hussey was one of the squad of eight men who captured the guerilla chief, Captain Allen, and two of his band near Gloucester Point, Va., and, later with a detachment of the command took part in the capture of General W.H. Lee, a nephew of General R.E. Lee, near South Ana Bridge, Va. These two noted officers, Lee and Allen, were held for a time as hostages for Captains Sawyer and Flynn, who were confined in Libby Prison and who were subsequently exchanged.

The regiment did hard fighting in the Shenandoah valley in 1864 under Sheridan. It was in that campaign that Alameda county lost one of her best citizens, Captain Charles S. Eigenbrodt, who was killed while leading his command in a cavalry charge near Charlestown, Va., and his remains were carried off the field by Captain Hussey and others who were near him when he fell. Captain Eigenbrodt will be remembered by the early citizens of Washington township as a genial, warm-hearted man, ever ready to respond to the call for aid from his fellow men. He gave $1000 to the lodge of I.O.O.F. at Alvarado for a library and when he bade his friends and neighbors good bye to go to the war there was general expression of regret. As a daring leader Captain Eigenbrodt had no superior.

Captain Hussey took part in the battles of Opequon Creek, Winchester, Fisher's Hill, Woodstock, Waynesboro and Cedar Creek. At Waynesboro his horse was shot under him. At Cedar Creek October 10, 1864, he was wounded by a minie ball while leading his company. He served eighteen months as an enlisted man and holds three commissions-second and first lieutenant and captain. He was mustered out of service July 20, 1865. Since his return to civil life he has been engaged in various occupations. For one term he served Alameda county most acceptably as sheriff.

Oakland Enquirer, Monday, April 23, 1894
[Interred at the National Cemetery, Presidio of San Francisco]

"ONE HUNDRED."

California's First Contribution to the Eastern Army.

The "California One Hundred" was enlisted in October and November, 1862, and in December was sent East by water. At Readville, Mass., they were drilled and supplied with horses, becoming a part of the Second Massachusetts Cavalry, in which were also four other companies of Californians who went East three months after the "One Hundred," making a total of 502 men. In nearly all of the cavalry engagements of the Eastern army, after its muster in, the Second Massachusetts bore an active and honorable part. Out of the 502 men enlisted in the five companies only 182 remained to be mustered out at the close of the war, thus showing the havoc three years of valiant service had wrought in their ranks.

Of the men who belonged to the One Hundred, here were the following named living in Oakland in August, 1890: Captain W.H.H. Hussey, Charles Roberts, D.W.C. Thompson, S.F. Tucker and Major E.E. Woodward.

Oakland Enquirer, Monday, April 23, 1894.

Company A
Major E. W. Woodward.

One of the most celebrated companies organized in this State for active service during the civil war was the "California Hundred." Among the first to enlist in this company was E.W. Woodward, now a resident of this city, where he is engaged in the real estate business. As soon as its organization was completed the "California Hundred" was transported to Massachusetts, where it was attached as Company A to the Second Massachusetts Cavalry, under Colonel Lowell, who was subsequently killed at Cedar Creek. The Second Massachusetts participated in all the campaigns under Sheridan in the Shenandoah valley.

For conspicuous bravery on the field of battle Mr. Woodward was recommended for promotion, and was commissioned as second lieutenant in the Twenty-fifth New York Cavalry. He served in the field for three years, participated in twenty battles, for a portion of the time under the command of General Custer, and at the close of the war, having attained the rank of major, was honorably discharged, July 7, 1865. Major Woodward is a prominent member if the Grand Army, and is not a little proud of having been one of the celebrated "California Hundred."

The corps served under Generals Halleck, Hooker, Meade and Sheridan; also in the Fourth Corps under General Keyes and General Warren of the Fifth, Wright of the Sixth, Hunter and Crook of the Eighth, Slocum of the Twelfth, Emory of the Nineteenth, Heinzelman and Auger of the Twenty-second, and Ord of the Twenty-fourth. At other times it was attached to the commands of Stoneman, Pleasanton, Torbet, Averill, Devens, Gibbs and Lowell.

Evening Tribune, Oakland, Tuesday, April 24, 1894.

❖❖❖
Company E

The funeral of **Stephen Esten** took place yesterday afternoon from Wessendorf & Staffler's undertaking parlors in the Y.M.C.A. building under the auspices of W.H.L. Wallace Post, G.A.R. of which he was a member. Mr. Esten was formerly of Boulder Creek but has been in a hospital at San Francisco, where he died of paralysis. His remains were brought to this city yesterday. The services were conducted by the G.A.R. and the deceased was interred in the G.A.R. plot at Evergreen cemetery. This is the third member of that post who has died within a month.

Santa Cruz Daily Sentinel, Wednesday, June 6, 1894.
Santa Cruz Surf, Wednesday, June 6, 1894.
[Interred at Evergreen Cemetery, Santa Cruz, California]

❖❖❖

1896
❖❖❖
Company F

ROBERTS - In Oakland, March 2, Charles Roberts, a native of Ohio, aged 55 years, 8 months and 24 days. (New York city papers please copy). Funeral services and interment strictly private.

The Chronicle, San Francisco, Tuesday, March 3, 1896.
The Bulletin, San Francisco, Tuesday, March 3, 1896
[Interred at Mountain View Cemetery, Oakland]

❖❖❖

1897
❖❖❖
Regimental Staff

General Caspar Crowninshield.

General Caspar Crowninshield died yesterday at his residence at 109 Commonwealth avenue *[Boston]* after a lingering illness. He was fifty-nine years old, and was a graduate of Harvard College in the class of 1860. He rowed bow oar in the varsity crew of that year, and was regarded as one of the crack oarsmen of his day. On July 10, 1861, he entered the Twentieth Massachusetts Infantry as captain, but changed to the cavalry branch of the service on Nov.

25 of the same year, when he became a captain of the First Massachusetts Cavalry, of which General Williams was then colonel and General Horace Binney Sargent lieutenant colonel. Captain Crowninshield became major of the Second Massachusetts Cavalry on Jan. 30, 1863, lieutenant colonel on March 1, 1864, and succeeded Colonel Charles Russell Lowell as commander of the regiment on Oct. 21, of the same year, after the latter's death at Cedar Creek. On March 13, 1865, Colonel Crowninshield was brevetted brigadier general "for gallant and meritorious services during the war," and on June 16 he resigned from the army.

His immediate family consists of two daughters, Mrs. George B. Peabody and Mrs. David N. Coolidge, Jr., and two sisters, Mrs. John Q. Adams and Mrs. Boyden.

The funeral service will be held at his residence, 109 Commonwealth avenue, tomorrow at noon. Among the delegations who will attend is the following from the Loyal Legion, of which General Crowninshield was a member: General Henry S. Russell, General Robert H. Stevenson, General Charles L. Pierson and Colonel William H. Forbes.

Evening Transcript, Boston, Monday, January 11, 1897
[Interred at Sears Memorial Chapel, Longwood, Boston, Massachusetts]

LOYAL LEGION IN MOURNING.

From his home at 109 Commonwealth avenue, the funeral of General Caspar Crowninshield took place at noon, today, the attendance of friends being large. The services, which were marked by the utmost simplicity, were conducted by Bishop Lawrence. There was no singing and there were no pall-bearers. The body was placed in the tomb at the Sears Memorial Chapel, Longwood.

Evening Transcript, Boston, Monday, January 11, 1897
Evening Transcript, Boston, Tuesday, January 12, 1897

Regimental

WILLIAM HATHAWAY FORBES.
Well-Known Resident of Milton Passes
Away at His Summer Home.

News was received in Boston last night of the death of Colonel William H. Forbes of Milton, at his summer home on Naushon Island, Buzzards Bay. Colonel Forbes had been ill for some time, and early in the season went to his home on Adams street, Milton. Colonel Forbes's death will be keenly felt in Milton, where he was one of the best-known residents, and is regretted by his many social and business associates in Boston. The remains will be brought to Milton for burial and services will probably be held at his late residence on Milton Hill.

William Hathaway Forbes was born on Nov. 1, 1840. He was the son of J. M. Forbes and a brother of J. Malcolm Forbes. He was fitted for college by E. S. Dixwell and H. L. Patten, and entered Harvard as a classmate of Oliver Wendell Holmes of the Supreme Court; J. K. Stone, the Catholic clergyman; C. C. Beaman, the law partner of William M. Evarts; Colonel N. P. Hallowell of the National Bank of Commerce; F. W. Haskell the Washington lawyer; W. P. Garrison son of W. L. Garrison; Lewis S. Dabney, the noted Boston lawyer; R. F. Bowditch, now professor in the medical school at Harvard; F. P. Gould of the Baptist Theological School at Newton; T. R. Robeson and John Ritchie.

Leaving college during the first junior term, he went into business in Boston in 1861. On Dec. 26, 1861, he was commissioned second lieutenant company E, First Massachusetts Cavalry, and served in South Carolina until July, 1862, afterwards going with the Army of the Potomac. He was promoted to first lieutenant Aug. 16, 1862, and on Jan. 1, 1863, to captain. He was made major of the Third Battalion, Second Massachusetts Cavalry, June 20, 1863. Having been taken by a party under Mosby, at Aldie, Va., July 6, 1864, he was held as a prisoner of war until Dec. 10 of that year, but was commissioned lieutenant colonel of his regiment on Oct. 28. He was honorably discharged May 15, 1865.

Mr. Forbes married Miss Edith Emerson, daughter of Ralph Waldo Emerson, the poet, Oct. 3, 1865, and was engaged in active business in Boston until 1887, for a number of years being with John M. Forbes & Co. He received the A. B. degree by vote of the corporation of Harvard College in 1872, and spent the spring and summer of that year in Europe. In 1887 Mr. Forbes resigned the presidency of the Bell Telephone Company, which he had held for eight years or more, remaining as a director. He was also a director in several other companies. He took an active interest in Milton Academy, and for many years was a member of its board of trustees. He was a member of several Boston clubs and took an active interest in yachting and outdoor sports. He was the owner of Meddler, one of the most famous stallions ever imported, and of the Duke of Magenta, another imported thoroughbred. He had several breeding farms in Milton, and kept two Arabian stallions, being interested in the development of this breed.

Colonel Forbes had eight children, Ralph Emerson, Edith, William Cameron, John Murray, Edward Waldo, Waldo Emerson, Ellen Randolph and Alexander. John Murray Forbes died on 1888, aged seventeen, and Ellen Randolph died in infancy.

In college Mr. Forbes was the chum of Colonel N. P. Hallowell, and although they were not in the same regiment in the war, they were ever close friends and companions. Colonel Hallowell says that one of the principal characteristics of Mr. Forbes was a broad-minded and generous nature. He was ever ready at college to help those who were struggling and on more than one occasion he sent home for money to assist young men in college who were deserving of aid. All through life this generosity was one of Mr. Forbes's most marked traits. He gave through the organized charities, and preferred to keep from his left hand the knowledge of what his right was doing. But he was never happier than when doing a generous act in behalf of some unfortunate who had appealed to him, and whose case he had investigated personally.

In other affairs of life he showed the same broad spirit, dealing liberally in business matters and taking broad ground upon public questions.

Evening Transcript, Boston, Tuesday, October 12, 1897

❖❖

1898

❖❖

Company L

Iowa Hill

Reported expressly for the Republican

Mr. **Jared S. Sparhawk** died at his home here on the 12th inst. of pneumonia. Deceased was only sick a short time. He was a California pioneer aged about 77 years. He served in the late war and lost three fingers in battle. He leaves a widow, two daughters and one son, all married, and residents of Iowa Hill, who have the sincere sympathy of the community.

Placer County Republican, Friday April 15, 1898
The Placer Herald, Auburn, Saturday, April 16, 1898

MOSBY'S COMMAND.
The Noted Confederate Raider will Lead a Company of Cavalry.
Colonel John S. Mosby, the famous Confederate raider of the Civil War, may yet have an opportunity to show his devotion to the stars and stripes. The man who telegraphed General Miles some months ago that "he had no influence but only a military record" when told to get the assistance of the Senators from his State when he volunteered his services at the outbreak of the war, is determined to show that he is still capable of leading a charge. As captain of the Light Cavalry Troop that is daily drilling in Kohler's Hall in Oakland, the old soldier is instilling the same vim that he showed when at the head of his "Raiders."

It is the intention of the company to recruit to the limit and present its services to the Government fully equipped and ready to proceed to the front. In this the members have the support of leading citizens of Oakland and this city. The company is composed of men who are expert with the rifle and on horseback, and many have had experience as cavalry men in Uncle Sam's service.

The men who are learning the first rudiments of cavalry drill are members of the best families in the Athenian City. Colonel Mosby's first lieutenant is Paul S. Luttrell, a son of the ex-Congressman. W.J. Tormey, the second lieutenant, has been in the cavalry service five years, during which time he has been in two engagements. At Wounded Knee he suffered a wound, and in another outbreak he was struck again.

Under the able drilling of their officers the men are being rapidly "licked" into shape and will soon be able to offer their services. They appreciate the fact that so far the cavalry has not been called into the field, but they hope to be chosen, as they will be able to offer a fully equipped company.

The Call, San Francisco, Friday, June 24, 1898

MOSBY'S HUSSARS.

Entertainment for the Benefit of the Equipment Fund and the Red Cross.
The military concert and ball to-morrow evening in Golden Gate Hall, 625 Sutter street, for the benefit of the equipment fund and the Red Cross Society, promises to be quite an attractive event. It will be given under the auspices of Troops A and B of Mosby's Hussars, who will march from the corner of Van Ness and Golden Gate avenues to the hall. Among the invited guests are Governor Budd, Mayor Phelan, Major General Otis, Colonel Sullivan and the executive committee of the Red Cross Society. The principal address of the evening will be delivered by Colonel John S. Mosby.

The committee of arrangements is composed of Captain E.A. Lorenzo, Lieutenant Milton Truett, Lieutenant W. Cottrell, Captain E.T. Furman, Lieutenant J.D. Graham, Lieutenant Lake, Corporal Fraja, Sergeant Brown, Sergeant Meyer, Corporal Russell and Privates A. Oberman, Fred O'Toole and F.L. Porfette.

All members of the Hussars are requested to meet at the armory, Tenth and Market streets, at 8 o'clock this morning to take part in to-days parade.

The Call, San Francisco, Monday, July 4, 1898

❖❖

1901

❖❖

Company E

SHELDON-In this city, May 29, Adelbert S. Sheldon, beloved husband of Mina Sheldon, a native of New York, aged 56 years, 7 months and 26 days.

The Chronicle, San Francisco, Thursday, May 30, 1901.
[Interred at the National Cemetery, Presidio of San Francisco]

❖❖

1902

❖❖

Company L

BEEBE-In this city, November 18, at the City and County Almshouse, Samuel J. Beebe, a native of Ohio, aged 67 years.

The Chronicle, San Francisco, Thursday, November 20, 1902
[Interred at the National Cemetery, Presidio of San Francisco]

❖❖

1903

❖❖

Company A

In Shelby Jan. 3, 1903, **Josephus Blake** aged 67 years. He was born in North Bangor, VT., removing with his parents in childhood to N.Y. State. While yet a young man he came to Michigan going onto Minnesota, and went from there with an invalid brother on a perilous journey to California with oxen and wagon, reaching their destination after many months of travel and great dangers. He afterwards went to South America, returning to California were he enlisted, but was credited to Massachusetts entering Co. A, 2nd regiment, Massachusetts cavalry, he was discharged Sept. 2, 1863. He was married first to Mary J. Merrill, and, came to Michigan making their home in Richland, where they lived until 1889 when they came to Shelby, where his wife died Jan. 1893; four children were born to them, two of whom died in infancy. The remaining two, Mrs. Luna Hale and Roy W. Blake are residents of Shelby. He married Mrs. Sarah Curtiss, Jan. 29, 1894 who with his children now mourn his loss. His health has never been good since he was in the army as the result of measles contracted while in the service. For several years he has often had severe attacks of illness which finally resulted in his death. He was a member of Shields Post No. 68 G.A.R., and his funeral service was conducted by them, the G.A.R. ladies society attending in a body. The funeral was held at the M.E. church Monday, the sermon being preached by Rev. J.W.H. Carlisle.

Oceana Herald, Shelby, Michigan, Saturday, January 3, 1903
[Interred at Mt. Hope Cemetery, Shelby, Michigan]

Company M

WILBURN - In this city, February 17, **James P. Wilburn**, beloved father of Mrs. H.B. Jerolaman, James S. and Frederick C. Wilburn, a native of Tennessee, aged 65 years, 11 months and 23 days. A member of John A. Dix Post, G.A.R., of San Jose.

　　　　Friends and acquaintances are respectfully invited to attend the funeral Friday, February 20, at 2 o'clock, from the funeral parlors of the H.F. Mass Company, 917 Mission street. Interment, National Cemetery, Presidio.

The Chronicle, San Francisco, Thursday, February 18, 1903.
[Interred at the National Cemetery, Presidio of San Francisco]

Company M

SOLDIERS' HOME.
FOUND DEAD IN STREET

Soldiers' Home. March 5. - The body of **Milo G. Ford** was found Wednesday evening near the "stump" in the vicinity of which the Southern Pacific home spur branched from the Santa Monica line. The body was lying in the road. It was removed to the Home, where an inquest was conducted by the Coroner this morning. A verdict of death by "senility" and "exposure" was returned. Ford was 75, and single. He served during the Civil War in the famous "California Hundred," which enlisted in this State, and was, upon its arrival in the East, merged in the Second Massachusetts Cavalry, which did service in the Army of the Potomac.

Los Angeles Daily Times, Friday, March 3, 1903
[Interred at the National Cemetery, Los Angeles]

THESE CAVALRYMEN WON LASTING FAME

California Hundred and Battalion Got to Front by Ruse and Fought Like Demons.

　　　　These organizations were raised under the following circumstances: There were a large number of young men in the State who desired to go East and enter the Army, and when it was found that the California volunteers were being kept on this Coast a proposition was made to the State of Massachusetts to raise a company here, take it East and credit it to the quota of the State, if the expenses of its organization and transportation were guaranteed. Massachusetts was paying large bounties for volunteers. This bounty, it was decided, should be paid into the company fund and used for the purpose of paying the expenses of the company.

On October 27, 1862, Captain J. Sewell Reed, received the necessary authority from Governor Andrews of Massachusetts, and on the following day recruiting commenced. Assembly Hall, located at the northwest corner of Kearny and Post streets, San Francisco, was made headquarters, and a man named H.H. Fillebrown was the first enrolled, on October 28, 1862. In three weeks over 500 men had offered themselves for enrollment. Just 100 were selected, and they were mustered into the United States service by Lieutenant-Colonel George H. Ringgold, U.S.A., at Platt's Hall December 10, 1862, and on December 11th sailed on the steamer Golden Age for the East.

The company went to Readville, near Boston, Mass., where it arrived January 4, 1863. The company was made Company A of the Second Massachusetts Cavalry, then consisting of a battalion of four companies. The Californians were soon mounted and sent to the front, arriving at Yorktown, Va., in February, 1863. The battalion was under command of Major Casper Crowninshield. After its arrival at Yorktown it performed picket and scouting duty, and had its first battle at South Anna Bridge, where seventy Californians and twenty Massachusetts men captured twenty-three of the Forty-fourth North Carolina Infantry in a dismounted charge upon their earthworks. In the fight the company lost Joseph B. Burdick, killed, and two seriously wounded.

The success attending the raising of the "California Hundred" and the large number presenting themselves for enlistment induced others to offer to raise four more companies under the same conditions. After considerable negotiations with the authorities in Washington and Massachusetts permission was received by Major D.W.C. Thompson to raise a battalion of four companies which were rapidly recruited. Upon the arrival of these companies at Readville they were also attached to the Second Massachusetts Cavalry and became Companies E, F, L and M of that regiment. The battalion, however, was soon moved to Washington, D.C., and attached to the Twenty-second Army Corps, then comprising the forces in that department. Its first duty was to stand picket at the outposts and to scout in front of the forts defending the national capital.

The Californians of this battalion had gone East in the hope of seeing active service, and never were men's hopes more completely fulfilled. The companies were sent along the Potomac to look out for the anticipated movement of Lee's forces into Maryland. The battalion cut across the river and made quick time through Virginia in pursuit of Mosby's guerrillas. The enemy escaped, but the Californians got much valuable experience. Joining the Army of the Potomac, under General Hooker, the battalion moved toward Gettysburg. It was detached and sent in pursuit of Stuart's Cavalry, which it caused much embarrassment. Being part of the forces sent on a reconnoissance of Virginia, the four companies, exclusively, fought a sharp engagement at Ashby's Gap on July 12th with a detachment of Confederates strongly intrenched, which resulted in driving the rebels from the gap and up the valley and enabling the command to accomplish the purposes of the reconnoissance. In this engagement Lieutenant John C. Norcross and several men were captured and hurried off, having gallantly charged through the enemy's ranks. Privates Walter S. Barnes and Heny P. Irving were killed in the gap and many of the battalion wounded. Many Confederate prisoners were taken.

In its first year the battalion was pitted against Mosby's, White's, Imboden's and Gilmore's men; they hunted them in summer and winter, day and night, mounted and dismounted, together and in squads, from the Blue Ridge to the Potomac, on every road and in almost every house in Loudon, Fairfax, Prince William and Fauquier counties. When a fair, square fight could be obtained the Californians were never beaten. If a small scouting party or isolated picket post could be pounced upon, or a detachment ambushed in the woods or going through a pass, the wily enemy were sometimes successful in such operations.

Now the companies were used in scouting the approaches to Washington and found all the fighting and sharp work they could attend to. Then the companies were moved into Maryland, where Union and Confederate forces were active and did good service in defending and rescuing wagon trains going to Harper's Ferry with supplies. A large force of guerrillas was utterly routed and broken up in a running fight at Sugar Loaf mountain. The battalion protected the line of communication until August 9th, when it was moved to Halltown and joined the Army of the Shenandoah under General Sheridan, uniting with the Third Brigade under command of General Merritt.

At daylight on the morning of August 10, 1864, the battalion marched with Sheridan's army up the valley toward Winchester, commencing on that day those brilliant and successful operations and almost daily battles against the enemy, which resulted on the evening of the memorable 19th of October, at Cedar Creek, in the ruin and almost total annihilation of Early's army. At Halltown, on August 26, 1864, Captain Charles S. Eigenbrodt, while gallantly leading his squadron in a charge against the enemy, was shot dead from his horse. Thus was lost to the battalion one of its bravest and best loved officers and to California one of its most patriotic citizens. On the next day and near the same field First Lieutenant Charles E. Meader was killed while fighting hand to hand - "too brave to retreat and too proud to surrender." He was then in command of the "California Hundred;" Captain Rufus W. Smith, formerly commander of the Light Guard of San Francisco, was killed while in command of his squadron at Cedar Creek, trying to check the then successful advance of the enemy.

After the close of the battle of Cedar Creek the battalion was with the advance, following up the defeated enemy, and many of the cannon captured and retaken from the rebels, that made the gallant Custer hug his General for joy, were halted and turned back by the sabres of the Californians.

On February 27th the battalion was in the saddle for one of the hardest marches made during the whole war - from Winchester to Petersburg - about 200 miles, through rain and mud, fighting the enemy all the way and destroying railroads, canals and other property. The command consisted of the first division of cavalry under General Devin, to which the battalion belonged; third division, under General Custer, with a small force of artillery, pontoons, etc., all under General Sheridan. On this march the battalion moved from Winchester up the valley, through Woodstock and Harrisburg, to Staunton and Waynesboro. At the latter place a battle was fought, resulting in the capture of the remnant of Early's army and a large amount of rebel supplies. The march was continued to Charlottesville, where the railroad and enemy's stores were destroyed; then to James river, destroying the canals and bridges over that river down to Goochland; then to the north of Richmond, across the South and North Anna rivers, down to White House Landing. The battalion assisted in charging and taking the railroad bridge across the South Anna with its defenses and cannon. From the White House the march was continued across the peninsula and over the James river in front of Petersburg, where the battalion went into camp on March 26th after one month of constant marching, fighting and skirmishing, destroying railroads, canals and the enemy's property beyond any immediate repair, and overcoming impediments of nature and the enemy seldom offered against the advance of troops.

The battalion marched from in front of Petersburg on March 29th and took part in the brilliant operations that resulted in the surrender of General Lee's army at Appomattox Courthouse on April 9, 1865. It formed a part General Gibb's brigade which attacked the enemy at Dinwiddie Courthouse and force him to retire. The battalion was commended by President Lincoln for its brave work at the fight at Five Forks, where it was the first inside the enemy's works. Here First Lieutenant Munger was killed.

On the morning of the memorable 9th of April, Sheridan's cavalry having formed in line of battle across Lee's line of retreat, the battalion was dismounted and deployed as skirmishers immediately in front of the enemy. When the army of Northern Virginia attempted to advance that morning it found every foot of the way stubbornly contested. For some time this spirited engagement was kept up, the rebels expecting to break through the cavalry and escape. While this was going on the Fifth, Twenty-fourth and part of the Twenty-fifth Corps came up and formed in the rear of the cavalry, which gradually moved to the right flank to allow them to come into action. When their long line of battle advanced, under General Ord, the veterans of the best rebel army, who had fought for four years vainly but too well, saw that their doom was sealed. They stopped firing and slowly fell back around Appomattox Courthouse, the Union troops following and hemming them in on all sides. Soon a white flag, in token of surrender, was presented to Sheridan's cavalry - an honor they well merited - and hostilities ceased. Early in the afternoon the battalion had the pleasure of witnessing the meeting of the General-in-Chief of the armies of the United States and the General-in-Chief of the rebel armies, and soon after the formal surrender of the army of Northern Virginia.

The battalion started to the assistance of Sherman in North Carolina, learned of the surrender of Johnston and returned to Petersburg, remaining there until May 10th, when it marched toward Washington. In the grand review at Washington May 23d the California colors were greeted with enthusiasm by the highest and bravest in the land. It remained on picket duty at Fairfax Courthouse until mustered out of the United States service on July 20, 1865.

Of the 400 officers and men mustered into the battalion at San Francisco only 148 remained to be mustered out at the final discharge. Many were killed in battle or died in the service; some were missing and unaccounted for; a large number were discharged from time to time on account of wounds or disability, and thirty of the enlisted men were promoted to commissioned officers in various regiments.

The veterans of the California Cavalry Battalion and California Hundred inscribed upon their colors the names of the following engagements in which they participated: Brookville, Ahsby's Gap, Coyle's Tavern, Little River Pike, Drainsville, Rectortown, Point of Rocks, Aldie, Frederick Pike, Tanallytown, Fort Reno, Fort Stephens, Rockville, Poolsville, Leesburg, Snicker's Gap, Knowland's Ford, Shepherdstown, Whitepost, Middletown, Strasburg, Kernstown, Winchester, Berryville Pike, Charlestown, Summit Point, Halltown, Berryville, Smithfield, Opequan Creek, Knoxford, Front Royal, Snake Mountain, Luray Courthouse, Mills Ford, Waynesboro, Mount Crawford, Tomsbrook, Cedar Creek, Madison Courthouse, Gordonsville, Charlottesville, South Anna, White Oak Road, Dinwiddie Courthouse, Five Forks, South Side Railroad, Devil's Ford, Sailor's Creek and Appomattox Courthouse.

How is that for a record?

The Chronicle, San Francisco, Monday, August 17, 1903
[This article was taken from the Reports to The Adjutant General, State of California, 1866 and 1867]

❖❖

Company A

BARNSTEAD-In this city, October 18, Thomas Delap, beloved husband of Catherine Barnstead, a native of Philadelphia, Pa., aged 66 years, 8 months and 28 days. Retired Sergeant of Police and Commander of Lincoln Post, No. 1, G. A. R.

Friends and acquaintances are respectfully invited to attend the funeral Wednesday, October 21, at 1 o'clock, from Assembly Hall, Pioneer building, Fourth street, between Mission and Market, under the auspices of Lincoln Post, No.1, G. A. R. Interment, National Cemetery. *[Presidio of San Francisco.]*

The Chronicle, San Francisco, Monday, October 19, 1903.

❖❖❖

1904
❖❖❖
Company E

SMITH-In this city, June 22, Leonard F., beloved husband of Maria D. Smith, a native of Pennsylvania, aged 81 years, 1 month and 16 days. (Honolulu papers please copy.)

Friends and acquaintenances are respectfully invited to attend the funeral services Sunday, June 26, at 1:30 o'clock, from Alcazar building, 114 O'Farrell street. Members of James A. Garfield Post, G. A. R.; Garfield Relief Corps, No. 21; Lincoln Relief Corps, No. 3. and Seven Pines Circle, No. 3, Ladies of the G. A. R., are respectfully invited to attend the internment, National Cemetery, Presidio. *[San Francisco]* Please omit flowers.

The Chronicle, San Francisco, Friday, June 24, 1904.

❖❖❖

1905
❖❖❖
Company A

M'INTOSH-In this city, June 9, Captain Isaac R. McIntosh, uncle of Mrs. Frank J. Falling, a native of Maine, aged 77 years.

Friends and acquaintances are respectfully invited to attend the funeral Sunday, June 11, at 2 o'clock, from Masonic Temple, corner of Post and Montgomery streets, under the auspices of California Lodge, No. 1, F. and A.M. Interment, National Cemetery. *[Presidio of San Francisco]*

The Chronicle, San Francisco, Sunday, June 9, 1905

❖❖❖
Company C
SUICIDE BY DROWNING.
———
John P. Glinn, a Veteran Jumped Into the Reservoir at Yountville Home.
———

John P. Glinn, an aged veteran of the Civil War, committed suicide Thursday afternoon at the Veteran's Home by drowning himself in the reservoir at the Home.

The body was recovered from the water Friday morning, and Coroner R.M. Keyser held an inquest on the remains Friday afternoon at the Home.

Glinn was 61 years of age and a native of Ireland. He served as an artillery-man in the Civil War, and came to the Veteran's home about 3 years ago. He left the Home about two months ago, and went to San Francisco to live, ceasing to be a member of the Home. Last Monday Glinn came back to the home and asked to be admitted to the institution again.

Thursday morning at about 11 o'clock he received word from the officers of the home that it would be necessary for him to make formal application for admission. This news, together with the fact that he had a spell of despondency from having been on a spree, led him to take his own life. He went up to the reservoir back of the Home, took off his hat and coat, laid them on the bank, and jumped in.

Chas. W. Mason, a veteran, saw the hat and coat on the bank of the reservoir Thursday night, and notified the authorities of the Home of the fact.

Glinn's body was recovered Friday forenoon. The jury rendered a verdict in accordance with the above facts.

Napa Daily Journal, Saturday, August 26, 1905
[Article in error, **Glynn,** *was a Farrier in Company C. He is Interred at the Veteran's Home Cemetery, Yountville, California]*

❖❖❖

1906

❖❖❖

Company F

VETERAN OF FIFTY BATTLES MEETS FINAL CONQUEROR
John Passage Passes Away Quickly, Succeeding Severe Stroke of Paralysis.

Retiring at his usual bed-time Thursday evening, with no premonition of impending death, John Passage, an old and highly respected resident of this city, suffered a hemorrhage of the brain accompanied by paralysis, at 11:30, so complete and severe in its visitation that he never rallied for a moment up to the time when death ensued Saturday morning at 3:15.

John Passage was born in Castile, Wyoming county, N. Y., Nov. 25, 1833, being next to the youngest of a family of ten children. At an early age he removed to Delavan, coming with the tide of emigration which swept the state in 1842, and making his boyhood home in and about this city. Succeeding the discovery of gold in California, he was among the first to cross the plains and locate in the Golden State, making the trip in 1852, but later returning.

At the outbreak of the civil war he was in California for the second time and volunteered from there, being a member of the famed "California Hundred," *[actually Co. F]* which was raised after the quota of the state had been filled, and could only get into the service by making up a part of the Massachusetts 2ⁿᵈ Cavalry, with whom however they continued to be known as the "Californians." During the last three years of the war he served in the Shenendoah Valley under Sheridan, participating in an even fifty battles, and being finally mustered out with the rank of first lieutenant, July 20ᵗʰ 1865, at Fairfax Court House, Va.

In 1874 he removed to Green, Iowa, where he established the Recorder, the first Democratic paper in Butler county, where he continued to reside until 1888, when he again sought Delavan as his home.

Under the second administration of Cleveland, he was appointed postmaster, serving from 1894 to 1898 in a manner that gave complete satisfaction to the patrons of the office.

He was married during a furlough, Feb. 2ⁿᵈ, 1865, to Miss Minnie Peets, of Turtle Prairie.

The deceased was a man of quiet, reserved demeanor, but fearless in the expression of his views. Of absolute integrity, he lived possessed of the entire respect of the community and died regretted by all.

The Delavan Enterprise, Delavan Wisconsin, Thursday, February 22, 1906
[Portions of this article have been deleted for the sake of brevity.]

1907

Company L

CAPTAIN T. H. MERRY DIES
AFTER A VERY SHORT ILLNESS

In the death of Captain T. H. Merry, who passed away last evening after an illness of several weeks, Santa Barbara loses a citizen who will be missed. Death was the result of kidney trouble which weakened the heart so that the physicians were unable to stimulate that organ and heart failure hastened the end.

Captain Merry was a native of New York, where he was born 67 years and three months ago. He had been in California since 1850 and in Santa Barbara for two years. He leaves a widow, three daughters, Mrs. D.M. Greenwell, Miss Genevieve and Miss Lenore Merry, one son, Edwin S. Merry, of San Francisco, a brother, William Laurence Merry, American minister to Costa Rica, Nicaragua, and Salvador, and a sister, Mrs. A.A. Banford of Los Gatos.

The funeral will take place from the family residence, 112 Kimberly avenue, Wednesday afternoon, under the auspices of Starr King Post, G. A. R., of which Captain Merry was a member.

Captain Merry was a graduate of Yale and later took a course and was graduated from the Yale school of law. He was admitted to the bar of San Francisco and subsequently moved to Ventura, where he practiced his profession.

Shortly after he had graduated from Santa Clara College, the civil war broke out and young Merry became a member of the California Battalion, a company of 100 men who equipped themselves at their own expense and went east and offered their services to the war department. Mr. Merry was assigned to the second Massachusetts cavalry and served to the end of the war when he was honorably discharged.

When he retired from the practice of his profession two years ago Captain Merry bought the Vishnu and took parties to the islands. There was no part of his life that he enjoyed as he did this passed on the sea and there are many who will shed a tear for the sailor-gentleman who has cast anchor in the harbor of eternal peace.

The Independent, Santa Barbara, Monday, October 21, 1907.
[Interred at Ocean View Section, Santa Barbara Cemetery]

1908

Company A

DEATH OF VETERAN OF "CALIFORNIA HUNDRED"

Richard Samuel, Who Fought in the Civil War, Passes Away.

Richard Samuel, one of the very few survivors of the famous "California Hundred" that represented this State in the Civil War and actually got into the thick of the fighting by uniting with a Massachusetts regiment, died at the Soldiers' Home at Yountville, in Napa county, Sunday night, aged 68.

Three months ago Samuels was attacked by what has proved a prolonged and fatal illness. It was his wish that he be taken to the soldiers' home and accordingly he was removed a week ago by his family and died among his comrades of the Civil War. Samuels will be given a soldier's funeral tomorrow at Yountville in keeping with his desire.

"Dick Sam," as he was affectionately called by his Grand Army comrades and intimate friends, was a native of Carrollton, Green county, Illinois. He came to California before he was of age and lived for a time along the Sacramento, below the Capital City, and later at what was then a small settlement near the inner reach of Tomales bay.

When war was declared he was 21 and eager to get to the front, where there would be fighting. The "California Hundred" was organized as a cavalry company, with that specific object in view, and "Dick Sam" was one of the little band of volunteers that made the long trip back to the New England States to offer their services as a company to unite with some Federal regiment that would get down to the firing line. And he was one of that historic few who actually fought for California during the Civil War.

Later he was married and lived in Chicago and was in the Government service there. About ten years ago the old love for California returned, and he moved back, bringing his family. They settled near Red Bluff, and there a few years since the elder daughter died. Before the fire, the family moved to Berkeley, where Mrs. Samuel and Miss Lucy Samuel of Le Conte avenue are the nearest surviving relatives.

Oakland Tribune, Tuesday, March 10, 1908.
[Interred at the Veteran's Cemetery, Yountville]

Company A

John L. Hunter, a veteran of the civil war, passed away at Josephine Friday and was buried Saturday. He was 78 years of age.

Georgetown Gazette, Thursday, April 23, 1908.
[Interred at Volcanoville, Ca.]

❖❖

Company L

Death Summons Eugene F. Loud

Ex-Congressman **Eugene F. Loud** died at the residence of his son-in-law, Captain J.J. Callundan, 1938 Post street late last night. The death of his wife and daughter within the last six months was a severe blow to him and he failed to survive the shock.

Loud was elected for six successive terms and served longer than any other member elected from California. Part of the time Loud served in Congress he held the position of chairman of the Committee on Post Offices and Postroads. In 1886 he was elected to the State Legislature with the largest majority ever received by any candidate in the Forty-third Assembly district, which he represented.

Loud participated in the battle of Gettysburg and was with General Sheridan in the Shenandoah valley. He fought in the bloody battles of Winchester, Cedar Creek, Tom's Brook, Fisher Hill, and in many minor engagements. In the winter of 1863 he rejoined the Army of the Potomac with the cavalry under Sheridan, and took part in all the engagements during the closing days of the war, including the memorable battles of Five Forks, Petersburg and Sailor creek, afterward being present at Appomattox Courthouse when General Lee surrendered. Although the regiment in which he served was in forty-three engagements during the war, he was only once slightly wounded, at Cedar creek, where his left hand was injured by a bullet from the other side.

Loud was well known in Masonic and friendly society circles and at various times held important offices in connection with these bodies. He lost his daughter, Mrs. Grace O'Connell, five months ago, and his wife on December 6th last. Both deaths told greatly on him and probably hastened his end. He was born at Ablington, Mass., March 12, 1817, of New England Stock, his ancestors having come to this country in 1630.

The funeral will take place Tuesday afternoon under the auspices of King Solomon Lodge, F. and A.M., and George H. Thomas Post, G.A.R.

The Chronicle, San Francisco, Sunday, December 20, 1908
(Interred at I.O.O.F. cemetery, Colma, California)

❖❖

1909

❖❖

Company A

WILLIAMS-At Allston, Jan. 29, suddenly, John H. Williams, 74 yrs, 15 dys.

Evening Transcript, Boston, Monday, February 1, 1909

Company E

Veteran Soldier Called to Rest
H.W. Mortimer, Long a Resident of This City Dies at His Home

H. W. Mortimer, for thirty years a familiar figure on the streets of San Francisco, died yesterday at his residence, 2030 Pierce street. Death was due to a feeble condition of health, augmented by a sudden attack of pneumonia. The attack is said to have greatly accelerated the fatal termination of his illness.

Mr. Mortimer was a member of the famous California One Hundred Battalion which left San Francisco January 15, 1863, and served until the end of the Civil War. At the close of the struggle he was appointed chief clerk of the War Department, and in 1897 served as Commander of Lincoln Post, Grand Army of the Republic.

He is survived by a widow and two sons, Frank C. Mortimer, assistant cashier of the First National Bank of Berkeley, and Charles S. Mortimer, who is now in Washington, D.C. His aged mother, Mrs. Amanda R. Cogswell of Oakland, also survives him.

For many years he was connected with the San Francisco office of the Liverpool and London and Globe Insurance Company.

Friends and acquaintances are respectfully invited to attend the funeral Wednesday, March 17, at 2 o'clock, from the mortuary chapel of the Golden Gate Undertaking Company, 2475 Mission street, near Twenty-first. Incineration, I.O.O.F. Cemetery. Remains at his late residence, 2030 Pierce street, until Wednesday.

The Chronicle, San Francisco, Monday, March 15, 1909.
The Chronicle, San Francisco, Tuesday, March 16, 1909.

Company M

STONE-In this city, June 1, Alvin W., beloved husband of Eliza F. Stone, and father of May, Rockwell and Raymond Stone, Mrs. George S. Pomeroy, Mrs. Harry Herbert, Mrs. Norman Trippe and the late Alvin M. Stone, a native of Massachusetts, aged 83 years, 4 months and 9 days. (San Jose papers, please copy).

Friends and acquaintances are respectfully invited to attend the funeral Thursday, June 3, at 9:30 o'clock, from his late residence, 369 Haight street. Interment private.

The Chronicle, San Francisco, Wednesday, June 2, 1909
[Interred at the National Cemetery, Presidio of San Francisco]

Company A

BENJAMIN-In this city, August 8, Colonel C. E. Benjamin.

Remains at the mortuary chapel of the Golden Gate Undertaking Company, 2475 Mission street, near Twenty-first.

The Chronicle, San Francisco, Tuesday, August 10, 1909.

1910

Company F

PAPWORTH-In this city, March 21, 1910, Alonzo Papworth, beloved husband of Alice Papworth, and father of Fred Papworth, Mrs. C. Enholmes and R. C. Papworth, a native of New York, aged 70 years, 5 months and 6 days.

Oakland Tribune, Wednesday, March 23, 1910
[Interred at Mountain View Cemetery, Oakland]

Company A

"Taps" Sound for War Veteran

JAMES WATSON, RESPECTED PIONEER HAS PASSED AWAY

Another California pioneer and civil war veteran has passed away. James Watson of this city had been in poor health for a long time, and Thursday last he answered the last roll call. He was born at Monterey, March 30, 1849, and came to this county when quite young, settling at Bolinas with his parents. He was one of the young men who went to the front and fought for the Union during the Civil War, serving with the famous California 100, under Sheridan.

Mr. Watson's father was an Englishman and his mother of Spanish descent. He leaves a widow and four sons, Edward, Eugene, Benjamin and James, and one daughter, Mrs. Agnes Hutto. He was a half brother of Peter, Henry and Charles Crane.

The funeral services were conducted from St. Rafaels's church with interment at Mt. Olivet.

The pall bearers were R. Kimsella, J.S. Kaneen, Peter Williams, Homer A. Ames, and T. J. Fallon.

The Marin Journal, San Rafael, Thursday, June 9, 1910.
[Interred at Mt. Olivet Cemetery, San Rafael]

1911

Company F

COCHRANE - The funeral services of Warren Cochrane, who died Monday (Oct. 29, 1911) in Ithaca, N.Y., were held yesterday afternoon at 2 o'clock at the chapel at the cutler undertaking parlors. Rev. Warren Goddard, pastor of the New Church (Swedenborg), officiated. The interment took place at the Pine Lake cemetery. Mr. Cochrane is survived by his wife, and son, Fernald, of Ithaca, N.Y., two sisters, Mrs. Clara Armstrong, of this city, and Mrs. H.A. Pershing, of South Bend. Mrs. Cochrane and son and Mr. Pershing attended the funeral, but Mrs. Pershing is at Logan, Utah, where a sister, Mrs. George H. Champ, died Tuesday, and was unable to be present.

LaPorte Argus Bulletin, LaPorte, Indiana, Friday, November 3, 1911
[Interred at Pine Lake Cemetery, LaPorte, Indiana]

❖❖

1912

❖❖

Company A

ROBINSON-In Santa Cruz May 21, William A. Robinson, a native of Massachusetts, aged 71 years and 9 months.

Friends and acquaintances are respectfully invited to attend the funeral services Thursday, May 23 at 1 o'clock, at the chapel of Cypress Lawn Cemetery.

The Chronicle, San Francisco, Thursday, May 23, 1912.
[Interred at Cypress Lawn Cemetery, San Francisco]

❖❖

1913

❖❖

Company A

DEMSEY. In Los Angeles, March 27, 1913, Dr. **C.F. Demsey** of Mojave, Cal., aged 75 years. Funeral services will be held at the chapel of Bresee Brothers, Friday at 1 o'clock.

Los Angeles Daily Times, Friday, March 28, 1913.
[Interred at Chapel of The Pines, Los Angeles]

❖❖

Company A

Colonel C. Mason Kinne Dies

Death Ends Yuletide Visit

Struck with heart failure during a Christmas morning visit to his daughter, Mrs. Clara Burnham of Bushnell Place, Berkeley, Colonel C. Mason Kinne, who resided at the Hotel Granada at 1000 Sutter street, died within a few moments of the attack yesterday. The death followed a Christmas tree entertainment which Colonel Kinne had planned for his grandchildren. He was 72 years of age.

A member of the famous California One Hundred and widely known in military circles, Colonel Kinne came to San Francisco in 1859, engaging in the insurance business just before the outbreak of the Civil War. He went East to join the Army of the North in a regiment that was later incorporated with the Second Massachusetts Cavalry. He served throughout the war as Adjutant-General., afterward returning to San Francisco to again take up his business connections. He had been a resident manager of a large insurance firm until his retirement two years ago.

As a soldier, Colonel Kinne had a host of friends in California. He kept up his military affiliations with an enthusiastic interest and served as Senior Vice-Commander of the Grand Army of the Republic and also as Commander of the California Loyal Legion. In the latter organization for the past thirty years he held the position of treasurer. He was a member of the Sons of the American Revolution and of Masonic orders.

A member of an old and well known New England family, he leaves many friends and relatives in New Jersey, New York and Connecticut. The widow, Elizabeth D'Arcy Kinne and two daughters, Mrs. W.I. Finch and Mrs. Clark Burnham of Berkeley, survive. A brother, Dr. Porter S. Kinne, lives at Paterson, New Jersey.

Private funeral services will be held Sunday from the Burnham home in Berkeley, and later services will be conducted at the Presidio by the Grand Army of the Republic and Loyal Legion.

The Chronicle, San Francisco, Friday, December 26, 1913.
[Interred at the National Cemetery, Presidio of San Francisco]

❖❖❖

1914

❖❖❖

Company A

HUSSEY-In this city, February 11, William H. H. Hussey, husband of Abigail Hussey, and father of Mrs. P.W. Lewis of Portland, Or., Mrs. R.L. Partington of Piedmont, Cal., Mrs. Dr. Fairweather of Honolulu and William and Edward Hussey of Portland, Or., a native of Ohio, aged 73 years, 5 months and 13 days. A member of Lincoln Post, No. 1, G. A. R., and the California Hundred.

Friends are invited to attend the funeral services, Friday, February 13, at 1 o'clock, at Gray's chapel, Geary and Divisadero streets. Interment, private.

The Chronicle, San Francisco, Thursday, February 12, 1914.
[Interred at the National Cemetery, Presidio of San Francisco]

❖❖❖

Company L

SEAGRAVE - In Alameda, Cal., May 4, at his late residence, 1831 Nason street, Mastick station, Edward Fletcher, dearly beloved husband of Sarah F. Seagrave, and father of Harry T., John C., William G., Frank E. and Joseph Seagrave, a native of Massachusetts, aged 78 years, 4 months and 17 days. A member of Lincoln Post, No. 1, and unity Lodge, No. 181, I.O.O.F.

Friends and acquaintances are respectfully invited to attend the funeral Wednesday, May 6, at 1:30 o'clock, from I.O.O.F. Hall, corner of Seventh and Market streets, where services will be held under the auspices of Unity Lodge, No. 181, I.O.O.F. Interment, Mount Olivet Cemetery, *[Colma]* by automobile.

The Chronicle, San Francisco, Tuesday, May 5, 1914
[Interred at Mt. Olivet Cemetery, Colma, California]

❖❖❖

Company E

W. H. STANIELS IS DEAD

WELL KNOWN VETERAN , WHO WAS CANDIDATE FOR NOMINATION FOR SHER-
IFF, PASSED AWAY AT VETERANS' HOME.

W. H. Staniels, a well known veteran, and a candidate at the primary election for the
nomination for Sheriff of Napa county, died suddenly on Thursday afternoon at the Veterans'
Home at Yountville.

He had been out in the hills hunting earlier in the day, and was seized with heart
failure shortly after his return, which resulted in his demise.

Napa Daily Journal, Friday, October 9, 1914.
[Interred at the Veteran's Cemetery, Yountville]

❖❖❖

1915

❖❖❖

ROSTER SHOWS SURVIVORS of CALIFORNIA CONTINGENT
Are Part of Famous Body of Men, Part of Second Massachusetts Volunteer Cavalry

A roster of the survivors of the famous California contingent of the Second Massachusetts Cavalry has been received by Colonel J. B. Fuller of this city. The roster was forwarded from Washington by Junius Thomas Turner, first sergeant of Troop E, and contains the
following names:

Major D.W.C. Thompson, Santa Rosa; Major E.W. Woodward, 1943 Forty-first avenue, Oakland; Edward Seagrave, San Francisco; H.C. Sherwin, Cambridge, Mass.; Samuel
Smith, Boston; H.C. Schrow, Evereet, Mass.; A. Loane, 1530 Golden Gate avenue, San Fran-
cisco; Captain Hugh Armstrong, Santa Monica; Frank Enos, 174 Randall street, San Francisco;
John Fletcher, Antioch; W.H. Lawrence, Los Gatos; Samuel W. Backus, Commissioner of Im-
migration, San Francisco; Captain Henry G. Burlingham, United States Pension Bureau; George
W. Buhrer, Willis, Mont.; George R. Boyle, Tuolumne county, Cal.; Alfred A. McLean, 218
Ellis street, San Francisco; Daniel K. McDougall, Salinas; Fred J. Quant, Madera; George W.
Towle, 112 Market street, San Francisco; B.R. Wildes, Leavenworth, Kansas; Junius Thomas
Turner, 414 B street, Washington; John Campbell, Alum Rock, San Jose, Cal.

The Chronicle, San Francisco, Sunday, August 29, 1915
[Junius T. Turner, Co. E; promoted 2ᵈ Lt. 2ᵈ Regt. Maryland Cavalry, Mar. 1864; Capt. Apr.
1865]

❖❖

1916

❖❖

MOSBY, REBEL RAIDER DIES AT 82 YEARS
Was the Most Famous Confederate Guerilla During the Civil War.
CAPTURED FEDERAL GENERAL.
Grant Saved Mosby From Hanging and Appointed Him Consul at Hong Kong

Washington, May 30 - Colonel **John S. Mosby**, the most famous Confederate raider of the Civil War, died here today after a long illness. He was a native of Virginia and was 82 years old.

Colonel Mosby dared death over fifty years ago when at the head of a band of a few hundred Confederate raiders he rode up and down the Shenandoah Valley, capturing outposts, destroying supply trains, and cutting off means of communication. It has been estimated that he often neutralized the force of over 15,000 Federals in the Valley.

Born in Powhatten County, Va., December 6, 1833, and graduated from the University of Virginia in 1852, he was practicing law in Bristol, Va., when the war broke out and he began his career in the Confederate Army. He proved his daring with such effect that he became a scout for General J.E.B. Stuart and led the celebrated raid around McClellan's army on the Chickahominy. In Richmond a year later he recruited an independent cavalry troop, which became famous as Mosby's Partisan Rangers. They became night riders and the terror of the Federal troops.

Mosby's most brilliant exploit was the capture of General Stoughton. On a March night in 1863 he, with thirty followers, rode through the Federal army to Fairfax Court House, only nineteen miles from Washington, where General Stoughton was asleep. Although surrounded by an army said to have been 17,000 strong, the rangers calmly kidnapped the general, his staff and many sentries, and turned them over to the Confederate authorities at Culpeper without having lost a man.

General Grant once later saved Mosby from hanging, and the two foes of the battlefield became staunch friends. Mosby stumped the State of Virginia for Grant during his Presidential campaign, and was rewarded with an appointment as consul at Hong Kong, a post which he held for seven years. When he returned to the United States, Mosby called on the surviving members of his rangers and, to his astonishment, he found that a large percentage of them had become ministers. In parting, their old colonel said; "Well, boys, if you fight the Devil like you fought the Yankees there will be something to record on Judgment Day."

He next became special land agent for the Government in Colorado, and from 1904 to 1910 he was an attorney in the Department of Justice. The closing years of his life were spent in lecturing and authorship. His home lay across the Potomac, at Warrenton, Va., but he was often seen in Washington, his white hair and strong Roman features making him a picturesque figure on the streets or lecture platform. He had written "Mosby's War Reminiscences," "The Dawn of the Real South," and "Stuart's Cavalry Campaign." He was also known as a Greek scholar.

"My military creed," he once declared, "is this: It is better to make a good run than a bad stand."

COL. MOSBY DIES; FAMOUS RAIDER IN CIVIL WAR
With 29 Men He Captured Gen. Stoughton in Fairfax County, Va.

Washington, May 30. - Colonel John Singleton Mosby, famous and daring Confederate raider of the Civil War, died here to-day after a lingering illness. He was eighty-two years old.

Death was due to infirmities superinduced by old age. He was conscious until about an hour before the end. Until six months ago, when he went into a sudden decline, Colonel Mosby was a familiar figure in the streets of the city.

The body will be shipped to his home in Warrenton, Va., where burial probably will be held Thursday. Several survivors of his noted command will act as pall-bearers. Colonel Mosby's death, coming as it did on Memorial Day, was affecting to many.

It was said that Colonel Mosby never participated in reunions of veterans, because twenty-two years ago when he attended one of his command at Alexandria, Va., he was so overcome with emotion that he was unable to speak. He is survived by a son, several daughters and sisters.

Few men in the Confederate Army were more conspicuous or interesting than Colonel Mosby. As a dashing raider his record was not approached even among the boldest of the Southern semi-guerillas. He was born in 1833. He received his early education at the University of Virginia.

STUDIED LAW IN JAIL.

Before completing his course he shot and wounded a fellow student who had insulted him. He was fined and imprisoned but later pardoned. While in jail he studied law and soon afterward was admitted to the bar. He married Miss Pauline Clark, daughter of a Congressman who was at one time United States Minister to a Central American nation.

At the beginning of the war Colonel Mosby enlisted in a company of cavalry under General J.E. Johnston. He served at Bull Run, in the Shenandoah Valley and along the Potomac. Later, General J.E.B. Stuart noticed his daring and made him a scout. He aided that officer in a bold raid on the rear of General McClellan's position on the Chickahominy in June, 1862.

In January, 1863, he crossed the Rappahannock and recruited a force of irregular cavalry. His celebrated partisan band soon came to be known and feared. Members were armed only with revolvers and bowie knives.

Colonel Mosby's greatest triumph came on March 8, 1863, when with twenty-nine men he slipped through the opposing lines and captured General Stoughton at his headquarters in Fairfax Court House, Va. Historians are unanimous in recording as his greatest service his prevention of Sheridan and Grant from effecting a junction.

SENT LOCK OF HAIR TO LINCOLN.

On one occasion it is related Colonel Mosby rode within sight of Washington and sent a lock of his hair to President Lincoln by a woman whom he met going to market in the city. The noted raider was promoted through the various grades to the rank of brigadier-general. He was wounded several times.

When General Lee finally surrendered at Appomattox there were many in the North who insisted that no mercy should be shown Colonel Mosby. A price of $5,000 was set upon his head. General Grant, however, refused to heed these demands. Colonel Mosby later declined to accept an office under General Grant when the latter became President. During the Hays administration he consented to become United States Consul at Hong Kong. Upon his return from China he settled in California, where he again took up the practice of law.

As a soldier, Colonel Mosby was a terrible disciplinarian. As a lawyer he was a shrewd reader of statutes.

Washington Post, Washington, D.C., Tuesday, May 30, 1916.
Loudon Mirror, Friday, Leesburg, June 2, 1916.
The Fauquier Democrat, Warrenton, Va., Saturday, June 3, 1916.
[Interred at Warrenton Cemetery, Warrenton, Va]

❖❖❖

Company A

FUNERAL OF F. J. QUANT
(From Monday's Daily)

Funeral services over the remains of the late Frederick J. Quant, Civil War veteran and resident of this city for many years, were held yesterday afternoon at three o'clock from the family residence, 412 South Lake street. Many friends of the old soldier were present, and there was an abundance of floral pieces. Rev. David H. McCullough, pastor of the Presbyterian church, conducted the services and the pall bearers were Charles A. Clark, R.L. Bennett, Peter Peterson, F.A. Wills, W.A. Moore and Frank Stevens. A quartet from the Presbyterian church sang. The casket was draped in an American flag.

At the close of the services at the grave, H.J. Williams sounded taps on his cornet, as the body of the veteran was lowered to its last resting place.

Madera Mercury, Friday, July 21, 1916.
[Interred at Arbor Vitae Cemetery, Madera]

❖❖❖

1917

❖❖❖

Company F

HARKINS-In Menlo Park, January 2, 1917. Major Charles Harkins, devoted husband of Mary S. Harkins, and loving father of Mary B., Elizabeth A., Catherine H., Charles L., Edward C., Dimetrio P. and Henry A. Harkins, a native of Ireland, aged 81 years, 4 months and 18 days.

Friends and acquaintances are respectfully invited to attend the funeral Friday, January 5, at 9:30 o'clock, from his late residence, Menlo Park; thence to the Church of the Nativity, where a requiem high mass will be celebrated for the repose of his soul, commencing at 10 o'clock. Internment, National Cemetery, Presidio, San Francisco.

The Chronicle, San Francisco, January 4, 1917.
[Interred at the National Cemetery, Presidio of San Francisco]

❖❖❖

Company E

CAMPBELL.-In Yountville, Cal., September 3, 1917, John T. Campbell, formerly of 2500 Alum Rock avenue, beloved husband of Elizabeth Campbell, father of Horace, Logan, Ben, Alice and Beatrice Campbell, a native of Branford, Canada, aged 80 years, 6 months and 17 days.

Friends are invited to attend the funeral today (Thursday) at 2 p.m. from the parlors of the San Jose Undertaking Co. 276 South Second street. Interment Oak Hill Cemetery. (Sacramento Bee please copy)

San Jose Mercury Herald, Thursday, September 6, 1917.
[Interred at Oak Hill Cemetery, San Jose]

❖❖

1918

❖❖❖

23 VETERANS OF NOTED CIVIL WAR UNIT STILL ALIVE
Figures Regarding Historic California Cavalry Battalion Made Public

---

ALL CHEERFUL FIGHTERS

Interesting Record of the "One Hundred" From This State is Told

---

Only twenty-three members of the historic California One Hundred and California Cavalry Battalion, the contingent from this State that made an enviable record with the 2d Regiment of Massachusetts in the Civil War, are alive today, according to figures prepared by Major Junius Thomas Taylor for General Samuel W. Backus, president of the board of directors of the Veterans' Home of California. Major Turner is the oldest of the survivors, having passed his ninety second birthday. He is still practicing law in Washington, D. C.

There were 558 men who entered the service in San Francisco when the two organizations which were later consolidated, were formed. Of this number, 160 were mustered out at the Fairfax, Va. Courthouse on July 20, 1865.

SURVIVORS NAMED

Those who survive are:
General Samuel W. Backus, president board of directors, Veterans' Home of California.
Captain Henry G. Burlingham, United States Pension Bureau.
George M. Boyle, Stent., Cal.
Captain Hiram E.W. Clark, Thorndike, Mass.
Erastus I. Enos, Elgin, Ia.
John Fletcher, Brentwood, Cal.
Charles H. Flournoy, Knoxville, Tenn.
Charles M. Jenkins, Los Angeles, Cal.
A. Loane, 1530 Golden Gate Avenue, San Francisco
William H. Lawrence, Los Gatos, Cal.
George W. Lee, 481 North Eleventh street, San Jose, Cal.
Delevan E. Moore, 1504 Cedar street, Milwaukee, Wis.
W. H. McNeil, 1022 North Nineteenth street, St. Joseph, Mo.

Daniel K. McDougal, Salinas, Cal.
Alfred A. McLean, 218 Ellis street, San Francisco
Major DeWitt Clinton Thompson, Santa Rosa, Cal.
Major Junius Thomas Turner, 414 B street, N.E., Washington, D.C.
George W. Towle, 112 Market street, San Francisco
Major E. W. Woodward, 1943 Forty-first avenue, Oakland, Cal.
Byron D. Gibbs, 20 Vine street, Ontario, Cal.
William Morris, Lakeport, Cal.
W. W. West. Lakeport, Cal.
Robert A. Campbell, 1014 Sixteenth street, Oakland, Cal.

GIVEN BAPTISM OF FIRE

The California One Hundred reached the field of action at Yorktown, Va., in February, 1863, and were immediately given their baptism of fire at Santa Ana *[South Anna]* bridge. The four companies of the "battalion" followed the "hundred" in July, and the two organizations became the first battalion of the 2d Massachusetts Cavalry. They were placed in such a position as to protect the national capital, and were far enough away from Washington to be fighting continually, General Backus says in an article describing the Activities of the Californians in the Civil War.

Mosby, writing of this battalion after the war, said: "They were the most cheerful fighters I ever met."

The Californians were at Appomattox Courthouse when Lee surrendered, and they were later mustered out after having seen two and a half years of hard fighting, which included more than fifty engagements.

The Chronicle, San Francisco, Wednesday, August 28, 1918.

❖❖❖

1919

❖❖❖
Regimental Staff

CAPT. DEWITT C. THOMPSON FAMOUS PIONEER, IS DEAD

Captain DeWitt Clinton Thompson, who arrived in San Francisco bay on the old steamship "California", the first steamer to enter San Francisco bay died at his country home north of Santa Rosa last evening at the advanced age of 92 years.

He is believed to be the last survivor of the historical old California which carried 500 passengers around the Horn.

Mr. Thompson was a native of Massachusetts where he was born September 1, 1826, and came to California February 28, 1848, and has resided here ever since. He lived with his daughter, Miss Marion Thompson, who gave him every attention during the last years of his life. Despite his age, Mr. Thompson maintained a wonderful physical and mental vitality and was in fairly good health for one of his age until quite recently.

The Press Democrat, Santa Rosa, Wednesday, May 14, 1919.

General Thompson Commanded Famous California Hundred

General DeWitt C. Thompson, whose death was recorded in these columns Wednesday morning, was commander of the California 100, a cavalry body which distinguished itself in the Civil War, being attached to the Army of the Potomac.

After returning to California, General Thompson lived for many years in Oakland and served for a time as adjutant-general of California and was also president of a bank in San Francisco for some time.

General Thompson came to Sonoma county and spent his declining years as a farmer, for some time residing on a ranch in the Mt. Olivet section, but more recently had resided on the Reid ranch, north of town, where he died.

In his active years General Thompson was a man of commanding figure, over six feet tall, with great energy and a strong will which made him a natural leader of men. For many years he had a wide circle of friends about San Francisco bay and throughout the State but at 93 he had naturally outlived most of them.

The Press Democrat, Santa Rosa, Thursday, May 15, 1919.
The Examiner, San Francisco, Friday, May 16, 1919.
[Interred at Mountain View Cemetery, Oakland]

1920

Company A

LOANE-In this city, January 13, 1920, Abraham, Husband of the late Matilda Loane, father of Albert S. Loane, Mrs. P.J. Donohue and Mrs. Alice deFerrari and brother of the late John M. Loane, a native of Ireland, aged 80 years. (Philadelphia papers please copy.)

Friends are invited to attend the funeral services Friday, at 2 o'clock P.M., from under the auspices of Apollo Lodge, No. 123, I.O.O.F., and interment, Greenlawn Cemetery. Remains at the parlors of Martin & Brown, 1515 Scott St., near Post.

The Chronicle, San Francisco, January 14, 1920.
[Interred at Greenlawn Cemetery, Colma]

Company L

ENOS-In this city, August 1, 1920, Frank Enos, beloved brother of Miss Helen M. Enos of Stevinson, *[Merced Co.]* Cal., aged 81 years. A member of Lipton Post, No. 1, G.A.R. Funeral, Friday, at 2 P.M., at the chapel of Letterman General Hospital, Funeral arrangements by Harry H. Valleno, U.S. Army mortician.

The Chronicle, San Francisco, Thursday, August 5, 1920
[Interred at the National Cemetery, Presidio of San Francisco]

Company A

Major Edwin W. Woodward Is Dead After Eventful Career

Veteran of Civil War Active in Civic Affairs for Great Many Years.

———————

Major Edwin W. Woodward, for 61 years a resident of Oakland, during which period he was at all times active in the political life of the county, died this morning at his home at 1943 Forty-first avenue. He was 81 years of age.

Although retired, he was active virtually until the time of his death. On Monday, he was stricken by a severe cold, which developed into pneumonia.

Major Woodward came to California in '59 and took up his residence in Weaverville, Trinity county, where he engaged in a general merchandise business in the early day gold town until the outbreak of the war in '61. Responding to the call for volunteers, he came to San Francisco and enlisted in the celebrated "California Hundred" the first company from California to report for active duty in the field.

RANKED AS MAJOR

For his services in the war he was successively ranked as lieutenant, as captain, and as major. The war saw him in active service up to the surrender of the Confederate forces at Appomattox.

Discharged from military service, he returned to California and ever since kept up his war associations by active work in the G. A. R. In 1893 he was elected commander of Lyon Post No. 8 and it was during his term as commander the G. A. R. memorial in Mountain View cemetery was subscribed for and unveiled.

MARRIED IN 1866

In '66 he married Miss Addie O. Rogers, daughter of the late proprietor of the Boston Journal. He returned to Oakland and the real estate partnership of Woodward & Taggart was formed. In '69 his wife died and sixteen years later he married Mary Anna Sands, his present widow.

About this time he moved to St. Helena in Napa county and there organized the Bank of St. Helena. He later returned to Oakland and formed a partnership with James Gamble, which, after a time, was moved to San Francisco. It was at the time of the fire in 1906 that he permanently returned to Oakland.

REAL ESTATE BUSINESS

Since then he had engaged in the real estate business in Fruitvale and the Melrose district in East Oakland, where he had his home.

Besides his widow, he is survived by five daughters. They are: Miss Edith L. Woodward, Dr. Grace Schilling, Mrs. Alexander Stewart, Mrs. Robert Moyle and Florence Aphearn.

Plans for one ceremonial have been taken in hand by local G. A. R. posts and a funeral with full military honors is to be accorded him.

Oakland Tribune, Wednesday, September 8, 1920
[Interred at Mountain View Cemetery, Oakland]

1921

Company A
Respected Pioneer Passes Away

George W. Towle passed away at his home on Mission avenue yesterday after an illness of a week from pneumonia.

Through his death San Rafael loses one of its most highly respected citizens, and the legal profession one of its leading members.

Mr. Towle came to San Rafael in 1876. Within a short time he was elected to the position of District Attorney of Marin county. Later he served as City Attorney of San Rafael. He was a member of the Grand Army of the Republic, having served in the Civil War with Company A, 2nd Massachusetts Infantry *[Cavalry]*, as a sergeant.

Since his retirement from public office in Marin county he had practiced law continuously in San Francisco, and was for many years the legal advisor for the Pacific Coast Steamship Company.

Mr. Towle had been one of the foremost figures for the betterment of San Rafael and had taken a keen interest in all public affairs.

Mrs. Towle passed away several years ago, leaving her husband and one daughter, Mrs. Kate Caroline Towle, who survives her father.

Mr. Towle and his daughter numbered among their closest friends many of the most highly respected families in Marin county. The deceased was 78 years of age and was born in Maine.

The funeral service will be held Saturday, with burial arrangements under the direction of the F.E. Sawyer Company.

The Marin Journal, San Rafael, Thursday, March 24, 1921.
[Interred at Mt. Tamalpais Cemetery, San Rafael]

Washington D.C.
September 26 '21

Mr. John Fletcher
  Dear Comrade.
    My Dear old John you do not know how delighted I am to receive a letter from you. It brings back so many incidents of our strenuous life from 1862 to 1865, and not a single day of it but what was honorable in the highest degree. The photo you send me of yourself and son are just splendid, and while I cannot see in your picture the old Soldier I knew nearly 60 years ago, I do see a great resemblance in your sons face to you as you then were. You certainly are a fine looking Father & Son.

This whole world is upside down and you and I will be gone a long time before peace and plenty prevails over the world again. In our own dear Country we are in a terrible mess. The last Administration pauperized the country for the next hundred years. I believe President Harding and party are doing the best they know how and have the interest of the nation at heart, but Capital & Labor are both selfish and not real friends of the government. What little time is left for you & me let us keep in the middle of the road and do the best we can.

I shall be pleased to hear from you when ever you can find time to write. Please give my love and best regards to Mrs. Houseman and to all your children, Grandchildren and Great Grandchildren. Yes every one and lots of love and good luck to your own dear self.

God bless you all

Henry G. Burlingham

Vallejo Naval & Historical Museum, Vallejo, California
[Henry G. Burlingham, Company A, mustered out as Capt. Co. G; John Fletcher, Company A,
mustered out as Sergeant.]

❖❖

1924

❖❖

Company A

HONORED VETERAN WELLS W. WEST CALLED BY DEATH

Death ended the long and commendable career of **Wells W. West**, at his home in west Lakeport on Monday. Mr. West had shown remarkable vitality for his years, although ailing and enfeebled in the past few months. He was 87 years, eight months and two days old.

Among the Argonauts who sought gold in the West in early days, Mr. West crossed the plains in 1853, and following an adventurous career of nine years in the mines of Amador county and on cattle ranches, he enlisted in one of the California Hundreds, as No. 96 in his troop. These were volunteer cavalrymen from California who made the long trip to serve for the North in the Civil War. William Morris was another Lake county man who served in one of these troops.

William Wallace West was born in Erie county, Pennsylvania, September 3, 1836. He spent his boyhood days in Illinois, and was a youth of 16 when he made the trip Westward by ox-team. Following his enlistment, in October, 1862, Mr. West and his comrades were transported by ship to the Isthmus of Panama and from there to New York. They were assigned as Co. A of the 2nd Massachusetts Cavalry, and in this company, Mr. West saw active service until July 20, 1865. When the company was mustered out, there were but 23 remaining of the original one hundred.

Following the war, Mr. West made his home in Missouri, and at LaClede, in that State, in 1867 he married Delilah J. Thompson, who survives him. Mr. West united with the Christian Church in October, 1872, which membership he faithfully and actively kept until his death.

The family lived in Missouri until 1878, then in Ellsworth, Kansas until 1882. In that summer the family moved to Lakeport, where Mr. and Mrs. West have made their home continuously since. Of the nine children born to their union, Maud passed away in February, 1917; Jessie in December, 1896; Ray, in February, 1899; and Dwight in January, 1889. The surviving children are M. Blanche, wife of Dr. G.W. Mallory of Santa Rosa; Lester W. West of Everett, Washington; Guy H. West of Santa Rosa; Cora L., wife of Charles A. Benson of Big Valley; Wirt M. West of Modesto. There are eleven grandchildren.

Mr. West followed the business of contracting and building during his mature years. Without taking much active part in public life, he was an upright and respected citizen, a man of bright mentality and devoted to his family. The bereaved relatives have the sympathy of a host of friends in their loss.

The funeral services will be held at the Christian Church tomorrow afternoon at 2:00 o'clock and entombment will be made in Hartley Cemetery.

Lake County Bee, Lakeport, Wednesday, May 7, 1924.
[Interred at Hartley Cemetery, Lakeport]

1926

H. G. BURLINGHAM
6600 Piney Branch Road
Washington, D,C,

Jany 7, 1926

My Dear Old Comrade, John Fletcher

       I am much pleased to receive a card from you showing you are still on top, God Bless you dear old John, I often think of you and of the times we had up in the Shenandoah Valley Va, 61 years ago. Well John you and I are about all thats left of the Cal100. You & I and W.R. Crumpton, Zanesville Ohio and Henry Sherwin Ayers Mass. I do not know of any others. I will be 90 ys of age next 5th of June and fairly well no fault to find. I was 44 years in the pension Bureau have been retired since July 1920. I sold my old house and moved here last September. My sister keeps house for me. We are about 5 miles north of the White house, out in the suburbs nicely located. I try to control myself and let it go at that for you and me there is little left for our enjoyment. I pray never to become a burden and am trying to live each day in the little sunshine that is afforded, thankful for the past, and with faith in Him who doeth all things well. But Dear John you and I have no fears having done our best for our Country and our fellow man. I trust you are quite well and still enjoy yourself in thinking over some of the events of long ago. Living in the past is about the only pleasure I enjoy and try each day not to worry. Seeing the sights of Washington so much enjoyed by visitors is no longer interesting to me. I try to exercise every day weather permitting, but enjoy my old Chair about as well as anything. Now it would be a great pleasure to see you John and swap a few lies about long ago, but this cannot be. Please remember me to all your family as your dear old faithful Comrade and true American. Good luck Good Bye and God Bless you John for ever.

H.G. Burlingham

Vallejo Naval & historical Museum, Vallejo, California

Santa Monica, Aug. 23, '26

Dear Comrade Fletcher:

       Received your letter inclosing snapshot for which many thanks. For a eighty odd year old man I must say that you are a winner. I don't suppose that you will hardly believe me but I will bet a doughnut that I could pick you out of a hundred men so keen is my memory for faces. And, you carry your young man's looks even today. Am I right in thinking that you are Quant's brother in law? It seems as though once he told me something to that effect. I saw a notice of the death of our Major D.W. Thompson in Santa Rosa and it said that he left a daughter. I wrote her and the letter was returned unopened. Do you know anything about his last days and why his name was not on our list of survivors? Please write me occasionally,

Yours   E.I. Drisko

Vallejo Naval & Historical Museum, Vallejo, California

❖❖
1927
❖❖
Company A

San Francisco May 22ⁿᵈ 1927

John Fletcher,
Dear Comrade;
I regret to inform you of the passing away of our comrade Captain Henry Burlingham, in Washington D.C. on May fourth, our ranks are fast thinning as we number nine. Captain Burlingham had attained the age of ninety one and till but two weeks before his death was in excellent spirits.

Yours truly.
(signed) Samuel W. Backus

Vallejo Naval & Historical Museum, Vallejo, California

❖❖
Company A

DEATH TAKES J. FLETCHER

John Fletcher, 88 year old Civil War veteran, who died at his home, 530 Monterey street last night after an illness, will be buried Saturday afternoon at 2 o'clock. Services which will be private, will be under the auspices of the Farragut Post, Grand Army of the Republic, and will take place at the residence. Interment will follow in the Masonic and Odd Fellows cemetery.

Fletcher, who was born in New York, came to Vallejo in 1859, and was considered one of the oldest pioneers of the city. He was, until the time of his death, the last surviving member of California's "100" troops which left here to take part in the Civil War.

The deceased made his home here with his grandson, Edward Houseman. Surviving him including his widow, Mrs. Mary Fletcher, are three sons and eight daughters, John Fletcher, of Oakland; Richard Fletcher, of San Francisco; Robert Fletcher, of Brentwood; Mrs. G. Houseman, of Vallejo; Mrs. F. Summer, of Oakland; Mrs. E. Smith, of Winters; Mrs. J. Wilkening, of Sacramento; Mrs. Earl Hudson, of Byron; Mrs. C. Mathewson, of Palo Alto, and Mrs. F. Burton, of Fresno. Several grand-children also survive.

The Vallejo Evening Chronicle, Thursday, December 15, 1927.
[Interred at Sunrise Memorial Cemetery, Vallejo]

❖❖

Company A

ARMSTRONG-Hugh Armstrong, Funeral services will be held Thursday Dec. 29, at 1:30 p.m., from the chapel of O.A. Kirkelle & Co. Interment Soldiers' Home cemetery.

Santa Monica Evening Outlook, Wednesday, December 28, 1927.
[Interred at the National Cemetery, Los Angeles]

1928

2502-16ᵗʰ St. Santa Monica, Calif., Feb. 6, '28.

My Dear Mrs. Houseman:

Just received your letter and hasten to thank you for writing me. I had already heard thru Gen. Backus of your father's passing and, of course, felt badly as it took one more of our fast dwindling band of old heroes. This leaves just eight of us and none of the "one hundred". Good old John. He was a good soldier and always ready to do his full duty. The snap shot that you sent me some time ago bore some of his young manhood looks and I could have picked him out of a hundred men. I have a great admiration for the "crack Cordon of California Cavalry" as we were known and doubt very much if a similar body of men could be found today. Again thanking you for writing, I am yours

E.I. Drisko

Vallejo Naval & Historical Museum, Vallejo, California
[Everard I. Drisko, Co. M; Mrs. Houseman, daughter of John Fletcher, Co. A]

1930

Company L

GEN. BACKUS, PIONEER, DIES

San Francisco, April 10.

General **Samuel W. Backus**, 85, senior past commander of the G. A. R., former postmaster and immigration commissioner, builder, soldier and clubman, died at his home, 1107 Jones street, early this morning following an illness of 12 days.

Funeral services will be private at the home Saturday morning and at Cypress Lawn cemetery.

Born in Pine Plains, N.Y., in 1844, General Backus was brought to California when only 5 years old.

At the age of 17 during the Civil war he joined the California Commandery battalion which later became the Second Massachusetts Cavalry of the Army of the Republic. When only 19 he was commissioned a second lieutenant and as such was chosen from 100 officers to escort President Lincoln into Richmond, Va., after its fall.

COMMANDED FORT

At the close of the war he was placed in command of Fort Bidwell for the winter of 1865, and 1866.

He resigned that year to enter the shipping and commission business here and for ten years operated one of the first regular lines of Oregon packets.

General Backus represented San Francisco in the last legislature under the old constitution and in 1880 was appointed adjutant general of the state militia by the late Senator George Perkins, at that time governor.

In 1886 he was named postmaster of San Francisco by President Harrison and reappointed four years later to serve until 1894.

After his resignation, General Backus formed the Western Expanded Metal and Fireproofing company here and for 20 years served as its president.

This was one of the first of its kind in the world and among the many buildings he contracted for were the Ferry building, the Fairmount Hotel, the Monadnock, Butler and Kohl buildings, still standing.

General Backus was nominated to the post of immigration commissioner here by President Taft and served two years in that capacity under President Wilson.

VARIED CAREER

Besides his many political, military and business activities, General Backus was for 24 years president of the board of directors of the Veterans Home at Yountville.

He was senior past commander of the G. A. R. in California, the senior past master of Occidental Lodge, F. & A. M. here, a Shriner, a Knight Templar and a member of the Union League and Commercial club.

He is survived by his widow, Mrs. Nellie G. S. Backus, who lives at the Jones street home, and one son, Sanborn Backus of St. Francis Wood.

General Backus had enjoyed unusually good health up to three months ago, when he caught cold and was confined to the house. He had been in bed, however, only 12 days before his death.

Oakland Tribune, Oakland, Saturday, April 12, 1930.
The Chronicle, San Francisco, Saturday, April 12, 1930.
[Interred at the National Cemetery, Presidio of San Francisco]

Backus

In the passing away of General Samuel W. Backus, which occurred at his home, 1107 Jones street, San Francisco, last Thursday, April 10th, the Home has lost one of its greatest and staunchest friends, one who for 48 years had worked hard and faithfully in its interests and improvements.

One of its inceptors and founders in 1882, with almost continuous service on its Board of Directors, of which, he was President for 24 years, and of which, up to the time of his retirement two years ago, he rarely missed a meeting, he labored hard and faithfully throughout nearly half a century, for the welfare and interests of the members of the Home, and it was only his rapidly failing health that forced him to resign from the Board of Directors last year.

General Backus served during the Civil War as a member of the First California Battalion, which afterwards became a part of the 2nd Massachusetts Cavalry. He served with distinction as a second lieutenant under General Phil Sheridan and was wounded in action. Later he was chosen as one of the hundred to escort President Lincoln into Richmond.

Born in Poughkeepse, New York, General Backus was brought to California in 1852 over the isthmus of Panama. At the close of the Civil War he returned to California and engaged in business. He served as Postmaster of San Francisco, under Presidents Harrison and Arthur and as Commissioner of Immigration under President Taft.

He is survived by his widow, Mrs. Nell Grant Backus, and a son, Sanborn Backus, both of San Francisco.

The funeral was from his residence in San Francisco, last Saturday, April 12, 1930.

The Napa Register, Tuesday, April 15, 1930

❖❖

1931

❖❖

Company L

M'LEAN, CIVIL WAR VET, DIES

Death yesterday ended the long career of **Andrew A. McLean**, 89, pioneer San Francisco printer and Civil War veteran.

McLean was prominently identified with the newspapers of early California and had made numerous friends during his 72 years as a member of the typographical union.

Twice he was wounded by rebel bullets. He fought at Gettysburg, he fought with Sheridan and he was at Appomattox when Lee surrendered. He remembered seeing President Lincoln on the breastworks at Fort Stevens.

Born in New York in 1841, McLean ran away from home as a boy of 11 and sailed around the Horn to California.

Following the Civil War he engaged in business for himself. He had maintained an office at 964A Market street for 47 years, re-establishing himself in the same place when the building was rebuilt after the fire in 1906.

He was a member of Lincoln Post No. 1, Grand Army of the Republic.

Surviving are a son, Alfred W. McLean, and two daughters, Mrs. Arthur Cooley and Mrs. Nelson Lansing.

The Examiner, San Francisco, Thursday, January 22, 1931
The Chronicle, San Francisco, Thursday, January 22, 1931
[Interred at Cypress Lawn Cemetery, Colma]

❖❖

1933

❖❖

Company E

Death Takes **C.V. Jenkins**
Supposed Oldest Settler Was Civil War Veteran With California Cavalry Battalion

Death came yesterday noon to Carl Van Jenkins, for eighty-five years a resident of Los Angeles believed to have been the oldest settler of the city. He died at his home, 1153 Santee street, after an illness of a week. Funeral services will be announced later.

Mr. Jenkins, who was born in Circleville, O, June 2, 1839, came to California when a boy. With his stepfather, George Dalton, Sr., he crossed the Isthmus of Panama and landed at San Pedro on March 9, 1850. He learned the printing trade and worked on the first paper in Los

Angeles, The Star. Later he was connected with other publications. At the outbreak of the Civil War he went with a California cavalry battalion of 500 which paid its own way to New York and enlisted as the Second Massachusetts Cavalry, participating in fifty battles of the war. Mr Jenkins was taken prisoner and was held in both Libby and Andersonville prisons, he being one of three who survived out of a company of 150. At the close of the war he returned to Los Angeles and was married to Miss Phoebe Sprague, who preceded him in death.

For seven years he was overseer of the water supply of Los Angeles and in the nineties acted as deputy United States Marshal. He lived on various ranches now located in the heart of the city. He had lived at the Santee street address more than forty years. All his relatives with the exception of a foster daughter, Juanita M. Olivera, are dead.

He was baptized a Catholic in the old Plaza Church when a boy and belonged to Post No. 55, G.A.R., and was a member of the Pioneer society.

The Times, Los Angeles, Sunday, January 29, 1933.
[Interred at Evergreen Memorial Cemetery, Los Angeles. Charles M. Jenkins (paper in error) was taken prisoner August 24, 1863 at Gooding's Tavern near Fairfax, Va. and was paroled from prison November 26, 1864.]

1935

SURVIVORS OF FAMED CIVIL WAR UNIT MEET HERE

Californians Who Shipped East In "63 Recall Old Battles, Adventures.

The last two survivors of the 558 young men in the famous California battalion, who sailed out of the Golden Gate 72 years ago for the Civil War, met here yesterday to talk of old times.

They are William H. Lawrence, 98 of San Jose, and William Morris 94, of Lakeport.

Reminiscences of brushes and ambuscades with Colonel Mosby's famed Confederate band of guerrillas, of service with Sheridan down the Shenandoah valley tossed back and forth as the aged but hearty warriors exchanged "remember whens."

COMRADES REUNITED.

Each had thought he was the "last man" of California's "famous five hundred" until Lawrence chanced to run across a newspaper article about Morris and the reunion followed.

They had strange parallels to their long lives since the March day of 1863 when they enlisted in San Francisco. Morris paying $80 stage fare down from the Trinity Mountain mines, where he was working. Lawrence hiking five miles to Alviso from Lawrence station, which his father founded in 1850, to board the bay steamer "Sophie McLean" to San Francisco.

"And we had to pay our own passage to the Atlantic seaboard", Lawrence recalls.

"Then we were mustered into the Second Massachusetts cavalry, and the fun began," chuckles Morris.

MOSBY CAPTURED BOTH.

Their chief job, it seems, was to keep track of the phantom Colonel Mosby and his band. Both fell victims to Colonel Mosby's habit of lying in ambush and picking off Yankee prisoners.

"We had 15 cavalry fights, before they captured me at Oil Tavern," says Morris.

"and they captured me at Drainsville, Virginia, with 25 other comrades." adds Lawrence.

"I was removed from Belle Island to Libby prison and then when they thought I was dying I was exchanged," continues Morris. "A month later I recovered consciousness in Boston and by a special order of the secretary of war I was able to rejoin my outfit in time to serve under Sheridan in the Shenandoah valley campaign.

ESCAPED, RECAPTURED.

"I did my best to get back and nearly got hung twice for trying," Lawrence recalls. "Conditions were so bad in the various Confederate prisons we were taken to - Libby prison, Andersonville, Savannah-that 21 of our unit of 25 died in the first seven months. I managed to escape and for three weeks worked across Georgia, almost to Sherman's lines, when they got me."

Of the 558 members of the California battalion, which was in 52 engagements during the war, only 181 were mustered out at its end. The rest were in their graves or in hospitals. "It was a fine bunch of men," Lawrence testifies.

"Yes," agrees Morris, "only one out of five who volunteered could pass the physical tests in San Francisco.

Both of the old warriors twice voted for Abraham Lincoln for president, and Lawrence also voted for him for senator when he ran against Douglas, in Illinois in 1858.

San Jose Mercury Herald, Sunday, May 5, 1935

❖❖❖

Company M

Funeral Services For Noted Civil War Comrade To Be Held Today.

LAST SEVEN G.A.R. VETS TO ATTEND LAWRENCE RITES

Funeral services for **William Howard Lawrence**, 98, widely known Civil War veteran of San Jose who died on the eve of Memorial day Thursday midnight, will be held at 2 o'clock today from the Curry and Gripenstraw parlors.

Santa Clara county's seven remaining Civil War veterans, who missed him in the seventeenth annual Memorial day observation yesterday, will take part in G.A.R. services at the Santa Clara cemetery for the last member of F.O.C. Ord post, G.A.R. of Los Gatos.

ONE MAN SURVIVES

Mourning him also is William Morris, 94, of Lakeport, who with Lawrence's passing, becomes "last man" of the famed California Battalion of 558 young men who sailed east 72 years ago to serve under General Sheridan in the campaigns of the Shenandoah valley. Captured by Mosby's guerrillas, Lawrence twice escaped from dismal southern prisons and was twice recaptured, missing hanging by a hair's breadth.

HERE SINCE 60's.

After the war, Lawrence returned to this valley to rejoin his parents who in 1850 located where Lawrence station, named for his father, now stands. The deceased was born in Massachusetts and first came to this valley in 1860.

Husband of the late Lottie E. Lawrence, he had three sons, two of whom survive. William C. Lawrence of Wrangel, Alaska; Albert H. Lawrence of Santiago, Chile, and the late Dr. G. Alfred Lawrence of New York..

San Jose Mercury Herald, Friday, May 31, 1935

[Interred at Mission City Memorial Park, Santa Clara]

1937

Company E

WM. MORRIS, NOTED VETERAN, ANSWERS FINAL ROLL CALL

Last Survivor of State's Battalion In Civil War, Passes At His Lakeport Home In 96th Year

California's lone survivor of enlisted men from this state in the Civil War, William Morris, beloved Lakeport citizen, passed to eternal sleep at his home in Lakeport Friday night. The grand old veteran was in his 96th year when he departed to join his comrades in a greater life where eternal peace is the much deserved reward.

Health Failed Of Late

Showing visible signs of the weakening of his former great physique, Mr. Morris had been ill at his home for two weeks prior to being stricken on Thursday night. He slumped into a comma in the early evening and Dr. Chas. Craig was summoned to attend him. Pneumonia was setting in. On Friday night at 10:45, death ensued. Mr. Morris passing quickly and peacefully. He failed to rally from the comma of the night before.

Name Will Go Into California history

The name of William Morris will go down into California history as a pioneer of the Golden West and the last of the historic California Battalion of 557 men who sailed from San Francisco to fight for the union in the Civil War in 1863.

Mr. Morris enlisted in February of that historic year and soon the battalion embarked on the frigate Constitution to Isthmus of Panama, was transshipped to the east coast and completed the journey to New York on the frigate Ocean Queen.

Only 36 of the original 557 men were alive when the last shot was fired at Appomattox. As stated, with the passing of Mr. Morris, the last survivor of this noted California battalion has passed on.

Born In Missouri

Born in Bates County, Missouri, on May 3, 1841, Mr. Morris crossed the plains as a driver of an ox team in a wagon party in the year 1857. He was a lad of 16 and accompanied his parents, Rev. Milton and Sarah Dodge Morris. The father was a Methodist minister.

The parents were the first white couple to be married within the boundaries of what is now Kansas.

Wm. Morris was 22 years of age when his country called for volunteers and he enlisted on the side of the Union, as stated.

After the eventful voyage on the frigates and arrival in New York, Mr. Morris went to Boston and was immediately sent to Washington. He was captured by Mosely in sight of Washington and sent to Belle Island and later Libby Prison.

Mr. Morris once stated to the Bee:

"I served until July 19, 1865, when I was exchanged for a Southern prisoner. I fought in 33 battles besides participating in many skirmishes. These included fights with Mosely's guerillas and Sheridan's celebrated charge at Winchester".

When Sheridan took charge of the military department, Mr. Morris was transferred to the Reserve Brigade of the first division of Sheridan's cavalry troops where he remained until discharged on July 21, at Fairfax, Virginia. He finally mustered out in Boston in August, 1865.

Entered College

He immediately went to Tabor, Iowa, where he entered college. On February 22, 1866, he married Miss Susanne Wilson. They lived in Fremont county, Iowa, twenty years where nine children were born to them, five of whom now survive, all residents of Lakeport.

After living several years in Kansas, the family came to California in 1890. They lived on Howell mountain in Napa county three years, then came to Lake county and settled in Scotts valley. In 1910 they removed to Lakeport and Mr. Morris built the family home on Eleventh street, where his death occurred last week.

Celebrated Golden Wedding In 1916

Mrs. Morris preceded her husband in death on Dec. 31, 1919. On February 22, 1916, the couple celebrated their gold wedding in Lakeport and a number of friends and relatives enjoyed the occasion, among who was the late Judge M.S. Sayre.

Surviving Children

The surviving children are the Misses Bessie and Olive Morris, Mrs. Sadie Hendricks, Mrs. Nellie Abercrombie and John Morris, all well known and respected citizens of Lakeport. Another daughter, Mrs. Helen Curry, wife of J.W. Curry, local furniture dealer, passed away in recent years.

Mr. Morris was exceptionally fond and proud of his children and their outstanding characters. He often spoke about them. And they will miss him. In their sadness, they have the deep sympathy of many friends.

Mr. Morris contributed articles for numerous newspaper in his younger days that appeared in the American Bee Journal, St. Helena Star, Falls City, Nebraska Journal, Toledo Blade and others.

Mr. Morris led a Christian life and abstained from liquor and tobacco. He was a good citizen and patriot. His mind was always clear and his memory was keen. He delighted in recounting his experiences in the war with the south. During the battles in which he fought he always carried his Bible.

Mr. Morris was relating an incident about his pocket Bible during the war. His superior officer was joshing him about it. So a short time later Mr. Morris presented the officer with a similar Bible. With a jest the officer placed it in his pocket at his left breast. A bullet later struck the Bible, tore a hole through the cover and pages but did not penetrate the flesh.

The officer was converted to the faith because of this incident. He always believed the little Bible had saved his life and no doubt it did on the occasion of the bullet.

San Jose Vet Was Next To Last

William H. Lawrence, who shared honors with Morris as a survivor of the California battalion, died at his home in San Jose on May 30, 1936. Several years before the passing of Lawrence the two veterans held a reunion in San Jose.

Last Rites Largely Attended

The last rites of Mr. Morris, which were largely attended, were conducted Monday afternoon at 2:00 o'clock at Jones Mortuary. Entombment took place at Hartley cemetery.

Lake County Bee, Lakeport, Thursday, December 16, 1937
[Interred at Hartley Cemetery, Lakeport]

Roll Call

ALTA CALIFORNIA

History of the California Hundred in Brief.

The friends of the gallant California Hundred, will read with interest the original muster roll of that now famous Company, with the remarks by their commander, giving the history of the Company in brief, which has been handed us for publication:

Captain J. Sewall Reed - Promoted Major. Killed in action with Mosby's guerrillas at Drainsville, Virginia, February 22d, 1864.

First Lieutenant Archibald McKendry - Promoted Captain of Company G, subsequently promoted Major, and mustered out as Colonel Commanding regiment.

Second Lieutenant John W. Sim -Discharged by Special Order of the War Department, at Vienna, Va., May 4th, 1864.

Armstrong, Hugh - Promoted to First Sergeant, subsequently to Lieutenant, and subsequently Captain, and mustered out as Captain of California Hundred.

Ackerman, Charles H. - Promoted Corporal, subsequently Sergeant, subsequently First Sergeant California Hundred.

Ackerman, James B. - Killed in charge at Halltown, Va., August 20th, 1864.

Allen, Henry W. - Transferred to Invalid Corps from Camp Windham, Va., July 20th, 1863.

Allen, E. Henry - Wounded in action at Rockville, Md. Died of wounds through neglect of Surgeon, in hospital at Washington, D.C., August 16th, 1864.

Allan, Charles - Promoted Sergeant, subsequently First Lieutenant of Fifth Mass. (Colored) Cavalry.

Anderson, George - Deserted August 2d, 1864; returned under President's Proclamation Act, April 4th, 1865.

Anthony, William G. - Promoted to Corporal, subsequently to Sergeant Company C.

Burdick, Joseph B. - Killed in action at South Anna Bridge, Va., June 26th, 1863.

Benjamin, Charles E. - Promoted Sergeant Company A, subsequently transferred to Non. Com. Staff, as Commissary Sergeant.

Barnstead, Thomas D. - Promoted to Sergeant Major, July 21st, 1865.

Balcom, Darnly O. -Transferred to Company G, promoted to Sergeant, subsequently to Second Lieutenant, and subsequently to First Lieutenant.

Burlingham, Henry G. - Promoted First Sergeant, subsequently Second Lieutenant, then to First Lieutenant and Adjutant, and mustered out as Captain of Company G.

Bumgardner, William H.H. - Promoted to Corporal. Died at farmhouse of wounds received in action with Mosby's guerrillas at Mount Zion Church, July 6th, 1864.

Balke, Charles - Promoted Corporal July 21st, 1865.

Baker, A. Frank - Deserted from Readville, Mass., subsequently returned, was restored to duty, deserted again from Falls Church, Va.

Beach, Nathan A. - Went home to Canada on furlough from Headquarters, Washington, D.C., and failed to return.

Briggs, Charles P. - Mustered out July 30th, 1865.

Blake, Josephus - Discharged in Boston, Mass., on account of bad eyesight, Sept. 1st, 1863.

Campbell, Edward B. - Promoted Corporal July 21st, 1865.

Carey, Jeremiah J. - Promoted Corporal July 1st, 1865.

Collins, Wm. W. - Promoted Second Lieutenant, Tenth New York Cavalry.

Corbett, Samuel J. - Promoted Corporal, subsequently reduced to the ranks, subsequently promoted Sergeant of Regimental Band- reduced to the ranks July 18th, 1865.

Cunningham, William - Mustered out July 20th, 1865, as Saddler.

Chalmers, John M. - Mustered out July 20th, 1865.

Chandler, William S. - Discharged from hospital at Washington, D.C., July 1865.

Crum, Henry - Promoted Sergeant, subsequently reduced to the ranks, subsequently promoted Corporal, then Sergeant.

Crumpton, Wesley R. - Promoted Corporal, reduced to the ranks, subsequently promoted Corporal, then Sergeant. First Sergeant of Company, promoted Second Lieutenant July 9th, 1865.

Davis, George F. - Promoted corporal, then sergeant, subsequently Second Lieutenant Fourth Massachusetts Cavalry.

Dewey, Charles S. - Deserted from Readville, Mass., February 27th, 1863.

Dearborn, Valorus - Promoted Corporal February, 1864. Killed in action at Opequan Creek, Shenandoah Valley, Va., September 13th, 1864.

Demsey, Cyrus F. - Taken prisoner by Mosby at Coyle's Tavern, Va., August 24th, 1864, subsequently exchanged and returned to Company, May 19th, 1865.

Doane, Gustavus C. - Promoted to Sergeant, subsequently reduced to ranks, subsequently promoted to First Lieutenant Mississippi Marine Brigade.

Ellett, Richard S. - Wounded in action at South Anna Bridge, Va., promoted from Hospital at Gloucester Point, Va., to Lieutenant Mississippi Marine Brigade.

Forbes, Alexander C. - Killed by accidental discharge of pistol, at Halltown, Va., August 9th, 1864.

Freeman, James - Deserted from Camp Windham, Va., August 1st, 1863.
Alias Alexander Purdy.

Fletcher, John - Promoted to Corporal, subsequently to Sergeant, captured in action on Opequan Creek, Va., August 10th, 1864, subsequently exchanged and returned to Company, May 21st, 1865, promoted Lieutenant July, 1865.

Gibbs, Byron D. - Promoted Corporal March 23d, 1865.

Goulding, George W. - Captured in action at Rockville, Md., July 13th, 1864, subsequently exchanged and returned to Company May 2d, 1865, promoted Corporal March 23d, 1865.

Hall, Frederick - Promoted Corporal November 1st, 1864, promoted Sergeant July 18th, 1865.

Hanscom, Samuel C. - Promoted Corporal. Killed in action near Mount Zion Church, Va., July 6th, 1864.

Hammerburg, William - Deserted from Readville, Md., January 26th, 1863.

Hill, Charles W. - Promoted at Gloucester Point, Va., to his old command, First Lieutenant First Missouri Cavalry.

Hill, John A. - Discharged for disability from Vienna, Va., April 1864.

Hilliard, William H.I. - Promoted Corporal, subsequently Sergeant, subsequently Second Lieutenant Company B.

Holt, George I. - Discharged from Hospital at Annapolis Junction, Md., June 10th, 1865.

Hunt, James A. - Discharged for disability, at Gloucester Point, Va., May 10th, 1863.

Hunter, John L. - Mustered out July 20th, 1865.

Hussey, William H.H. - Promoted to Corporal, subsequently to Sergeant, subsequently to Second Lieutenant Company C., mustered out as Captain.

Johnson, George M. - Mustered out July 20th, 1865.

Knowles, Frank - Deserted from Readville, Mass., January 26th, 1864.

Kinnie, Charles M. - Promoted Sergeant, subsequently to Lieutenant, subsequently to Captain and A.A.G. Reserve Brigade, First Division Cavalry.

Leighton, Alfred L. - Died of fever in Hospital, Washington, D.C., July 25th, 1863.

Lee, Alfred - Company Bugler. Died in Hospital at Vienna, Va., of brain fever, May 1st, 1864.

Legler, Charles - Mustered out July 20th, 1865.

Loane, Abraham - Captured in action with Mosby's Guerrillas at Mount Zion Church, Va., July 6th, 1864, subsequently exchanged, and discharged from Hospital at Readville, Mass., June, 1865.

Libby, Frank O. - Promoted Corporal, subsequently reduced to the ranks.

Locke, Benjamin - Promoted Corporal, and subsequently Sergeant.

Mazy, Henry - Mustered out July 20th, 1865.

Merriam, Jonathan - Captured at Rockville, Md., July 13th, 1864, subsequently exchanged, and discharged from Hospital at Readville, Mass., June, 1865.

McCarty, John - Killed in action at Coyles' Tavern, Va., August 24th, 1863.

McCarthy, John D. - Promoted Hospital Steward.

McIntosh, Isaac R. - Promoted Corporal, subsequently Sergeant, subsequently Lieutenant, then to Captain Company F.

McNeil, William H. - Promoted Corporal. Discharged by Special Orders A.G.O., June 20th, 1865.

Magary, Albert - Deserted from Readville, Mass., January 26th, 1863.

Nellis, E. - Deserted from Readville, Mass., Jan. 26th, 1863.

Nelson, H. - Deserted from Readville, Mass., Jan. 26th, 1863.

Nixon, John - Transferred to Company B. Killed by bushwhackers, while at a house near King and Queen's Court House, Va.

Owen, John W. - Promoted Corporal, subsequently Sergeant, subsequently Second Lieutenant, accidentally shot himself through the foot, and was discharged from Hospital, May, 1865.

Pelham, James W. - Discharged for disability from Hospital at Frederick, Md., June 4th, 1865.

Percy, William - Promoted Corporal, subsequently Sergeant, subsequently Lieutenant Fourth Mass. Cavalry, afterwards Captain.

Pool, Melbourne Z. - Mustered out July 20th, 1865 as Wagoner.

Parker, R.M. - Promoted Corporal, subsequently Lieutenant Fifth Mass. (Colored) Cavalry.

Powers, Charles H. - Promoted Sergeant, subsequently reduced to the ranks. Promoted Corporal July 21st, 1865.

Plummer, George - Promoted Corporal, subsequently Second Lieutenant. Mustered out as First Lieutenant California Hundred.

Quant, Frederick J. - Promoted Corporal, subsequently reduced to the ranks.

Rice, Hamilton - Deserted from Readville, Mass., subsequently arrested and discharged from Hospital, Washington, D.C.

Robinson, Wm. A. - Promoted Sergeant-Major, subsequently Lieutenant and Adjutant.

Rone, Carlos - Transferred to Invalid Corps, subsequently discharged from Hospital at Philadelphia, Penn., for disability.

Ross, Joshua C. - Mustered out July 20th, 1865.

Samuels, Richard C. - Mustered out July 20th, 1865.

Schrow, Henry - Promoted Corporal, discharged from Hospital at Washington, June 20th, 1865.

Sherwin, Henry C. - Promoted Corporal, subsequently Sergeant and Q.M. Sergeant of the Company.

Sivalls, Benson - Discharged for disability from the Hospital at Alexandria, Va., June, 1865.

Smith, Samuel, Jr. - Promoted Corporal and subsequently Sergeant.

Speight, Charles L. - Captured in action at Rockville, Md., July 13, 1864. Died in prison at Danville, Va., March 4, 1865.

Starr, William E. - Mustered out July 20th, 1865.

Sterling, Edward R. - Promoted Corporal, subsequently Sergeant, subsequently Lieutenant of the Fourth Mass. Cavalry.

Towle, George W. - Promoted Corporal, October, 1864. Promoted Sergeant July 18th, 1865.

Tubbs, Henry S.C. - Captured in action at Rockville, Md., July 13th, 1864, subsequently exchanged and returned to Company, May 21st, 1865. Promoted Corporal July 1st, 1865.

Thompson, George - Promoted Second Lieutenant Ninety-Sixth Regiment New York Infantry.

Verick, George W. - Died of wounds received in action at Coyles' Tavern, August 24th, 1863.

West, Wells W. - Mustered out July 20th, 1865.

Wheat, Jas. L. - Promoted Sergeant, subsequently Second Lieutenant Fifth Mass. (Colored) Cavalry, subsequently Captain.

White, Peter E. - Promoted Sergeant and Chief Bugler.

Williams, J.H. - Discharged for disability at Boston, Mass., October, 1863.

Winship, John - Mustered out July 20th, 1865.

Woodman, H.F. - Promoted to Corporal, subsequently to Sergeant, Company G., subsequently to Lieutenant, wounded in action at Waynesboro, Va., September 28th, 1864. Died of his wounds at Mount Jackson, Va

Woodward, E.W. - Promoted Second Lieutenant, Twenty-Fifth New York Cavalry, subsequently Captain.

Watson, James - Promoted Corporal November 1st, 1864, promoted Sergeant July 18th, 1865.

Alta California , San Francisco, Thursday, October 5, 1865

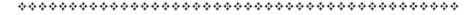

Major D.W.C. Thompson's Report to the Adjutant General-California 1867

Of the commissioned officers and enlisted men of the California Cavalry Battalion, as originally organized in San Francisco, January 15, 1863, with remarks relating to the services, promotion, wounds, death, discharge, etc. of each:

   Field Officer **Major DeWitt C. Thompson** - In command of the Battalion, from January 15th to July 15, 1863. In command of cavalry camp near Alexandria, Va., from July 15th to August 16, 1863. In command of Battalion in the field from August 16th to September 16, 1863. In command of "cavalry forces, Upper Potomac," from September 16, 1863, to August 9, 1864, embracing post at Edwards' Ferry and all troops between Washington and Point of Rocks, Md. Joined Army of the Shenandoah August 9th with detachments of 620 cavalry, which were ordered to their respective regiments. Resigned and honorably discharged by General Sheridan August 9, 1864.

EIGENBRODT'S COMPANY.

         Captain: Charles S. Eigenbrodt - In command of company from January 23d to April 17th. In command of squadron from April 17, 1863, to March 6, 1864. In command of Battalion at Muddy Branch Ford, and to the field from March 6th to August 26th. Killed in battle of Halltown, Va., August 25, 1864.

First Lieutenant: John C. Norcross - In company February, 1863. Taken prisoner in battle at Ashby's Gap July 12, 1863. Promoted Captain August 27, 1864. Exchanged April 1865. Mustered out July 20, 1865.

Second Lieutenant: Henry H. Crocker - In company February 1, 1863. Promoted First Lieutenant March 1, 1864. Promoted Captain September 3, 1864. Severely wounded in the battle of Cedar Creek, October 19, 1864. Mustered out July 20, 1865.

Enlisted men:
1. **Allen, George H.** - Mustered out July 20, 1865.
2. **Black, Thomas G.** - Discharged for disablity at Camp Brightwood, Washington, D.C., June 1863.
3. **Burnap, Oscar** - Shot through the chest by Mosby's guerillas while on picket near Hunter's Mills, Va., December 1863. Discharged on account of wounds, May, 1864.
4. **Barnes, Walter S.** - Killed in battle at Ashby's Gap, Va., July 12, 1863.
5. **Bishop, George** - Promoted to Sergeant. Wounded while on picket near Berryville, Va., August 20, 1864. Discharged for disability, July, 1865.
6. **Brossamer, Charles A.** - Discharged for disablity, from Hospital at Washington, September, 1865.
7. **Baker, Nelson J.** - Promoted to Corporal. Mustered out July 20, 1865.
8. **Boswell, John H.** - Discharged for disability, from camp at East Capitol Hill, May, 1863.
9. **Brickley, Richard T.** - Wounded in action at Ashby's Gap, July 12, 1863. Wounded at Vienna, Va., December, 1863. Discharged on account of wounds, at Cavalry Camp, Muddy Branch, Md., June, 15, 1864.
10. **Buhrer, George N.** - Promoted to Corporal and subsequently to Sergeant. Mustered out July 20, 1865.
11. **Blanchard, Oscar** - Taken prisoner on Fairfax Pike, October 19, 1863. Died a prisoner of war in Libby Prison, Richmond, Va.
12. **Brandon, John R.** - Died at Camp Meigs, Readville, Mass., May, 1863.
13. **Burns, Edward** - Transferred to the U.S. Navy, May, 1864.
14. **Blanche, Edgar N.** - Promoted to Corporal and subsequently Sergeant. Promoted to First Lieutenant Fifth Mass. Cavalry, February 8, 1864.
15. **Butcher, William T.** - Promoted Corporal and subsequently Sergeant. Killed in battle at Waynesboro, Va., September 28, 1864.
16. **Cain, John A.** -Promoted Corporal. Taken prisoner in action at Drainsville, Va., February 22, 1864. Exchanged April, 1865. Mustered out July 20, 1865.
17. **Christler, Hiram W.** - Died in Lincoln Hospital, Washington, D.C.
18. **Cheeney, William F.** - Mustered out while on detached service at Camp Meigs, Readville, Mass.
19. **Cobbey, Thomas W.** - Died a prisoner of war at Richmond, Va.
20. **Campbell, John T.** - Promoted to Corporal and subsequently to Sergeant Discharged on account of disability incurred by hard service, April, 1864.
21. **Cattrell, Robert J.** - Deserted while in the field against Early's army, near Rockville, Md., July 10, 1864.
22. **Clark, William B.** - Discharged for promotion in regiment Missouri Infantry Volunteers.
23. **Clarke, Hiram E.W.** - Promoted Sergeant March 19, 1863. Promoted to Second Lieutenant of company August 23, 1863.

24. **Crawford, Josiah H.** - Taken prisoner in action at Drainsville, Va., February 22, 1864. Exchanged April, 1865. Mustered out July 20, 1865.
25. **Campbell, Robert A.** - Mustered out July 20, 1865.
26. **Dyer, Andrew B.C.** - Teamster. Mustered out July 20, 1865.
27. **Davis, Asa M.** - Promoted Corporal. Killed in Sheridan's battle of Cedar Creek October 19, 1864.
28. **Eaten, Stephen H.** -Mustered out July 20, 1865.
29. **Enos, Erastus** - Blacksmith. Mustered out July 20, 1865.
30. **Flood, Stephen** - Promoted Corporal. Mustered out July 20, 1865.
31. **Fisher, Jackson** - Died a prisoner of war at Andersonville, Ga.
32. **Flourney, Charles H.** - Mustered out July 20, 1865. Re-enlisted as a clerk in War Department.
33. **Fencel, Henry C.W.** - Missing
34. **Goodfellow, John W.** - Promoted Corporal. Mustered out July 20, 1865.
35. **Griffing, Charles C.** - Bugler. Discharged for disability, from hospital at Frederick City, Md., June, 1865.
36. **Getty, Harry W.** - Deserted from camp at East Capitol Hill, Washington, D.C., May, 1865.
37. **Grover, Byron H.** - Killed in action at Drainsville, Va., February 22, 1864.
38. **Garrity, Thomas** - Taken prisoner in action at Ashby's Gap, July 12, 1863. Exchanged and returned to company, January, 1865. Mustered out July 20, 1865.
39. **Heitman, Charles H.** - Mustered out July 20, 1865.
40. **Holland, Henry** - Promoted to Assistant Surgeon, Battalion Maryland Cavalry, in May, 1863..
41. **Hood, John** - Taken prisoner near Upperville, Va., January, 1864, and paroled by Colonel Mosby. Promoted to Corporal. Mustered out July 20, 1865.
42. **Hepburn, James W.** - Promoted to Corporal; subsequently to Sergeant. Promoted to Second Lieutenent, California Cavalry, January 6, 1865. Mustered out with that regiment at expiration of service.
43. **Hamilton, Jasper A.** - Mustered out July 20, 1865.
44. **Irving, Harry P.** - Killed in battle at Ashby's Gap, July 12, 1863.
45. **Jones, John T.** - Deserted from cavalry camp, Muddy Branch, Md., February, 1864.
46. **Jenkins, Charles M.** - Promoted Corporal. Taken prisoner in action at Coyle's Tavern, August 25, 1863. Exchanged and joined the company in January, 1865. Promoted Sergeant. Mustered out July 20, 1865.
47. **Joy, Maurice** - Severely wounded in action at Ashby's Gap, July 12, 1863. Mustered out July 20, 1865.
48. **Kelly, Cains P.** - Promoted Corporal, and subsequently Sergeant. Promoted Second Lieutenent, July 9, 1865. Mustered out July 20, 1865.
49. **Lewis , Stephen** - Mustered out July 20, 1865.
50. **Lord, Thomas H.** - Discharged for disability at cavalry camp, Vienna, Va. January, 1864.
51. **Lunt, William P.** - Transferred to United States Navy, May, 1865.
52. **McEwen, Warren L.** - Discharged for disability at cavalry camp, Vienna, Va., January, 1864.
53. **McGuire, Arthur** - Transferred to Third California Infantry Volunteers.
54. **McCarrak, Joseph** - Deserted from cavalry camp Muddy Branch, Md. May, 1864.

55. **Merrill, Daniel E.** - Promoted Corporal, and subsequently Sergeant. Mustered out July 20, 1865.
56. **Moore, William H.**- Promoted Corporal. Severely wounded in action at Dinwiddie Court-house, Va., March 31, 1865. Discharged from hospital on account of wounds July, 1865.
57. **Mortimer, Harry W.** - Bugler. Mustered out July 20, 1865. Re enlisted as Clerk in War Department.
58. **Mihay, William** - Discharged for disability from hospital at Washington, D.C., July, 1863.
59. **Mallory, Abner T.** - Promoted Corporal, and subsequently Sergeant. Promoted to Second Lieutenant Fifth Massachusetts Cavalry, January 9, 1864. Promoted to First Lieutenant February 9, 1864. Mustered out October 31, 1865.
60. **Mossman, Judson A.** - Promoted Corporal. Taken prisoner in action at Drainsville, Va., February 22, 1864. Exchanged and returned to company January, 1865. Promoted Sergeant. Mustered out July 20, 1865.
61. **Moore, Delevan** - In brigade band. Mustered out July 20, 1865.
62. **Miller, James M.** - Deserted from camp near Dawsonville, Md., August 6, 1864.
63. **Manchester, Luman A.** - Promoted Sergeant. Taken prisoner in action at Rockville, Md., July 13,1864. Escaped from rebels near Staunton, Va., and returned to company. Mustered out July 20, 1865.
64. **Morrison, Walter** - Promoted to Sergeant, and subsequently to First Lieutenant in a regiment of Ohio Cavalry Volunteers.
65. **Manker, William A.** - Blacksmith. Taken prisoner in action at Coyles' Tavern, Va., August 25, 1863.Exchanged April, 1865. Mustered out July 20, 1865.
66. **Morris, William** - Taken prisoner in action at Coyles' Tavern, Va., August 25, 1863. Exchanged and returned to company May, 1864. Mustered out July 20, 1865.
67. **Mitchell, John T.** - Promoted Corporal, and subsequently Sergeant. Mustered out as private July 20, 1865.
68. **Myers, Randolph P.** - Wounded in action with Mosby's guerillas near Aldie, Va., February 6, 1864. Taken prisoner in action at Dinwiddie Court-house, March 31, 1865. Exchanged, and mustered out July 20, 1865.
69. **Millican, William W.** - Promoted Corporal. Taken prisoner in Action at Drainsvillle, Va., February 22, 1864. Died a prisoner of war at Andersonville, Ga.
70. **Ordway, John H.** - Mustered out July 20, 1865.
71. **Osts, John** - Taken prisoner in action at Drainsville, Va., February 22, 1864. Exchanged, and mustered out August, 1865.
72. **Partridge, Benjamin F.** - Promoted Corporal, and subsequently Sergeant. Promoted to Second Lieutenant, August 27, 1864. Promoted to Captain January 9, 1865. Mustered out July 20, 1865.
73. **Palmer, William T.** - Discharged for disability from hospital at Philadelphia June, 1865.
74. Pervis, Lawrence G. - Discharged for disability from hospital at Washington, D.C., June, 1865.
75. **Parris, Frank** - Taken prisoner in action at Drainsville February 22, 1864. Died a prisoner of war at Andersonville, Ga.
76. **Perry, Albert** - Brigade butcher. Mustered out July 20, 1865.
77. **Reese, James** - Deserted from Camp Meigs, Readville, Mass., April, 1863.
78. **Rodgers, Thomas L.** - Promoted Corporal. Mustered out July 20, 1865.
79. **Rhodes, Samuel H.** - Promoted Corporal. Taken prisoner in action at Rockville, Md., July 13, 1864. Escaped and returned to company. Mustered out July 20, 1865.

80. **Russell, Alvin H.** - Promoted Corporal and subsequently Sergeant. Killed in Sheridan's battle of Cedar Creek October 19, 1864.
81. **Sheldon, Joseph** - Mustered out July 20, 1865.
82. **Sheldon, Adelbert** - Saddler. Mustered out July 20, 1865.
83. **Sheldon, Aurelius B.** - Transferred to U.S. navy May, 1864.
84. **Shaw, William** - Deserted in New York city April 15, 1863.
85. **Spaulding, John** - Taken prisoner in action at Drainsville February 22, 1864. Died a prisoner of war at Andersonville, Ga.
86. **Silver, Harry** - In brigade band. Mustered out July 20, 1865.
86. **Straub, Edward** -Taken prisoner in action with guerillas near Leesburg, Va., May 1864. Escaped and returned to company. Mustered out July 20, 1865.
87. **Shaw, Sylvanus H.** - Promoted Sergeant. Discharged for disability, at Cavalry Camp, Muddy Branch, Md., May, 1864.
89. **Stevenson, John H.** - Mustered out July 20, 1865.
90. **Smith, Leonard F.** - Severely wounded in action at Rockville, Md., July 13, 1864. Mustered out July 20, 1865.
91. **Sarchet, Joseph B.** - Promoted Corporal. Mustered out July 20, 1865.
92. **Smith, John W.** - Wounded in the head in action at Ashby's Gap, July 12, 1863. Mustered out July 20, 1865.
93. **Sprague, James E.** - Teamster. Mustered out July 20, 1865.
94. **Saunders, Haulsey H.** - Farrier. Mustered out July 20, 1865.
95. **Towne, Nathan** - Mustered out July 20, 1865.
96. **Turnham, Albert B.** - Discharged for disability from hospital at Washington, D.C., August, 1863.
97. **Turner, Junius T.** - Promoted 1st Sergeant. Promoted to 2d Lieutenant in 1st Maryland Cavalry, then to First Lieutenant in same, and subsequently to Captain in Same. Mustered out September, 1865.
98. **Thompson, Lawrence** - Discharged for disability while on furlough in Iowa, July, 1864.
99. **Turner, Levi W.** - Promoted Corporal. Taken prisoner in action at Drainsville, February 22, 1864. Exchanged and returned to Company. Promoted 1st Sergeant. Mustered out July 20, 1865.
100. **Vuttee, Francis P.** - Promoted Corporal. Transferred to United States Navy, May, 1864.
101. **Venum, Hiram** - Taken prisoner in action at Ashby's Gap, July 12, 1863. Died a prisoner of war in Richmond, Va.
102. **Wilcox, George** - Taken prisoner in action at Drainsville, Va., February 22, 1864. Exchanged, April, 1865. Mustered out June, 1865.
103. **Williams, Benj. T.** - Promoted Sergeant. Killed in action at Waynesboro, Va., September 28, 1864.
104. **White, James A.** - Teamster. Mustered out July 20, 1865.
105. **Wescott, William** - Promoted Corporal. Wounded near Halltown, Va. Mustered out July 20, 1865.
106. **Wooster, Arthur J.** - Taken prisoner in action at Drainsville, Va., February 22, 1864. Exchanged April, 1865, and died in June, 1865, on account of ill-treatment at Andersonville prison.
107. **Walther, Jacob** - Died in hospital at Frederick City, Md., October, 1864.
108. **Wyatt, Henry H.** - Wounded in action at Drainsville, Va., February 22, 1864. Promoted Corporal, and subsequently Sergeant. Mustered out July 20, 1865.

ADAMS COMPANY.

Captain: Zabdiel B. Adams - In command of company June 25, 1863. In command of squadron from April 17, 1863 to March 2, 1864. Promoted March 2, 1864, to Major of Fifth Massachusetts Cavalry. Severely wounded in battle before Petersburg, Va., June 15, 1864. In Texas from July to November, 1865. Mustered out October 31, 1865.

First Lieutenant: William C. Manning - In company as First Lieutenant February 13, 1863. Promoted to Captain February 7, 1864. Wounded and taken prisoner in action at Drainsville, Va., February 22, 1864. Exchanged April 19, 1865. Promoted to Major June 8, 1865. Mustered out July 20, 1865.

Second Lieutenant: Josiah A. Baldwin - In company as Second Lieutenant February 1, 1863. Promoted to First Lieutenant February 5, 1864. Severely wounded and crippled in Sheridan's battle of Winchester September 19, 1864. Promoted to Captain October 20, 1864. Mustered out July 20, 1865..

Enlisted men:

1. **Abby, Samuel** - In Brigade Band. Mustered out July 20, 1865.
2. **Anderson, John** - Promoted to Corporal-subsequently to First Sergeant. Promoted to First Lieutenant Fifth Massachusetts Cavalry January 18, 1864. Promoted to Captain Fifth Massachusetts Cavalry July 5, 1864. Mustered out in Texas October 31, 1865.
3. **Anderson, John** - Missing.
4. **Ayer, Osborn** - Promoted to Corporal. Severely wounded in battle of Tom's Brook October 9, 1864. Discharged on account of wounds at Cloud's Mills in May, 1865.
5. **Baldwin, George E.** - Promoted to Corporal-subsequently to Sergeant. Promoted to Second Lieutenant April 29, 1865. Promoted to First Lieutenant July 16, 1865. Mustered out July 20, 1865.
6. **Babcock, Samuel W.** - Specially detailed as one of Sheridan's scouts in December, 1864, and served with that General until mustered out in August, 1865, at New Orleans.
7. **Backus, Samuel W.** - Promoted to Second Lieutenant in Second California Cavalry April 30, 1865. Mustered out with that regiment at expiration of service.
8. **Bard, James** - Wounded in action near Aldie, Va., July 30, 1863. Again wounded in action on Opequan creek in September, 1864. Promoted to Corporal. Mustered out July 20, 1865.
9. **Barron, Francis E.** - Mustered out July 20, 1865.
10. **Beebee, Samuel J. Jr.** - Promoted to Corporal. Mustered out July 20, 1865.
11. **Boggs, Daniel W.** - Severely wounded in action near Rectortown, April 30, 1864. Mustered out July 20, 1865.
12. **Boyle, George P.** - Mustered out July 20, 1865.
13. **Bruner, Edward D.** - Promoted to Corporal-subsequently to Sergeant. Promoted 2d Lieutenant, July 9, 1865. Mustered out July 20, 1865.
14. **Barnes, John** - Missing.
15. **Brown, Benjamin** - Promoted to Corporal-subsequently to Sergeant. Promoted to 2d Lieutenant, July 9, 1865. Mustered out July 20, 1865.
16. **Burns, Robert** - Killed in action at Waynesboro, Va., September 28, 1864.
17. **Carr, George** - Promoted to Corporal. Died of wounds received in action with Early's army in front of Fort Reno, Washington, D.C., July 12, 1864.
18. **Chaffee, Daniel K.** - Died at Lincoln Hospital, Washington, D.C., in June 1864.

19. **Chamberlin, Richard S.** - Severely wounded in Sheridan's battle of Cedar Creek, October 19, 1864. Mustered out July 20, 1865.
20. **Chandler, Seth** - Buglar-afterward in Brigade Band. Mustered out July 20, 1865.
21. **Clark, Charles A.** - Promoted to Sergeant. Killed in action near Rectortown, April 20, 1864.
22. **Clark, Levi K.** - Missing.
23. **Clark, John** - Severely wounded in action at Aldie, July 6, 1864. Mustered out July 20, 1865.
24. **Clawell, Robert** - Promoted to Corporal-had three horses killed under him in action during his service. Mustered out July 20, 1865.
25. **Coolidge, Henry H.** - Transferred to United States Navy in May, 1864.
26. **Dealing, Charles A.** - Taken prisoner in action near Berryville, August 13, 1864. Exchanged in April, 1865. Mustered out July 20, 1865.
27. **Elliott, William W.** - Missing.
28. **Enos, Frank** - Orderly to Brigade Commander. Mustered out July 20, 1865.
29. **Felch, John H.** - Wounded in action at Aldie, Va., July 6, 1864, and severely wounded in Sheridan's battle of Winchester, September 19, 1864. Mustered out July 20, 1865.
30. **Ferrill, David C.** - Severely wounded in action at Aldie, July 6, 1864. Discharged on account of wounds in May, 1865.
31. **Finley, John L.** - Promoted Corporal, subsequently Sergeant. Promoted to Second Lieutenant January 8, 1865. Promoted to First Lieutenant July 16, 1865. Mustered out July 20, 1865.
32. **Fogg, Nathan H.** - Wounded in action at Aldie, July 6, 1864. Mustered out July 20, 1865.
33. **Fostman, Henry** - Mustered out July 20, 1865.
34. **Fordham, Nathan C.** - In brigade band. Mustered out July 20, 1865.
35. **Gaskill, Aaron A.** - Missing.
36. **Green, Charles N.** - Mustered out July 20, 1865.
37. **Gudith, John D.** - Promoted to Corporal. Mustered out July 20, 1865
38. **Halsey, William F.** -Foragemaster. Mustered out July 20, 1865.
39. **Hanson ,William M.** - Ambulance driver. Mustered out July 20, 1865.
40. **Hardman, William H.** - Deserted from camp at East Capitol Hill in May, 1864.
41. **Harrington, George** - Mustered out July 20, 1865.
42. **Hatch, Richard A.**- Killed while on picket near Vienna, Va., May, 1864.
43. **Hawkins, James M.** - Buglar. Mustered out July 20, 1865.
44. **Howard, Amos H.** - Wounded in action on Little River pike, near Aldie, Va., July 30, 1863. Again wounded in action near Berryville, Va., August 13, 1864. Mustered out July 20, 1865.
45. **Howard, George E.** - Mustered out July 20, 1865.
46. **Howe, John W.** - Promoted to Corporal, and subsequently to Sergeant. Mustered out July 20, 1865.
47. **Hoxsie, Benjamin F.** - Specially detailed as one of Sheridan's scouts in December, 1864. Served with that General until mustered out in August, 1865 at New Orleans.
48. **Hudson, Charles** - Missing.
49. **Hull, Chauncey** - Discharged for disability from hospital at Washington in June 1863.
50. **Hunter, James P.** - Wounded in action at Waynesboro September 28, 1864. Died in hospital January, 1865

51. **Jones, Cyrus B.** - Wounded in skirmish with Mosby's guerillas near Lewinsville, Va., in December, 1863. Died in hospital at Vienna, Va., January, 1864.

52. **Keaton, Joseph Z.** - Blacksmith. Mustered out July 20, 1865.

53. **Kimball, Solon D.** - Taken prisoner in action at Rockville, Md., July 13, 1864. Exchanged April, 1865. Promoted to Corporal, and subsequently to Sergeant. Mustered out July 20, 1865.

54. **Kingsley, Edward H.** - Killed in action at Waynesboro, Va., September 28, 1864.

55. **Kuhls, Henry** - Promoted to Sergeant March 18, 1863. Promoted to Second Lieutenant February 5, 1864. Promoted to First Lieutenant March 25, 1864. Promoted to Captain August 31, 1864. Severely wounded in Sheridan's battle of Cedar Creek October 19, 1864. Taken prisoner in battle of Five Forks April 1, 1865. Exchanged in ten days. Mustered out July 20, 1865.

56. **Lane, Edward P.** - Promoted to Quartermaster Sergeant. Detailed on duty at Headquarters as Brigade Quartermaster. Mustered out July 20, 1865.

57. **Leonard, Patrick H.** - Missing.

58. **Lycan, William M.** - Discharged for disability from Cavalry Camp, Vienna, Va., in March, 1864.

59. **Larrien, Lorenzo D.** - Discharged for disability from Hospital at Washington, D.C., in 1864.

60. **Lee, George L. Jr.** - Deserted at New York April 15, 1853.

61. **Little, Hazen D.** - Killed in action on Little River Pike, near Aldie, Va., July 30, 1863.

62. **Long, Edward** - Deserted at Jersey City, May 18, 1863.

63. **Loud, Eugene** - Mustered out July 20, 1865.

64. **McCallon, John C.** - Mustered out July 20, 1865.

65. **McDougal, Daniel** - Wounded in action near Opequan creek, Shenandoah valley, August, 1864. Mustered out July 20, 1865.

66. **McKenny, John W.** - Severely wounded in action near Coyle's tavern, Va., August 25, 1863. Mustered out July 20, 1865.

67. **McFarland, Thomas** - Wounded in a hand to hand conflict, in which he sabered one of Mosby's guerillas. Promoted to Corporal. Mustered out at close of the war.

68. **McLean, Alfred A.** - Mustered out July 20, 1865.

69. **Maguire, Thomas F.** - Promoted to Sergeant. Mustered out July 20, 1865.

70. **Merry, Thomas H.** - Promoted to Com. Sergeant of another company. Mustered out July 20, 1865.

71. **Miller, John** - Missing.

72. **Moore, John** - Promoted to Corporal; subsequently to Sergeant. Mustered out July 20, 1865.

73. **Nystrom, Charles W.** - Promoted to Corporal. Taken prisoner in Sheridan's battle of Winchester, September 19, 1864. Exchanged in November, 1864. Promoted to Sergeant. Mustered out July 20, 1865.

74. **Parker, George W.** - Promoted to Corporal. Transferred to United States in May, 1864.

75. **Parker, William E.** - Promoted Corporal; subsequently to Sergeant. Promoted to Second Lieutenant, August 28, 1864. Promoted to First Lieutenant, January 8, 1865. Promoted to Captain June 16, 1865. Mustered out July 20, 1865.

76. **Peebles, James J.** - Promoted to Sergeant. Severely wounded in action at Aldie, July 6, 1864. Discharged on account of wounds at Remount Camp, Pleasant valley, Md., April 14, 1865.

77. **Pervine, Samuel** - Teamster. Mustered out July 20, 1865.

78. **Piquet, William** - Discharged at New York, April 15, 1863, on account of being under age.
79. **Pringle, William H.** - Promoted to Corporal. Taken prisoner in action near Berryville, Va., August 20, 1864. Died from the effects of imprisonment at Andersonville, Ga.
80. **Randall, James B.** - Taken prisoner in skirmish with Mosby's guerillas near Langley, Va., in December, 1863. Died a prisoner of war in Libby Prison, Richmond, Va.
81. **Reed, George W.** - Missing.
82. **Raymond, Peter** - Killed in action on Little River pike, near Aldie, Va., July 30, 1863.
83. **Rumery, Ezra D.** - Promoted to Corporal. Mustered out July 20, 1865.
84. **Sparohawk, Jared** - Promoted to Corporal. Severely wounded in Sheridan's battle of Cedar Creek, October 19, 1864. Discharged on account of wounds, March, 1865.
85. **Schroder, Henry** - Promoted to Corporal, subsequently to Sergeant. Mustered out July 20, 1865.
86. **Seagrave, Edward F.** -Taken prisoner in action on Little River pike, near Aldie, July 30, 1863. Recaptured a few days afterward. Wounded in Sheridan's battle of Cedar Creek, October 19, 1864. Promoted to Corporal. Mustered out July 20, 1865.
87. **Smedley, William W.** - Missing.
88. **Smith, Roswell R.** -Taken prisoner on raid to Ashby's Gap, July 13, 1863. Died a prisoner of war in Libby Prison, Richmond, Va.
89. **Smith, Albert J.** - Mustered out July 20, 1865.
90. **Spencer, Ebeneser** - Teamster. Mustered out July 20, 1865.
91. **Sponegle, James W.** - Mustered out July 20, 1865.
92. **Still, Alonzo D.** - Discharged for disability at Cavalry Camp, Vienna, Va., March, 1864.
93. **Swank, Lima** - Buglar. Wounded in action near Luray Court-house, September 24, 1864. Mustered out July 20, 1865.
94. **Switzer, George** -Teamster. Mustered out July 20, 1865.
95. **Tucker, Samuel F.** - Promoted to Sergeant, March 21, 1863. Promoted to Second Lieutenant, March 1, 1864. Promoted to First Lieutenant, September 30, 1864. Severely wounded in battle of Tom's Brook, October 8, 1864. Again severely wounded in battle of Five Forks, April 1, 1865. Discharged on account of wounds, June 1, 1865, as 1st Lieut. Of Company M.
96. **Taylor, John** - Missing.
97. **Townsend, Hiram** - Fell overboard from steamer Constitution on her passage to Panama, March 25, 1863.
98. **VanBenscoten, H.** - Saddler. Mustered out July 20, 1865.
99. **Van Hoosen, Jerome** - Blacksmith. Mustered out July 20, 1865.
100. **Waggoner, John H.** - Mustered out July 20, 1865.
101. **Washburn, Luman P.** - Promoted to Corporal. Died in camp at Vienna, Va., from wounds received while on picket.
102. **Weaver, Joseph** - Promoted to Corporal. Mustered out July 20, 1865.
103. **Weaver, William** - Ambulance driver. Mustered out July 20, 1865.
104. **Wildes, Bradstreet R.** - Promoted to Corporal. Subsequently to Sergeant. Mustered out July 20, 1865.
105. **Wilson, Frederick** - Missing.
106. **Wilson, Peter H.** - Killed accidentally in camp at Vienna, Va., May 2, 1864.
107. **Woodworth, Henry M.** - Dropped from the rolls at San Francisco in March, 1863.

MANNING'S COMPANY.

Captain: George A. Manning – In command of company January 29, 1863. Acting Adjutant Quartermaster and commander of Battalion from February 1st to April 17, 1863. In command of company from April 17, 1863, to February 22, 1864. Taken prisoner in action at Drainsville, Va., February 22, 1864. Exchanged April, 1865. Mustered out July 25, 1865.

First Lieutenant: Alvin W. Stone – Promoted from Second to First Lieutenant in February, 1863. In command of company on skirmish line in front of Fort Stevens July 11th and 12th, 1864. Mustered out on account of disability September 8, 1864.

Second Lieutenant: Hiram E. W. Clarke – Promoted from Company E to Second Lieutenant August 28, 1863. Promoted to Captain Fifth Michigan Cavalry February 25, 1864. Wounded in battle before Petersburg June 15, 1864. Mustered out in Texas October 31, 1865.

Enlisted men:

1. **Algie, Hugh** - Discharged on account of disability at Cavalry Camp. Muddy Branch, Md., in June, 1864.
2. **Allwell, Andrew** - Discharged on account of disability from hospital at Washington, D.C., in January, 1865.
3. **Benninger, Irwin J.** - Wounded in action near Berryville August 18, 1864. Mustered out July 10, 1865.
4. **Bluett, Joseph** - Mustered out July 20, 1865.
5. **Bucklin, Henry** - Discharged on account of disability at cavalry camp, Vienna,Va., in May, 1864.
6. **Barnes, George L.** - Killed in action near Difficult creek, Drainsville Pike, January 4, 1864.
7. **Babcock, Silas B.** - Discharged on account of disability at Camp Meigs, Readville, Mass., in May, 1864.
8. **Belnap, William D.** - Saddler. Promoted to Corporal. Mustered out July 20,1865.
9. **Bennett, Thomas** - Promoted to Sergeant. Transferred to Veteran Reserve Corps in September, 1863.
10. **Beal, Merrill C.** - Promoted to Corporal. Subsequently to First Sergeant. Killed in battle at Cedar creek October 19, 1864.
11. **Bell, William** - Taken prisoner in action at Drainsville, Va., February 22, 1864. Died a prisoner of war at Andersonville, Ga.
12. **Bixby, Samuel S.** - Blacksmith. Mustered out July 20, 1865.
13. **Blanchard, William E.** - Promoted to Commissary Sergeant. Mustered out July 20, 1865.
14. **Burke, Joseph H.** - Taken prisoner in action at Drainsville, Va., February 22, 1864. Died a prisoner of war at Andersonville, Ga.
15. **Clark, Richard** - Died in hospital at Alexandria, Va., August 5, 1863.
16. **Colman, John F.** - Mustered out July 20, 1865.
17. **Connelly, James** - Mustered out July 20, 1865.
18. **Cooper, Seth H.** - Severely wounded in the head while on picket near Hunter's Mills, Va., in December, 1863. Discharged on account of wounds in May, 1864.
19. **DeForrest, William F.** - Promoted to Corporal and subsequently to Sergeant. Severely wounded in the head while charging with his company in the action at Ashby's Gap, July 12, 1863. Discharged on account of wounds in September, 1863.
20. **Dexter, Henry H.** - Killed in action at Drainsvulle, Va., February 22, 1864.
21. **Dodd, Benjamin** - Missing.
22. **Dowell, John** - Deserted from camp at East Capitol Hill, Washington, D.C. in May, 1863.

23. **Dickson, Henry C.** - Transferred to Veteran Reserve Corps from Camp Brightwood in June, 1863.
24. **Eby, James N.** -Promoted to Corporal and subsequently to Commissary Sergeant. Mustered out July 20, 1865.
25. **Fair, William** - Promoted to Corporal. Deserted from Cavalry Camp, Dawsonville, Md., August 6, 1864.
26. **Ford, Milo G.** - Mustered out July 20, 1865.
27. **Ferrier, George W.** - Killed in action at Drainsville, Va., February 22, 1864.
28. **Foster, James** - Promoted to Corporal and subsequently to Sergeant. Promoted to 1st Lieutenant July 9, 1865. Mustered out July 20, 1865.
29. **Foster, Edward** - Mustered out July 20, 1865.
30. **Getens, Peter** - Missing.
31. **Goodrich, Henry M.** - Taken prisoner in action at Drainsville, Va., February 22, 1864. Escaped from Andersonville prison and joined company. Mustered out July 20, 1865.
32. **Gozzen, Herman** - Taken prisoner in action at Drainsville February 22, 1864. Died a prisoner of war at Andersonville, Ga.
33. **Hackett, Patrick J.** - Promoted to Corporal. Taken prisoner in action at Drainsville, February 22, 1864. Died a prisoner of war at Andersonville, Ga.
34. **Hallsted, Jacob W.** - Promoted to Corporal. Taken prisoner in action at Drainsville, February 22, 1864. Died a prisoner of war at Andersonville, Ga.
35. **Hayford, James B.** - Transferred to Veteran Reserve Corps from Camp Brightwood in June, 1863.
36. **Hill, John W.** - Wounded in a charge through Warrenton, Va., July 20, 1863. Discharged on account of disability at Vienna in January, 1864.
37. **Hughes, John** - Buglar. Transferred to United States Navy in May, 1864.
38. **Harbeck, Henry R.** - Taken prisoner while on picket at mouth of Monocacy river, July 5, 1864. Exchanged in April, 1865. Mustered out at Annapolis, Md.
39. **Howe, Wesley C.** - Promoted to Corporal and subsequently to Sergeant. Promoted to 2d Lieutenant March 25, 1864. Taken prisoner in Sheridan's battle of Winchester, September 19, 1864. Promoted to 1st Lieutenant January 8, 1865. Promoted to Captain July 9, 1865. Mustered out July 20, 1865.
40. **Jones, John** - Taken prisoner while on picket near Leesburg, Va., July 13, 1863. Died a prisoner of war at Andersonville, Ga.
41. **Jennings, William H.** - Promoted to Corporal. Mustered out July 20, 1865.
42. **Kehoe, James** - Deserted in New York City April 15, 1863.
43. **Knapp, David** - Taken prisoner in action at Drainsville February 22, 1864. Died a prisoner of war at Andersonville, Ga.
44. **Lawrence, William H.** - Promoted to Corporal. Taken prisoner in action at Drainsville, February 22, 1864. Exchanged and mustered out at Annapolis, Md.
45. **Lay, William J.** - Teamster. Mustered out July 20, 1865.
46. **Lee, George W.** - Taken prisoner in action at Drainsville, February 22, 1864. Exchanged in April, 1865. Mustered out at Annapolis, Md., June, 1865.
47. **Locke, John M.** - Promoted to Corporal and subsequently to Sergeant. Wounded in action at Drainsville, February 22, 1864. Mustered out July 20, 1865.
48. **McCann, John** - Promoted to Corporal, and subsequently to Sergeant. Mustered out July 20, 1865.
49. **McCammen, J.S.W.** - Killed in action at Drainsville, February 22, 1864.

50. **Mattox, Henry A.** - Acting Post Commissary Sergeant at Cavalry Camp, Muddy Branch, Md., and at Division Headquarters in the field. Mustered out July 20, 1865.
51. **Miles, Henry P.** - In Brigade Band. Mustered out July 20, 1865.
52. **Meacher, Charles P.** - Promoted to First Sergeant of Company March 19, 1863. Promoted to Second Lieutenant January 1, 1864. Promoted to First Lieutenant March 8, 1864. Killed in action at Halltown, Va., August 27, 1864, while in command of California Hundred.
53. **Merritt, Gilbert R.** - Promoted to Sergeant. Discharged on account of disability caused by broken leg.
54. **Morris, Joseph** - Transferred to United States Navy in May, 1864.
55. **Morris, Samuel N.** - Promoted to Corporal, and subsequently to Sergeant. Acting Sergeant Major, Cavalry Forces upper Potomac, from March 6 to August 9, 1864. Promoted to Second Lieutenant July 9, 1865. Mustered out July 20, 1865.
56. **Monroe, James** - Taken prisoner in action at Drainsville, February 22, 1864. Died prisoner of war at Andersonville, Ga.
57. **Neimeyer, Valentine** - Deserted in New York City April 15, 1863.
58. **Nichols, William** - Mustered out July 20, 1865.
59. **Parker, George W.** - Promoted to Corporal. Deserted while on furlough in May, 1864.
60. **Price, Edward** - Taken prisoner while in action at Drainsville, February 22, 1864. Died a prisoner of war at Andersonville, Ga., June 15, 1864.
61. **Roberts, Pulaski** - Discharged while on furlough in May, 1864.
62. **Robins, Charles** - Teamster. Mustered out July 20, 1865.
63. **Riley, Amos** - Promoted to Corporal. Taken prisoner hear Strasbury, Va., August 18, 1864. Exchanged in April, 1865. Mustered out July 20, 1865.
64. **Secin, Joseph** - Promoted to Corporal. Mustered out July 20, 1865.
65. **Shields, Joseph F.** - Deserted in New York city, August 15, 1863.
66. **Simonson, Anthony** - Taken prisoner in action at Drainsville, February 22, 1864. Died a prisoner of war at Andersonville, Ga.
67. **Smith, John P.** - Discharged on account of disability caused by railroad accident in May, 1863, at Readville, Mass.
68. **Smith, George E.** - Promoted to Corporal, subsequently to Sergeant. Mustered out July 20, 1865.
69. **Stocking, Edwin** - Promoted to Sergeant. Discharged on account of disability from hospital at Washington, D.C. Since died.
70. **Street, Pennalton** - Taken prisoner in action at Waynesboro, Va., September 28, 1864. Escaped and joined company. Mustered out July 20, 1865.
71. **Stevens, Thomas** - Taken prisoner in action at Drainsville, February 22, 1864. Died a prisoner of war at Andersonville, Ga.
72. **Stevens, Alfred** - Promoted to First Lieutenant in regiment United States colored Troops in Tennessee, May, 1864.
73. **Taylor, George** - Deserted at Camp East Capitol Hill, Washington, in May, 1863.
74. **Taylor, Archibald** - Taken prisoner in action at Drainsville, February 22, 1864. Died a prisoner of war at Andersonville, Ga.
75. **Thompson, Joseph W.** - Discharged for disability at Readville, Mass., in April, 1865.
76. **Varnum, Joseph B.** - Promoted to Commissary Sergeant of Company, March 19, 1863. Killed in action with Mosby's guerillas at Coyle's Tavern, August 25, 1863.
77. **VanVleet, DeWitt C.** - Taken prisoner in action at Ashby's Gap, July 12, 1863. Exhanged and discharged from Parole Camp, Annapolis, Md.

78. **VanSlyke, Peter** - Promoted to Corporal. Mustered out July 20, 1865.
79. **Warner, Isaac S.** - Promoted to Corporal, subsequently to Sergeant. Promoted to Second Lieutenant July 9, 1865. Mustered out July 20, 1865.
80. **Watson, David** - Promoted to Corporal. Mustered out July 20, 1865.
81. **Wilcox, William** - Mustered out July 20, 1865.
82. **Withrow, Abel A.** - Chief Buglar, afterward Sergeant of the Band. Mustered out July 20, 1865.
83. **Wood, Warren** - Mustered out July 20, 1865.
84. **Williams, Charles** - Promoted to Corporal. Mustered out as private July 20,1865.
85. **Wilson, William E.** - Promoted to Corporal, subsequently to Sergeant. Promoted to Second Lieutenant January 1, 1864. Mustered out July 20, 1865.
86. **Williams, John** - Taken prisoner while on picket near Fairfax Court-house, Va., August, 1863, and not heard from afterwards.
87. **Wilburn, James P.** - Promoted to Corporal. Severely wounded in action at Waynesboro, September 28, 1864. Discharged on account of loss of arm, January, 1865.

DE MERRITT'S COMPANY.

Captain: David A. DeMerritt - Resigned as Captain of Company F, Second California Cavalry, February 10, 1863, to command this company. In command of company from February 13th to June 10, 1863. Disabled on account of broken leg. In command of squadron from August 15th to September 15, 1863. Disabled on account of the hardships of field service. In command of squadron at Muddy Branch Ford from November 18th to December 24, 1863. Appointed Acting Inspecting General of Cavalry Brigade at Vienna, Va., December 24, 1863. Wounded in action at Rectortown, April 30, 1864. Mustered out, September 2, 1864, on account of disability.

First Lieutenant: Rufus W. Smith - In company as First Lieutenant February 1, 1863. In command of company during the absence of Captain DeMerritt. Promoted Captain, March 1, 1864. In command of "California Hundred" from March 1st to October 19, 1864. Killed in battle at Cedar creek, October 19, 1864.

Second Lieutenant: Horace B. Welch - In company as Second Lieutenant, March 19, 1863. Promoted to First Lieutenant of Fifth Massachusetts Cavalry, June 18, 1863. Promoted to Captain of Fifth Massachusetts Cavalry, February 3, 1864. In command of a squadron that entered Richmond, April 8, 1865. Mustered out in Texas, October 31, 1865.

Enlisted men:

1. **Barlow, Frank** - Mustered out July 20, 1865.
2. **Barr, George W.** - Transferred to regiment of Ohio Infantry Volunteers.
3. **Brown, James** - Deserted from Cavalry Camp, Muddy Branch, Md., in February, 1864.
4. **Boden, William C.** - Promoted to Corporal; subsequently to Sergeant. Deserted from Cavalry Camp, Muddy Branch, Md., March 14, 1864.
5. **Beeth, Benjamin F.** - Severely wounded in action at Aldie, July 6, 1864. Discharged on account of wounds.
6. **Bradford, Joseph L.** - Taken prisoner in action at Drainsville, July 22, 1864, and died a prisoner of war at Andersonville, Ga.
7. **Brown, Charles** - Promoted to Regimental Saddler, with the rank of Sergeant. Mustered out July 20, 1865.
8. **Cossell, Jackson** - Promoted Corporal, subsequently Sergeant. Taken prisoner in action at Rockville, Md., July 13, 1864. Exchanged in April, 1865. Mustered out July 20, 1865.

9. **Clay, George W.** - Died at Camp Brightwood, near Washington, in July, 1863.
10. **Coleman, James** - Discharged at Camp Meigs, in May, 1863, on account of being under age.
11. **Curtis, Charles** - Severely wounded in action at Aldie, July 6, 1864. Mustered out July 20, 1865. Now on half pension.
12. **Convery, Thomas** - Mustered out on account of disability at Washington, D.C., in November, 1865.
13. **Case, Chester** - Mustered out July 20, 1865.
14. **Cochran, Warren** - Promoted to Corporal. Taken prisoner in action at Rockville, Md., July 13, 1864. Escaped from Andersonville, Ga. Walked to Union lines in Tennessee and returned to company. Mustered out July 20, 1865.
15. **Cook, William F.** - Promoted to Quartermaster Sergeant. Mustered out July 20, 1865.
16. **Cook, Frederick** - Promoted to Corporal. Mustered out July 20, 1865.
17. **DeWald, Frederick** - Deserted from cavalry camp at Muddy Branch, Md. In February, 1864.
18. **Durab, John** - Discharged on account of disability at Frederick City, Md., in August, 1864.
19. **Day, Augustus D.** - Died in hospital at Washington, D.C.
18. **Enos, Frank** - Mustered out July 20, 1865.
19. **Fieldman, Julius** - Discharged for promotion to Second Lieutenant in New York Volunteers , at Vienna, Va., February, 1864.
20. **Foote, Charles D.** - Taken prisoner in Shenandoah Valley and exchanged. Mustered out July 20, 1865.
21. **Green, Samuel** - Left on furlough in December, 1864, and failed to return to company.
22. **Gray, Peleg C.** - Discharged for disability from hospital in Washington, December, 1863.
23. **Gaskill, Henry W.** - Discharged for disability from Hospital in Washington in April, 1864.
24. **Harding, James** - Promoted to Corporal. Wounded in action near Gordonsville, December, 1864. Mustered out July 20, 1865.
25. **Harkin, Charles** - Promoted to Corporal; subsequently to Second Lieutenant U.S. Colored Troops. Promoted to First Lieutenant in Regular Army.
26. **Hanson, Peter** - Taken prisoner in action at Coyle's Tavern, August 25, 1863, and died as prisoner of war, at Danville, N.C.
27. **Halligan, John T.** - Taken prisoner in action at Rectortown, April 30, 1864, and died a prisoner of war at Danville, N.C.
30. **Hiernan, Charles** - Promoted to Corporal. Mustered out July 20, 1865.
31. **Hann, John J.** - Promoted to Regimental Blacksmith, with the rank of Sergeant. Mustered out July 20, 1865.
32. **Hill, James** - Promoted to Corporal; subsequently to Sergeant. Severely wounded in action at Rockville, Md., July 13, 1864. Mustered out July 20, 1865.
33. **Johnson, Joseph W.** - Promoted to Sergeant. Taken prisoner in action at Rockville, Md., July 20, 1864. Exchanged in April, 1865. Mustered out July 20, 1865.
34. **Kercheval, Benjamin** - Promoted to Post Quartermaster Sergeant at Cavalry Camp, Muddy Branch, Md. Severely wounded in action at Rockville, Md., July 13, 1864. Mustered out July 20, 1865.
35. **Landis, Stephen F.** - Mustered out July 20, 1865.
36. **Logsdon, James** - Severely wounded in action at Aldie, July 6, 1864. Mustered out July 20, 1865.
37. **Lovejoy, Dana B.** - Company saddler. Mustered out July 20, 1865.
38. **Langley, Howell T.** - Wagonmaster. Mustered out July 20, 1865.

39. **Leach, Thomas** - Deserted while on picket at Conrad's Ferry, Md., in January, 1864.
40. **Munger, Lewis** - Promoted to Corporal, subsequently to Sergeant. Severely wounded in action at Winchester, September 19, 1864. Promoted to Second Lieutenant August 31, 1864. Promoted to First Lieutenant October 23, 1864. Killed in battle at Five Forks, April 1, 1865, while in command of his company.
41. **Maddox, Samuel B.** - Taken prisoner near Berryville, Va., August, 1864. Exchanged April, 1865. Mustered out July 20, 1865.
42. **McDonald, George** - Teamster. Mustered out July 20, 1865.
43. **McDonald, James** - Promoted to Corporal. Killed in action near Aldie, Va., July 6, 1864.
44. **McCarty. Lemuel** - Promoted to Sergeant. Specially detached as one of General Sheridan's scouts from November 1, 1864, until August, 1865. Mustered out in New Orleans.
45. **Marsh. William T.** - Promoted to Corporal. Taken prisoner in action at Rockville, Md., July 13, 1864. Died a prisoner of war in Richmond, Va.
46. **Morse, Charles F.** - Promoted to Sergeant. Taken prisoner in action at Rockville, Md., July 13, 1864. Died after exchange, at Annapolis, Md.
47. **Monroe, John** - Promoted to Corporal. Subsequently to Sergeant. Mustered out July 20, 1865.
48. **Miller, John** - Deserted from cavalry camp at Falls Church, Va., June, 1864.
49. **McGeehen, James** - Teamster. Mustered out July 20, 1865.
50. **O'Connell, John** - Promoted to Corporal. Severely wounded in action at Summit Point, Va., August 29, 1864. Promoted to Sergeant. Mustered out July 20, 1865.
51. **O'Brien, James** - Deserted from cavalry camp at Muddy Branch, Md. March 14, 1864.
52. **Passage, John** - Promoted to Corporal. Subsequently to Sergeant. Promoted to Second Lieutenant, September 3, 1864. Promoted to First Lieutenant, June 8, 1865. Mustered out July 20, 1865.
53. **Payne, Norman B.** - Transferred to Veteran Reserve Corps on account of disability, in September, 1864.
54. **Pendle, Morton M.** - Deserted to Mosby's guerillas while on picket at Conrad's Ferry, Md., January, 1864.
55. **Quirk, John J.** - Discharged for disability at Centerville, Va., August, 1863.
56. **Roberts, Charles** - Promoted to Corporal. Subsequently to Sergeant. Severely wounded in Sheridan's battle of Cedar Creek, October 19, 1864. Promoted to First Lieutenant, July 9, 1865. Mustered out July 20, 1865.
57. **Rawson, Benjamin F.** - Promoted to Sergeant. Discharged on account of disability while on furlough from Camp Russell, near Winchester, January, 1865.
58. **Rawson, Caleb H.** - Discharged on account of disability at cavalry camp, Vienna, August, 1864.
59. **Reed, John A.** - Ambulance driver. Afterward in band. Mustered out July 20, 1865.
60. **Reed, John K.** - Teamster. Mustered out July 20, 1865.
61. **Short, William H.** - Promoted to Corporal. Subsequently to Sergeant. Shot and severely wounded Mosby, the guerrilla chief, in action at Coyle's Tavern, Va., August 25, 1863. Promoted First Lieutenant United States Colored Infantry January, 1864. Subsequently promoted to Captain in same. Mustered out at expiration of service.
62. **Smith, Moses** - Mustered out July 20, 1865.
63. **Seymour, Dennis** - Promoted to Corporal. Mustered out July 20, 1865.
64. **Shiffer, James** - Mustered out July 20, 1865.

65. **Shiffer, John S.** - Promoted to Corporal. Killed in action at Opequan creek, September 7, 1864.

66. **Shurtleff, Oscar D.** - Promoted to Corporal. Severely wounded in the head action at Opequan creek, September 7, 1864. Promoted to Sergeant. Mustered out July 20, 1865.

67. **Small, George E.** - Killed in action at Opequan creek, September 7, 1864.

68. **Sutton, William H.** - Company Buglar. Mustered out July 20, 1865.

69. **Thayer, George F.** - Promoted to Corporal. Killed in battle of Five Forks, April 1, 1865.

70. **Terry, David E.** - Discharged on account of disability at Camp Brightwood in July 1863.

71. **Thomas, William B.** - Missing.

72. **Turner, John** -Teamster. Mustered out July 20, 1865.

73. **Thompson, Edward** - Promoted to Corporal. Subsequently to Sergeant. Promoted to Second Lieutenant August 31, 1864. Severely wounded Sheridan's battle of Winchester, September 19, 1864. Severely wounded in battle of Five Forks, April 1, 1865. Promoted to Captain May 27, 1865. Mustered out July 20, 1865.

74. **Wilson, George F.** - Promoted to Sergeant. Subsequently to Sergeant Major. Promoted to Second Lieutenant Fifth Massachusetts Cavalry March 2, 1864. Promoted to First Lieutenant Fifth Massachusetts Cavalry April 29, 1864. Mustered out September 6, 1865, on account of disability.

75. **Wilson, James R.** - Mustered out July 20, 1865.

76. **Williams, Robert H.** - Promoted to First Sergeant. Subsequently to Sergeant Major. Mustered out July 20, 1865.

77. **Williams, Andrew** - Promoted to Corporal. Died in hospital at Washington in January, 1865.

78. **Welsh, William S.** - Deserted from cavalry camp at Muddy Branch, Md., in February, 1864.

79. **Wagener, George** - Mustered out July 20, 1865.

80. **Wakefield, Elhana W.** - Promoted to First Sergeant. Severely wounded in battle at Tom's Brook, September 8, 1864. Discharged on account of wounds.

81. **Wiesgarber, Stephen** - Killed in Sheridan's battle of Cedar Creek, October 19, 1864.

82. **Whitcomb, Sylvester J.** - Promoted to Corporal. Severely wounded in battle of Five Forks, April 1, 1865. Mustered out July 20, 1865.

Sacramento Daily Union, Wednesday, December 18, 1867.

Pension Statements

Selected pension statements from Company A

PENSION PAPERS

If a soldier's war experiences are not recorded in a diary, letters or news accounts then his personal story may be forever lost. Pension papers however, can be a good source of these experiences recorded as testimony for a pension or increase in pension. The soldiers, their relatives or acquaintances testified in official documents to plead their case. The testimonies generally attest to a soldier's time spent in the service or to injuries incurred while in the service of their country. The following are excerpts from the Pension Records of which all the Hundred are available. These records are also a valuable resource for the researcher as they can contain addresses of the veterans, their families and friends. They may have the date and place of death listed. On a more personal note they tell of the physical appearance of the veteran and how time and the deprivations of war had taken their toll.

Henry W. Allen
Testimony of Henry W. Allen July 30th, 1879

Horse got frightened while riding as Orderly at night at some negros who were lying in the road throwing me on the Pomel of the Saddle. It was at the time of the Burning of the South Anna R. R. Bridge near Richmond was with Capt Stevens of Maj. Gen. Gettys staf at the time.

Darnley O. Balcom testifies: that I was a member of the same Company- The "California Hundred"- with Allen that, without actual knowledge, I yet am humanly certain that said Allen was a perfectly sound man when he enlisted- in Dec-1862 in San Francisco California- because every man of the Hundred was subjected to the most thorough examination by the US. Surgeon who examined us, and men very desirous of joining the organization, were rejected for the slightest physical defects, many of those who had signed the Roll, and were eager to go to the front were thrown out on very slight grounds because of the excess of applicants, hence I feel that I am right in saying, I Know that said Allen was a perfectly healthy and sound man when he enlisted December 10th 1862- had he not been he could not have become a member of the "California Hundred" afterward Compy "A" 2nd Mass Cavalry Vols.

Wiilliam G. Anthony
Testimony of John Connealy September 13, 1890,

I John Connealy was a private in Co. C 2nd Mass Cav. in 1864 and the Said William G. Anthony was Quartermaster Sergeant in the Same Company. I was well acquainted with him. While following up The Rebel Gen'l Early from Washington in July 1864, We became Engaged with the Enemy and at Rockvile, Md. where we had to dismount and Fight on foot in the Woods. While so Engaged we were Surrounded by the Enemy and in trying to force our way back through the Enemies lines we were overcome by the heat (it being a very hot day) and fell Exhausted. I was here taken prisoner and Saw William G. Anthony taken prisoner about ten feet away from me on the 13th of July 1864. I was in No 1 prison in Danville Va. with him and when the worst Cases were taken out of prison & carried about two miles to a Temporary Hospital on Maj. Milfords Farm. I was carried in Company with Sergeant Anthony. While there he was Suffering with bloody Flux and was reduced to something like a skeleton. he told me that he thought he would die here. there were Seventeen of us in the Temporary Hospital shed and all died but four. I was paroled in Company with the Said William G. Anthony on the 17th of October 1864, and was with him in Anapolis Md. until Jan. 1865. When I parted with him I was sent to Phila. Penn for treatment, I have not seen him since. he was a brave Soldier.

STATE OF NEW YORK
CERTIFICATE OF DEATH

1.Full name of deceased **William G. Anthony**
2. *Age* 53 *years* 11 *months* 20 *days*
9. *Date and Hour of Death Died on the* 3 *day of* May *1888*
Chief and Determing} Suicide by Shooting
Consecutive and Contributing} Aberation of mind

D. A. Sharpe, Coroner

Nathan Beach
MANUFACTURER OF LUMBER

North Derby, Vt. Nov. 16th 1906

V. Warner, Esq Commissioner of Pensions
Sir

In reply to yours of Sept 5th I have tried to find a comrad living who new of my condition while in the service but those who new me intimately have passed away. Joseph B. Burdick who shared the tent with me was killed in an engagement at South Anna River when we were charging up on to the embankment to destroy the R.R. Bridge and I carried him in front of me on my horse about a mile and a half to the wagon train- George W Verbick was killed in an engagement with Mosby near Coyles Tavern on the Centervill Pike when shot he fell over against me from his horse and went down he was a chum of mine. in this engagement my horse was shot & fell on me and caused a rupture there should be on file an affidavit from the Regimental Surgeon Dr. G who treated me while in the Hospital and several others from Dr. Keys Dr Ruff also from the board of examiners at Newport who examined me I think in 1885 There is also testimony in the offices of the Military Secretary, if any thing more is required to complete my case please advise and oblige

Yours respectfully
Nathan A Beach

Wlliam H. J. Hilliard
Officer's Certificate of Disability

Wm H. Forbes, Boston, Nov 13th 1877.

Wm H. J. Hilliard received a gunshot wound through his right shoulder in an engagement with the enemy (under Mosby) near Aldie Va. on the 6th day of July 1864. Said wound incapacitating him from duty as a soldier for about six months. Said Hilliard was under my command and received said wound when strictly in the line of duty *And that the said* Wm H. J. Hilliard was so far as I have knowledge and to the best of my belief a sound man *when he entered the service*

I have no interest in this claim.

W. H. Forbes late Lt Col 2 Massachusetts Cavalry

447

Charles E. Benjamin
Wm A. Robinson testifies:
Thos. D. Barnstead testifies:

That they were members of Co. A. 2d Mass. Vol. Cav. and know the above named claimant while he was a member of same Company. That they were present at Rockville Md. during an engagement in July 1864, and they know of their personal knowledge that the above mentioned claimant was wounded and taken prisoner and escaped and returned to the regiment. after wandering in the swamps two or three days and that he was wounded in the left leg at that time. That they know that the above named claimant had his right ankle injured by a kick from a horse at Falls Church Va. about Sept. 1864. That they know the above named injuries were not the result of vicious habits.

Thos D. Barnstead   W. A. Robinson {Private Co "A" and late 2d Lt.
Private Co "A" 2d Reg't Cav. Mass Vols.   2d Mass Cav

Hugh Armstrong
Sawtelle Los Angeles Co. Cal.
Oct. 29, 1904

Commissioner of Pensions
Washington D.C.

Dear Sir, Aug. 13, <u>1903</u> I made application for an increase of Pension No. of Certificate 1014986.
Issued when I was under 60 years of age. 1899.

I did not apply sooner in life as I was able to provide for myself and did not wish to add anything to the expense of the Government. Now my financial condition as well as physical have changed for the worse to such an extent that I feel that the great sacrafices I made for the nation entitle me to proper consideration, I being wholly unable to earn a living by "manual labor"

My service action in the field 1129 days as Private, Sergeant, 2d Lieutenant, 1st Lieutenant and Captain, by the time I was 24 years old, in the California 100. (Co. A 2d Mass. Cavy.) and Fremont Body Guard. Received no Bounty.

If I had $12.00 per month I would leave the Home and be no further expense to Country. Please grant if you can as I don't want to spend the short time I shall live in this place.

Yours obediently,
Hugh Armstrong
Late Capt. Cal. 100 Co. A 2 Mass Cav.

Hugh Armstrong
1916 Main St.
Ocean Park California
Oct. 6 -26

Pension Bureau
Washington D.C.
Gentlemen:-

I am so near blind that I cannot see to write for myself so I am dictating my wishes. I have not received the raise of pension to which I am entitled of by the act of July 1-26. I have been helpless & dependent upon my pension for several years and at the present time I am unable to get along without the help of an attendant. Please let me know why I have been forgotten.

Very sincerely yours
Hugh Armstrong

Samuel Corbett

June 19th, 1879

... received the following disability, to wit: At Dinwiddie Court House Va. on or about April 1st 1865 he was out as scout and was captured by rebels but escaped by racing his horse down a steep hill. During the ride his right stirrup strap broke throwing him to the ground fracturing his fourth and fifth ribs on right side, from which he has since suffered.

That on account of hard riding and exposure in Sheridans last campaign in Va from Feb. 27 to Apl. 9 1865 he contracted varicose veins in both legs near the knee-which have long since and do now disable him

Jerimiah J. Carey

Testimony of Alonzo C. Grout testifies:

on or about the last day of April, 1865, while in the line of duty, and without fault or improper conduct on his part, at or near Petersburg, State of Virginia said soldier was on duty as "Stable Guard" and shortly after he had taken his relief he came and awoke me asking me to take his brush and relieve him as he was feeling so badly that he could not continue his duty. He was suffering from a very bad cold which he contracted some time before with a very sore throat with sharp pains in his chest & side and a bad cough. and he continued to suffer from this trouble untill my discharge -July 12- 1865- I also saw said Carey twice while I resided in Rockford Ills. The last time in 1870 he was still suffering and in a very feeble & emaciated condition and he told me that he had never recovered from the affects of that "Spring Trip" (We were with Sheridan after Lee and then Johnson) and that he was sure that it would soon end his life and I firmly believe that it was the cause of his death

Henry Crum

April 7, 1887 Testifies: *That while in said service in the line of his duty at or near* Waynesboro *in the State of* Virginia *on or about the* 25 *day of* October 1864 He received a fracture of the Right leg below the knee while in action. His horse was shot from under him while guarding the amunition train, and when he fell, a wagon wheel ran over him and crushed his leg. Was treated at the Frederick City Hospital, Maryland.

George W. Goulding

State of Michigan
16 December 1890

I first knew him about fifteen years ago or more, I am a Dentist by profession, and have practiced said profession at East Saginaw Mich. for at least twenty-seven years and have pulled teeth for said Goulding from time to time since I first knew him and always on account of the teeth being loose caused by scurvy and they get loose & sore, and his jaws & face swell, and matterate. All the teeth that I have pulled for him were sound, but had to be pulled on account of scurvy. And I know of personal knowledge that said Goulding had scurvy during the year 1881, and that he has had said disease continuously every year since that date, and that he is now afflicted with said disease, and I pulled two teeth for him this day on that account.

Prescott Whipple

Alfred Lee

State of Massachusetts, County of Essex
Was intimately acquainted with Alfred F. Lee from the time of his birth until a few days before his death. He came to Massachusetts with "the California one hundred" so called early in 1863 and I saw him at the time in Newburyport and I know he married during his visit Anne M. Davis of Newburyport and was in this vicinity recruiting for the 2d Mass Cavalry several weeks. He then joined his regiment at Readville Mass and went to Old Point Comfort, Va. with his regiment. Later he was in Newburyport on sick parole, here he asked for an extension of his parole on account of sickness which being refused him he returned to his regiment at Vienna Va. on reaching there he was so sick that he was sent to Hospital where he died the next day. The body was brought to Newburyport the body having been embalmed by the Company. I saw the body and know it was the body of Alfred F. Lee. and saw it buried in Oak Hill Cemetary Newburyport.

January 25, 1890 George Colby

Abraham Loane

Aug. 1st 1890

Dr Mc Questin

Dear Sir

By your request

    I heare make a statement as near as my memory will permit taken to Andersonville Prison on the 27th day of July after being there a short time was taken with the bloddy flux, Itch, jaundice and Scurvy. I lost all my upper teeth and most of the lower ones. my joints ache continually my flesh has a numb feeling, at times the prick of a pin, or a pinch will not be felt, my memory is so poore I canot remember what happened the day prevous in fact I have not seen a well day since I was released from prison. The scars on my hips and rumps you have seen. That was caused from lying on the ground, while a prisoner that aught to satisfy every one what I have suffered and what I suffer to day

I remain your respectful
Abraham Loane
A, 2. Mass Cav..

William A. Robinson

San Francisco
5 Feb. 1879
...at Fairfax Court House Virginia on or about the 12th day of September 1863 he was riding a horse sick with "distemper" and "black tongue", back to Washington DC (with a detachment of the 2d Mass Cavalry on the same duty) the horses to be condemned, and while so riding the horse, with a rope around the neck of the horse, the head being so deseased, no bridle could be used, the horse stumbled and fell upon him (fracturing) his collar bone. The bone never properly united and he has ever since and does now suffer pain and lameness in shoulder, the arm is weak.

Henry Schrow

Boston, Mass. March 15, 1880
Corporal Schrow, while in the strict line of his duty, during a charge on the enemys picket, which was entrenched behind a fence, near Halltown, Va. on or about the 26 day of August

1864, received an injury of the head by being struck with the butt of a musket in the hands of one of the enemy. Further that I was an eye witness of the above being at the time Lieut Colonel of the Regiment and in comand of the Squardron which made the charge and I also saw Corporal Schrow immediately after this affair: that Lieut Meader who was in command of Company "A" was clubbed to death during the charge. Corporal Schrow was a most gallant and faithful soldier & certainly deserves a pension.

Caspar Crowninshield
Late Col, Second Regiment Cav'y Mass. Vols.

Henry S. C. Tubbs
February 18, 1867
...the circumstances of said wounds were that while on drill at Readville Massachusetts his horse became unmanageable and threw him and thus his collar bone was broken and his body badly bruised so much that he the said Henry S. C. Tubbs was unable to do duty with his company for three or four months. This occurred in the month of February 1863. During this same year while on duty in June 1865 while Reg't was stationed at Fairfax CH he was again badly injured, he was sent by the Col. of the Reg't with a dispatch to Washington, DC. While returning, his horse stumbled and he was thrown from him breaking his collar bone on the left side. From this time forward and while in the service the said Henry S. C. Tubbs was unable to perform full duty. I know too that until the time of said injuries he was a faithful and able bodyed soldier.

Hugh Armstrong
Late Capt. Co "A" 2d Mass. Cavy.

Muster Rolls

Transcribed from the original handwritten documents which were prepared quarterly.

Company A
From the 10th day of Dec 1862 to the 28th day of Feb 1863
This company was enlisted at San Francisco California by authority of Sect of War- Sailed from San Francisco Via Panama Dec 11th 1862. Arrived at New York Jan 3rd 1863. From New York to Readville Mass. Left Readville Mass Feb 11th 1863 for Fortress Monroe. Left Fortress Monroe Feb 19 for Gloucester Point Camp Grenshaw
Station: Gloucester Point, Va.

From the 28th day of Feb to 30th day of Apr 1863
From Gloucester Point Va and arrived at Fort Magruder Va April 19, 1863.
Station: Fort Magruder, Va.

From the 30th day of Apr to 30th day of June 1863
Marched from Fort Magruder to Gloucester Point Va May 14th 1863. June 19th 1863 under command of Col. Davis of the 12th Ills. Cavalry. Made a raid nearly to King & Queen Court House Va capturing Eight rebel prisoners, large number of stock &c. Marching 130 miles in three (3) days arriving in camp June 21st.
1863 - June 24th under command of Col Spear of the 11th Penn. Cavalry (with his Regt.) Moved in transports to the White House Landing. Thence June 25th toward Hannover Court House, and arrived at South Anna R.R. Bridge June 26th- To Companies of the 44th N. Carolina rebel troops guarded the bridge and the Company was ordered to dismount and fight on foot which was done and charged on the enemy in entrenchments, carrying them by Storm, capturing or killing all in conjunction with a squadron of the 11th Penn in their rear, mounted. This Company lost one (1) killed and one (1) wounded. Returned to the White House June 27th. Again marched with a column under Gen Getty nearly to a R.R. Bridge spanning the North Anna ~~Bridge~~ River and all returned to the White House and thence by order returned to Gloucester Point Va. with detachment of 2nd Mass Cavalry arriving July 10th 1863 via New Kent Court House and Williamsburg- The Company has assisted in capturing a rebel train of seventy (70) wagons and an appropriate number of mule teams and sets of Harness as also large number of rebel Cavalry Videttes and Pickets.
Station: None

From the 30th day of June to 30th day of Aug 1863
July 1st 1863, Marched from the White House on a search expedition being attached for the time being to the 11th Penn. Cavalry, Col Spear commanding: July 7th arrived at White House traveled 60 miles July 8th started for Yorktown Va. via Baltimore Cross Roads. New Kent Court House and Williamsburgh, arriving at Yorktown on the 10th at 10 'clock P.M. Same evening crossed the York River to our old camp at Gloucester Point. July 20th Capt Allen and 2 Privates of the Rebel Army were captured by six of our men. July 25th out on a scout to Gloucester ~~Point~~ Court House captured a large Rebel Mail several horses mules &c. July 27th started for Washington D.C. on board of steamer Juniata. July 28th arrived at Washington DC proceeded same evening to Camp Wyndham near Long Bridge Va. 31st July Private A. S. Laighton died in Hospital at ~~Camp Wyndham~~ Washington DC of Typhoid Fever. August 4th ordered to report for duty at Chain Bridge Va. arrived there same evening. Aug 11th left Chain

Bridge at 5 P.M. on a Scout. 14th arrived at Regimental Head Quarters near Centreville Va. 16th started on a scout at 6 o'clock A.M. arrived at camp the 20th bringing in several prisoners. August 24th a detachment of 32 men from the Regiment while returning from Washington DC leading 104 horses when about 3 miles north of Fairfax Court House was suddenly attacked by a force of 80 Rebels commanded by Mosby who were in ambush and by charging simultaneously on the front and rear and succeeded in capturing nearly all the horses after a short skirmish in which Private John McCarthy was instantly killed. Geo. W. Verick was mortally wounded and Cyrus P Dempsey was taken Prisoner. 28th out on a raid. Arrived in Camp August 30th 1863.
Station: Camp Lowell Near Centreville, Va.

From the 31st day of Aug to the 31st day of Oct 1863
On Sept 18th 63 Company marched to Washington City D.C. for horses for Company Regs and returned to camp at Centreville on the 19th Marched from Centreville Va. with Brigade in pursuit of Mosbeys Confederate Command. Through Aldie Leesburg and Hamilton to Snickersville and returned to Centreville Oct 5th Struck camp at Centreville Oct 5th marched to Fairfax Court House and went into camp Struck camp at Fairfax Court House Oct 9th Marched to Vienna Va and went into camp Company went in pursuit of the enemy Oct 19 returned to camp same day
Station: Vienna, Va.

From the 31st day of October 1863 to the 31st day of December 1863
Since last muster the Company have been engaged doing scouting and picket duty for the Army of Washington. Nov 29th the Company with a detachment of the 2nd Mass Cavy scouted through Aldie and Midleburg after the enemy and succeded in capturing Twenty - Six Again on Dec 29th the Company marching with Regt through Aldie by way of Philomont to Uperville pursuing the enemy captured 25 men of the 1st and 6th Virginia Confederate Cavalry returned to camp Dec 31st 1863
Station: Vienna, Va.

From the 31st day of December 1863 to the 29th day of February 1864
Since last muster in addition to its tour of picket and guard duty the Company has been out on several scouts and marches to Leesburg, Middleburg, Aldie & Drainsville, meeting small parties of guerrillas from time to time and assisting in their Capture. Of casualties there has been none until 22 February when Captain J. Sewall Reed commanding 2nd Battalion was killed in action with the enemy near Drainsville Va. The Company was not out at that time being in the 1st Battalion.
Station: Vienna, Va.

From the 29th day of February 1864 to the 30th day of April 1864
Company scouting through Fairfax and Louden Counties, Va besides doing Picket duty at Vienna Va. Company has been engaged in several skirmishes with the enemy near Leesburg and Aldie Va. Corporal Bumgardner wounded in skirmish near Aldie Va with Mosby's men.
Station: Vienna, Va.

From the 30th day of April 1864 to the 30th day of June 1864
Company changed Camp from Vienna Va to Falls Church Va May 1864 and has been employed scouting through Louden and Fairfax Counties Virginia
Station: Falls Church, Va.

From the 30th day June 1864 to the 31st day of August 1864
July 6th a detachment of the Comp attacked by party of Mosby's Guerrillas and lost 1 Corporal killed 4 Privates captured 1 Corporal died since of wounds July 10th Company broke camp at Falls Church and marched to Fort Reno DC July 11th & 12th skirmished with the enemy near Fort Reno DC July 13th fought the Enemy at Rockville, Md loosing 10 privates captured July 14th Skirmished with the Enemy at Poolville Md. Aug 11th skirmished with the enemy near Charlestown Va lost 1 Sergeant captured August 21st skirmished near Berryville- Aug 22nd skirmished in front of Charlestown August 26 charged the enemies line near Charlestown capturing 7 com officers & 67 men. Our loss 1 Private killed 1 Corporal wounded.
Station: Near Opequan Creek, Va.

From the 31st day of August 1864 to 31st day of October 1864
Active operations in Shenandoah Valley. Engaged in battle at Opequan and Winchester Va Sept 19th 1864. Cavalry fight in Luray Valley Sept 24th 1864 in which Private Phillip Baybutt captured a Rebel battle flag, and for which he was awarded a medal by Congress. Battle of Tumbling run Oct 9th 1864. Battle of Cedar Creek Va Oct 19th 1864, in which the Company lost its Commander.
Station: in the Field Near Cedar Creek

[In the entry for 31 Aug 64 to 31 Oct 64 it refers to the "Battle of Tumbling run" — Corbett refers to it as the "Battle of Tom's Creek; maps show a Tom's Brook just below Strasburg. Private Baybutt was not an original recruit, he enlisted and was mustered 24 Feb 1864 from Fairhaven, Mass]

From the 31st day of October 1864 to the 31st day of December 1864
Company engaged, guarding the operations of the construction party on the Harpers Ferry and Winchester Railroad. Dec 1st marched from Stevensons Station with command under Genl Merritt- on raid to Louden County Va.
Dec 19th marched from Camp Russell with command under Genl Torbett through Chester Gap, Little Washington and Madison Court House to Gordensville.
Dec 28th arrived and emcamped at Camp Russell.
Station: Camp Russell

From the 31st day of December 1864 to the 28th day of February 1865
Co. ordered into winter quarters near Winchester Va. Jany 10th 1865 remained in camp till Feby 27th 1865 when it broke camp and with the others of Sheridans Cavalry began the spring campaign.
Station: In the Field

From the 28th day of February 1865 to the 30th day of April 1865
March 1st to 18th in Sheridan's great raid from Winchester to White House during which the Co passed through Waynesboro, Rockfish Gap, Charlottsville, New Market, Columbia, Louisa Court House, Fredericks Hall, Hannover, King William Court House and engaged in destroying the Lynchburg & Richmond Canal & Va Central R.R. had several skirmishes with the enemy. April 1st assisted in the capture of South Side R.R. from 2nd to 9th was engaged with his Army in the last struggle & the surrender of Lees Army at last the backbone of the rebellion is broken 10th started for Petersburg Va which we reached by easy marching on the 20th remained in Camp till the 24th when we broke Camp and started for Johnsons Army heard of the

surrender of Johnsons Army on the 29th when near River Dan Camped on River Dan & on the 30th marched for Petersburg once more.
Station: In the Field

From the 30th day of April to the 30th day of June 1865 - missing.

<u>Company E</u>
From the 30th day of June to the 31st day of August 1863
Regt made a reconnaisance July 12th 1863 at Ashby Gap and had a skirmish in which two privates were killed and four privates were taken prisoners & four wounded Moved to Centreville July 22/63 Made several reconnaisances in Warrenton , Leesburg, Middleburg, & and surrounding country
The Co. having also did picket and scouting duty at Chain Bridge & near Fort Ethan Allen Dept of Potomac Aug 24/63 a party leading horses from Washington was attacked near Coyles Tavern & one Corp and two Privates taken prisoners.
Station: Vienna, Va.

> Chas S Eigenbrodt
> Capt Comdg Co

From the 31st day of August to the 31st Day of October 1863.
Did picket and Patrol duty on the Pike between Fairfax C.H. and Annandale from Sept 9th till October 10th 1863 during which time joined Col. Lowell with the greater portion of my command (leaving one Sergt and twelve men to guard my camp in the Pine Woods) on a scout to Leesburg Va on Sept 19 1863 - also on another scout to Snickers Gap October 2nd 1863 and again returned to Picket duty Va Camp. and then reported at Head Quarters at Cav. Camp 2nd Mass Cav. Vienna Va 10th October 1863 on the 18th Inst. while out on a scout with a portion of my command, and detachments from other Regiments fell in with a small party of Mosbys Guerillas under command of Lt. Williams *[Frank Williams]* also wounded near Stewarts old road 1 1/2 miles below Fairfax C.H. Killing one Mason *[Charles Mason]* and taking 3 prisoners viz: Jack Barnes, Dr. Stratton *[Dr. Ed Stratton]* and Harrover *[Robert Harrover]* & wounding Lt. Williams.

> Chas. S. Eigenbrodt
> Capt. Comdg.

Station: Vienna, Va.

From the 31st day of October to the 31st day of December 1863
Station: Vienna, Va.

From the 31st day of December to the 29th day of February 1864.
The company engaged in Picket and Scouting duty - on Feby 22nd 1864 near Drainsville Va in an engagement with Maj. Mosby lost 1st Lieut and 12 men prisoners and one wounded.
Station: Vienna, Va.

From the 29th day of February to the 30th day of April 1864.
From Camp Vienna Va; March 8th per Order Maj C.C. Crowinshield Comdg Regt. - The Captain Reptd for duty with his Company "E" to Major D.W.C. Thompson and have since been doing Picket and Patrol duty on the Maryland side of the Potomac River.
The Company Clothing account settled as to January 1st 1864.
Station: Muddy Branch, Md.

From the 30th day of April to the 30th day of June 1864.
The Company has been ardously employed in Picket, Patrol and Scouting duty in Maryland and Virginia since last muster.
Station: Muddy Branch, Md.

From the 30th day of June to the 31st day of August 1864.
Since last muster this Company with the Regiment has participated in all the operations of the Army, under Gen. Wright, in repelling the late Rebel invasion of Maryland and the Dist. of Co.; also in all the subsequent operations of the same army under Gen. Sheridan in the Shenandoah Valley, Va.
Station: Near Smithfield, Va.

From the 31st day of August to the 31st day of October 1864.
Since last muster the Company with the Regiment has participated in all the operations of the Army in the Shenandoah Valley, Va. under Gen Sheridan.
Station: Near Cedar Creek Shenandoah Valley, Va.

From the 31st day of October to the 31st day of December 1864.
During the month of Nov. 64 the Reserve Brigade 1st Cav. Division to which the 2nd Mass. Cav. is attached was employed in guarding the Construction Corp whilst Rebuilding the R.R. from Harpers Ferry to Winchester Va. E Co. assisted in that duty-Nov. 29-64 the Brigade started from Stephensons Station to join the Division in an expedition into Loudon Valley, Va. Dec. 4-64 Returned to Shenandoah Valley since which time the Brigade has been lying at Camp Russell near Winshester, Va.
Station: Camp Russell near Kernstown, Va.

From the 31st day of December, 1864 to the 28th Day of February 1865
Station: In the field

From the 28th day of February 1865 to the 30th Day of April 1865
Station: In the field

From the 30th Day of April 1865 to the 30th Day of June 1865
Station: Fairfax Court House

Company F
From enrollment to the 30th day of June 1863.
Commenced to Recruit in San Francisco January 30th 1863 - left San Francisco for New York March 23rd arrived at New York April 14th Started from New York for Readville Mass. on the 15th and arrived on the 16th - left Readville for Washington May 11th and arrived on the 16th Encamped East of Capitol Hill - on May 30th left Camp East of Capitol Hill and arrived at Brightwood were we encamped near Fort Stevens - June 11th went into Virginia in pursuit of Moseby - crossed the Potomac River on the 12th at Whites Ford and proceeded to Leesburgh from there we returned to Camp on the 13th - June 23rd removed Camp to Poolsville June 27th Proceeded in rear of Hookers army crossed the Monocacy and went to Knoxville where we encamped during the night - June 28th returned by way of Poolville to Rockville in pursuit of Stuart and reached Camp Poolville on the 30th.
Captain DeMerritt left San Francisco April 23rd 1863 with 49 men and arrived at New York May 15th left New York for Readville on the same day and arrived at Readville on the 16th left

Readville for Washington on the 5th and arrived at Camp Brightwood on the 7th.
Station: *[Not shown.]*

From the 30th day of June to the 31st day of August 1863.
July 3rd 1863 - Moved Camp from Poolesville to Seneca Creek. July 9th 1863 - Moved Camp to Brightwood - July 10th March to Wyndham and encamped during the night, 11th Marched through Fairfax and encamped at night near Aldie - July 12th through Middleburgh Upperville and Paris - Skirmish at Ashbys Gap - Drove Enemy through the Gap and over Shenandoah River - Returned through Union and encamped near Philmont - 13th passed through Leesburg and encamped near Drainsville - 14th passed by Falls Church - crossed Potomac River at Chain Bridge through George Town and arrived at Camp Brightwood about 12M same day removed Camp to Wyndham - 19th Removed Camp to Centreville Virga. - 30th Left Camp at Centreville about 8 P.M. and encamped that night behind the Church at Aldie - 31st Attacked Moseby and recaptured Sutlery Train - returned to Camp same day at 4 P.M. - August 15th Left Camp and marched to Gum Springs encamped there during the night - 17th Pursued Rebels at Aldie Capturing 3 - 19th
Captured 7 prisoners in Bull Run Mountains and returned to Camp - August 24th Detachment of Company attacked by Moseby between Washington and Fairfax Court House 2 men lost in action.
Station: Centreville, Va.

From the 31st day of August to the 31st day of October 1863.
Sept. 15th 1863
Removed Camp from Centreville - through Washington to Seneca - arriving there on the 19th.
Sept 22nd Removed Camp from Seneca to Edwards Ferry.
Station: Seneca and Edwards Ferry, Md.

From 31st day of October to the 31st day of December 1863
Nov. 16/63
Removed Camp from Edwards Ferry to Muddy Branch.
Station: Muddy Branch, Maryld.

From the 31st day of Dec 1863 to the 29th day of February 1864
Station: Muddy Branch Md

From the 29th day of February 1864 to the 30th day of April 1864
Station: Vienna Va

From the 30th day of April 1864 to the 30th day of June 1864
Station: Falls Church Va

From the 30th day of June 1864 to the 31st day of August 1864
Station: Camp Russell Va

From the 31st day of August 1864 to the 31st day of October 1864
Station: Camp Russell Va

From the 31st day of October 1864 to the 31st day of December 1864
Station: Camp Russell Va

From the 31st day of December 1864 to the 28th day of February 1865
Station: Camp Russell Va

From the 28th day of February 1865 to the 30th day of April 1865
Station: Near Petersburg Va

From the 30th day of April 1865 to the 30th day of June 1865
Station: Fairfax Court House

<u>Company L</u>
From enrollment to the 30th day of June 1863.
Commenced to Recruit at San Francisco Jany 26th 1863 up to Feb 17 had 61 men mustered into Service officers was mustered into U.S. Service March 18th 1863 Sailed from San Francisco March 23rd with 96 Enlisted Men arrived in N York April 14th Left for Readville April 15th arrived on the 16th Left Camp Meigs for Washington May 11th <u>via</u> Jersey City <u>Philadelphia</u> and <u>Baltimore</u> Went into Campsite East Capitol Hill May 16th Changed Camp from East Capitol Hill for Camp Brightwood May 30th June 4th one Commissioned Officer & 24 men on Patrol duty Stationed on the Georgetown Pike near <u>Beth Cedar Church</u> Patroled in the neighborhood of Cabin Johns Rockville and Norcutts Cross Roads Were relieved June 6th also 1 commissioned officer & 24 men doing Picket duty at Fort Lincoln June 11th left Camp Brightwood in pursuit of Guerillas by Great Falls Seneca and Poolesville Crossed the Potomac at Whites Ford the 12th inst Visited <u>Leesburg</u> <u>Balls Mills</u> <u>Aldie</u> and <u>Chantilly</u> Arrived at Camp via <u>Vianna</u> and <u>Chain</u> <u>Bridge</u> on the 13th June 23rd changed Camp from Brightwood to Poolesville 24th Company went to the Mouth of the Monocacy Picketing the River from that point to Edwards Ferry June 28th Returned to Poolesville and Marched with Command to Knoxville June 29th Returned to <u>Poolesville</u> and immediately marched in pursuit of <u>Stuarts</u> <u>Cavalry</u> via <u>Rockville</u> <u>Mcanicsville</u> <u>Brookville</u> <u>Cooksville</u> to near <u>Hoods</u> <u>Mills</u> where we remained June 30th 1863.
Station: *[Not shown.]*

From the 30th day of June to the 31st day of August 1863.
July 1st command ordered to Poolsville July 3rd Changed camp from Poolsville to Dawnsville *[Dawsonville]*. L Co doing Picket Duty on the Potomac from mouth of Monocacy to Gt Falls Co joined command at Brightwood on 10th on the 11th marched on reconnoisance via Long Bridge Fairfax C.H. Aldie Middleburg & Upperville reaching Paris & Ashby Gap July 12th had skirmish with the enemy driving them through the Gap. Co Lost 1 Private taken Prisoner 1 Musician wounded returned to Camp Brightwood July 14th July 15th changed camp to Alexandria July 18th joined Gen Kings Division command made a reconnoisance through Fairfax C.H. Fairfax Station Union Mills Buntsville Manassas to Centreville arriving July 19th July 20 marched via Sudleys Church Haymarket New Baltimore to Warrenton from thence via Cattlets & Burton Station to Centreville July 31st had skirmish with Mosbys Guerillas near Aldie Co Lost 2 Privates Killed 2 wounded 5 taken prisoners afterwards retaken losing all equipments. Head Quarters at Centreville up to Aug 31 During which time the Co has furnished daily details for Scouts &c to the utmost extent of its ability Aug 24 2 Privates with a Detachment with Horses from Alexandria were attacked by Mosbys Gain near Coyles Tavern Both escaped with their arms but lost horses and horse equipments 1 badly wounded
Station: Centreville, Va.

From the 31st day of August to the 31st day of October 1863.
Sept 2 Detachment from Co L with others march on expedition to Maryland via Leesburg and Point of Rocks return on the 4th Sept 8th Co made a reconnoisance in the neighborhood of Bull Run and Sudly Springs Sept 18h command made an expedition to Leesburg & vicinity returned by Mount Gibard Carters Ford Do—— Aldie and Gum Springs arrived in Camp 20th with 7 Prisoners & 5 Horses Oct 2nd command made reconnoisance to Leesburg Aldie Snickers Gap Grove Creek and other Small towns returned to Camp on the 5th 5th changed camp from Centreville to Fairfax C.H. Oct 9th changed camp to Vienna Corporal Washburn badly wounded by Guerillas near Tysons Oct 16 made reconnoisance in neighborhood of Gum Springs and Little River Pikes Oct 18 Command in readiness to move Detachment out constantly Patrolling this vicinity. Co have daily furnished large details for Picket & Scouting making the duty very arduous the men have but one night in Bed out of four have made good progress towards Building winter quarters and stables
Station: Vienna, Va.

From 31st day of October to the 31st day of December 1863
The Company has participated in frequent expeditions and scouts in pursuit of Moseby's men On the night of Dec 29th Private McFarlene was badly wounded in hand to hand encounter with a Guerrilla
Station: Vienna Va

From the 31st day of December to the 29th day of February 1864.
The Company have furnished the usual heavy details for Scout and Picket incidentally connected with this Department.
Station: Vienna, Va.

From the 29th day of February to the 30th day of April 1864.
Constant Scout & Picket duty - Averaging one nights sleep out of two - Apr 19th on Advance Guard near Aldie attacked & dispersed a party of Guerillas wounding one - Apr 20 Ran down & captured 5 Rebels with Horses & arms Apr 23 Chased Mosby's Command from Difficult Run thru Chantilly to Aldie Attacked & drove him from position in line capturing one of his officers wounding another - Apr 28 on Scout to Paris & Upperville Killed 2 & wounded 3 & captured 15 Rebels - prisoners Lost Sergt Clark killed.
Station: Vienna, Va.

From the 30th day of April to the 30th day of June 1864.
Company has been engaged in Constant Scout, Picket & Fatigue duty.
Station: Falls Church, Va.

From the 30th day of June to the 31st day of August 1864
Station: Camp near Halltown Va

From the 31st day of August to the 31st day of October 1864.
The Company has taken an active part in Sheridans Campaign in the valley.
Station: In Field Shenandoah Valley

From the 31st day of October to the 31st day of December 1864.
The Co. has taken an active part in Sheridans Campaign in the Valley and been engaged in forty (40) different engagements & skirmishes, including Opequan - Winchester - Luray - Waynesboro - The Cavalry Battle of Oct. 9th 64. Cedar Creek and the Raid on Gordonsville. Station: Camp Russell, Va.

From the 31st Day of December 1864 to the 28th Day of February 1865
Station: In the field

From the 28th Day of February to the 30th Day of April 1865
Station: In the field

From the 30th day of April to the 30th day of June 1865 - missing.

<u>Company M</u>
From date of enrollment to the 30th day of June 1863 missing.

From the 31st day of June to the 31st day of August 1863.
July 1st in Camp at Brightwood, July 2nd went to Acqueduct Bridge No 3 on Picket, dist 10 miles, July 6th Left 30 men there and proceed with balance Co to Camp near Seneca, 25 miles, Left Camp 8 P.M. 9th arrived at Camp Wyndham 6 P.M. 10th, 35 miles. Left Camp Wyndham 5 A.M. 11th on reconnoisance passed through Aldie Middleburgh Upperville Paris reaching Ashbys Gap 10 A.M. 12th had fight lost 2nd Lieut J.C. Norcross & 2 privates taken prisoners & Sergt DeForest wounded We took the Gap and went through to Shenandoah river retd through Gap went through Leesburgh and several other towns and retd to Camp Brightwood July 14th 6 P.M. dist 150 miles, 16th moved to Camp Wyndham 19th Started for reconnoisance, Hd Qrts at Centreville since 22nd, Company been continually on scout since, Sergt J.B. Varnum Killed in action Aug 24th 1863. Capt Manning on detached service since Aug 8th 1863. Station *[Not shown.]*

From the 31st day of August to the 31st day of October 1863.
Sept 1st the Company was stationed at Centreville Va where they were on Picket Duty and were continually on Scouts until Oct 5th when we moved to Fairfax C.H. Va Oct 9th moved from Fairfax C.H. Va Oct 9th to Vienna Va Where we have been stationed since. We have been doing Picket duty and Scouting since My enemy Company has been in several skirmishes during the time but have Lost no men Killed nor had any men wounded and but one man taken prisoner.

Geo. A. Manning
Capt. Co.M

Station: Vienna, Va.

From the 31st day of October to the 31st day of December 1863.
Since last muster have been stationed at Vienna Va doing Pickett and other duties, have made several Raids through Fairfax and Loudon Counties, been through Drainsville, Leesburgh, Aldie, Middleburgh, and Upperville and have been continually on duty the last two months, one man wounded Dec 21st.
Station: Vienna, Va.

From the 31st day of December to the 29th day of February 1864.

Since last muster have been Stationed at Vienna Va. doing Picket and other duties Have made several Raids through Fairfax and Loudon Counties been through Drainsville Leesburgh Aldie Middleburgh and Upperville and have been continually on duty In an Action with the Enemy (Mosbys Guerillas) near Drainsville February 22nd this Company lost 3 Privates Killed 2 Privates wounded and the Captain 3 Corporals and 22 Privates taken Prisoners.

Station: Vienna, Va.

From the 29th day of February to the 30th day of April 1864.

Since last muster - made a change of Stations from Vienna, Va. to Muddy Branch U.P. Md. March 8th Have done but little raiding but have been continually on fatigue and Police duties - nothing worthy of note transpiring.

Station: Muddy Branch, Md.

From the 30th day of April to the 30th day of June 1864.

Since last muster have been Stationed at Muddy Branch Upper Potomac Maryland - been constantly engaged Picketing the River raiding and scouting through Maryland and across the river to Leesburgh Va. building Block Houses.

Station: Muddy Branch, Md.

From the 30th day of June to the 31st day of August 1864.

Left Muddy Branch Md July 27th and joined Regt at Point of Rocks Md from thence to Shenandoah Valley and have been in Active service since under Genl Sheridan.

Station: Smithfield Shenand. Valley Va.

From the 31st day of August to the 31st day of October 1864.

Since last muster have been in active service under Genl Sheridan being engaged in several battles viz at Winchester, Laurey Valley, Waynesboro, Fishers Hill and Cedar Creek.

Station: Cedar Creek Shenandoah Valley

From the 31st day of October to the 31st day of December 1864.

Since last muster have been in Shenandoah Valley constantly on duty - raiding picketing &c &c.

Station: Camp Russell near Winchester Va.

From the 31st day of December to the 28th day of February 1865.

Since last muster have been at Camp Russell near Winchester Va - Raiding and Picketing.

Station: In the Field

From the 28th day of February to the 30th day of April 1865.

Left Camp Russell Va - Feb. 27 moving up the Valley and continuing with Maj. Gen.. Sheridan all thro his successful campaign.

Station: In the Field.

From the 30th day of April to the 30th day of June 1865.

Since last muster broke camp at Clouds Mills and came to Fairfax C.H. doing Guard and Fatigue duty.

Station: Fairfax C.H. Va.

Transcribed from muster rolls in the National Archives, Washington D.C.

Personnel Photos

*Charles R. Lowell-
Colonel of Regiment.
MOLLUS - USAMHI*

*Caspar Crowninshield- Major 1ˢᵗ Battalion.
Roger Hunt Collection at USAMHI*

*William Forbes- Major 3ʳᵈ Battalion.
MOLLUS-USAMHI*

*De Witt C. Thompson- Major 2ⁿᵈ
Battalion. Cal. State Parks-Sutter's
Fort State Historical Park*

Charles A. Humphreys- Chaplain. MOLLUS-USAMHI

J. Sewall Reed- Captain. MOLLUS-USAMHI

Co. A

Archibald McKendry- 1ˢᵗ Lieutenant. Cal. State Parks-Sutter's Fort State Historical Park

John W. Sim- 2ⁿᵈ Lieutenant. MOLLUS-USAMHI

Co. E

Charles S. Eignbrodt-Captain. Cal. State Parks-Sutter's Fort State Historical Park

John C. Norcross- 1ˢᵗ Lieutenant. Cal. State Parks-Sutter's Fort State Historical Park

Henry H. Crocker - 2ⁿᵈ Lieutenant. MOLLUS-USAMHI

Co. F

*David A. De Merritt- Captain. Cal. State Parks-
Sutter's Fort State Historical Park*

*Rufus W. Smith- 1ˢᵗ Lieutenant. MOLLUS-
USAMHI*

*Horace B. Welch- 2ⁿᵈ Lieutenant. Richard
K. Tibbals Collection at USAMHI*

Co. L

Zabdiel B. Adams- Captain. MOLLUS-USAMHI

William C. Manning- 1ˢᵗ Lieutenant. MOLLUS-USAMHI

Josiah A. Baldwin- 2ⁿᵈ Lieutenant. MOLLUS-USAMHI

Co. M

Alvin W. Stone- 1ˢᵗ Lieutenant. Cal. State Parks-Sutter's Fort State Historical Park

George A. Manning- Captain. MOLLUS-USAMHI

Hiram E. W. Clark- 2ⁿᵈ Lieutenant. MOLLUS-USAMHI

467

Bibliography

Diaries

Samuel W. Backus, Company L, 1863 - 1865
Brief, every other day or so, account of his personal activities, not to useful for research purposes. Re-written by him in 1908.
Source unknown, a photoopy is in the Editor's collection.

Samuel J. Corbett, Company A, 1862 - 1865
An excellent source, frequent entries concerning unit activities, personal experiences and opinions. Excerpts can be found in the 1864 and 1865 Sections.
Bancroft Library, Manuscript Collection, U.C. Berkeley

Valorus Dearborn, Company A, 1864
Year 1864 only, covers day to day experiences, weather, expenses; last entry, Sept. 11th. He was wounded in action at Opequon Creek and died in Field Hospital, Winchester, Sept.13, 1864.
Bancroft Library, Manuscript Collection, U.C. Berkeley

Frederick Quant, Company A, 1864 - 1865
A brief, day to day entry, similar to Corbett Diary, but not as descriptive. Both men were members of the Regimental Band and close friends. Covers January 64 to muster out at Readville, Mass., July 28, 1865.
Bancroft Library, Manuscript Collection, U.C. Berkeley

Charles Roberts, Company F, 1863.
An interesting account, day to day of his experiences in the mines and odd jobs in the Virginia City-Carson City area. A good description of his trip by stage over the Sierra to Sacramento and thence by boat to San Francisco to enlist in the California Battalion.
Huntington Library, Manuscript Collection, San Marino, California

Recollections

Harry W. Mortimer, Company E
A personal war history from his recollections as Regimental Clerk and Clerk at Headquarters, Reserve Brigade as well as Clerk in A.G.O. War Department, Washington, D.C. 1865-1866. Written ca. 1897. Lydia Luce Private collection.

George Plummer, Company A
Entitled "California In The War-The Hundred and Battalion" written ca. 1899 in Washington, D.C.. A brief, 12 page narrative of the California units.
Huntington Library, Manuscript Collection, San Marino, California.

George Washington Towle, Company A
Although manuscript is not dated, from references made in the text, it was written sometime between 1906 and Towle's death in March 24, 1921. A well written narrative of his experiences and fellow troopers; from his decision to enlist in the California Hundred to his "delivery" of the California Hundred's "Bear" Guidon and Colors to Sacramento, September, 1865.
Bancroft Library, Manuscript Collection, U.C. Berkeley.

Wells Wallace West, Company A
A brief narrative, written in 1921 at the age of 84. Describes his early life, his trip by wagon across country to California. His enlistment in the California Hundred and various experiences during his time of service to his mustering out at Readville, Mass., July 1865.
West & Benson Family Papers, Bancroft Library, Manuscript Collection, U.C. Berkeley.

Published Letters
All as published in newspapers of the time. They can be found at the date they were written within the body of the text.
Thomas DeLap Barnstead, Company A, Alta California, San Francisco
Charles P. Briggs, Company A, Napa County Reporter
Thomas H. Merry, Company L, Alta California, San Francisco
William H. Moore, Company E, Alta California, San Francisco

As well as several miscellaneous letters published in the Alta California; Evening Bulletin; Solano Herald; Boston Journal; Sacramento Daily Bee.

Letters
Caspar Crowninshield, Massachusetts Historical Society, Boston, Mass.
Robert Henry Williams, Co. F, Huntington Library, San Marino, Ca.
John Passage, Courtesy of Mary Paynter, Madison, Wis
Samuel Hanscom, Courtesy of Bruce MacAlpine, Concord, Mass.
Luman P. Washburn, Minnesota Historical Society, St. Paul, Minn.

For Further In Depth Reading
Alvord, Henry E. *"Early's Attack Upon Washington, July, 1864"*. Military Order of the Loyal Legion of the United States. War Papers No. 26, District of Columbia Commandery, 1897.
Backus, Samuel W. *"Californians in the Field, Historical Sketch of the Organization and Services of the California 'Hundred' and 'Battalion', 2d Massachusetts Cavalry"*. Military Order of the Loyal Legion of the United States. War Paper No. 4, California Commandery. 1889.
Bartol, Cyrus A. *"The Purchase By Blood: A Tribute to Brig.-Gen. Charles Russell Lowell, Jr."*. Spoken In The West Church, Oct. 30, 1864. Boston: John Wilson and Son, 1864.
Bowen, James L. *"Massachusetts In The War 1861-1865"*. Springfield, MA.: Clark W. Bryan, 1889.
Chandler, Robert J. *"The Velvet Glove: The Army During the Secession Crisis in California, 1860-1861"*. San Francisco: Journal of the West, 1981.
—-*"Vigilante Rebirth: The Civil War Union League"*. San Francisco: The Argonaut, Vol. 3, No. 1, 1992.
Cohen, Roger S. *"The Civil War In The Poolesville Area"*. Poolesville, MD: Montgomery County Historical Society, 1961.
Colwell, Wayne. *"The California Hundred"*. Stockton, CA: The Pacific Historian, Vol. 13, No. 3. University of The Pacific, 1969.
Crawford, J. Marshall. *"Mosby And His Men"* . New York: G.W. Carleton & Co., 1867.
Emerson, Edward W. *"Life and Letters of Charles Russell Lowell"*. Boston: Houghton Mifflin, 1907.
Fitzpatrick, Michael F. *"Jubal Early and the Californians"*. Civil War Times Illustrated, Vol. XXXVII No. 2, May 1998.
Harrison, Noel. *"The Sojourn of the Second Massachusetts Cavalry in Vienna"*. Northern Virginia Heritage, June 1985.

Higginson, Henry L. *"Massachusetts in the Army and Navy During the War of 1861 - 1865"*. Boston: Wright & Potter Printing Co., 1896.

Humphreys, Charles A. *"Field, Camp, Hospital and Prison In The Civil War, 1863-1865"*. Boston: Geo H. Ellis Co., 1918.

Hunt, Aurora. *"The Army of the Pacific"*. Glendale, CA: The Arthur H. Clark Co., 1951.

"The Image of War 1861-1865". The National Historical Society, Gettysburg, PA: Doubleday & Co., Inc. 1981.

Jones, Virgil C. *"Gray Ghosts and Rebel Raiders"*. New York: Galahad Books, 1995.

—-*"Ranger Mosby"*. McLean, VA: EPM Publications, 1972.

Keen, Hugh C. and Mewborn, Horace. *"43rd Battalion Virginia Cavalry Mosby's Command"*. Lynchburg, VA: H.E. Howard, Inc., 1993.

Kibby, Leo P. *"California Soldiers in the Civil War"*. California Historical Society Quarterly, December, 1961.

Kirsch, Robert and Murphy, William S. *"West of the West"*. New York: E.P. Dutton & Co., Inc., 1967.

Langellier, John and Colwell, Wayne. *"Cavaliers From California"*. Gateway Heritage, Winter 1984/1985. Missouri Historical Society.

Lewis, Thomas A. *"The Guns of Cedar Creek"*. New York: Harper & Row, 1988.

"Massachusetts Soldiers, Sailors, and Marines in the Civil War". Vol. VI, The Adjutant General, MA. Norwood, MA: Norwood Press, 1933.

McLean, James *"California Sabers"*. Indiana University Press.

"Memoirs of the War of '61, Colonel Charles Russell Lowell, Friends and Cousins". Boston: Geo. H. Ellis Co., 1920.

Mitchell, Adele H. *"The Letters of John S. Mosby"*. Stuart-Mosby Historical Society, 1986.

Morison, John H. *"Dying For Our Country, A Sermon on the Death of Capt. J. Sewall Reed and Rev. Thomas Starr King"*. Preached in the First Congregational Church in Milton, March 13, 1864. Boston: John Wilson and Son, 1864.

Morris, Roy Jr. *"Sheridan, The Life and Wars of General Phil Sheridan"*. New York: Crown Publishers, 1992.

Mosby, John S. *"Stuart's Cavalry in the Gettysburg Campaign"*. New York: Moffat, Yard & Company, 1908.

Orton, Richard H. *"Records of California Men in the War of The Rebellion 1861 To 1867"*. Sacramento, CA: J.D. Young, Supt. State Printing, 1890.

Parson, Thomas E. *"Bear Flag and Bay State in the Civil War"*. McFarland & Company, Inc.

Pier, Arthur S. *"Forbes, Telephone Pioneer"*. New York: Dodd, Mead & Company, 1953.

Riley, Roger D. *"California's Military Role in the Civil War"*. California Historian, Fall 1994.

Scott, Maj. John. *"Partisan Life with Col. John S. Mosby"*. New York: Harper & Brothers, 1867.

Siepel, Kevin H. *"The Life and Times of John Singleton Mosby"*. New York: St. Martin's Press,1983.

Thompson, D. W.C. *"California in the Rebellion"*. Military Order of the Loyal Legion of the United States, War Paper No. 8, Commandery of California, San Francisco, 1891.

Tibbals, Richard K. *"Go East, Young Man..."*. Military Images, Vol. V, No. 6, May-June 1984.

—-*"Thirty Years Later"*. Civil War Times Illustrated, Vol. XXV, No. 2, April 1986.

Vandiver, Frank. *"Jubal's Raid"*. New York: McGraw-Hill, Inc. 1960.

Wert, Jeffry D. *"From Winchester to Cedar Creek"*. Carlisle, PA. South Mountain Press, 1987.

—-*"Mosby's Rangers"*. New York: Simon and Schuster, 1990.

Williamson, James J. *"Mosby's Rangers"*. New York: Ralph B. Kenyon, 1896.

Cemetery Directory

The following is an incomplete and in progress directory of the interment of members of the CAL 100 & Battalion, as well as others of significance to the units.

Mt. Auburn Cemetery, Cambridge, Massachusetts
      Charles Russell Lowell   October 20, 1864

Mt. Hope Cemetery, Mattapan, Massachusetts
      J. Sewall Reed   February 22, 1864

Milton, Massachusetts
      William H. Forbes   October 11, 1897

Sears Memorial Chapel, Longwood, Boston, Massachusetts
      Caspar Crowninshield   January 10, 1897

Warrenton Cemetery, Warrenton, Virginia
      John S. Mosby   May 30, 1916

First Unitarian Church, San Francisco, California
      Thomas Starr King   March 4, 1864

National Cemetery, Arlington, Virginia

Philip H. Sheridan		August 5, 1888
William H. Bumgardner	(A)	July 6, 1864

National Cemetery, Los Angeles, California

Hugh Armstrong	(A)	December 27, 1927
George E. Baldwin	(L)	April 8, 1907
Robert Clawell	(L)	August 30, 1901
Milo G. Ford	(M)	March 1, 1903
Frank O. Libby	(A)	October 17, 1904
William N. Percy	(A)	June 4, 1895
Ebenezer Spencer	(L)	September 28, 1903
Joseph Weaver	(L)	April 9, 1902
Abel A. Withrow	(M)	February 8, 1911

National Cemetery, Presidio, San Francisco, California

Zabdial Adams	(L)	August 9, 1890
Samuel W. Backus	(L)	April 1, 1930
Josiah A. Baldwin	(L)	July 5, 1891
Thomas D. Barnstead	(A)	October 18, 1903
Samuel J. Beebe, Jr.	(L)	November 18, 1902
James M. Coleman	(F)	August 5, 1893
Samuel J. Corbett	(A)	November 12, 1891
Frank Enos	(L)	August 1, 1920
Charles Harkins	(F)	January 2, 1917
John A. Hill	(A)	December 1, 1869
William H. Hussey	(A)	February 11, 1914
C. Mason Kinne	(A)	December 25, 1913
Henry A. Mattox	(M)	September 20, 1884
Isaac R. McIntosh	(A)	June 9, 1905
Adelbert S. Sheldon	(E)	May 29, 1901
Leonard F. Smith	(E)	June 22, 1904
Alvin W. Stone	(M)	June 1, 1909
James P. Wilburn	(M)	February 17, 1903

National Cemetery, Danville, North Carolina

John F. Halligan	(F)	November 25, 1864
William S. Marsh	(F)	February 19, 1865
Francis E. Smith	(F)	February 1, 1865
Charles L. Spraight	(A)	March 4, 1865

National Cemetery, Richmond, Virginia

Roswell R. Smith	(L)	December 14, 1863
Hiram H. Vennum	(E)	December 25, 1863

National Cemetery, Winchester, Virginia

Joseph E. Burrill	(M)	May 5, 1865
Frank C. Griffin	(M)	April 23, 1865

Frederick H. Holden	(E)	April 19, 1865
John L. Moeglen	(M)	September 28, 1864
Alvin H. Russell	(E)	October 19, 1864
Jacob Walther	(E)	October 17, 1864
Stephen Weisberger	(F)	October 19, 1864

Angelus Rosedale Cemetery, Los Angeles, California

Francis E. Barron	(L)	September 18, 1917

Arbor Vitae Cemetery, Madera, California

Frederick J. Quant	(A)	July 16, 1916

Chapel of the Pines Columbarium, Los Angeles

Cyrus F. Demsey	(A)	March 27, 1913

Colfax California

James B. Hayford	(M)	1932

Crescent City, California

Edward Straub	(E)	December 26, 1907

Cypress Lawn, Colma, California

Henry H. Fillebrown	(A)	January 26, 1867
Alfred A. McLean	(L)	January 21, 1931
William A. Robinson	(A)	May 15, 1912

Downieville, California

Sylvanus Shaw	(E)	1906

Evergreen Cemetery, Compton

John C. Norcross	(E)	June 7, 1912

Evergreen Cemetery, Santa Cruz

Stephen H. Esten	(E)	June 6, 1894

Evergreen Memorial Park, Los Angeles, California

Charles M. Jenkins	(E)	January 28, 1933

Greenlawn, Colma, California

Abraham Loane	(A)	January 13, 1920

Hartley Cemetery, Lakeport, California

William Morris	(E)	December 10, 1937
Wells W. West	(A)	May 5, 1924

Holy Cross, Colma, California

Martin J. Acton	(L)	February 20, 1933

I.O.O.F. Cemetery, Colma, California

Eugene F. Loud	(L)	December 19, 1908
Harry W. Mortimer	(E)	March 14, 1909

I.O.O.F. Cemetery, Garden of Memories, Salinas, California

Daniel K. McDougall	(L)	May 3, 1923

Iowa Hill, California

Jared S. Sparhawk	(L)	April 12, 1898

Mission City Memorial Park, Santa Clara, California

William H. Lawrence	(M)	May 30, 1935

Mount Olivet Cemetery, Colma, California

Edward F. Seagrave	(L)	May 4, 1914

Mount Olivet Cemetery, San Rafael, California

James Watson	(A)	June 2, 1910

Mount Tamalpais Cemetery, San Rafael, California

George W. Towle	(A)	March 23, 1921

Mountain View Cemetery, Altadena, California

Robert H. Williams	(F)	December 30, 1904

Mountain View Cemetery, Oakland, California

Warren L. McEwen	(E)	December 12, 1890
Henry P. Miles	(M)	NA
Alonzo Papworth	(A)	March 21, 1910
Charles Roberts	(F)	March 2, 1896
DeWitt C. Thompson		May 13, 1919
Edwin W. Woodward	(A)	September 8, 1920

Oak Hill, San Jose, California

John T. Campbell	(E)	September 3, 1917

George W. Lee		(M)	June 20, 1923
Archibald McKendry	(A)	June 8, 1885	
Benson Sivalls		(A)	March 15, 1917

Pleasanton Memorial Gardens, Pleasanton, California

Henry Schroder		(L)	March 12, 1903

Rocklin District Cemetery, Rocklin, California

Stephen Landis		(F)	May 16, 1892

Russian River Cemetery, Ukiah, California

Charles Ackerman		(A)	March 4, 1892

Santa Barbara Cemetery, Santa Barbara, California

Benjamin W.C. Brown		(L)	July 9, 1883
Thomas H. Merry		(L)	October 20, 1907

Santa Cruz Memorial Park, Santa Cruz, California

George I. Holt		(A)	January 30, 1891

Suisun-Fairfield Cemetery, Fairfield, California

Benjamin F. Hoxie		(L)	December 9, 1884

Sunrise Memorial Park, Vallejo, California

John Fletcher		(A)	December 14, 1927

Sunset View, ElCerrito, California

Benjamin F. Rawson	(F)	March 24, 1917	

Tulocay Cemetery, Napa, California

Charles P. Briggs		(A)	January 3, 1885
William H. McNeill	(A)	April 5, 1920	

Volcanoville Cemetery, Volcanoville, California

John L. Hunter		(A)	April 17, 1908

Veterans Home Cemetery, Yountville, California

James Bard		(L)	May 13, 1905
Jackson Cossell		(F)	April 15, 1898
Charles W. Heitmann (aka Harloff)	(E)	NA	
John A. Reed		(F)	December 19, 1891
Richard C. Samuel		(A)	March 8, 1908
William H. Staniels	(E)	October 8, 1914	

Andersonville Prison, Georgia — **Grave No.**

Charles Atmore		(A)	September 26, 1864	9781
Newman L. Barnes (aka William)		(M)	June 7, 1864	1697
William Bell		(M)	September 7, 1864	8110
Oscar Blanchard		(E)	March 23, 1864	0109
Joseph Bradford		(F)	August 22, 1864	6512
Joseph H. Burke		(M)	May 21, 1864	1251
Alvin R. Coffin		(M)	August 11, 1864	5315
Jairus A. Dexter		(M)	July 27, 1864	4042
Jackson Fisher (aka John)		(E)	April 9, 1864	0441
Patrick Hackett (aka Haggert)	(M)	September 7, 1864	8056	
Jacob W. Halstead		(M)	March 25, 1864	0151
Edward P. Hamblin (aka H.P.)	(M)	June 8, 1864	1742	
John G. Harty		(M)	April 27, 1864	0766
John Jones	(M)	April 18, 1864	0603	
David Knapp		(M)	April 14, 1864	0554
William W. Millican	(E)	August 29, 1864	7178	
James Munroe (aka Monroe)		(M)	August 20, 1864	6235
John S. Nottage		(F)	September 30, 1864	10058
Frank Paris (aka Parriss)		(E)	August 11, 1864	5380
Edward Price		(M)	June 15, 1864	2008
James B. Randall		(L)	July 15, 1864	3358
Anthony Simonson		(M)	August 26, 1864	6957
George E. Small		(F)	January 15, 1865	NA
John Spaulding		(E)	June 19, 1864	2188
Thomas Z. Stevens		(M)	July 4, 1864	2881
Uriah Weymouth (aka Haymouth)		(M)	August 15, 1864	5789

Rock Creek Cemetery, Washington, D.C.
    Henry G. Burlingham   (A)   May 4, 1927
Savannah, Georgia
    Herman Gozzens   (M)   September, 1864
    Archibald Taylor   (M)   September, 1864
Lewiston, Idaho
    David Watson   (M)   October 3, 1895
Toponis, Idaho
    William H. Short   (F)   March 23, 1886
Greenfield Cemetery, Rockford, Illinois
    John Morse Locke   (M)   October 29, 1906
Pine Lake Cemetery, LaPorte, Indiana
    Warren Cochran   (F)   October 29, 1911
Gould's Cemetery, Milo, Maine
    William Cunningham   (A)   December 3, 1917
Annapolis, Maryland
Thomas W. Cobbey   (E)   December 28, 1863
Benjamin Thaxter   (D&L)   January 15, 1865
Mount Olivet Cemetery, Frederick, Maryland
    John Shiffer   (F)   September 19, 1864
    Jacob Walther   (E)   October 17, 1864
East Parsonsfield, Massachusetts
    Valorus Dearborn   (A)   September 13, 1864
Evergreen Cemetery, Brighton/Boston, Massachusetts
    John H. Williams   (A)   January 29, 1909
Georgetown, Massachusetts
    George Plummer   (A)   January 17, 1929
Oak Hill Cemetery, Newburyport, Massachusetts
    Alfred F. Lee   (A)   April 7, 1864
Mount Hope Cemetery, Shelby, Michigan
    Josephus Blake   (A)   January 3, 1903
Calvary Cemetery, St. Louis, Missouri
    Peter E. White   (A)   November 17, 1915
Sunset Hills, Bozeman, Montana
    Gustavus Doane   (A)   May 5, 1892
Blair Cemetery, Blair, Washington Co., Nebraska
    Bradstreet R. Wildes   (L)   NA
Guide Rock Cemetery, Webster Co. Nebraska
    Osborn Ayer   (L)   October 4, 1902
Washington Memorial (Mansfield) Cemetery, Washington, New Jersey
    Henry Crocker   (E)   March 27, 1913
Fairview Cemetery, Canton, New York
    Solon D. Kimball   (L)   1910
Greenwood Cemetery, Brooklyn, New York
    Charles S. Eigenbrodt   (E)   August 26, 1864
Mount Hope Cemetery, Rochester, New York
    William G. Anthony   (A)   May 3, 1888
Monroe Street Cemetery, Cleveland, Ohio
    David Chester Ferrel   (L)   May 12, 1906
Woodland Cemetery, Philadelphia, Pennsylvania
    Charles Rowe   (A)   April 20, 1886
New City Cemetery, Galveston, Texas
    William E. Parker   (L)   August 18, 1911
Mount Zion Church, Aldie/Leesburg, Virginia
    Samuel Hanscom   (A)   July 6, 1864
    James McDonald   (F)   "
Union Cemetery, Leesburg, Virginia
    Charles Clark   (L)   April 30, 1864
Spring Grove Cemetery, Delavan, Wisconsin
    John Passage   (F)   February 17, 1906

Index